Lecture Notes in Computer Science 1422
Edited by G. Goos, J. Hartmanis and J. van Leeuwen

Springer

*Berlin*
*Heidelberg*
*New York*
*Barcelona*
*Budapest*
*Hong Kong*
*London*
*Milan*
*Paris*
*Singapore*
*Tokyo*

Johan Jeuring (Ed.)

# Mathematics of Program Construction

4th International Conference, MPC'98
Marstrand, Sweden, June 15-17, 1998
Proceedings

Springer

Series Editors

Gerhard Goos, Karlsruhe University, Germany
Juris Hartmanis, Cornell University, NY, USA
Jan van Leeuwen, Utrecht University, The Netherlands

Volume Editor

Johan Jeuring
Utrecht University, Department of Computer Science
P.O. Box 80.089, 3508 TB Utrecht, The Netherlands
E-mail: johanj@cs.ruu.nl

Cataloging-in-Publication data applied for

**Die Deutsche Bibliothek - CIP-Einheitsaufnahme**

**Mathematics of program construction : 4th international conference ; proceedings / MPC '98, Marstrand, Sweden, June 15 - 17, 1998. Johan Jeuring (ed.). - Berlin ; Heidelberg ; New York ; Barcelona ; Budapest ; Hong Kong ; London ; Milan ; Paris ; Santa Clara ; Singapore ; Tokyo : Springer, 1998**
**(Lecture notes in computer science ; Vol. 1422)**
**ISBN 3-540-64591-8**

CR Subject Classification (1991): D.1-2, F.2-4, G.2

ISSN 0302-9743
ISBN 3-540-64591-8 Springer-Verlag Berlin Heidelberg New York



**Typesetting: Camera-ready by author**
**SPIN 10637451 06/3142 – 5 4 3 2 1 0 Printed on acid-free paper**

# Preface

This volume contains the papers selected for presentation at the 4th International Conference on Mathematics of Program Construction (MPC'98), which was held June 15-17, 1998 on the island Marstrand near Göteborg in Sweden.

The general theme of this series of conferences is the use of crisp, clear mathematics in the discovery and design of algorithms and in the development of corresponding software or hardware. The conference theme reflects the growing interest in formal, mathematically based methods for the construction of software and hardware. The goal of the MPC conferences is to report on and significantly advance the state of the art in this area. Previous conferences were held in 1989 at Twente, The Netherlands, organized by the Rijksuniversiteit Groningen, in 1992 at Oxford, United Kingdom, and in 1995 at Kloster Irsee, Germany, organized by Augsburg University. The proceedings of these conferences were published as LNCS 375, 669, and 947, respectively.

The program committee received 57 submissions, from which 17 were selected for presentation at the conference. Invited lectures were presented by David Harel, John Hughes, and Burghard von Karger.

**Acknowledgements**

I would like to express my gratitude to the members of the program committee and their referees for their care in reviewing and selecting from the submitted papers. I am also grateful to the members of the organization committee. The conference was sponsored by the NFR, the Swedish Natural Science Research Council.

April 1998 Johan Jeuring

# Organization

MPC'98 was organized by the department of Computing Science of Chalmers University of Technology and University of Göteborg.

## Program Committee

| | |
|---|---|
| Ralph-Johan Back | Finland |
| Roland Backhouse | The Netherlands |
| Richard Bird | UK |
| Eerke Boiten | UK |
| Dave Carrington | Australia |
| Robin Cockett | Canada |
| David Gries | USA |
| Lindsay Groves | New Zealand |
| Wim Hesselink | The Netherlands |
| Zhenjiang Hu | Japan |
| Barry Jay | Australia |
| Johan Jeuring | The Netherlands (Chair) |
| Dick Kieburtz | USA |
| Christian Lengauer | Germany |
| Lambert Meertens | The Netherlands |
| Sigurd Meldal | USA |
| Bernhard Möller | Germany |
| Chris Okasaki | USA |
| Jose Oliveira | Portugal |
| Ross Paterson | UK |
| Mary Sheeran | Sweden |
| Doug Smith | USA |

## Organization Committee

| | |
|---|---|
| Patrik Jansson | Chalmers University of Technology |
| Johan Jeuring | Utrecht University |
| Marie Larsson | Chalmers University of Technology |
| Mary Sheeran | Chalmers University of Technology |

## Referees

| | | |
|---|---|---|
| Y. Akama | M. Auguston | J. Barros |
| K. Asai | L. Barbosa | G. Barthe |

A. Bijlsma
M. Buechi
M. Butler
P. Casteran
M. Chakravarty
W. Chin
C. Colby
J. Collard
T. Coquand
S. Curtis
J. Derrick
R. Duke
T. Emerson
D. Espinosa
C. Fidge
G. Fisher
S. Fitzpatrick
H. van Gageldonk
S. Gorlatch
M. Haveraaen
I. Hayes
R. Hehner
M. Heisel
C. Herrmann
P. Jansson
M. Josephs
E. Kazmierczak
J. Knoop
V. Kriauciukas
N. Lesley
A. Liu
J. Liu
T. Lock
W. Luk
J. Lilius
N. Madhav
N. Madrid
B. Mahony
A. McIver
R. McPhee
M. Mendler
A. Mikhajlova
O. de Moor
A. Moran
C. Morgan
R. Nickson
P. Olveczky
O. Owe
J. Plosila
A. Poetzsch-Heffter
G. Renardel de Lavalette
P. Resende
B. Sanders
D. Sands
T. Santen
E. Sekerinski
K. Sere
B. Sufrin
D. Swierstra
J. Udding
I. Ulidowski
M. Utting
V. Vasconcelos
F. de Vries
W. Vogler
M. Walicki
N. Ward
C. Wedler
J. von Wright
E. Zehendner

## Sponsoring Institutions

NFR, the Swedish Natural Science Research Council.

# Table of Contents

## Invited Lectures



## Contributed Lectures

# On the Aesthetics of Diagrams

**(Summary of Talk)**

David Harel

The Weizmann Institute of Science
Rehovot, Israel
harel@wisdom.weizmann.ac.il

**Abstract** *Given the recent move towards visual languages in real-world system specification and design, the need for algorithmic procedures that produce clear and eye-pleasing layouts of complex diagrammatic entities arises in full force. This talk addresses a modest, yet still very difficult version of the problem, in which the diagrams are merely general undirected graphs with straight-line edges.*

## 1. A simulated annealing approach

A large amount of work on the problem of graph layout has been carried out in recent years, resulting in a number of sophisticated and powerful algorithms. Many of these are aimed at special cases of graphs, such as trees or planar graphs; others concentrate on special kinds of layouts, such as rectilinear grid drawings, or convex drawings. There have also been some attempts to solve the problem for general graphs. An extensive and detailed survey can be found in [BETT].

For several years, we have been participating in this effort. In 1989 we attempted to address the general problem of drawing nice-looking undirected straight-line graphs. The results appear in [DH]. Any proposed solution to this problem requires setting general criteria for the "quality" of the picture. One of our main objectives was to see if it were possible to define such criteria so that they apply to different types of graphs, but at the same time are generic enough to be subjected to a general optimization method. The approach in [DH] incorporates a small number of very simple criteria, such as distributing nodes away from each other while trying to keep edges short, minimizing edge-crossings, and keeping vertices from coming too close to edges. The optimization is carried out using simulated annealing [KGV], followed by a fine-tuning stage that does not allow the uphill moves typical to simulated annealing.

The system developed in [DH] performs well on small graphs, but becomes unsatisfactory when applied to graphs of over 30 vertices or so, especially with respect to minimizing edge crossings: planar graphs that do not result in planar layouts are particularly annoying. ([DH] also contains a comparison with the well-known spring method of Eades [E] and its derivatives.)

## 2 Heavy-duty preprocessing

Later, in [HS1], we designed and implemented a more involved algorithm, that carries out preprocessing steps designed to produce a topologically good, but not necessarily nice-looking layout, which is then subjected to a variant of the simulated annealing algorithm of [DH]. The system's results are better and faster than what the annealing approach is able to achieve on its own.

The basic idea in [HS1] is to use some rather intricate algorithms and heuristics — part known and part new — to first obtain a rough approximation of a drawing. These put special emphasis on minimizing edge crossing, but none on aesthetics. The intermediate result in then submited to a modified, downhill-only, version of the annealing system of [DH] for beautification according to the other criteria.

The system employs several phases. Phase A tests for planarity, and is carried out by the algorithm of [BL,LEC], using *PQ*-trees. The system then branches out to deal somewhat differently with planar and non-planar graphs. For planar graphs we carry out the following:

Phase $A$: Planarity testing.
Phase $B$: Planar embedding.
Phase $C$: Planar drawing.
Phase $D$: Randomized beautification.

Phase $B$ uses the *PQ*-trees-based algorithm presented in [CNAO] to construct a planar embedding, i.e., an ordered list of the neighbors of each vertex, which, if layed out appropriately in cyclic order around the vertex, leads to a planar drawing.

Phase $C$ then uses the embedding lists produced by the previous phase to actually draw the graph. The output is a planar drawing with (crossing-free) straight-line edges. To carry out this phase we had to design a special drawing algorithm, which generalizes the work of [FPP,CP]. This algorithm is rather technically involved, and we have devoted a separate paper to it [HS2]. Phase $D$ is the fine-tuning part of the simulated annealing system of [DH] (which doesn't allow uphill moves), slightly modified.

For non-planar graphs, the phases are as follows:

Phase $A$: Planarity testing.
Phase $B^-$: Extracting planar subgraph.
Phase $B$: Planar embedding.
Phase $B^+$: Reinserting removed edges.
Phase $C$: Planar drawing.
Phase $D'$: Extended randomized beautification.

Phase $B^-$ uses yet another application of the *PQ*-trees algorithm, described in [K,JTS], that attempts to find a maximal planar subgraph in the input graph, by eliminating as few edges as possible. The subgraph produced by this phase is then subjected to the planar embedding algorithm of phase $B$. Following this, phase $B^+$ reintroduces the eliminated edges, while trying to minimize the number of crossings that arise by doing so. At each crossing point a new vertex is inserted, yielding again a planar graph.[1]

This planar graph is then drawn in phase $C$, using the algorithm in [HS2], and is beautified by phase $D'$ in a manner similar to that of planar graphs. However, we have had to extend the randomized algorithm of [DH] with new components that try to overcome distortions introduced by phase $B^+$.

## 3 Performance

As far as planar graphs are concerned, the system of [HS1] achieves a significant improvement over the annealing system of [DH]. In general, planar graphs are always drawn planar. In fact, planar graphs with 50 vertices or so yield drawings that have a close-to-perfect look. The running time is also significantly improved, as the inherently slow annealing process is not burdened with having to find a solution, but only with "massaging" a topologically suitable layout into a nice-looking one. Phase D, however, is still by far the most time-consuming part of our system.

For graphs that can be made planar by extracting a small number of edges, the results are still good, and compared with the annealing system, the system of [HS1] has the advantage of being stable: In subsequent runs the results are much the same and are all fairly good, while in the annealing system results can vary widely from run to run — some are acceptable, and some are not.

For graphs that are far from planar (i.e., ones that require the elimination of more than 10 edges or so for planarization), improvements are still required, and the system's results can still be worse than a manually produced drawing, even for medium sized inputs.

Figures 1 and 2 illustrate a non-planar graph with 37 vertices and 76 edges. The planar subgraph algorithm of phase $B^-$ removed 9 edges; reinserting them in phase $B^+$ produced 13 dummy vertices, seen as bends on the edges in Figure 1, which is the intermediate result following phase C. The final result, with only 8 crossings (which is optimal), appears in Figure 2.

## 4 Future work

There are many directions for further work. At the moment, we are pursuing two.

One is to use a multi-level approach to the problem. We run an optimization on parts of the graph, carefully chosen according to multi-level criteria, and then combine the results. This process is carried out again and again, on increasingly higher levels of abstraction.

[1] We should mention the GIOTTO system of Tamassia, Di Battista and Batini [TBB]. They were interested in drawing diagrams using the *grid standard*, whereby vertices are placed at grid points and edges are rectilinear. While their goals are quite different from ours, there is similarity in the early stages: They have steps similar to our phases $A$ through $B^+$. However, the algorithms they use for these steps are different.

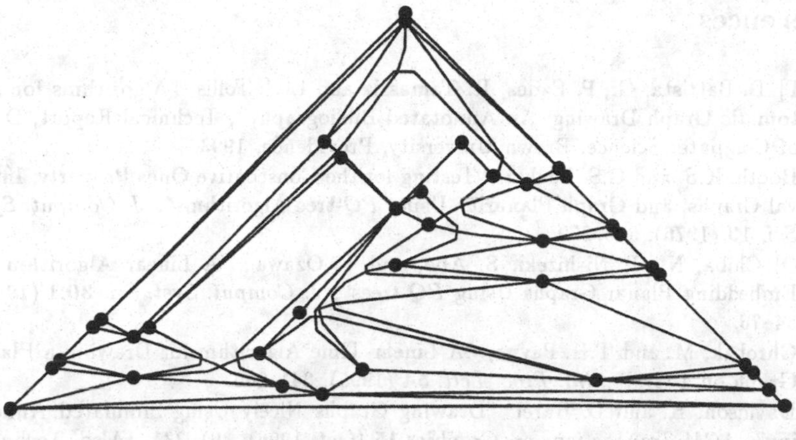

**Fig. 1.** Intermediate result for a non-planar graph of 37 vertices and 76 edges

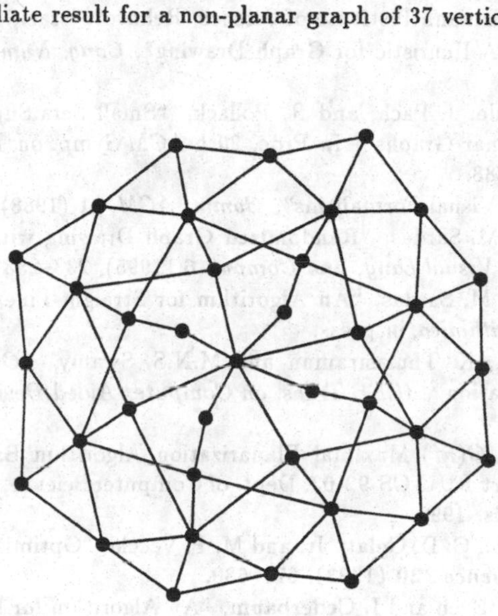

**Fig. 2.** Final result for the graph of Figure 1.

The other research direction is to try to deal with more complicated graphical objects, such as higraphs [H2]. Higraphs involve multi-level "blobs" that can intersect or enclose each other, as in Euler circles and Venn diagrams, and they employ a partitioning convention for representing Cartesian products, as well as inter-level edges or hyperedges. In contrast to ordinary graphs, here there are some very interesting problems that arise even before edges are considered. They have to do with the best shape for a blob, with how to embed *k* blobs in a larger blob, with what to do in terms of size and shape to cater for blobs that have different amounts of internal contents, and so on.

## References


[BETT] Di Battista, G., P. Eades, R. Tamassia and I. G. Tollis, "Algorithms for Automatic Graph Drawing: An Annotated Bibliography", Technical Report, Dept. of Computer Science, Brown University, Providence, 1993.

[BL] Booth, K.S. and G.S. Lueker, "Testing for the Consecutive Ones Property, Interval Graphs, and Graph Planarity Using *PQ*-tree Algorithms", *J. Comput. Syst. Sci.* **13** (1976), 335–379.

[CNAO] Chiba, N., T. Nishizeki, S. Abe, and T. Ozawa, "A Linear Algorithm for Embedding Planar Graphs Using *PQ*-trees", *J. Comput. Syst. Sci.* **30**:1 (1985), 54–76.

[CP] Chrobak, M. and T.H. Payne, "A Linear Time Algorithm for Drawing a Planar Graph on a Grid", *Inf. Proc. Lett.* **54** (1995), 241–246.

[DH] Davidson, R. and D. Harel, "Drawing Graphs Nicely Using Simulated Annealing", *ACM Transactions on Graphics* **15** (Oct. 1996), 301–331. (Also, Technical report, The Weizmann Institute of Science, Rehovot, Israel, 1989.)

[E] [E] Eades, P., "A Heuristic for Graph Drawing", *Cong. Numer.* **42** (1984), 149–160.

[FPP] Fraysseix, H. de, J. Pach, and R. Pollack, "Small Sets Supporting Fáry Embeddings of Planar Graphs", In *Proc. 20th ACM Symp. on Theory of Comput.*, pp. 426–433, 1988.

[H2] Harel, D., "On Visual Formalisms", *Comm. ACM* **31** (1988), 514–530.

[HS1] Harel, D. and M. Sardas, "Randomized Graph Drawing with Heavy-Duty Preprocessing", *J. Visual Lang. and Comput.* **6** (1995), 233–253.

[HS2] Harel, D., and M. Sardas, "An Algorithm for Straight-Line Drawing of Planar Graphs", *Algorithmica*, in press.

[JTS] Jayakumar, R., K. Thulasiraman and M.N.S. Swamy, "$O(n^2)$ Algorithm for Graph Planarization", *IEEE Trans. on Computer-Aided Design* **8**:3 (1989), 257–267.

[K] Kant, G., "An $O(n^2)$ Maximal Planarization Algorithm Based on *PQ*-trees", Technical Report RUU-CS-92-03, Dept. of Computer Science, Utrecht University, The Netherlands, 1992.

[KGV] Kirkpatrick, S., C. D. Gelatt Jr. and M. P. Vecchi, "Optimization by Simulated Annealing", *Science* **220** (1983), 671–680.

[LEC] Lempel, A., S. Even and I. Cederbaum, "An Algorithm for Planarity Testing of Graphs", In *Theory of Graphs: International Symposium* (P. Rosenstiehl, Ed.), Gordon and Breach, New York, 1967, pp. 215–232.

[TBB] Tamassia, R., G. Di Battista and C. Batini, "Automatic Graph Drawing and Readability of Diagrams", *IEEE Trans. on Systems, Man and Cybernetics*, **18** (1988), 61–79.

# Generalising Monads

John Hughes

Chalmers University of Technology and University of Göteborg
Göteborg, Sweden
rjmh@cs.chalmers.se

Phil Wadler's idea of using monads to structure purely functional programs has had a profound effect on the way libraries of combinators are designed in Haskell. By basing the signature of such a library on a monad, the designer gains access to a wide variety of possible implementations, and moreover enables the library to be used in conjunction with generic monadic code.

However, recently some combinator libraries have been designed that are inherently incompatible with the monad signature. Swierstra's library for LL-1 parsing is an interesting example. In this talk we propose another generic library signature, inspired by Kleisli categories, which is more general than the monad signature and can be used in the design of libraries such as Swierstra's that collect static information about computations.

# A Proof Rule for Control Loops

Burghard von Karger

Institut für Informatik und Praktische Mathematik
Christian-Albrechts-Universität Kiel
Preusserstraße 1–9, D–24105 Kiel, Germany

## 1 Introduction

Safety requirements are best expressed by describing behaviours that may *never* occur (for example explosions). If $Q$ is the description of a desaster then an implementation must solve the inequation

$$X \subseteq \overline{\oplus Q}\,,$$

where $\oplus$ means "in some arbitrary interval of time", the overbar is negation and $\subseteq$ denotes refinement. Plants are often controlled by looping programs that repeatedly cycle through a fixed set of production steps or alternate between a sensing phase and a correction phase. To ensure that a control program is safe we must therefore verify an inequation of the form

$$P^* \subseteq \overline{\oplus Q} \tag{1}$$

where the star operator denotes an arbitrary number of repetitions. The contribution of this article is a calculational rule for proving inequations of this form. Its formal statement and proof is given in *temporal algebra*, which is an algebraic calculus encompassing logics such as CTL, linear temporal logic, interval logic and the duration calculus. The first part of this paper (Sec. 2-4) gives a short introduction to temporal algebra; for a full treatment the reader is referred to [5]. In Sec. 5 we state the proof rule and establish its correctness. The next two sections extend the basic calculus with measures and durations. In Sec. 8 we give two examples that illustrate the use of our proof rule. The paper is concluded In Sec. 9 with a meta-theorem that reduces the verification of infinite loops to the verification of finite ones.

## 2 Time Diagrams

A single behaviour of a system may be described by a function that maps an interval in time (the observation interval) to the set of its possible states. Let us call such a function a time diagram. For simplicity, we assume that observation intervals are finite, closed, nonempty intervals of real numbers and that states are elements of a fixed set $\Sigma$.

Observation intervals must not be empty, but they may consist of a single point. For reasons that will become clear in a moment, a time diagram whose observation interval is a single point is called a *unit*. The left unit $\overleftarrow{x}$ of a time diagram $x : [a, b] \to \Sigma$ is defined to be the restriction of $x$ to the leftmost point of its observation interval, i.e. $dom\ \overleftarrow{x} = [a, a]$ and $\overleftarrow{x}(a) = x(a)$. The right unit $\overrightarrow{x}$ of $x$ is similarly obtained by restricting the observation interval to $[b, b]$. The sequential composition of two time diagrams $x$ and $y$ is defined when $\overrightarrow{x} = \overleftarrow{y}$. In this case we let $x; y =_{df} x \cup y$ which is again a time diagram. Thus the set of all time diagrams is an algebraic structure equipped with three operators (two unary and one partial binary) satisfying the following laws.

1. $x; y$ is defined if and only if $\overrightarrow{x} = \overleftarrow{y}$.
2. If $x; y$ is defined then $\overleftarrow{x; y} = \overleftarrow{x}$ and $\overrightarrow{x; y} = \overrightarrow{y}$.
3. Composition is associative (note that 1. and 2. imply that $(x; y); z$ is defined if and only if $x; (y; z)$ is defined).
4. If $e = \overleftarrow{x}$ or $e = \overrightarrow{x}$ then $\overleftarrow{e} = e = \overrightarrow{e}$.
5. $\overleftarrow{x}; x = x = x; \overrightarrow{x}$.

In other words, time diagrams are the arrows of a category (units being the objects). As a consequence, much of what follows holds not just for time diagrams but for many other models of computations as well. However, no understanding of categories is required to read this paper or to apply its results. In addition to 1.-5. there are just two properties of time diagrams that we shall need, namely local linearity and the reflection property.

6. Reflection: If $x; y$ is a unit then so is $y; x$
7. Local Linearity: If $x; y = x'; y'$ then there is a mediating element $z$ satisfying either $x; z = x'$ and $y = z; y'$ or $x = x'; z$ and $z; y = y'$.

We just mention a couple of other models of computation that satisfy 1.-7. The first one is the set all pairs of states with operations defined by$\overleftarrow{(x, y)} = (x, x) = \overrightarrow{(y, x)}$and $(x, y); (y, z) = (x, z)$. The second is the set of all finite sequences of letters drawn from an alphabet $A$ (with concatenation as composition and the empty sequence as the only unit). Many other models exists (see [1, 5]).

## 3 Sequential Algebra

A time diagram is the result of a single observation, or experiment, we might make on a machine. To describe a system fully, we require a set of time diagrams. Therefore, we lift the operations defined on individual time diagrams to sets and translate properties 1.-7. to corresponding laws at the set level.

If $P$ and $Q$ are sets of time diagrams then their composition is defined by

$$P; Q =_{df} \{x \mid \exists p \in P, q \in Q : x = p; q\}.$$

We often write $PQ$ in place of $P;Q$. Unlike the operation on individual time diagrams the composition of sets is total. The composition of sets of time diagrams is very much like the composition of relations (which is similarly defined by lifting the composition operator on pairs): It is associative and has a unit, namely

$$I =_{df} \{x \mid x \text{ is a unit}\}.$$

Unlike relations, sets of time diagrams do not have converses. To compensate for this deficiency we introduce two partial converse operations by

$$P;\text{-}Q =_{df} \{x \mid \exists p \in P, q \in Q : p; x = q\}$$

and

$$P\text{-};Q =_{df} \{x \mid \exists p \in P, q \in Q : x; q = p\}.$$

We rule that sequential composition binds stronger than either ;- or -; but we use this convention only when the semicolon is suppressed, i.e. we allow ourselves to write $PQ;\text{-}R$ but not $P;Q;\text{-}R$ because the latter expression is too easily misparsed. Set-theoretic union and intersection bind less strongly and complementation is denoted by an overbar. Equipped with these operations, the set of all sets of time diagrams is a *sequential algebra*, as defined below.

**3.1 Definition** A *sequential algebra* is a complete Boolean algebra $(\mathcal{S}, \cap, \cup, \bar{\ })$ with greatest element $U$ and least element $\mathsf{O}$, equipped with three additional binary operators (composition, left division and right division) satisfying the following axioms

$$(\mathcal{S}, ;) \text{ is a monoid with an identity } I \qquad \text{(Monoid)}$$

$$P\text{-};Q \cap R = \mathsf{O} \;\Leftrightarrow\; Q \cap PR = \mathsf{O} \;\Leftrightarrow\; Q;\text{-}R \cap P = \mathsf{O} \qquad \text{(Exchange)}$$

$$P(Q;\text{-}R) \subseteq PQ;\text{-}R \qquad \text{(Euclid)}$$

$$I;\text{-}P = P\text{-};I \qquad \text{(Reflection)}$$

The first three of these axioms follow from 1.-5. (so they hold for the power set of the set of arrows of any small category) and the reflection axiom follows from 6. More information on sequential algebras can be found in [1, 5, 6, 3]. Local linearity gives us an additional law (which is a stronger version of the Euclidean axiom).

$$PQ;\text{-}R = P(Q;\text{-}R) \cup P;\text{-}(R;\text{-}Q) \qquad \text{(Local Linearity)}$$

In the remainder of this section we list a number of laws that hold in every sequential algebra. The reader might tackle their proofs as exercises or look them up in [5].

**3.2 Euclid (dual version)** $(R\text{-};Q)P \subseteq R\text{-};QP$.

As a consequence, sequential algebra enjoys a perfect symmetry between left and right (or past and future), so that every law has not only a logical but also a time-wise dual. One can also show that, in the presence of the exchange axiom, the local linearity implies its temporal dual.

**3.3 Distributivity** Each of the operators ; and ;- and -; distributes (in each argument) over arbitrary unions. In particular, we have $\mathsf{O} = P;\mathsf{O} = P;\text{-}\mathsf{O}$ etc.

**3.4 Units of ;- and -;** $I$ is a one-sided unit of ;- and -; in the sense that $P;\text{-}I = P = I\text{-};P$.

**3.5 Dedekind law** $PQ \cap R \subseteq (P \cap R;\text{-}Q)\,(Q \cap P\text{-};R)$.

**3.6 Associativity of ;- and -;** $(P\text{-};Q);\text{-}R \;=\; P\text{-};(Q;\text{-}R)$.

**3.7 Fixed Points and Iterations** Since a sequential algebra is a complete lattice, every monotonic function $f$ has a least fixed point $\mu f$ and a great fixed point $\nu f$. The finite iteration operator is defined by

$$P^* \;=_{df}\; \mu_X(I \cup P;X)$$

where the right hand side denotes the lowest fixed point of the function that maps $X$ to $I \cup P;X$. We also use an infinite repetition operator which is defined by

$$P^\infty \;=_{df}\; \nu_X(P;X)\,.$$

We require the following rules for calculating with fixed points and iterations.

**3.8 $\mu$-Fusion** Assume that $\mathcal{L}$ is a complete lattice and that $f$, $g$ and $h$ are monotonic functions on $\mathcal{L}$. If $h$ distributes over all disjunctions then we have

$$h(\mu f) = \mu g \quad \Leftarrow \quad h \circ f = g \circ h\,.$$

**3.9 Tail Recursion** $\mu_X(Q \cup PX) \;=\; P^*Q$.

**3.10 Repetition Rule** $\nu_X(Q \cup PX) \;=\; P^*Q \cup P^\infty$.

# 4 Somewhere and Everywhere

Let $u$ and $v$ be time diagrams. We say that $u$ is a *subdiagram* of $v$ if the equation

$$x; u; y = v$$

can be solved. Every relation between time diagrams can be lifted. Let $P$ be a set of time diagrams. Then $\diamondplus P$ (*somewhere* $P$) is the set of all time diagrams that have a subdiagram in $P$.

$$\diamondplus P =_{df} \{x; u; y \mid x; u; y \text{ is defined and } u \in P\} \;=\; UPU.$$

The definition of $\diamondplus$ in terms of sequential composition is well-known from interval temporal logic and is used, for example, in [4, 7]. The dual modality (*everywhere* $P$) is defined by

$$\boxplus P =_{df} \overline{\diamondplus \overline{P}},$$

so $x \in \boxplus P$ just when all subdiagrams of $x$ are in $P$. The $\boxplus$ and $\diamondplus$ operators are referred to as *interval modalities.* The following properties are immediate from the definitions.

## 4.1 Basic Properties

1. $\diamondplus$ is universally disjunctive and $\boxplus$ is universally conjunctive;
2. $\diamondplus$ and $\boxplus$ are idempotent;
3. $\boxplus P \subseteq P \subseteq \diamondplus P$.

**4.2 Negative Modalities** We define the operators $\diamondminus$ and $\boxminus$ by

$$\diamondminus P = U\text{-}; P; \text{-}U \quad \text{and} \quad \boxminus P = \overline{\diamondminus \overline{P}}.$$

The following two Galois connections are the key to the proof of our rule for control loops.

$$\diamondplus P \subseteq Q \;\Leftrightarrow\; P \subseteq \boxminus Q \quad \text{and} \quad \diamondminus P \subseteq Q \;\Leftrightarrow\; P \subseteq \boxplus Q.$$

We mention a couple more laws that relate positive to negative modalities.

## 4.3 Dedekind

$$\diamondplus P \cap Q \subseteq \diamondplus(P \cap \diamondminus Q) \quad \text{and} \quad \diamondminus P \cap Q \subseteq \diamondminus(P \cap \diamondplus Q).$$

**4.4 Best of Both Worlds** If $P$ holds everywhere and $Q$ holds somewhere then they must hold together somewhere.

$$\boxplus P \cap \diamondplus Q \;\subseteq\; \diamondplus(P \cap Q).$$

# 5 The Proof Rule

Assume that we are asked to construct a control loop with body $P$ that is safe in the sense that repeated execution of $P$ will prevent the occurrence of a certain dangerous event $Q$. Then we must solve

$$P^* \subseteq \overline{\oplus Q}\,.$$

Since $\overline{\oplus Q} = \boxplus \overline{Q}$ we can apply the Galois correspondence between $\ominus$ and $\boxplus$ and rewrite the above to

$$\ominus P^* \subseteq \overline{Q}\,.$$

This inequation is more tractable than the previous one, because we have the following law for analyzing its left hand side.

**5.1 Theorem (Loop-Safety)** Assume that $\mathcal{S}$ is locally linear. Then we have

$$\begin{aligned} \ominus P^* &= \ominus I \cup \ominus P \cup (U\text{-};P);P^*;(P;\text{-}U) \\ &\subseteq \ominus(I \cup P \cup PP) \cup \oplus P\,. \end{aligned}$$

*Proof.*

$$\begin{aligned}
& \ominus P^* \\
= \quad & \{\text{ Definition of } \ominus \} \\
& U\text{-};P^*;\text{-}U \\
= \quad & \{\text{ Lemma 5.2 below }\} \\
& U\text{-};(I;\text{-}U \cup P^*(P;\text{-}U)) \\
= \quad & \{\text{ Distributivity, definition of } \ominus \} \\
& \ominus I \cup U\text{-};(P^*(P;\text{-}U)) \\
= \quad & \{\text{ Local linearity }\} \\
& \ominus I \cup (P^*\text{-};U)\text{-};(P;\text{-}U) \cup (U\text{-};P^*)(P;\text{-}U) \\
= \quad & \{\ P^*\text{-};U = U, \text{ definition of } \ominus \} \\
& \ominus I \cup \ominus P \cup (U\text{-};P^*)(P;\text{-}U) \\
= \quad & \{\text{ Lemma 5.2 below }\} \\
& \ominus I \cup \ominus P \cup (U\text{-};I)(P;\text{-}U) \cup (U\text{-};P)P^*(P;\text{-}U) \\
= \quad & \{\ (U\text{-};I)(P;\text{-}U) \subseteq U\text{-};(I(P;\text{-}U)) = \ominus P \text{ by Euclid }\} \\
& \ominus I \cup \ominus P \cup (U\text{-};P)P^*(P;U) \\
\subseteq \quad & \{\ P^* \subseteq I \cup \oplus P\ \} \\
& \ominus I \cup \ominus P \cup (U\text{-};P)(P;\text{-}U) \cup \oplus P \\
\subseteq \quad & \{\text{ Euclid (twice) }\} \\
& \ominus I \cup \ominus P \cup U\text{-};PP;\text{-}U \cup \oplus P \\
= \quad & \{\text{ Definition of } \ominus, \text{ Distributivity }\} \\
& \ominus(I \cup P \cup PP) \cup \oplus P\,.
\end{aligned}$$

■

The following lemma closes the gap in the last proof. It is a one-sided version of the preceding theorem.

**5.2 Lemma** Suppose that $\mathcal{S}$ is locally linear. Then we have

$$P^*;\text{-}U \;=\; I;\text{-}U \cup P^*(P;\text{-}U) \quad \text{and} \quad U\text{-};P^* \;=\; U\text{-};I \cup (U\text{-};P)P^* .$$

*Proof.* By symmetry, it is sufficient to prove the first equation.

$$\begin{array}{ll}
& P^*;\text{-}U \;=\; I;\text{-}U \cup P^*(P;\text{-}U) \\
\Leftarrow & \qquad \{\; P^* \;=\; I \cup \mu_X(P \cup PX)\,,\ \text{Distributivity} \;\} \\
& \mu_X(P \cup PX);\text{-}U \;=\; P^*(P;\text{-}U) \\
\Leftrightarrow & \qquad \{\; \text{Tail recursion rule 3.9} \;\} \\
& \mu_X(P \cup PX);\text{-}U \;=\; \mu_X(P;\text{-}U \;\cup\; PX) \\
\Leftarrow & \qquad \{\; \mu\text{-Fusion 3.8} \;\} \\
& \forall X :\ (P \cup PX);\text{-}U \;=\; P;\text{-}U \cup P(X;\text{-}U) \\
\Leftrightarrow & \qquad \{\; \text{Distributivity, local linearity} \;\} \\
& \forall X :\ P;\text{-}U \,\cup\, P(X;\text{-}U) \,\cup\, P;\text{-}(U;\text{-}X) \;=\; P;\text{-}U \,\cup\, P(X;\text{-}U) \\
\Leftrightarrow & \qquad \{\; P;\text{-}(U;\text{-}X) \subseteq P;\text{-}U \;\} \\
& \mathit{true}\,.
\end{array}$$

■

**5.3 Proof Rule** Using the Galois connection one more time we obtain the following proof rule:

$$P^* \subseteq \overline{\oplus Q} \qquad \Leftarrow \qquad I \cup P \cup PP \subseteq \overline{\oplus Q} \;\wedge\; Q \subseteq \overline{\oplus P}\,.$$

## 6 Measures

In order to be able to show some interesting examples we must enrich our calculus by a facility for reasoning about the length of intervals. For simplicity, we stick to the set of real numbers as our time domain, although all of the theory explained in this section, and the next, works for discrete time as well.

**6.1 The standard measure on time diagrams** The length of a time diagram $x : [a, b] \to \Sigma$ is given by

$$\mathit{length}(x) = b - a\,.$$

To lift this measure to the set level, we define a function $\ell : \mathbb{R}_{\geq 0} \to \mathcal{S}$ by

$$\ell(t) =_{df} \{x \mid \mathit{length}(x) = t\}\,.$$

The function $\ell$ has four characteristic properties.

1. **Uniqueness:** (Each observation has at most one length)

$$r \neq s \quad \Rightarrow \quad \ell(r) \cap \ell(s) \;=\; \mathsf{O}\,.$$

2. **Totality:** (Every observation has a length)

$$\bigcup_{r \in \mathbb{R}_{\geq 0}} \ell(r) \;=\; U\,.$$

3. **Additivity:**

$$\ell(r); \ell(s) \;=\; \ell(r+s)\,.$$

4. **Neutral Element:**

$$\ell(0) \;=\; I\,.$$

Notice that the last two conditions just say that $\ell$ is a monoid homomorphism.

**6.2 Abstract Measures** Now suppose $\mathcal{S}$ is an arbitrary sequential algebra and $\ell$ is a function from $\mathbb{R}_{\geq 0}$ to $\mathcal{S}$. Then we say that $\ell$ is

– a *pre-measure* if the first two properties hold (uniqueness and totality)

– a *measure* if the first three properties hold (uniqueness, totality and additivity)

– a *definite measure* if all four of the above properties hold.

**6.3 Lifting Operators** Any operation on real numbers can be lifted to pre-measures. Suppose $f$ is an $n$-ary operation on real numbers. Then an $n$-ary operator $\hat{f}$ on pre-measures is defined by

$$\hat{f}(\ell_1, \ldots, \ell_n)(r) =_{df} \bigcup\{\ell_1(s_1) \cap \ldots \cap \ell_n(s_n) \mid r = f(s_1, \ldots, s_n)\}\,.$$

For example, the sum of two pre-measures $\ell = \ell_1 \hat{+} \ell_2$ is defined by

$$\ell(r) = \bigcup_{r=s+t} \ell_1(s) \cap \ell_2(t)\,.$$

We have the following theorem.

**6.4 First Lifting Theorem** The set of all pre-measures is closed under all lifted operations. More precisely, if $\ell_1, \ldots, \ell_n$ are pre-measures and $f$ is an $n$-ary operation on real numbers then $\hat{f}(\ell_1, \ldots, \ell_n)$ is a pre-measure. ■

As a consequence, the hat operator maps operations on real numbers to operations on pre-measures. Notice that every real number can be regarded as a 0-ary function and consequently gives rise to a pre-measure. Thus the set of real numbers with all its operations is embedded into the set of pre-measures.

**6.5 Lifting Relations** Suppose $R$ is an $n$-ary relation on real numbers. Then $R$ may be lifted to a function that maps every $n$-tuple of pre-measures on a sequential algebra $\mathcal{S}$ to an element of $\mathcal{S}$.

$$\hat{R}(\ell_1, \ldots, \ell_n) =_{df} \bigcup\{\ell_1(r_1) \cap \ldots \cap \ell_n(r_n) \mid R(r_1,, \ldots, r_n)\}.$$

For example consider the case where $\mathcal{S}$ is the powerset of the set of all time diagrams and $R$ is the equality relation. We get

$$\begin{aligned}(\ell \hat{=} \hat{3}) &= \bigcup\{\ell(r_1) \cap \hat{3}(r_2) \mid r_1 = r_2\} = \bigcup_r \ell(r) \cap \hat{3}(r) = \ell(3) \\ &= \{x \mid \mathit{length}(x) = 3\}.\end{aligned}$$

**6.6 Validity** Next we may ask what algebraic properties of real numbers are preserved by lifting. For example, is lifted addition associative? The next theorem gives the strongest positive answer that one might hope for. Lifting has already been defined for operations and relations, and it extends naturally to expressions formed from variables, operations and relations. If $t$ is an expression, let $\hat{t}$ be the lifted expression (obtained by replacing each operation/relation by its lifted counterpart). A relational expression is valid if it evaluates to T for every possible assignment of real numbers to its variables. A lifted expression is valid if it evaluates to $\hat{\mathrm{T}}$ for every assignment of pre-measures to its variables. Then we have

**6.7 Second Lifting Theorem** Suppose $t$ is a relational expression. Then $t$ is valid if and only if $\hat{t}$ is valid. ■

The lifting theorems ensure that the theory of real numbers can be used freely for reasoning about expressions containing measures. There is no more need of making the lifting operator explicit, and we shall write it in invisible ink. To increase parsability we will keep parenthesis around expressions like $\ell = 3$. For example, the additivity axiom will be rendered as

$$(\ell = r); (\ell = s) = (\ell = r + s).$$

**6.8 Measure Algebra** A sequential algebra with a definite measure is called a *measure algebra*. The addition of a measure has a drastical effect on expressivity and reasoning power, because it allows us to introduce an ordering for the various chop points that occur in an expression like $PQ \cap RS \cap XY$ and then to apply case analysis. Dutertre has given a complete proof system for an interval logic with a measure [2]. All axioms and rules of Dutertre's system can be proved as theorems of measure algebra (see [5]). In order to illustrate the power of measure algebra we state and prove a couple of laws.

**6.9 Subtractivity and Antisymmetry** In a measure algebra we have, for all $r, s \geq 0$

$$(\ell = r);\text{-}(\ell = s) \;\subseteq\; (\ell = r - s)\,.$$

*Proof.*

$$(\ell = r);\text{-}(\ell = s) \subseteq (\ell = r - s)$$
$$\Leftarrow \qquad \{\text{ Totality of } \ell\ \}$$
$$(\ell = r);\text{-}(\ell = s) \subseteq \overline{(\ell = t)} \;\text{ for all } t \geq 0 \text{ with } t \neq r - s$$
$$\Leftrightarrow \qquad \{\text{ Exchange }\}$$
$$(\ell = r) \subseteq \overline{(\ell = t)(\ell = s)} \;\text{ for all } t \geq 0 \text{ with } t \neq r - s$$
$$\Leftrightarrow \qquad \{\text{ Additivity }\}$$
$$(\ell = r) \subseteq \overline{(\ell = t + s)} \;\text{ for all } t \geq 0 \text{ with } t \neq r - s$$
$$\Leftrightarrow \qquad \{\text{ Uniqueness of } \ell\ \}$$
$$\mathit{true}\,.$$

■

Since $(\ell = r) = \mathsf{O}$ for $r < 0$ we obtain the following antisymmetry law as a corollary (for an explanation why it is appropriate to to use the term antisymmetry here see [5]).

$$I;\text{-}U \;=\; I \;=\; U\text{-};I\,.$$

The antisymmetry law is required in the proof of several laws in the next section.

**6.10 A Synchronization Law** In every measure algebra we have

$$PQ \cap P'Q' \;=\; (P \cap P')(Q \cap Q') \quad \Leftarrow \quad \exists r : P \cup P' \subseteq (\ell = r)\,.$$

*Proof.* The inclusion from right to left follows from monotonicity. To prove the other inclusion, assume $P \cup P' \subseteq (\ell = r)$ and let $s \in \mathbb{R}_{\geq 0}$. Then we have

$$PQ \cap P'Q' \cap (\ell = s)$$
$$= \qquad \{\ P \cup P' \subseteq (\ell = r), \text{ definition of measures }\}$$
$$P(Q \cap (\ell = s - r)) \cap P'(Q' \cap (\ell = s - r))$$
$$= \qquad \{\text{ Let } R = Q \cap (\ell = r - s) \text{ and } R' = Q' \cap (\ell = r - s)\ \}$$
$$PR \cap P'R'$$
$$\subseteq \qquad \{\text{ Dedekind law }\}$$
$$(P \cap P'R';\text{-}R)\,(R \cap P\text{-};P'R')$$
$$= \qquad \{\text{ Local linearity }\}$$
$$(P \cap (P'(R';\text{-}R) \cup P';\text{-}(R;\text{-}R')))\,(R \cap ((P\text{-};P')R' \cup (P'\text{-};P);R'))$$
$$\subseteq \qquad \{\text{ Subtractivity }\}$$
$$(P \cap (P'(\ell = 0) \cup P';\text{-}(\ell = 0)))\,(R \cap ((\ell = 0)R' \cup (\ell = 0)\text{-};R'))$$
$$= \qquad \{\ \ell \text{ is definite and } I \text{ is a unit of composition and division }\}$$
$$(P \cap P')(R \cap R')\,.$$

Since the above calculation works for every $s \in \mathbb{R}_{\geq 0}$, totality of $\ell$ yields $PQ \cap P'Q' \subseteq (P \cap P')(Q \cap Q')$, as required. ■

# 7 Duration Algebra

We have seen that the addition of a measure greatly increases the power and expressivity of sequential algebra. Hoare, Ravn and Zhou observed that for some applications it is necessary to express the duration of a predicate in a given interval. For example, the specification of a gas burner may include a condition that gas must not be leaking for more than four seconds in any interval of length thirty. Requirements of this type can be expressed with the aid of integrals:

$$\boxplus((\ell \geq 30) \rightarrow (\textstyle\int \mathit{Leak} \leq 4))\,.$$

In this expression, $\int \mathit{Leak}$ is a measure and $(\int \mathit{Leak} \leq 4)$ is the set of all intervals that have no more than four seconds of leakage in them.

**7.1 Definition (Duration Algebra)** A *duration algebra* is a structure $(\mathcal{S}, \mathcal{B}, \int)$ where $\mathcal{S}$ is a sequential algebra, $\mathcal{B}$ is a complete Boolean algebra and $\int B$ assigns a measure $\int B$ to every $B \in \mathcal{B}$, subject to the following conditions:

1. Additivity: $\int(B \cup C) + \int(B \cap C) = \int B + \int C$.
2. $\int \mathtt{T}$ is definite: $(\int \mathtt{T} = 0) = I$ (where $\mathtt{T}$ is the largest element of $\mathcal{B}$).

The elements of $\mathcal{B}$ are called *states*. One possibility is to take $\mathcal{B} = \{B \mid B \subseteq I\}$.

**7.2 The "Holds" Operator** If $\mathcal{S}$ is a duration algebra we use the following abbbreviations (which are borrowed from duration logic [7]).

$$\ell =_{df} \textstyle\int \mathtt{T} \quad \text{and} \quad \lceil B \rceil =_{df} (\textstyle\int B = \ell) \cap (\ell > 0)\,.$$

The expression $\lceil B \rceil$ (pronounce: $B$ holds) describes the set of all non-unit time-diagrams that stay in state $B$ almost everywhere. Here is a set of useful laws for the holds operator:

1. Conjunctivity:

   $$\lceil B \cap C \rceil = \lceil B \rceil \cap \lceil C \rceil\,.$$

2. Exportability:

   $$\lceil B \rceil\,;\lceil B \rceil \subseteq \lceil B \rceil\,.$$

3. Importability: Assume that $P \subseteq (\ell > 0)$ and $Q \subseteq (\ell > 0)$. Then we have

   $$\lceil B \rceil \cap PQ = (\lceil B \rceil \cap P)(\lceil B \rceil \cap Q)\,.$$

4. Exclusion property: If $\neg B$ holds on some subinterval then $B$ does not hold on the entire interval

   $$\Diamond\lceil \neg B \rceil \subseteq \overline{\lceil B \rceil}\,.$$

5. Initial Exclusion: $B$ and $\neg B$ cannot both be true on an initial interval

$$\lceil \neg B \rceil ; U \subseteq \overline{\lceil B \rceil ; U}\,.$$

6. No overlap property:

$$\lceil B \rceil \cap \Diamond(P; \lceil \neg B \rceil ; Q) \subseteq \Diamond P \cap \Diamond Q\,.$$

# 8 Examples

In this section we give two examples where the proof rule for control loops can be applied. A further case study can be found in [5].

## 8.1 Unit Pulse

A unit pulse is a Boolean variable $B$ that can only be true for exactly one unit of time. Its specification is

$$\textit{unit-pulse-spec} =_{df} \boxplus Q \quad \text{where } Q =_{df} \lceil B \rceil \to \Diamond((\ell = 1) \cap \lceil B \rceil)\,,$$

i.e., every $B$-interval must be contained in a $B$-interval of length one. A first step towards an implementation eliminates the modal operator $\boxplus$ and the implication $\to$, because these are not admitted in any notation for implementation. Instead, we use the iteration operator.

$$\textit{unit-pulse-design} =_{df} P^* \quad \text{where } P =_{df} \lceil \neg B \rceil \; ; \; ((\ell = 1) \cap \lceil B \rceil)\,.$$

We must prove that the design is correct. This is achieved by the following calculation.

$$\begin{array}{ll}
 & \textit{unit-pulse-design} \subseteq \textit{unit-pulse-spec} \\
\Leftrightarrow & \qquad \{\text{ Definitions }\} \\
 & P^* \subseteq \boxplus Q \\
\Leftrightarrow & \qquad \{\text{ Proof Rule for Control Loops }\} \\
 & I \cup P \cup PP \subseteq \boxplus Q \quad \wedge \quad \Diamond P \subseteq Q \\
\Leftrightarrow & \qquad \{\ \Diamond P \subseteq Q \text{ follows from the exclusion property 7.2.4 }\} \\
 & I \cup P \cup PP \subseteq \boxplus Q \\
\Leftarrow & \qquad \{\text{ Galois connection }\} \\
 & \Diamond I \cup \Diamond(P \cup PP) \subseteq Q \\
\Leftarrow & \qquad \{\ \Diamond I = I \subseteq \overline{\lceil B \rceil}\ \} \\
 & \Diamond(P \cup PP) \subseteq Q \\
\Leftrightarrow & \qquad \{\text{ Shunting }\} \\
 & \lceil B \rceil \cap \Diamond(P \cup PP) \subseteq \Diamond((\ell = 1) \cap \lceil B \rceil) \\
\Leftrightarrow & \qquad \{\text{ No overlap property 7.2 (twice) }\} \\
 & \textit{true}\,. 
\end{array}$$

■

**8.2 Gas Burner**

The famous gas burner example has a safety requirement that gas must not be leaking for more than four seconds within any interval of thirty seconds.

$$\textit{gas-spec} =_{df} \boxplus\overline{Q} \quad \text{where} \quad Q =_{df} (\ell < 30) \cap (\textstyle\int \textit{Leak} > 4)\,.$$

This is implemented by

$$\textit{gas-design} =_{df} P^* \quad \text{where} \quad P =_{df} (\ell = 30) \cap (\textstyle\int \textit{Leak} \leq 2)\,.$$

*Proof.* As in the previous two example, we may apply the Loop-Safety Theorem to obtain the following two proof obligations:

$$\ominus(I \cup P \cup PP) \subseteq \overline{Q} \quad \text{and} \quad \oplus P \subseteq \overline{Q}\,.$$

The first claim follows from $\ominus(I \cup P \cup PP) \subseteq (\int \textit{Leak} \leq 4)$ and the second one from $\oplus P \subseteq (\ell \geq 30)$. ■

# 9 Safety of Infinite Control Loops

The loop safety theorem can be used to show the safety of finite repetitions. In this section we are going to explain why it can ensure the safety of infinite repetitions as well. Assume that $P$ is the body of a control loop $L$ that is supposed to repeat itself indefinitely. This situation may be described by the recursive equation

$$L = P; L\,.$$

Assume also that each execution of $P$ consumes at least one time unit

$$P \subseteq (\ell \geq 1)\,.$$

If $\mathbb{R}_{\geq 0}$ is the set of nonnegative real numbers, a simple induction shows that

$$L \subseteq (\ell \geq n) \quad \text{for all } n < \infty,$$

and, if $\ell$ is a measure in the sense of Sec. 6, we must conclude that $L = \mathsf{O}$. A natural remedy for this unfortunate mismatch of theory and reality is to admit the existence of infinite observations, so that we may have

$$L = P^\infty =_{df} \nu_X(P; X) \subseteq (\ell = \infty)\,.$$

In the following definition let $\mathbb{R}_\infty = \{r \in \mathbb{R} \mid r \geq 0\} \cup \{\infty\}$.

**9.1 Definition (Infinitary Measure)** Suppose $\mathcal{S}$ is a sequential algebra and $\ell$ is a function from $\mathbb{R}_\infty$ to $\mathcal{S}$. Then $\ell$ is an *infinitary measure* on $\mathcal{S}$ if the following conditions hold for all $r, s \in \mathbb{R}_\infty$:

1. **Uniqueness:** (Each observation has at most one length)

$$r \neq s \quad \Rightarrow \quad (\ell = r) \cap (\ell = s) \;=\; \mathsf{O}$$

2. **Totality:** (Every observation has a length)

$$\bigcup_{r \in \mathbb{R}_\infty} (\ell = r) \;=\; U\,.$$

3. **Additivity:**

$$\begin{array}{ll} (\ell = r); (\ell = s) = (\ell = r + s) & \text{if } r < \infty \text{ or } s = 0 \\ (\ell = \infty); (\ell = s) = \mathsf{O} & \text{if } s > 0\,. \end{array}$$

Note that we allow observations to be infinite to the right only. We might admit observations that are also infinite to the left, but that would make the additivity axiom more complicated.

From a programmer's point of view, the second clause of the additivity postulate may seem strange. If a program $P$ takes infinite time, then one ought to have $P; Q = P$ for every $Q$. The simplest solution to this problem is to distinguish between the composition of specifications and the composition of programs. The former is modelled by the composition operator of sequential algebra, and the latter is defined in terms of the former by

$$P \cdot Q \;=_{df}\; (P \cap (\ell = \infty)) \;\cup\; P; Q\,.$$

Thus the underlying theory need not be changed. We will not pursue this issue further here.

**9.2 Loop Safety Revisited** In the examples of the previous sections (Unit Pulse, Tracker, and Gas Burner) we established refinements of the form

$$P^* \subseteq \boxplus\overline{Q}\,,$$

where $P$ is the body of a control loop. But since a control loop is supposed to run indefinitely we really ought to have proved

$$P^\infty \subseteq \boxplus\overline{Q}\,.$$

The following theorem shows that under certain mild conditions on $P$ and $Q$ the former claim implies the latter. It formalizes the well-known fact that finite observations suffice for establishing safety properties. If $P$ is an element of a measure algebra then we say that $P$ is

- *non-Zeno* if $P \subseteq (\ell > \epsilon)$ for some $\epsilon > 0$ ($P$ does not contain arbitrarily short time diagrams)
- *finite* if $UP \subseteq (\ell < \infty)$ ($P$ contains no time diagram whose right end point is infinity).

**9.3 Theorem (Finite Refutability of Safety Properties)** If $P$ is non-Zeno and $Q$ is finite then

$$P^\infty \subseteq \boxplus\overline{Q} \quad \Leftarrow \quad P^* \subseteq \boxplus\overline{Q}.$$

*Proof.*

$$
\begin{array}{ll}
& P^\infty \subseteq \boxplus\overline{Q} \\
\Leftrightarrow & \quad \{ \text{ Galois Connection } \} \\
& \ominus P^\infty \subseteq \overline{Q} \\
\Leftrightarrow & \quad \{ \ominus X = U\text{-};X;\text{-}U \} \\
& U\text{-};P^\infty;\text{-}U \subseteq \overline{Q} \\
\Leftarrow & \quad \{ \text{ See lemma below (local linearity is used here) } \} \\
& U\text{-};(P^\infty \cup P^*;\text{-}U) \subseteq \overline{Q} \\
\Leftrightarrow & \quad \{ \text{ Distributivity, } U\text{-};P^*;\text{-}U = \ominus P^* \} \\
& U\text{-};P^\infty \cup \ominus P^* \subseteq \overline{Q} \\
\Leftrightarrow & \quad \{ \text{ Universal property of } \cup \} \\
& U\text{-};P^\infty \subseteq \overline{Q} \ \wedge\ \ominus P^* \subseteq \overline{Q} \\
\Leftrightarrow & \quad \{ \text{ Exchange, Galois Connection } \} \\
& UQ \subseteq \overline{P^\infty} \ \wedge\ P^* \subseteq \boxplus\overline{Q} \\
\Leftrightarrow & \quad \{ \text{ Assumptions on } P \text{ and } Q \} \\
& P^* \subseteq \boxplus\overline{Q}.
\end{array}
$$

■

The following lemma, which is an interesting rule for calculating with infinite loops in its own right, is required to complete the proof of the previous theorem.

**9.4 Lemma** $P^\infty;\text{-}U \subseteq P^*;\text{-}U \cup P^\infty$.

*Proof.* First we establish a recursive inequation for $P^\infty;\text{-}U$.

$$
\begin{array}{ll}
& P^\infty;\text{-}U \\
= & \quad \{ \text{ Definition of } P^\infty \} \\
& (P;P^\infty);\text{-}U \\
= & \quad \{ \text{ Local linearity } \} \\
& P;\text{-}(U;\text{-}P^\infty) \cup P;(P^\infty;\text{-}U) \\
\subseteq & \\
& P;\text{-}U \cup P;(P^\infty;\text{-}U).
\end{array}
$$

Now we are ready for the main calculation:

$$
\begin{array}{ll}
& P^\infty;\text{-}U \\
\subseteq & \quad \{ \text{ Induction, using the above } \} \\
& \nu_X(P;\text{-}U \cup P;X) \\
= & \quad \{ \text{ Repetition rule 3.10 } \} \\
& P^*;(P;\text{-}U) \cup P^\infty
\end{array}
$$

$$
\begin{array}{ll}
\subseteq & \{\text{ Euclid }\} \\
& (P^*;P);\text{-}U \cup P^\infty \\
\subseteq & \{\ P^*;P \subseteq P^*\ \} \\
& P^*;\text{-}U \cup P^\infty .
\end{array}
$$

■

It is interesting to note that the finite refutability theorem depends on local linearity.

## References


1. C.A.R. Hoare and B. von Karger. Sequential calculus. *Information Processing Letters*, 53:123–130, 1995.
2. B. Dutertre. On first order interval temporal logic. Technical Report CSD-TR-94-3, Royal Holloway University of London, November 1994.
3. P. Jipsen and R. Maddux. Nonrepresentable sequential algebras. *Logic Journal of the IGPL*, 5(4):565–574, 1997.
4. B. Moszkowski. Some very compositional temporal properties. In E.-R. Olderog, editor, *Programming Concepts, Methods and Calculi*, volume A-56 of *IFIP Transactions*. North-Holland, 1994.
5. B. von Karger. Temporal algebra. Habilitation Thesis, available through WWW `http://www.informatik.uni-kiel.de/~bvk/`, 1996.
6. B. von Karger and R. Berghammer. A relational model for temporal logic. *Logic Journal of the IGPL*, 6(2):157–173, 1998.
7. C. Zhou, C. A. R. Hoare, and A. P. Ravn. A calculus of durations. *Information Processing Letters*, 40:269–276, 1992.

# Relation-Algebraic Derivation of Spanning Tree Algorithms

Rudolf Berghammer, Burghard von Karger, and Andreas Wolf

Institut für Informatik und Praktische Mathematik
Christian-Albrechts-Universität Kiel
Preusserstraße 1–9, D–24105 Kiel, Germany

**Abstract.** We use Tarski's relational algebra to derive a series of algorithms for computing spanning trees of undirected graphs, including a variant of Prim's minimum spanning tree algorithm.

## 1 Introduction

The relational calculus has been very successful in the derivation and proof of algorithms for directed graphs. We claim that it is equally suitable for reasoning about undirected and even about weighted graphs. To prove our point we derive a series of increasingly powerful spanning tree algorithms which culminates in a variant of Prim's well-known algorithm for computing a spanning tree with minimal weight.

Directed graphs and relations are essentially the same, but there are (at least) two natural ways of representing undirected graphs as relations. The first possibility are symmetric relations on vertices, also known as *adjacence relations*. This representation has the advantage of simplicity; it is well suited for calculations. Alternatively we can use *incidence relations* between the set of edges and the set of vertices. Incidence relations are harder to calculate with but they are more easily generalized to multigraphs and weighted graphs. The two representations are linked by a Galois connection. Thus, we can derive a spanning tree algorithm for adjacence relations in the calculus of symmetric relations and then transform it into an algorithm for incidence relations, which can then be further refined into a minimum spanning tree algorithm.

The remainder of this paper is organized as follows. In Sec. 2 we derive a spanning tree algorithm for adjacency relations. Then in Sec. 3 we show how a Galois connection may be used for data reification. This procedure is instantiated in Sec. 4 to produce a spanning tree algorithm for incidence relations which in Sec. 5 is refined to a minimum spanning tree algorithm. Sec. 6 gives the proofs of various facts used in the derivations. In the appendix we explain how our programs can be implemented in the relational toolbox RelView.

## 2 Adjacence Relations

Given a connected (undirected) graph $G$, we are asked to compute a subgraph $T$ of $G$ with the following properties:

1. $T$ is connected and cycle-free ($T$ is a tree).
2. Every vertex of $G$ is also a vertex of $T$ ($T$ *spans* $G$).

Let us assume that $G$ is given as an *adjacence relation*, that is an irreflexive and symmetric relation on a set $V$ (the set of vertices), and that the output $T$ is required in the same format. Representing graphs as relations facilitates the *implementation* of algorithms, because relations can be encoded efficiently as Boolean matrices, linked lists, or binary decision diagrams. It also facilitates the *design* of algorithms, because relations are the objects of a concise algebraic calculus (which was formalized in 1941 by Tarski, see also [11, 4]). To advantage ourselves of these twin benefits let us translate the problem specification into the language of relations. We start with a couple of definitions that fix the notation and introduce some basic properties.

**Definition 1 (Relational Operators and Constants)** *We consider binary relations on the fixed set $V$. The largest and the smallest such relation are written as $\mathsf{L}$ and $\mathsf{O}$, respectively. Since we work in the fixed universe $V \times V$, every relation $R$ has a complement $\overline{R}$. The composition of two relations is denoted $RS$, and $R^{\cup}$ is the converse of $R$. The diagonal relation, which is the unit of composition, is written as $\mathsf{I}$. And, finally, $R^*$ is the transitive and reflexive closure of $R$.*

**Definition 2 (Properties of Relations)** *A relation $R$ is called* symmetric *if $R^{\cup} = R$,* asymmetric *if $R \cap R^{\cup} = \mathsf{O}$,* antisymmetric *if $R \cap R^{\cup} = \mathsf{I}$,* irreflexive *if $\mathsf{I} \cap R = \mathsf{O}$,* connected *if $R \neq \mathsf{O}$ and $R\mathsf{L}R \subseteq R^*$,* one-step-connected *if $R \neq \mathsf{O}$ and $R\mathsf{L}R \subseteq \mathsf{I} \cup R$.*

**Definition 3 (Symmetric Relations)** *For any $R \subseteq V \times V$ let $Symm(R)$ denote the set of all irreflexive and symmetric subrelations of $R$; this is a complete atomistic Boolean algebra. If $R, S \in Symm(\mathsf{L})$ we say that $R$* spans *$S$ if $R \subseteq S$ and $R\mathsf{L} = S\mathsf{L}$.*

**Definition 4 (Atoms and Edges)** *If $\mathcal{L}$ is a lattice and $R \in \mathcal{L}$ then $atoms_{\mathcal{L}}(R)$ denotes the set of atoms (minimal non-zero elements) that are below $R$. In particular, for $R \in Symm(\mathsf{L})$ the elements of $edges(R) =_{df} atoms_{Symm(L)}(R)$ are called its* edges.

In other words, edges are relations of the specific form $\{(v, w), (w, v)\}$ for distinct vertices $v$ and $w$. Note that every non-empty element of $Symm(\mathsf{L})$ contains at least one edge.

**Definition 5 (Bridges and Cycles)** *If $R \in Symm(\mathsf{L})$ and $e$ is an edge then $R$* bridges *$e$ if $e \subseteq R^*$. A relation $R \in Symm(\mathsf{L})$ is said to be* cycle-free *if no $e \in edges(R)$ is bridged by $R \cap \overline{e}$.*

Now assume that $G \in Symm(\mathsf{L})$ is connected. Our task is to discover a program $\pi$ that establishes the postcondition

$$T \text{ is connected and cycle-free} \wedge T \in Symm(G) \wedge T \text{ spans } G. \qquad (1)$$

If (1) holds then $T$ is called a *spanning tree* of $G$. It is, of course, understood that $G$ is the input of $\pi$ so that $\pi$ may not assign to $G$. The obvious candidate for an invariant property is

$$T \text{ is connected and cycle-free} \wedge T \in \mathit{Symm}(G)\,. \tag{2}$$

The following lemma shows that we can establish invariant (2) by assigning an arbitrary element of $\mathit{edges}(G)$ to $T$ (using the generalized assignment of the refinement calculus [9]).

**Lemma 6** *Edges are cycle-free and one-step-connected.*

We can now guess the following program outline:

$T :\in \mathit{edges}(G)$;
$\{\, T \text{ is connected and cycle-free} \wedge T \in \mathit{Symm}(G) \,\}$
`while` ... **do**
  $e :\in \mathit{edges}(G \cap \ldots)$;
  $T := T \cup e$
  $\{\, T \text{ is connected and cycle-free} \wedge T \in \mathit{Symm}(G) \,\}$
**od**
$\{\, T \text{ is a spanning tree of } G \,\}$

An annotated program, such as the above, is defined to be correct if every possible run through it satisfies all of the assertions. We assume that the reader is familiar with the proof rules for establishing correctness and also with the most elementary correctness-preserving transformations [5, 6]. The following lemma suggests a choice for the edge to be added in each iteration of the loop. Its proof is given in Sec. 6 (Lemmata 16 and 19).

**Lemma 7** *Let* $T \in \mathit{Symm}(\mathsf{L})$. *Then we have:*

1. *If* $T$ *is connected and* $x \in \mathit{edges}(T\mathsf{L} \cup \mathsf{L}T)$ *then* $T \cup x$ *is connected.*
2. *If* $T$ *is cycle-free and* $x \in \mathit{edges}(\overline{T\mathsf{L}} \cup \overline{\mathsf{L}T})$ *then* $T \cup x$ *is cycle-free.*

Thus, connectedness and cycle-freeness of $T$ can be preserved simultaneously by adding an edge in $(T\mathsf{L} \cup \mathsf{L}T) \cap (\overline{T\mathsf{L}} \cup \overline{\mathsf{L}T})$ This is precisely the *symmetric difference* of $T\mathsf{L}$ and $\mathsf{L}T$ and we will denote it $T\mathsf{L}\ \mathit{xor}\ \mathsf{L}T$. In order to pick an edge from $G \cap (T\mathsf{L}\ \mathit{xor}\ \mathsf{L}T)$, we must check that this relation is irreflexive, symmetric and non-empty. The first two properties follow immediately from the corresponding properties of $G$ and $T$. To ensure non-emptiness, we take it as the guard of the loop. Thus, we have proved correctness of the following program:

$T :\in \mathit{edge}(G)$;
`while` $G \cap (T\mathsf{L}\ \mathit{xor}\ \mathsf{L}T) \neq \mathsf{O}$ **do**
  $e :\in \mathit{edges}(G \cap (T\mathsf{L}\ \mathit{xor}\ \mathsf{L}T))$;
  $T := T \cup e$
**od**
$\{\, T \text{ is a spanning tree of } G \,\}$

Note that $T\mathsf{L}\ xor\ \mathsf{L}T \subseteq \overline{T\mathsf{L}} \cup \overline{\mathsf{L}T} \subseteq \overline{T}$, so that $T$ increases strictly. Since $T$ is bounded by $G$, termination is ensured (provided, of course, that $G$ is finite). The following lemma shows that invariant (2) and the exit condition of the previous program imply the required postcondition. For a proof see Lemma 20 in Sec. 6.

**Lemma 8** *Let $S, T \in Symm(\mathsf{L})$ such that $S$ is connected and $\mathsf{O} \neq T \subseteq S$. Then $(T\mathsf{L}\ xor\ \mathsf{L}T) \subseteq \overline{S}$ if and only if $\mathsf{L}S = \mathsf{L}T$ (i.e. $T$ spans $S$).*

Besides establishing the postcondition, this lemma permits us to simplify the exit condition. Thus, we have arrived at program

```
T :∈ edges(G);
while LG ≠ LT do
    e :∈ edges(G ∩ (TL xor LT));
    T := T ∪ e;                                  (3)
od
{ T is a spanning tree of G }
```

for computing a spanning tree $T$ of an adjacence relation $G$.

## 3 Changing the Representation

We ultimately aim at a minimum spanning tree algorithm for weighted graphs. Since a weight is a mapping on edges, it will be convenient to represent a graph as a set of edges, rather than a relation on vertices. The new representation may be isomorphic to the old one, but it does mean a change of data structure and consequently a substantial program modification. Moreover, there are many different ways of storing a set in a computer. To retain flexibility and avoid bias towards a specific implementation we will not commit ourselves to a fixed representation yet. Instead we will work in an arbitrary complete and atomistic lattice $\mathcal{E}$ that is linked to $Symm(G)$ by two mappings

$$\Delta : Symm(G) \to \mathcal{E} \qquad\qquad \Gamma : \mathcal{E} \to Symm(G)\,.$$

We require that $\Delta$ is an *embedding* (an injective mapping that distributes over arbitrary joins and meets) and that $\Gamma$ is its *lower adjoint* in the sense that $\Delta(\Gamma(p)) \supseteq p$ and $\Gamma(\Delta(R)) = R$ for every $p \in \mathcal{E}$ and $R \in Symm(G)$. The following lemma lists two simple consequences of these postulates for later use.

**Lemma 9** *1. Suppose that $e$ is an edge. Then $\Delta(e) \neq \mathsf{O}$ and $e = \Gamma(x)$ for every $x \in atoms_{\mathcal{E}}(\Delta(e))$.*
*2. Suppose $q$ is an atom of $r \in \mathcal{E}$. Then there is an edge $e$ of $\Gamma(r)$ such that $q \in atoms_{\mathcal{E}}(\Delta(e))$.*

Let $\mathsf{L}_{\mathcal{E}}$ denote the greatest element of $\mathcal{E}$. Then $\Delta(G) = \mathsf{L}_{\mathcal{E}}$ and $\Gamma(\mathsf{L}_{\mathcal{E}}) = G$. We will say that $p \in \mathcal{E}$ is a spanning tree of $\mathcal{E}$ if $\Gamma(p)$ is a spanning tree of $\Gamma(\mathsf{L}_{\mathcal{E}})$ in the sense defined by postcondition (1). Assume that $\Gamma(\mathsf{L}_{\mathcal{E}})$ is connected. Then we know from the previous section that the following program is correct:

```
G := Γ(L_E);
T :∈ edges(G);
p :∈ E;
while LG ≠ LT do
    e :∈ edges(G ∩ (TL xor LT));
    T := T ∪ e
od
{ Γ(p) = T  ⇒  p is a spanning tree of E }
```

We can eliminate the first assignment by replacing $G$ with $\Gamma(\mathsf{L}_{\mathcal{E}})$ throughout the rest of the program. To eliminate the antecedent from the postcondition we introduce the additional invariant $\Gamma(p) = T$, which we establish by refining the random assignment $p :\in \mathcal{E}$ and maintain by inserting an appropriate assignment to $p$. This is safe because $p$ is never used and we obtain the following program:

```
T :∈ edges(Γ(L_E));
p :∈ atoms_E(Δ(T));
{ Γ(p) = T }
while LΓ(L_E) ≠ LT do
    e :∈ edges(Γ(L_E) ∩ (TL xor LT));
    q :∈ atoms_E(Δ(e));
    T, p := T ∪ e, p ∪ q
    { Γ(p) = T }
od
{ p is a spanning tree of E }
```

The correctness of the first assertion follows from Lemma 9.1. To see that the parallel assignment to $T$ and $p$ preserves the new invariant we note that the assignment to $q$ establishes $e = \Gamma(q)$ (again by Lemma 9.1), whence we have $\Gamma(p \cup q) = \Gamma(p) \cup \Gamma(q) = T \cup e$. Now we can use the invariant to eliminate $T$ from all expressions. After that, $T$ becomes garbage, and all assignments to $T$ may be dropped. This results in the following program:

```
e :∈ edges(Γ(L_E));
p :∈ atoms_E(Δ(e));
while LΓ(L_E) ≠ LΓ(p) do
    e :∈ edges(Γ(L_E) ∩ (Γ(p)L xor LΓ(p)));
    q :∈ atoms_E(Δ(e));
    p := p ∪ q
od
{ p is a spanning tree of E }
```

By Lemma 9.2 a program piece of the form $e :\in \mathit{edges}(\Gamma(r))\,;\, q :\in \mathit{atoms}_{\mathcal{E}}(\Delta(e))$ can be refined to $e :\in \mathit{edges}(\Gamma(r))\,;\, q :\in \mathit{atoms}_{\mathcal{E}}(r)$. This transformation can be applied directly to the initialization. In order to exploit it also for the body of the loop we assume that we are given a mapping $f : \mathcal{E} \to \mathcal{E}$ with

$$\Gamma(\mathsf{L}_\mathcal{E}) \cap (\Gamma(p)\mathsf{L} \; xor \; \mathsf{L}\Gamma(p)) = \Gamma(f(p)) \,. \tag{4}$$

After applying the refinement, both assignments to $e$ can be scratched and the following program for computing a spanning tree $p$ of $\mathcal{E}$ remains:

$$\begin{array}{l} p :\in atoms_\mathcal{E}(\mathsf{L}_\mathcal{E}); \\ \mathtt{while}\ \mathsf{L}\Gamma(\mathsf{L}_\mathcal{E}) \neq \mathsf{L}\Gamma(p)\ \mathtt{do} \\ \quad t :\in atoms_\mathcal{E}(f(p)); \\ \quad p := p \cup t \\ \mathbf{od} \\ \{\ p \text{ is a spanning tree of } \mathcal{E}\ \} \end{array} \tag{5}$$

## 4 Incidence Structures and Multigraphs

We will now instantiate program (5) derived in the previous section by choosing a particular embedding $\Delta$, and exhibiting a mapping $f$ that satisfies (4). We thus obtain our third program, this time for a graph that is given as an incidence structure. In the next section, a further refinement will yield a minimum spanning tree algorithm for weighted graphs.

**Definition 10** *1. An* incidence structure $(V, E, M)$ *consists of a set* $V$ *(the vertices), a set* $E$ *(the edges), and an incidence relation* $M \subseteq E \times V$.

*2. The incidence structure* $(V, E, M)$ *is called a* multigraph *if we can write* $M = f \cup g$ *where* $f$ *and* $g$ *are disjoint functions in the relational sense*[1] *(i.e. every edge coincides with exactly two vertices).*

*3. The multigraph* $(V, E, M)$ *is a (proper)* graph *if,* $fg^\cup$ *is antisymmetric (i.e. no pair of vertices is connected by multiple edges).*

With every incidence structure $(V, E, M)$ we can associate an *adjacence* relation $G$ via $G =_{df} MM^\cup \cap \bar{\mathsf{I}}$ which is an irreflexive and symmetric relation on vertices. Now let $\mathcal{E} =_{df} \{p \subseteq E \times V \mid p\mathsf{L} = p\}$. Each $p \in \mathcal{E}$ represents a set of edges, which can be obtained by projecting $p$ to its first component. The required link between $\mathcal{E}$ and $Symm(G)$ is given by following mappings:

$$\begin{aligned} \Gamma(p) &= \{(x, y) \mid x \neq y \wedge \exists e \in E : (e, x), (e, y) \in M \cap p\} \\ &= (M \cap p)^\cup (M \cap p) \cap \bar{\mathsf{I}} \\ \Delta(R) &= \{e \mid \exists (x, y) \in R \,.\, (e, x), (e, y) \in M\} \times V \\ &= (\mathsf{I} \cap MRM^\cup)\mathsf{L}_\mathcal{E} \,. \end{aligned}$$

The following lemma states that $\Gamma$ and $\Delta$ do indeed enjoy the properties required for the derivation in the previous section. For its proof see Lemmata 26 through 29 in Sec. 6.

[1] We distinguish "meta level" mappings from the relation-algebraic (or: object level) notion of a function. A relation $f$ is a *function* if $f^\cup f \subseteq \mathsf{I}$ and $\mathsf{I} \subseteq ff^\cup$.

**Lemma 11** *1. If $(V, E, M)$ is a multigraph then $\Delta$ is an embedding and $\Gamma$ is its lower adjoint.*
*2. If $(V, E, M)$ is a proper graph then $\Delta$ is an isomorphism and $\Gamma$ is its inverse.*

Let us start with the case where $(V, E, M)$ is a proper graph. In this case, a spanning tree of $(V, E, M)$ is defined to be an element $p \in \mathcal{E}$ such that (1) is satisfied with $T = \Gamma(p)$ and $G = \Gamma(\mathsf{L}_{\mathcal{E}})$. The next lemma yields a mapping $f : \mathcal{E} \to \mathcal{E}$ that satisfies the condition (4). For a proof see Lemma 30 in Sec. 6.

**Lemma 12** $\Gamma(\mathsf{L}_{\mathcal{E}}) \cap (\Gamma(p)\mathsf{L}\ \mathit{xor}\ \mathsf{L}\Gamma(p)) = \Gamma(MM^{\cup}p \cap M\overline{M^{\cup}p})$ .

The mapping $\Gamma$ still occurs in the exit condition of (5). The following lemma allows us to eliminate $\Gamma$ completely from the entire program. For the proof see Lemma 22 in Sec. 6.

**Lemma 13** $\Gamma(p)\mathsf{L} = M^{\cup}p$ *and* $\mathsf{L}\Gamma(p) = p^{\cup}M$ .

Thus, we have derived the following program for computing a spanning tree of a proper graph $(V, E, M)$:

$$
\begin{array}{l}
p :\in \mathit{atoms}_{\mathcal{E}}(\mathsf{L}_{\mathcal{E}});\\
\texttt{while}\ \mathsf{L}_{\mathcal{E}}{}^{\cup}M \neq p^{\cup}M\ \texttt{do}\\
\quad t :\in \mathit{atoms}_{\mathcal{E}}(MM^{\cup}p \cap M\overline{M^{\cup}p});\\
\quad p := p \cup t\\
\texttt{od};\\
\{\ p \text{ is a spanning tree of } (V, E, M)\ \}
\end{array}
\qquad (6)
$$

This program does, in fact, also work for multigraphs. The only addition to the proof we need to make is to adapt the definition of a spanning tree: We must add the constraint that $p$ does not contain any double edges in the sense that $\Gamma(x) = \Gamma(y)$ implies $x = y$ for all $x, y \in \mathit{atoms}_{\mathcal{E}}(p)$. We leave it to the reader to check that this is an invariant of the above program.

## 5 Weighted Graphs

Let $(V, E, M)$ be a (proper) graph and assume that a weight $w(e) \in \mathbf{R}_{\geq 0}$ is assigned to every edge $e \in \mathit{atoms}_{\mathcal{E}}(\mathsf{L}_{\mathcal{E}})$. We are asked to compute a minimum spanning tree (i.e. one for which the sum of the weights of its edges is minimal). To reuse program (6) we have to strengthen its invariant. At the very least, we must require that after each cycle the tree computed so far is *contained* in a minimum spanning tree.

There are two points in program (6) where an edge is picked non-deterministically. It seems reasonable always to select the lightest edge available. Therefore, assume that we have at our disposal a mapping *least* : $\mathcal{E} \to \mathcal{E}$ that satisfies, for all elements $p \in \mathcal{E}$, the following implication:

$$q \in \mathit{atoms}_{\mathcal{E}}(\mathit{least}(p)) \land r \in \mathit{atoms}_{\mathcal{E}}(p) \quad \Rightarrow \quad w(q) \leq w(r)\,. \qquad (7)$$

Then the following lemma shows that the choice of the lightest edge will indeed establish and then preserve the desired invariant. This is a non-trivial fact and a proof in terms of points and paths can be found in [7], Theorems 4.3.1 through 4.3.3. We will give a point-free proof; see Lemmata 32 and 33 of Sec. 6.

**Lemma 14** *1. If $t \in atoms_{\mathcal{E}}(least(\mathsf{L}_{\mathcal{E}}))$ then $t$ is contained in a minimum spanning tree.*
*2. If $p$ is contained in a minimum spanning tree then $p \cup t$ is contained in a minimum spanning tree for all $t \in atoms_{\mathcal{E}}(least(MM^{\cup}p \cap M\overline{M^{\cup}p}))$.*

Thus, the following program is correct:

$$
\begin{array}{l}
p :\in atoms_{\mathcal{E}}(least(\mathsf{L}_{\mathcal{E}}));\\
\mathtt{while}\ \mathsf{L}_{\mathcal{E}}{}^{\cup}M \neq p^{\cup}M\ \mathtt{do}\\
\quad t :\in atoms_{\mathcal{E}}(least(MM^{\cup}p \cap M\overline{M^{\cup}p}));\\
\quad p := p \cup t\\
\quad \mathtt{od};\\
\{\ p \text{ is a minimum spanning tree of } (V,E,M) \text{ wrt. to } w\ \}
\end{array}
\tag{8}
$$

We still need to replace the implicit definition (7) of *least* with a closed relational expression. Let $W$ be the pre-order that $w$ induces on $E$. If $\rho$ is the order on real numbers and $w$ is conceived as function in the relational sense then $W$ can be defined by the formula $W =_{df} w\rho w^{\cup}$. The relational expression describing the set of all minimal elements of a set $p$ wrt a preorder $W$ is well-known (see [11]):

**Lemma 15** *If we define $least(p) =_{df} p \cap \overline{\overline{W}p}$ then (7) holds for every $p \in \mathcal{E}$.*

This completes the development of a minimum spanning tree algorithm. In the next section we will use Tarski's relational calculus for rigorously proving the lemmata used in its derivation. Before we do that, let us make some remarks on complexity. Assume $m$ and $n$ to be the number of edges resp. vertices of $(V,E,M)$. If we use the standard Boolean matrix implementation of relations and their operations then program (8) runs in time $O(m^2 * n)$. However, if we implement relations by successor lists and compute the set of edges described by $MM^{\cup}p \cap M\overline{M^{\cup}p}$ (i.e., the "neighbour edges" of the tree constructed so far) incrementally, then a refinement with quadratic run time complexity can be obtained. This program is a variant of Prim's spanning tree algorithm [10] which relies on a similar optimization.

# 6 Relation-Algebraic Proofs

We believe that programs should be proved even more rigorously than most other mathematical theorems. For one thing, programming errors can be costly. Also program correctnes proofs do not tend to be read by many people, so that the social process of eliminating errors works less well than in general mathematics. Ideally, program proofs are conducted in a formal calculus where each step can be checked mechanically.

The calculus of annotated programs is one such framework. We have used it quite informally here, because this is a scientific paper and not a program documentation. In real life, the development should be performed within a proof assistant which relieves the programmer from the burden of copying the entire program at each transformation step while generating the proof obligations that must be discharged for its justification. These proof obligations are the various lemmata scattered throughout the preceding sections. Their nature varies greatly with the problem domain and it is not likely that a general-purpose theory will always be adequate for their treatment.

The data in our programs are relations and graphs. These structures are the objects of another formal calculus, known as the algebra of relations [11, 4]. Unlike the calculus of annotated programs, relational algebra is well-suited to rigorous pen-and-paper reasoning[2]. Therefore, it can (and should) be used for giving precise proofs of graph-theoretical statements, even in a scientific paper.

### 6.1 Relational Algebra

We have already described the operators and constants of relational algebra in Sec. 2. In the following, we collect some basic facts on relations. Their proofs are straight-forward set-theoretic arguments. Alternatively, they may be derived from Tarski's axiomatization of relations, but then some of them require, in addition, the so-called Point Axiom. This can't be avoided, because our programs rely on being able to pick an element from any non-empty set.

- Composition is associative, monotonic, has identity $\mathsf{I}$ and is $\cup$-distributive.
- Transposition distributes over all Boolean operators. Moreover, we have $R^{\cup\cup} = R$ and $(RS)^{\cup} = S^{\cup}R^{\cup}$.
- Schröder equivalences: $PQ \subseteq \overline{R} \;\Leftrightarrow\; P^{\cup}R \subseteq \overline{Q} \;\Leftrightarrow\; RQ^{\cup} \subseteq \overline{P}$.
- Dedekind laws: $P \cap QR \subseteq Q(Q^{\cup}P \cap R)$ and $P \cap QR \subseteq (PR^{\cup} \cap Q)R$.
- Tarski's rule: If $R \neq \mathsf{O}$ then $\mathsf{L}R\mathsf{L} = \mathsf{L}$.
- Distributivity of functions: If $f$ is a function then $f(R \cap S) = fR \cap fS$ and $(R \cap S)f^{\cup} = Rf^{\cup} \cap Sf^{\cup}$.
- Dedekind laws for functions: If $f$ is a function then $f^{\cup}(R \cap fS) = f^{\cup}R \cap S$ and $(R \cap Sf^{\cup})f = Rf \cap S$.
- Identity transposition rule: $\mathsf{I} \cap R = \mathsf{I} \cap R^{\cup}$.
- Tail recursion rule: If $T \subseteq X$ and $XS \subseteq X$ then $TS^* \subseteq X$.
- If the relation $R \in \mathit{Symm}(L)$ is cycle-free then $A^* \cap B^* = (A \cap B)^*$ for all $A, B \in \mathit{Symm}(R)$.
- Star decomposition rule: If $R$ is one-step-connected then $(S \cup R)^* = S^* \cup S^*RS^*$.
- Singling out rows: If $a\mathsf{L} = a$ then $(a \cap R)S = a \cap RS$.
- Rectangle rule: $a \cap b^{\cup} = ab^{\cup}$ provided $a\mathsf{L} = a$ and $b\mathsf{L} = b$.

[2] This does not mean that relation-algebraic proofs cannot or should not be developed or checked with computer assistance. In fact, there exists an excellent tool for doing just that [3].

- Vector[3] identity rules: If $a\mathsf{L} = a$ then $(R \cap a^{\cup}) = R(\mathsf{I} \cap a)$. Conversely, if $b \subseteq \mathsf{I}$ then $Rb = R \cap (b\mathsf{L})^{\cup}$.
- Vector negation rule: If $a\mathsf{L} = a$ then also $\overline{a}\mathsf{L} = \overline{a}$.
- Vector associativity rule: If $a\mathsf{L} = a$ then $(R \cap a^{\cup})S = R(S \cap a)$.

## 6.2 Adjacence Relations

The purpose of this section is to present the proofs of Sec. 2.

**Lemma 16** *If $T \in Symm(\mathsf{L})$ is connected and $x \in edges(T\mathsf{L} \cup \mathsf{L}T)$ then $T \cup x$ is connected.*

*Proof.*

$$
\begin{array}{ll}
 & T \cup x \text{ is connected} \\
\Leftrightarrow & \quad \{\text{Definition 2}\} \\
 & (T \cup x)\mathsf{L}(T \cup x) \subseteq (T \cup x)^* \\
\Leftrightarrow & \quad \{\text{Distributivity, connectedness of } T \text{ and } x\} \\
 & T\mathsf{L}x \cup x\mathsf{L}T \subseteq (T \cup x)^* \\
\Leftrightarrow & \quad \{x, T, \text{ and } \mathsf{L} \text{ are symmetric}\} \\
 & T\mathsf{L}x \subseteq (T \cup x)^* \\
\Leftrightarrow & \quad \{x = (x \cap T\mathsf{L}) \cup (x \cap \mathsf{L}T), \text{ distributivity}\} \\
 & T\mathsf{L}(x \cap \mathsf{L}T) \cup T\mathsf{L}(x \cap T\mathsf{L}) \subseteq (T \cup x)^* \\
\Leftrightarrow & \quad \{T\mathsf{L}(x \cap \mathsf{L}T) \subseteq T\mathsf{L}T \subseteq T^* \text{ since } T \text{ is connected}\} \\
 & T\mathsf{L}(x \cap T\mathsf{L}) \subseteq (T \cup x)^* \\
\Leftarrow & \quad \{\text{Vector associativity rule, } (T\mathsf{L})^{\cup} = \mathsf{L}T\} \\
 & T\mathsf{L}Tx \subseteq (T \cup x)^* \\
\Leftrightarrow & \quad \{T \text{ is connected}\} \\
 & \mathit{true}.
\end{array}
$$

■

**Lemma 17 (Bridge Exchange)** *Assume that $S \in Symm(\mathsf{L})$ bridges neither of the edges $x$ and $y$. Then $S \cup x$ bridges $y$ if and only if $S \cup y$ bridges $x$.*

*Proof.*

$$
\begin{array}{ll}
 & S \cup x \text{ bridges } y \\
\Leftrightarrow & \quad \{\text{Definition 5}\} \\
 & y \subseteq (S \cup x)^* \\
\Leftrightarrow & \quad \{y \text{ is an edge and } (S \cup x)^* \text{ is symmetric}\} \\
 & y \cap (S \cup x)^* \neq \mathsf{O} \\
\Leftrightarrow & \quad \{\text{Star decomposition, edges are one-step-connected}\} \\
 & y \cap (S^* \cup S^*xS^*) \neq \mathsf{O} \\
\Leftrightarrow & \quad \{S \text{ does not bridge } y, \text{ so } y \cap S^* = \mathsf{O}\} \\
 & y \cap S^*xS^* \neq \mathsf{O}
\end{array}
$$

[3] A relation $R$ is called a *vector* if $R\mathsf{L} = R$.

$\Leftrightarrow$ {Schröder equivalences (twice)}

$S^{*\cup} y S^{*\cup} \cap x \neq \mathsf{O}$

$\Leftrightarrow$ {$S$ is symmetric}

$S^* y S^* \cap x \neq \mathsf{O}$

$\Leftrightarrow$ {Reverse first four steps}

$S \cup y$ bridges $x$. ■

**Lemma 18** *Assume that $T \in Symm(\mathsf{L})$ is cycle-free and that $x$ is an edge which is not bridged by $T$. Then $T \cup x$ is cycle-free.*

*Proof.* Let $y \in edges(T \cup x)$; we have to show that $(T \cup x) \cap \overline{y}$ does not bridge $y$. We may assume that $y \neq x$. Since $x$ and $y$ are edges, it follows that $x \cap y = \mathsf{O}$ whence $y \subseteq T$. Let $S =_{df} T \cap \overline{y}$. Since $x$ is not bridged by $T$ and $T = S \cup y$ the bridge exchange lemma implies that $y$ is not bridged by $S \cup x$. ■

**Lemma 19** *Assume that $T \in Symm(\mathsf{L})$ is cycle-free and $x \in edges(\overline{T\mathsf{L}} \cup \overline{\mathsf{L}T})$. Then $T \cup x$ is cycle-free.*

*Proof.* We note that $T$ does not bridge $x$ for otherwise we get $x \subseteq \bar{\mathsf{I}} \cap T^* \subseteq TT^* \subseteq T\mathsf{L} \cap \mathsf{L}T$, contrary to assumption. Now Lemma 18 applies. ■

**Lemma 20** *Let $S, T \in Symm(\mathsf{L})$ such that $S$ is connected and $\mathsf{O} \neq T \subseteq S$. Then $(T\mathsf{L}\ xor\ \mathsf{L}T) \subseteq \overline{S}$ if and only if $\mathsf{L}S = \mathsf{L}T$.*

*Proof.* The implication from right to left is very easy, and we leave it to the reader. For the other implication, assume that $(T\mathsf{L}\ xor\ \mathsf{L}T) \subseteq \overline{S}$. We start with

$\mathsf{L}TS$

$\subseteq$ {$TS = TS \cap \mathsf{L}$, Dedekind law}

$\mathsf{L}T(S \cap T^{\cup}\mathsf{L})$

$\subseteq$ {Symmetry of $T$ and $S \subseteq \overline{T\mathsf{L}\ xor\ \mathsf{L}T} \subseteq \overline{T\mathsf{L}} \cup \mathsf{L}T$}

$\mathsf{L}T\mathsf{L}T$

$\subseteq$

$\mathsf{L}T$.

as auxiliary result. Since $T \subseteq S$ the following calculation completes the proof:

$\mathsf{L}S$

$=$ {Tarski's Rule, $TT \neq \mathsf{O}$ as $T \neq \mathsf{O}$ symmetric}

$\mathsf{L}TT\mathsf{L}S$

$\subseteq$ {$T \subseteq S$}

$\mathsf{L}TS\mathsf{L}S$

$\subseteq$ {$S$ is connected}

$\mathsf{L}TS^*$

$\subseteq$ {$TS^* \subseteq \mathsf{L}T$ by auxiliary result and tail recursion}

$\mathsf{L}T$. ■

## 6.3 Incidence Structures and Multigraphs

In the following, we assume that $(V, E, M)$ is a multigraph. Then $M = f \cup g$ where $f$ and $g$ are disjoint functions from $E$ to $V$. We let the variables $p$ and $q$ range over $\mathcal{E} = \{r \subseteq E \times V \mid r\mathsf{L} = r\}$. They can be thought of as denoting sets of edges.

**Lemma 21** $\Gamma(p) = (f \cap p)^{\cup} g \cup (g \cap p)^{\cup} f = f^{\cup}(\mathsf{I} \cap p) g \cup g^{\cup}(\mathsf{I} \cap p) f\,.$

*Proof.*

$$\begin{aligned}
& \Gamma(p) \\
= \quad & \{\text{Definition of } \Gamma\text{, vector associativity}\} \\
& \bar{\mathsf{I}} \cap (M \cap p)^{\cup} M \\
= \quad & \{M = f \cup g\text{, distributivity}\} \\
& \bar{\mathsf{I}} \cap ((f \cap p)^{\cup} f \cup (f \cap p)^{\cup} g \cup (g \cap p)^{\cup} f \cup (g \cap p)^{\cup} g) \\
= \quad & \{f^{\cup} f \subseteq \mathsf{I} \text{ and } g^{\cup} g \subseteq \mathsf{I} \text{ since } f \text{ and } g \text{ are a functions}\} \\
& \bar{\mathsf{I}} \cap ((f \cap p)^{\cup} g \cup (g \cap p)^{\cup} f) \\
= \quad & \{f^{\cup} g \subseteq \bar{\mathsf{I}} \text{ and } g^{\cup} f \subseteq \bar{\mathsf{I}} \text{ since } f, g \text{ are disjoint (Schröder)}\} \\
& (f \cap p)^{\cup} g \cup (g \cap p)^{\cup} f \\
= \quad & \{\text{Vector identity rule}\} \\
& f^{\cup}(\mathsf{I} \cap p) g \;\cup\; g^{\cup}(\mathsf{I} \cap p) f\,.
\end{aligned}$$

∎

**Lemma 22** *$M^{\cup} p = \Gamma(p)\mathsf{L}$ and $p^{\cup} M = \mathsf{L}\Gamma(p)$.*

*Proof.* Since $\Gamma(p)$ is symmetric, these equations are equivalent and we only show the first one.

$$\begin{aligned}
& M^{\cup} p \\
= \quad & \{M = f \cup g\text{, distributivity}\} \\
& f^{\cup} p \cup g^{\cup} p \\
= \quad & \{\text{Vector associativity}\} \\
& (f \cap p)^{\cup} \mathsf{L} \cup (g \cap p)^{\cup} \mathsf{L} \\
= \quad & \{f\mathsf{L} = \mathsf{L} \text{ and } g\mathsf{L} = \mathsf{L} \text{ since } f \text{ and } g \text{ are total}\} \\
& (f \cap p)^{\cup} g\mathsf{L} \cup (g \cap p)^{\cup} f\mathsf{L} \\
= \quad & \{\text{Distributivity, Lemma 21}\} \\
& \Gamma(p)\mathsf{L}\,.
\end{aligned}$$

∎

**Lemma 23** *Let $a \subseteq V \times V$ with $a\mathsf{L} = a$. Then $\Gamma(Ma) = (a \cup a^{\cup}) \cap \Gamma(\mathsf{L}_{\mathcal{E}})$.*

*Proof.*

$$\begin{aligned}
& \Gamma(Ma) \\
= \quad & \{\text{Lemma 21}\} \\
& (f \cap Ma)^{\cup} g \;\cup\; (g \cap Ma)^{\cup} f \\
= \quad & \{M = f \cup g\text{, distributivity}\} \\
& (f \cap fa)^{\cup} g \;\cup\; (g \cap fa)^{\cup} f \;\cup\; (f \cap ga)^{\cup} g \;\cup\; (g \cap ga)^{\cup} f
\end{aligned}$$

$$
\begin{aligned}
= &\quad \{\text{Distributivity of functions}\}\\
&(f(\mathsf{I}\cap a))^{\cup}g \,\cup\, (g\cap fa)^{\cup}f \,\cup\, (f\cap ga)^{\cup}g \,\cup\, (g(\mathsf{I}\cap a))^{\cup}f\\
= &\quad \{\text{Distributivity of transposition}\}\\
&(\mathsf{I}\cap a)f^{\cup}g \,\cup\, (g^{\cup}\cap a^{\cup}f^{\cup})f \,\cup\, (f^{\cup}\cap a^{\cup}g^{\cup})g \,\cup\, (\mathsf{I}\cap a)g^{\cup}f\\
= &\quad \{\text{Singling out rows, Dedekind law of functions}\}\\
&(a\cap f^{\cup}g) \,\cup\, (g^{\cup}f\cap a^{\cup}) \,\cup\, (f^{\cup}g\cap a^{\cup}) \,\cup\, (a\cap g^{\cup}f)\\
= &\quad \{\text{Boolean algebra}\}\\
&(a\cup a^{\cup}) \,\cap\, (f^{\cup}g\cup g^{\cup}f)\\
= &\quad \{\text{Lemma 21}\}\\
&(a\cup a^{\cup}) \,\cap\, \Gamma^{\cup}(\mathsf{L}_{\mathcal{E}})\,.
\end{aligned}
$$

■

**Lemma 24** *Let $a, b \subseteq V \times V$ with $a\mathsf{L} = a$ and $b\mathsf{L} = b$. Then we have the distributivity property $\Gamma(Ma) \cap \Gamma(Mb) = \Gamma(Ma \cap Mb)$.*

*Proof.* The inclusion from right to left follows from the fact that $\Gamma$ is monotonic. By Lemma 23 the other inclusion equivales

$$\Gamma(\mathsf{L}_{\mathcal{E}}) \cap (a \cup a^{\cup}) \cap (b \cup b^{\cup}) \;\subseteq\; \Gamma(Ma \cap Mb)\,.$$

Since every relation in the image of $\Gamma$ is symmetric it is sufficient to prove

$$\Gamma(\mathsf{L}_{\mathcal{E}}) \cap a \cap b \;\subseteq\; \Gamma(Ma \cap Mb)$$

and

$$\Gamma(\mathsf{L}_{\mathcal{E}}) \cap a \cap b^{\cup} \;\subseteq\; \Gamma(Ma \cap Mb)\,.$$

The first of these two inclusions is immediate from Lemma 23 (with $a \cap b$ in place of $a$) and monotonicity; the following calculation yields the second one:

$$
\begin{aligned}
&a\cap b^{\cup}\cap\Gamma(\mathsf{L}_{\mathcal{E}})\\
= &\quad \{\text{Rectangle rule, definition of } \Gamma\}\\
&ab^{\cup}\cap M^{\cup}M\cap\overline{\mathsf{I}}\\
\subseteq &\quad \{\text{Dedekind laws (twice)}\}\\
&M^{\cup}(Mab^{\cup}M^{\cup}\cap\mathsf{I})M\cap\overline{\mathsf{I}}\\
= &\quad \{\text{Rectangle rule}\}\\
&M^{\cup}(Ma\cap(Mb)^{\cup}\cap\mathsf{I})M\cap\overline{\mathsf{I}}\\
= &\quad \{\text{Identity transposition rule}\}\\
&M^{\cup}(Ma\cap Mb\cap\mathsf{I})M\cap\overline{\mathsf{I}}\\
= &\quad \{\text{Vector identity rule}\}\\
&(M\cap Ma\cap Mb)^{\cup}M\cap\overline{\mathsf{I}}\\
= &\quad \{\text{Definition of } \Gamma\}\\
&\Gamma(Ma\cap Mb)\,.
\end{aligned}
$$

■

**Lemma 25** *If $R \in Symm(G)$ then $\Delta(R) = (\mathsf{I} \cap fRg^{\cup})\mathsf{L}_{\mathcal{E}}$.*

*Proof.* By definition, we have $\Delta(R) = (\mathsf{I} \cap MRM^{\cup})\mathsf{L}_{\mathcal{E}}$. Next we substitute $f \cup g$ for the relation $M$ and multiply out. Then two of the four resulting terms vanish, e.g. $\mathsf{I} \cap fRf^{\cup} \subseteq f(f^{\cup}f \cap R)f^{\cup} \subseteq f(\mathsf{I} \cap R)f^{\cup} = \mathsf{O}$. The remaining two terms are equal, because of the identity transposition rule. ∎

**Lemma 26** *The mapping $\Delta : Symm(G) \to \mathcal{E}$ distributes over all meets and joins.*

*Proof.* By the previous lemma we have

$$\Delta = (x \mapsto (\mathsf{I} \cap x)\mathsf{L}_{\mathcal{E}}) \circ (x \mapsto fx) \circ (x \mapsto xg^{\cup})$$

and each of the three mappings on the right hand side distributes over all meets and joins (recall that $f$ and $g$ are functions). ∎

**Lemma 27** *$\Delta(\Gamma(p)) \supseteq p$ for every $p \in \mathcal{E}$.*

*Proof.*

$$\begin{aligned}
& \Delta(\Gamma(p)) \\
= \quad & \{\text{Lemma 25}\} \\
& (\mathsf{I} \cap f\Gamma(p)g^{\cup})\mathsf{L}_{\mathcal{E}} \\
\supseteq \quad & \{\text{Lemma 21}\} \\
& (\mathsf{I} \cap ff^{\cup}(\mathsf{I} \cap p)gg^{\cup})\mathsf{L}_{\mathcal{E}} \\
\supseteq \quad & \{ff^{\cup} \supseteq \mathsf{I} \text{ and } gg^{\cup} \supseteq \mathsf{I} \text{ because } f \text{ and } g \text{ are functions}\} \\
& (\mathsf{I} \cap p)\mathsf{L}_{\mathcal{E}} \\
= \quad & \{\text{Vector identity rule}\} \\
& p\,.
\end{aligned}$$

∎

**Lemma 28** *$\Gamma(\Delta(R)) = R$ for every $R \in Symm(\Gamma(\mathsf{L}_{\mathcal{E}}))$.*

*Proof.*

$$\begin{aligned}
& \Gamma(\Delta(R)) \\
= \quad & \{\text{Lemma 21}\} \\
& f^{\cup}(\mathsf{I} \cap \Delta(R))g \cup g^{\cup}(\mathsf{I} \cap \Delta(R))f \\
= \quad & \{\text{Lemma 25}\} \\
& f^{\cup}(\mathsf{I} \cap fRg^{\cup})g \cup g^{\cup}(\mathsf{I} \cap gRf^{\cup})f \\
= \quad & \{\text{Dedekind law for functions}\} \\
& f^{\cup}(g \cap fR) \cup g^{\cup}(f \cap gR) \\
= \quad & \{\text{Dedekind law for functions}\} \\
& (f^{\cup}g \cap R) \cup (g^{\cup}f \cap R) \\
= \quad & \{\text{Lemma 21, distributivity}\} \\
& R \cap \Gamma(\mathsf{L}_{\mathcal{E}}) \\
= \quad & \{R \in Symm(\Gamma(\mathsf{L}_{\mathcal{E}}))\} \\
& R\,.
\end{aligned}$$

∎

**Lemma 29** *If* $(V, E, M)$ *is a graph then* $\Delta(\Gamma(p)) \subseteq p$.

*Proof.* Before we start with the main calculation we show that $R(p \cup \mathsf{I})R \cap \mathsf{I} \subseteq p$ for every antisymmetric relation $R$:

$$
\begin{array}{ll}
 & R(p \cup \mathsf{I})R \cap \mathsf{I} \\
\subseteq & \quad \{\text{Use Dedekind to factor out } (p \cup \mathsf{I})R\} \\
 & (R \cap ((p \cap \mathsf{I})R)^{\cup})\,(p \cup \mathsf{I})\,R \\
\subseteq & \quad \{\text{Monotonicity}\} \\
 & (R \cap R^{\cup})p\mathsf{L} \\
\subseteq & \quad \{R \text{ is antisymmetric, } p\mathsf{L} = p\} \\
 & p\,.
\end{array}
$$

In the following calculation the above result is used with $R = fg^{\cup}$ (which is antisymmetric by Def. 10).

$$
\begin{array}{ll}
 & \Delta(\Gamma(p)) \\
= & \quad \{\text{Lemma 25}\} \\
 & (\mathsf{I} \cap f\Gamma(p)g^{\cup})\mathsf{L}_{\mathcal{E}} \\
= & \quad \{\text{Lemma 21, distributivity}\} \\
 & (\mathsf{I} \cap (ff^{\cup}(p \cap \mathsf{I})gg^{\cup})\mathsf{L}_{\mathcal{E}} \;\cup\; (\mathsf{I} \cap (fg^{\cup}(p \cap \mathsf{I})fg^{\cup}))\mathsf{L}_{\mathcal{E}} \\
\subseteq & \quad \{ff^{\cup} \subseteq \mathsf{I} \text{ and } gg^{\cup} \subseteq \mathsf{I} \text{ and auxiliary result}\} \\
 & (\mathsf{I} \cap p)\mathsf{L}_{\mathcal{E}} \\
\subseteq & \quad \{\text{Vector identity law}\} \\
 & p\,.
\end{array}
$$

■

**Lemma 30** *Let* $a =_{df} \Gamma(p)\mathsf{L}$. *Then* $\Gamma(\mathsf{L}_{\mathcal{E}}) \cap (a \mathbin{xor} a^{\cup}) = \Gamma(MM^{\cup}p \cap M\overline{M^{\cup}p})$.

*Proof.*

$$
\begin{array}{ll}
 & \Gamma(\mathsf{L}_{\mathcal{E}}) \cap (a \mathbin{xor} a^{\cup}) \\
= & \quad \{\text{Definition of } xor\} \\
 & \Gamma(\mathsf{L}_{\mathcal{E}}) \cap (a \cup a^{\cup}) \cap (\overline{a} \cup \overline{a}^{\cup}) \\
= & \quad \{\text{Lemma 23 (note that } \overline{a}\mathsf{L} = \overline{a} \text{ by vector negation)}\} \\
 & \Gamma(Ma) \cap \Gamma(M\overline{a}) \\
= & \quad \{\text{Lemma 24}\} \\
 & \Gamma(Ma \cap M\overline{a}) \\
= & \quad \{\text{Lemma 22}\} \\
 & \Gamma(MM^{\cup}p \cap M\overline{M^{\cup}p})\,.
\end{array}
$$

■

## 6.4 Weighted Graphs

Assume that $\mathsf{L} = V \times V$ is finite and that $T \in \mathit{Symm}(\mathsf{L})$ is cycle-free. Then the transitive-reflexive closure operator is a universally conjunctive mapping from $\mathit{Symm}(T)$ to the lattice of all subrelations of $T^*$. It follows that we can define a lower adjoint, i.e. a mapping that maps each $S \subseteq T^*$ to some $S^{[T]} \in Symm(T)$ such that the following Galois connection holds:

$$S \subseteq R^* \quad \Leftrightarrow \quad S^{[T]} \subseteq R \quad \text{for all } S \subseteq T^* \text{ and } R \in Symm(T)\,. \qquad (9)$$

An element $x$ of a basis of a vector space may be replaced with a different vector $y$ provided $x$ is needed for expressing $y$ as a linear combination of basis vectors. Similarly, an element $x$ of a spanning tree may be replaced with $y$ if $y$ is needed for bridging $p$:

**Lemma 31 (Edge Replacement)** *Suppose that $Q$ is a spanning tree of $G$ and let $x \in edges(G)$. If $y \in edges(x^{[Q]})$ then $(Q \cap \overline{y}) \cup x$ is a spanning tree of $G$.*

*Proof.* For convenience, let $S = Q \cap \overline{y}$. We have assumed that $y \subseteq x^{[Q]}$, so $x^{[Q]} \not\subseteq Q \cap \overline{y}$ and the Galois connection (9) yields $x \not\subseteq S^*$. In other words, $S$ does not bridge $x$, and Lemma 18 implies that $S \cup x$ is cycle-free. Moreover, the bridge exchange lemma tells us that $S \cup x$ bridges $y$. It follows that $Q^* = (S \cup x)^*$ and we conclude that $S \cup x$ is, indeed, a spanning tree. ∎

For the rest of the section we assume that $(V, E, M)$ is a proper graph with adjacency relation $G$. Then $\Gamma : \mathcal{E} \to Symm(G)$ is an isomorphism and $\Delta$ is its inverse (see the definitions in Sec. 4 and Lemma 11). Moreover, a weight mapping $w$ and a mapping *least* satisfying (7) are assumed to be given.

**Lemma 32** *If $t \in atoms_{\mathcal{E}}(least(\mathsf{L}_{\mathcal{E}}))$ then $t$ is contained in a minimum spanning tree.*

*Proof.* Let $q$ be a spanning tree of $\mathcal{E}$ and let $G =_{df} \Gamma(\mathsf{L}_{\mathcal{E}})$, $Q =_{df} \Gamma(q)$ and $x =_{df} \Gamma(t)$. Since $\Gamma$ is an isomorphism, $x$ is an edge. Moreover $Q$ is a spanning tree of $G$ and therefore bridges $x$. Thus, we may pick $y \in edges(x^{[Q]})$. Since $\Gamma$ is an isomorphism, we have $y = \Gamma(s)$ for some $s \in atoms_{\mathcal{E}}(q)$. By the edge replacement lemma, $(Q \cap \overline{y}) \cup x$ is another spanning tree of $G$ and it follows that $(q \cap \overline{s}) \cup t$ is a spanning tree of $\mathcal{E}$. By (7) we have $w(t) \leq w(s)$ so this new spanning tree is also minimal. ∎

**Lemma 33** *Assume that $p$ is contained in a minimum spanning tree $q$ and that $t \in atoms_{\mathcal{E}}(least(MM^{\cup}p \cap \overline{MM^{\cup}p}))$. Then also $p \cup t$ is contained in a minimum spanning tree.*

*Proof.* Let $P =_{df} \Gamma(p)$, $G =_{df} \Gamma(\mathsf{L}_{\mathcal{E}})$, $Q =_{df} \Gamma(q)$ and $x =_{df} \Gamma(t)$. Since $\Gamma$ maps atoms to edges, Lemma 30 implies $x \in edges(G \cap (P\mathsf{L} \; xor \; \mathsf{L}P))$. Let $R =_{df} x^{[Q]}$, so that $x \subseteq R^*$ by the Galois connection (9). Define

$$R_1 =_{df} R \cap (P\mathsf{L} \cup \mathsf{L}P) \qquad R_2 =_{df} R \cap (\overline{P\mathsf{L}} \cup \overline{\mathsf{L}P})\,.$$

Obviously, $R = R_1 \cup R_2$. We claim that $R_1 \cap R_2 \neq \mathsf{O}$. Assume false. Then

$$R_1 R_2 \subseteq (R \cap \overline{R_2})(R \cap \overline{R_1}) \subseteq \mathsf{L}P\overline{P\mathsf{L}} = \mathsf{O}$$

and, similarly, $R_2R_1 = \mathsf{O}$, whence

$$x \subseteq R^* = (R_1 \cup R_2)^* = R_1^* \cup R_2^* .$$

But $x$ is an edge and $R_1$ and $R_2$ are symmmetric, so $x \subseteq R_1^*$ or $x \subseteq R_2^*$. Now the Galois connection (9) implies $x^{[Q]} \subseteq R_1$ or $x^{[Q]} \subseteq R_2$. Since $R = x^{[Q]}$ and $R_1 \cap R_2 = \mathsf{O}$ it follows that $R_1 = \mathsf{O}$ or $R_2 = \mathsf{O}$. But if, say, $R_1 = \mathsf{O}$ then

$$x \subseteq (R^* \cap \bar{\mathsf{I}}) \cap (P\mathsf{L} \cup \mathsf{L}P) = \mathsf{O} ,$$

and a similar contradiction follows from $R_2 = \mathsf{O}$.

Thus, we have established $R_1 \cap R_2 \neq \mathsf{O}$. Now let $y \in edges(R_1 \cap R_2)$. Then we have that $y \neq x$ and $y \in edges(G \cap (P\mathsf{L}\ xor\ \mathsf{L}P))$. By the edge replacement lemma, $(Q \cap \overline{y}) \cup x$ is a spanning tree of $G$ wich contains $P \cup x$. Just like in the previous proof we take $s \in atoms_{\mathcal{E}}(q)$ with $\Gamma(s) = y$ and it follows that $(q \cap \overline{s}) \cup t$ is a minimum spanning tree of $\mathcal{E}$ which contains $p \cup t$. ∎

## 7 Discussion

The length of our proofs may seem somewhat out of proportion with the difficulty of our results, and it is legitimate to question the adequacy of the relational method for deriving graph-theoretic algorithms. For one thing, the higher level of rigorousness imposed by the relational calculus has required us to explicitly prove a number of statements which the graphical intuition of the mathematician would have dismissed as obvious. But if you look through the proofs you will also find that many of the calculations deal with the properties of the Galois correspondence between incidence and adjacence relations. These results are not specific to spanning trees and should therefore be reusable. The present article is a first attempt at using relational algebra to develop algorithms on undirected and weighted graphs and we expect subsequent work to be more efficient.

There is another approach to the computation of spanning trees, which uses matroids rather than relations. It is based on the observation that the set of all cycle-free subgraphs of a graph forms a matroid (a family of sets that is closed under formation of subsets and satisfies a condition analogous to the well-known Steinitz exchange theorem for linearly independent subsets of a vector space). A spanning tree is a maximal element of this matroid. To find a spanning tree, start with $T$ being the empty set of edges and repeatedly add edges to $T$ while maintaining the invariant that $T$ is an element of the matroid (i.e. $T$ is a forest). Like ours, this scheme generalizes to weighted graphs; it leads to Kruskal's well-known algorithm for computing a minimum spanning tree [8].

It is worth noting that both Prim's and Kruskal's algorithm are "greedy" in the sense that each iteration of the loop adds exactly an edge to the tree resp. forest that will preserve the invariant. Unlike Prim's algorithm, Kruskal's algorithm does not maintain connectedness. When $T$ is represented as a relation the lack of connectedness makes it harder to find an edge whose addition will preserve the invariant. Kruskal solved this problem by introducing a special data structure for representing forests, but that is a different story.

*Acknowledgements* We thank J. Ravelo for discussions on the proof of the bridge exchange lemma and also acknowledge the contribution of the anonymous referees.

## References

1. Berghammer R., Schmidt G.: RELVIEW – A computer system for the manipulation of relations. In: Nivat M., et al. (eds.): Proc. AMAST '93, Workshops in Computing, Springer Verlag, 405-406 (1993)
2. Berghammer R., von Karger B., Ulke C.: Relation-algebraic analysis of Petri nets with RELVIEW. In: Margaria T., Steffen B. (eds.): Proc. TACAS '96, LNCS 1055, Springer Verlag, 49-69 (1996)
3. Hattensperger, C.: Computer-aided proofs in relational algebras (in German). Dissertation, Faculty of Computer Science, University of German Forces Munich (1997)
4. Brink C., Kahl W., Schmidt G. (eds.): Relational methods in computer science. Advances in Computing Science, Springer Verlag (1997)
5. Dijkstra E.W.: A discipline of programming. Prentice-Hall (1976)
6. Gries D.: The science of computer programming. Springer Verlag (1981)
7. Jungnickel D.: Graphen, Netzwerke und Algorithmen. BI Wissenschaftsverlag, 3rd ed. (1994)
8. Kruskal J.B.: On the shortest spanning subtree of a graph and the travelling salesman problem. Proc. AMS 7, 48-50 (1956)
9. Morgan C., Vickers T. (eds.): On the refinement calculus. Springer Verlag (1994)
10. Prim R.C.: Shortest connection networks and some generalizations. Bell Syst. Tech. J. 36, 1389-1401 (1957)
11. Schmidt G., Ströhlein T.: Relations and graphs. Discrete Mathematics for Computer Scientists, EATCS Monographs on Theoretical Computer Science, Springer Verlag (1993)

# Appendix: Implementation

Relational algebra has a fixed and surprisingly small set of operations which – in the case of finite carrier sets – can be implemented very efficiently using Boolean arrays, predecessor resp. successor lists, or binary decision diagrams, for example. At Kiel University we have developed a visual computer system for calculating with relations, called RelView [1, 2]. It is written in the C programming language and makes full use of the X-windows graphical user interface. For more information on the RelView system, see the Web page http://www.informatik.uni-kiel.de/~progsys/relview.html.

The main purpose of RelView is the evaluation of relational terms which are constructed from the relations of its workspace using pre-defined operations and tests, user-defined relational mappings, and user-defined relational programs. A RelView program is much like a function procedure in Pascal or Modula 2, except that its basic data types are only relations. For example, our final program

(8) for computing a minimum spanning tree in RelView looks as follows:

```
Prim(M,W)
  DECL least(W,v) = -(-W*v);
       L, p, t
  BEG  L = L(M);
       p = point(least(W,L));
       WHILE -eq(L^*M,p^*M) DO
         t = point(least(W,M*M^*p & M*-(M^*p)));
         p = p | t OD
       RETURN p
  END.
```

Let us now look at a concrete example. In RelView all data are modeled as binary relations, which can be visualized as Boolean matrices. The input consists of two such matrices, say **M** and **W**, where **M** is the incidence relation of $(V, E, M)$ with 14 vertices and 19 edges, and **W** is the pre-order $W \subseteq E \times E$ defined by the edge weights. RelView displays **M** and **W** as follows:

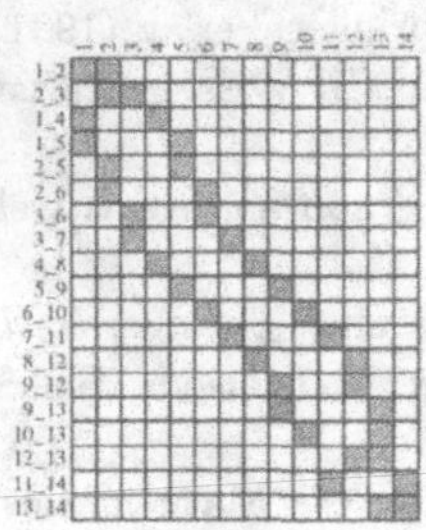

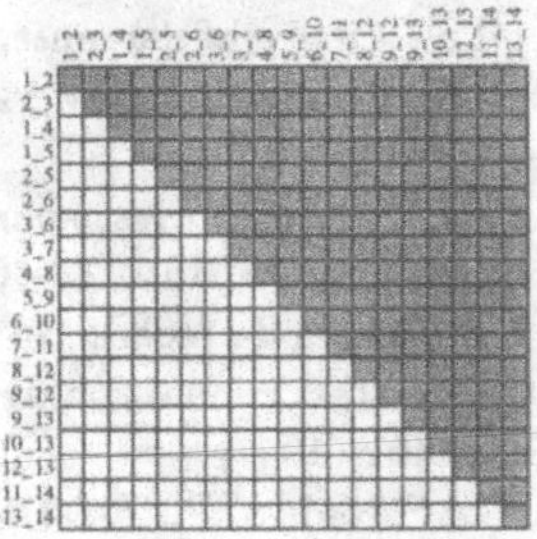

To increase legibility, we have instructed RelView to label the rows and columns of **M** and **W**. Vertices are simply numbered from 1 to 14, whereas each edge is labeled by the set of its vertices.

Next we ask RelView to evaluate the relational term **Prim(M,W)** and to put the edge labels on the rows of the result. On the relation window of the system we see the following $19 \times 14$ Boolean vector **p**. It represents a minimum spanning tree $p \subseteq E \times V$ of $(V, E, M)$ wrt. the pre-order $W$:

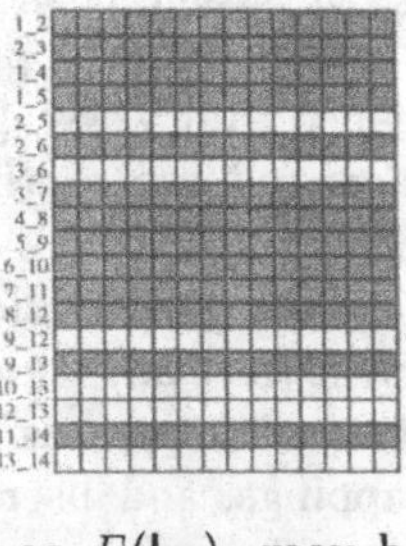

Homogeneous relations, such as $\Gamma(\mathsf{L}_\mathcal{E})$, may be visualized as directed graphs and RelView offers several sophisticated algorithms for drawing them nicely.

Moreover, a subrelation such as $\Gamma(p)$, may be visualized by printing its elements as bold arrows. To do this, we first ask RELVIEW to compute $G = \Gamma(\mathsf{L}_\mathcal{E}) \subseteq V \times V$ and $T = \Gamma(p) \subseteq V \times V$ according to the definition in Sec. 4. After adding the vertex labels to the rows and columns we obtain the following two $14 \times 14$ Boolean matrices **Gamma_G** and **Gamma_p** on the system's relation window:

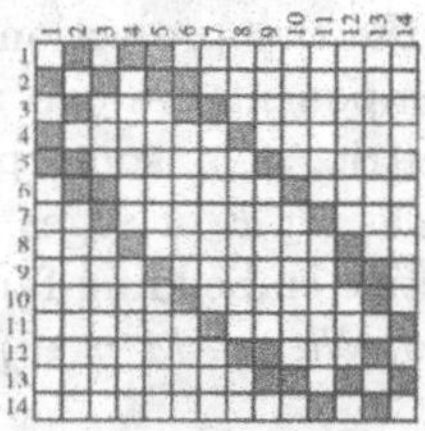

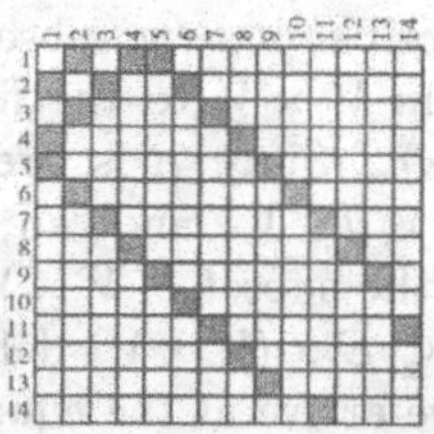

Then we ask the RELVIEW system to print the Boolean matrix **Gamma_G** as a graph while highlighting the subgraph corresponding to the matrix **Gamma_p**. The result is the following picture on the graph window of RELVIEW. It shows the graph that was given as input and a minimum spanning tree.

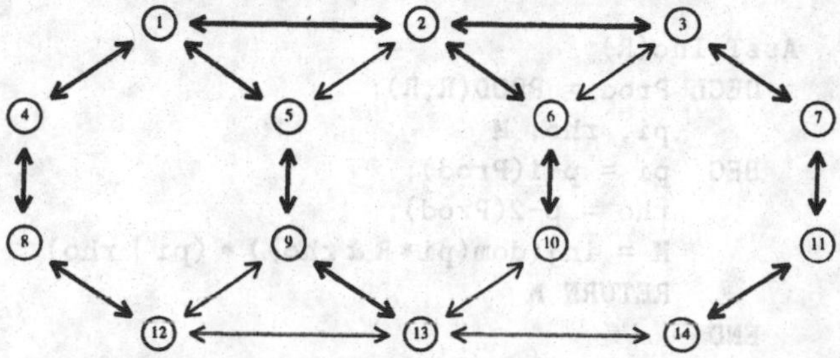

If we use the tree drawing algorithm of RELVIEW to draw the Boolean matrix **Gamma_p**, then we get the following picture:

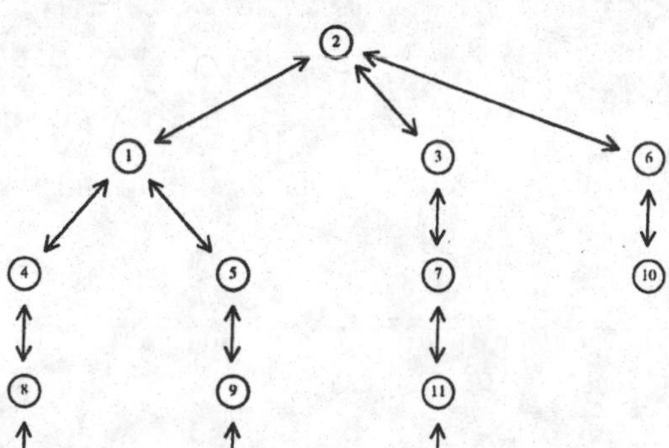

The graphical representation of relations lends itself to visual editing and the most intuitive way of inputting an adjacence relation is to draw its graph on

RELVIEW's graph window. In the following we discuss how an incidence relation can be computed from its adjacence relation, so that also incidence relations can be fed into the system as graphs.

So assume we are given an irreflexive and asymmetric relation $R \subseteq V \times V$. We will now construct a relational expression for the incidence relation $M$ of $(V, E, M)$ such that $M^{\mathsf{U}} M \cap \bar{\mathsf{I}} = R \cup R^{\mathsf{U}}$. First, we compute from $R$ a vector $v$ which describes it as a subset of $V \times V$. Using the two projection functions $\pi$ and $\rho$ from $V \times V$ to the first resp. second component, we can write $v$ as $v = (\pi R \cap \rho)\mathsf{L}$. Since $R$ is irreflexive and asymmetric, it is isomorphic to the set $\{\{x, y\} \mid x, y \in V\}$ and can, therefore, be taken as set $E$ of edges. With this choice, $E$ is the subset of $V \times V$ given by the injective embedding function (see [11]) $inj(v) \subseteq E \times (V \times V)$ defined by the vector $v$. We get $M = inj(v)(\pi \cup \rho)$ and, thus, we arrive at the equation

$$M = inj((\pi R \cap \rho)\mathsf{L})(\pi \cup \rho).$$

RELVIEW knows about product spaces and their projection functions. The computation of the injective embedding function from a given non-empty vector is also implemented. With the aid of these features we can write

```
AssToInc(R)
  DECL Prod = PROD(R,R);
       pi, rho, M
  BEG  pi = p-1(Prod);
       rho = p-2(Prod);
       M = inj(dom(pi*R & rho)) * (pi | rho)
       RETURN M
  END
```

as RELVIEW program for converting an adjacence relation $R$ into an incidence relation $M$.

# An Application of Program Derivation Techniques to 18th-Century Mathematics

**dedicated to Prof. Dr F.E.J. Kruseman Aretz**

A. Bijlsma

Department of Mathematics and Computing Science
Eindhoven University of Technology
P.O. Box 513, 5600 MB Eindhoven, The Netherlands
lexb@win.tue.nl

**Abstract.** Program derivation methodology is applied to reconstruct Euler's proof that every prime congruent to 1 modulo 4 is the sum of two squares.

## 1 Introduction

This note presents a derivation of one of the proofs given by Euler [4] of the famous theorem that every prime congruent to 1 modulo 4 is the sum of two squares—an observation commonly credited to Fermat but attributed to Girard [5] in [2]. The proof seems to be of methodological interest because it demonstrates that the techniques for program derivation developed by computing science have matured to a level where a proof that originally took many years to find may now be constructed with a minimum of invention. Incidentally, the proof also furnishes a counterexample to Dijkstra's remark [3] that all known methods of factorization are nonconstructive. (It does so because writing a prime as $x^2 + y^2$ is equivalent to factorizing it as $(x + i \cdot y) \cdot (x - i \cdot y)$ in $\mathbf{Z}[i]$.) Of course, this note does not provide any information on the way mathematics was actually done in the 18th century.

In what follows, we shall depart from established mathematical notation in one respect. The assertion that $x$ and $y$ differ by a multiple of $k$ will be written as

$$x =_k y$$

rather than

$$x \equiv y \pmod{k} \quad .$$

There are two reasons for this decision: the classical notation is too confusing in the presence of logical equivalence, and equational reasoning demands an infix operator for the equivalence relation involved. The use of an equality sign is acceptable since a weak form of Leibniz' rule is present: if $f$ is a polynomial over the integers,

$$x =_k y \Rightarrow f.x =_k f.y \tag{1}$$

for integer $x, y$ and positive integer $k$.

## 2 First approximation

We are looking for a constructive proof: given a prime $p$ with $p =_4 1$, we want to find $x, y$ such that

$$x^2 + y^2 = p \quad . \tag{2}$$

(It is not difficult to show [1] that (2) determines $x, y$ uniquely up to minus signs and interchanges, but we shall make no use of this.)

Our first approximation is produced by the most commonly used technique in program derivation: we replace a constant by a variable, and consider

$$P0: \quad x^2 + y^2 = k \cdot p$$

as invariant of a repetition to be constructed. The chosen constant is acceptable because is easy to see when $P0$ implies the desired postcondition (2), namely when $k = 1$; and because $P0$ is easily initialized, namely by

$$x,\ y,\ k := p,\ 0,\ p \quad .$$

Progress towards the postcondition will be made by decreasing $k$. In order to be able to take $k$ as the variant function, we strengthen the invariant by

$$P1: \quad k \geq 1 \quad .$$

## 3 Invariance of *P*0

To be able to guarantee invariance of $P0$ as $k$ is decreased, we need a method to transform a sum of two squares into a smaller one, while retaining the divisibility by $p$. Here our starting point is the observation that a sum of two squares constitutes the square of the absolute value of a complex number. This gives

$$\begin{array}{ll} & (x^2 + y^2) \cdot (u^2 + v^2) \\ = & \quad \{\text{introduce complex numbers}\} \\ & |x + i \cdot y|^2 \cdot |u + i \cdot v|^2 \\ = & \quad \{\text{distribution}\} \\ & |(x + i \cdot y) \cdot (u + i \cdot v)|^2 \\ = & \quad \{\text{multiplication}\} \\ & |(x \cdot u - y \cdot v) + i \cdot (x \cdot v + y \cdot u)|^2 \\ = & \quad \{\text{eliminate complex numbers}\} \\ & (x \cdot u - y \cdot v)^2 + (x \cdot v + y \cdot u)^2 \quad , \end{array}$$

so

$$(x^2 + y^2) \cdot (u^2 + v^2) = (x \cdot u - y \cdot v)^2 + (x \cdot v + y \cdot u)^2 \quad . \tag{3}$$

To number theorists, the occurrence of this identity does not come as a surprise: in fact, it constitutes the proof of the theorem that the set of sums of two squares is closed under multiplication, which logically and chronologically precedes Girard's theorem.

Inspired by (3), we investigate an assignment of the form

$$x,\ y := x\cdot u - y\cdot v,\ x\cdot v + y\cdot u \quad .$$

For any $k'$, we have

$$\begin{array}{ll} & P0(k,\ x,\ y := k',\ x\cdot u - y\cdot v,\ x\cdot v + y\cdot u) \\ \equiv & \quad \{\text{substitution}\} \\ & (x\cdot u - y\cdot v)^2 + (x\cdot v + y\cdot u)^2 = k'\cdot p \\ \equiv & \quad \{(3)\} \\ & (x^2+y^2)\cdot(u^2+v^2) = k'\cdot p \\ \equiv & \quad \{P0\} \\ & k\cdot p\cdot(u^2+v^2) = k'\cdot p \\ \equiv & \quad \{\} \\ & k' = k\cdot(u^2+v^2) \quad . \end{array}$$

We conclude that, for arbitrary $u, v$, predicate $P0$ is invariant under

$$k,\ x,\ y := k\cdot(u^2+v^2),\ x\cdot u - y\cdot v,\ x\cdot v + y\cdot u \quad .$$

Because this assignment must decrease $k$, we are led to the condition

$$u^2 + v^2 < 1 \quad . \tag{4}$$

Equation (4) does not have any interesting solutions in integers, since $u, v = 0, 0$ is hopeless in view of $P1$. However, there is no need for $u$ and $v$ to be integer: the derivation given above works equally well for rational $u$ and $v$, provided the expressions on the right hand side of the assignment are integers. Let us formalize this condition: putting $u = a/c$ and $v = b/c$, we find that the values assigned to $x, y, k$ are integers if

$$c \mid x\cdot a - y\cdot b \quad , \tag{5}$$
$$c \mid x\cdot b + y\cdot a \quad , \tag{6}$$
$$c^2 \mid k\cdot(a^2+b^2) \quad . \tag{7}$$

(The symbol | is pronounced as 'divides'.) In terms of $a, b, c$, equation (4) may be reformulated as

$$a^2 + b^2 < c^2 \quad . \tag{8}$$

To ensure invariance of $P0$ while decreasing $k$, it suffices to find a solution to (5) through (8) and then to perform the assignment

$$k,\ x,\ y := k\cdot(a^2+b^2)/c^2,\ (x\cdot a - y\cdot b)/c,\ (x\cdot b + y\cdot a)/c \quad .$$

First we look at (7). There, $c$ must not be chosen relatively prime to $k$: if it is, it follows that

$$\begin{array}{ll} & (7) \\ \equiv & \quad \{\} \end{array}$$

$$
\begin{array}{ll}
 & c^2 \mid k \cdot (a^2+b^2) \\
\equiv & \quad \{c \text{ and } k \text{ relatively prime}\} \\
 & c^2 \mid a^2+b^2 \\
\equiv & \quad \{(8)\} \\
 & a^2+b^2 = 0 \quad ,
\end{array}
$$

and we have already rejected this solution in view of $P1$. Hence $c$ and $k$ must have a nontrivial factor in common. But since we know nothing of the multiplicative structure of $k$, and indeed $k$ may well be prime, the obvious way to achieve this is to take $c = k$. With this choice, we have

$$
\begin{array}{ll}
 & (7) \\
\equiv & \quad \{c = k\} \\
 & k \mid a^2+b^2 \\
\equiv & \quad \{\} \\
 & a^2+b^2 =_k 0 \\
\equiv & \quad \{P0, \text{ as the only relevant information on } k \text{ we have}\} \\
 & a^2+b^2 =_k x^2+y^2 \\
\Leftarrow & \quad \{(1)\} \\
 & a =_k y \wedge b =_k x \quad .
\end{array}
$$

In the last line, we might equally well have decided to associate $a$ with $x$ and $b$ with $y$, as is suggested by the order of the alphabet. However, consideration of (5) shows why we have made the right choice.

$$
\begin{array}{ll}
 & (5) \\
\equiv & \quad \{c = k\} \\
 & k \mid x \cdot a - y \cdot b \\
\equiv & \quad \{\} \\
 & x \cdot a - y \cdot b =_k 0 \\
\equiv & \quad \{\} \\
 & x \cdot a - y \cdot b =_k x \cdot y - y \cdot x \\
\Leftarrow & \quad \{(1)\} \\
 & a =_k y \wedge b =_k x \quad .
\end{array}
$$

And we are in luck, for also

$$
\begin{array}{ll}
 & (6) \\
\equiv & \quad \{c = k\} \\
 & k \mid x \cdot b + y \cdot a \\
\equiv & \quad \{\} \\
 & x \cdot b + y \cdot a =_k 0 \\
\equiv & \quad \{P0\} \\
 & x \cdot b + y \cdot a =_k x^2+y^2 \\
\Leftarrow & \quad \{(1)\} \\
 & a =_k y \wedge b =_k x \quad .
\end{array}
$$

The choice $c = k$ thus allows us to dispense with (5) through (7), provided we take $a$ and $b$ such that $a =_k y$ and $b =_k x$. We are left with (8).

$$
\begin{array}{ll}
 & (8) \\
\equiv & \qquad \{c = k\} \\
 & a^2 + b^2 < k^2 \\
\Leftarrow & \qquad \{\text{dividing the obligation equally between } a \text{ and } b\} \\
 & |a| < k/\sqrt{2} \ \wedge \ |b| < k/\sqrt{2} \ .
\end{array}
$$

We conclude that equations (5) through (8) are satisfied if $a$ and $b$ are chosen such that

$$a =_k y \ \wedge \ |a| < k/\sqrt{2} \ , \tag{9}$$

$$b =_k x \ \wedge \ |b| < k/\sqrt{2} \ . \tag{10}$$

An explicit solution of (9) and (10) is easy to find: for instance, one of several solutions of (9) is given by

$$a = \begin{cases} y \bmod k & \text{if } y \bmod k < k/2 \ , \\ y \bmod k - k & \text{if } y \bmod k \geq k/2 \ . \end{cases}$$

However, we have no need for a definition that is any more specific than (9).

The conclusion of the preceding calculations may be formulated as follows: $k$ is decreased and $P0$ is kept invariant by the statements

$$
\begin{array}{l}
\ \ a: \ \ a =_k y \ \wedge \ |a| < k/\sqrt{2} \\
; b: \ \ b =_k x \ \wedge \ |b| < k/\sqrt{2} \\
; k, \ x, \ y := (a^2 + b^2)/k, \ (x \cdot a - y \cdot b)/k, \ (x \cdot b + y \cdot a)/k \ \ .
\end{array}
$$

## 4 Invariance of $P1$

For $a$ and $b$ chosen as in the preceding section, we have

$$k \mid a^2 + b^2 \ , \tag{11}$$

$$a =_k y \ \wedge \ b =_k x \ \ . \tag{12}$$

Under assumption of (11), (12), and (the repetition's guard) $k \neq 1$, we have

$$
\begin{array}{ll}
 & P1(k := (a^2 + b^2)/k) \\
\equiv & \qquad \{\text{substitution}\} \\
 & (a^2 + b^2)/k \geq 1 \\
\equiv & \qquad \{(11)\} \\
 & \neg(a^2 + b^2 = 0) \\
\equiv & \qquad \{\} \\
 & \neg(a = 0 \ \wedge \ b = 0) \\
\Leftarrow & \qquad \{(12)\} \\
 & \neg(k \mid x \ \wedge \ k \mid y) \\
\Leftarrow & \qquad \{\} \\
 & \neg(k^2 \mid x^2 + y^2) \\
\equiv & \qquad \{P0\}
\end{array}
$$

$$
\begin{array}{ll}
 & \neg(k^2 \mid k \cdot p) \\
\equiv & \qquad \{\} \\
 & \neg(k \mid p) \\
\Leftarrow & \qquad \{k \neq 1 \text{ and } p \text{ is prime}\} \\
 & k \neq p \ .
\end{array}
$$

Since it is very difficult to ensure invariance of $k \neq p$ under $k := (a^2 + b^2)/k$, we decide to strengthen the invariant of the repetition by

$$P2: \quad k < p \ .$$

As we have already shown $k$ to decrease in each iteration, invariance of $P2$ is trivial. However, the original initialization does not establish $P2$ and we are forced to replace it.

## 5 Initialization

The standard way to construct an initialization is to choose an 'easy' value, say 0 or 1, for one of the variables, and to calculate the corresponding values of the other variables. In the case under consideration, choosing $k = 1$ is useless, since that takes us back to the original postcondition. The problem being symmetric in $x$ and $y$, it suffices to consider start values for $y$.

Initialization of $P0..2$ with $y = 0$ turns out to be impossible, as the diligent reader can easily check. So we consider $y = 1$. This leads to

$$
\begin{array}{ll}
 & P0(y := 1) \\
\equiv & \qquad \{\text{substitution}\} \\
 & x^2 + 1 = k \cdot p \\
\equiv & \qquad \{\} \\
 & x^2 =_p -1 \ \wedge \ k = (x^2 + 1)/p \ .
\end{array}
$$

Hence $k := (x^2 + 1)/p$ establishes $P0(y := 1)$ provided $x$ is chosen such that $x^2 =_p -1$. This value of $k$ is obviously positive, so $P1$ is established as well. As to $P2$, we have

$$
\begin{array}{ll}
 & (k < p)(k := (x^2 + 1)/p) \\
\equiv & \qquad \{\text{substitution}\} \\
 & x^2 + 1 < p^2 \\
\Leftarrow & \qquad \{(p-1)^2 + 1 < p^2 \text{ since } p \geq 2\} \\
 & 1 \leq x < p \ .
\end{array}
$$

Our final proof obligation is the existence of an $x$ satisfying

$$1 \leq x < p \ \wedge \ x^2 =_p -1 \ . \tag{13}$$

Here our derivation could end, for it so happens that the existence of an $x$ satisfying (13) is a very famous theorem in number theory, known as the First

Supplement to the Law of Quadratic Reprocity. But for completeness' sake, we supply a proof—one that was originally devised by Lagrange [6].

When we look at the proof obligation (13), the property $(=_p\, -1)$ brings to mind *Wilson's theorem:* for prime $p$,

$$(p-1)! =_p -1 \quad . \tag{14}$$

(An easy proof can be found in, for instance, [1].) Taking Wilson's theorem as our point of departure, we have for odd $p$, with $n$ short for $(p-1)/2$,

$$\begin{array}{ll}
 & -1 \\
=_p & \quad \{(14)\} \\
 & (p-1)! \\
= & \quad \{\text{definition of factorial}\} \\
 & (\Pi\, j : 1 \leq j < p : j) \\
= & \quad \{\text{domain split}\} \\
 & (\Pi\, j : 1 \leq j \leq n : j) \cdot (\Pi\, j : n < j < p : j) \\
= & \quad \{\text{factorial} \parallel \text{dummy transformation } j := p - j\} \\
 & n! \cdot (\Pi\, j : 0 < j < p - n : p - j) \\
\doteq & \quad \{n = p - n - 1\} \\
 & n! \cdot (\Pi\, j : 1 \leq j \leq n : p - j) \\
=_p & \quad \{p - j =_p -j\} \\
 & n! \cdot (\Pi\, j : 1 \leq j \leq n : -j) \\
= & \quad \{\text{distribution of } - \text{ over } \Pi\} \\
 & n! \cdot (-1)^n \cdot (\Pi\, j : 1 \leq j \leq n : j) \\
= & \quad \{\text{factorial}\} \\
 & (-1)^n \cdot n!^2 \\
= & \quad \{\text{provided } p =_4 1\} \\
 & n!^2 \quad .
\end{array}$$

Notice that the last step in the derivation is the first time that the condition $p =_4 1$ plays a role.

We conclude that (13) is established by the assignment

$$x := ((p-1)/2)! \ \mathbf{mod}\ p$$

for $p$ a prime with $p =_4 1$. Inserting this into the algorithm, we obtain the following constructive proof:

$$\begin{array}{l}
\quad x := ((p-1)/2)! \ \mathbf{mod}\ p \\
\ ,\ k := (x^2 + 1)/p \\
\ ;\ y := 1 \\
\ ;\ \{\text{inv } P0 : \ x^2 + y^2 = k \cdot p \ \ , \\
\qquad\quad P1 : \ k \geq 1 \ \ , \\
\qquad\quad P2 : \ k < p \ \ ; \\
\quad\ \ \text{bd } k \\
\quad \} \\
\quad \mathbf{do}\ k \neq 1 \rightarrow a : \ a =_k y \wedge |a| < k/\sqrt{2}
\end{array}$$

$$; b: \quad b =_k x \wedge |b| < k/\sqrt{2}$$
$$; k, x, y := (a^2 + b^2)/k, (x \cdot a - y \cdot b)/k, (x \cdot b + y \cdot a)/k$$

**od** .

*Acknowledgement* The ETAC read a previous version of this note and suggested several improvements in the presentation.

## References

1. H. Davenport, *The higher arithmetic*, 6th ed. Cambridge University Press, 1992.
2. L.E. Dickson, *History of the theory of numbers*, vol. II. Carnegie Institute, Washington, 1919. Repr. Chelsea, New York, 1966.
3. E.W. Dijkstra, *A derivation of a proof by D. Zagier*. EWD1154, August 1993.
4. L. Euler, 'Novae demonstrationes circa resolutionem numerorum in quadrata'. *Acta Eruditorium Lipsiae* (1773), 193.
5. A. Girard (ed.), *L'Arithmétique de Simon Stevin*. Leiden, 1625.
6. J.L. Lagrange, 'Démonstration d'un théorème nouveau concernant les nombres premiers', *Nouv. Mém. Acad. Roy. Berlin* **2** (1773), 125–337.

# Nested Datatypes

Richard Bird[1] and Lambert Meertens[2]

[1] Programming Research Group, Oxford University
Wolfson Building, Parks Road, Oxford, OX1 3QD, UK
bird@comlab.ox.ac.uk
[2] CWI and Department of Computer Science, Utrecht University,
P.O. Box 94079, 1090 GB Amsterdam, The Netherlands
lambert@cwi.nl

**Abstract.** A nested datatype, also known as a *non-regular* datatype, is a parametrised datatype whose declaration involves different instances of the accompanying type parameters. Nested datatypes have been mostly ignored in functional programming until recently, but they are turning out to be both theoretically important and useful in practice. The aim of this paper is to suggest a functorial semantics for such datatypes, with an associated calculational theory that mirrors and extends the standard theory for regular datatypes. Though elegant and generic, the proposed approach appears more limited than one would like, and some of the limitations are discussed.

> Hark, by the bird's song ye may learn the nest.
> TENNYSON *The Marriage of Geraint*

## 1 Introduction

Consider the following three datatype definitions, all of which are legal Haskell declarations:

**data** *List a* = *NilL* | *ConsL* (*a*, *List a*)
**data** *Nest a* = *NilN* | *ConsN* (*a*, *Nest* (*a*, *a*))
**data** *Bush a* = *NilB* | *ConsB* (*a*, *Bush* (*Bush a*))

The first type, *List a*, describes the familiar type of cons-lists. Elements of the second type *Nest a* are like cons-lists, but the lists are not homogeneous: each step down the list, entries are "squared". For example, using brackets and commas instead of the constructors *NilN* and *ConsN*, one value of type *Nest Int* is

$$[7, (1,2), ((6,7),(7,4)), (((2,5),(7,1)),((3,8),(9,3)))]$$

This nest has four entries which, taken together, contain fifteen integers.

In the third type *Bush a*, at each step down the list, entries are "bushed". For example, one value of type *Bush Int* is

```
[4,
  [8, [5], [[3]]],
  [[7], [], [[[7]]]],
  [[[], [[0]]]]
]
```

This bush contains four entries, the first of which is an element of *Int*, the second an element of *Bush Int*, the third an element of *Bush* (*Bush Int*), and so on. In general, the $n$-th entry (counting from 0) of a list of type *Bush a* has type $Bush^n\ a$.

The datatype *List a* is an example of a so-called *regular* datatype, while *Nest a* and *Bush a* are examples of *non-regular* datatypes. Mycroft [17] calls such schemes *polymorphic recursions*. We prefer the term *nested* datatypes. In a regular datatype declaration, occurrences of the declared type on the right-hand side of the defining equation are restricted to copies of the left-hand side, so the recursion is "tail recursive". In a nested datatype declaration, occurrences of the datatype on the right-hand side appear with different instances of the accompanying type parameter(s), so the recursion is "nested".

In a language like Haskell or ML, with a Hindley-Milner type discipline, it is simply not possible to define all the useful functions one would like over a nested datatype, even though such datatype declarations are themselves perfectly legal. This remark applies even to recent extensions of such languages (in particular, Haskell 1.4), in which one is allowed to declare the types of problematic functions, and to use the type system for checking rather than inferring types. To be sure, a larger class of functions can now be defined, but one still cannot define important generic functions, such as *fold*, over nested types.

On the other hand, the most recent versions of Hugs and GHC (the Glasgow Haskell Compiler) both support so-called *rank-2* type signatures, in which one can universally quantify over type constructors as well as types (see [20]). By using such signatures one can construct most of the functions over nested datatypes that one wants. We will return to this point below. However, rank-2 type signatures are not yet part of standard Haskell.

The upshot of the current situation is that nested datatypes have been rather neglected in functional programming. However, they are conceptually important and evidence is emerging (e.g. [3, 18, 19]) of their usefulness in functional data structure design. A brief illustration of what they can offer is given in Section 2.

Regular datatypes, on the other hand, are the bread and butter of functional programming. Recent work on *polytypic* programming (e.g. [2, 9, 15]) has systematised the mathematics of program construction with regular datatypes by focusing on a small number of generic operators, such as *fold*, that can be defined for all such types. The basic idea, reviewed below, is to define a regular datatype as an initial object in a category of $F$-algebras for an appropriate functor $F$. Indeed, this idea appeared much earlier in the categorical literature, for instance in [10]. As a consequence, polytypic programs are parametrised by one or more regular functors. Different instances of these functors yield the concrete programs we know and love.

The main aim of this paper is to investigate what form an appropriate functorial semantics for nested datatypes might take, thereby putting more 'poly' into 'polytypic'. The most appealing idea is to replace first-order functors with higher-order functors over functor categories. In part, the calculational theory remains much the same. However, there are limitations with this approach, in that some expressive power seems to be lost, and some care is needed in order that the standard functorial semantics of regular datatypes may be recovered as a special case. It is important to note that we will not consider datatype declarations containing function spaces in this paper; see [6, 16] for ways of dealing with function spaces in datatype declarations.

## 2 An example

Let us begin with a small example to show the potential of nested datatypes. The example was suggested to us by Oege de Moor. In the De Bruijn notation for lambda expressions, bound variables introduced by lambda abstractions are represented by natural numbers. An occurrence of a number $n$ in an expression represents the bound variable introduced by the $n$-th nested lambda abstraction. For example, $\underline{0}\,(\underline{1}\,\underline{1})$ represents the lambda term

$$\lambda x.\lambda y.x\,(y\,y)$$

On the other hand, $\underline{0}\,(w\,\underline{1})$ represents the lambda term

$$\lambda x.\lambda y.x\,(w\,y)$$

in which $w$ is a free variable.

One way to capture this scheme is to use a nested datatype:

**data** *Term a* = *Var a* | *App* (*Term a*, *Term a*) | *Abs* (*Term* (*Bind a*))
**data** *Bind a* = *Zero* | *Succ a*

Elements of *Term a* are either free variables (of type *Var a*), applications, or abstractions. In an abstraction, the outermost bound variable is represented by *Var Zero*, the next by *Var* (*Succ Zero*), and so on. Free variables in an abstraction containing $n$ nested bindings have type $Var\,(Succ^n\,a)$. The type *Term a* is nested because *Bind a* appears as a parameter of *Term* on the right-hand side of the declaration.

For example, $\lambda x.\lambda y.x\,(w\,y)$ may be represented by the following term of type *Term Char*:

*Abs* (*Abs* (*App* (*Var Zero*, *App* (*Var* (*Succ* (*Succ* 'w')), *Var* (*Succ Zero*)))))

The closed lambda terms – those containing no free variables – are elements of *Term Empty*, where *Empty* is the empty type containing no members.

The function *abstract*, which takes a term and a variable and abstracts over that variable, can be defined in the following way:

*abstract* :: (*Term a*, *a*) → *Term a*
*abstract* (*t*, *x*) = *Abs* (*lift* (*t*, *x*))

The function *lift* is defined by

$$
\begin{aligned}
&\mathit{lift} && :: (\mathit{Term}\,a, a) \to \mathit{Term}\,(\mathit{Bind}\,a)\\
&\mathit{lift}\,(\mathit{Var}\,y, x) && = \mathbf{if}\ x = y\ \mathbf{then}\ \mathit{Var}\,\mathit{Zero}\ \mathbf{else}\ \mathit{Var}\,(\mathit{Succ}\,y)\\
&\mathit{lift}\,(\mathit{App}\,(u, v), x) && = \mathit{App}\,(\mathit{lift}\,(u, x), \mathit{lift}\,(v, x))\\
&\mathit{lift}\,(\mathit{Abs}\,t, x) && = \mathit{Abs}\,(\mathit{lift}\,(t, \mathit{Succ}\,x))
\end{aligned}
$$

The $\beta$-reduction of a term is implemented by

$$
\begin{aligned}
&\mathit{reduce} && :: (\mathit{Term}\,a, \mathit{Term}\,a) \to \mathit{Term}\,a\\
&\mathit{reduce}\,(\mathit{Abs}\,s, t) && = \mathit{subst}\,(s, t)
\end{aligned}
$$

where

$$
\begin{aligned}
&\mathit{subst} && :: (\mathit{Term}\,(\mathit{Bind}\,a), \mathit{Term}\,a) \to \mathit{Term}\,a\\
&\mathit{subst}\,(\mathit{Var}\,\mathit{Zero}, t) && = t\\
&\mathit{subst}\,(\mathit{Var}\,(\mathit{Succ}\,x), t) && = \mathit{Var}\,x\\
&\mathit{subst}\,(\mathit{App}\,(u, v), t) && = \mathit{App}\,(\mathit{subst}\,(u, t), \mathit{subst}\,(v, t))\\
&\mathit{subst}\,(\mathit{Abs}\,s, t) && = \mathit{Abs}\,(\mathit{subst}\,(s, \mathit{term}\,\mathit{Succ}\,t))
\end{aligned}
$$

The function *term f* maps *f* over a term:

$$
\begin{aligned}
&\mathit{term} && :: (a \to b) \to (\mathit{Term}\,a \to \mathit{Term}\,b)\\
&\mathit{term}\,f\,(\mathit{Var}\,x) && = \mathit{Var}\,(f\,x)\\
&\mathit{term}\,f\,(\mathit{App}\,(u, v)) && = \mathit{App}\,(\mathit{term}\,f\,u, \mathit{term}\,f\,v)\\
&\mathit{term}\,f\,(\mathit{Abs}\,t) && = \mathit{Abs}\,(\mathit{term}\,(\mathit{bind}\,f)\,t)
\end{aligned}
$$

The subsidiary function *bind f* maps *f* over elements of *Bind a*:

$$
\begin{aligned}
&\mathit{bind} && :: (a \to b) \to (\mathit{Bind}\,a \to \mathit{Bind}\,b)\\
&\mathit{bind}\,f\,\mathit{Zero} && = \mathit{Zero}\\
&\mathit{bind}\,f\,(\mathit{Succ}\,x) && = \mathit{Succ}\,(f\,x)
\end{aligned}
$$

It is a routine induction to show that

$$\mathit{reduce}\,(\mathit{abstract}\,(t, x), \mathit{Var}\,x) = t$$

for all terms $t$ of type *Term a* and all $x$ of type $a$.

Modulo the requirement that $a$ and *Bind a* be declared as equality types (because elements are compared for equality in the definition of *lift*) the programs above are acceptable to Haskell 1.4, provided the type signatures are included as part of the definitions.

## 3 Datatypes as initial algebras

The standard semantics (see e.g. [8, 10]) of inductive datatypes parametrised by $n$ type parameters employs functors of type $\mathbf{C} \times \cdots \times \mathbf{C} \to \mathbf{C}$, where the product has $n+1$ occurrences of $\mathbf{C}$. For simplicity, we will consider only the case $n = 1$. The category $\mathbf{C}$ cannot be arbitrary: essentially, it has to contain finite sums and products, and colimits of all ascending chains. The category **Fun** (also known as **Set**), whose objects are sets and whose arrows are typed total functions, has everything needed to make the theory work.

To illustrate, the declaration of *List* as a datatype is associated with a binary functor $F$ whose action on objects of $\mathbf{C} \times \mathbf{C}$ is defined by

$$F(a, b) = 1 + a \times b$$

Introducing the unary functor $F_a$, where $F_a(b) = F(a, b)$, the declaration of $List\ a$ can now be rewritten in the form

$$\mathbf{data}\ List\ a \xleftarrow{\alpha_a} F_a(List\ a)$$

in which $\alpha_a :: F_a(List\ a) \to List\ a$. For the particular functor $F$ associated with *List*, the arrow $\alpha_a$ takes the form $(NilL_a, ConsL_a)$, where $NilL_a :: 1 \to List\ a$ and $ConsL_a :: a \times List\ a \to List\ a$. This declaration can can be interpreted as the assertion that the arrow $\alpha_a$ and the object $List\ a$ are the "least" values with this typing. More precisely, given any arrow

$$f :: F_a(b) \to b$$

the assertion is that there is a unique arrow $h :: List\ a \to b$ satisfying the equation

$$h \cdot \alpha_a = f \cdot F(id_a, h)$$

The unique arrow $h$ is denoted by $fold\, f$. The arrow $h$ is also called a *catamorphism*, and the notation $(\!|f|\!)$ is also used for $fold\, f$. In algebraic terms, $List\ a$ is the carrier of the *initial* algebra $\alpha_a$ of the functor $F_a$ and $fold\, f$ is the unique $F_a$-homomorphism from the initial algebra to $f$.

A surprising number of consequences flow from this characterisation. In particular, $fold\ \alpha_a$ is the identity arrow on $List\ a$. Also, one can show that $\alpha_a$ is an isomorphism, with inverse $fold\,(F(id_a, \alpha_a))$. As a result, one can interpret the declaration of *List* as the assertion that, up to isomorphism, $List\ a$ is the least fixed point of the equation $x = F(a, x)$.

The type constructor *List* can itself can be made into a functor by defining its action on an arrow $f : a \to b$ by

$$list\, f = fold\,(\alpha_b \cdot F(f, id))$$

In functional programming $list\, f$ is written $map\, f$. Expanding the definition of *fold*, we have

$$list\, f \cdot \alpha_a = \alpha_b \cdot F(f, list\, f)$$

This equation states that $\alpha$ is a natural transformation of type $\alpha :: G \to List$, where $G\,a = F(a, List\ a)$.

The most important consequence of the characterisation is that it allows one to introduce new functions by structural recursion over a datatype. As a simple example, $fold\,(zero, plus)$ sums the elements of a list of numbers.

Functors built from constant functors, type functors (like *List*), the identity and projection functors, using coproduct, product, and composition operations, are called *regular* functors. For further details of the approach, consult, e.g., [12] or [1].

For *Nest* and *Bush* the theory above breaks down. For example, introducing $Q\, a = a \times a$ for the squaring functor, the corresponding functorial declaration for *Nest* would be

$$\textbf{data}\ Nest\ a \xleftarrow{\alpha_a} F(a, Nest\,(Q\,a))$$

where $F$ is as before, and $\alpha_a$ applies *NilN* to left components and *ConsN* to right components. However, it is not clear over what class of algebras $\alpha_a$ can be asserted to be initial.

## 4 A higher-order semantics

There is an appealing semantics for dealing with datatypes such as *Nest* and *Bush*, which, however, has certain limitations. We will give the scheme, then point out the limitations, and then give an alternative scheme that overcomes some of them.

The idea is to use higher-order functors of type

$$Nat(\mathbf{C}) \to Nat(\mathbf{C}),$$

where $Nat(\mathbf{C})$ is the category whose objects are functors of type $\mathbf{C} \to \mathbf{C}$ and whose arrows are natural transformations. We will use calligraphic letters for higher-order functors, and small Greek letters for natural transformations. Again, the category $\mathbf{C}$ cannot be arbitrary, but taking $\mathbf{C} = \mathbf{Fun}$ gives everything one needs. Here are three examples.

*Example 1.* The declaration of *List* can be associated with a higher-order functor $\mathcal{F}$ defined on objects (functors) by

$$\mathcal{F}(F)(a) = 1 + a \times F(a)$$
$$\mathcal{F}(F)(f) = id_1 + f \times F(f)$$

These equations define $\mathcal{F}(F)$ to be a functor for each functor $F$. The functor $\mathcal{F}$ can be expressed more briefly in the form

$$\mathcal{F}(F) = K1 + Id \times F$$

The constant functor $K\,a$ delivers the object $a$ for all objects and the arrow $id_a$ for all arrows, and *Id* denotes the identity functor. The coproduct $(+)$ and product $(\times)$ operations are applied pointwise.

The action of $\mathcal{F}$ on arrows (natural transformations) is defined in a similar style by

$$\mathcal{F}(\eta) = id_{K1} + id \times \eta$$

Here, $id_{K1}$ delivers the identity arrow $id_1$ for each object of $\mathbf{C}$. If $\eta :: F \to G$, then $\mathcal{F}(\eta) :: \mathcal{F}(F) \to \mathcal{F}(G)$. We have $\mathcal{F}(id) = id$, and $\mathcal{F}(\eta \cdot \psi) = \mathcal{F}(\eta) \cdot \mathcal{F}(\psi)$, so $\mathcal{F}$ is itself a functor.

The previous declaration of *List* can now be written in the form

$$\textbf{data } List \xleftarrow{\alpha} \mathcal{F}(List)$$

and interpreted as the assertion that $\alpha$ is the initial $\mathcal{F}$-algebra.

*Example 2.* The declaration of *Nest* is associated with a functor $\mathcal{F}$, defined on objects (functors) by

$$\mathcal{F}(F)(a) = 1 + a \times F(Qa)$$
$$\mathcal{F}(F)(f) = id_1 + f \times F(Qf)$$

where $Q$ is the squaring functor. More briefly,

$$\mathcal{F}(F) = K1 + Id \times (F \cdot Q)$$

where $F \cdot Q$ denotes the (functor) composition of $F$ and $Q$. Where convenient, we will also write this composition as $FQ$ for brevity.

The action of $\mathcal{F}$ on arrows (natural transformations) is defined by

$$\mathcal{F}(\eta) = id_{K1} + id \times \eta Q$$

where $\eta Q :: FQ \to GQ$ if $\eta :: F \to G$.

*Example 3.* The declaration of *Bush* is associated with a functor $\mathcal{F}$, defined on functors by

$$\mathcal{F}(F) = K1 + Id \times (F \cdot F)$$

and on natural transformations by

$$\mathcal{F}(\eta) = id_{K1} + id \times (\eta \star \eta)$$

The operator $\star$ denotes the horizontal composition of two natural transformations. If $\theta :: F \to G$ and $\psi :: H \to N$, then $\theta \star \psi :: FH \to GN$ is defined by $\theta \star \psi = \theta N \cdot F\psi$. In particular, if $\eta :: F \to G$, then $\eta \star \eta :: FF \to GG$.

Consider again the declaration of *Nest* given in the Introduction, and rewrite it in the form

$$\textbf{data } Nest \xleftarrow{\alpha} \mathcal{F}(Nest)$$

The assertion that $\alpha$ is the initial $\mathcal{F}$-algebra means that for any arrow $\varphi :: \mathcal{F}(F) \to F$, there is a unique arrow $\theta :: Nest \to F$ satisfying the equation

$$\theta \cdot \alpha = \varphi \cdot \mathcal{F}(\theta).$$

The unique arrow $\theta$ is again denoted by *fold* $\varphi$.

We can express the equation above in Haskell. Note that for the particular functor $\mathcal{F}$ associated with *Nest*, the arrow $\varphi$ takes the form $\varphi = (\varepsilon, \psi)$, where $\varepsilon :: K1 \to F$ and $\psi :: Id \times FQ \to F$. For any type $a$, the component $\varepsilon_a$ is an arrow delivering a constant $e$ of type $F\,a$, while $\psi_a$ is an arrow $f$ of type $(a, F(a,a)) \to F(a)$. Hence we can write

$$\begin{aligned} &\mathit{fold}\,(e,f)\;\mathit{NilN} &&= e \\ &\mathit{fold}\,(e,f)\,(\mathit{ConsN}\,(x,xps)) &&= f(x, \mathit{fold}\,(e,f)\;xps) \end{aligned}$$

However, no principal type can be inferred for *fold* under the Hindley-Milner type discipline, so the use of *fold* in programs is denied us. Moreover, it is not possible to express the type of *fold* in any form that is acceptable to a standard Haskell type checker. On the other hand, in GHC (The Glasgow Haskell Compiler) one can declare the type of *fold* by using a rank-2 type signature:

$$\mathit{fold} :: (\forall f.\forall b.\,((\forall a.f\,a), (\forall a.(a, f(a,a)) \to f\,a)) \to \mathit{Nest}\;b \to f\,b)$$

This declaration uses both local universal quantification and abstraction over a type constructor. Such a signature is called a rank-2 type signature. With this asserted type, the function *fold* passes the GHC type-checker.

Observe that in the proposed functorial scheme, unlike the previous one for regular datatypes, the operator *fold* takes natural transformations to natural transformations. In particular, the fact that *Nest* is a functor is part of the assertion that *Nest* is the least fixed point of $\mathcal{F}$. The arrow *nest f* cannot be defined as an instance of *fold* since it is not a natural transformation of the right type.

The typing $\alpha :: \mathcal{F}(\mathit{Nest}) \to \mathit{Nest}$ means that, given $f :: a \to b$, the following equation holds:

$$\mathit{nest}\,f \cdot \alpha_a = \alpha_b \cdot \mathcal{F}(\mathit{nest})\,f$$

We can express this equation at the point level by

$$\begin{aligned} &\mathit{nest}\,f\;\mathit{NilN} &&= \mathit{NilN} \\ &\mathit{nest}\,f\,(\mathit{ConsN}\,(x,xps)) &&= \mathit{ConsN}\,(f\,x, \mathit{nest}\,(\mathit{square}\,f)\;xps) \end{aligned}$$

where $\mathit{square}\,f\,(x,y) = (f\,x, f\,y)$ is the action on arrows of the functor $Q$. The fact that *nest* is uniquely defined by these equations is therefore a consequence of the assertion that $\alpha$ is a natural transformation.

Exactly the same characterisation works for *Bush*. In particular, the arrow *bush f* satisfies

$$\begin{aligned} &\mathit{bush}\,f\;\mathit{NilB} &&= \mathit{NilB} \\ &\mathit{bush}\,f\,(\mathit{ConsB}\,(x,xbs)) &&= \mathit{ConsB}\,(f\,x, \mathit{bush}\,(\mathit{bush}\,f)\;xbs) \end{aligned}$$

## 5 Examples

To illustrate the use of folds over *Nest* and *Bush*, define $\tau :: Q \to \mathit{List}$ by

$$\tau(x,y) = [x,y]$$

Using $\tau$ and the natural transformation $\mathit{concat} :: \mathit{List} \cdot \mathit{List} \to \mathit{List}$, we have $\mathit{concat} \cdot \mathit{list}\,\tau :: \mathit{List} \cdot Q \to \mathit{List}$, and so

$$\alpha_{\mathit{List}} \cdot \mathcal{F}(\mathit{concat} \cdot \mathit{list}\,\tau) :: \mathcal{F}(\mathit{List}) \to \mathit{List}$$

where $\mathcal{F}(F) = K1 + Id \times FQ$ is the higher-order functor associated with *Nest*. The function *listify*, defined by

$$listify = fold\,(\alpha_{List} \cdot \mathcal{F}(concat \cdot list\,\tau))$$

therefore has type *listify* :: *Nest* → *List*. For example, *listify* takes

$$[0, (1, 1), ((2, 2), (3, 3))] \quad \text{to} \quad [0, 1, 1, 2, 2, 3, 3]$$

The converse function *nestify* :: *List* → *Nest* can be defined by

$$nestify = fold\,(\alpha_{Nest} \cdot \mathcal{F}(nest\,\delta))$$

where $\mathcal{F}(F) = K1 + Id \times F$ is the higher-order functor associated with *List*, and $\delta\,a = (a, a)$ has type $\delta :: Id \to Q$. For example, *nestify* takes

$$[0, 1, 2] \quad \text{to} \quad [0, (1, 1), ((2, 2), (2, 2))]$$

For another example, define $\sigma :: Q \to Bush$ by

$$\sigma(x, y) = [x, [y]]$$

Then $bush\,\sigma :: Bush \cdot Q \to Bush \cdot Bush$, and so

$$\alpha_{Bush} \cdot \mathcal{F}(bush\,\sigma) :: \mathcal{F}(Bush) \to Bush$$

where $\mathcal{F}(F) = K1 + Id \times FQ$ is the functor associated with *Nest*. Hence

$$bushify = fold\,(\alpha_{Bush} \cdot \mathcal{F}(bush\,\sigma))$$

has type *bushify* :: *Nest* → *Bush*. For example, *bushify* sends

$$[1, (2, 3), ((4, 5), (6, 7))] \quad \text{to} \quad [1, [2, [3]], [[4, [5]], [[6, [7]]]]]$$

## 6 The problem

The basic problem with the higher-order approach described above concerns expressive power. Part of the problem is that it does not generalise the standard semantics for regular datatypes; in particular, it does not enable us to make use of the standard instances of *fold* over such datatypes. To see why not, let us compare the two semantics for the datatype *List*.

Under the standard semantics, $fold\,f :: List\,a \to b$ when $f :: 1 + a \times b \to b$. For example,

$$fold\,(zero, plus) :: List\,Int \to Int$$

sums a list of integers, where $zero :: 1 \to Int$ is a constant delivering 0, and $plus :: Int \times Int \to Int$ is binary addition.

As another example,

$$fold\,(nil, cat) :: List\,(List\,a) \to List\,a$$

concatenates a list of lists; this function was called *concat* above. The binary operator *cat* has type $cat :: List\ a \times List\ a \to List\ a$ and concatenates two lists.

Under the new semantics, $fold\ \varphi :: List \to F$ when $\varphi :: K1 + Id \times F \to F$. We can no longer sum a list of integers with such a fold because *plus* is not a natural transformation of the right type. For $fold\ (zero, plus)$ to be well-typed we require that *plus* has type $plus :: Id \times KInt \to KInt$. Thus,

$$plus_a :: a \times Int \to Int$$

for all $a$, and so *plus* would have to ignore its first argument.

Even worse, we cannot define $concat :: List \cdot List \to List$ as an instance of *fold*, even though it is a natural transformation. The binary concatenation operator *cat* does not have type

$$cat :: Id \times List \to List$$

because again it would have to ignore its first argument. Hence $fold\ (nil, cat)$ is not well-typed.

On the other hand, $\alpha_{Nest} \cdot \mathcal{F}(nest\ \delta)$ does have type $K1 + Id \times Nest \to Nest$, so the definition of *nestify* given in the previous section is legitimate.

Putting the problem another way, in the standard semantics, $fold\ f$ is defined by providing an arrow $f :: F(a, b) \to b$ for a fixed $a$ and $b$; we cannot in general elevate $f$ to a natural transformation that is parametric in $a$.

## 7 An alternative

Fortunately, for lists and other regular datatypes, there is a way out of this particular difficulty. Using the isomorphism defining *List*, the functor $List \cdot F$ satisfies the isomorphism

$$List \cdot F \cong (K1 + Id \times List) \cdot F \cong K1 + F \times (List \cdot F)$$

Hence $List \cdot F$ is isomorphic to the "higher-order" datatype $Listr\ F$, declared by

$$\textbf{data}\ Listr\ F \xleftarrow{\alpha} K1 + F \times Listr\ F$$

We can write the functor on the right as $\mathcal{F}(F, Listr\ F)$, where $\mathcal{F}$ now is a higher-order binary functor of type

$$Nat(\mathbf{C}) \times Nat(\mathbf{C}) \to Nat(\mathbf{C})$$

Over the higher-order datatype $Listr\ F$, the natural transformation $fold\ \varphi$ takes an arrow $\varphi :: K1 + F \times G \to G$, and has type $fold\ \varphi :: Listr\ F \to G$. If we change $Listr\ F$ to $List \cdot F$ in this signature, we have a useful fold operator for lists. In particular,

$$fold\ (zero, plus) :: List \cdot KInt \to KInt$$

since $(zero, plus) :: K1 + KInt \times KInt \to KInt$. The arrow $fold\ (zero, plus)$ of $Nat(\mathbf{C})$ is a natural transformation; since $List \cdot KInt = K(List\ Int)$, its component for any $a$ is the standard fold $fold\ (zero, plus) :: List\ Int \to Int$.

By a similar device, all folds in the standard semantics are definable as folds in the new semantics, simply by lifting the associated algebra to be a natural transformation between constant functors.

More precisely, define *Type a* to be the least fixed point of a regular functor $F_a$, where $F_a(b) = F(a, b)$. Furthermore, define *Typer G* to be the least fixed point of $\mathcal{F}_G$, where $\mathcal{F}_G(H) = \mathcal{F}(G, H)$ and $\mathcal{F}(G, H)x = F(Gx, Hx)$ for all objects $x$. Take an algebra $f :: F(a, b) \to b$, and construct the natural transformation $\varphi :: \mathcal{F}(Ka, Kb) \to Kb$ by setting $\varphi = Kf$. This is type correct since

$$\mathcal{F}(Ka, Kb)x = F(Ka(x), Kb(x)) = F(a, b) \quad \text{and} \quad Kb(x) = b$$

Then $\mathit{fold}\, f :: \mathit{Type}\, a \to b$, and $\mathit{fold}\, \varphi :: \mathit{Typer}\, Ka \to Kb$ satisfy

$$\mathit{fold}\, \varphi = K(\mathit{fold}\, f)$$

under the isomorphism $\mathit{Typer}\, Ka = K(\mathit{Type}\, a)$.

Thus, not only do we generalise from the defining expression for *List* by replacing occurrences of *List* by $G$, we also generalise by replacing occurrences of *Id* by a functor $F$.

However, the same idea does *not* work for nested datatypes such as *Nest*. This time we have

$$\mathit{Nest} \cdot F \cong (K1 + \mathit{Id} \times (\mathit{Nest} \cdot Q)) \cdot F \cong K1 + F \times (\mathit{Nest} \cdot Q \cdot F)$$

The type $\mathit{Nest} \cdot F$ is quite different from the datatype defined by

$$\textbf{data}\ \mathit{Nestr}\, F \xleftarrow{\alpha} K1 + F \times ((\mathit{Nestr}\, F) \cdot Q)$$

For example, *Nest* (*List a*) is the type of nests of lists over $a$, so the $n$-th entry of such a nest has type $Q^n\,(\mathit{List}\, a)$. On the other hand the $n$-th entry of a nest of type *Nestr List a* has type $\mathit{List}\,(Q^n\, a)$.

Even more dramatically, the type *Nest Int* gives a nest of integers, but *Nestr KInt b* is isomorphic to ordinary lists of integers for all $b$. More generally, *Nestr Ka* is the constant functor $K(\mathit{List}\, a)$.

On the other hand, we have $\mathit{Nest} = \mathit{Nestr}\, \mathit{Id}$, so the higher-order view is indeed a generalisation of the previous one.

## 8 Reductions

Replacing higher-order unary functors by higher-order binary functors enables us to integrate the standard theory of regular datatypes into the proposed scheme. Unfortunately, while the higher-order approach is elegant and generic, it seems limited in the scope of its applicability to nested datatypes, which is restricted to folding with natural transformations. For example, one cannot sum a nest of integers with a fold over nests. Such a computation is an instance of a useful general pattern called a *reduction*. It is possible to define reductions completely generically for all regular types (see [15]), but we do not know at present whether the same can be done for nested datatypes.

One way to sum a nest of integers is by first listifying the nest and then summing the result with a fold over lists. More generally, this strategy can be used to reduce a nest with an arbitrary binary operator $\oplus$ and a seed $e$. For example,

$$[x_0, (x_1, x_2), ((x_3, x_4), (x_5, x_6))]$$

reduces to

$$x_0 \oplus (x_1 \oplus (x_2 \oplus \cdots \oplus (x_6 \oplus e)))$$

It can be argued that this strategy for reducing over nests is unsatisfactory because the structure of the nest entries is not reflected in the way in which $\oplus$ is applied. Better is to introduce a second operator $\otimes$ and reduce the nest above to

$$x_0 \otimes ((x_1 \oplus x_2) \otimes (((x_3 \oplus x_4) \oplus (x_5 \oplus x_6)) \otimes e))$$

By taking $\otimes$ to be $\oplus$, we obtain another way of reducing a nest.

The above pattern of computation can be factored as a fold over lists after a reduction to a list:

$$\mathit{fold}\,(e, \otimes) \cdot \mathit{reduce}\,(\oplus)$$

With $(\oplus) :: Q\ a \to a$, the function $\mathit{reduce}\,(\oplus)$ has type $\mathit{Nest}\ a \to \mathit{List}\ a$. For example, applied to the nest above, $\mathit{reduce}\,(\oplus)$ produces

$$[x_0,\ x_1 \oplus x_2,\ (x_3 \oplus x_4) \oplus (x_5 \oplus x_6)]$$

There is no problem with defining *reduce*. In a functional style we can define

$$\begin{aligned} &\mathit{reduce\ op\ NilN} &&= \mathit{NilL} \\ &\mathit{reduce\ op}\,(\mathit{ConsN}\,(x, \mathit{xps})) &&= \mathit{ConsL}\,(x, \mathit{reduce\ op}\,(\mathit{nest\ op\ xps})) \end{aligned}$$

In effect, *reduce op* applies the following sequence of functions to the corresponding entries of a nest:

$$[\mathit{id},\ \mathit{op},\ \mathit{op} \cdot \mathit{square\ op},\ \mathit{op} \cdot \mathit{square\ op} \cdot \mathit{square}\,(\mathit{square\ op}), \ldots]$$

The $n$-th element of this sequence has type $Q^n\ a \to a$ when $\mathit{op} :: Q\ a \to a$.

The reduction of a bush proceeds differently:

$$\begin{aligned} &\mathit{reduce}\,(e, \mathit{op})\ \mathit{NilB} = e \\ &\mathit{reduce}\,(e, \mathit{op})\,(\mathit{ConsB}\,(x, \mathit{xbs})) = \\ &\qquad \mathit{op}\,(x, \mathit{reduce}\,(e, \mathit{op})\,(\mathit{bush}\,(\mathit{reduce}\,(e, \mathit{op}))\ \mathit{xbs})) \end{aligned}$$

At present we see no systematic way of unifying reductions over nested datatypes, nor of relating them to the folds of previous sections.

## 9 Another approach

There is a way that higher-order folds and the reductions of the previous section can be unified, but whether or not the method is desirable from a calculational point of view remains to be seen. It requires a different and more complicated notion of folding over a nested datatpe, one that involves an *infinite* sequence of appropriate algebras to replace the infinite sequence of differently typed instances of the constructors of the datatype. We will briefly sketch the construction for the type *Nest a*.

The basic idea is to provide an infinite sequence of algebras to replace the constructor $\alpha = (\mathit{NilN}, \mathit{ConsN})$ of *Nest*, one for each instance

$$\alpha :: F(Q^n\, a, \mathit{Nest}\,(Q^{n+1}\, a)) \rightarrow \mathit{Nest}\,(Q^n\, a)$$

where $n$ is a natural number and $F(a, b) = 1 + a \times b$. For regular datatypes the application of *fold f* to a term can be viewed as the systematic replacement of the constructors by corresponding components of $f$, followed by an evaluation of the result. The same idea is adopted here for nested datatypes. However, whereas for regular datatypes each occurrence of a constructor in a term has the same typing, the same is not true for nested datatypes, hence the need to provide a collection of replacements.

In more detail, consider the datatype *NestAlgs* defined by

$$\mathbf{data}\ \mathit{NestAlgs}\ G\,(a, b) = \mathit{Cons}\,(F(a, G(Qb)) \rightarrow Gb, \mathit{NestAlgs}\ G\,(Qa, Qb))$$

The datatype *NestAlgs* is a *coinductive*, infinite, nested datatype. The $n$-th entry of a value of type $\mathit{NestAlgs}\ G\,(a, b)$ is an algebra of type

$$F(Q^n\, a, G(Q^{n+1}\, b)) \rightarrow G(Q^n\, b)$$

Now for $fs :: \mathit{NestAlgs}\ G\,(a, b)$, define $\mathit{fold}\,fs :: \mathit{Nest}\ a \rightarrow Gb$ by the equation

$$\mathit{fold}\,fs \cdot \alpha = \mathit{head}\,fs \cdot F(id, \mathit{fold}\,(\mathit{tail}\,fs))$$

where

$$\begin{aligned} \mathit{head}\,(\mathit{Cons}\,(f, fs)) &= f \\ \mathit{tail}\,(\mathit{Cons}\,(f, fs)) &= fs \end{aligned}$$

Equivalently,

$$\mathit{fold}\,(\mathit{Cons}\,(f, fs)) \cdot \alpha = f \cdot F(id, \mathit{fold}\,fs)$$

To illustrate this style of *fold*, suppose $f :: a \rightarrow b$ and define $\mathit{generate}\,f :: \mathit{NestAlgs}\ \mathit{Nest}\,(a, b)$ by

$$\mathit{generate}\,f = \mathit{Cons}\,(\alpha \cdot F(f, id), \mathit{generate}\,(\mathit{square}\,f))$$

Then $\mathit{fold}\,(\mathit{generate}\,f) :: \mathit{Nest}\ a \rightarrow \mathit{Nest}\ b$, and in fact

$$\mathit{nest}\,f = \mathit{fold}\,(\mathit{generate}\,f)$$

The functorial action of *Nest* on arrows can therefore be recovered as a fold. The proof of $nest\,(f \cdot g) = nest\,f \cdot nest\,g$ makes use of coinduction.

As another example, suppose $\varphi :: \mathcal{F}(Id, GQ) \to G$ is a natural transformation, where $\mathcal{F}(M, N)a = F(Ma, Na)$. Define $repeat\,\varphi :: NestAlgs\; G$ by

$$repeat\,\varphi = Cons\,(\varphi, repeat\,\varphi Q)$$

For each type $a$ we have $(repeat\,\varphi)_a :: NestAlgs\; G\,(a, a)$. The relationship between the higher-order folds of the previous sections and the current style of folds is that

$$fold\,\varphi = fold\,(repeat\,\varphi)$$

In particular, $fold\,(repeat\,\alpha) = id :: Nest \to Nest$.

We can also define reductions as an instance of the new folds. Suppose $f :: F(a, a) \to a$, so $f = (f_0, f_1)$, where $f_1 :: Qa \to a$. Define $redalgs\,f :: NestAlgs\; Ka\,(a, b)$ by

$$\begin{aligned} redalgs\,f &= red\;id \\ \textbf{where}\; red\,k &= Cons\,(f \cdot F(k, id), red\,(f_1 \cdot square\,k)) \end{aligned}$$

We have $fold\,(redalgs\,f) :: Nest\;a \to a$, and we claim that

$$reduce\,f = fold\,(redalgs\,f)$$

## 10 Conclusions

The results of this investigation into nested datatypes are still incomplete and in several aspects unsatisfactory. The higher-order folds are attractive, and the corresponding calculational theory is familiar, but they seem to lack sufficient expressive power. The approach sketched in the previous section for *Nest* is more general, but brings in more machinery. Furthermore, it is not clear what the right extension is to other nested datatypes such as *Bush*.

We have also ignored one crucial question in the foregoing discussion, namely, what is the guarantee that functors such as *Nest* and *Nestr* do in fact exist as least fixed points of their defining equations? The categorical incantation ensuring the existence of an initial $F$-algebra in a co-complete category $\mathbf{C}$ is that, provided $F$ is co-continuous, it is the colimit of the chain

$$0 \hookrightarrow F0 \hookrightarrow FF0 \hookrightarrow \cdots$$

The category **Fun** has everything needed to make this incantation work: **Fun** is co-complete (in fact, bi-complete) and all regular functors $F$ on **Fun** are co-continuous. The proof for polynomial functors can be found in [14], and the extension to type functors is in [13].

Moreover, the category *Nat* (**Fun**) inherits co-completeness from the base category **Fun** (see [11, 7]). We believe that all regular higher-order functors are co-continuous, though we have not yet found a proof of this in the literature, so the existence of datatypes like *Nest* and *Bush* is not likely to be problematic.

If we adopt the higher-order approach, then there is a need to give a systematic account of reductions over a nested datatype. If the alternative method of the previous section proves more useful, then there is a need to give a systematic account of the method, not only for an arbitrary inductive nested datatype, but also for coinductive nested datatypes.

Finally, in [4] (see also [5]) the idea was proposed that a datatype was a certain kind of functor called a *relator*, together with a membership relation. It needs to be seen how the notion of membership can be extended to nested datatypes

**Acknowledgements**

The authors would like to thank Ian Bayley, Jeremy Gibbons, Oege de Moor, Mark Jones, and Simon Peyton Jones for comments and discussions on the work. A particular debt is owed to Ross Paterson, who commented on an earlier draft of the paper. Thanks are also due to the anonymous referees who suggested numerous improvements.

## References

1. R. Bird and O. de Moor. *Algebra of Programming*. International Series in Computing Science. Prentice Hall, 1996.
2. R. S. Bird, P. F. Hoogendijk, and O. De Moor. Generic programming with relations and functors. *Journal of Functional Programming*, 6(1):1–28, 1996.
3. R.H. Connelly and F. Lockwood Morris. A generalisation of the trie data structure. *Mathematical Structures in Computer Science*, 5(3):381–418, 1995.
4. Oege de Moor and Paul Hoogendijk. What is a datatype? Technical Report 96/16, Department of Maths and Computing Science, Eindhoven University of Technology, 1996.
5. Paul Hoogendijk. *A Generic theory of Data Types*. Ph.D Thesis, Eindhoven University of Technology, 1997.
6. L. Fegaras and T. Sheard. Revisiting catamorphisms over datatypes with embedded functions. In *23rd ACM SIGPLAN-SIGACT Symposium on Principles of Programming Languages*. Association for Computing Machinery, 1996.
7. Peter Freyd. Algebraically complete categories. Springer-Verlag Lecture Notes in Mathematics, vol 1488, 95–104, 1990.
8. T. Hagino. *Category theoretic approach to data types*. PhD thesis, Laboratory for Foundations of Computer Science, University of Edinburgh, UK, 1987. Technical Report ECS-LFCS-87-38.
9. J. Jeuring. Polytypic pattern matching. In S. Peyton Jones, editor, *Functional Programming and Computer Architecture*, pages 238–248. Association for Computing Machinery, 1995.
10. J. Lambek. A fixpoint theorem for complete categories. *Mathematische Zeitschrift*, 103:151–161, 1968.
11. Saunders Mac Lane. Categories for the Working Mathematician. Graduate Texts in Mathematics. Springer-Verlag, 1971.
12. G. Malcolm. Data structures and program transformation. *Science of Computer Programming*, 14(2–3):255–279, 1990.

13. G. Malcolm. Algebraic Data Types and Program Transformation. Ph.D thesis, University of Groningen, The Netherlands, 1990.
14. E.G. Manes and M.A. Arbib. *Algebraic Approaches to Program Semantics*. Texts and Monographs in Computing Science. Springer-Verlag, 1986.
15. Lambert Meertens. Calculate polytypically! In Herbert Kuchen and S. Doaitse Swierstra, editors, *Programming Languages: Implementations Logics, and Programs Proceedings Eighth International Symposium PLILP '96*, volume 1140 of *LNCS*, pages 1–16. Springer-Verlag, 1996.
16. E. Meijer and G. Hutton. Bananas in space: extending fold and unfold to exponential types. In S. Peyton Jones, editor, *Functional Progamming Languages and Computer Architecture*, pages 324–333. Association for Computing Machinery, 1995.
17. A. Mycroft. Polymorphic type schemes and recursive definitions. In *International Symposium on Programming*, volume LNCS 167, pages 217–228. Springer-Verlag, 1984.
18. C. Okasaki. *Purely Functional Data Structures*. Ph.D thesis, School of Computer Science, Carnegie Mellon University, 1996.
19. C. Okasaki. Catenable double-ended queues. In *Proceedings of the 1997 ACM SIGPLAN International Conference on Functional Programming (ICFP '97)*, pages 66–74. ACM, 1997.
20. S. Peyton Jones and J. Launchbury. Explicit quantification in Haskell. See: `http://www.dcs.gla.ac.uk/people/personal/simonpj/`.

# An Approach to Object-Orientation in Action Systems

Marcello M. Bonsangue[1], Joost N. Kok[1], and Kaisa Sere[2]

[1] Department of Computer Science, Rijks Universiteit Leiden
P.O. Box 9512, NL-2300 RA Leiden, The Netherlands
marcello@cs.leidenuniv.nl and joost@cs.leidenuniv.nl

[2] Department of Computer Science, Åbo Akademi University
Turku Centre for Computer Science, FIN-20520 Turku, Finland
Kaisa.Sere@abo.fi

**Abstract.** We extend the action system formalism with a notion of objects that can be dynamically created, active and distributed. With this extension we can model class-based systems as action systems. Moreover, as the introduced constructs can be translated into ordinary action systems, we can use the theory developed for action systems, especially the refinement calculus, even for class-based systems. We show how inheritance can be modelled in different ways via class refinement. Refining a class with an other class within the refinement calculus ensures that the original behavior of the class is maintained throughout the refinements. Finally, we show how to reuse refinements and entire class modules in a refinement step.

## 1 Introduction

Object-oriented programming offers a very clear way to structure large systems by encapsulating data and operations into objects, by grouping objects into classes, and by dynamically binding operations to program code. In contrast to the popularity reached by some object-oriented programming languages, there is no general agreement on their formal computational model.

We propose an approach to object-orientation based on action systems, so called OO-action systems. We take a class-based approach to object orientation: OO-action systems model classes and instances of classes, i.e. objects, are created at run time. The objects themselves can be *distributed* and *active*. Communication between objects takes place via remote procedure calls and shared variables.

We show how an OO-action system, i.e. a specification of some classes, is translated into an ordinary action system [BK83]: methods correspond to exportable procedures, attributes to shared and local variables, object variables to local variables, and classes to entire action systems. Moreover, object constructors correspond to initialization statements of an action system. A collection of classes is translated into a parallel composition of ordinary action systems. This translation allows us to use most of the theory built around action systems even when designing OO-action systems. As a side effect we get a mechanism to add processes to action systems, a desirable feature now missing from the formalism.

Action systems are designed stepwise within the refinement calculus [BS96]. We therefore define the notion of *refinement* for OO-action systems within the refinement calculus. The notion we want to preserve by refinement is total correctness if we are interested only on the input-output behaviour of the system, and trace correctness if we are interested on its reactive behaviour. We develop proof rules to be used when designing and reasoning about OO-action systems. The correctness of the rules is shown by appealing to the standard rules of the refinement calculus. The rules can be used to refine both methods, actions, and the constructors of a class.

When we refine a class with another class, the refined class can inherit methods and attributes from the original class. New attributes can be introduced in a refinement step and some methods can be overridden by the refined methods. As our objects are active, a refinement step can introduce additional autonomous behavior in the form of new actions in the class. Class refinement ensures that each set of successful computation with respect to the global variable satisfied by the original class is also satisfied by the refined class. Methods have the same interface throughout the refinement steps. Hence, so called interface refinement can only take place via shared variables.

One of the most useful features of object-orientation is the idea of reuse. OO-action systems employ this idea in two ways. Refinement via inheritance naturally models reuse of code. We additionally show that we can reuse refinement steps in our derivations.

*Related work* Action systems were originally proposed as a formalism for developing parallel and distributed systems [BK83]. They have similarities with e.g. UNITY-programs [CM88], in particular with the ImpUNITY formalism [UK95]. The action systems formalism has been recently extended from its original form in various ways, also towards object-orientation. Järvinen and Kurki-Suonio [JK91] develop their DisCo framework as a specification language for object-oriented systems. Back et al. [BBS97] show how objects are added into Action-Oberon, an Oberon-like language for parallel programming.

The OO-action system formalism is related with POOL [ABKR86,ABKR89] because objects are created dynamically, and their name can be assigned to variables. Furthermore, objects are active and distributed, hence, several objects are executed in parallel. The first model incorporating active objects was the actor model [Hew77,Agh86]. Moreover, CCS and the $\pi$-calculus, have been used to give a semantics to POOL-type parallel object-oriented languages [Jon93,Wal95]. Recently several formalisms and languages have been proposed that offer active objects, e.g. Oblique [Car95] which supports distributed object-oriented computation and Oblets [BN96] which are written in Oblique and which have a family of Web browsers capable of running Oblets.

We reason about OO-action systems in the framework of the refinement calculus. The refinement calculus and related calculi [Mor88,Mor87] have become popular foundations for program construction and for reasoning about specifications and implementations that meet their specifications. The refinement calculus uses weakest precondition predicate transformers as the semantic basis. Also Naumann [Nau94] uses predicate transformers to define a semantics for an Oberon-like object-oriented language with specification constructs. Moreover, Abadi and Leino develop a Hoare-style logic for reasoning about object-oriented programs [AL97]. Alternative frameworks for reasoning about object oriented systems include TLA [Lam91] used for reasoning about DisCo specifications, and coalgebras, used for automatic reasoning on CCSL and JAVA classes [HHJT98].

The way we define inheritance or sub-typing as class refinement is based on data refinement for action systems [Bac90,BS94,SW97]. Class refinement in the data refinement framework has also been studied by Mikhajlova and Sekerinski [MS97]. They construct new classes by inheritance and overriding, but do not consider the addition of new methods. Moreover, their objects are not active and distributed as ours are. Class refinement between Z specifications for object-oriented programs has also been reported in the literature [LH92,Str95].

*Overview* We proceed as follows. In Section 2 we describe the action system formalism and how they can be composed in parallel. We also briefly describe the refinement calculus for action systems. In Section 3 we introduce the OO-action systems, a formalism for the specification and development of object-oriented systems. To illustrate the formalism we present two examples of OO-action systems, one describing a phone company and another specifying the prime numbers sieve. In Section 4 we give a computational interpretation of OO-action systems in terms of standard action systems. Based on this interpretation in Section 5 we give rules for the refinement of OO-action systems. We show that we can reuse refinement step in Section 6. In Section 7 we give some examples of refinement steps for one of the two OO-action systems introduced in Section 3. We end in Section 8 with some concluding remarks.

## 2 Actions and action systems

Let *Var* be a countable set of *variables* and assume that each variable in *Var* is associated with a nonempty set of *values*. A *state* is a function mapping variables to values in their respective associated set of values. We denote by *true* the predicate on *Var* which holds for every state, and by *false* the predicate on *Var* which holds for no state. Given a predicate $\mathcal{P}$, a list of variables $x$, and a list of values $v$ we denote by $\mathcal{P}[x/v]$ the predicate which holds for those states $s$ such that $\mathcal{P}$ holds for $s[x/v]$, where $s[x/v]$ is the state which is defined as $s$ but for the variables $x$ which are mapped to values $v$.

A *conjunctive predicate transformer* is a function $\pi$ mapping predicates to predicates such that, for every nonempty index set $I$,

$$\pi(\bigwedge\{\mathcal{P}_i \mid i \in I\}) = \bigwedge\{\pi(\mathcal{P}_i) \mid i \in I\}\,.$$

Conjunctive predicate transformers form the semantic domains for statements interpreted by means of a *weakest precondition* semantics [Dij76].

We consider the following language of *actions* defined by the grammar

$$A ::= abort \mid skip \mid x := v \mid b \rightarrow A \mid p \mid A \,;\, A \mid [\!]_I A_i\,.$$

Here $x$ is a list of variables, $v$ a list of values (possibly resulting from the evaluation of a list of expressions), $b$ a predicate, $p$ a procedure name, and $I$ an index set ranged over by $i$. Intuitively, '*abort*' is the action which always deadlocks, '*skip*' is a stuttering action, '$x := v$' is a multiple assignment, '$b \rightarrow A$' is a guarded action, '$p$' is a procedure call, '$A_1 ; A_2$' is the sequential composition of two actions '$A_1$' and '$A_2$', and '$[\!]_I A_i$' is the nondeterministic choice among actions '$A_i$' for $i \in I$. Given a nonempty set $V$ of values and a variable $x$, we denote by '$x :\in V$' an abbreviation for the nondeterministic assignment '$[\!]_{v \in V} x := v$'.

A procedure declaration $p = P$ consists of a header $p$ and an action $P$, the body of the procedure. Given a declaration for each procedure, we define the weakest precondition semantics of the above language in a standard way [Dij76,Bac90] defined as the least conjunctive predicate transformer such that, for any predicate $\mathcal{P}$,

$$\begin{array}{llll} wp(abort, \mathcal{P}) & = false & wp(skip, \mathcal{P}) & = \mathcal{P} \\ wp(x := v, \mathcal{P}) & = \mathcal{P}[x/v] & wp(b \rightarrow A, \mathcal{P}) & = b \Rightarrow wp(A, \mathcal{P}) \\ wp(p, \mathcal{P}) & = wp(P, \mathcal{P}) & wp(A_1 ; A_2, \mathcal{P}) & = wp(A_1, wp(A_2, \mathcal{P})) \\ wp([\!]_I A_i, \mathcal{P}) & = \forall i \in I. wp(A_i, \mathcal{P})\,, & & \end{array}$$

where $P$ is the action denoting the body of the procedure $p$. The details of the definition of the above function is studied elsewhere [BK94].

In the sequel we will need the following notions. An action $A$ is *enabled* in a given state if its *guard*

$$gd(A) = \neg\, wp(A, false)$$

holds in that state. An action $A$ *cannot enable* another action $B$ whenever

$$wp(A, true) = true \;\text{ and }\; \neg\, gd(B) \Rightarrow wp(A, \neg\, gd(B))\,.$$

Moreover, $A$ *cannot disable* $B$ whenever

$$wp(A, true) = true \;\text{ and }\; gd(B) \Rightarrow wp(A, gd(B))\,.$$

## 2.1 Refinement of actions

An action $A$ is *refined* by another action $A'$, denoted $A \leq A'$, if, whenever $A$ establishes a certain postcondition, so does $A'$:

$$A \leq A' \text{ if and only if } \forall \mathcal{P}. wp(A, \mathcal{P}) \Rightarrow wp(A', \mathcal{P})\,.$$

Together with the monotonicity of the weakest precondition predicate transformers this implies that $A'$ is less nondeterministic than $A$ or it may behave miraculously, i.e. it may establish the postcondition *false*. Note that the refinement relation is reflexive and transitive.

If we need to change the state space in a refinement, we can use the following technique due to Hoare [Hoa72]. Let $A$ be an action that refers to the variables $x$ and $y$, and $A'$ be an action referring to the variable $x'$ and $y$. We say that the action $A$ is *data refined* by the action $A'$ using an *abstraction relation* $R(x, x', y)$ between the abstract variables $x$, the concrete variables $x'$ and the common variables $y$, if

$$\forall \mathcal{P}.R \wedge wp(A, \mathcal{P}) \Rightarrow wp(A', \exists x.R \wedge \mathcal{P}),$$

where $\mathcal{P}$ is a predicate on the variables $x$ and $y$, and $\exists x.R \wedge \mathcal{P}$ is a predicate on the variables $x'$ and $y$. Note that the common variables $y$ are not changed. We denote by $A \leq_R A'$, the refinement of $A$ by $A'$ using the abstraction relation $R$. Data refinement as described here is also called *downward simulation*. It may strengthen the guards of an action, decrease nondeterminism and increase termination. Note carefully that refinement and data refinement are related notions in the sense that the above data refinement relation can be defined in term of the ordinary refinement relation using special commands to encode abstraction relations [Wri94].

## 2.2 Action systems

An *action system* is a set of actions operating on local and global variables. First, the variables are created and initialized. Then, repeatedly, enabled actions are chosen and executed. Actions operating on disjoint sets of variables can be executed in parallel. The computation terminates if no action is enabled, otherwise it continues infinitely. Syntactically, an action system $\mathcal{A}$ is a statement of the form

$$\begin{array}{lll} \mathcal{A} = \; [\![ & \textbf{var} & y^* := y0 \,;\, x := x0 \\ & \textbf{proc} & p_1^* = P_1 \,;\, \cdots \,;\, p_n^* = P_n \,; \\ & & q_1 = Q_1 \,;\, \cdots \,;\, q_m = Q_m \\ & \textbf{do} & \|_I \, A_i \; \textbf{od} \\ ]\!] & & \end{array}$$

An action system provides a declaration section for variables and one for procedures. Here $y$ is a list of *global variables*, marked with an asterisk $*$, that can be used locally by $\mathcal{A}$ and also by other action systems when put in parallel with $\mathcal{A}$. The variables in the list $x$ are *local* to $\mathcal{A}$. The global variables $y$ get initial values $y0$ and the local variables $x$ get initial values $x0$. Local variables that are declared but not initialized get an arbitrary initial value in their respective sets of associated values. We assume that $x$ and $y$ are disjoint.

Procedures marked with an asterisk $*$ in a procedure declaration $p_i = P_i$ are *exportable*: they can be called by the actions of $\mathcal{A}$ or by actions of some other action systems when put in parallel with $\mathcal{A}$. A procedure declared in $q_i = Q_i$ is *local* and can be called only by actions of $\mathcal{A}$. A procedure $p$ with body $P$ is said to be *locally enabled* if only actions of $\mathcal{A}$ (possibly containing a procedure call $p$) can enable or disable the action $P$.

*Actions* of the action system $\mathcal{A}$ are the actions $A_i$ for all $i \in I$ and all bodies of the procedures (both exportable and local) declared in $\mathcal{A}$. They can be any statement of our language of actions defined above, can refer to variables which are not declared in $\mathcal{A}$ but globally declared in an other action systems to be put in parallel with $\mathcal{A}$, and can contain procedure calls to procedure declared exportable in an other action systems to be put in parallel with $\mathcal{A}$. Since the nondeterministic choice $\|_I A_i$ is included as an operator on actions, we can confine ourselves to action systems with a body consisting of only a single action. Actions are atomic, meaning that if an action $A_k$, for $k \in I$, is chosen for execution then it is executed to completion without any interference from the other actions $A_i$ of the system. This ensures that a parallel execution of an action system gives the same results of a sequential non-deterministic execution.

Next we define the parallel composition of action systems. Let $I$ be a non-empty index set, and consider the action systems $\mathcal{A}_i$, for $i \in I$,

$$\begin{array}{lll} \mathcal{A}_i = [\![ & \textbf{var} & y_i^* := y0_i \ ; \ x_i := x0_i \\ & \textbf{proc} & p_{i,1}^* = P_{i,1} \ ; \cdots ; \ p_{i,n_i}^* = P_{i,n_i} \ ; \\ & & q_{i,1} = Q_{i,1} \ ; \cdots ; \ q_{i,m_i} = Q_{i,m_i} \\ & \textbf{do} \ A_i \ \textbf{od} & \\ ]\!] & & \end{array}$$

where the global variables, the local variables, the headers of the exportable procedures, and the headers of the local procedures declared in each action system $\mathcal{A}_i$ are required to be distinct. We define the the *parallel composition* $\|_I \mathcal{A}_i$ of the action systems $\mathcal{A}_i$ to be the action system

$$\begin{array}{lll} \|_I \mathcal{A}_i = [\![ & \textbf{var} & y^* := y0 \ ; \ x := x0 \\ & \textbf{proc} & p^* = P \ ; \ q = Q \\ & \textbf{do} \ \|_I \ A_i \ \textbf{od} & \\ ]\!] & & \end{array}$$

where $y$ is the list obtained by concatenating all lists of global variables $y_i$, $x$ is the list obtained by concatenating all lists of local variables $x_i$, $p = P$ is list containing the declarations of all the exportable procedures of every $\mathcal{A}_i$, and finally $q = Q$ is the list containing the declarations of all the local procedures of every $\mathcal{A}_i$. The initial values of the variables and the actions in $\|_I \mathcal{A}_i$ consist of the initial values and the actions of the original systems.

Since actions of an action system $\mathcal{A}$ may contain calls to procedure not declared in $\mathcal{A}$, in order to formally define the behaviour of $\mathcal{A}$ we need the following notion. An action system $\mathcal{E}$ is called a *full context* of an action system $\mathcal{A}$ if the actions of $\mathcal{E}$ contains only calls to procedures either declared in $\mathcal{E}$ or declared exportable in $\mathcal{A}$, and the actions of $\mathcal{A}$ contains only calls to procedure either declared in $\mathcal{A}$ or declared exportable in $\mathcal{E}$.

Action system in parallel with a full context can be considered as a command of the refinement calculus [Bac90]. This view allows for reasoning about the total correctness of the system. Indeed, data refinement for action systems, as described below, implies, for any full context, data refinement of the corresponding commands in the refinement calculus [SW97].

The behaviour of an action system in parallel with a full context considered as a reactive system is described by means of set of computations, that is, set of finite or infinite sequences of states restricted only to the global variables, without finite repetition of the same state (finite stuttering), and possibly terminating with a special symbol to denote abortion. A refinement relation for action systems as reactive systems can be defined as follows: an action system $\mathcal{A}$ is *trace refined* by an action system $\mathcal{A}'$ if for any full context $\mathcal{E}$ of $\mathcal{A}$ and $\mathcal{A}'$, whenever $\mathcal{A} \parallel \mathcal{E}$ cannot produce a computation which aborts then each computation of $\mathcal{A}' \parallel \mathcal{E}$ is also a computation of $\mathcal{A} \parallel \mathcal{E}$ [Bac90]. Data refinement for action systems, as described below, is justified via trace refinement.

### 2.3 Data refinement of action systems

Next we consider data refinement in the context of action systems. Let $\mathcal{A}$ be the action system

$$\begin{array}{rll} \mathcal{A} = |[ & \textbf{var} & y^* := y0 \,;\, x := x0 \\ & \textbf{proc} & p_1^* = P_1 \,;\, \cdots \,;\, p_n^* = P_n \,; \\ & & q_1 = Q_1 \,;\, \cdots \,;\, q_m = Q_m \\ & \textbf{do}\ A\ \textbf{od} & \\ & ]| & \end{array}$$

with every global procedure locally enabled, and let

$$\begin{array}{rll} \mathcal{A}' = |[ & \textbf{var} & y^* := y0 \,;\, x' := x0' \\ & \textbf{proc} & p_1^* = P_1' \,;\, \cdots \,;\, p_n^* = P_n' \,; \\ & & r_1^* = R_1 \,;\, \cdots \,;\, r_h^* = R_h \,; \\ & & s_1 = S_1 \,;\, \cdots \,;\, s_k = S_k \\ & \textbf{do}\ A' \parallel H\ \textbf{od} & \\ & ]| & \end{array}$$

We say that $\mathcal{A}$ is *data refined* by the action $\mathcal{A}'$ using an abstraction relation $R(x, x', y)$, denoted by $\mathcal{A} \preceq_R \mathcal{A}'$, if we have that

(1) Initialization: $R(x0, x0', y0)$,
(2) Procedures: $P_i \leq_R P_i'$,
(3) Enabledness: $R \wedge gd(P_i) \Rightarrow gd(P_i') \vee gd(A') \vee gd(H)$,
(4) Main actions: $A \leq_R A'$
(5) Continuation: $R \wedge gd(A) \Rightarrow gd(A') \vee gd(H)$,
(6) Auxiliary actions: $\textit{skip} \leq_R H$,
(7) Internal convergence: $R \Rightarrow wp(\textbf{ do } H \textbf{ od }, \textit{true})$,
(8) Non-interference: $R \wedge wp(B, \textit{true}) \Rightarrow wp(B, R)$ for every action $B$ of another action system $\mathcal{B}$ which can occur in a parallel composition with A.

In case of procedures with parameters we require that the formal parameters of the procedures are not changed in the refinement step [SW97].

The idea is that local variables $x$ in $A$ are replaced by $x'$ in $A'$. Due to this replacement, the action $A$ is changed into the action $A'$, and the procedure bodies $P_i$ of each exportable procedure $p_i$ is changed into $P_i'$. Some new computations on the local variables $x'$ may be added to the system in terms of the action $H$. Local procedures may be changed and new exportable procedures $r_i$ may be added to the system. Clearly they may use global variables. However, by (4) the procedures called by the action $A'$ use global variables essentially in the same way as some statements of the action $A$, whereas by (6) the procedures called by the action $H$ do not change the content of any global variables.

Informally, in order to prove a data refinement between two action systems we require that

(1) the abstraction relation is established by the initialization of the variables,
(2) the body $P_i$ of each exportable procedure $p_i$ is data refined as action by the respective body $P_i'$ using $R$,
(3) if $R$ holds then enabledness of the body of a global procedure in $\mathcal{A}$ is either preserved or an action in $\mathcal{A}'$ is enabled,
(4) the action $A$ is data refined by $A'$ using $R$,
(5) if $R$ holds then enabledness of the action $A$ is preserved by $A' \parallel H$,
(6) some new computations may be added by the action $H$ but they do not involve global variables,
(7) if $R$ holds then the new computations added by the action $H$ terminates,
(8) any context preserves the relation $R$.

Relying on the definition of data refinement of action systems we have that for two action systems $\mathcal{A}$ and $\mathcal{A}'$ and abstraction relation $R$, if $\mathcal{A} \preceq_R \mathcal{A}'$ then $\mathcal{A}$ is trace refined by $\mathcal{A}'$. The correctness of this statement can be proved in a similar way as Theorem 2 of Sere and Walden [SW97], who also consider procedures with parameters.

## 3 OO-action systems

In this section we introduce our action based formalism for object-oriented systems, the so-called OO-action systems. An OO-action system consists of a finite set of classes, each class specifying the behaviour of objects that are dynamically created and executed in parallel. A class contains a description (attributes) of the local and shared variables of the object instances of the class, some pointers (object variables) to object instances of possibly other classes, the operations (methods) that can be applied to object instances of the class, the internal operations (procedure) of object instances of the class, and a description of the actions to be executed when an object instance of the class is created.

Before introducing the notion of class, we need to define some basic building blocks. Let *CName* be a fixed set of class names. We define the set *OName* of valid names for objects, ranged over by $o$, by the following grammar:

$$o ::= c(root) \mid c(o, i),$$

where $i$ runs over the natural numbers and $c$ over the set *CName* of class names. Hence a name of an object is either $c(root)$, or a class name together with an object name and a number. The intended meaning is that the object $c(o,i)$ is an instance of a class with name $c$ and it is the $(i+1)$-th object created by the object named $o$. The name $c(root)$ is the name of an object, instance of a class with name $c$, that starts the execution.

We will also consider a fixed set *Attr* of attributes and assume that each attribute is associated with a nonempty set of *values*; and a fixed set of object variables *OVar* assumed to be disjoint from *Attr*. The only valid values for object variables are the constant *self* and the names for objects in *OName*.

The actions of a class are defined by the following grammar:

$$A ::= abort \mid skip \mid x := v \mid n := o \mid new(c) \mid n := new(c) \mid kill(n) \mid kill(self) \mid b \rightarrow A \mid p \mid n.m \mid self.m \mid A \,;\, A \mid \|_I A_i \,.$$

Here $x$ is a list of attributes, $n$ is an object variable, $v$ a list of values, $o$ is an object name or the constant *self* (both possibly resulting from the evaluation of an expression), $c$ is a class name, $b$ a predicate (possibly on attributes and object variables and referring to the constant *self*), $p$ is a procedure name and $m$ is a method name. Intuitively, '$n$:=$o$' stores the object name $o$ into the object variable $n$, '$n.m$' is a call of the method $m$ of the object the name of which is stored in the object variable $n$, '$self.m$' is a call of the method $m$ of declared in the same object. Note that method calls are always prefixed by an object variables or by the constant *self*. There are two object destructors '$kill(n)$' and '$kill(self)$', and two object constructors '$new(c)$' and '$n := new(c)$'. The latter assigns the name of the newly created instance of the class $c$ to the object variable $n$.

A *class* is a pair $\langle c, C\rangle$, where $c \in CName$ is the *name* of the class and $C$ is its *body*, that is, a statement of the form

$$\begin{array}{ll} C = |[ & \textbf{attr} \quad y^* := y0 \,;\, x := x0 \\ & \textbf{obj} \quad n \\ & \textbf{meth} \quad m_1 = M_1 \,;\, \cdots ;\, m_h = M_h \\ & \textbf{proc} \quad p_1 = P_1 \,;\, \cdots ;\, p_k = P_k \\ & \textbf{do}\ A\ \textbf{od} \\ ]| & \end{array}$$

A class body consists of an action of the above grammar and of four declaration sections. In the attribute declaration the ***shared attributes*** in the list $y$, marked with an asterisk $*$, describe the variables to be shared among all active objects. Therefore they can be used by instances of the class $C$ and also by objects instances of other classes. Initially they get values $y0$. The ***local attributes*** in the list $x$ describe variables that are local to an object instance of the class, meaning that they can only be used by the instance itself. The variables are initialized to the values $x0$. We assume that $x$ and $y$ are disjoint.

The list $n$ of *object variables* describes a special kind of variables local to an object instance of the class. They contain names of objects and are used for calling methods of other objects. We assume that the lists $x$, $y$ and $n$ are pairwise disjoint.

A *method* $m_i = M_i$ describes a procedure of an object instance of the class. They can be called by actions of the object itself or by actions of another object instance of possibly another class. A method consists of an header '$m$' and a body '$M$'. The latter is an action of the above grammar.

A *procedure* $p_i = P_i$ describes a procedure that is local to the object instances of the class. It can be called only by actions of the object itself. Like a method, it consists of an header '$p$' and an action forming the body '$P$'.

An *action* of a class is a description of the actions to be executed when the object instance of the class is activated. It can refer to attributes which are declared shared in another class, and to the object variables and the local attributes declared within the class itself. It can contain procedure calls only to procedure declared in the class and method calls of the form $n.m$ to methods declared in another class. Methods calls ***self***$.m$ are allow only if $m$ is a method declared in the class. The constant ***self*** is used to indicate the name of the instance of the class. As for action systems actions are atomic.

An *OO-action system OO* consists of a finite set of classes

$$OO = \{\langle c_1, C_1\rangle, ..., \langle c_n, C_n\rangle\}$$

such that the shared attributes declared in each $C_i$ are distinct and actions in each $C_i$ or bodies of methods and procedures declared in each $C_i$ do not contain *new* statements referring to class names not used by classes in $OO$. Local attributes, object variables, methods, and procedures are not required to be distinct. There are some classes in $OO$, marked with an asterisk $*$, that serve as roots. Execution starts by the creation of one object instance of each of these classes. Each object, when created, chooses enabled actions and execute them. Actions operating on disjoint sets of local and shared attributes, and object variables can be executed in parallel. They can also create or kill other objects. Actions of different active objects can be executed in parallel if they are operating on disjoint sets of shared attributes. Objects can interact by means of the shared attributes and by executing methods of other objects.

### 3.1 An example: the prime number sieve

Our first example of OO-action systems is the (rather standard) prime number sieve which typically illustrates the dynamical binding of operations to program code. An object of the class $\langle \mathit{Driver}, \mathit{Dr}\rangle$ generates an infinite increasing sequence of natural numbers, which it feeds into a chain of object instances of the class $\langle \mathit{Prime}, \mathit{Pr}\rangle$. Each of those object stores in the variable $\mathit{prime}[n]$ the first number it receives (always a prime number greater than 1) and from the rest of the numbers it passes only those numbers that are not divisible by $\mathit{prime}[n]$. The OO-action system is defined as follows:

$$\{\langle \mathit{Driver}, \mathit{Dr}\rangle^*, \langle \mathit{Prime}, \mathit{Pr}\rangle\}\,.$$

The computation starts with an object instance of the class *Driver*.

Below we describe the body of the class *Driver*. It introduces two shared attributes *prime*[1] and *counter*. The first one stores the first prime number, and will never be changed by any object. It is introduced only for sake of completeness. The other shared attribute is used to count the number of primes that are already found plus one. Since the system starts with the first prime number stored in the attribute *prime*[1], *counter* is initially set to 2. The local attribute *number* is used to generate an infinite increasing sequence of natural numbers.

$$
\begin{array}{lll}
Dr = \| [ & \textbf{attr} & prime[1]^* := 1 \; ; \; counter^* := 2 \\
 & & number := 1 \; ; \; created := false \\
 & \textbf{obj} & first \\
 & \textbf{do} & \\
 & & \quad \neg created \rightarrow first := new(Prime) \; ; \; created := true \\
 & & \| \; created \rightarrow number := number + 1 \; ; \; first.Sieve(number) \\
 & \textbf{od} & \\
 ] \| & &
\end{array}
$$

Next we define the body of the class *Prime*. It declares an infinite number of shared attributes *prime*[*n*] where the *n*-th prime number will be stored. The class has only one method which is repeatedly executed by the object which creates an instance of *Prime*. The computation proceeds in a pipelined way: when a new prime number is found then a new object is created and pipelined.

$$
\begin{array}{lll}
Pr = \| [ & \textbf{attr} & prime[2]^* := 0 \; ; \cdots ; \; prime[n]^* := 0 \; ; \cdots \\
 & & p := 0 \; ; \; created := false \\
 & \textbf{obj} & next \\
 & \textbf{meth} & Sieve(z) = (\neg created \rightarrow prime[counter] := z; \\
 & & \qquad\qquad p := counter \; ; \; counter := counter + 1; \\
 & & \qquad\qquad next := new(Prime) \; ; \; created := true \\
 & & \qquad \| \; created \wedge z \textbf{ mod } prime[p] = 0 \rightarrow skip \\
 & & \qquad \| \; created \wedge z \textbf{ mod } prime[p] \neq 0 \rightarrow next.Sieve(z)) \\
 ] \| & &
\end{array}
$$

Here the local attribute *p* is used as a pointer to the prime array remembering where the objects has stored the prime number associated with its creation.

### 3.2 Another example: a phone company

As a second example of an OO-action system we describe a phone company with many phones that can call each other. The system consists of two classes, one named *PhonoCompany* and another one named *Phone*:

$$\{\langle PhoneCompany, PC\rangle^*, \langle Phone, Ph\rangle\}$$

The execution starts with the creation of one phone company (the class is marked with an asterisk) and then an arbitrary number of phones may start their activity.

The body *PC* of the class *PhoneCompany* is described below. It models a company that can create new phones (when the variable *allow_new_phones* is true). When a new phone is created, it is added to the phonebook (a set of integers represented by the shared attribute *phonebook*) that contains phone numbers. The link between a phone number $i$ and the name of the phone is kept in the object variable $names[i]$. After a phone is created, the name of the phone company where it has been registered in is told to the phone. This is done by the phone company by calling the method *where* of the created phone. Each phone company offers a service *give_name* to the phones: given a phone number, it will give the name of the phone (in a result parameter).

$$
\begin{array}{lll}
PC = [\![ & \textbf{attr} & phones^* := 0 \; ; phonebook^* := \emptyset; \\
 & & allow\_new\_phones := true \\
 & \textbf{obj} & entry \; ; names[1] \; ; \cdots ; names[n] \; ; \cdots \\
 & \textbf{meth} & Give\_name(x, n) = n := names[x] \\
 & \textbf{proc} & Update(n) = (\, phones := phones + 1; \\
 & & \qquad\qquad\qquad phonebook := phonebook \cup \{phones\}; \\
 & & \qquad\qquad\qquad names[phones] := n \,) \\
 & \textbf{do} & \\
 & & \quad allow\_new\_phones \rightarrow entry := new(Phone); \\
 & & \qquad\qquad\qquad Update(entry); \\
 & & \qquad\qquad\qquad entry.Where(self) \\
 & & [\!]\; allow\_new\_phones :\in \{true, false\} \\
 & \textbf{od} & \\
]\!] & &
\end{array}
$$

Here the variable *phones* stores the number of phones registered at the company, and *entry* is the name of the new phone to be register in the phonebook.

Next we describe the body *Ph* of the class *Phone*. Each phone has a variable *number* which stores for the caller the number of the phone to which it is currently connected, or, if the phone is not connected, the number of the last phone it called.

$$
\begin{array}{lll}
Ph = [\![ & \textbf{attr} & number := -1; \\
 & & idle := trueregistered := false \\
 & \textbf{obj} & company \; ; callee \\
 & \textbf{meth} & Accept\_call\_from(n) = (\, idle \wedge n \neq self \rightarrow idle := false; \\
 & & \qquad\qquad\qquad\qquad\qquad\qquad callee := n \,) \\
 & & Where(y) = (company := y \; ; registered := true) \\
 & & Return = idle := true \\
 & \textbf{proc} & Call = (\, number :\in phonebook; \\
 & & \qquad company.Give\_name(number, callee); \\
 & & \qquad callee.Accept\_call\_from(self) \; ; idle := false) \\
 & \textbf{do} & \\
 & & \quad idle \wedge registered \rightarrow Call \\
 & & [\!]\; \neg idle \rightarrow callee.Return \; ; idle := true \\
 & \textbf{od} & \\
]\!] & &
\end{array}
$$

Phones have two actions, one for calling other phones and another one for ending a call. Only a registered phone in an idle state may call another phone. In this case a number is selected from the phonebook and the name of the corresponding object is obtained by the company via the method *Give_name* and stored in the object variable *callee*. If the phone *callee* is idle then both phones are connected and enter in a not-idle state. One of the two phones can now break the connection and both phones return in their idle state.

### 3.3 Composing OO-action systems

Let $OO_1$ and $OO_2$ be two OO-action systems where the shared attributes declared in each class in $OO_1$ are distinct from the shared attributes declared in each class in $OO_2$. Furthermore, assume that the class names used by the classes in $OO_1$ are distinct from the class names used by the classes in $OO_2$. We define the *parallel composition* $OO_1 \parallel OO_2$ of $OO_1$ and $OO_2$ to be the OO-action system $OO_1 \cup OO_2$, where a class in $OO_1 \parallel OO_2$ is marked by an asterisk $*$ if it is marked by an asterisk $*$ in either $OO_1$ or $OO_2$.

## 4 The computational model

Computationally, an OO-action system can be represented by a parallel composition of infinitely many action systems, each of them used either for initializing the global variables of a class, or for representing instances of classes. The action and procedure bodies of each of these action systems are guarded by a local boolean variable *start*. It is set to true only when that instance becomes an active object and it is set to false when the object is deactivated. The constructors $new(c)$ and $n := new(c)$ and the destructors $kill(n)$ and $kill(self)$ are replaced by remote procedure calls that act on the variable *start*.

We define the semantic model of an OO-action system in three steps. In the first step we translate every action $A$ of a class $\langle c, C\rangle$ into an action $A_o$ of an action system. This translation is parametric with respect to the name of the object $o$ where the action has to be executed. In the second step we associate to each class $\langle c, C\rangle$ an action system $\mathcal{A}(c)$ obtained as the parallel composition of an action system $\mathcal{A}(c(root))$ with all the action systems $\mathcal{A}(c(o,i))$ for $o \in OName$ and $i \in \mathbb{N}$. The first action system initializes the global variables of the class and, if the class is marked by an asterisk, starts executing an action of the first object instance of the class. The action systems $\mathcal{A}(c(o,i))$ for $o \in OName$ and $i \in \mathbb{N}$ represent all possible object instances of the class $\langle c, C\rangle$. Finally, in the third step we translate an OO-action system $OO$ into an single action system $\mathcal{A}(OO)$ obtained by putting in parallel the action systems $\mathcal{A}(c)$ for each class $\langle c, C\rangle \in OO$ .

### 4.1 Translating class-actions

For fixed and disjoint sets *Attr* and *OVar* of attributes and object variables let us consider a set *Var* of variables containing $x$, $o.x$, and $o.n$ for each $x \in Attr$,

$n \in OVar$ and object name $o \in OName$. Furthermore, let us assume that $o.start$ and $o.count$ are in $Var$ but not in $Attr$ and $OVar$ for each object name $o \in OName$. The set of values associated with the variables $x$ and $o.x$ are the same as for the set of values associated with the attribute $x$, while $OName$ is the set of value associated with every variable of the form $o.n$.

We start with the translation of an action of a class. Let $o$ be an object name in $OName$, and $A$ be an action of some class with local attributes $x$, object variables $n$ and local procedures $p$. Define the action $A_o$ as the result of consecutively applying the following steps:

1. replace the constant *self* by the name $o$,
2. replace every local attribute $x$ by $o.x$,
3. replace every call to a local procedure $p$ by $o.p$,
4. replace every method call $n.p$, for some object variable $n$, by the statement
$$\|_{u \in OName}(n = u) \rightarrow u.p\,,$$
5. replace every action $new(c)$ by the statement
$$(\|_{i \in \mathbb{N}}(o.count = i) \rightarrow c(o,i).init)\ ;\ o.count := o.count + 1\,,$$
6. replace every $n := new(c)$ by the statement
$$(\|_{i \in \mathbb{N}}(o.count = i) \rightarrow n := c(o,i)\ ;\ c(o,i).init)\ ;\ o.count := o.count + 1\,,$$
7. replace every $kill(n)$ by the statement
$$\|_{u \in OName}(n = u) \rightarrow u.stop\,,$$
8. replace every $kill(o)$ by the procedure call $o.stop$
9. replace every object variable $n$ by $o.n$.

The idea is that the name $o$ is the name of an object instance of a class where the action $A_o$ has to be executed. Since this action must be an action in the format required by the syntax of action systems, we substitute the constant *self* by the name of the object. Local attributes and object variables become ordinary variables. Locality of these variables is obtained by prefixing them with the name of the object $o$. The same is applied also to local procedures. Every method call becomes a call to a remote procedure. Since the name of the object where the procedure is declared is known only at run-time, we need to quantify the procedure call over all possible object names. Note that, in the first step, a method call prefixed by the constant *self* is replaced by a procedure call declared exportable in the object itself. The actions $new(c)$ and $n := new(c)$ are both replaced by a call to the remote procedure $c(o,i).init$ followed by an increment of the local variable $o.count$. The procedure $c(o,i).init$ is declared in the i-th object instance of the class $c$ created by the object named $o$, where $i$ is a number stored in $o.count$. Since this number is known only at run-time, we quantify over all possible values of $o.count$, that is, over all natural numbers.

The procedure $c(o,i).\mathit{init}$ has the task of setting the boolean flag $c(o,i).\mathit{start}$ to true, so that the computation of the object named $c(o,i)$ may start. The action $\mathit{kill}(n)$ is replaced by a call to the remote procedure $u.\mathit{stop}$ declared in the object named $u$, where $u$ is the object name stored in $n$. This name is known only at run-time. Similarly, the action $\mathit{kill}(\mathit{self})$ is replaced by a call to the procedure $o.\mathit{stop}$. The effect of the procedure $u.\mathit{stop}$ is to set the flag $u.\mathit{start}$ of the object named $u$ to false interrupting its computation.

## 4.2 Translating classes

We now translate a single class $\langle c, \mathcal{C}\rangle$ into an action system $\mathcal{A}(c)$. Let $\mathcal{C}$ be the class body

$$
\begin{array}{ll}
[\![ & \mathbf{attr}\ \ y^* := y0\ ;\ x := x0 \\
& \mathbf{obj}\ \ n \\
& \mathbf{meth}\ m_1 = M_1\ ;\ \cdots\ ;\ m_h = M_h \\
& \mathbf{proc}\ \ p_1 = P_1\ ;\ \cdots\ ;\ p_k = P_k \\
& \mathbf{do}\ A\ \mathbf{od} \\
]\!] &
\end{array}
$$

We begin with the definition of the action system $\mathcal{A}(c(\mathit{root}))$ containing the declaration and initialization of all global variables corresponding to the shared attributes of the class $c$ and the actions to be initially executed in case the class $\langle c, \mathcal{C}\rangle$ is marked with an asterisk $*$. If the class is not marked by an asterisk then

$$\mathcal{A}(c(\mathit{root})) = [\![\ \mathbf{var}\ y^* := y0\ ]\!]\ ,$$

otherwise

$$
\begin{array}{lll}
\mathcal{A}(c(\mathit{root})) = [\![ & \mathbf{var} & y^* := y0; \\
& & c(\mathit{root}).\mathit{start} := \mathit{true}\ ;\ c(\mathit{root}).\mathit{count} := 0; \\
& & c(\mathit{root}).x := x0\ ;\ c(\mathit{root}).n \\
& \mathbf{proc} & c(\mathit{root}).\mathit{stop}^* = (c(\mathit{root}).\mathit{start} := \mathit{false}); \\
& & c(\mathit{root}).m_1^* = (c(\mathit{root}).\mathit{start} \rightarrow M_{1_{c(\mathit{root})}}); \\
& & \vdots \\
& & c(\mathit{root}).m_h^* = (c(\mathit{root}).\mathit{start} \rightarrow M_{h_{c(\mathit{root})}}); \\
& & c(\mathit{root}).p_1 = P_{1_{c(\mathit{root})}}\ ;\ \cdots\ ;\ c(\mathit{root}).p_k = P_{k_{c(\mathit{root})}} \\
& \multicolumn{2}{l}{\mathbf{do}\ c(\mathit{root}).\mathit{start} \rightarrow A_{c(\mathit{root})}\ \mathbf{od}} \\
]\!] & &
\end{array}
$$

In case the class $\langle c, \mathcal{C}\rangle$ is not marked by an asterisk, the action system $\mathcal{A}(c(\mathit{root}))$ is used only to transform the shared attributes of the class into global variables. Therefore $\mathcal{A}(c(\mathit{root}))$ has no declaration section for procedures and no action in its body. If the class $\langle c, \mathcal{C}\rangle$ is marked by an asterisk $*$, the shared attributes of the class are transformed into global variables of the action system $\mathcal{A}(c(\mathit{root}))$, and every action $A$, method body $M$ and procedure body $P$ of the class are translated into actions $A_{c(\mathit{root})}$, $M_{c(\mathit{root})}$ and $P_{c(\mathit{root})}$, respectively. Actions and methods are also guarded by the local variable $c(\mathit{root}).\mathit{start}$ which is initially set to true; it can be set to false only when the object is deactivated by means of a call of the exportable procedure $c(\mathit{root}).\mathit{stop}$. Local attributes and object variables of the class are treated as local variables. There is an extra local variable $c(\mathit{root}).\mathit{count}$ which is used to store the number of objects created by $\mathcal{A}(c(\mathit{root}))$.

Next we define, for each $o \in \mathit{OName}$ and $i \in \mathbb{N}$, the action system $\mathcal{A}(c(o,i))$ that describes the behaviour of the $i$-th object instance of the class $\langle c, \mathcal{C}\rangle$ created by the object named $o$:

$$
\begin{array}{lll}
\mathcal{A}(c(o,i)) = |[ & \textbf{var} & c(o,i).\mathit{start} := \mathit{false}\ ;\ c(o,i).\mathit{count} := 0;\\
& & c(o,i).x := x0\ ;\ c(o,i).n\\
& \textbf{proc} & c(o,i).\mathit{init}^* = (c(o,i).\mathit{start} := \mathit{true});\\
& & c(o,i).\mathit{stop}^* = (c(o,i).\mathit{start} := \mathit{false});\\
& & c(o,i).m_1^* = (c(o,i).\mathit{start} \to M_{1_{c(o,i)}});\\
& & \vdots\\
& & c(o,i).m_h^* = (c(o,i).\mathit{start} \to M_{h_{c(o,i)}});\\
& & c(o,i).p_1 = P_{1_{c(o,i)}}\ ;\cdots ;\ c(o,i).p_k = P_{k_{c(o,i)}}\\
& \multicolumn{2}{l}{\textbf{do}\ c(o,i).\mathit{start} \to A_{c(o,i)}\ \textbf{od}}\\
]| & &
\end{array}
$$

The action system $\mathcal{A}(c(o,i))$ is defined in a similar way as for the action system $\mathcal{A}(c(\mathit{root}))$ when the class $c$ is marked by an asterisk. There are no global variables corresponding to the shared attributes, because they are declared only in the action system $\mathcal{A}(c(\mathit{root}))$. Moreover, the local variable $c(o,i).\mathit{start}$ is initially set to false: it will be set to true only when the object is created and set to false when the object is deactivated. The value of the variable $c(o,i).\mathit{start}$ can only be changed by a remote call to the exportable procedures $c(o,i).\mathit{init}$ and $c(o,i).\mathit{stop}$.

The action system $\mathcal{A}(c)$ describing the behaviour of the class $\langle c, \mathcal{C}\rangle$ is defined by

$$\mathcal{A}(c) = \mathcal{A}(c(\mathit{root})) \parallel (\parallel_{\mathit{OName}\times\mathbb{N}} \mathcal{A}(c(o,i)))\,.$$

Clashes of variables and procedure names are avoided in the above definition by declaring global variables only in the action system $\mathcal{A}(c(\mathit{root}))$ and by prefixing each local variable and procedure name by the name of the object instance of the class.

## 4.3 Translating OO-action systems

In the last step we define the action system $\mathcal{A}(\mathit{OO})$ for an OO-action system $\mathit{OO} = \{\langle c_1, \mathcal{C}_1\rangle, ..., \langle c_n, \mathcal{C}_n\rangle\}$:

$$\mathcal{A}(\mathit{OO}) = (\mathcal{A}(c_1) \parallel \cdots \parallel \mathcal{A}(c_n))\,.$$

The action system $\mathcal{A}(\mathit{OO})$ is a parallel composition of all possible instance of the classes composing the OO-action system $\mathit{OO}$. The execution starts with an action from an action system $\mathcal{A}(c(root))$ for some class $\langle c, \mathcal{C}\rangle \in OO$ marked by an asterisk. Initially, only the actions generated from the marked classes are potentially enabled.

The following theorem is an immediate consequence of the translation above and the definition of parallel composition between OO-action systems.

**Theorem 1.** *Let $OO_1 \parallel OO_2$ be the OO-action system obtained as the parallel composition of two OO-action systems $OO_1$ and $OO_2$. Then $\mathcal{A}(OO_1 \parallel OO_2) = \mathcal{A}(OO_1) \parallel \mathcal{A}(OO_2)$.*

## 5 Refining OO-action systems

A refinement relation between OO-action systems can be obtained by translating them into ordinary action systems. For two OO-action systems $OO$ and $OO'$ we say that $OO$ is refined by $OO'$, denoted by

$$OO \sqsubseteq OO'$$

if there exists an abstraction relation $R$ such that

$$\mathcal{A}(OO) \preceq_R \mathcal{A}(OO').$$

The idea is that in an OO-action system only the values of the shared attributes are visible. Since shared attributes are translated into global variables, refinement between two OO-action systems preserves the behavior of the original system with respect to these variables.

In this section we give a number of rules that can be applied directly between OO-action system without translating them into action systems. The justification for all the refinement rules below is based on this translation.

*Class refinement* We start by a simple rule which allows to substitute a class in an OO-action system by a refinement of that class. We say that a class $\langle c, \mathcal{C}\rangle$ with

$$
\begin{array}{lll}
\mathcal{C} = [\![ & \textbf{attr} & y^* := y0 \;;\; x := x0 \\
& \textbf{obj} & n \\
& \textbf{meth} & m_1 = M_1 \;;\; \cdots \;;\; m_h = M_h \\
& \textbf{proc} & p_1 = P_1 \;;\; \cdots \;;\; p_k = P_k \\
& \textbf{do}\ A\ \textbf{od} & \\
]\!] & &
\end{array}
$$

is *class-refined* by a class $\langle c', \mathcal{C}'\rangle$ with

$$
\begin{array}{lll}
\mathcal{C}' = [\![ & \textbf{attr} & y^* := y0 \;;\; x' := x0' \\
& \textbf{obj} & n \\
& \textbf{meth} & m_1 = M_1' \;;\; \cdots \;;\; m_h = M_h' \\
& \textbf{proc} & q_1 = Q_1 \;;\; \cdots \;;\; q_j = Q_j \\
& \textbf{do}\ A'\ \textbf{od} & \\
]\!] & &
\end{array}
$$

if $c = c'$ and there exists a relation $R(x, x', y)$ between the attributes $x$ and $x'$ and the shared attributes $y$ such that,

1. $\mathcal{A}(c(root)) \preceq_{R_{c(root)}} \mathcal{A}(c'(root))$, and
2. for each $o \in OName$ and $i \in \mathbb{N}$, $\mathcal{A}(c(o,i)) \preceq_{R_{c(o,i)}} \mathcal{A}(c'(o,i))$.

Here, for $o \in OName$, $R_o$ is the relation obtained by translating each attribute $x$ and $x'$ in $o.x$ and $o.x'$, respectively. If a class $\langle c, C \rangle$ is refined by another class $\langle c, C' \rangle$ then we call the class $\langle c, C' \rangle$ a ***subclass*** of $\langle c, C \rangle$ and $\langle c, C \rangle$ a ***superclass*** of $\langle c, C' \rangle$.

Because the relation $R$ does not refer to the object variables $n$ and the variables $c(o,i).start$ and $c(o,i).count$, and because all relations $R_o$ are distinct, class-refinement implies that $\mathcal{A}(c) \preceq_{R'} \mathcal{A}(c')$, where $R'$ is the union of all relations $R_{c(root)}$ and $R_{c(o,i)}$, for $o \in OName$ and $i \in \mathbb{N}$. This justifies the following rule.

**Rule 1.** *Let OO be an OO-action system such that $\langle c, C \rangle \in OO$. Let also $\langle c, C' \rangle$ be another class (which cannot be in OO because a class with the name c is already in it) such that $\langle c, C \rangle$ is class-refined by $\langle c, C' \rangle$. Then*

$$OO \sqsubseteq OO' = OO \setminus \{\langle C, C \rangle\} \cup \{\langle C, C' \rangle\},$$

*where the class $\langle c, C' \rangle$ is marked with an asterisk $*$ in OO' if the class $\langle c, C \rangle$ is marked with an asterisk $*$ in OO.*

*Introducing new classes* Next we give a rule which allows an OO-action system to duplicate one of its classes. The class which is duplicated can then be refined according to the previous rule obtaining a subclass. This may be useful because the superclass can have variables that are used by the refined class or some other class might share them. Moreover, some clients might use the superclass, and some others the subclass as will be made clear later in this section.

**Rule 2.** *Let OO be an OO-action system such that $\langle c, C \rangle \in OO$ and assume $c' \in CName$ is a class name not used in OO. Let $C'$ be a copy of $C$ without declaration of shared attributes. Then*

$$OO \sqsubseteq OO \cup \{\langle c', C' \rangle\},$$

*where the class $\langle c', C' \rangle$ is not marked by an asterisk.*

This rule can be justified as follows. The idea is that we refine within an iterative command an action $A$ by the action $A \,\|\, g \rightarrow A'$, where $g$ is a boolean variable initially set to false and which cannot be set to true by $A$. Informally, introducing a new class $\langle c', C' \rangle$ means that new actions and new exportable procedures are now introduced in the action system $\mathcal{A}(OO)$. However, these actions and procedure bodies are guarded by a boolean variable which is initially set to false. Only if the environment calls the procedure $c'(o,i).init$ for some $o \in OName$ and $i \in \mathbb{N}$ can this guard be set to true. But this procedure can only be called if a statement $new(c')$ or $n := new(c')$ is present in the action of some other class in $OO$. Since the class name $c'$ is not used in $OO$ such *new* statements cannot be present in any class of $OO$. For a similar reason, no full context of $\mathcal{A}(OO)$ can call any procedure $c'(o,i).init$.

*Removing a class* A converse of the above rule is possible. A class that has no declaration of shared attributes, that is not marked by an asterisk, and such that no other class refers to it can be safely removed from an OO-action system.

**Rule 3.** *Let $\langle c, \mathcal{C}\rangle$ be a class of an OO-action system $OO$ such that no shared attributes are declared in $\mathcal{C}$, it is not marked by an asterisk, and for all other classes $\langle c', \mathcal{C}'\rangle \in OO$ with $c' \neq c$ no statement $new(c)$ or $n := new(c)$ is present in the actions of $\mathcal{C}'$. Then*

$$OO \sqsubseteq OO \setminus \{\langle c, \mathcal{C}\rangle\}.$$

This rule can be justified in a similar way as the Rule 2. Note that each class introduced by Rule 2 can be safely removed by the above rule obtaining the original OO-action system. Similarly, each class removed by the above rule can be re-introduced by Rule 2 obtaining the original OO-action system.

*Refining new statements* In a refinement we are interested only in the values of the shared attributes. It is of no importance which object acts on which attributes. Hence it is unobservable if an object is an instance of a class named $c$ or of another class $d$ if both classes have the same body (except for the list of shared attributes declared, which must be disjoint).

**Rule 4.** *Let $OO$ be an OO-action system and assume the $\langle c, \mathcal{C}\rangle$ and $\langle c', \mathcal{C}'\rangle$ are two classes in $OO$ such that $\mathcal{C}'$ is a copy of $\mathcal{C}$ except for declaration of the shared attributes which are distinct. Let $\langle d, \mathcal{D}\rangle$ be a class in $OO$ and define $\mathcal{D}'$ to be as $\mathcal{D}$ but where some of the occurrences of $new(c)$ have been replaced either by $new(c')$ or by $new(c) \parallel new(c')$, and some of the of the occurrences of $n{:=}new(c)$ have been replaced either by $n := new(c')$ or by $n := new(c) \parallel n := new(c')$. Then*

$$OO \sqsubseteq OO \setminus \{\langle d, \mathcal{D}\rangle\} \cup \{\langle d, \mathcal{D}'\rangle\}.$$

*The class $\langle d, \mathcal{D}'\rangle$ is marked by an asterisk only if $\langle d, \mathcal{D}\rangle$ is marked by an asterisk in $OO$.*

The above rule can be justified by an argument similar to the following. Assume $p_1$ and $p_2$ are two procedures with the same body. If $A$ is an action containing a call to the procedure $p_1$ then it can be refined by an action $A'$ where $p_2$ or $p_1 \parallel p_2$ substitutes $p_1$.

*Client refinement* Rule 4 can be used in combination with the previous rules to model explicit client refinement as follows: we change the name of the class to be refined by creating a new class (Rule 2), then change the appropriate clients to refer to the newly created class by refining the *new* statements (Rule 4). Finally, we can refine the newly created class (Rule 1). In this case in an OO-action system we have both the superclass and the subclasses of the same original class.

To model implicit client refinement we can use Rule 1: we replace in an OO-action system a class with another class refining it without changing the name of the class. In this way every client of the superclass becomes implicitly a client of the subclass.

*Inheritance and overriding* Rule 1 for class refinement models inheritance in a limited manner: the new class $\langle c, C' \rangle$ inherits all the methods $m$ as well as the local procedures $q$ from its superclass $\langle c, C \rangle$. Method overriding takes place via refinement, as the bodies of the procedures declared in $C$ might change in the refinement step. Using this rule no new global methods are provided by the subclass $C'$. The formal parameters of the methods are not to be changed in a refinement step.

A special case of Rule 1, the superposition rule [BS92,BS94], could be used instead of the above, more general data refinement rule. In superposition we do not remove old attributes, only new attributes are added into a class. Hence, a subclass would work with all attributes declared in the superclass and with some new, added attributes.

*Introducing new methods* Next we give a rule for the introduction of new methods. The idea is similar as for the Rule 2 for the introduction of new classes. Indeed a local procedure $p$ of a class $\langle c, C \rangle$ can be made a method without any observable change of the behaviour of the system, because only actions of $C$ can call the new method $p$.

**Rule 5.** *Let $\langle c, C \rangle$ be a class in an OO-action system $OO$, and let $C'$ be as $C$ except that some local procedures of $C$ are now declared as methods. Then*

$$OO \sqsubseteq OO \setminus \{\langle c, C \rangle\} \cup \{\langle c, C' \rangle\}.$$

*The class $\langle c, C' \rangle$ is marked by an asterisk only if $\langle c, C \rangle$ is marked by an asterisk in $OO$.*

This rule can be easily justified by the fact that an action system is always refined by an equivalent one where we make some local procedures global.

*Merging classes* Let $OO$ be an OO-action system, and let $\langle c_1, C_1 \rangle$ and $\langle c_2, C_2 \rangle$ be two classes in $OO$ where

$$
\begin{array}{llll}
C_1 = |[ & \textbf{attr} & y^* := y0 \,;\, x := x0 \\
& \textbf{obj} & n \\
& \textbf{meth} & m_1 = M_1 \,;\, \cdots ;\, m_h = M_h \\
& \textbf{proc} & p_1 = P_1 \,;\, \cdots ;\, p_k = P_h \\
& \textbf{do}\ A_1\ \textbf{od} \\
]| \\
\end{array}
\qquad
\begin{array}{llll}
C_2 = |[ & \textbf{attr} & z^* := z0 \,;\, w := w0 \\
& \textbf{obj} & n' \\
& \textbf{meth} & r_1 = R_1 \,;\, \cdots ;\, r_i = R_i \\
& \textbf{proc} & q_1 = Q_1 \,;\, \cdots ;\, q_j = Q_j \\
& \textbf{do}\ A_2\ \textbf{od} \\
]| \\
\end{array}
$$

Since both classes are in $OO$ it follows that the list of shared attributes $y$ and $z$ are disjoint. Furthermore, we assume that the lists of local attributes $x$ and object variables $n$ are disjoint from $w$ and $n'$, and that the methods $m$ and procedures $p$ are distinct from the methods $r$ and the procedures $q$.

Then we have the following rule that allows us to introduce a class into an OO-action system by merging two classes together.

**Rule 6.** *Let OO be an OO-action system, and let $\langle c_1, C_1\rangle$ and $\langle c_2, C_2\rangle$ be two classes in OO as above. Let also c be a class name not used by the classes in OO. Then*

$$OO \sqsubseteq OO' \cup \{\langle c, C\rangle\}$$

*where*

$$\begin{array}{lll} C = [\![ & \textbf{attr} & x := x0 \,;\, w := w0 \\ & \textbf{obj} & n \,;\, n' \\ & \textbf{meth} & m_1 = M_1 \,;\cdots;\, m_h = M_h; \\ & & r_1 = R_1 \,;\cdots;\, r_i = R_i \\ & \textbf{proc} & p_1 = P_1 \,;\cdots;\, p_k = P_h; \\ & & q_1 = Q_1 \,;\cdots;\, q_j = Q_j \\ & \textbf{do}\ A_1 \,[\!]\, A_2\ \textbf{od} & \\ ]\!] & & \end{array}$$

*and $OO'$ is obtained by replacing some occurrences of $new(c_1)$ ; $new(c_2)$ by $new(c)$ in the actions of the classes in OO.*

The converse rule for splitting a class in two is more problematic: a local procedure of one of the classes may need to become a method in order for an action of the other class to call it; but this introduces the problem of which object instance should be considered. Also conditions on the constant *self* should be given in order to preserve its intended meaning.

## 6 Reusing refinements and classes

In the above rules for class refinement the goal was to reuse existing classes and use them via inheritance. Let us now look at how to reuse classes in a different way, namely reuse refinements between classes.

*Reusing refinements* Consider a class $\langle c, C\rangle$ with

$$\begin{array}{lll} C = [\![ & \textbf{attr} & y^* := y0 \,;\, x := x0 \\ & \textbf{obj} & n \\ & \textbf{meth} & m_1 = M_1 \,;\cdots;\, m_h = M_h \\ & \textbf{proc} & p_1 = P_1 \,;\cdots;\, p_k = P_k \\ & \textbf{do}\ A\ \textbf{od} & \\ ]\!] & & \end{array}$$

and assume that $\langle c, C\rangle$ is *class-refined* by a class $\langle c, C'\rangle$ with

$$\begin{array}{lll} C' = [\![ & \textbf{attr} & y^* := y0 \,;\, x' := x0' \\ & \textbf{obj} & n \\ & \textbf{meth} & m_1 = M_1' \,;\cdots;\, m_h = M_h' \\ & \textbf{proc} & p_1' = Q_1' \,;\cdots;\, p_j' = P_j' \\ & \textbf{do}\ A'\ \textbf{od} & \\ ]\!] & & \end{array}$$

This refinement step can be reused when the body of the class $\langle c, \mathcal{C} \rangle$ is 'inside' another class $\langle d, \mathcal{D} \rangle$ where

$$\begin{array}{rll} \mathcal{D} = [\![ & \textbf{attr} & y^* := y0 \; ; \; x := x0; \\ & & z^* := z0 \; ; \; w := w0 \\ & \textbf{obj} & n; \\ & & n' \\ & \textbf{meth} & m_1 = M_1 \; ; \cdots ; \; m_h = M_h; \\ & & r_1 = R_1 \; ; \cdots ; \; r_i = R_i \\ & \textbf{proc} & p_1 = P_1 \; ; \cdots ; \; p_k = P_k; \\ & & q_1 = Q_1 \; ; \cdots ; \; q_l = Q_l \\ & \multicolumn{2}{l}{\textbf{do } A \, [\!] \, B \textbf{ od}} \\ ]\!] & & \end{array}$$

Hence, the class $\langle d, \mathcal{D} \rangle$ extends the class $\langle c, \mathcal{C} \rangle$ because it has new shared attributes $z$, local attributes $w$, name variables $n'$, methods $r$, local procedures $q$, and a new action $B$.

Because the class $\langle c, \mathcal{C} \rangle$ is *class-refined* by the class $\langle c, \mathcal{C}' \rangle$, the class $\langle d, \mathcal{D} \rangle$ extending $\langle c, \mathcal{C} \rangle$ is *class-refined* by the class $\langle d, \mathcal{D}' \rangle$, where

$$\begin{array}{rll} \mathcal{D}' = [\![ & \textbf{attr} & y^* := y0 \; ; \; x' := x0'; \\ & & z^* := z0 \; ; \; w := w0 \\ & \textbf{obj} & n; \\ & & n' \\ & \textbf{meth} & m_1 = M_1' \; ; \cdots ; \; m_h = M_h'; \\ & & r_1 = R_1 \; ; \cdots ; \; r_i = R_i \\ & \textbf{proc} & p_1' = P_1' \; ; \cdots ; \; p_j' = P_j'; \\ & & q_1 = Q_1 \; ; \cdots ; \; q_l = Q_l \\ & \multicolumn{2}{l}{\textbf{do } A' \, [\!] \, B \textbf{ od}} \\ ]\!] & & \end{array}$$

provided that the action $B$ does not contain calls to procedures $p_1 \cdots p_k$. Hence, we can reuse the proof of a refinement of a class $\langle c, \mathcal{C} \rangle$ for classes $\langle d, \mathcal{D} \rangle$ with $\mathcal{D}$ syntactically including $\mathcal{C}$. In particular this can be used to prove that class refinement does not depend on class names.

*Reusing a set of classes* Let $OO$ and $OO'$ be two OO-action systems such that $OO \sqsubseteq OO'$ and let $\langle c, \mathcal{C} \rangle$ be a class in $OO$ marked with an asterisk such that there exists a class $\langle c, \mathcal{C}' \rangle \in OO'$ with the same name $c$ and also marked with an asterisk $*$. Let now $\langle d, \mathcal{D} \rangle$ be another class such that the name $d$ is not used in both $OO$ and $OO'$. Then

$$\{\langle d, \mathcal{D} \rangle^*\} \cup OO \sqsubseteq \{\langle d, \mathcal{D} \rangle^*\} \cup OO' ,$$

where the class $\langle c, \mathcal{C} \rangle \in OO$ and $\langle c, \mathcal{C}' \rangle \in OO'$ are not marked with an asterisk. Notice that actions of the class $\langle d, \mathcal{D} \rangle$ may or may not contain the statements '$new(c)$' or '$n := new(c)$'. Hence, the behaviour of the new OO-action system can be completely different from the behaviour of the action systems $OO$ and $OO'$.

In the above case we have reused an entire OO-action system $OO$ and made it part of a bigger OO-action system. We can interpret the above so that entire class specifications are modules that can be (re)used by other class specifications.

## 7 Examples of refinement

In this section we give some examples of refinement of the OO-action systems modelling a simple phone company introduced in Section 3.2. We want to refine the system in order to allow for two kind of phones: ordinary phones and payphones. The latter must be managed by a separate company. All phone companies start their activity only after the government creates them. For sake of brevity we omit the details of the refinement steps and present only the results.

We begin with refining the body of the class $\langle Phone, Ph\rangle$. We introduce a new type of phone $PPh$, a so-called payphone. It has a *credit* variable, which can recharge itself. If there is no credit, then the phone is not working in the sense that it cannot initiate phone calls. However, when there is no credit, then it is still possible to receive calls. In the description below of $PPh$ we do not write the bodies of procedures and methods of the class which are not changed with respect to their definition in $Ph$.

$$
\begin{array}{lll}
PPh = [\![ & \textbf{attr} & number := -1; \\
 & & idle := true \; ; \; registered := false \; ; \; credit := 0 \\
 & \textbf{obj} & company \; ; \; callee \\
 & \textbf{meth} & Accept\_call\_from(n) = \cdots \\
 & & Where(y) = \cdots \\
 & & Return = \cdots \\
 & \textbf{proc} & Call = \cdots \\
 & \textbf{do} & \\
 & \multicolumn{2}{l}{\quad idle \wedge registered \wedge credit > 0 \rightarrow Call \; ; \; credit := credit - 1} \\
 & \multicolumn{2}{l}{\quad [\!]\; \neg idle \rightarrow callee.Return \; ; \; idle := true} \\
 & \multicolumn{2}{l}{\quad [\!]\; credit := credit + 1} \\
 & \textbf{od} & \\
]\!] & &
\end{array}
$$

It is not hard to see that the class $\langle Phone, PPh\rangle$ refines the class $\langle Phone, Ph\rangle$. Hence, using Rule 1 we have

$$
\begin{array}{c}
\{\langle PhoneCompany, PC\rangle^*, \langle Phone, Ph\rangle\} \\
\sqsubseteq \\
\{\langle PhoneCompany, PC\rangle^*, \langle Phone, PPh\rangle\}\,.
\end{array}
$$

In order to have two kinds of phones (normal phones and payphones) in the same system we can use Rules 2 and 1. Indeed first we can introduce a class $\langle PayPhone, Ph\rangle$ using Rule 2 and then we can refine the system replacing $Ph$ with the above $PPh$ in the class named *PayPhone* obtaining the refinement

$$
\begin{array}{c}
\{\langle PhoneCompany, PC\rangle^*, \langle Phone, Ph\rangle\} \\
\sqsubseteq \\
\{\langle PhoneCompany, PC\rangle^*, \langle Phone, Ph\rangle, \langle PayPhone, PPh\rangle\}\,.
\end{array}
$$

Note that the payphones are not (yet) connected to the rest of the system, in the sense that no instances of the class *PayPhone* may be created by the above system. To solve this problem we introduce in a similar way a second phone company $\langle PhoneCompany2, PC2\rangle$, where $PC2$ is a copy of $PC$ but without the declaration of the shared attributes ***phones*** and ***phonebook*** and where phones are replaced by payphones in the object constructor *new*. As before, we do not write down the bodies of procedures and methods of $PC2$ which are not changed with respect to their definition in $PC$:

$$
\begin{array}{l}
PC2 = \;[\![ \; \textbf{attr} \;\; allow\_new\_phones := true \\
\qquad\qquad \textbf{obj} \;\; entry \,;\, names[1] \,;\, \cdots \,;\, names[n] \,;\, \cdots \\
\qquad\qquad \textbf{meth} \;\; Give\_name(x, n) = \cdots \\
\qquad\qquad \textbf{proc} \;\; Update(n) = \cdots \\
\qquad\qquad \textbf{do} \\
\qquad\qquad\qquad allow\_new\_phones \rightarrow entry := new(PayPhone); \\
\qquad\qquad\qquad\qquad\qquad\qquad\qquad Update(entry); \\
\qquad\qquad\qquad\qquad\qquad\qquad\qquad entry.Where(self) \\
\qquad\qquad\quad [\!]\; allow\_new\_phones :\in \{true, false\} \\
\qquad\qquad \textbf{od} \\
\qquad\quad ]\!]
\end{array}
$$

Using Rules 2, 1, and 4 we have obtained the following refinement:

$$
\begin{array}{c}
\{\langle PhoneCompany, PC\rangle^*, \langle Phone, Ph\rangle\} \\
\sqsubseteq \\
\{\langle PhoneCompany, PC\rangle^*, \langle PhoneCompany2, PC2\rangle, \\
\langle Phone, Ph\rangle, \langle PayPhone, PPh\rangle\}\,.
\end{array}
$$

Now object instance of the class *PayPhone* may be created by instances of the class *PhoneCompany2*. In order to create an instance of this class we make the following two steps. First we apply the rule for reusing a set of classes and add a new class *Government* which creates two instances of the same phone company ***PhoneCompany***. Then we refine the government in order to create an instance of both phone companies. Define the body of the class *Government* as follows

$$Gvt = [\![\; \textbf{do}\; new(PhoneCompany) \,;\, new(PhoneCompany) \,;\, kill(self)\; \textbf{od}\; ]\!]$$

Basically, a *Government* creates two instances of the same kind of phone company and then terminates its activity. By reuse of a set of classes we have

$$
\begin{array}{c}
\{\langle Government, Gvt\rangle^*, \langle PhoneCompany, PC\rangle, \langle Phone, Ph\rangle\} \\
\sqsubseteq \\
\{\langle Government, Gvt\rangle^*, \langle PhoneCompany, PC\rangle, \langle PhoneCompany2, PC2\rangle \\
\langle Phone, Ph\rangle, \langle PayPhone, PPh\rangle\}
\end{array}
$$

In the second step we refine *Gvt* by *Gvt'* replacing one *new(PhoneCompany)* by *new(PhoneCompany2)*:

$$Gvt' = [\![\; \textbf{do}\; new(PhoneCompany) \,;\, new(PhoneCompany2) \,;\, kill(self)\; \textbf{od}\; ]\!]$$

Using Rule 4, we conclude with the last refinement

$$\{\langle Government, Gvt\rangle^*, \langle PhoneCompany, PC\rangle, \langle Phone, Ph\rangle\}$$
$$\sqsubseteq$$
$$\{\langle Government, Gvt'\rangle^*, \langle PhoneCompany, PC\rangle, \langle PhoneCompany2, PC2\rangle$$
$$\langle Phone, Ph\rangle, \langle PayPhone, PPh\rangle\}$$

## 8 Concluding remarks

We have extended the action systems framework with objects and defined a new language, OO-action systems. The formal semantics of the new language is given by translating the OO-action systems into ordinary action systems. Moreover, we defined a refinement relation between OO-action systems and gave a number of refinement rules expressing inheritance and reuse of code and refinements.

Also Back et al. [BBS97] give the formal semantics for their Action-Oberon by reducing them to ordinary action systems. Instead of translating the system into an infinite number of objects as we do here (although they mention this possibility), they use a data structure which keeps information about each object, inheritance history and focus on the $n$-ary communication between objects which participate in actions.

Bailes and Duke [BD91] define a notion of ecological refinement between pairs of classes and their environments. Our refinement notion between classes conforms to theirs in the sense that both define the refinement as a relation between the externally visible behaviours of the systems. Moreover, also our environment (the clients) can change during refinement steps as allowed by the ecological refinement.

There seems to be a close connection between our computational model of OO-action systems and the way action systems are modeled [Wal97] within the B Method [Abr96]. Both formalisms give names to action systems and their refinements as well as their global variables are treated in a similar way. This connection might prove useful as it potentially allows us to use the tool support of the B-Method on OO-action systems. This is, however, left for future studies.

Observe that we do not consider interface refinement in this paper. Hence, all the methods of the subclass appear the same as those of the superclass to a specific client class the formal parameters of the procedures being identical. Interface refinement in the context of class refinement has been studied e.g. by Mikhajlova and Sekerinski [MS97]. This problem is left for future research.

Finally, it would be interesting to study both an operational and a denotational semantics of OO-action systems without translating them into action systems, using, for example, the work of America et al. [ABKR86,ABKR89].

*Acknowledgments* The authors are grateful to Robin Milner for his suggestion to use the theory of remote procedures of action systems for object-oriented systems. We would also like to thank Martin Büchi, Marina Waldén and Jockum von Wright for their comments and several discussions on the contents of this paper. We are very much indebted to the anonymous referees, who have written detailed reports, pointing out some errors and suggesting ways of improving the presentation. The work of Kaisa Sere is supported by the Academy of Finland and the work of Marcello Bonsangue is supported by the *Stichting Informatica Onderzoek in Nederland* within the context of the project no. 612-33-007 'Formal methods and refinement for *Co*ordination *L*anguages'.

## References

[ABKR86] P. America, J.W. de Bakker, J.N. Kok, and J.J.M.M. Rutten. Operational semantics of a parallel object-oriented language. In *Proceedings of the 13th Annual ACM Symposium on Principles of Programming Languages*, pages 194–208, 1986.

[ABKR89] P. America, J.W. de Bakker, J.N. Kok, and J.J.M.M. Rutten. Denotational semantics of a parallel object-oriented language. *Information and Computation*, 83(2):152–205, 1989.

[Abr96] J.-R. Abrial. *The B-Book.* Cambridge University Press, 1996.

[Agh86] G. Agha. *Actors: A Model of Concurrent Computation in Distributed Systems.* MIT Press, 1986.

[AL97] M. Abadi and K.R.M. Leino. A logic of object-oriented programs. In *Theory and Practice of Software Development, TAPSOFT'97*, volume 1214 of *Lecture Notes in Computer Science*, Springer-Verlag, 1997.

[Bac80] R.-J.R. Back. *Correctness Preserving Program Refinements: Proof Theory and Applications.* Volume 131 of *Mathematical Centre Tracts.* Mathematical Centre, Amsterdam, 1980.

[Bac87] R.J.R. Back. Procedural abstraction in the refinement calculus. Technical Report, Åbo Akademi University, Department of Computer Science, Turku, Finland 1987.

[Bac90] R.J.R. Back. Refinement calculus, part II: parallel and reactive programs. In J.W. de Bakker, W.-P. de Roever, and G. Rozenberg, editors, *Stepwise Refinement of Distributed Systems: Models, Formalisms, Correctness*, volume 430 of *Lecture Notes in Computer Science*, pages 67–93, Springer-Verlag, 1990.

[BBS97] R.J.R. Back, M. Büchi, and E. Sekerinski. Action-based concurrence and synchronization for objects. In *Proceedings of the 4th AMAST Workshop on Real-Time Systems, Concurrent, and Distributed Software, Ciutad de Mallorca*, Springer-Verlag, 1997.

[BD91] C. Bailes and R. Duke. The Ecology of class refinement. In J.M. Morris and C. Shaw, editors, *Proceedings of the 4th Refinement Workshop*, January 1991, Cambridge, UK. *Workshops in Computing*, pp. 185–196, Springer Verlag.

[BK83] R.J.R. Back and R. Kurki-Suonio. Decentralization of process nets with centralized control. *Distributed Computing*, 3(2):73–87, 1983.

[BK94] M.M. Bonsangue and J.N. Kok. The weakest precondition calculus: recursion and duality. *Formal Aspects of Computing*, 6A:788–800, 1994.

[BN96] M.H. Brown and M.A. Najork. Distributed active objects. SRC Research Report 141a, DEC Palo Alto CA, 1996.

[BS92] R.J.R. Back and K. Sere. Superposition refinement of parallel algorithms. In Parker, K.R. and Rose, editors, *Proceedings of the IFIP Working Conference on Formal Description Techniques - IV*, pages 475–494. North-Holland Publishing Company, 1992.

[BS94] R.J.R. Back and K. Sere. Action systems with synchronous communication. In E.-R. Olderog, editor, *Proceedings of the IFIP Working Conference on Programming Concepts, Methods and Calculi*, IFIP Transactions A-56, pages 107–126, North-Holland Publishing Company, 1994.

[BS96] R.J.R. Back and K. Sere. From action systems to modular systems. *Software - Concepts and Tools*, 17, Springer Verlag, 1996.

[Car95] L. Cardelli. A language with distributed scope. *Computing Systems* 8(1):27–29, 1995.

[CM88] K.M.Chandy and J. Misra. *Parallel Program Design: A Foundation.* Addison-Wesley, 1988.

[Dij76] E.W. Dijkstra. *A Discipline of Programming.* Prentice–Hall International, 1976.

[Hew77] C. Hewitt. Viewing control structures as patterns of passing messages. *Artificial Intelligence* 8(3), 1977.

[HHJT98] U. Hensel, M. Huisman, B. Jacobs, and H. Tews. Reasoning about classes in object-oriented languages: logical models and tools. To appear in *Proceedings of ESOP/ETAPS 1998, Lecture Notes in Computer Science*, Springer-Verlag, 1998.

[Hoa72] C.A.R. Hoare. Proofs of correctness of data representation. *Acta Informatica*, 1(4):271–281, 1972.

[JK91] H.-M. Järvinen and R. Kurki-Suonio. DisCo specification language: marriage of actions and objects. In *Proceedings of the 11th International Conference on Distributed Computing Systems*, IEEE Computer Society Press, pages 142-151, 1991.

[Jon93] C.B. Jones. A $\pi$-calculus semantics for an object-based design notation. In *Proceedings of CONCUR'93*, volume 715 of *Lecture Notes in Computer Science*, Springer-Verlag, 1993.

[Lam91] L. Lamport. The temporal logic of actions. Research report 79, DEC Systems research Center, 1991. To appear in *ACM Transactions on Programming Languages and Systems.*

[LH92] K. Lano and H. Haughton. Reasoning and refinement in object-oriented specification languages. In *European Conference on Object-Oriented Programming'92*, volume 615 of *Lecture Notes in Computer Science*, Springer-Verlag 1992.

[MS97] A. Mikhajlova and E. Sekerinski. Class refinement and interface refinement in object-oriented programs. In *Proceedings of the Fourth International Formal Methods Europe Symposium (FME'97)*, volume 1313 of *Lecture Notes in Computer Science*, Springer-Verlag, 1997.

[Mor88] C. Morgan. The specification statement. *ACM Transactions on Programming Languages and Systems* 10:3, pages 403–419, 1988.

[Mor87] J.M. Morris. A theoretical basis for stepwise refinement and the programming calculus. *Science of Computer Programming*, 9:287–306, 1987.

[Nau94] D.A. Naumann. Predicate transformer semantics of an Oberon-like language. In E.-R. Olderog, editor, *Proceedings of the IFIP Working Conference on Programming Concepts, Methods and Calculi*, IFIP Transactions A-56, North-Holland Publishing Company, 1994.

[Str95] B. Strulo. How firing conditions help inheritance. In J.P. Bowen and M.G. Hinchey, editors, *ZUM'95: The Z Formal Specification Notation*, volume 967 of *Lecture Notes in Computer Science*, Springer-Verlag 1995.

[SW97] K. Sere and M. Waldén. Data refinement of remote procedures. In M. Abadi and T. Ito, editors, *Proceedings of the International Symposium on Theoretical Aspects of Computer Software (TACS'97), Sendai, Japan*, volume 1281 of *Lecture Notes in Computer Science*, pages 267–294, Springer-Verlag, 1997.

[UK95] R.T. Udink and J.N. Kok. ImpUNITY: UNITY with Procedures and Local Variables. In *Proceedings of Mathematics of Program Construction '95*, volume 947 of *Lecture Notes in Computer Science*. Springer-Verlag, 1995.

[Wal95] D.J. Walker. Objects in the $\pi$-calculus. *Information and Computation*, 116(2):253–271, 1995.

[Wal97] M. Waldén. Layering distributed algorithms. Technical report No 121, Turku Centre for Computer Science, Turku, Finland, 1997. To appear in *Proceedings of the 2nd B conference*, France, April 1998.

[Wri94] J. von Wright. The lattice of data refinement. *Acta Informatica*, 31(2):105–135, 1994.

# Layered Graph Traversals and Hamiltonian Path Problems – An Algebraic Approach

Thomas Brunn[1], Bernhard Möller[2], and Martin Russling[3]

[1] Feilmeier, Junker & Co. (Institut für Wirtschafts- und Versicherungsmathematik GmbH), München
[2] Institut für Informatik, Universität Augsburg
[3] R. Böker Unternehmensgruppe AG, München

**Abstract.** Using an algebra of paths we present abstract algebraic derivations for two problem classes concerning graphs, viz. layer oriented traversal and computing sets of Hamiltonian paths. In the first case, we are even able to abstract to the very general setting of Kleene algebras. Applications include reachability and a shortest path problem as well as topological sorting and finding maximum cardinality matchings.

## 1 Introduction

Starting out from ideas in [Möller 91] the paper [Möller, Russling 93] presented algebraic derivations of a few graph algorithms. While there the algorithms were treated separate from each other, in [Russling 96a,Russling 96b] a systematization into classes of graph algorithm was achieved. For each class a schematic algorithm was derived; the problems in the class are then solvable by instantiations of that schematic algorithm.

This topic has been further pursued in [Brunn 97], which contains two innovations. In the case of layer-oriented graph traversal the case of a set of starting *nodes* was generalized to that of a set of starting *paths*. This allowed dropping one essential assumption in the earlier developments, made the overall derivation smoother and led to a simplified algorithm. Second, in the case of Hamiltonian path problems, a significant new application of the general scheme was found, viz. that of computing maximum cardinality matchings.

Next to presenting the above-mentioned two classes and some of their instances, in the present paper we are able to abstract the derivation of the layer-oriented traversal algorithm to typed Kleene algebras; even the efficiency improvement can be performed at this very abstract level.

## 2 Graphs and Path Languages

### 2.1 Formal Languages and Relations

Consider a finite alphabet $A$. The set of all words over $A$ is denoted by $A^*$ and the empty word by $\varepsilon$. A *(formal) language* $V$ is a subset of $A^*$. For simplicity

This research was partially funded by Esprit Working Group 8533 — NADA: New Hardware Design Methods we identify a singleton set with its only element and a word of length 1 with its only letter. The set of non-empty words is $A^+ \stackrel{\text{def}}{=} A^*\backslash\varepsilon$. Concatenation is denoted by $\bullet$; it is associative and has $\varepsilon$ as its neutral element.

In connection with graph algorithms the letters of $A$ are interpreted as nodes. The words of a language are used to represent paths in that graph: the nodes are listed in the order of traversal. The *length* of a word $w$ is the number of letters in $w$ and is denoted by $\|w\|$.

A *relation* is a language $R$ in which all words have equal length. This length is called the *arity* of the relation, in symbols $\operatorname{ar} R$. The empty relation $\emptyset$ has all arities. Unary relations can be interpreted as sets of nodes, whereas binary relations represent sets of edges. The binary *identity relation* is

$$I \stackrel{\text{def}}{=} \{a \bullet a : a \in A\} ,$$

whereas $A \bullet A$ is the *universal relation* on $A$.

## 2.2 Pointwise Extension

The operations on languages we are going to define in the next section will first be explained for single words and then lifted pointwise to languages.

The *pointwise extension* of an operation $f : A^* \to \mathcal{P}(A^*)$ is denoted by the same symbol $f$ and has the functionality $f : \mathcal{P}(A^*) \to \mathcal{P}(A^*)$. It is defined by

$$f(U) \stackrel{\text{def}}{=} \bigcup_{x \in U} f(x)$$

for $U \subseteq A^*$. This definition implies that the extension is *universally disjunctive*, i.e., distributes over arbitrary unions, is *strict* w.r.t. $\emptyset$, i.e., satisfies $f(\emptyset) = \emptyset$, and is monotonic w.r.t. $\subseteq$.

Moreover, linear laws for $f$, i.e., equational laws in which all variables occur exactly once on both sides of the equality sign, are inherited by the pointwise extension.

The pointwise extension generalizes in a straightforward way to operations with more than one argument.

## 2.3 Join and Composition

For words $s$ and $t$ over alphabet $A$ we define their **join** $s \bowtie t$ and their **composition** $s\,;t$ by

$$\varepsilon \bowtie s = \emptyset = s \bowtie \varepsilon , \quad \varepsilon\,; s = \emptyset = s\,; \varepsilon ,$$

and, for $s, t \in A^*$ and $x, y \in A$, by

$$(s \bullet x) \bowtie (y \bullet t) \stackrel{\text{def}}{=} \begin{cases} s \bullet x \bullet t & \text{if } x = y , \\ \emptyset & \text{otherwise} , \end{cases}$$

$$(s \bullet x)\ ;\ (y \bullet t) \stackrel{\text{def}}{=} \begin{cases} s \bullet t & \text{if } x = y , \\ \emptyset & \text{otherwise} . \end{cases}$$

These operations provide two different ways of "gluing" two words together upon a one-letter overlap: join preserves one copy of the overlap, whereas composition erases it. Again, they are extended pointwise to languages. On binary relations, composition coincides with usual relational composition (see e.g. [Schmidt, Ströhlein 93]). To save parentheses we use the convention that $\bullet$, $\bowtie$ and ; bind stronger than all set-theoretic operations.

To exemplify the close connection between join and composition further, we consider a binary relation $R \subseteq A \bullet A$ modeling the edges of a directed graph with node set $A$. Then

$$R \bowtie R = \{x \bullet z \bullet y \ : \ x \bullet z \in R \wedge z \bullet y \in R\} \ ,$$
$$R \,; R = \{x \bullet y \ : \ x \bullet z \in R \wedge z \bullet y \in R\} \ .$$

Thus, the relation $R \bowtie S$ consists of exactly those paths $x \bullet z \bullet y$ which result from gluing two edges together at a common intermediate node. The composition $R\,;R$ is an abstraction of this; it just states whether there is a path from $x$ to $y$ via some intermediate point without making that point explicit. Iterating this observation shows that the relations

$$R,\ R \bowtie R,\ R \bowtie (R \bowtie R), \ldots$$

consist of the paths with exactly $1, 2, 3, \ldots$ edges in the directed graph associated with $R$, whereas the relations

$$R,\ R\,;R,\ R\,;(R\,;R), \ldots$$

just state existence of these paths between pairs of vertices.

The pointwise extension of join yields the following result for unary relations $S$ and $T$:

$$S \bowtie T = S \cap T \ . \qquad (1)$$

Finally, we have the associativities (see [Möller 93] for further ones)

$$\left.\begin{array}{ll} U \bowtie (V \bowtie W) = (U \bowtie V) \bowtie W \ , & \\ U \bullet (V \bowtie W) = (U \bullet V) \bowtie W & \Leftarrow V \cap \varepsilon = \emptyset \ , \\ U \bowtie (V \bullet W) = (U \bowtie V) \bullet W & \Leftarrow V \cap \varepsilon = \emptyset \ , \end{array}\right\} \qquad (2)$$

# 3 Kleene Algebras and Closures

## 3.1 Kleene Algebras

A *Kleene algebra* (cf. [Conway 71]) is a quintuple $(S, \Sigma, \cdot, 0, 1)$ consisting of a set $S$, operations $\Sigma : \mathcal{P}(S) \to S$ and $\cdot : S \bullet S \to S$ as well as elements $0, 1 \in S$ such that $(S, \cdot, 1)$ is a monoid and

$$\begin{array}{lll} \Sigma\emptyset &= 0 \ , & \\ \Sigma\{x\} &= x & (x \in S) \ , \\ \Sigma(\cup \mathcal{K}) &= \Sigma\{\Sigma K : K \in \mathcal{K}\} & (\mathcal{K} \subseteq \mathcal{P}(S)) \ , \\ \Sigma(K \cdot L) &= (\Sigma K) \cdot (\Sigma L) & (K, L \in \mathcal{P}(S)) \ , \end{array}$$

where $\cdot$ in the latter equation is the pointwise extension of the original $\cdot$ operation. The definition implies that $\cdot$ is strict w.r.t. 0:

$$0 \cdot x = 0 = x \cdot 0 .$$

In connection with graph algorithms one often considers the related structure of a *closed semiring* (see e.g. [Aho et al. 74]). It differs from a Kleene algebra in that $\Sigma K$ is only required to exist for *countable* $K$; moreover, idempotence of $+$ is not postulated. So every Kleene algebra is a closed semiring, but not vice versa.

Examples of Kleene algebras are given by

$$LAN \stackrel{\text{def}}{=} (\mathcal{P}(A^*), \bigcup, \bullet, \emptyset, \varepsilon) ,$$
$$REL \stackrel{\text{def}}{=} (\mathcal{P}(A \bullet A), \bigcup, ;, \emptyset, I) ,$$
$$PAT \stackrel{\text{def}}{=} (\mathcal{P}(A^*), \bigcup, \bowtie, \emptyset, A \cup \varepsilon) .$$

For a Kleene algebra one can define a partial order as follows:

$$x \leq y \stackrel{\text{def}}{\Leftrightarrow} x + y = y , \tag{3}$$

where

$$x + y \stackrel{\text{def}}{=} \Sigma\{x, y\} . \tag{4}$$

Then $(S, \leq)$ forms a complete lattice. We denote the greatest element of that lattice by $\top$. In the above examples $\leq$ coincides with $\subseteq$.

Let $\mu$ denote the least fixpoint operator in a complete lattice. With its help we can define an improper closure operator $.^*$ by

$$x^* \stackrel{\text{def}}{=} \mu y . 1 + x \cdot y , \tag{5}$$

and a proper closure operator $.^+$ by

$$x^+ \stackrel{\text{def}}{=} \mu y . x + x \cdot y .$$

### 3.2 Path Closure

For a directed graph with node set $A$ and edge set $R \subseteq A \bullet A$ we define the *path closure* $R^{\leadsto}$ to be the improper closure $R^*$ in the Kleene algebra $PAT$. Since $\bowtie$ is universally disjunctive and hence chain-continuous, we know from [Kleene 52] that

$$R^{\leadsto} = \bigcup_{i \in \mathbb{N}} {}^{i}R ,$$

where

$${}^{0}R \stackrel{\text{def}}{=} A \cup \varepsilon , \tag{6}$$
$${}^{i+1}R \stackrel{\text{def}}{=} R \bowtie {}^{i}R . \tag{7}$$

Hence ${}^{i}R$ is the relation consisting of all paths of length $i$.

It should be mentioned that the closures $R^*$ and $R^+$ of a binary relation in $REL$ are the reflexive-transitive closure and transitive closure, resp.

## 3.3 Typed Kleene Algebras

A *subidentity* of a Kleene algebra is an element $x$ with $x \leq 1$. We call a Kleene algebra *pre-typed* if all its subidentities are idempotent, i.e., if $x \leq 1 \Rightarrow x \cdot x = x$. The subidentities then play the role of types. Moreover, restriction and co-restriction of an element $a$ to a subtype $x$ are given by $x \cdot a$ and $a \cdot x$, resp. We have

$$x, y \leq 1 \Rightarrow x \cdot y = x \sqcap y \ ,$$

i.e., the infimum of two types is their product.

We call a pre-typed Kleene algebra *typed* if it is a boolean algebra and the restriction operations distribute through arbitrary meets of subtypes, i.e., if we have for all sets $K$ of subidentities and all $a \in S$ that

$$(\sqcap K) \cdot a = \sqcap(K \cdot a) \ \wedge \ a \cdot (\sqcap K) = \sqcap(a \cdot K) \ .$$

Then the subidentities are called *types*.

In a typed Kleene algebra we can define, for $a \in S$, the *domain* $\ulcorner a$ and *co-domain* $a\urcorner$ via the Galois connections ($y$ ranges over subidentities only!)

$$\begin{aligned} \ulcorner a \leq y &\overset{\text{def}}{\Leftrightarrow} a \leq y \cdot \top \ , \\ a\urcorner \leq y &\overset{\text{def}}{\Leftrightarrow} a \leq \top \cdot y \ . \end{aligned}$$

By this, the operations $\ulcorner\_$ and $\_\urcorner$ are universally disjunctive and hence monotonic and strict. Moreover, we can show the usual properties of domain and co-domain (see [Möller 98]):

$$\left.\begin{array}{rlrl} \ulcorner a &= \sqcap\{x : x \leq 1 \wedge x \cdot a = a\} \ , & & \\ a\urcorner &= \sqcap\{y : y \leq 1 \wedge a \cdot y = a\} \ , & & \\ x \leq 1 &\Rightarrow \ulcorner x = x = x\urcorner \ , & & \\ \ulcorner(\ulcorner a) &= \ulcorner a \ , & (a\urcorner)\urcorner &= a\urcorner \ , \\ \ulcorner(a \cdot b) &= \ulcorner(a \cdot \ulcorner b) \ , & (a \cdot b)\urcorner &= (a\urcorner \cdot b)\urcorner \ , \\ \ulcorner(\ulcorner a \cdot b) &= \ulcorner a \sqcap \ulcorner b \ , & (a \cdot b\urcorner)\urcorner &= a\urcorner \sqcap b\urcorner \ , \\ \ulcorner a \leq \ulcorner b &\Rightarrow \ulcorner(a \cdot c) \leq \ulcorner(b \cdot c) \ , & a\urcorner \leq b\urcorner &\Rightarrow (a \cdot c)\urcorner \leq (b \cdot c)\urcorner \ . \end{array}\right\} \quad (8)$$

Our Kleene algebras *LAN*, *REL* and *PAT* are all typed. In *REL* we have, as usual,

$$\ulcorner R = R ; \top \cap I \ \wedge \ R\urcorner = \top ; R \cap I \ .$$

In *LAN* we have

$$\ulcorner U = U\urcorner = \begin{cases} \varepsilon \text{ if } U \neq \emptyset, \\ \emptyset \text{ otherwise.} \end{cases}$$

Finally, most relevant for our applications, in *PAT* we get

$$\ulcorner U = \mathit{first}(U) \ \wedge \ U\urcorner = \mathit{last}(U) \ ,$$

where *first* and *last* are the pointwise extensions of the operations given by

$$\begin{aligned} \mathit{first}(\varepsilon) \overset{\text{def}}{=} \mathit{last}(\varepsilon) &\overset{\text{def}}{=} \varepsilon \ , \\ \mathit{first}(a \bullet s) \overset{\text{def}}{=} a \ , \qquad \mathit{last}(s \bullet a) &\overset{\text{def}}{=} a \ , \end{aligned}$$

for $a \in A, s \in A^*$.

### 3.4 Truth Values and Assertions

The elements 1 and 0 of a Kleene algebra can play the roles of the truth values "true" and "false". Expressions that yield one of these values are therefore also called *assertions* (see e.g. [Möller 96]). The assertion 0 means not only "false", but also "undefined".

Negation is defined by

$$\neg 0 \stackrel{\text{def}}{=} 1 \,, \qquad \neg 1 \stackrel{\text{def}}{=} 0 \,.$$

Then for an assertion $b$ and an element $c$ we have

$$b \cdot c = c \cdot b = \begin{cases} c \text{ if } b = 1 \,, \\ 0 \text{ if } b = 0 \,. \end{cases}$$

In the sequel, for emphasis we shall always use the generic $\cdot$ when connecting assertions with expressions, regardless of the concrete Kleene algebra we are working in.

Note that 0 and 1 are types. The conjunction of types and hence assertions $a, b$ is their infimum $a \sqcap b$ or, equivalently, their product $a \cdot b$; their disjunction is their sum $a + b$. We write $a \wedge b$ for $a \sqcap b$ and $a \vee b$ for $a + b$.

Using assertions we can construct a conditional and a guarded expression:

$$\begin{aligned} &\textsf{if } b \textsf{ then } c \textsf{ else } d \textsf{ fi} \stackrel{\text{def}}{=} b \cdot c \,+\, \neg b \cdot d \,, \\ &\textsf{if } b_1 \textsf{ then } c_1 \,[\!]\, \cdots \,[\!]\, b_n \textsf{ then } c_n \textsf{ fi} \stackrel{\text{def}}{=} \sum_{i=1}^{n} b_i \cdot c_i \,. \end{aligned}$$

for assertions $b, b_i$ and elements $c, c_i, d$. Note that the conditional is monotonic only in $c$ and $d$. So recursions over the condition $b$ need not be well-defined. A property we are going to use in the sequel is

$$\textsf{if } b \textsf{ then } d \textsf{ else if } c \textsf{ then } d \textsf{ else } e \textsf{ fi fi} = \textsf{if } b \vee c \textsf{ then } d \textsf{ else } e \textsf{ fi} \tag{9}$$

for assertions $b, c$ and elements $d, e$.

In connection with recursions, assertions play the role of invariants as known from imperative programming. See [Möller 96] for rules for strengthening and weakening such invariants; invariant introduction and elimination are, of course, particular cases.

### 3.5 Filters

A particular case of assertions in the Kleene algebra *LAN* are filters. Given a parameterized assertion $B : A^* \to \{\emptyset, \varepsilon\}$, the filter $B \triangleleft$ is defined on words by

$$B \triangleleft w = B(w) \bullet w = \begin{cases} w \text{ if } B(w) = \varepsilon \,, \\ \emptyset \text{ if } B(w) = \emptyset \,. \end{cases}$$

The pointwise extension $B \lhd W$ of the filter to a language $W$ yields those elements of $W$ that satisfy $B$:

$$B \lhd W = \{w : w \in W \land B(w)\} \ .$$

This operation distributes through $\cap$ and $\cup$:

$$\begin{aligned} B \lhd (V \cap W) &= B \lhd V \cap B \lhd W \ , \\ B \lhd (V \cup W) &= B \lhd V \cup B \lhd W \ . \end{aligned}$$

By *filter promotion* we mean an application of the laws

$$\left.\begin{aligned} \bigcup_{x \in U} B(x) \cdot E(x) &= \bigcup_{x \in B \lhd U} E(x) \ , \\ \bigcup_{x \in U} F(x \cap V) &= \bigcup_{x \in U \cap V} F(x) \ , \end{aligned}\right\} \tag{10}$$

provided $F(\emptyset) = \emptyset$.

## 4 A General Graph Problem Class

Consider now a graph over node set $A$. We define a general graph processing operation $E$ by

$$E(f,g)(W) \stackrel{\text{def}}{=} g(f(W)) \ , \tag{11}$$

where

- $W \subseteq A^*$ is a subset depending on the structure of the particular application. It might, e.g., be the set of all finite paths in the graph.
- $f : A^* \to M$ is an *abstraction* function from words to a "valuation" set $M$ which might e.g. be the set of natural numbers if we are interested in counting edges in a path. $f$ is extended pointwise to sets of words and hence is distributive, monotonic and strict.
- $g : \mathcal{P}(M) \to \mathcal{P}(M)$ is a *selection* function. It acts globally on $f(W)$, e.g., selects the minimum in the case of sets of natural numbers, and hence *is not* defined as a pointwise extension. Rather we assume the properties

  $$\begin{aligned} &\text{(GEN1)} \quad g(K) \subseteq K \ , \\ &\text{(GEN2)} \quad g(K \cup L) = g(g(K) \cup g(L)) \ \text{(weak distributivity)}, \end{aligned}$$

  for $K, L \subseteq M$.

Weak distributivity means that $g$ may be applied to subsets without changing the overall result. Note that (GEN2) implies idempotence of $g$ and (GEN2) is equivalent to

$$\text{(GEN2')} \quad g(K \cup L) = g(K \cup g(L)).$$

If $g$ is a filter ($B \lhd$), then (GEN1) and (GEN2) hold automatically. The advantage of defining $g$ not generally as a filter gives us the flexibility of admitting non-distributive operations like the minimum. This difference in algebraic properties explains why we use two separate functions $f$ and $g$ rather than their combination into a single one.

The general operation $E$ comprises quite a diversity of graph problems, embodied by different choices of $W$ and additional constraints on $f$ and $g$.

But we now abstract even further, moving away from the particular case of graphs. Assume that $(S, \Sigma, \cdot, 0, 1)$ is a typed Kleene algebra. We define the general operation $E$ by

$$E(f,g)(w) \stackrel{\text{def}}{=} g(f(w)) \tag{12}$$

where

- $w \in S$ is a fixed element of $S$,
- $f : S \to \mathcal{P}(M)$ is a disjunctive ***abstraction*** function with some set $M$ of "valuations", where a function $f$ from a Kleene algebra into an upper semilattice is *disjunctive* if it distributes through $+$, i.e., satisfies $f(x+y) = f(x) \sqcup f(y)$,
- $g : \mathcal{P}(M) \to \mathcal{P}(M)$ is a ***selection*** satisfying the properties

  (GEN1) $g(K) \subseteq K$ ,
  (GEN2) $g(K \cup L) = g(g(K) \cup g(L))$ (weak distributivity),

  for $K, L \subseteq M$.

## 5 Layer Oriented Graph Traversals

A number of problems use the set of all paths starting in a set $S$ and ending in a set $T$ of nodes.

For some of these problems we define in this section a class, derive a basic algorithm and apply it to examples. At the end of this section we show how a more efficient version of the basic algorithm can be developed.

### 5.1 Definition

As mentioned above, we choose for $W$ the set of all paths that start in end points of $S$ and end in starting points of $T$, i.e., we set in (12) $W = S \bowtie R^{\rightsquigarrow} \bowtie T$ and specify a graph traversal operation $F$ by

$$F(f,g)(S,R,T) \stackrel{\text{def}}{=} E(f,g)(S \bowtie R^{\rightsquigarrow} \bowtie T) = g(f(S \bowtie R^{\rightsquigarrow} \bowtie T)) \ ,$$

with $S, T \subseteq A^*$ and $R \subseteq A \bullet A$. Note that, contrary to [Russling 96b] we do not choose $S$ and $T$ as subsets of $A$. This eases the recursion step for the basic algorithm, as is shown in the next section.

We replace this graph theoretic formulation by one for general typed Kleene algebras. Here the definition of $F$ reads

$$F(f,g)(a,b,c) \stackrel{\text{def}}{=} E(f,g)(a \cdot b^* \cdot c) = g(f(a \cdot b^* \cdot c)) \ ,$$

with $a, b, c \in S$.

## 5.2 Derivation of the Basic Algorithm

We now want to find a recursion equation for $F$. We calculate

$$\begin{aligned}
& F(f,g)(a,b,c) \\
= \quad & \{\!\![\ \text{definition}\ ]\!\!\} \\
& g(f(a\cdot b^*\cdot c)) \\
= \quad & \{\!\![\ \text{idempotence of } \cup\ ]\!\!\} \\
& g(f(a\cdot b^*\cdot c)\cup f(a\cdot b^*\cdot c)) \\
= \quad & \{\!\![\ (5)\ ]\!\!\} \\
& g(f(a\cdot(1+b\cdot b^*)\cdot c)\cup f(a\cdot b^*\cdot c)) \\
= \quad & \{\!\![\ \text{distributivity and neutrality}\ ]\!\!\} \\
& g(f(a\cdot c+a\cdot b\cdot b^*\cdot c)\cup f(a\cdot b^*\cdot c)) \\
= \quad & \{\!\![\ \text{associativity of + and disjunctivity of } f \text{ twice}\ ]\!\!\} \\
& g(f(a\cdot c)\cup f(a\cdot b\cdot b^*\cdot c+a\cdot b^*\cdot c)) \\
= \quad & \{\!\![\ \text{distributivity}\ ]\!\!\} \\
& g(f(a\cdot c)\cup f((a\cdot b+a)\cdot b^*\cdot c)) \\
= \quad & \{\!\![\ \text{(GEN2') and commutativity of +}\ ]\!\!\} \\
& g(f(a\cdot c)\cup g(f((a+a\cdot b)\cdot b^*\cdot c))) \\
= \quad & \{\!\![\ \text{definition}\ ]\!\!\} \\
& g(f(a\cdot c)\cup F(f,g)(a+a\cdot b,\ b,\ c))\ .
\end{aligned}$$

## 5.3 Termination Cases

We prepare the introduction of termination cases by deriving another form of $F$:

$$\begin{aligned}
& F(f,g)(a,b,c) \\
= \quad & \{\!\![\ \text{definition}\ ]\!\!\} \\
& g(f(a\cdot b^*\cdot c)) \\
= \quad & \{\!\![\ \text{by (5) we have } b^*=1+b^*\ ]\!\!\} \\
& g(f(a\cdot(1+b^*)\cdot c)) \\
= \quad & \{\!\![\ \text{distributivity and neutrality}\ ]\!\!\} \\
& g(f(a\cdot c+a\cdot b^*\cdot c)) \\
= \quad & \{\!\![\ \text{disjunctivity of } f\ ]\!\!\} \\
& g(f(a\cdot c)\cup f(a\cdot b^*\cdot c))\ . \qquad (13)
\end{aligned}$$

Motivated by the graph theoretical applications we now postulate some conditions about $f$ and $g$:

$$\begin{array}{ll}(\text{LAY1}) & \ulcorner c \leq a\urcorner \Rightarrow g(f(a\cdot c)\cup f(a\cdot u\cdot c)) = g(f(a\cdot c))\ ,\\ (\text{LAY2}) & (a\cdot u)\urcorner \leq a\urcorner \Rightarrow g(f(a\cdot c)\cup f(a\cdot u\cdot c)) = g(f(a\cdot c))\ ,\end{array}$$

with $a, c, u \in S$. When dealing with graph problems, $\ulcorner c \leq a\urcorner$ is the case where the set of starting nodes of $c$ already is contained in the set of end nodes of $a$. The condition $(a\cdot u)\urcorner \leq a\urcorner$ means that by further traversal of the graph along $u$ no new end nodes are reached. In both cases the second use of the abstraction $f$ should give no new information and be ignored by $g$.

**Case 1:** $\ulcorner c \leq a\urcorner$. Then we get by (LAY1) that

$$(13) = g(f(a\cdot c))\ .$$

For the second case we need the following lemma:

**Lemma 1.** For $a, b \in S$ one has $(a\cdot b)\urcorner \leq a\urcorner \Rightarrow (a\cdot b^*)\urcorner \leq a\urcorner$.

**Proof:** We apply Lemma 1 (Closure Induction) of [Möller 93] with continuous predicate $P[x] \stackrel{\text{def}}{\Leftrightarrow} (a\cdot x)\urcorner \leq a\urcorner$ and $z = b$. Then we need to show $\forall\, c : P[c] \Rightarrow P[b\cdot c]$:

$$\begin{array}{ll} & (a\cdot(b\cdot c))\urcorner \\ = & \quad \{\!\!\{\text{ associativity }\}\!\!\} \\ & ((a\cdot b)\cdot c)\urcorner \\ \leq & \quad \{\!\!\{\text{ assumption and (8) }\}\!\!\} \\ & (a\cdot c)\urcorner \\ \leq & \quad \{\!\!\{\ P[c]\ \}\!\!\} \\ & a\urcorner \end{array}$$

From this and $P[1] \Leftrightarrow (a\cdot 1)\urcorner \leq a\urcorner$ we obtain the result. ■

Now we can proceed with

**Case 2:** $(a\cdot b)\urcorner \leq a\urcorner$. Then by Lemma 1 and (LAY2) we get again

$$(13) = g(f(a\cdot c))\ .$$

In sum we have derived the following basic algorithm:

$$\begin{array}{rl} F(f,g)(a,b,c) = & \textsf{if}\ \ulcorner c \leq a\urcorner \ \vee\ (a\cdot b)\urcorner \leq a\urcorner \\ & \textsf{then}\ g(f(a\cdot c)) \\ & \textsf{else}\ g(f(a\cdot c)\ \cup\ F(f,g)(a+a\cdot b,\ b,\ c))\ \textsf{fi}\ . \end{array} \tag{14}$$

This terminates whenever the set of types in the underlying Kleene algebra is upward noetherian, i.e, has no infinite $\leq$-ascending chains. This is always the case in $LAN$, whereas in $REL$ and $PAT$ it holds only if $A$ is finite. A suitable termination measure is $a^{\urcorner}$, since

$$(a + a \cdot b)^{\urcorner} = a^{\urcorner} + (a \cdot b)^{\urcorner} \geq a^{\urcorner}$$

and

$$(a + a \cdot b)^{\urcorner} = a^{\urcorner} \Leftrightarrow (a \cdot b)^{\urcorner} \leq a^{\urcorner} .$$

## 5.4 Applications

**Reachability** Our first example is the problem to compute, given an edge set $R \subseteq A \bullet A$ and a set $S \subseteq A$ of nodes the set of all nodes which are reachable from $S$. We first give a solution in the Kleene algebra $PAT$ and choose $f \stackrel{\text{def}}{=} \_^{\urcorner}$, $g \stackrel{\text{def}}{=} id$, $c \stackrel{\text{def}}{=} A$ and define, for $S \subseteq A^{+}$,

$$reach(S) \stackrel{\text{def}}{=} F(\_^{\urcorner}, id)(S, R, A) .$$

It is easily checked that $\_^{\urcorner}$ and $id$ satisfy the required conditions.

By our definitions we can now solve the reachability problem recursively:

$$
\begin{array}{ll}
& reach(S) \\
= & \quad \{\!\![ \text{ definition } ]\!\!\} \\
& F(\_^{\urcorner}, id)(S, R, A) \\
= & \quad \{\!\![ \text{ (14) } ]\!\!\} \\
& \text{if } {}^{\ulcorner}A \subseteq S^{\urcorner} \vee (S \bowtie R)^{\urcorner} \subseteq S^{\urcorner} \\
& \quad \text{then } (S \bowtie A)^{\urcorner} \\
& \quad \text{else } (S \bowtie A)^{\urcorner} \cup reach(S \cup S \bowtie R) \text{ fi} \\
= & \quad \{\!\![ \text{ (1),(8) } ]\!\!\} \\
& \text{if } A \subseteq S^{\urcorner} \vee (S \bowtie R)^{\urcorner} \subseteq S^{\urcorner} \\
& \quad \text{then } S^{\urcorner} \\
& \quad \text{else } S^{\urcorner} \cup reach(S \cup S \bowtie R) \text{ fi} \\
= & \quad \{\!\![ A \subseteq S^{\urcorner} \Rightarrow A = S^{\urcorner} \Rightarrow (S \bowtie R)^{\urcorner} \subseteq S^{\urcorner} ]\!\!\} \\
& \text{if } (S \bowtie R)^{\urcorner} \subseteq S^{\urcorner} \\
& \quad \text{then } S^{\urcorner} \\
& \quad \text{else } S^{\urcorner} \cup reach(S \cup S \bowtie R) \text{ fi} .
\end{array}
$$

Alternatively, we can solve the reachability problem in $REL$ by setting, for $Q \subseteq A$

$$relreach(Q) \stackrel{\text{def}}{=} F(\_^{\urcorner}, id)(I_Q, R, I_A) .$$

Again the required conditions are easily shown. The resulting algorithm is

$$\begin{array}{l} relreach(Q) = rr(I_Q) \ , \\ rr(S) = \\ \quad \textsf{if } (S\,;R)^{\urcorner} \subseteq S^{\urcorner} \\ \qquad \textsf{then } S^{\urcorner} \\ \qquad \textsf{else } S^{\urcorner} \cup rr(S \cup S\,;R) \textsf{ fi} \ . \end{array}$$

**Shortest Connecting Path** We define, in $PAT$,

$$shortestpaths(S,T) \stackrel{\text{def}}{=} F(id, minpaths)(S,R,T) \ ,$$

with

$$\begin{array}{l} minpaths(U) \stackrel{\text{def}}{=} \textsf{let } ml = min(\|U\|) \textsf{ in } lg(ml) \triangleleft U \ , \\ lg(n)(x) = (\|x\| = n) \ . \end{array}$$

Here we use the pointwise extension of $\|\_\|$ to languages. Hence *minpaths* selects from a set of words the ones with the least number of letters. Again the conditions (GEN) and (LAY1,LAY2) are satisfied. Therefore we have the following algorithm for computing the shortest path between a set $S$ and the node $y$:

$$\begin{array}{ll} & shortestpaths(S,y) \\ = & \{\!\!\{ \text{ definition } \}\!\!\} \\ & F(id, minpaths)(S,R,y) \\ = & \{\!\!\{ \text{ (14) } \}\!\!\} \\ & \textsf{if } {}^{\ulcorner}y \subseteq S^{\urcorner} \vee (S \bowtie R)^{\urcorner} \subseteq S^{\urcorner} \\ & \quad \textsf{then } minpaths(S \bowtie y) \\ & \quad \textsf{else } minpaths(S \bowtie y \cup shortestpaths(S \cup S \bowtie R, y)) \textsf{ fi} \\ = & \{\!\!\{ \text{ set theory, (9) } \}\!\!\} \\ & \textsf{if } y \in S^{\urcorner} \\ & \quad \textsf{then } minpaths(S \bowtie y) \\ & \quad \textsf{else if } (S \bowtie R)^{\urcorner} \subseteq S^{\urcorner} \\ & \qquad\qquad \textsf{then } minpaths(S \bowtie y) \\ & \qquad\qquad \textsf{else } minpaths(S \bowtie y \cup shortestpaths(S \cup S \bowtie R, y)) \textsf{ fi fi} \\ = & \{\!\!\{ \ y \notin S^{\urcorner} \Rightarrow S \bowtie y = \emptyset \ \}\!\!\} \\ & \textsf{if } y \in S^{\urcorner} \\ & \quad \textsf{then } minpaths(S \bowtie y) \\ & \quad \textsf{else if } (S \bowtie R)^{\urcorner} \subseteq S^{\urcorner} \\ & \qquad\qquad \textsf{then } minpaths(\emptyset) \\ & \qquad\qquad \textsf{else } minpaths(shortestpaths(S \cup S \bowtie R, y)) \textsf{ fi fi} \ . \end{array}$$

Since *minpaths* is defined via a filter, we have

$$minpaths(\emptyset) = \emptyset \ .$$

We now simplify the second else-branch.

$$
\begin{aligned}
& \textit{minpaths}(\textit{shortestpaths}(S \cup S \bowtie R, y)) \\
= \quad & \{\!\!\{ \text{ definition of } \textit{shortestpaths} \ \}\!\!\} \\
& \textit{minpaths}(F(\textit{id}, \textit{minpaths})(S \cup S \bowtie R, R, y)) \\
= \quad & \{\!\!\{ \text{ definition of } F \ \}\!\!\} \\
& \textit{minpaths}(\textit{minpaths}(\textit{id}(S \cup S \bowtie R, y))) \\
= \quad & \{\!\!\{ \text{ idempotence of } \textit{minpaths} \ \}\!\!\} \\
& \textit{minpaths}(\textit{id}(S \cup S \bowtie R, y)) \\
= \quad & \{\!\!\{ \text{ definition of } F \ \}\!\!\} \\
& F(\textit{id}, \textit{minpaths})(S \cup S \bowtie R, R, y) \\
= \quad & \{\!\!\{ \text{ definition of } \textit{shortestpaths} \ \}\!\!\} \\
& \textit{shortestpaths}(S \cup S \bowtie R, y) \ .
\end{aligned}
$$

Altogether,

$$
\begin{array}{l}
\textit{shortestpaths}(S, y) = \\
\quad \text{if } y \in S^{\urcorner} \\
\quad\quad \text{then } \textit{minpaths}(S \bowtie y) \\
\quad\quad \text{else if } (S \bowtie R)^{\urcorner} \subseteq S^{\urcorner} \\
\quad\quad\quad \text{then } \emptyset \\
\quad\quad\quad \text{else } \textit{shortestpaths}(S \cup S \bowtie R, y) \text{ fi fi} \ .
\end{array}
$$

Note that, in view of the law $(a \cdot b)^{\urcorner} = (a^{\urcorner} \cdot b)^{\urcorner}$ in (8), we only need to carry along $S^{\urcorner}$ rather than all of $S$. Together with the efficiency improvement in the next subsection this brings the algorithm down to a complexity of $O(|A| + |R|)$.

## 5.5 Improved Efficiency

In graph applications, the parameter $a$ in algorithm (14) carries all paths of the graph which have already been visited during the layered traversal from the starting set. We shall now improve the efficiency of the algorithm by introducing an additional parameter $u$ that contains all already computed paths, while $a$ carries only those paths whose last node has not been visited by any other path. This can again be done in the more general framework of typed Kleene algebras.

We define, using an assertion,

$$F_{\mathit{eff}}(f, g)(a, b, c, u) = (a^{\urcorner} \sqcap u^{\urcorner} = 0) \cdot F(f, g)(a + u, b, c) \ .$$

From this we get immediately

$$F(f, g)(a, b, c) = F_{\mathit{eff}}(f, g)(a, b, c, 0) \ . \tag{15}$$

Let now $v \stackrel{\text{def}}{=} a + u$ and assume $a^\urcorner \sqcap u^\urcorner = 0$. By (14) and (15) we get the following termination case:

$$\begin{array}{l} \ulcorner c \leq v^\urcorner \ \vee \ (v \cdot b)^\urcorner \leq v^\urcorner \Rightarrow \\ F_{\mathit{eff}}(f,g)(a,b,c,u) = g(f(v \cdot c)) \ . \end{array}$$

The recursive case looks as follows:

$$\begin{array}{ll}
& F_{\mathit{eff}}(f,g)(a,b,c,u) \\
= & \quad \{\!\![ \text{ definitions } ]\!\!\} \\
& F(f,g)(v,b,c) \\
= & \quad \{\!\![ \text{ (14) } ]\!\!\} \\
& g(f(v \cdot c) + g(f((v + v \cdot b) \cdot b^* \cdot c))) \\
= & \quad \{\!\![ \text{ let } b_1 = b \cdot v^\urcorner, b_2 = b \backslash b_1 \ ]\!\!\} \\
& g(f(v \cdot b) + g(f((v + v \cdot (b_1 + b_2)) \cdot b^* \cdot c))) \\
= & \quad \{\!\![ \text{ distributivity and disjunctivity of } f \text{, commutativity} \\
& \quad\quad \text{and associativity of } + \text{, several times (GEN2') } ]\!\!\} \\
& g(f(v \cdot b) + f(v \cdot b_2 \cdot b^* \cdot c) + g(f(v \cdot b^* \cdot c) + f(v \cdot b_1 \cdot b^* \cdot c))) \\
= & \quad \{\!\![ \text{ definition of } b_1 \text{, (8), (LAY2) } ]\!\!\} \\
& g(f(v \cdot b) + f(v \cdot b_2 \cdot b^* \cdot c) + g(f(v \cdot b^* \cdot c))) \\
= & \quad \{\!\![ \text{ (GEN2') twice, commutativity of } + \text{ and distributivity } ]\!\!\} \\
& g(f(v \cdot b) + g(f((v + v \cdot b_2) \cdot b^* \cdot c))) \\
= & \quad \{\!\![ \text{ definition of } F \ ]\!\!\} \\
& g(f(v \cdot b) + F(f,g)(v + v \cdot b_2, b, c)) \\
= & \quad \{\!\![ \text{ definition of } F_{\mathit{eff}} \ ]\!\!\} \\
& g(f(v \cdot b) + F_{\mathit{eff}}(f,g)(v \cdot b_2, b, c, v)) \ .
\end{array}$$

It is easy to see that the recursive call preserves the invariant. In sum we get

$$\begin{array}{l}
F_{\mathit{eff}}(f,g)(a,b,c,u) = \\
\quad \textsf{let } v = a + u \\
\quad\quad\ b_1 = b \cdot v^\urcorner \\
\quad\quad\ b_2 = b \backslash b_1 \\
\quad \textsf{in } (a^\urcorner \sqcap u^\urcorner = 0) \cdot \\
\quad\quad \textsf{if } \ulcorner c \leq v^\urcorner \ \vee \ (v \cdot b)^\urcorner \leq v^\urcorner \\
\quad\quad\quad \textsf{then } g(f(v \cdot c)) \\
\quad\quad\quad \textsf{else } g(f(v \cdot c) + F_{\mathit{eff}}(f,g)(v \cdot b_2, b, c, v)) \textsf{ fi } .
\end{array} \tag{16}$$

One checks easily that we can strengthen the invariant by the conjunct $u \cdot b_2 \leq a + u$. With its help, we can simplify the algorithm to

$$
\begin{array}{ll}
F_{eff2}(f,g)(a,b,c,u) = & \\
\quad \text{let } v = a + u & (17)\\
\qquad b_1 = b \cdot v^{\urcorner} & \\
\qquad b_2 = b \backslash b_1 & \\
\quad \text{in } (a^{\urcorner} \sqcap u^{\urcorner} = 0 \wedge u \cdot b_2 \leq v) \cdot & \\
\qquad \text{if } {}^{\ulcorner}c \leq v^{\urcorner} \vee (a \cdot b_2)^{\urcorner} \leq v^{\urcorner} & \\
\qquad\quad \text{then } g(f(v \cdot c)) & \\
\qquad\quad \text{else } g(f(v \cdot c) + F_{eff2}(f,g)(a \cdot b_2, b, c, v)) \text{ fi } . &
\end{array}
$$

Here the expensive computation of $v \cdot b_2$ is reduced to that of $a \cdot b_2$.

# 6 Hamiltonian Path Problems

In this section we define a class of graph problems for the case where the set of nodes is ordered. An order can be given by a binary relation between the nodes or by a permutation of the node set. Since permutations are Hamiltonian paths, the latter will serve as the basis of our further considerations.

## 6.1 Definition

In 1859 Sir William Hamilton suggested the game "around the world ": the points of a dodecahedron were named after cities and the task of the game was to plan a round trip along the edges of the dodecahedron such that each city was visited exactly once.

A *Hamiltonian path* for an alphabet $A$ and a binary relation $R \subseteq A \bullet A$ is a path which traverses each node of the respective graph exactly once. Hence the set of Hamiltonian paths is defined as follows:

$$
\mathit{hamiltonianpaths} \stackrel{\text{def}}{=} \mathit{perms}(A) \cap R^{\rightsquigarrow} ,
$$

with

$$
\begin{aligned}
\mathit{perms}(\emptyset) &\stackrel{\text{def}}{=} \varepsilon , \\
\mathit{perms}(S) &\stackrel{\text{def}}{=} \bigcup_{x \in S} x \bullet \mathit{perms}(S \backslash x)
\end{aligned}
$$

for $S \neq \emptyset$. This set of Hamiltonian paths is, as mentioned above, the underlying language of the instantiation of our general operation we want to specify now. As selection function we use in this section a filter operation $B \triangleleft$. In the sequel, when a recursive equation for *hamiltonianpaths* is available, we do not want to apply the test $B$ only to the paths in the end result. This would be inefficient, since in this way we would compute many paths which in the end would be filtered out again by $B$. To avoid this we require that $B$ be suffix closed, a property which is defined as follows:

An assertion $B(u)$ is *suffix closed* for a language $U \subseteq A^*$ iff for all $v \bullet w \in U$ with $\|w\| \geq 1$ one has

$$
B(v \bullet w) \leq B(w) , \tag{18}
$$

i.e., $B(v \bullet w)$ implies $B(w)$. If then $B$ doesn't hold for a non-empty suffix of a repetition free path then it doesn't hold for the complete path either. A path or a word is *repetition free* if no node or no letter appears twice or more in it.

Therefore we choose in (11) $W \stackrel{\text{def}}{=} perms(A) \cap R^{\leadsto}$, $f \stackrel{\text{def}}{=} id$ and $g \stackrel{\text{def}}{=} B \triangleleft$ and obtain in this way the Hamiltonian path operation $H$ as

$$H(B) \stackrel{\text{def}}{=} E(perms(A) \cap R^{\leadsto})(id, B) = B \triangleleft hamiltonianpaths \ ,$$

with the condition that

(HAM) $B$ is a suffix closed assertion for the set of all repetition free paths.

## 6.2 Derivation of the Basic Algorithm

To derive a basic algorithm for this problem class we need a recursive version of *hamiltonianpaths*. To this end we generalize *hamiltonianpaths* in the following way:

$$hamiltonianpaths = hp(|A|) \ .$$

*hp* computes the set of repetition free paths of length $n$:

$$hp(n) \stackrel{\text{def}}{=} partperms(n) \cap R^{\leadsto} \ ,$$

where $partperms(n)$ is the set of partial permutations of length $n$:

$$partperms(n) \stackrel{\text{def}}{=} \bigcup_{T \subseteq A \wedge |T|=n} perms(T) \ .$$

One sees easily that $n > |A|$ implies $partperms(n) = \emptyset$ and hence

$$hp(n) = \emptyset \ .$$

Moreover, $n \leq |A|$ implies ar $partperms(n) = n$ and hence, for $n \geq 1$,

$$hp(n) = partperms(n) \cap {}^{n-1}R \ . \qquad (19)$$

In the sequel we denote the set of letters occurring in a word $p$ by $set(p)$. we omit the straightforward inductive definition of *set* but note that it is extended pointwise to languages. Define now, for $U \subseteq A^*$,

$$non(U) \stackrel{\text{def}}{=} A \backslash set(U) \ .$$

For the transformation into recursive form we need an auxiliary lemma:

**Lemma 2.** For $n \neq 0$ one has

$$partperms(n) = \bigcup_{T \subseteq A \wedge |T|=n-1} non(T) \bullet perms(T) \ .$$

**Proof:** see [Russling 96b]. ■

Now we can perform a case distinction for *partperms*.

**Case 1:** $n = 0$. From the definitions we obtain immediately

$$partperms(0) = \varepsilon \ .$$

**Case 2:** $n \geq 1$.

$$\begin{aligned}
& partperms(n) \\
= \quad & \{\!\!\{ \text{ Lemma 2 } \}\!\!\} \\
& \bigcup_{T \subseteq A \wedge |T|=n-1} non(T) \bullet perms(T) \\
= \quad & \{\!\!\{ \text{ pointwise extension and } p \in perms(T) \Rightarrow set(p) = T \ \}\!\!\} \\
& \bigcup_{T \subseteq A \wedge |T|=n-1} \ \bigcup_{p \in perms(T)} non(p) \bullet p \\
= \quad & \{\!\!\{ \text{ definition of } partperms \ \}\!\!\} \\
& \bigcup_{p \in partperms(n-1)} non(p) \bullet p \ .
\end{aligned}$$

We extend the case distinction to *hp*.

**Case 1:** $n = 0$. From the definitions we obtain immediately

$$hp(0) = \varepsilon \ .$$

**Case 2:** $n = 1$. From (19) we get

$$hp(1) = A \ .$$

For the next case we need

**Lemma 3.** For $S \subseteq A$ and $R \subseteq A \bullet A$ one has:

$$S \bullet U \cap R \bowtie V = S \bowtie R \bowtie (U \cap V).$$

**Proof:** see [Russling 96a]. ■

**Case 3:** $n > 1$.

$$\begin{aligned}
& hp(n) \\
= \quad & \{\!\!\{ \ (19) \ \}\!\!\} \\
& partperms(n) \cap {}^{n-1}R \\
= \quad & \{\!\!\{ \text{ case distinction of } partperms \text{ and } (7) \ \}\!\!\} \\
& \Big( \bigcup_{p \in partperms(n-1)} non(p) \bullet p \Big) \cap R \bowtie {}^{n-2}R
\end{aligned}$$

$$= \quad \{\!\!\{ \text{ distributivity } \}\!\!\}$$

$$\bigcup_{p \in partperms(n-1)} non(p) \bullet p \cap R \bowtie {}^{n-2}R$$

$$= \quad \{\!\!\{ \text{ Lemma 3 } \}\!\!\}$$

$$\bigcup_{p \in partperms(n-1)} non(p) \bowtie R \bowtie (p \cap {}^{n-2}R)$$

$$= \quad \{\!\!\{ \text{ filter promotion (10) } \}\!\!\}$$

$$\bigcup_{p \in partperms(n-1) \cap {}^{n-2}R} non(p) \bowtie R \bowtie p$$

$$= \quad \{\!\!\{ \text{ (19) } \}\!\!\}$$

$$\bigcup_{p \in hp(n-1)} non(p) \bowtie R \bowtie p.$$

In sum we get for *hp*:

$$\begin{aligned} hp(n) = \ & \mathsf{if}\ n = 0\ \mathsf{then}\ \varepsilon \\ & [\!]\ n = 1\ \mathsf{then}\ A \\ & [\!]\ n > 1\ \mathsf{then} \bigcup_{p \in hp(n-1)} non(p) \bowtie R \bowtie p\ \mathsf{fi}. \end{aligned} \tag{20}$$

Termination is guaranteed by the decreasing parameter $n$.

Analogously to ***hamiltonianpaths*** we generalize the Hamiltonian path operation $H$ to an operation $HP$ which computes the set of repetition free paths of length $n$ that satisfy $B$:

$$HP(B)(n) \stackrel{\text{def}}{=} B \lhd hp(n) \ . \tag{21}$$

Because of

$$H(B) = HP(B)(|A|) \tag{22}$$

we perform also for $HP$ a case distinction.

**Case 1:** $n = 0$. From the definition of $HP$ and (20) we get immediately

$$HP(B)(0) = B \lhd \varepsilon \ .$$

**Case 2:** $n = 1$. Again, the definition and (20) yield

$$HP(B)(1) = B \lhd A \ .$$

**Case 3:** $n > 1$.

$$HP(B)(n)$$

$$= \quad \{\!\!\{ \text{ definition } \}\!\!\}$$

$$B \lhd hp(n)$$

$$
\begin{aligned}
= \quad & \{\!\!\{ (20) \}\!\!\} \\
& B \lhd \bigcup_{p \in hp(n-1)} non(p) \bowtie R \bowtie p \\
= \quad & \{\!\!\{ \text{distributivity} \}\!\!\} \\
& \bigcup_{p \in hp(n-1)} B \lhd (non(p) \bowtie R \bowtie p) \\
= \quad & \{\!\!\{ \text{(HAM) B is suffix closed} \Rightarrow \\
& \quad \text{for } q \in non(p) \bowtie R \bowtie p : B(q) \leq B(p) \}\!\!\} \\
& \bigcup_{p \in hp(n-1)} (B \lhd (non(p) \bowtie R \bowtie p)) \cdot B(p) \\
= \quad & \{\!\!\{ \text{filter promotion (10)} \}\!\!\} \\
& \bigcup_{p \in B \lhd hp(n-1)} B \lhd (non(p) \bowtie R \bowtie p) \\
= \quad & \{\!\!\{ \text{definition} \}\!\!\} \\
& \bigcup_{p \in HP(n-1)} B \lhd (non(p) \bowtie R \bowtie p) \; .
\end{aligned}
$$

In sum we have

$$
\begin{aligned}
HP(B)(n) = & \text{ if } n = 0 \text{ then } B \lhd \varepsilon \\
& [\!] \; n = 1 \text{ then } B \lhd A \\
& [\!] \; n > 1 \text{ then } \bigcup_{p \in HP(B)(n-1)} B \lhd (non(p) \bowtie R \bowtie p) \text{ fi} \; .
\end{aligned} \tag{23}
$$

For $A \neq \emptyset$ the algorithm starts with all paths of length 1, i.e., the nodes that satisfy $B$. It then repeatedly attaches to the front ends of the already obtained paths those nodes which have not yet been used and still maintain $B$. Because of its way of traversing the graph in which every visit of a node may lead to many others the algorithm is also known as a *hydramorphism* after the hydra from Greek Mythology.

A derivation of a more efficient version of the basic algorithm can be found in [Russling 96b].

## 6.3 Applications

**Topological Sorting** We now want to study the problem of topologically sorting a set $A$ w.r.t. a relation $Q \subseteq A \bullet A$. A *topological sorting* of $A$ is a permutation of the $A$ such that for arbitrary $a, b \in A$ one has: if $a \bullet b \in Q$ then $a$ must occur in the sorting before $b$.

We first want to attack the problem from the rear and compute the set of all relations which are admissible for a given sorting $s \in perms(A)$: The first letter of $s$ may be in relation $Q$ with any other letter, the next one with all those which occur after it and so on. So we can define the greatest admissible relation inductively by

$$allowedrel(\varepsilon) \stackrel{\text{def}}{=} \emptyset,$$
$$allowedrel(a \bullet w) \stackrel{\text{def}}{=} a \bullet set(w) \cup allowedrel(w) \ ,$$

with $a \in A$ and $w \in A^*$ so that $a \bullet w$ is repetition free. A permutation $w \in perms(A)$ is therefore a topological sorting w.r.t. $Q$ iff $Q \subseteq allowedrel(w)$.

We are now in the position to solve the problem by application of the Hamiltonian path operation choosing $R \stackrel{\text{def}}{=} A \bullet A$, i.e., first admitting all permutations and then incorporating $Q$ into a filter operation to check $Q \subseteq allowedrel(w)$.

This assertion is, however, not suffix closed, because it is not applicable to partial permutations. Hence we must extend it to the assertion $consistent(Q)(w)$ which checks $Q$ also for a suffix of a topological sorting as admissible relation:

$$consistent(Q)(w) \stackrel{\text{def}}{=} Q \subseteq allowedrel(w) \cup non(w) \bullet A \ .$$

This means that no restriction is placed on points outside $set(w)$. Note that for $w \in perms(A)$ one obviously has

$$consistent(Q)(w) = Q \subseteq allowedrel(w) \ .$$

For the following Lemma we introduce the set of sinks relative to relation $Q$ and set $B \subseteq A$ by

$$sinks(Q)(B) \stackrel{\text{def}}{=} \{a \in B : Q \cap a \bullet B = \emptyset\} \ .$$

**Lemma 4.** For $a \in A, t \in A^*$ and $a \bullet t \in \bigcup_{i \in \mathbb{N}} hp(i)$ we have

$$consistent(Q)(a \bullet t) = consistent(Q)(t) \wedge a \in sinks(Q)(non(t)) \ .$$

In particular, $consistent(Q)$ is suffix-closed on $\bigcup_{i \in \mathbb{N}} hp(i)$.

**Proof:** We calculate,

$$\begin{aligned}
& consistent(Q)(a \bullet t) \\
= \quad & \{\!\!\{ \text{ definition of } consistent \ \}\!\!\} \\
& Q \subseteq allowedrel(a \bullet t) \cup non(a \bullet t) \bullet A \\
= \quad & \{\!\!\{ \text{ definition of } allowedrel \text{ and set theory } \}\!\!\} \\
& Q \subseteq allowedrel(t) \cup a \bullet set(t) \cup non(a \bullet t) \bullet A \\
= \quad & \{\!\!\{ \text{ set theory } \}\!\!\} \\
& Q \subseteq allowedrel(t) \cup a \bullet A \cup non(a \bullet t) \bullet A \ \wedge \\
& Q \cap a \bullet non(t) = \emptyset
\end{aligned}$$

$$
\begin{aligned}
= \quad & \{\!\![\ \text{set theory, definition of } \textit{non} \text{ and distributivity}\ ]\!\!\} \\
& Q \subseteq \textit{allowedrel}(t) \cup \textit{non}(t) \bullet A \ \wedge \\
& Q \cap a \bullet \textit{non}(t) = \emptyset \\
= \quad & \{\!\![\ \text{definition of } \textit{consistent}\text{, definition of } \textit{sinks}, \\
& \quad \text{since } a \bullet t \text{ is repetition-free and hence } a \in \textit{non}(t)\ ]\!\!\} \\
& \textit{consistent}(Q)(t) \wedge a \in \textit{sinks}(Q)(\textit{non}(t)) \ .
\end{aligned}
$$

Thus $\textit{consistent}(a \bullet t) \leq \textit{consistent}(t)$. ∎

Now we specify, for $Q \subseteq A{\bullet}A$ and $R \stackrel{\text{def}}{=} A{\bullet}A$, the set of topological sortings of $A$ w.r.t. $Q$ by

$$\textit{topsort} \stackrel{\text{def}}{=} H(\textit{consistent}(Q)) = \textit{consistent}(Q) \triangleleft \textit{perms}(A) \ .$$

Using (22) we define, with $R = A \bullet A$,

$$\textit{conshp}(n) \stackrel{\text{def}}{=} HP(\textit{consistent}(Q))(n) = \textit{consistent}(Q) \triangleleft \textit{hp}(n) \ .$$

Hence we have the following intermediary result:

$\textit{topsort} = \textit{conshp}(|A|)$ ,

$$
\begin{aligned}
\textit{conshp}(n) = \ & \textbf{if } n = 0 \textbf{ then } \textit{consistent}(Q) \triangleleft \varepsilon \\
& [\!]\ n = 1 \textbf{ then } \textit{consistent}(Q) \triangleleft A \\
& [\!]\ n > 1 \textbf{ then } \bigcup_{p \in \textit{conshp}(n-1)} \textit{consistent}(Q) \triangleleft (\textit{non}(p) \bowtie R \bowtie p) \textbf{ fi} \ .
\end{aligned} \tag{24}
$$

**Case 1:** $n = 0$. From the definition of *consistent* we get immediately

$$\textit{conshp}(0) = \varepsilon \ .$$

**Case 2:** $n = 1$.

$$
\begin{aligned}
& a \in \textit{conshp}(1) \\
= \quad & \{\!\![\ \text{by (24) and definition of } \textit{consistent}\ ]\!\!\} \\
& Q \subseteq \textit{allowedrel}(a) \cup \textit{non}(a) \bullet A \\
= \quad & \{\!\![\ \text{definition of } \textit{allowedrel}\ ]\!\!\} \\
& Q \subseteq \textit{non}(a) \bullet A \\
= \quad & \{\!\![\ \text{set theory}\ ]\!\!\} \\
& a \bullet A \cap Q = \emptyset \\
= \quad & \{\!\![\ \text{definition of } \textit{sinks}\ ]\!\!\} \\
& a \in \textit{sinks}(Q)(A) \ .
\end{aligned}
$$

**Case 3:** $n > 1$. We first calculate within (24)

$$
\begin{array}{ll}
& non(p) \bowtie R \bowtie p \\
= & \{\!\!\{ \text{ by } R = A \bullet A \text{ and associativity (2) } \}\!\!\} \\
& non(p) \bowtie A \bullet A \bowtie p \\
= & \{\!\!\{ \text{ neutrality twice } \}\!\!\} \\
& non(p) \bullet p \; .
\end{array}
$$

Now, for $p \in conshp(n-1)$ and $x \in non(p)$

$$
\begin{array}{ll}
& consistent(Q)(x \bullet p) \\
= & \{\!\!\{ \text{ Lemma 4 } \}\!\!\} \\
& consistent(Q)(p) \wedge x \in sinks(Q)(non(p)) \\
= & \{\!\!\{ \; p \in conshp(n-1) = consistent(Q) \triangleleft hp(n-1), \\
& \quad \text{hence } consistent(Q)(p) \; \}\!\!\} \\
& x \in sinks(Q)(non(p)) \; ,
\end{array}
$$

so that by filter promotion (10) and pointwise extension we can in (24) reduce the expression for $n > 1$ to

$$\bigcup_{p \in conshp(n-1)} sinks(Q)(non(p)) \bullet p \; .$$

Altogether,

$$
\begin{array}{rl}
conshp(n) = & \mathsf{if}\; n = 0 \;\mathsf{then}\; \varepsilon \\
& [\!]\; n = 1 \;\mathsf{then}\; sinks(Q)(A) \\
& [\!]\; n > 1 \;\mathsf{then}\; \bigcup_{p \in conshp(n-1)} sinks(Q)(non(p)) \bullet p \;\mathsf{fi}\; .
\end{array} \tag{25}
$$

This is the standard removal-of-sinks algorithm. It can be implemented in complexity $O(|A|+|Q|)$ using an array of adjacency lists and in-degrees together with a linked list of relative sinks. A formal treatment of the array of in-degrees can be found in [Möller, Russling 93] in connection with an algorithm for cycle detection.

**The Maximal Matching Problem in Directed, Bipartite Graphs** Assume an alphabet $A$ and a binary relation $R \subseteq A \bullet A$. In the sequel we consider *bipartite* directed graphs. This means that there are subsets $U, V \subseteq A$ with $A = U \cup V$, $U \cap V = \emptyset$ and $R \subseteq U \bullet V$. One may wonder why we did not include the summand $V \bullet U$ as well. However, we will work with the symmetric closure of our relations anyway.

A matching is a subset of the edges with the property that each node of the graph may be at most once starting point or end point of an edge of the matching.

More precisely, $M \subseteq R$ is a *matching* if $\forall\, m \in M : ends(M \backslash m) \cap ends(m) = \emptyset$, where

$$ends(\varepsilon) = \emptyset$$
$$ends(a) = \{a\}$$
$$ends(a \bullet u \bullet b) = \{a\} \cup \{b\},$$

for $a, b \in A, u \in A^*$. The function *ends* is extended pointwise to languages.

The *maximal matching problem* consists in finding matchings with maximal cardinality $|M|$.

In the sequel we do not derive an algorithm for this problem from scratch. Rather we show that one subalgorithm of the standard solution is another particular instance of the general Hamiltonian operation.

By $\overleftrightarrow{M}$ we now denote the symmetric closure of $M$. A path $x_0 \bullet x_1 \bullet \cdots \bullet x_n \in R^{\rightsquigarrow}$ of vertices is an *alternating chain* w.r.t. $M$ if the pairs $x_i \bullet x_{i+1}$ alternatingly lie within and without of $\overleftrightarrow{M}$. Formally, the assertion $alter(M)(w)$ is inductively defined by

$$\begin{aligned}
alter(M)(\varepsilon) &= 0\ ,\\
alter(M)(a) &= 1\ ,\\
alter(M)(a \bullet b) &= a \bullet b \in \overleftrightarrow{R}\\
alter(M)(a \bullet b \bullet c) &= (a \bullet b \in \overleftrightarrow{R} \setminus \overleftrightarrow{M} \wedge b \bullet c \in \overleftrightarrow{M}) \vee\\
&\phantom{=}\ (a \bullet b \in \overleftrightarrow{M} \wedge b \bullet c \in \overleftrightarrow{R} \setminus \overleftrightarrow{M})\\
alter(M)(a \bullet b \bullet c \bullet u) &= alter(M)(a \bullet b \bullet c) \wedge\\
&\phantom{=}\ alter(M)(b \bullet c \bullet u)\ ,
\end{aligned}$$

for $a, b, c \in A$ and $u \in A^*$. By this inductive definition, $alter(M)$ is obviously suffix closed.

A node $a$ is *isolated* if it is not touched by any edge in $M$, i.e., if $x \notin ends(M)$. Formally,

$$isolated(M) \stackrel{\text{def}}{=} A \backslash ends(M)\ .$$

An alternating chain is *increasing* if its extremal nodes $x_0$ and $x_n$ are isolated. Note that the length of an increasing chain always is odd and the starting and end points do not lie both in $U$ nor both in $V$. If there now exists an increasing chain for a matching $M$, then one can construct a larger matching by omitting all edges of the chain that are contained in the matching and adds those edges of the chain which were not yet contained in $M$. For this we use the function

$$symdiff(M, c) \stackrel{\text{def}}{=} edges(c) \backslash M \cup M \backslash edges(c) \tag{26}$$

where

$$edges(\varepsilon) \stackrel{\text{def}}{=} \emptyset \stackrel{\text{def}}{=} edges(a)\ ,$$
$$edges(a \bullet b \bullet c) \stackrel{\text{def}}{=} a \bullet b \cup edges(b \bullet c)\ .$$

The fact that using an increasing chain one can construct a larger matching leads to the following recursive approach. In an auxiliary function $G$ we compute for an arbitrary matching the set of corresponding increasing chains (function:

*calc_aac*). If this set is empty the matching is maximal. Otherwise one computes a larger matching by *symdiff* and calls $G$ with the new matching as argument. Additional arguments of $G$ are the sets of isolated nodes of $U$ and $V$; they allow an efficient computation of the increasing alternating chains. $G$ is initially called with the empty set, $U$ and $V$. The correctness of the algorithm is established by

**Theorem 5.** A matching has maximal cardinality iff no increasing chain exists for it.

For the proof see e.g. [Biggs 89]. Therefore we have the specification

$$\mathit{maxmatch} \stackrel{\text{def}}{=} G(\emptyset, U, V)$$

where

$$\begin{array}{l} G(M,U,V) \stackrel{\text{def}}{=} \\ \textsf{let } \mathit{aac} = \mathit{calc\_aac}(M,U,V) \\ \textsf{in if } \mathit{aac} = \emptyset \\ \quad\quad \textsf{then } M \\ \quad\quad \textsf{else } \bigcup\limits_{c \in \mathit{aac}} G(\mathit{symdiff}(M,c), U \backslash \ulcorner c, V \backslash c \urcorner) \textsf{ fi} . \end{array} \tag{27}$$

The core of this function is the computation of the increasing alternating chains. Since an alternating chain orders the nodes in a certain way, we can solve this problem using the generalization $HP$ of the Hamiltonian path operation $H$.

To this end we define

$$\mathit{calc\_aac}(M,U,V) \stackrel{\text{def}}{=} \mathit{increasingchain}(M,U,V) \lhd \mathit{altchain}(M) \ .$$

*altchain* computes all alternating paths of the graph corresponding to $\overleftrightarrow{R}$. The extension of $R$ to its symmetric closure is necessary, since otherwise, by the bipartiteness assumption for $R$, we could not construct any alternating chains. We compute an alternating chain of length $n$ as a Hamiltonian path of length $n$ and specify:

$$\mathit{altchain}(M) \stackrel{\text{def}}{=} \bigcup_{n=2}^{|A|} HP(\mathit{alter}(M))(n) \ .$$

For the complete computation of *calc_aac* we have to filter out from the intermediate result those increasing chains which start in $U$ and end in $V$. This is done by the assertion $\mathit{increasingchain}(M,U,V)(w)$:

$$\begin{array}{l} \mathit{increasingchain}(M,U,V)(w) \stackrel{\text{def}}{\Leftrightarrow} \\ \quad \|w\| \geq 2 \wedge \ulcorner w \subseteq \mathit{isolated}(M) \cap U \wedge \\ \quad w\urcorner \subseteq \mathit{isolated}(M) \cap V \ . \end{array} \tag{28}$$

The computation of *altchain* with the union of all alternating chains of lengths 2 up to $|A|$ is inefficient, however, since the chains with length $n-1$ are used again for the computation of the chains with length $n$. Hence it is better to adapt the basic algorithm (23) so that it yields alternating chains of arbitrary length. Since a chain contains at least two nodes, we shall make the case $n = 2$ the termination case. Moreover, we change the end node set, i.e., we start the construction of the chains not with nodes from $A$ but with nodes from $isolated(M) \cap V$, since all chains whose last nodes are not from this set will be eliminated from the result by *increasingchain* anyway.

In sum we obtain therefore:

$$
\begin{array}{l}
calc\_aac(M,U,V) = \\
\quad increasingchain(M,U,V) \lhd alc(M, isolated(M) \cap V)(|A|) \ ,
\end{array}
$$

$$
\begin{array}{l}
alc(M,S)(n) = \\
\quad \textsf{if } n < 2 \textsf{ then } \emptyset \\
\quad [\!]\ n = 2 \textsf{ then } alter(M) \lhd (R \bowtie S) \\
\quad [\!]\ n > 2 \textsf{ then let } W = alc(M,S)(n-1) \\
\quad \textsf{in} \qquad W \cup \bigcup\limits_{p \in W \wedge \|p\| = n-1} alter(M) \lhd (non(p) \bowtie R \bowtie p) \textsf{ fi} \ .
\end{array}
\qquad (29)
$$

## 7 Conclusion

We have presented derivations of schematic algorithms for two classes of graph problems. In particular, the class of Hamiltonian path problems presents a wide variety of applications, among which finding maximum cardinality matchings is the most advanced. Further instances of this class can be found in [Russling 96b].

In the case of layer oriented traversals it was surprising how far the abstract framework of typed Kleene algebras carries. The axiomatization used there is much weaker than that of relational or sequential calculus.

It is to be hoped that a similar treatment of other graph algorithm classes can be found.

**Acknowledgement** The derivation of the maximal matching algorithm was inspired by [Berghammer]. The anoymous referees provided a number of quite helpful comments.

## References

[Aho et al. 74] A.V. Aho, J.E. Hopcroft, J.D. Ullman: The design and analysis of computer algorithms. Reading, Mass.: Addison Wesley 1974

[Berghammer] R. Berghammer: unpublished manuscript

[Biggs 89] Biggs: Discrete Mathematics. Oxford: Clarendon Press 1989

[Brunn 97] T. Brunn: Deduktiver Entwurf und funktionale Programmierung von Graphenalgorithmen. Institut für Informatik, Universität Augsburg, Diplomarbeit, August 1997

[Conway 71] J.H. Conway: Regular algebra and finite machines. London: Chapman and Hall 1971

[Kleene 52] S.C. Kleene: Introduction to metamathematics. New York: van Nostrand 1952

[Möller 91] B. Möller: Relations as a program development language. In: B. Möller (ed.): Constructing programs from specifications. Proc. IFIP TC2/WG 2.1 Working Conference on Constructing Programs from Specifications, Pacific Grove, CA, USA, 13–16 May 1991. Amsterdam: North-Holland 1991, 373–397

[Möller 93] B. Möller: Derivation of graph and pointer algorithms. In: B. Möller, H.A. Partsch, S.A. Schuman (eds.): Formal program development. Proc. IFIP TC2/WG2.1 State of Art Seminar, Rio de Janeiro, Jan. 1992. Lecture Notes in Computer Science **755**. Berlin: Springer 1993, 123–160

[Möller 96] B. Möller: Assertions and recursions. In: G. Dowek, J. Heering, K. Meinke, B. Möller (eds.): Higher order algebra, logic and term rewriting. Second International Workshop, Paderborn, Sept. 21-22, 1995. Lecture Notes in Computer Science **1074**. Berlin: Springer 1996, 163–184

[Möller 98] B. Möller: Typed Kleene algebras. Institut für Informatik, Universität Augsburg, Technical Report 1998-3, April 1998

[Möller, Russling 93] B. Möller, M. Russling: Shorter paths to graph algorithms. In: R.S. Bird, C.C. Morgan, J.C.P. Woodcock (eds.): Mathematics of Program Construction. Lecture Notes in Computer Science **669**. Berlin: Springer 1993, 250–268. Extended version: Science of Computer Programming **22**, 157–180 (1994)

[Russling 96a] M. Russling: Deriving a class of layer-oriented graph algorithms. Science of Computer Programming **26**, 117-132 (1996).

[Russling 96b] M. Russling: Deriving general schemes for classes of graph algorithms. Augsburger Mathematisch-Naturwissenschaftliche Schriften, Band 13 (1996).

[Schmidt, Ströhlein 93] G. Schmidt, T. Ströhlein: Relations and graphs. Discrete Mathematics for Computer Scientists. EATCS Monographs on Theoretical Computer Science. Berlin: Springer 1993

# A Unifying Framework for Correct Program Construction*

Henning Dierks and Michael Schenke
e-mail: {dierks,schenke}@informatik.uni-oldenburg.de
University of Oldenburg, Germany

**Abstract.** We present a description technique for the correct construction of programs that allows us to define terms like refinement, model-checking, and synthesis as special operations within this framework. From that meta-view on program constructions both advantages and disadvantages of all methods mentioned become clear. Furthermore, it becomes clear that an incremental program construction seems to be the most suitable method to construct programs. To demonstrate this incremental construction method we present a real-time case study.

## 1 Introduction

The most popular methods in computer science for construction of correct programs are refinement, synthesis, and model-checking. Each method has its own research groups, communities, and conferences, although they are dealing with the same problem: how to prove a program correct?

The reason why there are different methods is simple: none of them is perfect. Each method has its advantages and disadvantages. In this paper we will present a common framework for correct program construction in which many known methods can be represented. The main idea is that all methods justify their correctness by semantics of both program and specification and their aim is to find a program that refines the specification with respect to the semantics.

Main purpose of this common model is to recognise the significant difference between these methods and the reasons for their advantages and disadvantages. Moreover, from this model we can derive a new concept of program construction which is a reasonable compromise. Basically this method changes specification and program simultaneously in a way that the specification may be *weakened*. This idea of weakening a specification in a correct way enables the designer to reach subsets of the specification language for which mechanical support like model-checking or synthesis exist.

The paper is organised as follows: In Sect. 2 we introduce the uniform model for program construction. The rest of the paper deals with an example of our

* This research was partially supported by the German Ministry for Education and Research (BMBF) as part of the project UniForM under grant No. FKZ 01 IS 521 B3.

proposed construction method. Firstly, we introduce the interval based real-time logic Duration Calculus [7, 6] in Sect. 3 which is used as the specification language for our case study "quasi-fair scheduler" (Sect. 4). In Sect. 5 we introduce the notion of PLC-Automata [2, 3] which serves as our target language in the development process. Finally, Sect. 6 demonstrates the incremental construction of a PLC-Automaton out of a specification in a subset of Duration Calculus.

It should go without saying that DC and PLC-Automata are only special examples of our framework. The construction of correct implementations along the lines of this paper, in which the difference between the simple refinement, synthesis etc. approaches are overcome, is also possible in other formalisms.

## 2 The Common Framework

To establish correctness of a program with respect to a specification one has to show that the program refines the specification. To this end both programs and specifications have a common semantical basis. It is often the case that the semantics of the program is in the same language as the specification. Main purpose of the semantics is to enable mathematical reasoning.

In mathematical notation we have a specification language $\mathcal{S}$, a programming language $\mathcal{P}$ and a semantical domain $\mathcal{D}$. Furthermore, we have two semantic functions $[\![\cdot]\!]_{\mathcal{S}} : \mathcal{S} \longrightarrow 2^{\mathcal{D}}$ and $[\![\cdot]\!]_{\mathcal{P}} : \mathcal{P} \longrightarrow 2^{\mathcal{D}}$ where $2^{\mathcal{D}}$ denotes the powerset of $\mathcal{D}$. A usual definition is that $P \in \mathcal{P}$ *refines* $S \in \mathcal{S}$ $(P \Rrightarrow S)$, if

$$[\![P]\!]_{\mathcal{P}} \subset_{\mathcal{D}} [\![S]\!]_{\mathcal{S}}.$$

In the same way one defines that a specification $S'$ refines the specification $S$ (cf. Fig. 1):

$$S' \Rrightarrow S \stackrel{\text{df}}{=} [\![S']\!]_{\mathcal{S}} \subset_{\mathcal{D}} [\![S]\!]_{\mathcal{S}}$$

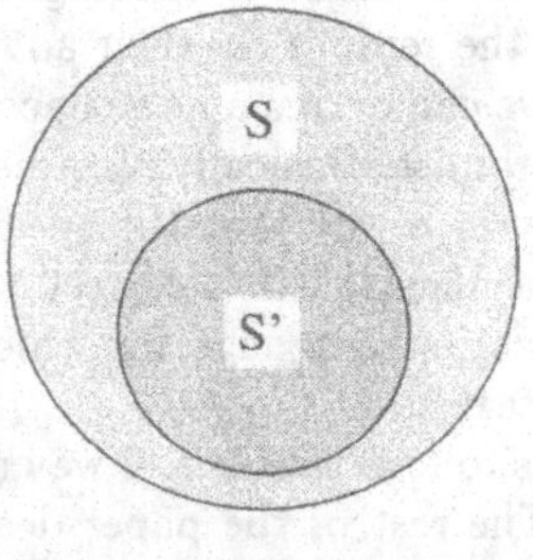


**Fig. 1.** The ordinary view of the refinement relation

In our common model we observe pairs consisting of a specification and a program because during the construction of a program we have to reflect both. Starting the construction process with a pair $(S, P)$ the task we have to solve is: Find a program that is more deterministic than $P$ and fulfils the specification $S$. Now a refinement of this task could strengthen the specification $S$ or make the program $P$ more deterministic.

**Definition 1.** Given the specification $S, S' \in \mathcal{S}$ and programs $P, P' \in \mathcal{P}$ we say that $(S', P')$ *refines* $(S, P)$ if the intersection of the semantics of $S'$ and $P'$ is a subset of the intersection of the semantics of $S$ and $P$. In symbols:

$$(S', P') \Rrightarrow (S, P) \overset{\text{df}}{=} [\![S']\!]_{\mathcal{S}} \cap [\![P']\!]_{\mathcal{P}} \subset_{\mathcal{D}} [\![S]\!]_{\mathcal{S}} \cap [\![P]\!]_{\mathcal{P}}$$

□

Hence, this definition allows a simultaneous change of both specification and program in one refinement step. For example, it holds

$$(S_1, P') \Rrightarrow (S_1 \wedge S_2, P)$$

provided that $[\![P']\!]_{\mathcal{P}} \subset_{\mathcal{D}} [\![S_2]\!]_{\mathcal{S}} \cap [\![P]\!]_{\mathcal{P}}$, which means that $P'$ is a refinement of $P$ and fulfils $S_2$. But Def. 1 allows even refinement steps that neither strengthen the specification nor make the program more deterministic. In Fig. 2 such a situation is depicted: $S'$ is not a subset of $S$ and $P'$ is not a subset of $P$.

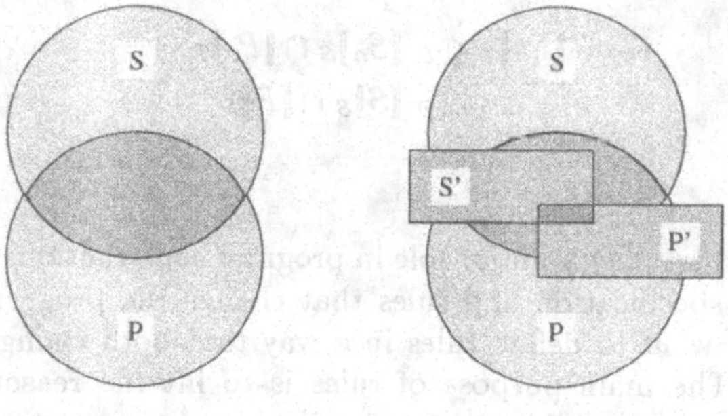


**Fig. 2.** The new refinement relation
LHS: the specification $S$ and the program $P$. RHS: $(S', P')$ refines $(S, P)$ because $S' \cap P'$ is contained in $S \cap P$.

The advantage of the new refinement paradigm is that it allows greater flexibility during the development. It often proves useful to shift requirements from $S$ to $P$. This will be done in the steps in Sect. 6.

**Definition 2.** Suppose $S, S_0, \ldots, S_n \in \mathcal{S}$ and $P, P_0, \ldots, P_n \in \mathcal{P}$. We call a pair $(S, P)$ *correct* if

$$[\![P]\!]_{\mathcal{P}} \subset_{\mathcal{D}} [\![S]\!]_{\mathcal{S}}$$

holds. A sequence of pairs $((S_0, P_0), \ldots, (S_n, P_n))$ is called a *refinement path* if for each $i \in \{1, \ldots, n\}$ $(S_i, P_i)$ refines $(S_{i-1}, P_{i-1})$. This refinement path is called *correct* if at least the last pair $(S_n, P_n)$ is correct. □

The definition of a correct refinement path is restricted to the last pair, because what we are looking for is a correct pair. This must bave been constructed only at the end of the refinement path.

The task of the construction of a correct program with respect to a specification $S$ can now be viewed as a quest for a correct refinement path that starts with $(S, P_{\mathsf{true}})$ where $P_{\mathsf{true}}$ is the complete nondeterministic program, i.e. $[\![P_{\mathsf{true}}]\!]_{\mathcal{P}} = \mathcal{D}$

**Lemma 3.** *Suppose that* $((S, P), (S_1, P_1), \ldots, (S_n, P_n))$ *is a correct refinement path, then*

$$P_n \Rrightarrow S \quad \textit{and} \quad P_n \Rrightarrow P$$

*hold (in the traditional sense).* □

*Proof.* Due to the definition of a refinement path and the transitivity of $\Rrightarrow$

$$(S_n, P_n) \Rrightarrow (S, P)$$

is clear. By the correctness of $(S_n, P_n)$ and the definition of $\Rrightarrow$ we have

$$\begin{aligned} [\![P_n]\!]_{\mathcal{P}} &\subset_{\mathcal{D}} [\![S_n]\!]_{\mathcal{S}} \cap [\![P_n]\!]_{\mathcal{P}} \\ &\subset_{\mathcal{D}} [\![S]\!]_{\mathcal{S}} \cap [\![P]\!]_{\mathcal{P}} \end{aligned}$$

□

Transformation rules play a major role in program construction. There are rules that change the specification and rules that change the program. In our combined setting we want to define rules in a way that both changes can be done simultaneously. The main purpose of rules is to lift the reasoning about the correctness of a refinement from the semantical level to a syntactical level.

**Definition 4.** A relation $R \subset (\mathcal{S} \times \mathcal{P}) \times (\mathcal{S} \times \mathcal{P})$ is called *transformation rule*, if for all pairs $(S, P), (S', P') \in \mathcal{S} \times \mathcal{P}$ with $(S, P) R (S', P')$ the following holds:

$$(S', P') \Rrightarrow (S, P)$$

Suppose $S_0, \ldots, S_n \in \mathcal{S}$, $P_0, \ldots, P_n \in \mathcal{P}$, and $R_1, \ldots, R_n$ are transformation rules with $(S_{i-1}, P_{i-1}) R_i (S_i, P_i)$ for all $i = 1, \ldots, n$. We use the following notation to abbreviate this situation:

$$(S_0, P_0) \xrightarrow{R_1} (S_1, P_1) \xrightarrow{R_2} \cdots \xrightarrow{R_n} (S_n, P_n)$$

□

Note that this definition of a transformation rule differs from the usual concept of rules. It uses the ***instances of all rule applications*** to define a rule.

From that generalised definition of rules we can specify different kinds of rule applications:

**Definition 5.** Let $S, S' \in \mathcal{S}$, $P, P' \in \mathcal{P}$, and $R$ a transformation rule.

a) $(S, P) \xrightarrow{R} (S', P')$ is a ***synthesising*** rule application, if $[\![P']\!]_{\mathcal{P}} \Rrightarrow [\![P]\!]_{\mathcal{P}}$ and $[\![P]\!]_{\mathcal{P}} \neq [\![P']\!]_{\mathcal{P}}$ holds.
b) $(S, P) \xrightarrow{R} (S', P')$ is a ***specification refining*** rule application, if $[\![S']\!]_{\mathcal{S}} \Rrightarrow [\![S]\!]_{\mathcal{S}}$ and $[\![S]\!]_{\mathcal{S}} \neq [\![S']\!]_{\mathcal{S}}$ holds.
c) $(S, P) \xrightarrow{R} (S', P')$ is a ***specification weakening*** rule application, if $[\![P']\!]_{\mathcal{P}} \Rrightarrow [\![P]\!]_{\mathcal{P}}$, $[\![S]\!]_{\mathcal{S}} \Rrightarrow [\![S']\!]_{\mathcal{S}}$, and $[\![S]\!]_{\mathcal{S}} \neq [\![S']\!]_{\mathcal{S}}$ hold.

We call $R$ ***synthesising (specification refining, specification weakening) rule*** if every application of $R$ is a synthesising (specification refining, specification weakening) rule application. □

The specification weakening rules are very interesting. These rules remove non-determinism of the program and weaken the specification in one step. This makes the remaining task of program construction easier. The reasons are twofold:

- Since the program is now more deterministic and more specified there is less ambiguity left how to implement the remaining specification.
- Since the specification is weakened it is easier to implement it.

As usual, in our setting the specification part of an $(S, P)$-pair describes what remains to be implemented, $P$ describes parts whose implementation is already fixed.

## 2.1 Transformational Refinement in the Unifying Framework

Traditional transformational refinement approaches like the ProCoS-method [1] start with a specification $S$ and use rules to refine this specification into one that can be translated directly into source-code. To enable the last step, the program constructs of the target language $\mathcal{P}$ are contained in the specification language $\mathcal{S}$ such that there is a mixture of specification and programming language. The refinement process stops when a specification is reached which contains program language constructs only.

From this approach several problems arise:

- It is often the case that the specification language and the programming language are quite different. Hence, it is very complicated to find a common semantical domain where both semantics and the semantics of the mixture of the languages can be expressed in an appropriate way.
- Typically the specification refining rules are not very powerful. Thus one needs a lot of refinement steps to come from a specification down to a program.

– The degree of automation is relatively small, that means if tool support is given then its usage is very interactive.

One major advantage of a transformational approach is that one can use arbitrary languages and logics as long as there is a common semantical basis.

In our framework the transformational refinement process looks like this

$$(S_0, P_{\mathbf{true}}) \xrightarrow{R_1} (S_1, P_{\mathbf{true}}) \xrightarrow{R_2} \dots \xrightarrow{R_n} (S_n, P_{\mathbf{true}}) \xrightarrow{R_{shift}} (S_n, S_n)$$

where $S_0, \dots, S_n \in \mathcal{S}$ and $R_1, \dots, R_n$ are specification refining rules, that are not synthesising. The last rule $R_{shift}$ replaces $P_{\mathbf{true}}$ by the specification $S_n$. This rule is applicable if the specification is in the programming language, i.e. $S_n \in \mathcal{P}$. Note that $(S_n, S_n)$ is correct.

From the viewpoint of our unifying framework one can derive the advantages and disadvantages of transformational refinement. The mixture of two languages with different purposes usually demands a relatively complex semantics. To separate both languages seems to be more natural and need not lead to these semantical problems. One result of a complex semantics as it is often necessary for transformational approaches within wide spectrum languages is a more complicated reasoning within this semantics to prove rules and application conditions. Especially, the usage of automated reasoning is restricted or at least difficult.

## 2.2 Synthesis Approaches in the Unifying Framework

Synthesis approaches try to get a program from a specification without user interaction. That means an algorithm $P$ is used that translates a specification $S \in \mathcal{S}$ to a program $P(S) \in \mathcal{P}$. The correctness of this transformation is guaranteed by the correctness of the synthesis algorithm $P$.

Advantages of synthesis approaches are:

- they are completely automated and
- only one general proof is needed namely the correctness of the algorithm has to be proven.

Disadvantages are:

- the expressiveness of the specification language is restricted by the scope of the synthesis algorithm and
- the algorithm is shown to deliver correct result, but the user has no influence on the result if more than one result is possible. Possibly, the delivered solution is suboptimal.

In our framework a synthesis approach tries to solve the problem of correct program construction in just one step:

$$(S, P_{\mathbf{true}}) \xrightarrow{R_{syn}} (S, P(S))$$

where $S \in \mathcal{S}$ is a specification and $R_{syn}$ denotes the rule that describes the synthesis algorithm. $P(S) \in \mathcal{P}$ is the result of the synthesis and $(S, P(S))$ is correct. Considering synthesis approaches in the unifying framework we can make the following observations:

- The expressiveness of $\mathcal{S}$ is at most as high as the expressiveness of $\mathcal{P}$ and the synthesis algorithm is only a compiler.
- All other advantages and disadvantages mentioned above of synthesis approaches can be derived within our model.

## 2.3 Model-Checking Approaches in the Unifying Framework

Model-Checking approaches use a decidable logic as the semantical basis for both specification and programming language. They check for a given specification and program whether the semantics of the program refines the semantics of the specification. Like the synthesis approach the model-checking approach is a one-step approach in our framework.

Advantages of Model-Checking are:

- Like the synthesis approach model-checking is completely automatic.
- The user can check an arbitrary program against a specification.

Disadvantages of Model-Checking exist, too:

- The calculus in which the semantics are expressed has to be decidable. Furthermore, the complexity of deciding a formula is very important for the efficiency of the model-checking. That restricts the expressiveness of the logics and hence the expressiveness of the languages used. That means there is a trade-off between expressiveness of the calculus and the efficiency of the model-checking.
- The user has to invent a program that possibly fulfils the specification before the model-check process is started.

In our framework model-checking is simply the test whether a pair of specification and program is correct or not. In this sense there is no application of a rule to gain a program from the specification. This reflects the invent-and-verify paradigm of model-checking.

## 2.4 How should an ideal approach of program construction look like?

An ideal approach to construct correct programs should be completely automatic and should require a specification only. This seems to be the description of the synthesis approach. But the disadvantages of synthesis like the inherent low level of abstraction of the specification language should be overcome by the ideal approach. Hence, a mixed approach seems appropriate: A specification language with a high level of abstraction in comparison to the programming language.

But a non-trivial subset of this specification language should be the source for a synthesis algorithm. Furthermore, a non-trivial subset of the semantic calculus should be decidable and as much language constructs as possible of both specification language and programming language should be semantically expressed in that decidable sublanguage of the calculus.

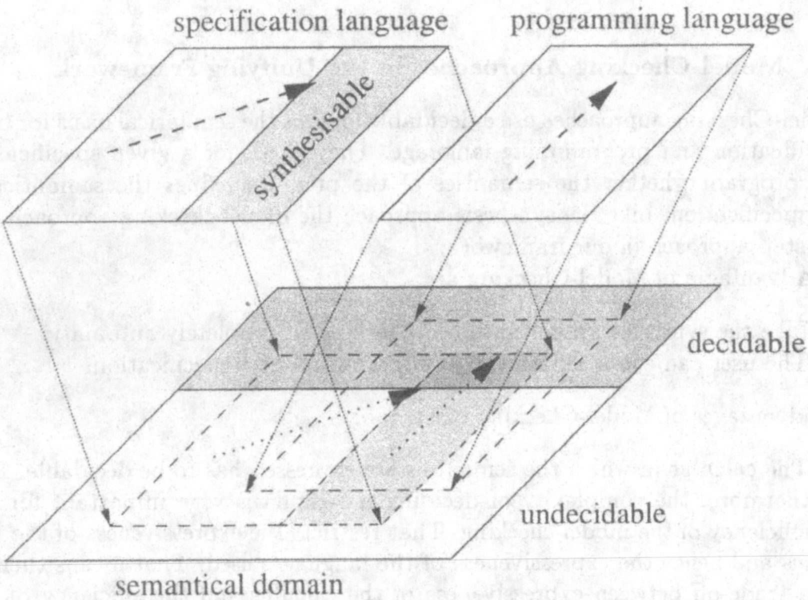


**Fig. 3.** an ideal approach of program construction

What has to be done first is the transformation of specification and program into these sublanguages where synthesis or model-checking apply. To this end it is important that both specification weakening and specification refining rules are used to remove constructs of the specification language that do not belong to the automatically supported sublanguages. Figure 3 demonstrates the relations between calculus, specification and programming language. The aim of this approach is to reach a mechanised region by specification weakening steps. That means that the aim of the transformational part of the program construction is to remove those parts of the specification that are not synthesisable or to transform both specification and program until a stage is reached such that the solution of the remaining problems can be supported by a model-checker (cf Fig.4).

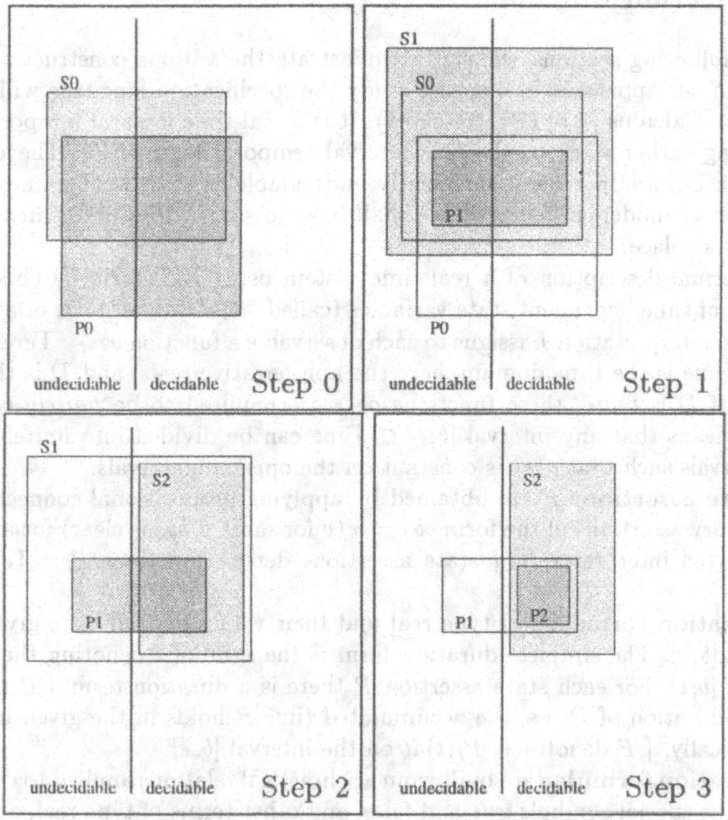


**Fig. 4. example path of an ideal approach**
**From Step 0 to Step 1 a specification weakening rule is applied: $S1$ is weaker than $S0$. Now a specification refining rule is applicable which refines $S1$ by $S2$. The latter is in the decidable subset. From Step 2 to Step 3 a synthesizing step removes some nondeterminism of the program such that the result $P2$ is in the decidable subset, too. Now the decision algorithm is applicable to prove that $(S2, P2)$ is correct.**

# 3 Duration Calculus

In the following sections we shall demonstrate the various construction techniques of our approach. In our case study the specification language will be the Duration Calculus [7,6] (DC for short). It is a real-time interval temporal logic extending earlier work on discrete interval temporal logic of [5]. The requirements in DC are in general sufficiently undecidable as to prevent an automatic synthesis or model-checking. So we shall have to start with a refinement phase in the first place.

A formal description of a real-time system using DC starts by choosing a number of time-dependent state variables (called "observables") *obs* of a certain type. An interpretation $I$ assigns to each observable a function $obs_I : \mathsf{Time} \longrightarrow D$ where Time is the time domain, here the non-negative reals, and $D$ is the type of *obs*. If $D$ is finite, these functions $obs_I$ are required to be *finitely variable*, which means that any interval $[b,e] \subset \mathsf{Time}$ can be divided into finitely many subintervals such that $obs_I$ is constant on the open subintervals.

**State assertions** $P$ are obtained by applying propositional connectives to elementary assertions of the form $obs = v$ ($v$ for short if *obs* is clear) for a $v \in D$. For a given interpretation $I$ state assertions denote functions $P_I : \mathsf{Time} \longrightarrow \{0,1\}$.

**Duration terms** are of type real and their values depend on a given time interval $[b,e]$. The simplest duration term is the symbol $\ell$ denoting the length $e-b$ of $[b,e]$. For each state assertion $P$ there is a duration term $\int P$ measuring the duration of $P$, i.e. the accumulated time $P$ holds in the given interval. Semantically, $\int P$ denotes $\int_b^e P_I(t)dt$ on the interval $[b,e]$.

**Duration formulae** are built from arithmetical relations applied to duration terms, the special symbols true and false, and other terms of type real, and they are closed under propositional connectives and quantification over rigid variables. Their truth values depend on a given interval. We use $F$ for a typical duration formula. true and false evaluate to true resp. false on every given interval. Further basic duration formulae are:

**Relation over Durations:** For example, $\int P = k$ expresses that the *duration* of the state assertion $P$ in $[b,e]$ is $k$.

**Chop:** The composite duration formula $F_1; F_2$ (read as $F_1$ *chop* $F_2$) holds in $[b,e]$ if this interval can be divided into an initial subinterval $[b,m]$ where $F_1$ holds and a final subinterval $[m,e]$ where $F_2$ holds.

Besides this basic syntax various abbreviations are used:

$$
\begin{array}{lrcl}
\text{point interval:} & \lceil\rceil & \stackrel{\text{df}}{=} & \ell = 0 \\
\text{everywhere:} & \lceil P \rceil & \stackrel{\text{df}}{=} & \int P = \ell \wedge \ell > 0 \\
\text{somewhere:} & \Diamond F & \stackrel{\text{df}}{=} & \mathsf{true}; F; \mathsf{true} \\
\text{always:} & \Box F & \stackrel{\text{df}}{=} & \neg\Diamond\neg F \\
 & F^t & \stackrel{\text{df}}{=} & (F \wedge \ell = t) \\
 & F^{\sim t} & \stackrel{\text{df}}{=} & (F \wedge \ell \sim t) \\
 & & & \text{with } \sim \in \{<, \leq, >, \geq\}
\end{array}
$$

A duration formula $F$ *holds* in an interpretation $I$ if $F$ evaluates to true in $I$ and every interval of the form $[0,t]$ with $t \in \mathsf{Time}$. If convenient, we use $F$ to describe a set of interpretations namely all interpretations in which $F$ holds.

The following so-called ***standard forms*** are useful to describe dynamic behaviour:

followed-by: $F \longrightarrow \lceil P \rceil \stackrel{\text{df}}{=} \Box\neg(F; \lceil \neg P \rceil)$

timed leads-to: $F \stackrel{t}{\longrightarrow} \lceil P \rceil \stackrel{\text{df}}{=} (F \wedge \ell = t) \longrightarrow \lceil P \rceil$

timed up-to: $F \stackrel{\leq t}{\longrightarrow} \lceil P \rceil \stackrel{\text{df}}{=} (F \wedge \ell \leq t) \longrightarrow \lceil P \rceil$

To avoid parentheses the following precedence rules are used:

1. $\int$
2. real operators
3. real predicates
4. $\neg, \Box, \Diamond$
5. ;
6. $\wedge, \vee$
7. $\Longrightarrow, \longrightarrow, \stackrel{\leq t}{\longrightarrow}, \stackrel{t}{\longrightarrow}$
8. quantification

During the ProCoS-project [1] a subset of Duration Calculus formulas called "Implementables" was discovered that is useful for the specification of reactive systems in an operational style. The Implementables consist of all formulas of one of the following patterns:

$$\begin{aligned}
\text{Initialisation: } & \lceil\rceil \vee \lceil \pi \rceil; \mathsf{true} \\
\text{Sequencing: } & \lceil \pi \rceil \longrightarrow \lceil \pi \vee \pi_1 \vee \ldots \vee \pi_n \rceil \\
\text{Unbounded Stability: } & \lceil \neg(\pi) \rceil; \lceil \pi \wedge (\phi_1 \vee \ldots \vee \phi_m) \rceil \longrightarrow \lceil \pi \vee \pi_1 \vee \ldots \vee \pi_n \rceil \\
\text{Bounded Stability: } & \lceil \neg(\pi) \rceil; \lceil \pi \wedge (\phi_1 \vee \ldots \vee \phi_m) \rceil \stackrel{\leq t}{\longrightarrow} \lceil \pi \vee \pi_1 \vee \ldots \vee \pi_n \rceil \\
\text{Progress: } & \lceil \pi \wedge (\phi_1 \vee \ldots \vee \phi_m) \rceil \stackrel{t}{\longrightarrow} \lceil \neg(\pi) \rceil
\end{aligned}$$

where $\pi, \pi_1, \ldots, \pi_n$ are states of the system, $\phi_1, \ldots, \phi_m$ are inputs to that system, $m, n \geq 0$ are natural numbers and $t > 0$ is a positive real.

## 4 A quasi-fair scheduler

The following case study of a scheduler gives an example how the various types of transformation rules can be mixed on the various levels of abstraction. We shall start with a formal requirement in DC to a scheduler $SCHED_w$, which in our general setting has to be conceived as $(SCHED_w, \mathsf{true})$. Then a scheduling strategy is specified in DC and shown that this set of formulae implies $SCHED_w$, a step which in our approach is interpreted as aspecification refinement. Later synthesis steps will be applied to this formalised scheduling strategy which finally lead to an implementation.

Assume we have $n$ processes $P_1, \ldots, P_n$ which want to have access to some critical resource $R$. From the view of the scheduler $P_i$ can be in exactly one of three states: $p_i nrm$ (normal working mode), $p_i rdy$ (access to $R$ requested, process is waiting), $p_i run$ (process is using $R$ exclusively). These are $(P1)-(P4)$ of the following formal assumptions on the processes. Initially, the process is in its normal working mode $(P5)$. From this mode no direct access to $R$ is possible, access has to be requested before $(P6)$ and afterwards it may be granted $(P7)$. From $p_i run$ every successor state is possible $(P8)$.

$$
\begin{array}{ll}
(P1) & \forall i : \Box\,(p_i nrm \vee p_i rdy \vee p_i run) \\
(P2) & \forall i : \Box\,(p_i nrm \Rightarrow \neg(p_i rdy \vee p_i run)) \\
(P3) & \forall i : \Box\,(p_i rdy \Rightarrow \neg(p_i nrm \vee p_i run)) \\
(P4) & \forall i : \Box\,(p_i run \Rightarrow \neg(p_i nrm \vee p_i rdy)) \\
(P5) & \forall i : \lceil\rceil \vee \lceil p_i nrm\rceil; \mathsf{true} \\
(P6) & \forall i : \lceil p_i nrm\rceil \longrightarrow \lceil p_i nrm \vee p_i rdy\rceil \\
(P7) & \forall i : \lceil p_i rdy\rceil \longrightarrow \lceil p_i rdy \vee p_i run\rceil \\
(P8) & \forall i : \lceil p_i run\rceil \longrightarrow \lceil p_i run \vee p_i nrm \vee p_i rdy\rceil
\end{array}
$$

In connection with $(P1)$, $(P8)$ is equivalent to **true** and can hence be disregarded.

The fair scheduler requires that in each interval for each processor the ratio of waiting time to waiting plus running time is the same, provided that it is not normal throughout.

$$
SCHED_f \;\equiv\; \forall i,j : \Box\Big(\big(\textstyle\int(p_i run \vee p_i rdy) \neq 0 \wedge \int(p_j run \vee p_j rdy) \neq 0\big) \Rightarrow
\frac{\int p_i run}{\int(p_i run \vee p_i rdy)} = \frac{\int p_j run}{\int(p_j run \vee p_j rdy)}\Big)
$$

Unfortunately, this scheduler is not implementable, for example if arbitrarily small intervals are considered. That is why we design a scheduler $sched(d,c)$ with two parameters $d$ and $c$ by the definition

$$
SCHED \;\equiv\; \forall i : \Box\Big(\big(\ell \geq d \wedge \textstyle\int(p_i run \vee p_i rdy) \neq 0\big) \Rightarrow
\bigwedge_i \frac{\int p_i run}{\int(p_i run \vee p_i rdy)} > c\,\frac{1}{n}\Big)
$$

saying that for each sufficiently large interval for each processor the ratio of waiting time to waiting plus running time is bigger than a constant multiple $c$ of what would be the processor's fair share of access time to the resource. It is quite obvious that this scheduler is not implementable for $c \geq 1$. At first we give an impression of the possible implementations of $sched(d,c)$ by time slices for the various choices of $c$ and $d$.

In Fig. 5 we assume that we have $n = 3$ processors which are all either running or ready to run. Processors 2 and 3 are ready to run whenever they are not actually running.

Consider for example the first five slices of processor 3. There the ratio between running time and running or ready time is $1/5$. So including a certain amount of time for reloading we are on the safe side if $c = 1/2$ is chosen. If a $c$ is specified which is closer to 1 we shall have to use smaller time slices than ones of length $d/n$, as has been done in the drawing.

| | | | | | | |
|---|---|---|---|---|---|---|
| 1 | *run* | *rdy* | *rdy* | *run* | *rdy* | *rdy* |
| 2 | *rdy* | *run* | *rdy* | *rdy* | *run* | *rdy* |
| 3 | *rdy* | *rdy* | *run* | *rdy* | *rdy* | *run* |

**Fig. 5.**

Having given the requirements for $SCHED_f$ or $SCHED$ we are, considering our framework, in the situation that no automatic steps are applicable. Hence we start with a traditional refinement step: We (intelligently) guess a scheduling strategy and are obliged to show that it fulfils the scheduling requirements.

We are aiming at an implementation in which the processes which are ready to run or running are administered in a queue. The state space of the scheduler is $\{go, wt, ch\} \times Q$ where $Q$ is the set of all possible queues, *go* means that some process is running or just about to run, in *wt* the running process is about to be deactivated or has just been deactivated and *ch* is the phase between deactivation of one and activation of another process. In the beginning of *ch* the queue is shortened and at its end the processes which have become ready since the last activation are included in the queue. In the following, head and tail of the queue will be abbreviated by *hd* and *tl*. Formally, our scheduling strategy is

$$STRATEGY \equiv \bigwedge_{i=1}^{8} P\,i \wedge \bigwedge_{i=1}^{4} S\,i \wedge \bigwedge_{i=1}^{6} C\,i \wedge \bigwedge_{i=1}^{5} G\,i \wedge \bigwedge_{i=1}^{3} W\,i$$

with $P\,i$ as above and the other requirements as follows:

$$\begin{array}{ll}
(S1) & \lceil \neg(p_i rdy) \rceil ; \lceil p_i rdy \wedge (i \neq hd(\langle q \rangle) \vee (ch, \langle q \rangle) \vee (wt, \langle q \rangle)) \rceil \longrightarrow \lceil p_i rdy \rceil \\
(S2) & \lceil \neg(p_{hd(\langle q \rangle)} run) \rceil ; \lceil p_{hd(\langle q \rangle)} run \wedge (go, \langle q \rangle) \rceil \longrightarrow \lceil p_{hd(\langle q \rangle)} run \rceil \\
(S3) & \lceil p_{hd(\langle q \rangle)} rdy \wedge (go, \langle q \rangle) \rceil \xrightarrow{\varepsilon} \lceil \neg(p_{hd(\langle q \rangle)} rdy) \rceil \\
(S4) & \lceil p_i run \wedge (i \neq hd(\langle q \rangle) \vee (ch, \langle q \rangle) \vee (wt, \langle q \rangle)) \rceil \xrightarrow{\varepsilon} \lceil \neg(p_i run) \rceil
\end{array}$$

Readiness of a process $i$ is maintained until $i$ is the head of the queue and *go* holds. A process remains running as long as *go* holds, $(S1), (S2)$. $(S3)$ and $(S4)$ say that the process must change its state as soon as the scheduler state fulfils the side conditions.

$$
\begin{array}{ll}
(C1) & \lceil\rceil \vee \lceil(ch, \langle\rangle)\rceil; \mathsf{true} \\
(C2) & \lceil(ch, \langle q\rangle)\rceil \longrightarrow \lceil(ch, \langle q\rangle) \vee (go, \langle q'\rangle)\rceil \\
 & \quad \text{with } \langle q'\rangle = \langle q\rangle.\langle q''\rangle, \langle q\rangle \cap \langle q''\rangle = \emptyset \\
(C3) & \lceil\neg((ch, \langle q\rangle))\rceil; \lceil(ch, \langle q\rangle) \wedge p_i rdy\rceil \longrightarrow \lceil(ch, \langle q\rangle) \vee \bigvee_{i\in\langle q.q'\rangle}(go, \langle q.q'\rangle)\rceil \\
(C4) & \lceil\neg((ch, \langle q\rangle))\rceil; \lceil(ch, \langle q\rangle) \wedge \bigwedge_i \neg p_i rdy\rceil \longrightarrow \lceil(ch, \langle q\rangle)\rceil \\
(C5) & \lceil(ch, \langle q\rangle) \wedge p_i rdy\rceil \xrightarrow{\varepsilon} \lceil\neg((ch, \langle q\rangle))\rceil \\
(C6) & \lceil\neg((ch, \langle q\rangle))\rceil; \lceil(ch, \langle q\rangle) \wedge \neg p_i rdy\rceil \longrightarrow \lceil(ch, \langle q\rangle) \vee \bigvee_{i\notin\langle q'\rangle}(go, \langle q.q'\rangle)\rceil
\end{array}
$$

Initially no process is activated or about to be activated, $(C1)$. State $ch$ is maintained as long as no process becomes ready, $(C4)$, but $ch$ has to be left as soon as some process becomes ready, $(C5)$. In the next state $go$ must hold, $(C2)$. After $ch$ the queue is extended by those processes which have become ready but are not yet in the queue, $(C3), (C6)$. Here and in the following we feel free to use set theoretical notation for queues, provided no misunderstanding is possible.

$$
\begin{array}{ll}
(G1) & \lceil(go, \langle q\rangle)\rceil \longrightarrow \lceil(go, \langle q\rangle) \vee (wt, \langle q\rangle)\rceil \\
(G2) & \lceil\neg((go, \langle q\rangle))\rceil; \lceil(go, \langle q\rangle) \wedge \neg p_{hd(\langle q\rangle)} nrm\rceil \xrightarrow{\leq dl} \lceil(go, \langle q\rangle)\rceil \\
(G3) & \lceil(go, \langle q\rangle) \wedge p_{hd(\langle q\rangle)} nrm\rceil \xrightarrow{\varepsilon} \lceil\neg((go, \langle q\rangle))\rceil \\
(G4) & \lceil(go, \langle q\rangle) \wedge p_i rdy\rceil \xrightarrow{dl+\varepsilon} \lceil\neg((go, \langle q\rangle))\rceil \text{ with } hd(\langle q\rangle) \neq i \\
(G5) & \lceil\neg((go, \langle q\rangle))\rceil; \lceil(go, \langle q\rangle) \wedge \neg p_{hd(\langle q\rangle)} nrm \wedge \bigwedge_{i\neq hd(\langle q\rangle)} \neg p_i rdy\rceil \longrightarrow \lceil(go, \langle q\rangle)\rceil
\end{array}
$$

In the state $go$ the first process in the queue is guaranteed the use of the resource for some delay time $dl$, unless it voluntarily relinquishes its use by becoming normal, $(G2)$. However, if some other process becomes ready, the head process will be deactivated after that time, $(G4)$, also if it no longer needs the resource and chooses to go into the normal state, $(G3)$. In the next state $wt$ will hold. If no competing process becomes ready the scheduler state remains the same, until the head process voluntarily becomes normal, $(G5)$.

$$
\begin{array}{ll}
(W1) & \lceil(wt, \langle q\rangle)\rceil \longrightarrow \lceil(wt, \langle q\rangle) \vee (ch, \langle tl(\langle q\rangle)\rangle)\rceil \\
(W2) & \lceil\neg((wt, \langle q\rangle))\rceil; \lceil(wt, \langle q\rangle) \wedge p_{hd(\langle q\rangle)} run\rceil \longrightarrow \lceil(wt, \langle q\rangle)\rceil \\
(W3) & \lceil(wt, \langle q\rangle) \wedge \neg p_{hd(\langle q\rangle)} run\rceil \xrightarrow{\varepsilon} \lceil\neg((wt, \langle q\rangle))\rceil
\end{array}
$$

State $wt$ is upheld as long as the head process is running, $(W2)$. But thereafter the state must be left, $(W3)$. In the successor state $ch$ holds and the head is removed from the queue, $(W1)$.

Now we are going to try to prove the scheduler correct, formally this means $STRATEGY \Rightarrow SCHED$ which in our approach is reinterpreted as

$$(STRATEGY, P_{\mathsf{true}}) \Rrightarrow (SCHED, P_{\mathsf{true}})$$

Actually, we shall prove that under $STRATEGY$ holds

$$(1) \quad \lceil p_j rdy\rceil \xrightarrow{3\varepsilon + (n+1)(dl+5\varepsilon)} \lceil p_j run\rceil$$

The main tool in the proof of (1) will be the formulae (2) which intuitively say that, when a process $j$ is waiting in the queue for access to the resource $R$ which is occupied by some process $i$, then after some time (at most $dl + 5\varepsilon$ seconds) either the access to $R$ is granted to $j$ or another process $k$ is running and $j$ has advanced by at least one place in the queue. If $j$ has just become ready then after $dl + 5\varepsilon$ seconds it is contained in the queue.

$$\begin{aligned}(2)\quad & \Box\,(\lceil p_i run \wedge p_j rdy \wedge rank_j = r > 1\rceil ; \ell > 0 \ \wedge\ \ell > dl + 5\varepsilon \ \Rightarrow \\ & \qquad \ell \leq dl + 5\varepsilon ; \lceil p_k run \wedge k \neq i \wedge rank_j < r\rceil ; \mathsf{true}), \\ & \Box\,(\lceil p_i run \wedge p_j rdy \wedge rank_j = 1\rceil ; \ell > 0 \ \wedge\ \ell > dl + 5\varepsilon \ \Rightarrow \\ & \qquad \ell \leq dl + 5\varepsilon ; \lceil p_j run\rceil ; \mathsf{true}) \quad \text{and} \\ & \Box\,(\lceil p_i run \wedge p_j rdy \wedge rank_j = 0\rceil ; \ell > 0 \ \wedge\ \ell > dl + 5\varepsilon \ \Rightarrow \\ & \qquad \ell \leq dl + 5\varepsilon ; \lceil p_k run \wedge rank_j > 0\rceil ; \mathsf{true})\end{aligned}$$

In these formulae let $rank_j = k$, iff $j$ is the $k$-th element of $\langle q\rangle$, in particular $rank_j = 1 \iff hd(\langle q\rangle) = i$. For $j \notin \langle q\rangle$ we put $rank_j = 0$.

We start our investigations with

$$(*) \quad \Box(\lceil i \in \langle q\rangle\rceil \ \Rightarrow\ \lceil p_i rdy \vee p_i run \vee (wt, \langle q\rangle)\rceil)$$

Proof of $(*)$: By $(C2)$, $(G1)$ and $(W1)$ the queue can only be extended at the change from $(ch, \langle q\rangle)$ to $(go, \langle q'\rangle)$. In this case by $(C6)$ a process $i$ can enter the queue only if $p_i rdy$ holds. By $(S1)$ this is maintained until $(go, \langle q\rangle)$ holds for some $q$ with $i = hd(\langle q\rangle)$. $(P7)$ and $(S2)$ then guarantee $p_i run$, thereafter by $(G1)$ we have $(wt, \langle q\rangle)$. But $(W1)$ says that this state can only be left towards $(ch, \langle tl(\langle q\rangle)\rangle)$, and then $i$, having been the head of the queue is removed. This establishes $(*)$.

We shall also need

$$(**) \quad \Box(\lceil (go, \langle q\rangle) \vee (wt, \langle q\rangle)\rceil \ \Rightarrow\ \lceil q \neq \emptyset\rceil)$$

Proof of $(**)$: We proceed by induction on the number of state changes. By $(C1)$ initially the claim is true.

By $(C2)$, $(G1)$ and $(W1)$ the state cycles through $(ch, \langle q\rangle)$, $(go, \langle q\rangle)$ and $(wt, \langle q\rangle)$ for appropriate $q$. Assume after the $n$-th state change we have reached $(ch, \langle q\rangle)$, then by $(C4)$ this state is maintained until one process is ready. In this case $(C3)$ guarantees that in the successor state $(go, \langle q\rangle)$ the queue is not empty.

If after the $n$-th state change the state is $(go, \langle q\rangle)$, then by induction the queue is not empty. And so is the queue in the successor state by $(G1)$.

If after the $n$-th state change the state is $(wt, \langle q\rangle)$, the successor state is $(ch, \langle tl(\langle q\rangle)\rangle)$ and nothing is to prove. This ends the proof of $(**)$.

Now we prove (2) as follows: Let $I$ an interval with

$$I \models (\lceil p_i run \wedge p_j rdy\rceil ; \ell > 0).$$

In the case of $j \in q$ let $rank_j = r$. We shall chop off subintervals $I_j$ from the beginning of $I$ and estimate their maximal length. Figure 6 shows the situation which will be the result of our reflections:

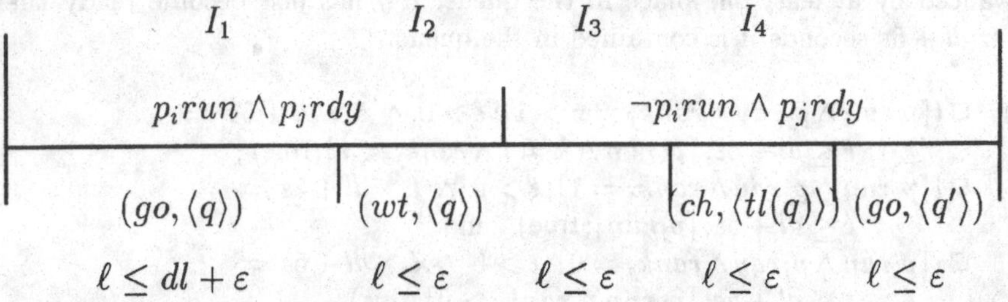


**Fig. 6.**

At first we remark that by $(P5)$ – $(P8)$ process $i$ must have been ready before running. By $(S1)$ the state $p_i rdy$ is maintained unless the state is $(go, \langle q \rangle)$ and $hd(\langle q \rangle) = i$. So without loss of generality we may assume the following situation:

$$I \models \lceil (go, \langle q \rangle) \wedge hd(\langle q \rangle) = i \rceil; \mathsf{true}$$

and there is an interval $I'$ immediately preceding $I$ with

$$I' \models \lceil p_i rdy \wedge (go, \langle q \rangle) \wedge hd(\langle q \rangle) = i \rceil.$$

By $(S2)$ the state $p_i run$ is maintained as long as $(go, \langle q \rangle)$ holds and so is $p_j rdy$ by $(S1)$. By $(G4)$ the state $(go, \langle q \rangle)$ must be left after at most $dl + \varepsilon$ seconds. Formally, we can decompose $I$ into $I_1; I^1$ with

$$I_1 \models \lceil (go, \langle q \rangle) \rceil \wedge \ell \leq dl + \varepsilon \quad \text{and} \quad I^1 \models \lceil \neg (go, \langle q \rangle) \rceil; \mathsf{true}.$$

By $(G1)$ the initial state in $I^1$ is $(wt, \langle q \rangle)$, which by $(W2)$ is maintained as long as $p_i run$ holds. By $(S4)$ and $(W3)$ we chop $I^1$ into $I_2; I_3; I^2$ with

$$\begin{aligned} I_2 &\models \lceil p_i run \wedge (wt, \langle q \rangle) \rceil \wedge \ell \leq \varepsilon, \\ I_3 &\models \lceil \neg p_i run \wedge (wt, \langle q \rangle) \rceil \wedge \ell \leq \varepsilon \quad \text{and} \\ I^2 &\models \lceil \neg p_i run \wedge \neg (wt, \langle q \rangle) \rceil; \mathsf{true}. \end{aligned}$$

By $(W1)$ we get $I^2 \models \lceil (ch, \langle tl(q) \rangle) \rceil; \mathsf{true}$ and in particular

$$I^2 \models \lceil rank_j = r - 1 \rceil; \mathsf{true}$$

in the case that $j \in q$ with $rank_j = r$ has held before. By $(S1)$ holds $I_2 \models \lceil p_j rdy \rceil$, $I_3 \models \lceil p_j rdy \rceil$ and $I^2 \models \lceil p_j rdy \rceil; \mathsf{true}$. By $(C5)$ hence $I^2$ can be chopped into $I^2 = I_4; I^3$ with

$$I_4 \models \lceil (ch, \langle tl(q)\rangle)\rceil \wedge \ell \leq \varepsilon \quad \text{and} \quad I^3 \models \lceil \neg(ch, \langle tl(q)\rangle)\rceil; \text{true}.$$

More precisely, by $(C3)$ there is a $\langle q'\rangle$ with $\langle q'\rangle = tl(q).\langle q''\rangle$ for some $\langle q''\rangle$ such that $I^3 \models \lceil (go, \langle q'\rangle)\rceil; \text{true}$. $(C3)$ also says that $j$ is contained in $\langle q''\rangle$ if $j$ has not been in $q$ before. Due to $I_3 \models \lceil p_j rdy\rceil$, $(S1)$ and $(P7)$ we have $I_4 \models \lceil p_j rdy\rceil$. From $(C3)$ we conclude that $\langle q'\rangle$ is not empty. Let $k = hd(q')$. By $(*)$ then $I_4 \models \lceil p_k rdy \vee p_k run\rceil$. Because of $I_2 \models \lceil p_i run\rceil$ and $(S1)$ we obtain $I_4 \models \lceil p_k rdy\rceil$. Then by $(S3)$ holds

$$I^3 \models (\lceil \neg p_k run\rceil \wedge \ell \leq \varepsilon); \lceil p_k run\rceil; \text{true}.$$

This establishes (2) for all three cases.

Now (1) is a conclusion from (2) obtained by induction over the rank: At first we have to give an estimation how long it takes to establish the preconditions of (2) when $j$ becomes ready. Since our case distinction in (2) concerning the rank of $j$ is complete, we may assume as the worst situation that none of the processes is actually running. We claim that it lasts at most $3\varepsilon$ seconds until one process has accessed the resource. In order to prove the claim we take an interval $I$ with

$$I \models \lceil p_j rdy \wedge \textstyle\bigwedge_k \neg p_k run\rceil; \text{true} \wedge \ell \geq 3\varepsilon.$$

We have to show

(3) $I \models \text{true}; \lceil p_k run\rceil; \text{true}$

for some $k$.

After having established (3) we can show (1) as follows:
If $j$ becomes ready it lasts at worst $3\varepsilon$ seconds until one process is running, after another $dl + 5\varepsilon$ seconds it is $i \in q$, in the worst case with rank $n$. After at most further $n - 1$ iterations its rank is 1 and after a final $dl + 5\varepsilon$ seconds the process is running.

We are left with the task to show (3). At first we additionally assume that initially in $I$ the queue $q$ is not empty. Let $i = hd(q)$. By $(*)$ and our main assumption for (3) we are left with the two possibilities $p_i rdy$ and $(wt, \langle q\rangle)$. If the initial state in $I$ is $(wt, \langle q\rangle)$ by $(W3)$ and $(W1)$ after $\varepsilon$ seconds the state is $(ch, \langle q'\rangle)$ for some $q'$. By $(C5)$ and $(C2)$ after another $\varepsilon$ seconds the state is $(go, \langle q''\rangle)$ for some $q''$. By $(**)$ the queue is not empty. Hence by $(*)$ we have that in each of the two above possibilities after at most $2\varepsilon$ seconds holds $p_{hd(q)} rdy$. By $(S3)$ and $(P3)$ hence after at most $3\varepsilon$ seconds one process is running.

If initially in $I$ the queue $q$ is empty, then by $(**)$ initially in $I$ holds $(ch, \langle q\rangle)$. By $(C5)$ and $(C2)$ after another $\varepsilon$ seconds the state is $(go, \langle q'\rangle)$ for some $q'$, and by $(C3)$ it is $i$ contained in $q'$. Again by $(S3)$ and $(P3)$ after another at most $\varepsilon$ seconds one process is running.

This establishes (3) and fills the final gap in the proof of (1).

The question now is: *Is* (1) *sufficient to prove* $SCHED$? The answer is no, because $SCHED$ is still not implementable in contrast to our intuition. The reason is the following: Assume a process $i$ has been ready for as long as possible, eg. the $3\varepsilon + (n+1)\,(dl+5\varepsilon)$ seconds from (1). Then nothing stops $i$ from releasing the resource after $\varepsilon$ seconds and becoming ready again after another $\varepsilon$ seconds. In general, comparably long ready intervals may be interrupted by arbitrarily small running and normal phases. Nevertheless we think that the scheduler we have specified is fairly fair, because a normal phase indicates that the process has had access to the resource for at least some time (by $(G2)$ this minimum time is $dl$) or until it has its task completed (by going back to $p_q nrm$). So a reasonable formula for a weaker scheduler is

$$SCHED_w \;\equiv\; \forall i:\; \Box\Big((\ell \geq d \wedge \textstyle\int(p_i run \vee p_i rdy) \neq 0) \;\Rightarrow$$
$$(\Diamond p_i nrm \quad \vee \quad \textstyle\bigwedge_i \frac{\int p_i run}{\int(p_i run \vee p_i rdy)} \; > c\,\frac{1}{n})\Big)$$

By some simple arguments and arithmetical calculations $SCHED_w$ can be derived from (1) and two sideconditions which give an estimation for $c$ and $d$:

$$c \;<\; \frac{1}{2}\,\frac{n\,dl}{3\varepsilon \,+\, (n+1)\,(dl+5\varepsilon)} \quad \text{and} \quad d \;>\; (n+2)\,(dl+5\varepsilon)$$

So altogether the result of the refinement is

$$(STRATEGY, P_{\mathsf{true}}) \;\Rrightarrow\; (SCHED_w, P_{\mathsf{true}})$$

and in the following sections $STRATEGY$ will further be treated by a synthesis algorithm.

## 5 PLC-Automata

In the UniForM-project [4] we made the experience that automaton-like pictures can serve as a common basis for computer scientists and engineers. The latter have a intuitive understanding of these pictures. Therefore, we formalised the notion of "PLC-Automaton" and defined a formal semantics for it in DC that is consistent to the translation of PLC-Automata into PLC-source-code. But PLC-Automata are not especially tailored to PLCs. In fact, PLC-Automata are an abstract representation of a machine that periodically polls the input and has the possibility of measuring time. In [2] a compilation function to PLC source code is given.

Figure 7 gives an example of a PLC-Automaton. It shows an automaton with three states ($\{q_0, q_1, q_2\}$) and outputs $\{\mathtt{A}, \mathtt{B}, \mathtt{C}\}$, that reacts to inputs of the alphabet $\{\mathtt{x}, \mathtt{y}\}$. Every state has two annotations in the graphical representation. The upper one denotes the output of the state, thus in state $q_0$ the output is $\mathtt{A}$ and in state $q_2$ the output is $\mathtt{C}$. The lower annotation is either 0 or a pair consisting of a real number $d > 0$ and a nonempty subset $S$ of inputs.

The operational behaviour is as follows: If the second annotation of a state $q$ is 0, the PLC-Automaton reacts in every cycle to the inputs that are read and

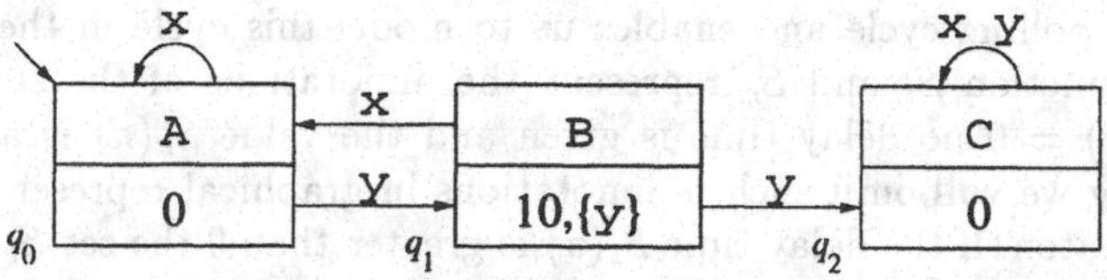


**Fig. 7.** An example of a PLC-Automaton.

behaves according to the transition relation. If the second annotation of $q$ is a pair $(d, S)$, the PLC-Automaton checks in every cycle the input $i$ according to these parameters. If $i$ is not in $S$ the automaton reacts immediately according to the transition relation. If $i$ is in $S$ and the current state does not hold longer than $d$, the input will be ignored and the automaton remains in state $q$. If $i$ is in $S$ and state $q$ held longer than $d$ the PLC-Automaton will react on $i$ according to the transition relation.

The PLC-Automaton in Fig. 7 thus behaves as follows: It starts in state $q_0$ and remains there as long as it reads only the input **x**. The first time it reads **y** it changes to state $q_1$. In $q_1$ the automaton reacts to the input **x** by changing the state back to $q_0$ independently of the time it stayed in state $q_1$. It reacts to the input **y** by changing the state to $q_2$ provided that $q_1$ holds longer than 10 seconds. If this transition takes place the automaton enters $q_2$ and remains there forever. Hence, we know that the automaton changes its output to C when **y** holds a little bit longer than 10 seconds (the cycle time has to be considered).

We formalise this graphic notation using an automaton-like structure extended by some components:

**Definition 6.** A tuple $\mathcal{A} = (Q, \Sigma, \delta, \pi_0, \varepsilon, S_t, S_e, \Omega, \omega)$ is a *PLC-Automaton* if

- $Q$ is a nonempty, finite set of *states*,
- $\Sigma$ is a nonempty, finite set of *inputs*,
- $\delta$ is a function of type $Q \times \Sigma \longrightarrow Q$ (*transition function*),
- $\pi_0 \in Q$ is the *initial state*,
- $\varepsilon > 0$ is the *upper bound* for a cycle,
- $S_t$ is a function of type $Q \longrightarrow \mathbb{R}_{\geq 0}$ assigning to each state $\pi$ a *delay time* how long the inputs contained in $S_e(\pi)$ should be ignored,
- $S_e$ is a function of type $Q \longrightarrow \mathcal{P}(\Sigma) \setminus \{\emptyset\}$ assigning to each state a set of *delayed inputs*,[1]
- $\Omega$ is a nonempty, finite set of *outputs*, and
- $\omega$ is a function of type $Q \longrightarrow \Omega$ (*output function*)

The components $Q$, $\Sigma$, $\delta$, and $q_0$ are as for usual finite state automata. The additional components are needed to model a polling behaviour and to enrich the language for dealing with real-time aspects. The $\varepsilon$ represents the upper

[1] If $S_t(\pi) = 0$ the set $S_e(\pi)$ can be arbitrarily chosen. The single 0 represents this in the graphical notation (cf. Fig. 7).

bound for a polling cycle and enables us to model this cycle in the semantics. The delay function $S_t$ and $S_e$ represent the annotations of the states. In the case of $S_t(\pi) = 0$ no delay time is given and the value $S_e(\pi)$ is arbitrary. In the following we will omit such 0-annotations in graphical representations of a PLC-Automaton. If the delay time $S_t(\pi)$ is greater than 0 the set $S_e(\pi)$ denotes the set of inputs for which the delay time is valid.

The DC-semantics of a PLC-Automaton $\mathcal{A} = (Q, \Sigma, \delta, \pi_0, \varepsilon, S_e, S_t, \Omega, \omega)$ is given by the conjunction of the following predicates in the observables $\mathsf{state} : \mathsf{Time} \longrightarrow Q$, $\mathsf{input} : \mathsf{Time} \longrightarrow \Sigma$ and $\mathsf{output} : \mathsf{Time} \longrightarrow \Omega$. First of all, the start of the automaton in the proper initial state is expressed by:

$$\lceil\rceil \vee \lceil \pi_0 \rceil ; \mathsf{true}. \tag{1}$$

Note that $\lceil \pi_0 \rceil$ is an abbreviation of $\lceil \mathsf{state} = \pi_0 \rceil$. The transition function, the cyclic behaviour, and the output is modelled by the following formulas where we use $A$ as an abbreviation for $\mathsf{input} \in A$ resp. $\delta(\pi, A)$ for $\mathsf{state} \in \{\delta(\pi, a) | a \in A\}$.

$$\lceil \neg\pi \rceil ; \lceil \pi \wedge A \rceil \longrightarrow \lceil \pi \vee \delta(\pi, A) \rceil \tag{2}$$
$$\lceil \pi \wedge A \rceil \xrightarrow{\varepsilon} \lceil \pi \vee \delta(\pi, A) \rceil \tag{3}$$
$$\Box(\lceil \pi \rceil \Longrightarrow \lceil \omega(\pi) \rceil) \tag{4}$$

where $A$ ranges over sets with $\emptyset \neq A \subseteq \Sigma$. For states without delay requirement ($S_t(\pi) = 0$) we postulate:

$$\lceil \pi \wedge A \rceil \xrightarrow{2\varepsilon} \lceil \delta(\pi, A) \rceil \tag{5}$$
$$\pi \notin \delta(\pi, A) \Longrightarrow \lceil \neg\pi \rceil ; \lceil \pi \wedge A \rceil^{=\varepsilon} \longrightarrow \lceil \neg\pi \rceil \tag{6}$$

For states with delay requirement ($S_t(\pi) > 0$) we have:

$$\lceil \pi \rceil ; \lceil \pi \wedge A \rceil^{=2\varepsilon} \xrightarrow{2\varepsilon + S_t(\pi)} \lceil \delta(\pi, A) \rceil \tag{7}$$
$$\lceil \neg\pi \rceil ; \lceil \pi \wedge A \rceil \xrightarrow{\leq S_t(\pi)} \lceil \pi \vee \delta(\pi, A \setminus S_e(\pi)) \rceil \tag{8}$$
$$\lceil \neg\pi \rceil ; \lceil \pi \rceil ; \lceil \pi \wedge A \rceil^{=\varepsilon} \xrightarrow{\leq S_t(\pi)} \lceil \pi \vee \delta(\pi, A \setminus S_e(\pi)) \rceil \tag{9}$$
$$A \cap S_e(\pi) = \emptyset \Longrightarrow \lceil \pi \wedge A \rceil \xrightarrow{2\varepsilon} \lceil \delta(\pi, A) \rceil \tag{10}$$
$$A \cap S_e(\pi) = \emptyset \Longrightarrow \lceil \neg\pi \rceil ; \lceil \pi \wedge A \rceil^{=\varepsilon} \longrightarrow \lceil \neg\pi \rceil \tag{11}$$

## 6 Synthesis

In Sect. 4 we have proven that the specification of the scheduler fulfils its constraints provided that the processes behave as specified. In this section we construct a program that implements the specification for the scheduler. To this end we use an algorithm in [3] that works for specifications given in terms of DC-Implementables and produces PLC-Automata as output.

This algorithm describes how to change a given PLC-Automaton such that a certain Implementable is fulfilled. That means that an Implementable can be removed from the specification if the corresponding step of the algorithm has been performed. Thus, each step which removes an Implementable is a specification weakening step.

Instead of explaining this algorithm in detail we demonstrate its behaviour by the application to our scheduler specification. The first step of the algorithm determines the states of the PLC-Automaton from the set of Implementables by recognising both the states mentioned and the bounded stabilities used. This yields the state space given below. Note that on the left hand side the specification is mentioned which should be met. The right hand side contains the description of the program developed so far.

Each of the following steps (except the first one) is a specification weakening step (and hence synthesising), where by each time some of the conjuncts of *STRATEGY* are removed in favour of a strengthening of the already developed implementation. We start with $(STRATEGY, P_{\mathsf{true}})$ and in the first step get:

(C1)
(C2)
(C3)
(C4)
(C5)
(C6)
(G1)
(G2)
(G3)
(G4)
(G5)
(W1)
(W2)
(W3)

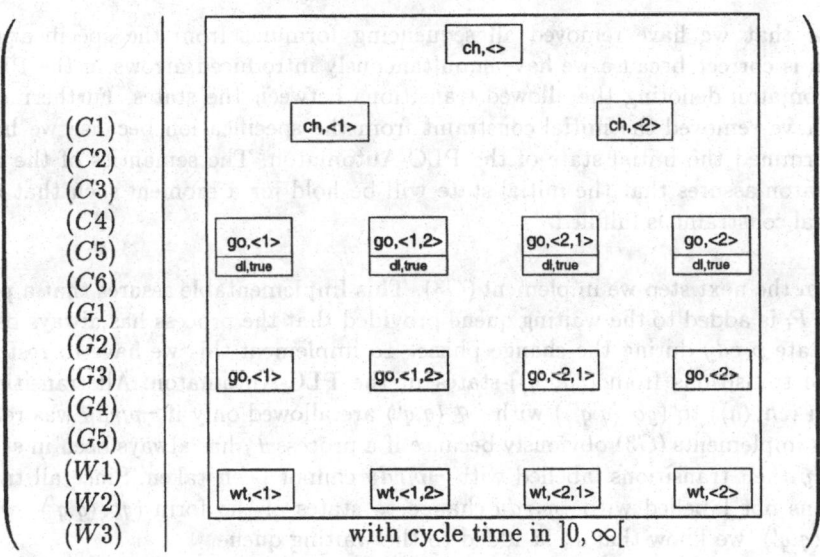

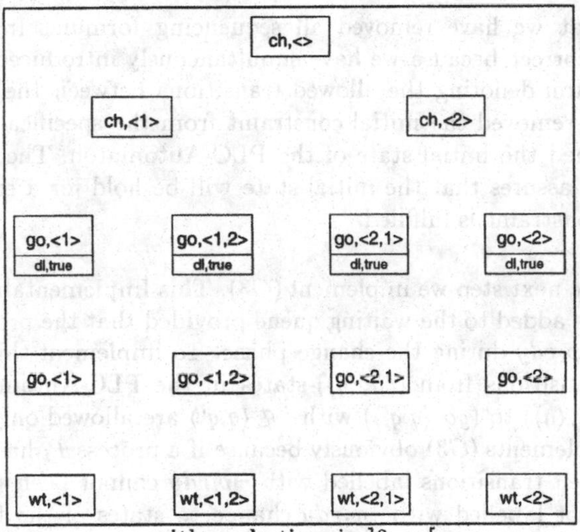

with cycle time in $]0, \infty[$

Thus, the first step does not change the specification itself. Only the program has changed. Note that in the implementing automaton all transitions are allowed at this stage of development.

By the sequencing formulas ($C2$), ($G1$), and ($W1$) the specification restricts the possible changes of states. Hence, the next step restricts the transition relation according to the sequencing formulas:

$(C3)$
$(C4)$
$(C5)$
$(C6)$
$(G2)$
$(G3)$
$(G4)$
$(G5)$
$(W2)$
$(W3)$

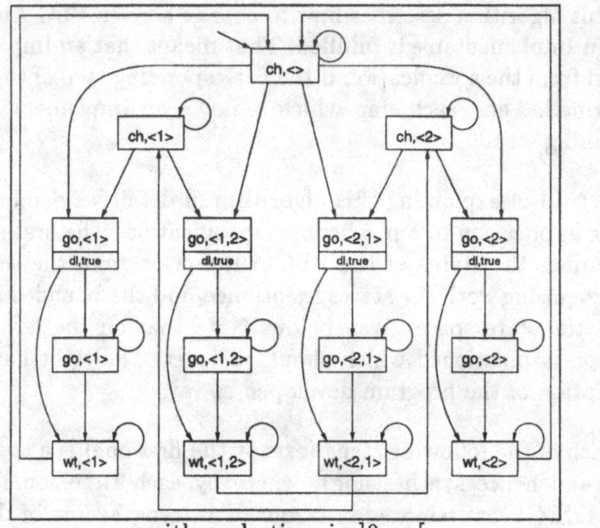


with cycle time in $]0, \infty[$

Note that we have removed all sequencing formulas from the specification. This is correct because we have simultaneously introduced arrows in the PLC-Automaton denoting the allowed transitions between the states. Furthermore, we have removed the initial constraint from the specification because we have determined the initial state of the PLC-Automaton. The semantics of the automaton assures that the initial state will be hold for a moment such that the initial constraint is fulfilled.

In the next step we implement $(C3)$. This Implementable assures that a process $P_i$ is added to the waiting queue provided that the process has always been in state $p_i rdy$ during the change phase. To implement this we have to restrict some transitions from $(ch, \langle q \rangle)$-states in the PLC-Automaton: All transitions from $(ch, \langle q \rangle)$ to $(go, \langle q.q' \rangle)$ with $i \notin \langle q.q' \rangle$ are allowed only if $\neg p_i rdy$ was read. This implements $(C3)$ obviously because if a process $P_i$ has always been in state $p_i rdy$ then transitions labelled with $\neg p_i rdy$ cannot been taken. Since all transitions not labelled with $\neg p_i rdy$ change to states of the form $(go, \langle q.q' \rangle)$ with $i \in \langle q.q' \rangle$, we know that $P_i$ is added to the waiting queue.

The result is given below where the constraint $(C3)$ is already removed from the specification and the corresponding constraints are added to some transitions.

(C4)
(C5)
(C6)

(G2)
(G3)
(G4)
(G5)

(W2)
(W3)

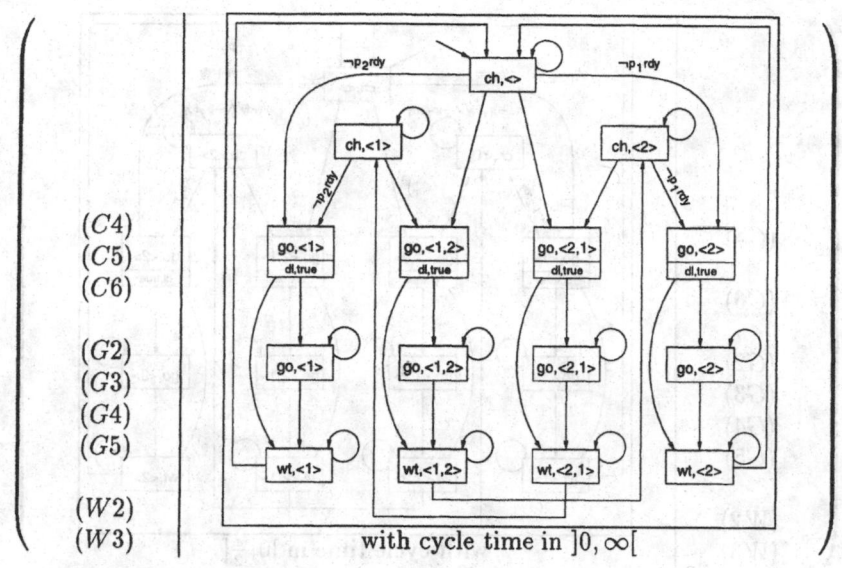

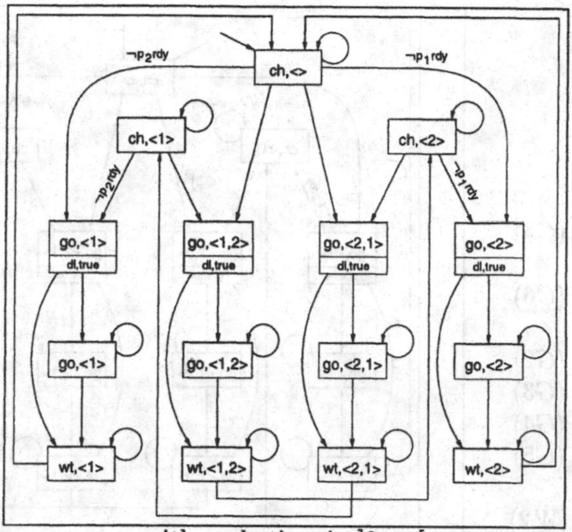


with cycle time in $]0, \infty[$

Note that all unlabelled transitions are implicitly labelled with **true**. Now we deal with $(C5)$. This progress constraint forces the system to leave a state $(ch, \langle q \rangle)$ within $\varepsilon$ seconds provided that a process $P_i$ is always in $p_i rdy$ during these $\varepsilon$ seconds. To implement this behaviour by our PLC-Automaton we have to introduce restrictions on the loops for all $(ch, \langle q \rangle)$-states: We add the label $\neg p_i rdy$ to all loops of such states for each $i$. Furthermore, we have to restrict the cycle time *ct* of the PLC-Automaton. We know from the semantics that it is assured that the automaton will react at least once to the input within $2ct$ seconds. Hence we restrict the cycle time such that it is less than $\frac{\varepsilon}{2}$.

(C4)
(C6)
(G2)
(G3)
(G4)
(G5)
(W2)
(W3)

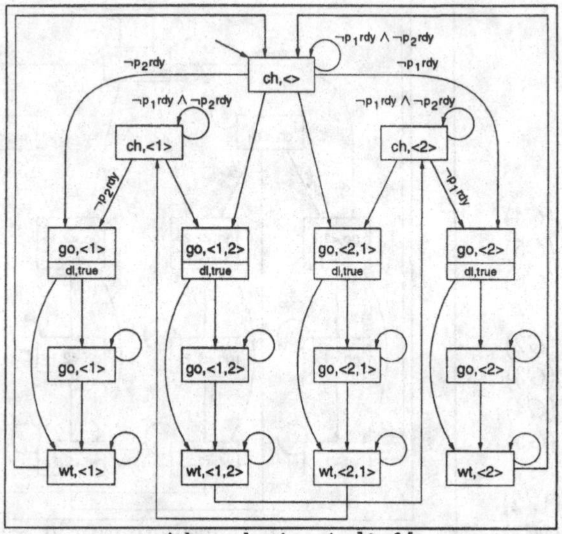


with cycle time in $]0, \frac{\varepsilon}{2}[$

Implementing $(C6)$ by our PLC-Automaton is done similarly to $(C3)$: We have to prevent changes from $(ch, \langle q\rangle)$ to $(go, \langle q.q'\rangle)$ with $i \in q'$ if $\neg p_i rdy$ was valid during the whole $(ch, \langle q\rangle)$-phase. This is possible by adding labels of the form $p_i rdy$ to transitions from $(ch, \langle q\rangle)$ to $(go, \langle q.q'\rangle)$ with $i \in q'$. This yields the following pair of specification and program:

(C4)
(G2)
(G3)
(G4)
(G5)
(W2)
(W3)

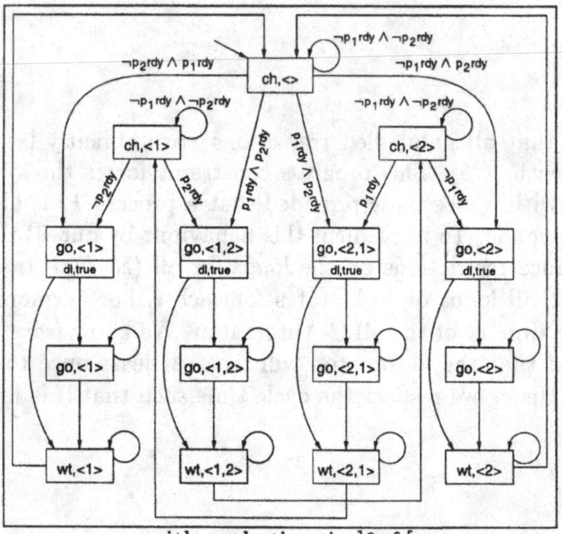


with cycle time in $]0, \frac{\varepsilon}{2}[$

Finally among the constraints for the $(ch, \langle q\rangle)$-states, we deal now with $(C4)$. Again we can implement this unbounded stability be introducing labels to some transitions that leave the corresponding states. In this case we have to add the label $\bigvee_i p_i rdy$ to all leaving transitions. Below is the result of this step with some simplifications of the labels.

(G2)
(G3)
(G4)
(G5)

(W2)
(W3)

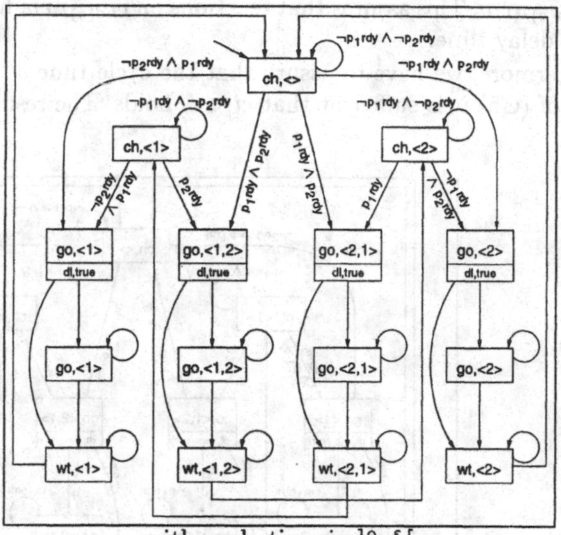


with cycle time in $]0, \frac{\varepsilon}{2}[$

The Implementable $(G2)$ forbids that the system leaves the $(go, \langle q \rangle)$-states within the first $dl$ seconds provided that the process $P_{hd(q)}$ is not in $p_{hd(q)}nrm$. Therefore, we label transitions from the first $(go, \langle q \rangle)$-states (that means with delay $dl$) to $(wt, \langle q \rangle)$ with $p_{hd(q)}nrm$. Due to the boundedness of $(G2)$ this has to be done for the delayed $(go, \langle q \rangle)$-states only.

(G3)
(G4)
(G5)

(W2)
(W3)

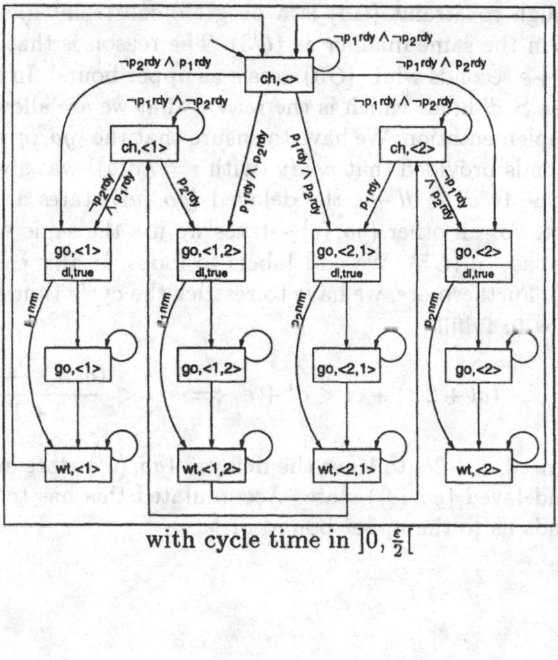


with cycle time in $]0, \frac{\varepsilon}{2}[$

To implement ($G3$) we have to assure that there is no transition from a $(go, \langle q \rangle)$-state to a $(go, \langle q \rangle)$-state that can happen under $p_{hd(q)}nrm$. Hence, we label all such transitions with $\neg p_{hd(q)}nrm$. Additionally, we have to prevent that the delay time *dl* is valid in such cases. To this end we change the delay predicate into $\neg p_{hd(q)}nrm$. This assures that reactions on $p_{hd(q)}nrm$ happen independently from the delay time.

Furthermore, we have to assure that the cycle time *ct* is fast enough. As in the case of ($C5$) it is sufficient that $ct < \frac{\varepsilon}{2}$ holds. The result of this step is:

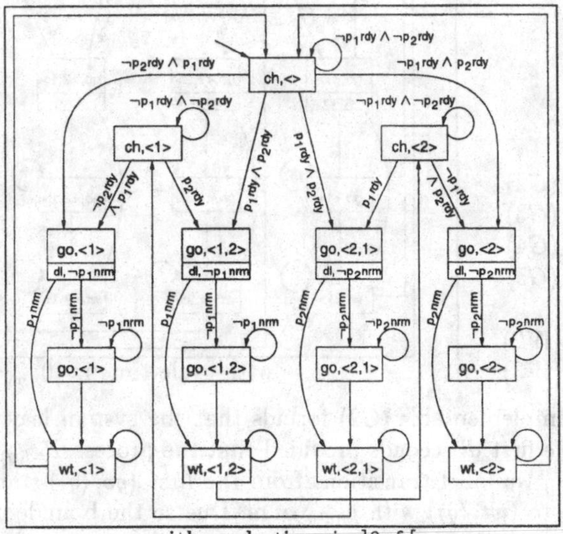


($G4$)
($G5$)
($W2$)
($W3$)

with cycle time in $]0, \frac{\varepsilon}{2}[$

Although constraint ($G4$) is a progress constraint like ($G3$), we implement ($G4$) not in the same manner as ($G3$). The reason is that ($G4$) forces reactions within $dl + \varepsilon$ seconds while ($G3$) uses $\varepsilon$ as upper bound. In the first case we know that $dl + \varepsilon > dl$ holds which is the reason that we are allowed to choose another way of implementation: We have to ensure that the $(go, \langle q \rangle)$-states are left within $dl + \varepsilon$ seconds provided that $p_i rdy$ (with $i \neq hd(q)$) was always valid during that period. Due to $dl < dl + \varepsilon$ the delayed $(go, \langle q \rangle)$-states are not affected by this constraint. For all other $(go, \langle q \rangle)$-states we use the same way to implement this as in the case of ($C5$): We add labels to loops. In this case we add $p_i rdy$ with $i \neq hd(q)$. Furthermore, we have to restrict the cycle time *ct* accordingly: In this case *ct* has to fulfill

$$(dl + 2ct) + ct < dl + \varepsilon \iff ct < \frac{(dl + \varepsilon) - dl}{2 + 1} = \frac{\varepsilon}{3}$$

since we need $dl + 2ct$ to leave the delayed $(go, \langle q \rangle)$-state and another *ct* to react in the undelayed $(go, \langle q \rangle)$-state. Accumulated this has to be faster than $dl + \varepsilon$ which leads us to the upper bound of $\frac{\varepsilon}{3}$.

(G5)
(W2)
(W3)

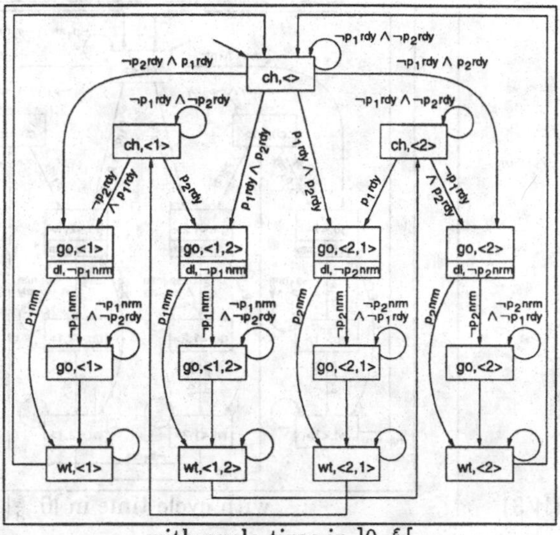


with cycle time in $]0, \frac{\varepsilon}{3}[$

$(G5)$ can be implemented similarly as all unbounded stabilities by introducing corresponding constraints on all $(go, \langle q \rangle)$-leaving transitions. In this case we have to add the label $p_{hd(q)}nrm \vee \bigvee_{i \neq hd(q)} p_i rdy$. Note that the label $p_{hd(q)}nrm \wedge (p_{hd(q)}nrm \vee \bigvee_{i \neq hd(q)} p_i rdy)$ can be simplified to $p_{hd(q)}nrm$.

(W2)
(W3)

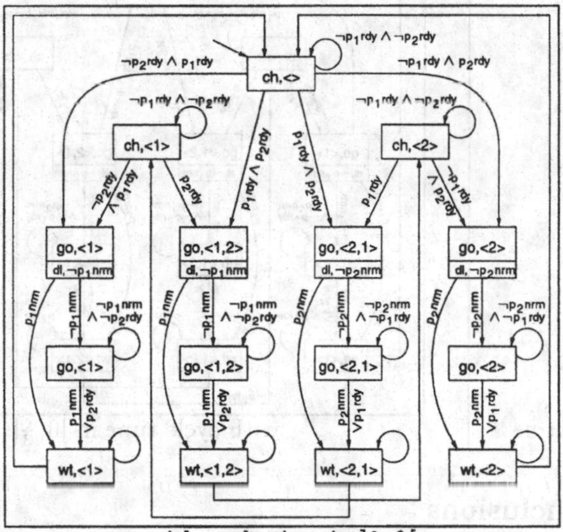


with cycle time in $]0, \frac{\varepsilon}{3}[$

Now only constraints for the waiting states of the scheduler are left. In the same way as several times before we implement the unbounded stability $(W2)$ by adding the label $\neg p_{hd(q)}run$ to all $(wt, \langle q \rangle)$-leaving transitions.

(W3)

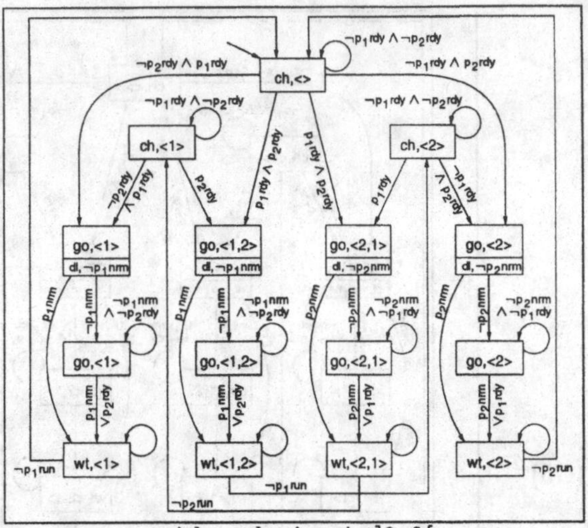


with cycle time in $]0, \frac{\varepsilon}{3}[$

The last step in handled as ($C5$): We add to all $(wt, \langle q \rangle)$-loops the constraint $p_{hd(q)}run$. The cycle time $ct$ has to fulfill $ct < \frac{\varepsilon}{2}$ which is already true.

true

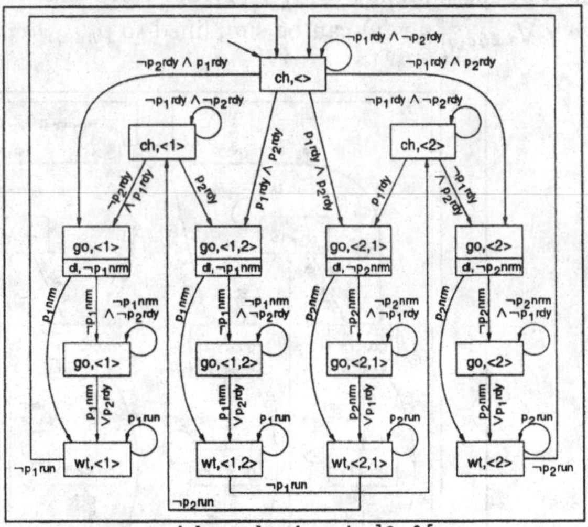


with cycle time in $]0, \frac{\varepsilon}{3}[$

## 7 Conclusions

In the present paper we have proposed a unifying view on several traditional construction methods. A new refinement notion allows to combine techniques like refinement, synthesis, and model-checking. This combination of otherwise incompatible steps makes it possible to strictly separate those parts of the development process which can be automatically treated from parts which require the user's interaction. It turns out that the different parts can be treated by different development methods.

Our framework has been exhibited by means of the logical requirements' language DC and PLC-Automata as the implementation device. In concreto, we started with abstract scheduler requirements which by refinement (reinterpreted in our setting) were transformed into a subset of DC, which now can automatically be transformed into PLC-Automata. This latter transformation is base on specification weakening steps.

To the best of our knowledge the proposed formalism is the first in which specification weakening and refinement are compatible. In our example we did not need model-checking, but it is easily conceivable that after initially unimplementable requirements the whole task is split into subtasks which can be treated by different methods.

## References

1. J. Bowen, C.A.R. Hoare, H. Langmaack, E.-R. Olderog, and A.P. Ravn. *ProCoS II: A ProCoS II Project Final Report*, chapter 7, pages 76–99. Number 59 in Bulletin of the EATCS. European Association for Theoretical Computer Science, June 1996.
2. H. Dierks. PLC-Automata: A New Class of Implementable Real-Time Automata. In M. Bertran and T. Rus, editors, *ARTS'97*, volume 1231 of *Lecture Notes in Computer Science*, pages 111–125, Mallorca, Spain, May 1997. Springer-Verlag.
3. H. Dierks. Synthesising Controllers from Real-Time Specifications. In *Tenth International Symposium on System Synthesis*, pages 126–133. IEEE CS Press, September 1997.
4. B. Krieg-Brückner, J. Peleska, E.-R. Olderog, et al. UniForM — Universal Formal Methods Workbench. In *Statusseminar des BMBF Softwaretechnologie*, pages 357–378. BMBF, Berlin, 1996.
5. B. Moszkowski. A Temporal Logic for Multilevel Reasoning about Hardware. *IEEE Computer*, 18(2):10–19, 1985.
6. Zhou Chaochen. Duration Calculi: An overview. In D. Bjørner, M. Broy, and I.V. Pottosin, editors, *Formal Methods in Programming and Their Application*, volume 735 of *Lecture Notes in Computer Science*, pages 256–266. Springer-Verlag, 1993.
7. Zhou Chaochen, C.A.R. Hoare, and A.P. Ravn. A Calculus of Durations. *Inform. Proc. Letters*, 40/5:269–276, 1991.

# Computation Calculus

## Bridging a Formalization Gap

Rutger M. Dijkstra

Rijksuniversiteit Groningen

**Abstract.** We present an algebra that seeks to bridge the gap between programming formalisms that have a high level of abstraction and the operational interpretations these formalisms have been designed to be sound for.
In order to *prove* a high level formalism sound for its intended operational interpretation, one needs a mathematical handle on the latter. To this end we design the computation calculus. As an expression mechanism, it is sufficiently transparent to avoid begging the question. As an algebra, it is quite powerful and relatively simple.

## 0 Introduction

For reasoning about (imperative style) programs, lots of extensions of predicate calculus or logic are in circulation: Hoare-logic, *wp*-calculus, temporal logics of various kinds, UNITY-logic, etc. All these extensions enrich the language of predicate calculus with 'primitives' intended to capture some operational aspects of programs. E.g. in *wp*-calculus

*wp.s.q* : holds in those initial states for which every execution of program $s$ terminates in a state satisfying the predicate $q$,

in linear time temporal logic

$\mathbf{G}\,s$ : holds for those computations (i.e. infinite sequences of states) for which every suffix satisfies $s$,

or for a UNITY program

*wlt.q* : holds in those (initial) states for which every computation of the program contains at least one state satisfying the predicate $q$.

The verbal right-hand sides above are 'intended operational interpretation' without any formal status: they serve only to translate operational intentions into the formalism. In order to actually prove properties of programs, the formalisms supply rules in the form of postulates, definitions, axioms, inference rules, and so forth. E.g.

(a) $wp.(S\,;T).q \;=\; wp.S.(wp.T.q)$

(b) $\vdash \mathbf{G}(s \Rightarrow \mathbf{X}\,s) \;\Rightarrow\; (s \Rightarrow \mathbf{G}\,s)$

(c) $wlt.q \;=\; \langle \boldsymbol{\mu}\, x :: \langle \exists\, S :: \langle \boldsymbol{\nu}\, y :: q \vee (\langle \forall\, T :: wp.T.y \rangle \wedge wp.S.x) \rangle \rangle \rangle$

This is where the problems start. Although for many of the rules it is quite clear that they are indeed adequate for the intended operational interpretation

—see (a)— this is by no means always the case —see (c). This distance between intended interpretation and mathematical formalization is what we call "the formalization gap". If large, the formalization gap can become a serious problem, since it means that the things we write down do not necessarily mean what we think they do.

In this paper we develop an algebra that we call "the computation calculus" and that is intended to bridge this formalization gap. The idea is that intended operational interpretations can be expressed succinctly in the computation calculus and that characterizations on a higher level of abstraction can subsequently be derived from that. E.g. for the predicate transformer *wlt*, we would ideally like to be able to derive the fixpoint expression in (c) from some 'direct' formalization of the intended operational interpretation.

We abstract the computation calculus from a simple model of computations. Thus, we start with a model wherein we *define* some operators satisfying certain properties. Subsequently we forget the definitions and *postulate* the relevant properties. This ensures that all results in our algebra are valid for the model and it provides a clear view on the properties we use thereof, i.e. the assumptions we rely on.

The procedure we follow is incremental for both the model and the algebra. We begin with a model that is far too general and we extract from that some very elementary insights that we capture in our postulates. As we become more ambitious in the things we want to prove, we may find that our algebra is not yet strong enough. We then add what is missing to the algebra and impose, if necessary, the appropriate restrictions on the model.

After the initial exploration of the basics, the first slightly more ambitious target we aim for is the pre-/postcondition semantics of simple sequential programs. The biggest hurdle to overcome here is the treatment of (tail-) recursion. Subsequently, we prepare the ground for higher targets by enriching our algebra with some insights concerning atomic computations. This leaves us with an algebra that is very powerful indeed: subsuming various temporal logics. We end with a short discussion on UNITY.

We build on top of the predicate calculus of E.W. Dijkstra and C.S. Scholten [3] augmented with whatever facts from lattice theory we have use for, in particular the fixpoint calculus as explored by R.C. Backhouse, J.C.S.P. van der Woude, and colleagues [13]. Some highlights of this calculus are listed in the appendix.

Readers familiar with relation algebra in any form, the sequential calculus of B. von Karger and C.A.R. Hoare [9], or any of various temporal logics may recognise where we got our inspiration from. However, unfamiliarity with these fields should not stand in the way of understanding our algebra.

## 1 Basics of the Model

Our model is in essence taken from Johan Lukkien's PhD-thesis [11]. A "program (fragment)" or "statement" operates on a set of *states*. Starting a statement in some initial state results in a sequence of (atomic) steps each of which ends in a new state. We call the sequence of states traversed during the execution the *computation* generated by the statement. Computations can be finite or infinite but not empty (0 steps means that the initial state is also the final state, i.e. generates a singleton computation). So we have:

$\mathcal{S}$ : the state space; a nonempty set the elements of which we call 'states'.

$\mathcal{C}$ : the computation space; a set of nonempty, finite or infinite sequences of states that we call 'computations'.

We identify a statement with the computations it can generate. More precisely, we consider a statement to be the predicate on computations that holds for exactly those computations it can generate. Thus, statements are elements of the set *CPred* that is defined as

**Definition 0.** $CPred = \mathcal{C} \to \mathbb{B}$ .

This provides a standard model for the predicate calculus as developed in [3] where all the boolean operators are lifted:

$$(s \Rightarrow t).\tau \;\equiv\; (s.\tau \Rightarrow t.\tau), \quad \langle \forall i :: s.i \rangle.\tau \;\equiv\; \langle \forall i :: s.i.\tau \rangle, \quad \text{etc},$$

and the everywhere-operator quantifies universally over all computations:

$$[\, s \,] \equiv \langle \forall \tau :: s.\tau \rangle .$$

We extend the predicate algebra with sequential composition. With $\#$, $\uparrow$, and $\downarrow$ denoting the list operations 'length', 'take', and 'drop' respectively, we define:

**Definition 1.** For all predicates $s$ and $t$ and computations $\tau$

$$(s\,;t).\tau \;\equiv\; (\#\tau = \infty \wedge s.\tau) \vee \langle \exists n : n < \#\tau : s.(\tau \uparrow n{+}1) \wedge t.(\tau \downarrow n) \rangle .$$

Note the 'one point overlap' between $\tau \uparrow n{+}1$ and $\tau \downarrow n$, which reflects that the final state of the $s$-subcomputation is the initial state of the $t$-subcomputation.

In order for the right-hand side of (1) to be well typed, the sequences $\tau \uparrow n{+}1$ and $\tau \downarrow n$ must be computations for all $n$ in the range. We therefore impose on $\mathcal{C}$ the restriction that it satisfies:

**Requirement 2.** Nonempty segments of computations are computations.

Sequential composition is universally disjunctive in its first argument, positively disjunctive in its second argument, and associative. Moreover it has the (left- and right-) neutral element $\mathbb{1}$ given by:

**Definition 3.** $\mathbb{1}.\tau \;\equiv\; \#\tau = 1 \quad$ for all $\tau$.

Not distinguishing between a singleton computation and the single state it consists of, the singleton computations are a subset of $\mathcal{S}$. We assume that $\mathcal{S}$ does not contain states that do not partake in any computation:

**Requirement 4.** "no junk": $\mathcal{S} \subseteq \mathcal{C}$

This means that $\mathbb{1}$ is the characteristic predicate of our state space and that we can identify predicates on the state space with predicates that hold only for singleton 'computations'.

## 2 Basics of the Algebra

The computation calculus is an algebra on objects of the type *CPred* and it is an extension of the predicate calculus, i.e.

**Postulate 5.** *CPred* is a predicate algebra.

Postulate (5) means that we import all the postulates for the predicate calculus from [3]. These postulates characterise exactly a complete boolean lattice with the order $[\_ \Rightarrow \_]$ and the boolean operators denoting the various lattice operations.

The first extensions we introduce are a further binary operator and an extra constant:

$;\ :\ CPred^2 \to CPred$ and $\mathbb{1}\ :\ CPred$,

and these additional ingredients satisfy:

**Postulates 6.**

(i) ; is universally disjunctive in its first and positively disjunctive in its second argument.

(ii) ; is associative and $\mathbb{1}$ is its neutral element.

These postulates amount to little more than that our calculus is what Roland Backhouse calls a "semi-regular (boolean) algebra". This is a very general structure, so there would appear to be little of consequence to be deducible from these postulates alone. For the moment, however, they are all we've got. Some standard consequences that we do not care to list as separate results are that composition is monotonic in both arguments and has *false* as a left-zero element.

Life becomes more interesting with the introduction of some vocabulary:

**Definition 7.** $p$ is a state predicate $\equiv [p \Rightarrow \mathbb{1}]$ for all $p$.

As noted in the previous section, these correspond with predicates on our state space. For state predicates we record the highly useful

**Facts 8.** *State-restriction rules.*

(i) $p\,;s \;=\; p\,;true \wedge s$, and

(ii) $s\,;p \;=\; s \wedge true;p$ for all $s$, and all state predicates $p$.

*Proof.* We show only the first. On account of monotonicity it suffices to prove '$\Leftarrow$' and this follows after shunting from the observation that:

$p\,;s \vee \neg s$

$\Leftarrow$ { $p$ is a state predicate }

$p\,;s \vee p\,;\neg s$

$=$ { ; over $\vee$, excluded middle }

$p\,;true$.

□

The state-restriction rules express that by pre-/postfixing a state predicate $p$ to a predicate $s$, we obtain a characterisation of those $s$ computations for which the initial/final state state satisfies $p$. We proceed by exploring the consequences of requiring the final state to satisfy *false*, i.e. be non-existent. Instantiating state restriction rule (8.ii) with $p := \textit{false}$ yields

$$s\,;\textit{false} \;=\; s \wedge \textit{true};\textit{false}\,.$$

Interpreting *true*; *false* in the model, we find that this predicate holds exactly for the infinite ("eternal") computations. We introduce names for this constant and for its negation (which of course characterises the finite computations) and we introduce some more vocabulary.

**Definitions 9.**

$\mathtt{E},\mathtt{F} : \textit{CPred},\quad \mathtt{E} = \textit{true};\textit{false}$ and $\mathtt{F} = \neg\mathtt{E}$.

$s$ is eternal $\equiv [\, s \Rightarrow \mathtt{E}\,]$ and $s$ is finite $\equiv [\, s \Rightarrow \mathtt{F}\,]$ for all $s$.

Exploring to what extent our modest postulates allow us to confirm our expectations concerning finite and infinite behaviour, we are not at all disappointed.

**Etudes 10.** Leaving universal quantification over the free variables understood:

(i) $s\,;\textit{false} \,=\, s \wedge \mathtt{E}$,

(ii) $[\, s \Rightarrow \mathtt{E}\,] \;\Rightarrow\; s\,;t \,=\, s$,

(iii) $[\, 1\!\!1 \Rightarrow \mathtt{F}\,],\;\; \mathtt{F};\mathtt{F} = \mathtt{F}$,

(iv) $s\,;t \;=\; (s \wedge \mathtt{E}) \vee (s \wedge \mathtt{F})\,;t$,

(v) $s\,;t \wedge \mathtt{F} \;=\; (s \wedge \mathtt{F});(t \wedge \mathtt{F})$, and

(vi) $s\,;t \wedge \mathtt{E} \;=\; (s \wedge \mathtt{E}) \vee (s \wedge \mathtt{F});(t \wedge \mathtt{E})$.

So, as modest as our current postulates are, there is more in them than one might think at first glance.

## 3 Hoare-triples and 'Leads-to'

Let $s$ be some statement, let $p$ and $q$ be state predicates. The Hoare-triple $\{p\}\, s\, \{q\}$ asserts that every $s$-computation for which the initial state satisfies $p$ terminates in a final state satisfying $q$. The $s$-computations with an initial state satisfying $p$ are given by $p\,;s$ and the computations that terminate in a state satisfying $q$ are given by $\mathtt{F}\,;q$. Thus, the Hoare-triple can be translated into our algebra as:

(a) $[\, p\,;s \Rightarrow \mathtt{F}\,;q\,]$.

Now, let $u$ be some UNITY program. In UNITY —where the program under consideration is left implicit— the assertion $p \mapsto q$ expresses that every $u$-computation for which the initial state satisfies $p$ has some state satisfying $q$. Since the computations that have a state satisfying $q$ are those that satisfy $\mathtt{F}\,;q\,;\textit{true}$, this can be rendered in our algebra as

(b) $[\, p\,;u \Rightarrow \mathtt{F}\,;q\,;\textit{true}\,]$.

Considered as equations in the unknown $p$ of the type 'state predicate', the weakest solution of (a) is *wp.s.q* and the weakest solution of (b) is *wlt.q*. So we would like to be able to give closed expressions for these weakest solutions in our algebra. To this end, we take a closer look at the universe of state predicates.

## 4 State Predicates and Computation Quantifiers

We devote some special attention to the universe of state predicates. The first thing to do is naming this universe:

**Definition 11.** $p \in SPred \;\equiv\; [p \Rightarrow \mathbb{1}]$ for all predicates $p$.

One immediate consequence of this definition is that $(SPred, [\_ \Rightarrow \_])$ is also a complete boolean lattice. From the encompassing lattice, it inherits all the lattice operations that it is closed under, i.e. existential quantification, disjunction, and conjunction. The other lattice operations on *SPred* —we use only negation and universal quantification— are easily defined in terms of the corresponding ones on *CPred*:

**Definitions 12.** $\sim : SPred \to SPred$ and $\forall\!\!\!\forall : \mathcal{P}.SPred \to SPred$,

$$\sim p \;=\; \neg p \wedge \mathbb{1} \quad\text{and}\quad \langle \forall\!\!\!\forall i :: p.i \rangle \;=\; \langle \forall i :: p.i \rangle \wedge \mathbb{1}\,.$$

With these operators (and $\mathbb{1}$ playing the rôle of *true*) *SPred* is yet another predicate algebra.

For a state predicate $p$, the computations with an initial state satisfying $p$ are characterised by $p\,;true$. For the restriction of $\_\,;true$ to state predicates we introduce special notation, the 'initially-operator':

**Definition 13.** $\bullet : SPred \to CPred,\quad \bullet p \;=\; p\,;true\,.$

The reason for introducing this almost redundant operator is that it enjoys some properties not enjoyed by $\_\,;true$ in general. In particular

**Fact 14.** $\bullet\!\sim\! p \;=\; \neg\bullet p$ for all $p$.

*Proof.* By ping-pong argument.

Ping: $[\bullet\!\sim\! p \;\Rightarrow\; \neg\bullet p]$

$=$ { shunt, definition (13) }

$[p\,;true \wedge \sim p\,;true \;\Rightarrow\; false]$

$=$ { state restriction (8) (thrice) }

$[(p \wedge \sim p)\,;true \;\Rightarrow\; false]$

$=$ { predicate calculus }

$[false\,;true \;\Rightarrow\; false]$

$=$ { universal disjunctivity of ; }

$true\,.$

Pong: $[\neg\bullet p \;\Rightarrow\; \bullet\!\sim\! p]$

$=$ { shunt, definition (13) }

$[true \;\Rightarrow\; p\,;true \vee \sim p\,;true]$

$=$ { ; over $\vee$ }

$[true \;\Rightarrow\; (p \vee \sim p)\,;true]$

$=$ { predicate calculus }

$[true \;\Rightarrow\; \mathbb{1}\,;true]$

$=$ { neutrality of $\mathbb{1}$ }

$true\,.$

□

Combining the fact that the initially-operator inherits universal disjunctivity from $\_\,;true$ with fact (14), we now find that it is universally conjunctive as well. Consequently, the initially-operator has both an upper adjoint and a lower adjoint. We introduce operators denoting these adjoints:

**Definitions 15.** $\mathcal{A}, \mathcal{E} : CPred \to SPred$,

$[\bullet p \Rightarrow s] \;\equiv\; [p \Rightarrow \mathcal{A} s]$ and

$[\mathcal{E} s \Rightarrow p] \;\equiv\; [s \Rightarrow \bullet p]$ for all $s$ and all state predicates $p$.

These operators are, in essence, the "trace quantifiers" from the branching-time temporal logic CTL*. Their interpretation is elementary:

- $\mathcal{A}\,s$ holds in those initial states for which every computation satisfies $s$ and
- $\mathcal{E}\,s$ holds in those initial states for which at least one computation satisfies $s$.

We call these operators the universal and existential computation quantifier respectively.

Using the universal computation quantifier, we can now lay our hands on the weakest solution of the Hoare-triple equation (a) from the previous section:

$$
\begin{aligned}
& [\,p\,;s \;\Rightarrow\; \mathtt{F}\,;q\,] \\
=\;& \quad \{ \text{ state restriction } \} \\
& [\,p\,;\mathit{true} \wedge s \;\Rightarrow\; \mathtt{F}\,;q\,] \\
=\;& \quad \{ \text{ definition (13) and shunting } \} \\
& [\,\bullet p \;\Rightarrow\; (s \Rightarrow \mathtt{F}\,;q)\,] \\
=\;& \quad \{ \text{ definition (15) } \} \\
& [\,p \;\Rightarrow\; \mathcal{A}(s \Rightarrow \mathtt{F}\,;q)\,]\,.
\end{aligned}
$$

Since $\mathcal{A}\,(s \Rightarrow \mathtt{F}\,;q)$ is a state predicate, it is the weakest solution for $p$. As a succinct description of the intended operational interpretation of $wp.s.q$, we consider this a highly satisfactory solution: $\mathcal{A}\,(s \Rightarrow \mathtt{F}\,;q)$ expresses quite clearly that "every $s$-computation terminates in a state satisfying $q$", which is indeed what $wp.s.q$ is supposed to mean.

The computation quantifiers are not only in name and notation suggestive of quantifiers, but also in their algebraic properties:

**Etudes 16.** Leaving universal quantification over the free variables understood:

(i) "de Morgan": $\sim\mathcal{E}\,s \;=\; \mathcal{A}\neg s$

(ii) $\mathcal{A}\,\langle\forall i :: s.i\rangle \;=\; \langle\forall i :: \mathcal{A}\,s.i\rangle\,.$

(iii) $\mathcal{E}\,\langle\exists i :: s.i\rangle \;=\; \langle\exists i :: \mathcal{E}\,s.i\rangle\,.$

(iv) $\mathcal{A}\,\mathit{false} \;=\; \mathit{false}$ and $\mathcal{E}\,\mathit{true} \;=\; \mathbb{1}\,.$

(v) $\mathcal{A}\,\bullet p = p = \mathcal{E}\,\bullet p\,.$

(vi) $p \vee \mathcal{A}\,s \;=\; \mathcal{A}\,(\bullet p \vee s)$ and $p \wedge \mathcal{E}\,s \;=\; \mathcal{E}\,(\bullet p \wedge s)\,.$

(vii) $p \wedge \mathcal{A}\,s \;=\; \mathcal{A}\,(\bullet p \wedge s)$ and $p \vee \mathcal{E}\,s \;=\; \mathcal{E}\,(\bullet p \vee s)$

For the restriction of $\mathit{true}\,;\_$ to $\mathit{SPred}$, one might expect properties that are similar to those of the initially-operator. However, since composition is only positively disjunctive in its second argument, the situation is slightly more complicated:

**Etude 17.** $\mathit{true}\,;\!\sim\! p \;=\; \neg(\mathtt{F}\,;p)$ for all state predicates $p$.

Thus, as functions of the type $\mathit{SPred} \rightarrow \mathit{CPred}$, the prefixes $\mathit{true}\,;\_$ and $\mathtt{F}\,;\_$ are each others dual. It follows that the one is as conjunctive as the other is disjunctive. Now, $\mathit{true}\,;\_$ is positively disjunctive while $\mathtt{F}\,;\_$ is, on account of $\mathtt{F}$ being finite, universally disjunctive; hence

**Facts 18.** As functions of the type $\mathit{SPred} \rightarrow \mathit{CPred}$

(i) $\mathit{true}\,;\_$ is universally conjunctive, and

(ii) $\mathtt{F}\,;\_$ is positively conjunctive.

# 5 Weakest Preconditions

In the precondition semantics of Dijkstra and Scholten [3] a statement $s$ is characterised by two state-predicate transformers, $wp.s$ and $wlp.s$. We introduce these functions into our algebra via their intended interpretation.

**Definitions 19.** For all $s$ and state predicates $q$

(i) $wp.s.q \;=\; \mathcal{A}\,(s \Rightarrow \mathtt{F}\,;q)$, and

(ii) $wlp.s.q = \mathcal{A}\,(s \Rightarrow \mathit{true}\,;q)$.

Now that we have included the weakest preconditions in our algebra, we may seek to *prove*, as theorems in our algebra, facts that Dijkstra and Scholten *postulate*.

Since $\mathcal{A}$ is universally conjunctive (16.ii), it follows from respectively (18) and state-restriction rule (8.ii) that

**Facts 20.** for all $s$

(i) $wp.s$ is positively conjunctive and $wlp.s$ is universally conjunctive.

(ii) $wp.s.q \;=\; wp.s.\mathbb{1} \wedge wlp.s.q$ for all state predicates $q$.

Dijkstra and Scholten impose these as "healthiness conditions": properties that a pair $(wp.s, wlp.s)$ should satisfy in order to qualify as a reasonable definition of statement $s$. Since we can prove these properties from the intended interpretation, anything else would, indeed, be quite unhealthy.

From the universal conjunctivity of $\mathcal{A}$ and predicate calculus, we also get

**Facts 21.** *Non-deterministic choice.* For all functions $s$ and state predicates $q$

(i) $wp.\langle \exists i :: s.i \rangle.q \;=\; \langle \forall i :: wp.(s.i).q \rangle$ and

(ii) $wlp.\langle \exists i :: s.i \rangle.q \;=\; \langle \forall i :: wlp.(s.i).q \rangle$.

These equalities are what W. H. Hesselink [8] uses to define "non-deterministic choice". A moment of reflection should suffice to see that, in our model, non-deterministic choice is, indeed, captured by existential quantification.

Further exploration of the preconditions is greatly simplified by the following two observations

**Fact 22.** $wlp.s \;=\; wp.(s \wedge \mathtt{F})$ for all $s$.

**Fact 23.** *wp-dualisation.* $\sim wp.s.q \;=\; \mathcal{E}\,(s\,;\sim q)$ for all $s$ and state predicates $q$.

The first of these follows immediately from the definitions and the fact that $\mathit{true}\,;q = \mathtt{E} \vee \mathtt{F}\,;q$ (see (10.iv)). The second is established using state restriction and dualities (16.i) and (17).

Our next natural target consists of the preconditions of sequential compositions. This is the point where we finally reach the limit of our very modest initial postulates. Following [3], we expect

**Facts 24.** *Compositionality of the preconditions.*

(i) $wp.(s\,;t).q = wp.s.(wp.t.q)$ and

(ii) $wlp.(s\,;t).q \;=\; wlp.s.(wlp.t.q)$ for all $s$, $t$ and state predicates $q$.

Using (22) and (10.v), we find the second of these to be equal to the first instantiated with $s, t := (s \wedge \mathtt{F}), (t \wedge \mathtt{F})$, so we need to consider the first only. Attempting to verify (24.i) we observe —with the types of the dummies understood—

$\langle \forall s,t,q :: wp.(s\,;t).q \;=\; wp.s.(wp.t.q) \;\rangle$

$= \quad \{$ negating both sides and (23) (thrice) $\}$

$\langle \forall s,t,q :: \mathcal{E}\,(s\,;t\,;\sim q) \;=\; \mathcal{E}\,(s\,;\mathcal{E}\,(t\,;\sim q))\;\rangle$

$= \quad \{$ mutual instantiation: $q = \sim\mathbb{1}$ and $t := t\,;\sim q$ respectively $\}$

$\langle \forall s,t :: \mathcal{E}\,(s\,;t) \;=\; \mathcal{E}\,(s\,;\mathcal{E}\,t)\;\rangle$

and here we get stuck. The last line is not provable because, as we will see, it need not —yet— be true in our model.

We make the compositionality of the preconditions a theorem of our algebra by adding the last line in the preceding calculation to our postulates.

**Postulate 25.** *Composition rule.* $\mathcal{E}\,(s\,;t) = \mathcal{E}\,(s\,;\mathcal{E}\,t)$ for all $s$ and $t$.

In the next section we check what this postulate means for our model, thereby establishing both that it is reasonable and that it is independent of the previous postulates. However, we gave the composition rule in its simplest, rather than its weakest form. In order to facilitate the analysis of the next section, we request that the reader verifies that postulate (25) follows from the —evidently weaker—

**Fact 25′.** $[\,\mathcal{E}\,(s\,;\mathcal{E}\,t) \Rightarrow \mathcal{E}\,(s\,;t)\,]$ for all finite $s$ and all $t$.

This is the rule that we now have a closer look at in our model.

## 6 Composition in the Model

In our model of computations, the meaning of the existential computation quantifier is that, for any predicate $s$ and any state $\pi$:

$$(\mathcal{E}\,s).\pi \;=\; \langle \exists \sigma : \pi = \sigma.0 : s.\sigma \rangle\,.$$

In order to keep the analysis of the composition rule in our model palatable, we introduce two abbreviations:

$$\sigma \bowtie \tau \;\equiv\; \#\sigma < \infty \;\wedge\; \mathrm{last}.\sigma \;=\; \tau.0 \quad (\text{where } \mathrm{last}.\sigma \;=\; \sigma.(\#\sigma - 1)\,)$$

$$\rho \simeq \sigma\cdot\tau \;\equiv\; \langle \exists n : n < \#\rho : \sigma = \rho{\uparrow}n{+}1 \;\wedge\; \tau = \rho{\downarrow}n \rangle$$

("$\sigma$ fits $\tau$" and "$\rho$ consists of $\sigma$ followed by $\tau$"). Now, (25′) states that

$$(\mathcal{E}\,(s\,;\mathcal{E}\,t)).\pi \;\Rightarrow\; (\mathcal{E}\,(s\,;t)).\pi \quad \text{for all finite } s\text{, all } t\text{, and all states } \pi,$$

and spelling out the antecedent and consequent in isolation yields —after a considerable amount of juggling—

$$(\mathcal{E}\,(s\,;\mathcal{E}\,t)).\pi \equiv \langle \exists \sigma,\tau : \;\pi = \sigma.0 \;\wedge\; s.\sigma \;\wedge\; t.\tau : \;\sigma \bowtie \tau \;\rangle$$

$$(\mathcal{E}\,(s\,;t)).\pi \quad\equiv \langle \exists \sigma,\tau : \;\pi = \sigma.0 \;\wedge\; s.\sigma \;\wedge\; t.\tau : \;\langle \exists \rho :: \rho \simeq \sigma\cdot\tau \rangle\;\rangle\,.$$

Comparing the two right-hand sides we find that the question of whether (25′) holds in our model boils down to the question of whether

(∗) $\quad \sigma \bowtie \tau \Rightarrow \langle \exists \rho :: \rho \simeq \sigma\cdot\tau \rangle$ for all $\sigma$ and $\tau$.

Is this reasonable? Can we prove it? Well, since $\sigma \bowtie \tau$ means that the final state of the finite computation $\sigma$ coincides with the initial state of the computation $\tau$, it is easily seen that there is a (unique) sequence of states $\rho$ such that $\rho \simeq \sigma\cdot\tau$: just "paste" $\sigma$ and $\tau$ together with one point overlap. However, the dummy $\rho$ in (∗) ranges over our computation space $\mathcal{C}$ rather than over arbitrary sequences of states, thus (∗) expresses that our computation space is closed under "pasting".

The current restrictions on our computation space do not allow us to conclude this. Hence, if we find it reasonable, we have to require it explicitly. We do find it reasonable, so we impose on $\mathcal{C}$ the further restriction that

**Requirement 26.** $\mathcal{C}$ is closed under "pasting", i.e.

$$\sigma \bowtie \tau \;\Rightarrow\; \langle \exists \rho : \rho \in \mathcal{C} : \rho \simeq \sigma \cdot \tau \rangle \quad \text{for all } \sigma \text{ and } \tau \text{ in } \mathcal{C}.$$

## 7 Iterators

So far, the expressive power of our algebra is rather limited. We increase the expressive power —considerably— by the introduction of two more unary operators. We import the definitions of these operators from relational calculus

**Definitions 27.** $\_^*, \_^\infty$: *CPred* → *CPred*,

$$s^* = \langle \mu x :: s\,;x \vee \mathbb{1} \rangle \text{ and } s^\infty = \langle \nu x :: s\,;x \rangle \quad \text{for all } s.$$

We call these operators the "finite iterator" and "infinite iterator" respectively and they bind stronger than negation and the computation quantifiers.

The operational interpretation of $s^*$ is "$s$ repeated any finite number of times" and we could also have defined it by $s^* = \langle \exists n :: s^n \rangle$ (with exponentiation defined as usual: $s^0 = \mathbb{1}$ and $s^{n+1} = s\,;s^n$). The finite iterator enjoys all the algebraic properties one would expect from a Kleene-star. Since re-exploring these properties is not all that exciting, we refrain from doing so; a fine treatment of general Kleene-stars based on fixpoint calculus can be found in [13]. Here, we simply state the properties we use where the need arises.

We make an exception to this rule for two observations concerning $\_^*$ and the constant F, since the latter is highly specific for our algebra.

**Etudes 28.** For all $s$

(i) $[\, s \Rightarrow \mathsf{F} \,] \Rightarrow [\, s^* \Rightarrow \mathsf{F} \,]$ and

(ii) $s^* \wedge \mathsf{F} = (s \wedge \mathsf{F})^*$.

(Hint: the first follows from the second and the latter is screaming for fixpoint fusion —see appendix.)

The operational interpretation of $s^\infty$ is "$s$ repeated forever" and we know of no closed expression for it other than the weakest fixpoint given above. Although this operator is less well known, we treat it the same as the previous one. The algebraic properties of $\_^\infty$ are similar to those of $\_^*$ and, on the whole, unsurprising. An exhaustive treatment of $\_^\infty$ in the context of relational calculus can be found in [5].

Two things should be noted about the operational interpretation of $s^\infty$. The first is that "forever" does not necessarily mean "infinitely often". The reader may verify that $[\, s^*;(s \wedge \mathsf{E}) \Rightarrow s^\infty ]$, so $s^\infty$ includes finite repetitions that get stuck in an eternal $s$-subcomputation.

The second thing to note is, at first glance, surprising. For a state predicate $p$, one easily establishes that $p^\infty = p\,;$ *true*, which means that "$p$ forever" is the same as "$p$ once and then anything at all". The point here is that singleton computations are computations that do not take place; they involve 0 computation steps and, hence, take no time. Consequently, $p^\infty$ yields a kind of short-circuit loop wherein repeating $p$ "forever" still takes no time and is followed by something completely unpredictable. Since the latter may be for instance $\mathbb{1}$, "forever" may be over in a flash.

Clearly, such short-circuits can not arise in $s^\infty$-computations if all $s$-computations are 'real' computations doing some honest work, i.e. consist of at least one atomic step. In that case, $s^\infty$ holds no more surprises and "$s$ forever" indeed takes forever:

**Fact 29.** $[\, s \Rightarrow \neg\mathbb{1} \,] \;\Rightarrow\; [\, s^\infty \Rightarrow \mathtt{E} \,]$ for all $s$.

Well... in the model that is. Fact (29) is readily verified in the model we are abstracting our algebra from. However, all our current postulates are valid in relational calculus as well and, in that context, (29) is simply not true (no, $\neq$ is really not well-founded). Since the observation that infinite loops do not terminate is not entirely insignificant, we add (29) to our postulates. But before we do so, we eliminate the infinite iterator from it:

$$\begin{aligned}
& \langle \forall s : [\, s \Rightarrow \neg\mathbb{1} \,] : [\, s^\infty \Rightarrow \mathtt{E} \,] \rangle \\
= \;& \{\ _^\infty \text{ is monotonic, predicate calculus } \} \\
& [\, (\neg\mathbb{1})^\infty \;\Rightarrow\; \mathtt{E} \,] \\
= \;& \{\ \text{definition (27) and Knaster-Tarski } \} \\
& [\, \langle \exists s : [\, s \Rightarrow \neg\mathbb{1} ; s \,] : s \rangle \;\Rightarrow\; \mathtt{E} \,] \\
= \;& \{\ \text{predicate calculus } \} \\
& \langle \forall s : [\, s \Rightarrow \neg\mathbb{1} ; s \,] : [\, s \Rightarrow \mathtt{E} \,] \rangle
\end{aligned}$$

and this is what we take for our new postulate.

**Postulate 30.** *Accumulation rule.* $[\, s \Rightarrow \neg\mathbb{1} ; s \,] \;\Rightarrow\; [\, s \Rightarrow \mathtt{E} \,]$ for all $s$.

Since the premiss of (29) pops up regularly, we conclude this section with the introduction of adjective for it:

**Definition 31.** $s$ is active $\equiv [\, s \Rightarrow \neg\mathbb{1} \,]$ for all $s$.

## 8 Tail-recursion

In computing, life starts with recursion and recursion starts with tail-recursion. In this section we have a look at a 'procedure' $r$ defined recursively in terms of some active $s$ and some $t$ as:

$(*) \qquad r = s ; r \vee t\,,$

i.e. $r$ is a choice ($\vee$) between a recursive case ($s\,; r$) and a base case ($t$).

*Remark.* That $s$ is active amounts to the assumption that at least one atomic step separates any two executions of $r$. Operationally, this is inescapable, because the repetition involves at least one jump. So the assumption involves no significant loss of generality. Without this assumption, we'd have what is known as 'unguarded recursion' and some of the things below would fall apart as a result of short-circuit loops.

One problem with definition $(*)$ is that the equation fails to determine $r$ uniquely. Arguably one of the more important aspects of the iterators is that these give us closed expressions for both extreme solutions for $r$ from $(*)$. The proofs of both of the equalities below are standard examples of the use of fixpoint fusion.

**Fact 32.** *Tail-recursion theorem.* For all $s$ and $t$

$$\langle \mu\, x :: s\,;x \vee t\rangle = s^*;t \quad \text{and} \quad \langle \nu\, x :: s\,;x \vee t\rangle = s^*;t \;\vee\; s^\infty .$$

Which, if any, of these two do we consider $r$ to be? Operationally, we'd expect that executing $r$ either leads to the base case after a number of unfoldings ($s^*;t$) or results in infinite recursion ($s^\infty$). So the weakest solution is the 'operational' one. That recursion leads to ***weakest*** fixpoints is quite reasonable: it simply means that everything not explicitly excluded from the range of possibilities is, indeed, possible.

Generalising Dijkstra and Scholten's treatment of the repetition or applying Hesselink's theory of general recursion leads us to expect

**Facts 33.** For all active $s$, all $t$, and all state predicates $q$

(i) $\quad wp.\langle \nu\, x :: s\,;x \vee t\rangle.q \;=\; \langle \mu\, y :: wp.s.y \;\wedge\; wp.t.q\rangle$ and

(ii) $\quad wlp.\langle \nu\, x :: s\,;x \vee t\rangle.q \;=\; \langle \nu\, y :: wlp.s.y \;\wedge\; wlp.t.q\rangle$ .

Let's see whether we can confirm this. The closed form of the tail-recursion theorem suggests that we have a look at the iterators in isolation first and we begin with the finite iterator. For any $s$ and state predicate $q$, we calculate:

$wp.s^*.q$

$=\quad$ { $wp$-dualisation (23) }

$\sim\mathcal{E}\,(s^*;\sim q)$

$=\quad$ { tail recursion theorem (32) }

$\sim\mathcal{E}\,\langle \mu\, x :: s\,;x \vee \sim q\rangle$

$=\quad$ { $\mathcal{E}$ is universally disjunctive. Heading for fixpoint fusion, we calculate for any $x$ and $y$ such that $\mathcal{E}\,x = y$

$\qquad\mathcal{E}\,(s\,;x \;\vee\; \sim q)$

$\qquad=\quad$ { $\mathcal{E}$ over $\vee$, composition rule (25) }

$\qquad\mathcal{E}\,(s\,;\mathcal{E}\,x) \;\vee\; \mathcal{E}\sim q$

$\qquad=\quad$ { $\mathcal{E}\,x = y$ (given) and $\mathcal{E}\sim q = \sim q$ (etude) }

$\qquad\mathcal{E}\,(s\,;y) \;\vee\; \sim q$ .

Thus, we can now apply fixpoint fusion. }

$\sim\langle \mu\, y :: \mathcal{E}\,(s\,;y) \;\vee\; \sim q\rangle$

$=\quad$ { fixpoint dualisation, de Morgan, and $wp$-dualisation (23) }

$\langle \nu\, y :: wp.s.y \;\wedge\; q\rangle$ .

Using (22) and (28.ii), the equality we just derived can be transformed into the corresponding one for the liberal precondition. So we have

**Facts 34.** For all $s$ and state predicates $q$

(i) $\quad wp.s^*.q \;=\; \langle \nu y :: wp.s.y \;\wedge\; q \rangle$ and

(ii) $\quad wlp.s^*.q = \langle \nu y :: wlp.s.y \;\wedge\; q \rangle$.

In essence, this takes care of (33.ii). Using the closed form from the tail-recursion theorem and the rules for the liberal preconditions of disjunctions (21), compositions (24), and finite iterations (above), we get

$$wlp.\langle \nu x :: s\,;x \vee t \rangle.q = \langle \nu y :: wlp.s.y \;\wedge\; wlp.t.q \rangle \;\wedge\; wlp.s^{\infty}.q\,.$$

Since $s$ is active, $s^{\infty}$ is eternal by (29) and hence (using (22)) $wlp.s^{\infty}.q = \mathbb{1}$. Consequently, the final conjunct above vanishes. Note that this final conjunct would not vanish, and indeed (33.ii) would be false, if $s$ were not active.

The equality of (33.i) is less straightforward. Using the same recipe as above, we get for the left-hand side of (33.i)

$$wp.\langle \nu x :: s\,;x \vee t \rangle.q = \langle \nu y :: wp.s.y \;\wedge\; wp.t.q \rangle \;\wedge\; wp.s^{\infty}.q\,,$$

whereas, using fixpoint fusion, we get for the right-hand side of (33.i)

$$\langle \mu y :: wp.s.y \;\wedge\; wp.t.q \rangle \;=\; \langle \nu y :: wp.s.y \;\wedge\; wp.t.q \rangle \;\wedge\; \langle \mu y :: wp.s.y \rangle\,.$$

Thus, we'd be done if we can establish the equality of the two final conjuncts on the right (which amounts to our original proof obligation with $t := \mathit{false}$). Now

$$\begin{aligned}
& wp.s^{\infty}.q \;=\; \langle \mu y :: wp.s.y \rangle \\
= \quad & \{ \text{ dualisation; } s^{\infty};{\sim}q = s^{\infty} \text{ by (10.ii) since } s^{\infty} \text{ is eternal } \} \\
& \mathcal{E}\, s^{\infty} \;=\; \langle \nu y :: \mathcal{E}(s\,;y) \rangle \\
= \quad & \{ \text{ `}\Rightarrow\text{' is an immediate consequence of fixpoint induction } \} \\
& [\, \langle \nu y :: \mathcal{E}(s\,;y) \rangle \;\Rightarrow\; \mathcal{E}\, s^{\infty} ] \\
= \quad & \{ \text{ Knaster-Tarski and predicate calculus } \} \\
& \langle \forall y : [\, y \Rightarrow \mathcal{E}\,(s\,;y) \,] : [\, y \Rightarrow \mathcal{E}\, s^{\infty} ] \rangle\,.
\end{aligned}$$

Sadly, this is not —yet— provable because it need not —yet— be true in our model. We did leave room in our model for the ***possibility*** of computations being eternal, but nothing in our current assumptions allows the conclusion that our computation space ***actually contains*** eternal computations. If all computations were finite, the term in the last line above would almost always be false, but the same wouldn't hold for the range.

The point is that the non-liberal precondition distinguishes itself from the liberal one by also guaranteeing termination. If certain eternal computations are *a priori* excluded from the range of possibilities, it may well be that a precondition that is weaker than the strongest fixpoint in (33.i) would be sufficient.

We don't believe in magic termination and we make our scepticism explicit by adding yet another postulate to our algebra.

**Postulate 35.** *Cycle rule.* $[\, p \Rightarrow \mathcal{E}\,(s\,;p) \,] \;\Rightarrow\; [\, p \Rightarrow \mathcal{E}\, s^{\infty} ]$ for all $p$ and $s$.

(This brings the total of our postulates up to (5), (6), (25), (30), and (35).)

Before we check what this means for our model, we record the fixpoint equality we had rewritten to yield the cycle rule (see preceding calculation):

**Fact 36.** $\mathcal{E}\, s^{\infty} = \langle \nu y :: \mathcal{E}\,(s\,;y) \rangle$ for all $s$.

And now we have a look at the model.

## 9 Cycles in the Model

Let $p$ and $s$ satisfy $[p \Rightarrow \mathcal{E}\,(s\,;p)]$, i.e. the antecedent of the cycle rule. We would like to establish the consequent of the cycle rule: $[\,p \Rightarrow \mathcal{E}\,s^\infty]$, i.e. every $p$-state is initial for some $s^\infty$-computation. Roughly, the reasoning goes as follows.

For every initial state satisfying $p$ we have, on account of $[\,p \Rightarrow \mathcal{E}\,(s\,;p)\,]$ an $s$-computation that, if finite, ends with a state that satisfies $p$ again. If existent, this final state is initial for another such $s$-computation which fits the previous one and, hence can be pasted to it. Repeating the process indefinitely or until an infinite $s$-computation is encountered, now yields our $s^\infty$-computation.

Well, almost but not quite. Our 'computation-under-construction' converges to a sequence of states that would, indeed, be an $s^\infty$-computation *if only it were a computation*. But nothing in the current assumptions about $\mathcal{C}$ allows us to conclude the latter: $\mathcal{C} = \mathcal{S}^+$ would satisfy all restrictions nicely.

We remedy the situation by imposing yet another restriction on our model

**Requirement 37.** $\mathcal{C}$ is "limit closed", i.e.

every nonempty subset of $\mathcal{C}$ that is linear w.r.t the prefix-order has an upper bound in $\mathcal{C}$ (upper bound w.r.t to the prefix-order, naturally).

It should be noted that the limit closedness is stronger than necessary for ensuring the validity of the cycle rule. Putting it the other way around: the cycle rule is too weak to capture limit closedness in its full generality. We make do with the cycle rule because it is simple and it suffices for almost everything we want. Notable exceptions to the latter are general (mutual) recursion and UNITY programs with infinite assign sections.

## 10 Temporal Logic and Atomic Steps

Having dealt to our satisfaction with the pre-/postcondition semantics of simple imperative programs, we now raise our sights. In pre-/postcondition semantics, the only things that interest us in a program are, for every initial state, the reachable final states and the possibility of non-termination. This is OK as long as these are the only things that matter.

There are, however, situations in which what happens in the course of program execution is also relevant or is all that is relevant. In particular, this is the case if programs are supposed to interact (with a user or with other programs). In such cases, we want to be able to specify run-time behaviour.

Various temporal logics have been designed precisely for this purpose. We have already mentioned the "branching time" temporal logic CTL* from Emerson and Srinivasan [7], which is the logic from which we have borrowed our computation quantifiers. CTL* is an extension of another logic: the "linear time" temporal logic LTL from Manna and Pnueli [12]. In fact, the trace quantifiers that we borrowed are exactly what CTL* adds to LTL.

The language of LTL extends standard logic with a handful of temporal operators intended to be used to specify behaviour in time. The single most important of these is the unary "next-time operator" **X**: a computation satisfies **X** $s$ if the the computation that follows the first atomic step satisfies $s$.

There are two reasons why this is an operator of fundamental importance. Firstly, all the other temporal operators of LTL can be expressed in terms of it. Hence, **X** is all we need to obtain the full expressive power of LTL. Secondly and more importantly, this operator makes the grain of atomicity explicit and doing so is essential for reasoning about parallel programs with interleaving semantics.

So we add the next-operation to our algebra. There is, however, a slight difference between LTL and our algebra. Where LTL is designed to be sound for models containing eternal computations only, the model that we are abstracting our algebra from contains finite computations as well. In particular, our computation space contains atomic computations. Consequently, we can add "next" as a constant instead of an operator.

An atomic computation is a computation of length 2 and, after introducing the predicate X that holds for exactly these:

**Definition 38.** $\mathtt{X}.\tau \;\equiv\; \#\tau = 2$ ,

we can express the next-operation of LTL as $\mathbf{X}\, s \;=\; \mathtt{X}\,;s$.

To add X to the computation calculus, we need some algebraic characterisation of it. The first thing we note is that X ; *true* holds exactly for the non-singleton computations, i.e.

(a) $[\,\mathbb{1} \not\equiv \mathtt{X}\,;\mathit{true}\,]$ .

From this fact it can be inferred that singleton computations do not satisfy X and that atomic steps do. However, (a) also holds for $\mathtt{X} := \neg\mathbb{1}$ —it follows from (a) that this is so— thus, we still have to capture the fact that computations of length greater than 2 do not satisfy X. For a non-singleton computation, the X-prefix is finite and unique, therefore, the remainder of the computation is also unique:

(b) $[\,\mathtt{X}\,;s \;\wedge\; \mathtt{X}\,;\neg s \;\Rightarrow\; \mathit{false}\,]$ for all $s$ .

Models for our current postulates can be constructed wherein (a)∧(b), as an equation in the unknown X, has no solutions. (But doing so is a sizable exercise.) Hence, we have to add this to our postulates.

Right at the beginning, we required that our state space be contained in our computation space. This does not exclude the possibility of states that occur *only* in a singleton computation. In fact, a computation space consisting of nothing else but singleton computations satisfies all the restrictions we imposed so far.

Since we consider this an undesirable degeneration of our model, we replace the no-junk property by the stronger requirement that

**Requirement 39.** An atomic step is possible for every initial state,

which can be rendered algebraically as

(c) $\mathcal{E}\,\mathtt{X} \;=\; \mathbb{1}$ .

## 11 Atomicity and Temporal Logic

We extend our algebra with a new constant

$\texttt{X} : CPred$

and this constant satisfies the following properties.

**Postulates 40.** *Atomicity rules.*

(i) $[\,\mathbb{1} \not\equiv \texttt{X}\,;\mathit{true}\,]$.

(ii) $[\,\texttt{X}\,; s \,\wedge\, \texttt{X}\,; \neg s \;\Rightarrow\; \mathit{false}\,]$ for all $s$.

(iii) $\mathcal{E}\,\texttt{X} \;=\; \mathbb{1}$.

We list some elementary consequences of these postulates:

**Facts 41.**

(i) $[\,\texttt{X} \Rightarrow \neg\mathbb{1} \wedge \texttt{F}\,]$.

(ii) $\texttt{X}^{\infty} = \texttt{E}$ and $\texttt{X}^{*} = \texttt{F}$.

(iii) $\neg(\texttt{X}\,; s) \;=\; \texttt{X}\,; \neg s \,\vee\, \mathbb{1}$ for all $s$.

(iv) $\texttt{X}\,;\_$ is positively conjunctive.

*Proofs.* That $\texttt{X}$ is active and finite —i.e. (i)— follows respectively from (40.i) and from (40.ii) with $s := \mathit{true}$. From (i, (29) and (28.i), we immediately obtain '⇒' for the two equalities in (ii) and the reverse implications are established by

$$
\begin{array}{ll}
\quad [\,\texttt{E} \Rightarrow \texttt{X}^{\infty}\,] & \\
\Leftarrow \quad \{\text{ fixpoint induction }\} & \\
\quad [\,\texttt{E} \Rightarrow \texttt{X}\,; \texttt{E}\,] & \\
= \quad \{\text{ definition (9) of } \texttt{E}\ \} & \\
\quad [\,\texttt{E} \Rightarrow \texttt{X}\,; \mathit{true}; \mathit{false}\,] & \\
= \quad \{\text{ (10.i) and postulate (40.i) }\} & \\
\quad [\,\texttt{E} \Rightarrow \neg\mathbb{1} \wedge \texttt{E}\,] & \\
= \quad \{\ \texttt{E} \text{ is active }\} & \\
\quad \mathit{true}\,. &
\end{array}
\qquad
\begin{array}{ll}
\quad [\,\texttt{X}^{*} \Leftarrow \texttt{F}\,] & \\
= \quad \{\text{ predicate calculus }\} & \\
\quad [\,\texttt{X}^{*} \vee \texttt{E}\,] & \\
= \quad \{\text{ neutralities and } \texttt{E} = \texttt{X}^{\infty}\ \} & \\
\quad [\,\mathit{true} \;\Rightarrow\; \texttt{X}^{*}; \mathbb{1} \,\vee\, \texttt{X}^{\infty}\,] & \\
\Leftarrow \quad \{\text{ (32) and fixpoint induction }\} & \\
\quad [\,\mathit{true} \Rightarrow \texttt{X}\,; \mathit{true} \,\vee\, \mathbb{1}\,] & \\
= \quad \{\text{ (40.i), predicate calculus }\} & \\
\quad \mathit{true}\,. &
\end{array}
$$

The proof of (iii) is left to the reader and (iv) is an immediate consequence thereof. □

With the constant $\texttt{X}$, we have the full expressive power of LTL at our disposal (the full expressive power of CTL* in fact). The other temporal operators of LTL are "some-time", "always", and "until". Since we have no use for "until" we refrain from introducing it. The "some-time" operator is something we already have: it is the prefix $\texttt{F}\,;\_$. In order to be in accordance with the axiomatisation of LTL, this operator should satisfy

**Fact 42.** $\texttt{F}\,; s \;=\; \langle \mu\, x :: \texttt{X}\,; x \,\vee\, s\,\rangle$ for all $s$,

which follows immediately from (41.ii) and the tail-recursion theorem (32). The most salient algebraic properties of "some time" are captured by

**Fact 43.** $\texttt{F}\,;\_$ is a universally disjunctive closure.

which follows from (10.i) and (10.iii).

We define "always" as the dual of "some time":

**Definition 44.** $\texttt{G} : CPred \to CPred$, $\;\texttt{G}\,s \;=\; \neg(\texttt{F}\,; \neg s)$ for all $s$.

On account of being the dual of a universally disjunctive closure:

**Fact 45.** $\mathtt{G}$ is a universally conjunctive interior.

The axiomatisation of LTL for the always-operator boils down to the fixpoint characterisation $\mathtt{G}\,s = \langle \nu x :: \mathtt{X}\,; x \wedge s \rangle$, but —since our computations may be finite— this doesn't hold in our algebra. Instead, dualising (42) and simplifying the result with (41.iii) yields

**Fact 46.** $\mathtt{G}\,s \;=\; \langle \nu x :: (\mathtt{X}\,; x \vee \mathbb{1}) \wedge s \rangle$ for all $s$.

If $s$ is eternal, $(\mathtt{X}\,; x \vee \mathbb{1}) \wedge s = \mathtt{X}\,; x \wedge s$ since $\mathbb{1}$ is finite. So, in that case, the above fixpoint characterisation reduces to the one of LTL.

Taking care of the cosmetic differences necessary to cater for the existence of finite computations, the entire axiomatisation of LTL can now be proved correct; so our algebra subsumes this logic completely. The reader may wonder how we fare with CTL*, but there is nothing to subsume here since CTL* has no axiomatisation that we know of. Emerson and Srinivasan [7] do give an axiomatisation for a (small) segment of CTL* and those axioms and inference rules are, indeed, all provable in our algebra (postulate (40.iii) is essential here).

## 12 Persistence

The fixpoints of the interior operator $\mathtt{G}$ are of particular interest: they occur frequently and are pleasant to work with. We call these predicates 'persistent':

**Definition 47.** $s$ is persistent $\equiv s = \mathtt{G}\,s$ for all $s$.

Since $\mathtt{G}$ is strengthening, the mathematical content of this equality consists of the implication $[\, s \Rightarrow \mathtt{G}\,s \,]$.

If a computation has some persistent property, all of its suffixes have that same property. This inheritance is something we frequently exploit and the following rule makes it algebraically explicit.

**Fact 48.** *Persistence rule.*

$$[\, t\,; u \wedge s \Rightarrow t\,;(u \wedge s) \,] \text{ for all persistent } s \text{ and all } t \text{ and } u.$$

*Proof.* This follows after shunting from the observation that:

$$\begin{array}{ll}
 & t\,; u \\
= & \{\ (10.\text{iv})\ \} \\
 & (t \wedge \mathtt{E}) \vee (t \wedge \mathtt{F})\,; u \\
= & \{\ \text{excluded middle and distribution}\ \} \\
 & (t \wedge \mathtt{E}) \vee (t \wedge \mathtt{F})\,;(s \wedge u) \vee (t \wedge \mathtt{F})\,;(\neg s \wedge u) \\
\Rightarrow & \{\ (10.\text{iv}),\ \text{monotonicity}\ \} \\
 & t\,;(s \wedge u) \vee \mathtt{F}\,;\neg s \\
= & \{\ \mathtt{F}\,;\neg s = \neg\,\mathtt{G}\,s,\ \ s \text{ is persistent}\ \} \\
 & t\,;(s \wedge u) \vee \neg s\,.
\end{array}$$

□

Using the persistence rule in any particular circumstance requires that we establish the persistence of the particular instance of $s$ involved. Obviously, a direct proof of $[\, s \Rightarrow \mathtt{G}\, s \,]$ would do, but there are cheaper alternatives. The first and cheapest is induction on the syntax; from the idempotency, universal conjunctivity, and monotonicity of G respectively, it follows that

**Facts 49.** For all $s$ and functions $t$

(i) $\mathtt{G}\, s$ is persistent, and

(ii) $\langle \forall i :: t.i \text{ is persistent} \rangle \Rightarrow \langle \forall i :: t.i \rangle$ and $\langle \exists i :: t.i \rangle$ are persistent.

The second cheap way for establishing persistence consists of weakening the proof obligation $[\, s \Rightarrow \mathtt{G}\, s \,]$ using (46) and fixpoint induction to $[\, s \Rightarrow \mathtt{X} ; s \vee \mathbb{1} \,]$. In the —usual— case that $s$ is active, the final '$\ldots \vee \mathbb{1}$' vanishes and this strategy boils down to

**Fact 50.** $s$ is persistent $\Leftarrow [\, s \Rightarrow \mathtt{X} ; s \,]$ for all $s$.

As an easy consequence of the persistence rule, we get a relation between the always-operator G and the infinite iterator $\_^\infty$. For any $s$ we have that

$$\begin{array}{ll} & \mathtt{G}(s ; \mathit{true}) \\ = & \{\ \mathtt{G} \text{ is strengthening } \} \\ & s ; \mathit{true} \wedge \mathtt{G}(s ; \mathit{true}) \\ \Rightarrow & \{\ \mathtt{G}(s ; \mathit{true}) \text{ is persistent, persistence rule (48) } \} \\ & s ; \mathtt{G}(s ; \mathit{true}) , \end{array}$$

from which we conclude —by fixpoint induction— that $[\, \mathtt{G}(s ; \mathit{true}) \Rightarrow s^\infty \,]$. Asking ourselves the question under which conditions the reverse implication —and hence equality— would hold, we first note that $\mathtt{G}(s ; \mathit{true}) = s^\infty$ implies that $s^\infty$ is persistent. Thus the latter is a necessary condition for the reverse implication to hold. It is also sufficient:

$$\begin{array}{ll} & [\, \mathtt{G}(s ; \mathit{true}) \Leftarrow s^\infty \,] \\ = & \{\ s^\infty \text{ is persistent and unfolding } \} \\ & [\, \mathtt{G}(s ; \mathit{true}) \Leftarrow \mathtt{G}(s ; s^\infty) \,] \\ = & \{\ \text{monotonicity } \} \\ & \mathit{true} . \end{array}$$

So we have found

**Facts 51.** For all $s$

(i) $[\, \mathtt{G}(s ; \mathit{true}) \Rightarrow s^\infty \,]$

(ii) $\mathtt{G}(s ; \mathit{true}) = s^\infty \ \equiv\ s^\infty$ is persistent.

## 13 Atomic Actions

An atomic action is a statement generating only single-step computations:

**Definition 52.** $a$ is atomic $\equiv [\, a \Rightarrow \mathtt{X} \,]$ for all $a$.

Atomic actions satisfy a property that is similar to the state restriction rule (8.i) for state predicates.

**Fact 53.** *Atomic split.* $a\,;s \;=\; a\,;\mathit{true} \wedge \mathtt{X}\,;s$ for all atomic $a$ and all $s$.

*Proof.* On account of monotonicity it suffices to prove '$\Leftarrow$' and this follows after shunting from the observation that:

$$
\begin{array}{ll}
 & a\,;s \vee \neg(\mathtt{X}\,;s) \\
\Leftarrow & \{ \text{ postulate (40.ii) } \} \\
 & a\,;s \vee \mathtt{X}\,;\neg s \\
\Leftarrow & \{\ a \text{ is atomic, ; over } \vee\text{, excluded middle } \} \\
 & a\,;\mathit{true}\,.
\end{array}
$$

□

When reasoning on the atomic level, we occasionally need the following stronger version of the atomic split.

**Fact 54.** *Abide rule.* For all atomic $a$ and $b$ and all $s$ and $t$

$$a\,;s \wedge b\,;t \;=\; (a \wedge b)\,;(s \wedge t)\,.$$

Since our algebra is by now quite powerful, one might expect the verification of the abide rule to be unproblematic. Sadly, it is not. Using the atomic split, one readily verifies that it suffices to prove the abide rule for $s$ and $t$ both equal to *true*, but then we get stuck.

The problem is that the validity of the abide rule in the model depends upon a property of the prefix order $\preceq$ that our current postulates don't address:

$$\langle \exists \rho :: \sigma \preceq \rho \wedge \tau \preceq \rho \rangle \;\Rightarrow\; \sigma \preceq \tau \vee \tau \preceq \sigma \quad \text{for all computations } \sigma \text{ and } \tau\,.$$

In [9], something akin to this is called "local linearity".

This brings us to the final postulate of our algebra.

**Postulate 55.** *Linearity.* For all $s$ and $t$

$$[\, s\,;\mathit{true} \wedge t\,;\mathit{true} \;\Rightarrow\; (s\,;\mathit{true} \wedge t)\,;\mathit{true} \vee (s \wedge t\,;\mathit{true})\,;\mathit{true}\,]\,.$$

We leave it to the reader to prove the abide rule from this.

The growing number of postulates is making it increasingly difficult to find alternative models and we have not been able to construct a model that establishes that our final postulate doesn't follow from the rest. Still, we are reasonably confident that it does not.

## 14 UNITY

The need for formal support for operational reasoning was driven home to us in the course of our explorations of UNITY. State-predicate transformers for UNITY with a straightforward operational interpretation often have an intractable mathematical characterisation, which makes the correctness of such a characterisation a non trivial theorem.

In this section we briefly discuss UNITY. A full-blown analysis far exceeds the scope of this paper; instead, we give just an impression of how all the machinery we have developed can be used in such an analysis.

A UNITY program is given by a nonempty finite set of atomic actions $A$. Execution of the program results in an infinite sequence of steps such that

– each step consists of the execution of some action from $A$, and
– every action in $A$ is executed infinitely often.
Defining *stp* by $stp = \langle \exists a : a \in A : a \rangle$, the computations described above are those that
– consist of an infinite sequence of *stp*-steps, and
– contain, for every $a \in A$, an infinite number of $a$-steps.
From the definition of *stp* it follows that *stp* is atomic and that $[\, a \Rightarrow stp \,]$ for all $a \in A$. These consequences are all we ever need and, therefore, all that we require in the formal characterisation of UNITY computations. We give some equivalent characterisations; the reader may choose the one that he/she considers to be most convincing as *the* definition.

**Definition 56.** For any atomic *stp* and nonempty finite set $A$ such that $[\, a \Rightarrow stp \,]$ for all $a \in A$, we define —with the range $a \in A$ understood—

(i) $\quad unity.stp.A \;=\; \mathtt{G}(stp\,;true) \wedge \langle \forall a :: \mathtt{G}(\mathtt{F}\,;a\,;true) \rangle$
(ii) $\quad\quad = \; stp^{\infty} \wedge \langle \forall a :: (\mathtt{F}\,;a)^{\infty} \rangle$
(iii) $\quad\quad = \; \langle \forall a :: (stp^{*};a)^{\infty} \rangle$

The first two are direct translations into mathematics of the English description given above. The verification that these two are equal is reasonably straightforward using (51) and (50).

The third is the starting point for most of the predicate-transformer semantics and is easily seen to imply the other two. In order to see that it also follows, let $u = unity.stp.A$ as defined by the first two. That $[\, u \Rightarrow \langle \forall a :: (stp^{*};a)^{\infty} \rangle \,]$ follows by fixpoint induction from the observation that

$$[\, u \Rightarrow stp^{*};a\,;u \,] \text{ for all } a\,,$$

which we establish as follows:

$\quad stp^{*};a\,;u$
$\Leftarrow \quad$ { $u$ is persistent, persistence rule (48) }
$\quad stp^{*};a\,;true \wedge u$
$\Leftarrow \quad$ { $[\, b^{\infty} \wedge \mathtt{F}\,;t \Rightarrow b^{*};t \,]$ for all atomic $b$ and all $t$ (etude) }
$\quad stp^{\infty} \wedge \mathtt{F}\,;a\,;true \wedge u$
$= \quad$ { $u$ implies the other two conjuncts }
$\quad u\,.$

For the rest of this section we assume that *stp* and $A$ satisfy the premisses of definition (56) and that $u = unity.stp.A$.

In UNITY logic, as it was designed by Chandy and Misra [1], progress of a unity program is captured by the relation $\mapsto$ ("leads to") on state predicates. Operationally, $p \mapsto q$ means that in any $u$-computation, every state satisfying $p$ is succeeded eventually — possibly simultaneously— by some state satisfying $q$. Carefully transcribing this into our algebra yields

**Definition 57.** $p \mapsto q \equiv [\, u \Rightarrow \mathtt{G}(\bullet p \Rightarrow \mathtt{F}\,;\bullet q) \,]$ for all $p$ and $q$.

For any $q$, we calculate the weakest $p$ that leads to $q$:

$\quad p \mapsto q$

$=\quad \{$ definition (57) $\}$
$[\, u \Rightarrow \mathtt{G}(\bullet p \Rightarrow \mathtt{F}\,;\bullet q)\,]$
$=\quad \{$ $u$ is persistent, i.e. "open" w.r.t. to the interior operator $\mathtt{G}$ $\}$
$[\, u \Rightarrow (\bullet p \Rightarrow \mathtt{F}\,;\bullet q)\,]$
$=\quad \{$ shunt twice $\}$
$[\,\bullet p \Rightarrow (u \Rightarrow \mathtt{F}\,;\bullet q)\,]$
$=\quad \{$ definition (15) of $\mathcal{A}$ $\}$
$[\, p \Rightarrow \mathcal{A}(u \Rightarrow \mathtt{F}\,;\bullet q)\,]\,.$

So, we now get that

**Fact 58.** $p \mapsto q \equiv [\, p \Rightarrow \mathit{wlt}.q\,]$ for all $p$ and $q$,
where the state-predicate transformer *wlt* is given by

**Definition 59.** $\mathit{wlt}.q = \mathcal{A}(u \Rightarrow \mathtt{F}\,;\bullet q)$ for all state predicates $q$.

Spelling out the right-hand side in English, we get

*wlt.q* : holds in those initial states for which every $u$-computation contains at least one state satisfying $q$,

which is essentially what we wrote in the introduction.

The formal definition of the predicate transformer *wlt* given by Jutla, Knapp, and Rao [10] is an intractable double fixpoint expression which, in [6], we showed to be equivalent to

**Fact 60.** $\mathit{wlt}.q = \langle \mu\, x :: \langle \exists\, a :: \langle \nu\, y :: q \vee (\mathit{wp.stp.y} \wedge \mathit{wp.a.x})\,\rangle\,\rangle\,\rangle$ for all $q$.

The computation calculus has been designed to enable us to derive characterisations such as (60) from definitions such as (59). The actual derivation consists of many pages of intricate calculations and we refrain from giving it here.

The predicate transformer *wlt* is not the only tool of the trade in UNITY theory. Two others are

**Definition 61.** For any state-predicate $q$

(i) $\mathit{wst}.q = \mathcal{A}(u \Rightarrow \mathtt{G}\bullet q)$ and

(ii) $\mathit{wta}.q = \mathcal{A}(u \Rightarrow \mathtt{F}\,;\mathtt{G}\bullet q)\,.$

The predicate transformer *wst* ('weakest stable') is characterised by Chandy and Sanders [2] via

**Fact 62.** $\mathit{wst}.q = \langle \nu\, y :: \mathit{wp.stp.y} \wedge q\,\rangle$ for all $q$.

Upon trying to prove (62) from (61.i), we found that we need to assume $\mathcal{E}\, u = \mathbb{1}$ for that. This follows from $\mathcal{E}\, a = \mathbb{1}$ for all $a$ and, since totality of all the actions is a running assumption in UNITY, this is not a serious restriction; however, that it is essential for (62) to be correct had hitherto escaped our notice entirely.

The predicate transformer *wta* ('weakest to-always') is introduced by Sanders and the present author in [4] via

**Fact 63.** $\mathit{wst}.q = \langle \mu\, x :: \mathit{wlt}.(\mathit{wst}.(x \vee q))\,\rangle\,.$

There, a verbal argument is given for the correspondence with the operational interpretation (61.ii). This verbal argument can be rendered algebraically as a proof in the computation calculus.

## 15 Summary and Concluding Remarks

We developed the computation calculus as we went along and, consequently, the ingredients are scattered throughout the text. So let us summarise. The sum total of the postulates that make up the computation calculus is :

the basic postulates (5) and (6),
the composition rule (25),
the accumulation rule (30),
the cycle rule (35),
the atomicity rules (40), and
linearity (55).

That's it. While, in general, we'd like the algebras we use to be less complex, we feel that this is reasonably modest in view of what it achieves. We covered the precondition semantics for sequential programs of Dijkstra and Scholten. We have subsumed the linear time temporal logic of Manna and Pnueli. We have subsumed the language of CTL* and, while this "logic" has no proof system — that we know of— our algebra does give a handle on these expressions. Finally, the calculus as a whole is powerful enough for a mathematically explicit analysis of UNITY, which is something no other formalism enabled us to do.

Also scattered throughout the text are the restriction on our computation space ensuring that it provides a model for the computation calculus. We rendered these restrictions informally as:

Nonempty segments of computations are computations
$\mathcal{C}$ is closed under "pasting"
$\mathcal{C}$ is limit closed
$\mathcal{C}$ contains an atomic step for every initial state

(Note that requirement (4), i.e. that every state constitutes a singleton computation, is subsumed by the first and last of this list.) Put the other way around, the computation calculus is 'sound' for the class of computation spaces satisfying these four 'healthiness properties'.

We consider these healthiness requirements to be quite reasonable, so we can live with the fact that the applicability of our algebra is restricted to computation spaces satisfying them. In fact, now that we have this list explicitly in front of us, we can see that the list constitutes assumptions that we used to make implicitly and without always being fully aware of it.

## A On Fixpoint Calculus, Closures and Interiors

In our explorations of the computation calculus, we make heavy use of fixpoint calculus [13]. For a monotonic predicate transformer $f$ we use $\langle \mu\, x :: f.x \rangle$ to denote the strongest fixpoint and $\langle \nu\, x :: f.x \rangle$ to denote the weakest fixpoint. We list the essential rules (for $\mu$ only).

Leaving universal quantification over the free variables and monotonicity of the functions understood:

*Theorem of Knaster-Tarski*

$$\langle \mu x :: f.x \rangle = \langle \forall x : [\, f.x \Rightarrow x \,] : x \rangle .$$

*(Un-)folding*

$$\langle \mu x :: f.x \rangle = f.\langle \mu x :: f.x \rangle .$$

*Fixpoint induction*

$$[\, f.x \Rightarrow x \,] \Rightarrow [\, \langle \mu x :: f.x \rangle \Rightarrow x \,] .$$

*Monotonicity*

$$\langle \forall x :: [\, f.x \Rightarrow g.x \,] \rangle \Rightarrow [\, \langle \mu x :: f.x \rangle \Rightarrow \langle \mu x :: g.x \rangle \,] .$$

*Fixpoint rolling*

$$f.\langle \mu x :: g.(f.x) \rangle = \langle \mu x :: f.(g.x) \rangle .$$

*Dualisation*

$$\neg \langle \mu x :: f.x \rangle = \langle \nu x :: \neg f.(\neg x) \rangle .$$

*Fixpoint fusion* For universally disjunctive $f$

$$f.\langle \mu x :: g.x \rangle = \langle \mu y :: h.y \rangle \;\Leftarrow\; \langle \forall x,y : f.x = y \;:\; f.(g.x) = h.y \rangle .$$

*Diagonal rule*

$$\langle \mu x :: \langle \mu y :: f.(x,y) \rangle \rangle = \langle \mu x :: f.(x,x) \rangle .$$

We also make some use of familiarity with 'closures' and 'interiors'. These are predicate transformers enjoying a cocktail of properties:

$f$ is a closure $\equiv$ $f$ is monotonic, idempotent and weakening,

$f$ is an interior $\equiv$ $f$ is monotonic, idempotent and strengthening.

The most frequently exploited algebraic properties thereof are

$[\, f.x \Rightarrow f.y \,] \equiv [\, x \Rightarrow f.y \,]$ if $f$ is a closure, and

$[\, f.x \Rightarrow f.y \,] \equiv [\, f.x \Rightarrow y \,]$ if $f$ is an interior.

# References


1. K. Mani Chandy and Jayadev Misra. Parallel Program Design, a foundation. Addison-Wesley, 1988.
2. K. Mani Chandy and Beverly A. Sanders. Conjunctive predicate transformers for reasoning about concurrent computation. Science of Computer Programming, 24:129–148, 1995.
3. Edsger W. Dijkstra and Carel S. Scholten. Predicate Calculus and Program Semantics. Texts and Monographs in Computer Science. Springer Verlag New York Inc., 1990.
4. Rutger M. Dijkstra and Beverly A. Sanders. A predicate transformer for the progress property 'to-always'. Formal Aspects of Computing, 9:270–282, 1997.
5. Rutger M. Dijkstra. Relational calculus and relational program semantics. CS-R9408, University of Groningen, 1994.
6. Rutger M. Dijkstra. DUALITY: a simple formalism for the analysis of UNITY. Formal Aspects of Computing, 7:353–388, 1995.

7. E. Allen Emerson and Jai Srinivasan. Branching time temporal logic. In: W.P. de Roever J.W. de Bakker and G. Rozenberger, editors, Linear Time, Branching Time, and Partial Order in Logics and Models for Concurrency, pages 123–172. Springer-Verlag, 1989. LNCS 354.
8. Wim H. Hesselink. Programs, Recursion and Unbounded Choice. Cambridge Tracts in Theoretical Computer Science. Cambridge University Press, 1992.
9. B. von Karger and C.A.R. Hoare. Sequential calculus. Information Processing Letters, 53:123–130, 1995.
10. E. Knapp, C.S. Jutla, and J.R. Rao. A predicate transformer approach to semantics of parallel programs. In: Proceedings of the 8th Annual ACM symposium on Principles of Distributed Computing, pages 249–263. ACM Press, 1989.
11. Johan J. Lukkien. Parallel Program Design and Generalized Weakest Preconditions. PhD thesis, Rijksuniversiteit Groningen, 1990.
12. Z. Manna and A. Pnueli. Verification of concurrent programs: a temporal proof system. In: J.W. de Bakker and J. van Leeuwen, editors, Foundations Of Computer Science. Distributed Systems: part 2, Semantics and Logic, pages 163–255. Mathematisch Centrum, Amsterdam, 1983. Mathematical Centre Tracts 159.
13. Mathematics of Program Construction Group. Fix-point calculus. Information Processing Letters, 53:131–136, 1995.

# An Elementary Derivation of the Alternating Bit Protocol

W.H.J. Feijen[0], A.J.M. van Gasteren[0] and Birgit Schieder[1]

[0] Department of Mathematics and Computing Science, Eindhoven University of Technology, 5600 MB Eindhoven, The Netherlands, {wf,vangasteren}@win.tue.nl

[1] Institut für Informatik, Technische Universität München, 80290 München, Germany, schieder@informatik.tu-muenchen.de

**Abstract.** The famous alternating bit protocol is an algorithm for transmitting a sequence of data through a so-called faulty channel, i.e. a channel that can lose or duplicate injected data. The established literature provides a wealth of treatments and plenty of a-posteriori correctness proofs of the protocol; derivations of the algorithm, however, are very rare. The prime purpose of this note is to provide such a derivation from first principles, using the theory of Owicki and Gries as the only tool for reasoning about parallel programs.

**Keywords.** Program derivation, multiprogramming, the theory of Owicki and Gries, multibounds, faulty channels, the alternating bit protocol.

## 0 Introduction

We consider the problem of deriving an algorithm for the correct transmission of a sequence of data from a sender to a receiver through a so-called faulty channel. The type of faulty channel considered here is a uni-directional channel that can hold at most one message at a time and that can "misbehave" in that it can lose or duplicate a message injected into the channel, so that either no or several copies of the message arrive at the receiver. However, the channel does not persist in losing: if a sufficiently long stream of messages is injected, then at least one of them will arrive at the receiver. Similarly, the channel does not persist in duplicating. A more precise specification of the problem and of faulty channels will be given later.

This note contains three technical sections. In the first section we present some preliminaries, such as a brief summary of the theory of Owicki and Gries; we do so for the sake of completeness. In section 2 we give a more precise description of faulty channels, and, finally, in section 3 we formally specify the programming problem and derive a solution.

# 1 Preliminaries

## 1.0 The theory of Owicki and Gries, in brief

The theory of Owicki and Gries [OG76, Dij82, Schn97] was developed to formally address the partial correctness of parallel programs — or: multiprograms, as we call them —. Simplicity is its greatest asset. Here we only give a rudimentary presentation, confining ourselves to what is needed in what follows.

A multiprogram is a set of sequential programs, to be called the components of the multiprogram. Each component is built out of atomic statements (, i.e. statements the execution of which takes place indivisibly, without interference). A component may be annotated with assertions in the way familiar from sequential programming [Hoa69]. Informally,

> an assertion in a component is correct whenever it is established by the component in which it occurs—it is *locally* correct—and maintained by all atomic statements of the other components—it is *globally* correct—.

Phrased more formally, an assertion $P$ is established by $\{Q\}\ S$, i.e. by atomic statement $S$ with pre-assertion $Q$, whenever $\{Q\}\ S\ \{P\}$ is a valid Hoare-triple, and it is maintained by such a $\{Q\}\ S$ whenever $\{P \wedge Q\}\ S\ \{P\}$ is a valid Hoare-triple.

A rule that we use very frequently to prove global correctness of assertions is the utterly simple

**Rule of Widening**

> For integers $x$ and $y$, condition $x \leq y$ is maintained by descents* of $x$ and ascents of $y$.

**End** .

Of course, Widening comes in many variations. More in general, a condition like $F.x \leq G.y$ is, for instance, maintained by $y := z$ whenever $G.y \leq G.z$.

A notion that is of general importance in multiprogramming is the notion of a system invariant. A system invariant is a condition that holds initially (i.e. at the start of the multiprogram's execution) and that is maintained by each atomic statement of each component. Thus, a system invariant holds "everywhere" in the multiprogram: it is a correct pre- and post-assertion of each atomic statement.

Local correctness of an assertion $B$ will often be established by a so-called guarded skip: **if** $B \rightarrow$ ***skip*** **fi**, whose semantics — in Hoare-triple format — is given by

$$\{Q\}\ \textbf{if}\ B \rightarrow \textbf{\textit{skip}}\ \textbf{fi}\ \{R\} \quad \equiv \quad [Q \Rightarrow (B \Rightarrow R)] \quad .$$

Thus, program fragment **if** $B \rightarrow$ ***skip*** **fi** indeed establishes $B$.

---

* A "descent" is a "non-increase"; an "ascent" a "non-decrease".

We will return to guarded skips shortly. Here we conclude with a simple rule allowing us to change the guard of a guarded skip.

**Rule of Guard Strengthening**

Strengthening the guard of a guarded skip does not affect the correctness of the annotation.

**End** .

(For a proof, note that every proof obligation involving guarded skip **if** $B \rightarrow$ ***skip*** **fi** has shape $\{Q\}$ **if** $B \rightarrow$ ***skip*** **fi** $\{R\}$, i.e. $[Q \Rightarrow (B \Rightarrow R)]$, a proof obligation that becomes weaker when $B$ is strengthened.)

## 1.1 Synchronization and Total Deadlock

Correct cooperation of the components of a multiprogram usually requires synchronization. Our main means for achieving synchronization is the guarded skip, **if** $B \rightarrow$ ***skip*** **fi**, just introduced. Operationally, it behaves like **do** $\neg B \rightarrow$ ***skip*** **od**. (Hence its capacity for synchronization.)

Incorporating guarded skips — or any other synchronization primitives — brings about the danger of components getting stuck. In the extreme case, ***all*** components get stuck in a guarded skip. Then the system can no longer generate state changes, so that the components will remain stuck forever: there is "total deadlock".

The canonical way of proving the absence of total deadlock is to show that, when all components are engaged in the execution of a guarded skip, the state of the system is such that at least one of the corresponding guards is true. (In our solution to the present programming problem it so happens that the absence of total deadlock will be obvious.)

## 1.2 Individual Progress and the Multibound

Even if there is no total deadlock, there is the danger of an ***individual*** component getting stuck at a guarded skip forever, due to unfortunate joint activities of other components. Showing the absence of this "danger of individual starvation", i.e. showing individual progress, is in general far more difficult than proving absence of total deadlock.

There is a particular class of designs, however, for which individual progress can be shown at a bargain, because it is possible to show that if any component gets stuck forever, so do all the others. We illustrate this by means of the following small example.

Consider a two-component multiprogram that, projected on the changes of integer variables $x$ and $y$, has shape**

$$* [\ x := x + 1\ ] \quad || \quad * [\ y := y + 1\ ] \qquad ,$$

** $*[\ S\ ]$ is short for **do** *true* $\rightarrow S$ **od**.

and suppose that (by the rest of the code) the components are synchronized such that, for some $K$ and $L$, relation $MB$, given by

$$MB: \quad x \leq K + y \ \wedge \ y \leq L + x \qquad ,$$

is a system invariant. Then, if the $y$-component gets stuck so will the $x$-component, and vice versa. Consequently, there are only two possible scenarios with regard to progress, viz.

either both components get stuck, which means total deadlock
or each component makes individual progress.

As a result, the presence of a ***multibound*** like $MB$ and components of the shape indicated above means that individual progress follows from the absence of total deadlock. As will become clear later, the algorithm that we are about to develop will provide such a multibound. Before starting the development, however, we first have to become more explicit about faulty channels.

## 2 Faulty channels

For the following discussion it is vital to realize that in our computational model we assume weak fairness, that is we assume that each component of a multiprogram proceeds with an unknown but positive and finite speed. In particular, for terminating statement $S$, a component of the form

$$*[\ S\ ]$$

will produce a sequence of $S$-events of unbounded length; i.e. at any moment in time we can be certain *that* a next $S$ will be produced within a finite period of time (although we don't know *when* it will be generated).

We now consider the three-component multiprogram

$$\begin{array}{l} \textit{Pre}:\ x = 0 \ \wedge \ p = 0 \\ \text{A}: *[\ x := x + 1\ ] \\ \text{F}:\ *[\ p := x\ ] \\ \text{B}:\ *[\ \textit{print}(p)\ ] \qquad , \end{array}$$

where *Pre* — the precondition — describes the initial state of the multiprogram. Apparently, component $F$ is engaged in communication with both $A$ and $B$. Let us encode these communications more explicitly, for instance by CSP-like constructs for synchronous message passing over perfect links [Hoa78, Mar81, Mar85]. To that end we split $F$ into two components: component $AF$ for communication with $A$ via (perfect) link *af*, and $FB$ for communication with $B$ via *fb*. We thus arrive at the following four-component multiprogram

$$\begin{array}{ll} \textit{Pre}: & x = 0 \ \wedge \ h = 0 \ \wedge \ p = 0 \\ \text{A}: & *[\, x := x+1 \,] \\ \text{AF}: & *[\, \textit{af}?h \,] \\ \text{FB}: & *[\, \textit{fb}!h \,] \\ \text{B}: & *[\, \textit{print}(p) \,] \end{array}$$

Component $A$'s communication via link ***af*** and $B$'s communication via ***fb*** have remained implicit. We do assume, however, that *every now and then* (for instance, when a time-out is generated or a new data item is produced, etc.) component $A$ sends a message into $F$ by performing an $af!x$. Similarly, we assume that $B$ will perform $fb?p$ with positive frequency. We also assume that $A$ and $B$ do so at moments entirely determined by themselves.

With this in mind we now argue why $F$, i.e. the pair $(AF, FB)$, can be "blamed" for the faultiness in the transmission of the data stream from $A$ to $B$.

The pair $(AF, FB)$ produces an interleaving of events $af?h$ and $fb!h$. If such an interleaving contains two consecutive events $af?h$, then apparently $A$ has sent two messages to $F$, the first one of which is lost due to the interleaving chosen by $F$. Thus $F$ can lose messages ***autonomously.*** However, $F$ will not persist in losing, because within a finite period of time an event $fb!h$ will take place — which will be matched by a receipt of $B$.

In exactly the same way $F$, i.e. the pair $(AF, FB)$, may generate two consecutive events $fb!h$, implying the arrival of a duplicate at $B$. As a result, channel $(AF, FB)$ can autonomously, outside our control, lose and duplicate data, but will not persist in doing so. That is, it is a faulty channel.

The reason why we prefer to encode it in the way we did, viz. as $*[\, p := x \,]$, is that $*[\, p := x \,]$ can behave exactly like $(AF, FB)$, while at the same time it is far simpler to deal with in our formalism.

# 3 Problem statement and program derivation

The problem to be solved can be described as follows. We consider a component $A$ that extracts an infinite stream of data from an outside world. Since for our problem it is irrelevant where the data come from, we consider a simplified component $A$ that produces the stream of data itself; and since for our problem it is irrelevant what the data are like, we consider yet a simpler component $A$ that produces the sequence of natural numbers.

We also consider a component $B$ that ejects an infinite stream of data into some outside world, for instance by printing it. The task that we face is to synchronize the two components in such a way that $B$ prints exactly what is produced by $A$, and this subject to the handicap that $A$ and $B$ can only communicate via faulty channels.

We will develop a solution in three stages. First we specify the problem, and derive a solution under the assumption that direct communication between components $A$ and $B$ is allowed (i.e. $A$ and $B$ can inspect each other's state). Then we introduce the faulty channels and adjust the solution accordingly, and, finally, we transform the resulting program into one that uses boolean variables only, thereby arriving at the Alternating Bit Protocol.

## 3.0 A solution using direct communication

Our starting point is multiprogram

| *Pre*: $x = 0$ | |
|---|---|
| A: $*[\ x := x+1\ ]$ | B: $*[\ print(x)\ ]$ |

and our task is to synchronize the components in such a way that $B$ prints the sequence of natural numbers.

In order to cast this specification into a more formal and workable shape, we *temporarily* equip $B$ with *clairvoyance* by letting it produce the same sequence as $A$ does. To that end we introduce an auxiliary variable $y$ and transform the multiprogram into***

| *Pre*: $x = 0 \ \wedge\ y = 0$ | |
|---|---|
| A: $*[\ x := x+1\ ]$ | B: $*[\ \{?\ x = y\}$<br>$print(x)$<br>$;\ y := y+1$<br>$]$ |

It should be clear now that $B$ prints the sequence of natural numbers — as required — provided we can see to the correctness of pre-assertion $x = y$ of $print(x)$. The programming task ahead of us is to develop additional code that makes this assertion correct. By the time we are finished, we should also have eliminated all references to clairvoyance, as embodied by variable $y$.

* *
*

It is common practice to rewrite an equality like $x = y$ as the conjunction of $x \leq y$ and $y \leq x$. We establish $x \leq y$ by making it a system invariant and $y \leq x$ — which is globally correct: $x := x+1$ is Widening — by means of guarded skip **if** $y \leq x \rightarrow$ *skip* **fi**. Thus we arrive at our first approximation, which reads:

*** The query in front of an assertion is a clerical device reminding us that we still have to ensure the correctness of that assertion. We will also encounter queried invariants.

| |
|---|
| *Pre*: $x = 0 \ \wedge \ y = 0$ |
| A: $*[\, x := x+1 \,]$ |
| B: $*[$ **if** $y \leq x \rightarrow$ ***skip*** **fi**<br>; $\{x = y\}\{x \leq y\}\{y \leq x\}$<br>*print*$(x)$<br>; $y := y+1$<br>$]$ |
| *Inv*: ? $P_0 : \ \ x \leq y$ |

What remains to be done is to see to the invariance of $P_0$. Relation $P_0$ can only be violated by statement $x := x + 1$ in $A$, and in order to prevent this we require that $x+1 \leq y$ be a correct pre-assertion to $x := x+1$. This pre-assertion, in turn, is straightforwardly handled by guarded skip **if** $x + 1 \leq y \rightarrow$ ***skip*** **fi**, and so $P_0$ has been dealt with. In passing we note, that $y \leq x + 1$ is a system invariant as well, and thus we arrive at

| |
|---|
| *Pre*: $x = 0 \ \wedge \ y = 0$ |
| A: $*[$ **if** $x + 1 \leq y \rightarrow$ ***skip*** **fi**<br>; $\{x + 1 \leq y\}$<br>$x := x + 1$<br>$]$ |
| B: $*[$ **if** $y \leq x \rightarrow$ ***skip*** **fi**<br>; $\{x = y\}$<br>*print*$(x)$<br>; $y := y+1$<br>$]$ |
| *Inv*: $P_0 : \ x \leq y$<br>$P_1 : \ y \leq x + 1$ |

Finally, note that $P_0 \wedge P_1$ is a proper multibound for the above multiprogram.

### 3.1 Introducing the faulty channels

If we now disallow the direct communication between $A$ and $B$, component $B$ can no longer inspect variable $x$, and, similarly, $A$ is denied access to $y$. So we plug in two (faulty) channels, viz.

$F: \ \ *[\, p := x \,] \quad ,$

for transmitting the value of $x$ from $A$ to $B$, and

$G: \ \ *[\, q := y \,] \quad ,$

for transmitting the value of $y$ from $B$ to $A$. Along with this change in architecture, ***all*** occurrences of $x$ in the program text of $B$ have to be replaced by $p$, and all occurrences of $y$ in $A$ by $q$. So we have to change guard $y \leq x$ and statement $print(x)$ in $B$ and guard $x+1 \leq y$ in $A$. In this process, however, we wish to retain the correctness of the annotation.

We deal with the replacement of the guards first. The Rule of Guard Strengthening tells us that we are safe if the guards are strengthened. So we can replace guard $y \leq x$ in $B$ by $y \leq p$, whenever we can rely on the validity of

$$P_2: \quad p \leq x \quad ,$$

and we will see to $P_2$ by making it a system invariant. To this end, note that both $x := x+1$ in $A$ and $p := x$ in new component $F$ maintain $P_2$ (Widening).

Similarly, we replace guard $x+1 \leq y$ in $A$ by $x+1 \leq q$, while seeing to the system invariance of

$$P_3: \quad q \leq y \quad .$$

Thus we arrive at the following version, in which — on the fly — we introduce a number of queried items for later usage,

| |
|---|
| *Pre*: $x=0 \ \wedge\ y=0 \ \wedge\ p=0 \ \wedge\ q=0$ |
| A: $*$[ **if** $x+1 \leq q \rightarrow$ ***skip*** **fi**<br>; $\{?\ x+1 \leq q\}$<br>$x := x+1$<br>] |
| F: $*$[ $p := x$ ] |
| B: $*$[ **if** $y \leq p \rightarrow$ ***skip*** **fi** $\{x = y\}$<br>; $\{?\ y \leq p\}$ ***print***$(x)$<br>; $y := y+1$<br>] |
| G: $*$[ $q := y$ ] |
| *Inv*: $P_0: \ x \leq y$<br>$P_1: \ y \leq x+1$<br>$P_2: \ p \leq x$<br>$P_3: \ q \leq y$<br>$?\ P_4: \ x \leq q$<br>$?\ P_5: \ y \leq p+1$ |

Apart from $P_2$ and $P_3$, the unqueried assertions and invariants are inherited from the previous version of our multiprogram. $P_2$ and $P_3$ themselves were (briefly) dealt with above.

As for the queried items, we observe that assertion $y \leq p$ in $B$ is locally correct thanks to the preceding guarded skip and, thanks to $P_2$, it is globally correct as well: $p := x$ in $F$ is a Widening. For assertion $x + 1 \leq q$ in $A$, the argument is entirely similar. The invariance of $P_4$ and $P_5$ can now be left to the reader.

Also, observe that $P_2 \wedge P_0$ implies the invariance of $p \leq y$, so that, in $B$, assertion $y \leq p$ can be strengthened into $y = p$. Because of co-assertion $x = y$, we also have $x = p$, so that $print(x)$ can now be replaced by $print(p)$.

Finally, we deal with progress. If both $A$ and $B$ are stuck in their guarded skips, the rest of the system — $F$ and $G$ — will reach a state in which $p = x \;\wedge\; q = y$ stably holds. In that state, one of the guards — $x + 1 \leq q$ and $y \leq p$ — is stably true. So there is no total deadlock. Furthermore, since $A$ and $B$ are still coupled by their multibound $P_0 \wedge P_1$, individual progress is guaranteed as well.

Summarizing the above, retaining just what will be needed later, we arrive at

| |
|---|
| *Pre*: $x = 0 \;\wedge\; y = 0 \;\wedge\; p = 0 \;\wedge\; q = 0$ |
| A: $*$[ **if** $x + 1 \leq q \rightarrow$ ***skip*** **fi**<br>; $\{x + 1 \leq q\}$ $x := x + 1$<br>] |
| F: $*$[ $p := x$ ] |
| B: $*$[ **if** $y \leq p \rightarrow$ ***skip*** **fi**<br>; $\{y = p\}$ $print(p)$<br>; $y := y + 1$<br>] |
| G: $*$[ $q := y$ ] |
| *Inv*: $p \leq x \leq q \leq y \leq p + 1$ |

A basis for the ABP

## 3.2 The Alternating Bit Protocol

For the final transformation of our multiprogram, we observe that the "control" of the program only depends on the differences $x - q$ — in $A$'s guard — and $y - p$ — in $B$'s guard —. Invariant *Inv* shows that these differences are only two-valued, which means that by a coordinate transformation we can achieve that the program runs under control of boolean variables only. For this coordinate transformation we propose coupling invariants†

$Q_0 : \; c \equiv g \equiv x + 1 \leq q$ , and

$Q_1 : \; d \equiv f \equiv y \leq p$ ,

† "≡" is an associative operator, [DS90].

with $c$ — like $x$ — private to (i.e. can only be changed by) $A$
$d$ — like $y$ — private to $B$
$f$ — like $p$ — private to $F$, and
$g$ — like $q$ — private to $G$.

**Remark** The choice of $Q_0$ and $Q_1$, i.e. of the boolean expressions that are to replace the guards in $A$ and $B$, was motivated by the equivalence of expressions $\neg(a \equiv b)$ and $\neg a \equiv b$: component $A$, for instance, can now flip the value of the whole expression $c \equiv g$ by just flipping its own private variable $c$.
**End** Remark.

For the invariance of $Q_0$ and $Q_1$, we have to investigate — and possibly adjust — all assignments to $x$, $y$, $p$, and $q$. (Note that each assignment affects only one of them.)

**Re** $x := x + 1$ in $A$
For the invariance of $Q_0$, we propose to replace $x := x + 1$ by $c, x := C, x + 1$ and to calculate a suitable expression $C$:

$(c, x := C, x + 1).Q_0$
$\equiv$ {substitution}
$C \equiv g \equiv x + 2 \leq q$
$\equiv$ {from *Inv* : $q \leq x + 1$}
$C \equiv g \equiv \mathit{false}$
$\equiv$ $\{Q_0\}$
$C \equiv c \equiv x + 1 \leq q \equiv \mathit{false}$
$\equiv$ $\{x + 1 \leq q$ is pre-assertion of $x := x + 1\}$
$C \equiv \neg c$ .

Hence — not too amazingly — a flipping of $c$ along with the increment of $x$ does the job.

**Re** $y := y + 1$ in $B$
Very similarly, $y := y + 1$ is replaced by $d, y := \neg d, y + 1$.

**Re** $p := x$ in $F$
The invariance of $Q_1$ under $p := x$ may require an adjustment of $f$. The only two possible adjustments being $f := c$ and $f := \neg c$, we first try the former:

$(f, p := c, x).Q_1$
$\equiv$ {substitution}
$d \equiv c \equiv y \leq x$
$\equiv$ {invariant $Q_2$, introduced below}
*true* .

Invariant $Q_2$, given by
$Q_2 : \ d \equiv c \equiv y \leq x$ ,
will be dealt with shortly.

**Re** $q := y$ in $G$

Very similarly, $Q_0$ is maintained by $g, q := \neg d, y$, since $(g, q := \neg d, y).Q_0$ equivales $Q_2$ as well.

**End** of Re's.

Finally, we deal with $Q_2$. We only have to consider $c, x := \neg c, x+1$ in $A$ and $d, y := \neg d, y+1$ in $B$. As for the former, we calculate

$$
\begin{array}{ll}
 & (c, x := \neg c, x+1).Q_2 \\
\equiv & \quad \{\text{substitution}\} \\
 & d \;\equiv\; \neg c \;\equiv\; y \leq x+1 \\
\equiv & \quad \{\text{from } \mathit{Inv}: \quad y \leq x+1\} \\
 & \neg(d \equiv c) \\
\equiv & \quad \{Q_2\} \\
 & x < y \\
\equiv & \quad \{x+1 \leq q \leq y, \text{ from } \mathit{Inv} \text{ and pre-assertion of } c, x := \neg c, x+1\} \\
 & \mathit{true}
\end{array}
$$

Likewise, statement $d, y := \neg d, y+1$ maintains $Q_2$.

In summary, we have now arrived at

| |
|---|
| *Pre*: $x = 0 \;\wedge\; y = 0 \;\wedge\; p = 0 \;\wedge\; q = 0 \;\wedge\; c \;\wedge\; \neg g \;\wedge\; d \;\wedge\; f$ |
| A: $*$[ **if** $c \equiv g \rightarrow$ *skip* **fi**<br>; $c, x := \neg c, x+1$<br>] |
| F: $*$[ $f, p := c, x$ ] |
| B: $*$[ **if** $d \equiv f \rightarrow$ *skip* **fi**<br>; *print*$(p)$<br>; $d, y := \neg d, y+1$<br>] |
| G: $*$[ $g, q := \neg d, y$ ] |

The (Concurrent) Alternating Bit Protocol

Observe the compelling symmetry exhibited by this program.

Finally, we can eliminate variable $y$ and its offspring $q$ from the program text, since they do not contribute to the computation. The resulting algorithm is known as the (Concurrent) Alternating Bit Protocol — see e.g. [BSW69, CM88, Mil89, Bro92, vdSn95] —.

## 4 Final Remarks

In the past few years, more and more evidence has been created that it is possible to formally derive multiprograms with the aid of the (simple) theory of Owicki and Gries — see e.g. [Moe93, vdSom94, FG97] —. At some point, then, it becomes inevitable that one starts tackling more tricky algorithms, such as the famous Alternating Bit Protocol.

When carrying out this experiment, however, we decided to reduce the problem to its bare essentials — knowing that this should make the logical structure of the design much more transparent —. That is why, in our treatment, we abstracted from all details of the data stream to be transmitted, just identifying it with the sequence of natural numbers (number $i$ in this sequence standing for the $i^{th}$ message in the stream). And that is why for faulty channels we took the most rudimentary model that we could think of (viz. the autonomously operating component $*[\ p := x\ ]$ ), — a model that was heavily inspired by those used in [CM88] and [vdSn95].

We would never have thought of submitting this note for publication, had not the experiment turned out to be so extremely and unexpectedly simple and illuminating. Thanks to the simplifications it has become clear that the Alternating Bit Protocol is not a "tricky" algorithm at all, but a simple and obvious adaptation of the two-phase handshake protocol (i.e. of the simplest protocol for data transmission available): the adaptation consists in inserting faulty channels between the sending and the receiving component and in equipping the sender and receiver with facilities enabling them to regularly deposit messages into those channels. A further benefit of the simplifications that we have carried out is that there is no need any more to remember the algorithm in all its details, because, should the need arise, it can now be re-derived at any time and at any place.

## Acknowledgements

In Eindhoven, the members of the Eindhoven Tuesday Afternoon Club provided comments on every part of the design. We are particularly grateful to Frans W. van der Sommen, who conjectured the adequacy of our model of faulty channels. From outside the club, Johan L. Lukkien has been willing to discuss this model and this text with us. In Munich, Manfred Broy pointed out that we had to be more explicit about our fairness assumptions and Ursula Hinkel provided many constructive remarks concerning presentation; Michael Streichsbier did the LaTeX-ing. We are grateful to all these people

## References

[BSW69] K.A. Bartlett, R.A. Scantlebury, and P.T. Wilkinson. A note on reliable full-duplex transmission over half-duplex links. *Communications of the ACM*, 12(5): 260–261, 1969.

[Bro92] M. Broy. Functional Specification of Time Sensitive Communicating Systems. In Manfred Broy, editor, *Proceedings of the NATO Advanced Study Institute on Programming and Mathematical Method, held at Marktoberdorf 1990*, pages 325–367. Springer, Berlin Heidelberg, 1992.

[CM88] K. Mani Chandy and Jayadev Misra. *Parallel Program Design: A Foundation.* Addison-Wesley, Amsterdam, 1988.

[Dij82] Edsger W. Dijkstra. A Personal Summary of the Gries-Owicki Theory. In *Selected Writings on Computing: A Personal Perspective.* Springer-Verlag, New York, 1982.

[DS90] Edsger W. Dijkstra and Carel S. Scholten. *Predicate Calculus and Program Semantics.* Springer-Verlag, New York, 1990.

[FG97] W.H.J. Feijen and A.J.M. van Gasteren. On a Method for the Formal Design of Multiprograms. In Manfred Broy and Birgit Schieder, editors, *Proceedings of the NATO Advanced Study Institute on Mathematical Methods in Program Development, held at Marktoberdorf 1996*, pages 53–82. Springer-Verlag, Berlin Heidelberg, 1997.

[Hoa69] C.A.R. Hoare. An Axiomatic Basis for Computer Programming. *Communications of the ACM*, 12(10): 576–580 and 583, October 1969.

[Hoa78] C.A.R. Hoare. Communicating Sequential Processes. *Communications of the ACM*, 21(8): 666–677, 1978.

[Mar81] A.J. Martin. An Axiomatic Definition of Synchronization Primitives. *Acta Informatica*, 16: 219–235, 1981.

[Mar85] A.J. Martin. The probe: an addition to communication primitives. *Information Processing Letters*, 20: 125–130 and 21: 107, 1985.

[Mil89] Robin Milner. *Communication and Concurrency.* Prentice-Hall International, UK, 1989.

[Moe93] Perry D. Moerland. Exercises in Multiprogramming. Computing Science Notes 93/07, Department of Computing Science, Eindhoven University of Technology, 1993.

[OG76] S. Owicki and D. Gries. An Axiomatic Proof Technique for Parallel Programs I. *Acta Informatica*, 6: 319–340, 1976.

[Schn97] F.B. Schneider. *On Concurrent Programming.* Graduate Texts in Computer Science. Springer, 1997.

[vdSom94] F.W. van der Sommen. Multiprogram Derivations. Master's Thesis, Department of Computing Science, Eindhoven University of Technology, 1994.

[vdSn95] Jan L.A. van de Snepscheut. The Sliding-Window Protocol Revisited. *Formal Aspects of Computing*, 7: 3–17, 1995.

# A Set-Theoretic Model for Real-Time Specification and Reasoning

C. J. Fidge[1], I. J. Hayes[1,2], A. P. Martin[1], and A. K. Wabenhorst[1]

[1] Software Verification Research Centre, and
[2] Department of Computer Science and Electrical Engineering,
The University of Queensland, Queensland 4072, Australia
cjf@it.uq.edu.au ianh@csee.uq.edu.au
apm@ecs.soton.ac.uk akw@it.uq.edu.au

**Abstract.** Timed-trace formalisms have emerged as a powerful method for specifying and reasoning about concurrent real-time systems. We present a simple variant which builds methodically on set theory, and is thus suitable for use by programmers with little formal methods experience.

## 1 Introduction

Following an intensive period of research, formal methods for modelling real-time systems are now starting to mature. One of the most successful approaches has been to model real-time systems via time-varying functions—this accords with the way dynamic behaviour of time-dependent processes is modelled in the physical sciences. Prominent examples include the *Duration Calculus* [20], the *Temporal Agent Model* [15], and the *timed refinement calculus* [9]. Despite many superficial differences, these languages offer similar capabilities and collectively form part of the family of 'timed trace' formalisms.

Our overall goal is to address the dual challenge of making formal methods accessible to practising computer programmers, and of devising practical tools to support the application of formal methods in software engineering. Although successful in their own right, the timed-trace formalisms are intimidating for programmers who have little formal methods experience. Furthermore, they require unconventional reasoning methods, so it is not immediately clear how to upgrade existing tools to support them.

In this paper we present a timed-trace formalism that builds methodically on set theory. It borrows the best features of the above-named formalisms, yet introduces as few new operators as possible. The approach is compatible with the popular Z specification notation [17] so that programmers already familiar with Z will be able to learn it quickly, and so that tools that support Z-like languages can be upgraded to support the notation. (The timed-trace formalisms already do have Z-based definitions [4, 5, 1] and the Duration Calculus's reasoning methods have been implemented in a theorem prover [16], but the outcomes are discouragingly complex.)

The timed-trace formalisms each consist of two parts, a mathematical notation for specifying and reasoning about requirements on timed traces [6, 5], and a refinement formalism for structuring specifications and developing designs and programs [8, 15]. Here we consider the former only. Section 2 defines our notation, Section 3 summarises some of its laws, and Section 4 presents a small example.

## 2 A Mathematical Notation for Timed-Trace Predicates

In earlier work, Millerchip et al. defined a simple set-theoretic notation for concisely expressing properties of time intervals and used it to undertake a substantial case study [11]. Duddy et al. then expanded this definition with operators for accessing interval endpoints [5]. Elsewhere, the Duration Calculus [6], Temporal Agent Model [15], and their predecessors [12], showed how a 'chop' operator can form the basis of an effective real-time modelling and reasoning capability. Here we build on these previous methods by combining Millerchip et al.'s interval definitions with a chop operator. We use Z-like mathematical notation throughout.

### 2.1 Time

Let the absolute time domain $\mathbb{T}$ be continuous, as modelled by the real numbers $\mathbb{R}$ [7, 20]. (We assume the availability of real numbers in Z [19].)

**Definition 1 (Time)**

$$\mathbb{T} == \mathbb{R}$$

□

A common alternative is to use the non-negative reals $\mathbb{R}_+$, with time 0 taken to be the moment at which we start observing the system [13]. The definitions below work equally well with this type.

Another alternative is to assume a discrete time, represented by the integers or natural numbers. This is often suggested for digital systems [6]. However we note that such systems are merely a special case. They can be modelled as continuous systems, with a real-valued time domain, in which values change only at whole multiples of some *sampling period* [3].

### 2.2 Time Intervals

Time intervals are represented as the set of all times between some infimum $a$ and supremum $z$ [11].

**Definition 2 (Time intervals)** *The left-open, right-closed interval between values a (exclusive) and z (inclusive), both of type* $\mathbb{T}$*, is defined as*

$$(a \ldots z] == \{t : \mathbb{T} \mid a < t \leqslant z\}.$$

*Similarly for left and right-open* $(a \ldots z)$*, left and right-closed* $[a \ldots z]$*, and left-closed, right-open* $[a \ldots z)$ *endpoint brackets.*

□

This is consistent with mathematical tradition for real intervals. Syntactically, we use special brackets and thus write '$(a \ldots z)$', rather than the usual '$(a, z)$', to avoid ambiguities between intervals and pairs.

Intervals defined in this way are all bounded. In the literature, unbounded intervals are often introduced by leaving one argument blank, or using the infinity symbol. For instance, the open interval from $a$ onwards may be written $(a, )$ or $(a, \infty)$, meaning $\{t : \mathbb{T} \mid a < t\}$. We could define equivalent notations here, but do not need to because we introduce operators below that allow unbounded properties to be expressed via unbounded unions of bounded intervals.

## 2.3 All Time Intervals

The set $\mathbb{I}$ of all (bounded) time intervals is defined as all non-empty sets of times constructable using the above interval brackets [5].

**Definition 3 (All time intervals)**

$$\begin{aligned}\mathbb{I} == & \{a, z : \mathbb{T} \mid a < z \bullet (a \ldots z)\} \cup \\ & \{a, z : \mathbb{T} \mid a < z \bullet [a \ldots z)\} \cup \\ & \{a, z : \mathbb{T} \mid a < z \bullet (a \ldots z]\} \cup \\ & \{a, z : \mathbb{T} \mid a \leqslant z \bullet [a \ldots z]\}\end{aligned}$$

□

The empty set is not a meaningful time interval. The shortest possible interval is a single point, denoted by a closed interval with identical endpoints. For instance, $[7 \ldots 7] = \{7\}$ is a single-point interval with duration zero. Note that $(7 \ldots 7)$ is *not* a valid interval, since it denotes the empty set.

## 2.4 Timed Traces

The central feature of the timed-trace formalisms is their use of functions from the time domain to model the dynamic behaviour of observable system properties [7, 13, 15].

**Definition 4 (Timed traces)** *Each variable v in a system, which may take on values from some type V, is modelled as a total function from the time domain to V:*

$$v : \mathbb{T} \rightarrow V.$$

□

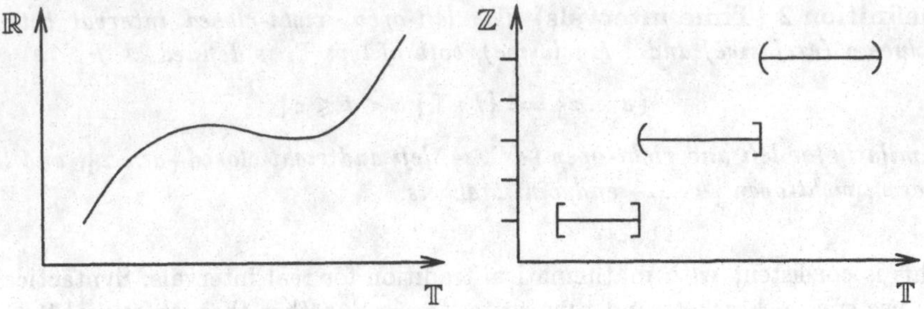


**Fig. 1.** Timed-trace graphs for continuous (left) and discrete (right) range types.

As shown in Figure 1, range type $V$ has a significant impact on the shape of the graph defined by such a trace. If $V$ is the real numbers, as is usually the case when modelling properties of the physical environment, the graph of $v$ may be a smooth curve. If $V$ is a discrete type, as is usually the case when modelling properties of digital hardware devices or computer program variables, the graph of $v$ will exhibit a stepped pattern.

We have assumed that all timed traces are *total* functions. Earlier, Duddy et al. went to considerable lengths to accommodate partial functions, so that times when the observed variable does not have *any* well-defined value could be modelled by omitting such times from the domain [5, 7]. Here we instead represent times when a variable is ill-defined through underspecification of the range at that time. This is slightly weaker than Duddy et al.'s approach, since a partial function can capture the notion that sampling $v$ when it is ill-defined may return a value outside type $V$. Nevertheless, this capability can be simulated when using total functions by adding a distinguished 'not-in-type' value $\perp$ to $V$. Similarly, the Duration Calculus uses a 'defined almost everywhere' assumption which allows for a countable number of points of undefinedness in any observation interval [20]. Again we use a simpler approach and just assume that variables are defined everywhere.

For example, given a continuous type $\mathit{Celsius} == \mathbb{R}$, and a discrete type $\mathit{Switch} ::= \mathit{On} \mid \mathit{Off}$, the temperature of a room may be declared as

$$\mathit{temp} : \mathbb{T} \rightarrow \mathit{Celsius} \,,$$

and the state of an air-conditioner as

$$\mathit{aircond} : \mathbb{T} \rightarrow \mathit{Switch} \,.$$

## 2.5 Avoiding References to Time

An important feature of the Duration and timed refinement calculi is their provision for *lifting* predicates on timed traces [4, 5]. This mechanism makes it possible to elide most explicit references to the time domain when accessing timed-trace variables, thus supporting concise specifications. For example, given a *Celsius*-valued constant *TooHot*, we may wish to write

$$TooHot < temp$$

to express the notion that the temperature is uncomfortably warm, even though *temp* is not a number, but a function. The lifting mechanisms account for this by creating overloaded versions of boolean and arithmetic operators to act on functions, as well as single values. Unfortunately, the general definitions of these lifting procedures are quite complex [4,5]. Therefore, we instead use the simple substitution-based approach advocated by Millerchip et al [11].

**Definition 5 (Time instantiation)** *Let P be an expression containing free occurrences of timed-trace variables $\tilde{v}$, and t be a value of type $\mathbb{T}$. Then we define instantiation of expression P at time t as*

$$P \mathbin{@} t == P[\tilde{v}(t)/\tilde{v}]\,,$$

*where $P[\tilde{v}(t)/\tilde{v}]$ is expression P with any free occurrence 'v' of a timed-trace variable from $\tilde{v}$,* which is not dereferenced, *replaced by 'v(t)'. Appropriate renaming may be needed if t occurs bound in P.*
□

In effect, this is a context-sensitive generalisation of the standard notion of syntactic substitution, relying on knowledge of which identifiers have been declared as timed traces. Care must be taken to recognise *implicit* dereferencing of timed-trace variables via, for example, relational image brackets, domain restriction and exclusion operators, integration and differentiation operators, and so on.

For example,

$$(TooHot < temp) \mathbin{@} 3 = TooHot < temp(3)\,.$$

On the right, *temp* has been explicitly dereferenced by 3 because it was declared as a timed trace, but not dereferenced. Non-timed-trace constant *TooHot* is unchanged.

This special form of substitution is the only operator we introduce that differs substantially from the Z specification language.

## 2.6 Sets of Time Intervals

We can now introduce our principal specification modelling tool, brackets for defining the set of all time intervals during which some predicate is (everywhere) true [11]. We also use the opportunity to introduce notations for features of the intervals themselves, specifically their infimum $\alpha$, supromum $\omega$, and duration $\delta$. For instance, given a positive $\mathbb{T}$-valued constant *TooLong*, we may wish to write

$$TooHot < temp \land TooLong \leqslant \delta$$

to express the notion that the temperature has been too high for too long a period.

Sets of time intervals are expressed by special brackets as follows.

**Definition 6 (Sets of time intervals)** *Given a predicate $P$, containing free occurrences of timed-trace variables $\tilde{v}$, we define all left-open, right-closed intervals during which $P$ is true as*

$$(P] == \{\alpha, \omega : \mathbb{T} \mid \alpha < \omega \wedge (\forall \tau : (\alpha \ldots \omega] \bullet P[\omega - \alpha / \delta] \mathbin{@} \tau) \bullet (\alpha \ldots \omega]\}.$$

*Similarly for left and right-open $(P)$, left-closed, right-open $[P)$, and, with the condition $\alpha \leqslant \omega$, left and right-closed $[P]$ brackets.*

□

In other words, these brackets return all intervals with infimum $\alpha$ and supremem $\omega$ during which predicate $P$ is true at every time $\tau$ in the interval. (We assume $\tau$ does not occur in $P$.) If $P$ does not hold over any such interval the empty set is returned. Syntactically, the brackets overload the time interval brackets introduced in Section 2.2, but are distinguished by the absence of the '...' separator.

The time-instantiation operator @ is used in Definition 6 so that $P$ may contain non-dereferenced occurrences of timed-trace variables. Furthermore, our definition allows times $\alpha$ and $\omega$ to appear free in $P$—they are bound to the infimum and supremum of the interval, respectively. A similar, but considerably more complicated, capability is achieved in the Duration and timed refinement calculi by lifting terms with respect to intervals, rather than times, and allowing functions on the *interval* domain to appear in $P$ [5, 4].

Duration $\delta$ is supported by Definition 6 as a shorthand for the difference between the infimum and supremum. Its occurrences in $P$ are syntactically replaced by expression $\omega - \alpha$. The $\delta$ notation is not fundamental, however the need to refer to the duration of an interval occurs so frequently that it is worth including this redundancy. In the Duration Calculus the much-used *length* operator $\ell$ serves the same role [13].

For example,

$$\begin{aligned} &(\mathit{TooHot} < \mathit{temp} \wedge \mathit{TooLong} \leqslant \delta) \\ &= \{\alpha, \omega : \mathbb{T} \mid \alpha < \omega \wedge (\forall \tau : (\alpha \ldots \omega) \bullet \mathit{TooHot} < \mathit{temp}(\tau) \wedge \\ &\qquad \mathit{TooLong} \leqslant \omega - \alpha) \bullet (\alpha \ldots \omega)\} \end{aligned}$$

defines the set of all open intervals during which the temperature is too high for too long.

In use, the brackets defined above appear similar to the $\lceil P \rceil$ brackets used by the Duration Calculus [20]. However, $\lceil P \rceil$ denotes not a set of intervals, but a *formula* which must be interpreted in the context of a particular interval [6]. Also, we have a slightly stronger notion of equivalence. In the Duration Calculus $\lceil P \rceil = \lceil Q \rceil$ tells us that properties $P$ and $Q$ hold for the same duration within each fixed interval, whereas in our notation $(P) = (Q)$ says that $P$ and $Q$ are both true everywhere on the same (open) intervals. We allow values to be observed at all points, and make a distinction between open and closed endpoints. The Duration Calculus's 'almost everywhere' assumption means that values may not be observable on some points, and, because it is concerned only with comparing interval lengths, the Duration Calculus treats endpoint closure as unimportant.

## 2.7 Unspecified Endpoints

So far we have made endpoints explicit, since this is consistent with mathematical convention for describing intervals. In writing specifications, however, which may involve a degree of deliberate underspecification, we sometimes do not care whether endpoints are open or closed. Interval set brackets that allow for either an open or closed endpoint are defined trivially.

**Definition 7 (Unspecified endpoints)** *Given a predicate $P$, the set of all right-open intervals during which $P$ is true is defined as*

$$\llbracket P) == [P) \cup (P) .$$

*Similarly for sets of right-closed $\llbracket P]$, left-open $(P \rrbracket$, and left-closed $[P \rrbracket$ intervals. Sets of intervals where neither endpoint is specified are defined as*

$$\llbracket P \rrbracket == (P) \cup [P] \cup (P] \cup [P) .$$

□

In practice, specific endpoint brackets are typically used for properties which are fixed in absolute time—in such situations knowing whether the endpoint is included or not can be significant. Unspecified endpoint brackets are usually used for relating system properties where the particular times at which they occur is unimportant. The style of specification promoted by the Duration Calculus also reminds us that endpoint closure is irrelevant for properties dependent on interval lengths only.

## 2.8 Operators on Sets of Intervals

Since properties are expressed as sets of time intervals, conventional set operators can be used for manipulating them. However, an extra, frequently-needed capability is an operator for connecting intervals end-to-end, in order to support reasoning about sequences of behaviours [12, 20, 15]. (In interval logics this concept is called "chop" because it divides a temporal property into two subintervals [12].) Let $\mathbb{P}$ denote powerset.

**Definition 8 (Concatenation)** *Concatenation of intervals from two sets is defined via the binary operator ';'.*

$$\_ ; \_ : \mathbb{P}\mathbb{I} \times \mathbb{P}\mathbb{I} \to \mathbb{P}\mathbb{I}$$

$$\begin{aligned} &\forall X, Y : \mathbb{P}\mathbb{I} \bullet \\ &\quad X ; Y = \{x : X;\ y : Y;\ z : \mathbb{I} \mid z = x \cup y \\ &\qquad\qquad \wedge (\forall t_1 : x;\ t_2 : y \bullet t_1 < t_2) \bullet z\} \end{aligned}$$

□

In other words, an interval $x$ from the left-hand set can be joined to an interval $y$ from the right-hand set, to form a new interval $z$, if $x$ occurs strictly before $y$, and the two intervals meet *exactly*, with no overlap or gap [5]. Allowing a point of overlap [12] would prevent us from using this operator to mark those times when a predicate changes between true and false. Alternatively, allowing an undefined point between the intervals [11] would be inconsistent with our use of total functions. Importantly, whenever two intervals are joined in this way, the supremum of the left-hand interval *equals* the infimum of the right-hand one.

For example, a requirement that the air-conditioner is on at the end of any open interval where the temperature has been excessive for too long can be expressed by the following Z predicate.

$$\llparenthesis \mathit{TooHot} < \mathit{temp} \land \mathit{TooLong} \leqslant \delta \rrparenthesis \subseteq \llparenthesis \mathrm{true} ]\!] \,;\, [\![ \mathit{aircond} = \mathit{On} \rrparenthesis$$

Notice the use of unspecified brackets so that we are not troubled by the endpoints used by the concatenation operator to join the intervals. Either an open-closed or closed-open concatenation is allowed. In this way concatenation can be made insensitive to endpoints. (Since the '$\mathit{aircond} = \mathit{On}$' interval is open on the right, it must have a non-zero duration, regardless of its left-hand endpoint.)

Many other useful operators for manipulating intervals could be defined, but are not fundamental. For instance, a prominent feature of the timed refinement calculus, missing from our notation, is the concept of *maximal interval covers* [11, 5]. There '$\llparenthesis\!| P \rrparenthesis$' is used to define those intervals which are maximal on the left with respect to $P$. That is, they begin at the moment $P$ first *became* true, and thus cannot be extended any further left. However we observe that specifications relying on this operator can always be equivalently expressed using concatenation, albeit more verbosely, using the '$\llparenthesis \neg P ]\!] ; \llparenthesis P \rrparenthesis$' approach frequently found in Duration Calculus specifications to mark moments when some property changes from false to true or vice versa [20].

## 3 Laws

In this section we present a selection of laws applicable to reasoning about the above specification notation. Of course, we inherit all the usual properties of set theory [2] for reasoning about both time intervals and sets of intervals. Below we introduce laws for reasoning about interval brackets and the concatenation operator. In doing so, we adapt some of the well-established laws defined for interval logic and the Duration Calculus [14, 6].

### 3.1 Properties of Sets of Time Intervals

The following laws show how logical expressions relate to interval set brackets. Let $P$, $Q$ and $R$ be predicates containing (possibly non-dereferenced) occurrences of timed-trace variables $\tilde{v}$. Unless otherwise stated, they may also contain free occurrences of $\alpha$, $\omega$ and $\delta$.

The first law tells us how predicates and sets of intervals are related.

**Law 1 (Monotonicity)** *If, for all $\alpha$, $\omega$, $\delta$ and $\tau$ of type $\mathbb{T}$, where $\delta = \omega - \alpha$ and $\alpha \leqslant \tau \leqslant \omega$, it is the case that*

$$P @ \tau \Rightarrow Q @ \tau ,$$

*then*

$$⦃P⦄ \subseteq ⦃Q⦄ .$$

□

From Law 1 and properties of the subset operator we can derive many other useful laws. For instance, if it is always the case that $P @ \tau \Leftrightarrow Q @ \tau$ then we may conclude $⦃P⦄ = ⦃Q⦄$. Also, thanks to the transitivity of the subset relation [2, p. 22], we gain an especially useful property. If $⦃P⦄ \subseteq ⦃Q⦄$, then for a predicate $P'$, *stronger* than $P$, we can conclude $⦃P'⦄ \subseteq ⦃Q⦄$. Similarly, for a predicate $Q'$, *weaker* than $Q$, we can conclude $⦃P⦄ \subseteq ⦃Q'⦄$.

For generality, Law 1 used unspecified endpoint brackets. In this, and other laws below, we also implicitly assume *specialisations* for specific endpoints via set difference [2, p. 23]. For instance, if $⦃P⦄ \subseteq ⦃Q⦄$ then we may also conclude $(P⦄ \subseteq (Q⦄$, by subtracting all left-closed intervals from both sides, and so on.

We can identify two extreme cases of interval specification.

**Law 2 (True and false)**

$$⦃true⦄ = \mathbb{I}$$
$$⦃false⦄ = \varnothing$$

□

Thus we can express the notion that some property $P$ is true in any interval by stating $⦃P⦄ = \mathbb{I}$. We also observe that if a property is true everywhere it is false nowhere: $⦃P⦄ = \mathbb{I} \Leftrightarrow ⦃\neg P⦄ = \varnothing$.

Further laws show how other logic and set operators relate. For instance, conjunction and intersection interact in an obvious way.

**Law 3 (And)**

$$⦃P⦄ \cap ⦃Q⦄ = ⦃P \wedge Q⦄$$

□

From Law 3 and the definition of subset [2, p. 21], we gain another useful property. If $⦃P \wedge Q⦄ \subseteq ⦃R⦄$, then we may conclude $⦃P \wedge Q⦄ \subseteq ⦃Q \wedge R⦄$, thus allowing predicates on the left to be used on the right.

The relationship between disjunction and union is weaker, however.

**Law 4 (Or)**

$$⦃P⦄ \cup ⦃Q⦄ \subseteq ⦃P \vee Q⦄$$

□

To see the cause of the asymmetry consider a situation where $P$ is true throughout interval $\lceil 1 \ldots 10 \rceil$, but at no other times, and $Q$ is similarly true everywhere in $\lceil 5 \ldots 15 \rceil$ only. In this case, interval $\lceil 3 \ldots 14 \rceil$ is a member of the right-hand side of Law 4 but not the left, so we cannot strengthen the inequality.

Another asymmetric relationship holds between negation and set difference.

**Law 5 (Not)**

$$[\![\neg P]\!] \subseteq \mathbb{I} \setminus [\![P]\!]$$

□

To illustrate the asymmetry consider the situation where $P$ is false at all times except time 1. In this case, interval $(0 \ldots 2)$ is a member of the right-hand side above, but not the left.

## 3.2 Properties of Concatenation

The following laws show how concatenation interacts with other set operators. Let $S$, $T$, $U$ and $V$ be sets of time intervals, i.e., elements of type $\mathbb{P}\mathbb{I}$.

From Definition 8 we can derive the following fundamental laws [14, p. 41].

**Law 6 (Concatenation monotonicity)** *If*

$$S \subseteq S' \ \ \textit{and} \ \ T \subseteq T',$$

*then*

$$S \,;\, T \subseteq S' \,;\, T'.$$

□

**Law 7 (Concatenation associativity)**

$$(S \,;\, T) \,;\, U = S \,;\, (T \,;\, U)$$

□

Definition 8 also tells us that the empty set of intervals acts as the zero of the concatenation operator. It thus serves the same role as formula '*false*' in the Duration Calculus [14, p. 41].

**Law 8 (Concatenation zero)**

$$S \,;\, \varnothing = \varnothing \,;\, S = \varnothing$$

□

Concatenation distributes over union [14, p. 41].

**Law 9 (Concatenate union)**

$$(S \cup T) ; U = (S ; U) \cup (T ; U)$$
$$S ; (T \cup U) = (S ; T) \cup (S ; U)$$

□

The equivalent law for intersection is weaker, however.

**Law 10 (Concatenate intersection)**

$$(S \cap T) ; U \subseteq (S ; U) \cap (T ; U)$$
$$S ; (T \cap U) \subseteq (S ; T) \cap (S ; U)$$

□

Ravn suggests the following example to illustrate the asymmetry [14, p. 42]:

$$((\llparenthesis \delta = 1 \rrparenthesis \cap \llparenthesis \delta < 1 \rrparenthesis) ; [\text{true}\rrparenthesis \not\supseteq (\llparenthesis \delta = 1 \rrparenthesis ; [\text{true}\rrparenthesis) \cap (\llparenthesis \delta < 1 \rrparenthesis ; [\text{true}\rrparenthesis) .$$

We can easily find intervals to satisfy the right-hand side. However, because $\llparenthesis \delta = 1 \rrparenthesis \cap \llparenthesis \delta < 1 \rrparenthesis = \varnothing$, due to the contradictory requirements on the duration, the left-hand side is empty.

A symmetric law for distributing concatenation over intersection can be provided for intervals of fixed length, however [14, pp. 41–2].

**Law 11 (Concatenate fixed intersection)** *If $r$ is a non-negative value of type $\mathbb{T}$, then*

$$((S \cap \llbracket \delta = r \rrparenthesis) ; T) \cap ((U \cap \llbracket \delta = r \rrparenthesis) ; V) = (S \cap U \cap \llbracket \delta = r \rrparenthesis) ; (T \cap V)$$

*and*

$$(S ; (U \cap \llparenthesis \delta = r \rrbracket)) \cap (T ; (V \cap \llparenthesis \delta = r \rrbracket)) = (S \cap T) ; (U \cap V \cap \llparenthesis \delta = r \rrbracket) .$$

*Similarly in the first case with the $\llbracket \cdot\cdot \rrparenthesis$ brackets replaced by $\llbracket \cdot\cdot ]$, and in the second case with the $\llparenthesis \cdot\cdot \rrbracket$ brackets replaced by $[ \cdot\cdot \rrbracket$.*

□

The restriction on $\delta$ serves to fix the lengths of the intervals so that the two concatenations on the left occur at the same time. A specific endpoint is needed where the concatenations occur to ensure that the two pairs of intervals are joined with the same open-closed or closed-open combination.

Other useful properties of concatenation also rely on the lengths of intervals. An interval can be composed of two subintervals, provided that it does not have zero duration [14, p. 45].

**Law 12 (Concatenate property)** *If $\alpha$, $\omega$ and $\delta$ do not occur free in $P$, then*

$$\llbracket P \wedge 0 < \delta \rrbracket = \llbracket P \rrbracket ; \llbracket P \rrbracket .$$

□

In specialisations of this law where the intervals on the left have open endpoints, and hence non-zero duration, we can omit the condition on $\delta$ and just state $\lparen P \rrbracket = \lparen P \rrbracket\,;\, \llbracket P \rrbracket$, and so on. Law 12 restricts the appearance of $\alpha$, $\omega$ and $\delta$ in predicate $P$ because, in general, the *same* time-dependent predicate cannot appear on both sides of the concatenation operator. For instance, it is clear that $\llbracket \delta = 6 \rrbracket$ is not equal to $\llbracket \delta = 6 \rrbracket\,;\, \llbracket \delta = 6 \rrbracket$.

A variant of Law 12 shows how concatenation relates to duration [14, p. 44].

**Law 13 (Concatenate duration)** *If $\alpha$, $\omega$ and $\delta$ do not occur free in $P$, and $r$ and $s$ are non-negative values of type $\mathbb{T}$, where* $r > 0$ or $s > 0$, *then*

$$\llbracket P \wedge \delta = r + s \rrbracket = \llbracket P \wedge \delta = r \rrbracket\,;\, \llbracket P \wedge \delta = s \rrbracket\,.$$

□

# 4 Example

As a concrete example we present a proof that a specified property is achieved via a periodic design. This is a common situation in embedded real-time devices that repeatedly sample some value, process it, and output the result.

## 4.1 Specifications

Consider the specification of a speedometer. Its input consists of a voltage $v$, proportional to the velocity of the vehicle, produced by an axle-mounted sensor. The required output is an estimate $s$ of the vehicle's speed. We assume the system is calibrated so that a satisfactory value for $s$ is calculated easily by multiplying $v$ by some constant $M$.

| $M : \mathbb{R}_+$ [Multiplier for estimating speed from voltage]

We consider the value of output $s$ to be acceptable if it differs from $v * M$ by no more than some error $E$.

| $E : \mathbb{R}_+$ [Acceptable error magnitude]

To describe the times when speed $s$ has an acceptable value, we introduce an auxiliary, $\{0, 1\}$-valued 'good-speed' function $g$, which equals 1 only when speed $s$ is within the acceptable range. Let $\mathbb{D}$ denote the set of differentiable real-to-real functions, i.e., continuous functions with graphs for which a unique tangent exists at all points [18, pp. 32–3]. Let $\mathbb{S}$ be the set of integrable real-to-real functions, i.e., those that exhibit bounded piecewise continuity [18, p. 182]. Boundedness means that there is some finite constant greater than the magnitude of the function at all points. Piecewise continuity requires that any interval can be partitioned into a finite sequence of nonoverlapping open subintervals over each of which the function is continuous. For some number $a$ and non-negative number $b$, let $a \pm b == \{c : \mathbb{R} \mid a - b \leqslant c \leqslant a + b\}$.

*InputOutput*

$v : \mathbb{D}$ [Input voltage]
$s : \mathbb{T} \to \mathbb{R}$ [Output speed]
$g : \mathbb{S} \cap (\mathbb{T} \to \{0,1\})$ [Auxiliary good-speed function]

---

$[\![g = 1 \Leftrightarrow s \in v * M \pm E]\!] = \mathbb{I}$

In other words, in all time intervals, $g$ equals 1 if and only if speed $s$ stays within the acceptable error bounds.

Since it would be unreasonable to expect the system to produce acceptable values at *all* times, we merely require that in any observation interval of length at least $I$, that there will be acceptable outputs for some proportion $P$ of the time.

$I : \mathbb{T}$ [Minimum observation interval]
$P : \mathbb{R}$ [Acceptable proportion of good output times]

---

$0 < I$
$0 < P < 1$

The system is required to produce good outputs only after starting time 0, to allow for initialisation activities. The overall requirement is then expressed as follows. Let $\int_a^b f$ denote the integral of function $f$ between times $a$ and $b$ [18, p. 174].

*SpeedOk*

*InputOutput*

---

$\{\!\!\{0 \leqslant \alpha \wedge I \leqslant \delta\}\!\!\} \subseteq \{\!\!\{\delta * P \leqslant \int_\alpha^\omega g\}\!\!\}$

This exploits the fact that in intervals where function $g$ is everywhere equal 1, the integral of $g$ also equals the duration of the interval. The Duration Calculus makes extensive use of this property by making all predicates $\{0,1\}$-valued, so that integrals and durations are interchangeable [20].

To make a solution to this requirement feasible we need an assumption about the maximum acceleration of the vehicle, and hence worst-case rate of change of the voltage $v$. The magnitude of the voltage's rate of change is assumed to be no greater than some constant $R$.

$R : \mathbb{R}_+$ [Worst-case voltage rate of change]

The following assumption states that this is true in any interval after starting time 0. Let $f'$ denote the derivative of function $f$ [18, p. 33]. (This notation should not be confused with the priming convention used when expressing state-machine models in Z.)

*VoltageRate*

$v : \mathbb{D}$

---

$[\![0 \leqslant \alpha]\!] \subseteq [\![|v'| \leqslant R]\!]$

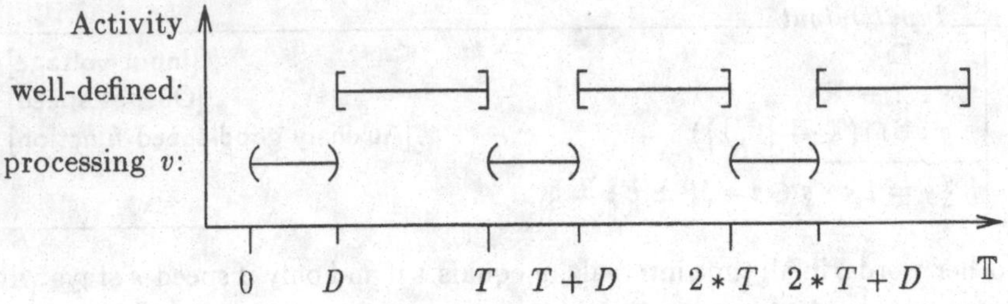


**Fig. 2.** Behaviour of periodic speedometer.

We now propose a solution to the above requirement in the form of a periodic behaviour, with period $T$ and relative deadline $D$.

| | |
|---|---|
| $T : \mathbb{T}$ | [Period] |
| $D : \mathbb{T}$ | [Deadline relative to start of period] |
| $0 < D < T$ | |

As shown in Figure 2, the intention is that the system will start processing voltage $v$ after the start of each period, producing a new value for speed $s$ by the deadline. In every period there is therefore an initial open interval of duration $D$ during which input $v$ will be sampled, and the value of output $s$ may be ill-defined. In the remainder of the period, output $s$ must equal $M$ times the sampled value of $v$. Thus, in the $n^{\text{th}}$ period, speed $s$ will be well-defined for at least the closed interval from time $n * T + D$ to $(n+1) * T$. Let $f(\!| S |\!)$ be the image of set $S$ through function $f$.

*Speedometer*
*InputOutput*

$$\{n : \mathbb{N} \bullet \lceil n * T + D \ldots (n+1) * T \rceil\} \subseteq \lceil s/M \in v(\!| \lfloor \alpha - D \ldots \alpha \rfloor |\!) \rceil$$

The set on the left consists of all closed intervals during which $s$ should be well defined. It can be expressed equivalently without the set-comprehension brackets as $\lceil \exists n : \mathbb{N} \bullet \alpha = n * T + D \wedge \delta = T - D \rceil$. On the right, acceptable values of $s$ in such intervals are defined, relative to values of $v$. Notice that interval $\lfloor \alpha - D \ldots \alpha \rfloor$, used to define the times when $v$ may be sampled, lies *outside* the enclosing $\lceil \cdot \rceil$ brackets. Such expressive power is one of the advantages of making the current infimum and supremum explicitly accessible.

### 4.2 Proof

Our task now is to show that the design expressed by *Speedometer* satisfies requirement *SpeedOk* in the presence of assumption *VoltageRate* [13]. In other words, we must prove that

$$(\mathit{Speedometer} \wedge \mathit{VoltageRate}) \Rightarrow \mathit{SpeedOk}\,.$$

As a first step we use the concatenation operator to extend the speedometer property to cover an entire period, not just the part after the deadline. To do this we prefix an open interval of duration $D$.

$$
\begin{array}{l}
\textit{Speedometer} \\
\Rightarrow \text{`by Law 6'} \\
\quad (\!\!-\delta = D-\!\!)\,;\{n:\mathbb{N}\bullet [\!\!-n*T+D\ldots(n+1)*T-\!\!]\} \\
\subseteq (\!\!-\delta = D-\!\!)\,;[\!\!-s/M \in v(\!|(\!\!-\alpha - D\ldots\alpha-\!\!)|\!)-\!\!] \\
\Leftrightarrow \text{`by Definition 8'} \\
\quad \{n:\mathbb{N}\bullet (\!\!-n*T\ldots(n+1)*T-\!\!]\} \\
\subseteq (\!\!-\delta = D-\!\!)\,;[\!\!-s/M \in v(\!|(\!\!-\alpha - D\ldots\alpha-\!\!)|\!)-\!\!]
\end{array} \qquad (1)
$$

Next, we wish to determine how the input voltage $v$ behaves during a period. To do so, we firstly observe that

$$\{n:\mathbb{N}\bullet (\!\!-n*T\ldots(n+1)*T-\!\!]\} \subseteq (\!\!-\delta = T-\!\!]\,, \qquad (2)$$

which tells us the length of each period, and

$$\{n:\mathbb{N}\bullet (\!\!-n*T\ldots(n+1)*T-\!\!]\} \subseteq [\![0 \leqslant \alpha]\!]\,, \qquad (3)$$

which tells us the earliest starting time of each period. The second of these can be combined with the overall assumption to determine how $v$ may change in a period.

$$
\begin{array}{l}
(3) \wedge \textit{VoltageRate} \\
\Rightarrow \text{`by transitivity of subset and set difference'} \\
\{n:\mathbb{N}\bullet (\!\!-n*T\ldots(n+1)*T-\!\!]\} \subseteq (\!\!-|v'| \leqslant R-\!\!]
\end{array} \qquad (4)
$$

This known rate-of-change can then be partitioned into the two subintervals of interest in each period.

$$
\begin{array}{l}
(2) \wedge (4) \Rightarrow \text{`by absorption [10, p. 71]'} \\
\qquad \{n:\mathbb{N}\bullet (\!\!-n*T\ldots(n+1)*T-\!\!]\} \\
\quad \subseteq (\!\!-|v'| \leqslant R-\!\!] \cap (\!\!-\delta = T-\!\!] \\
\quad = \text{`by Law 3'} \\
\qquad (\!\!-|v'| \leqslant R \wedge \delta = T-\!\!] \\
\quad = \text{`by Law 13'} \\
\qquad (\!\!-|v'| \leqslant R \wedge \delta = D-\!\!)\,;[\!\!-|v'| \leqslant R \wedge \delta = T - D-\!\!]
\end{array} \qquad (5)
$$

For each subinterval of each period, we now know how voltage $v$ behaves, and how speed $s$ is defined in terms of $v$. These two pieces of information are combined as follows.

$$
\begin{aligned}
&(1) \wedge (5) \Rightarrow \text{`by absorption'} \\
&\qquad \{n : \mathbb{N} \bullet (\!\lceil n * T \ldots (n+1) * T \rceil\!]\} \\
&\qquad \subseteq ((\!\lceil \delta = D \rceil\!) \,;\, [\!\lceil s/M \in v\llparenthesis (\!\lceil \alpha - D \ldots \alpha \rceil\!) \rrparenthesis \rceil\!]) \cap \\
&\qquad\quad ((\!\lceil |v'| \leqslant R \wedge \delta = D \rceil\!) \,;\, [\!\lceil |v'| \leqslant R \wedge \delta = T - D \rceil\!]) \\
&\qquad = \text{`by Law 3'} \\
&\qquad\quad ((\!\lceil \delta = D \rceil\!) \,;\, [\!\lceil s/M \in v\llparenthesis (\!\lceil \alpha - D \ldots \alpha \rceil\!) \rrparenthesis \rceil\!]) \cap \\
&\qquad\quad (((\!\lceil |v'| \leqslant R \rceil\!) \cap (\!\lceil \delta = D \rceil\!)) \,;\, [\!\lceil |v'| \leqslant R \wedge \delta = T - D \rceil\!]) \\
&\qquad = \text{`by Law 11'} \\
&\qquad\quad ((\!\lceil |v'| \leqslant R \rceil\!) \cap (\!\lceil \delta = D \rceil\!)) \,; \\
&\qquad\quad ([\!\lceil s/M \in v\llparenthesis (\!\lceil \alpha - D \ldots \alpha \rceil\!) \rrparenthesis \rceil\!] \cap [\!\lceil |v'| \leqslant R \wedge \delta = T - D \rceil\!]) \\
&\qquad = \text{`by Law 3'} \\
&\qquad\quad (\!\lceil |v'| \leqslant R \wedge \delta = D \rceil\!) \,; \\
&\qquad\quad [\!\lceil s/M \in v\llparenthesis (\!\lceil \alpha - D \ldots \alpha \rceil\!) \rrparenthesis \wedge |v'| \leqslant R \wedge \delta = T - D \rceil\!] \qquad (6)
\end{aligned}
$$

We then use the behaviour of voltage $v$, and the known durations, to determine how stale the value of $s$ may be. Firstly we express the rate of change as a property relative to the point where the concatenation occurs. Notice the use of expressions in which $v$ occurs in both dereferenced and non-dereferenced instances.

$$
\begin{aligned}
&(6) \Rightarrow \text{`by Laws 1 and 6'} \\
&\qquad \{n : \mathbb{N} \bullet (\!\lceil n * T \ldots (n+1) * T \rceil\!]\} \\
&\qquad \subseteq (\!\lceil v \in v(\omega) \pm D * R \wedge \delta = D \rceil\!) \,; \\
&\qquad\quad [\!\lceil s/M \in v\llparenthesis (\!\lceil \alpha - D \ldots \alpha \rceil\!) \rrparenthesis \wedge v(\alpha) \in v \pm (T - D) * R \rceil\!] \\
&\qquad = \text{`by Definition 6'} \\
&\qquad\quad (\!\lceil v\llparenthesis (\!\lceil \omega - D \ldots \omega \rceil\!) \rrparenthesis \subseteq v(\omega) \pm D * R \wedge \delta = D \rceil\!) \,; \\
&\qquad\quad [\!\lceil s/M \in v\llparenthesis (\!\lceil \alpha - D \ldots \alpha \rceil\!) \rrparenthesis \wedge v(\alpha) \in v \pm (T - D) * R \rceil\!] \qquad (7)
\end{aligned}
$$

We then exploit the fact that time $\omega$ for an interval on the left-hand side of a concatenation equals time $\alpha$ for the right-hand one.

$$
\begin{aligned}
&(7) \Rightarrow \text{`by Definition 8 and Laws 1 and 6'} \\
&\qquad \{n : \mathbb{N} \bullet (\!\lceil n * T \ldots (n+1) * T \rceil\!]\} \\
&\qquad \subseteq (\!\lceil \delta = D \rceil\!) \,;\, [\!\lceil s/M \in v(\alpha) \pm D * R \wedge v(\alpha) \in v \pm (T - D) * R \rceil\!] \\
&\qquad \subseteq \text{`by Laws 1 and 6'} \\
&\qquad\quad (\!\lceil \delta = D \rceil\!) \,;\, [\!\lceil s \in v * M \pm T * R * M \rceil\!] \qquad (8)
\end{aligned}
$$

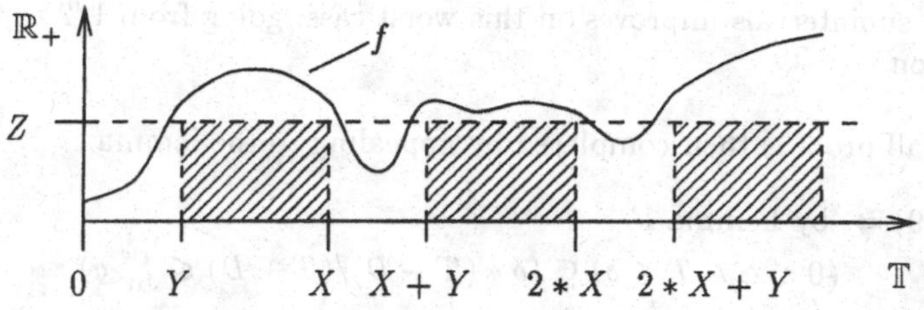


**Fig. 3.** A behaviour of function $f$ consistent with the condition for Lemma 1.

The definition of auxiliary function $g$ can be used to simplify this predicate.

$$
\begin{aligned}
&(8) \wedge \mathit{InputOutput} \\
&\Rightarrow \text{`by Laws 1 and 6'} \\
&\qquad \{n : \mathbb{N} \bullet \lceil n * T \mathbin{...} (n+1) * T \rceil\} \subseteq \lceil \delta = D \rceil \mathbin{;} \lceil g = 1 \rceil \qquad (9)
\end{aligned}
$$

This step introduces proviso $T * R * M \leqslant E$, relating the sampling period and input rate of change to the acceptable error. A smaller acceptable error will require a faster sampling rate, or a slower rate of change, as one would expect.

Having proven a property of the system relative to fixed intervals, we need a way of generalising its applicability. To do this we introduce the following lemma which uses integration to extend repetitive properties to longer intervals.

**Lemma 1.** *Let $f$ be a non-negative function of type $\mathbb{R} \rightarrow \mathbb{R}_+$. Also let $X$ and $Y$ be non-negative values of type $\mathbb{T}$, where $Y \leqslant X$, and $Z$ be a non-negative real value. If*

$$\{n : \mathbb{N} \bullet [\![ n * X \mathbin{...} (n+1) * X ]\!]\} \subseteq [\![ \delta = Y ]\!] \mathbin{;} [\![ Z \leqslant f ]\!]$$

*then*

$$[\![ 0 \leqslant \alpha \wedge X \leqslant \delta ]\!] \subseteq [\![ \delta * Z * (X - Y)/(X + Y) \leqslant \textstyle\int_\alpha^\omega f ]\!] .$$

□

In other words, we initially know that in every period, of duration $X$, the value of $f$ is always at least $Z$, except for an initial 'undefined' subinterval of duration $Y$. In Figure 3 we can see that $f$ does not enter the shaded areas. From this we wish to conclude that in any interval, of duration at least $X$, the integral of $f$ will be at least the duration times $Z * (X - Y)/(X + Y)$.

*Proof outline* Since $f$ equals at least $Z$ for at least $X - Y$ time units in any one period, term $Z * (X - Y)$ represents the *least* integral of $f$ in a period. Term $X + Y$ is the duration of a worst-case observation interval. This is one covering two undefined subintervals, but only one defined subinterval. The first such worst-case interval is $\lceil 0 \mathbin{...} X + Y \rceil$. In longer observation intervals, that similarly begin and end with whole undefined subintervals, the ratio of defined

to undefined subintervals improves on this worst case, going from 1/2 to 2/3 to 3/4, and so on.
□

The overall proof is then completed by appealing to the lemma.

$$\begin{aligned} & (9) \Rightarrow \text{`by Lemma 1'} \\ & \quad \lbrace 0 \leqslant \alpha \wedge T \leqslant \delta \rbrace \subseteq \lbrace \delta * (T - D)/(T + D) \leqslant \textstyle\int_\alpha^\omega g \rbrace \\ & \Rightarrow \text{`by definition'} \\ & \quad \mathit{SpeedOk} \end{aligned} \tag{10}$$

The last step introduces provisos $T \leqslant I$ and $P \leqslant (T - D)/(T + D)$. The first of these tells us that the period must be no greater than the minimum observation interval. The second relates the deadline and period to the proportion of time during which good values can be observed. As the value of deadline $D$ approaches the period $T$, it reduces the possible proportion $P$ of 'good' time. Again, this matches our intuitions, since a larger deadline relative to the period allows output $s$ to be ill-defined for longer intervals.

Thus, if we satisfy the provisos on the system constants introduced during steps (9) and (10), we can finally conclude that our proposed design does indeed satisfy its specification.

## 5 Conclusion

We have introduced a set-theoretic model for specification and reasoning using timed traces. It embodies many features found in previous real-time formalisms, yet requires little specialised mathematical knowledge, so should be amenable to industrial uptake by programmers with minimal formal methods experience, and representable in existing formal development tools. The definitions avoid the usual need for implicit expression lifting with respect to intervals by making the current interval endpoints explicitly accessible. At the time of writing we are extending the set of laws with rules for induction, and starting work on a theorem-prover representation of the model.

**Acknowledgements** We gratefully acknowledge our debt to unpublished work by Keith Duddy, Luke Everett, Brendan Mahony and Colin Millerchip for inspiring the overall approach adopted in this paper. We wish to thank Graeme Smith and the anonymous referees for their many helpful comments on this work. This research is funded by the Information Technology Division of the Defence Science and Technology Organisation.

## References

1. S. Atkinson and D. Scholefield. Transformational vs reactive refinement in real-time systems. *Information Processing Letters*, 55:201–210, 1995.

2. E. J. Billington, D. Donovan, B. D. Jones, S. Oates-Williams, and A. Street. *Discrete Mathematics: Logic and Structures.* Longman, 1990.
3. J. G. Bollinger and N. A. Duffie. *Computer Control of Machines and Processes.* Addison-Wesley, 1988.
4. S. M. Brien, M. Engel, He Jifeng, A. Ravn, and H. Rischel. Z description of duration calculus. Draft, Oxford University Computing Laboratory, August 1993.
5. K. Duddy, L. Everett, C. Millerchip, B. Mahony, and I. J. Hayes. Z-based notation for the specification of timing properties. Draft, Department of Computer Science, University of Queensland, June 1995.
6. M. R. Hansen and Zhou Chaochen. Duration calculus: Logical foundations. *Formal Aspects of Computing,* 9(3):283–330, 1997.
7. B. Mahony and I. J. Hayes. Using continuous real functions to model timed histories. In *Proc. Sixth Australian Software Engineering Conference (ASWEC'91),* Sydney, July 1991.
8. B. P. Mahony. The refinement calculus and data-flow processes. In *Proc. Second Australasian Refinement Workshop,* pages 1–28, Brisbane, September 1992.
9. B. P. Mahony and I. J. Hayes. A case-study in timed refinement: A mine pump. *IEEE Transactions on Software Engineering,* 18(9):817–826, September 1992.
10. A. Margaris. *First Order Mathematical Logic.* Blaisdell, 1967.
11. C. Millerchip, B. Mahony, and I. J. Hayes. The generic problem competition: A whole system specification of the boiler system. Software Verification Research Centre, University of Queensland, June 1993.
12. B. Moszkowski. *Executing Temporal Logic Programs.* Cambridge University Press, 1986.
13. E.-R. Olderog, A. P. Ravn, and J. U. Skakkebæk. Refining system requirements to program specifications. In C. Heitmeyer and D. Mandrioli, editors, *Formal Methods for Real-Time Computing,* volume 5 of *Trends in Software,* chapter 5, pages 107–134. Wiley, 1996.
14. A. P. Ravn. *Design of Embedded Real-Time Computing Systems.* PhD thesis, Department of Computer Science, Technical University of Denmark, 1995.
15. D. Scholefield, H. Zedan, and He Jifeng. A specification-oriented semantics for the refinement of real-time systems. *Theoretical Computer Science,* 131:219–241, 1994.
16. J. U. Skakkebæk. *A Verification Assistant for a Real-Time Logic.* PhD thesis, Department of Computer Science, Technical University of Denmark, 1994.
17. J. M. Spivey. *The Z Notation: A Reference Manual.* Prentice Hall International, 1989.
18. G. B. Thomas, Jr. *Calculus and Analytic Geometry.* Addison-Wesley, 4th edition, 1968.
19. S. H. Valentine. An algebraic introduction of real numbers into Z. In H. Habrias, editor, *7th International Conference on: Putting into practice methods and tools for information system design, Z Twenty Years On — What is its Future?,* Nantes, France, October 1995.
20. Zhou Chaochen. Duration calculi: An overview. In D. Bjorner, M. Broy, and I. Pottosin, editors, *Formal Methods in Programming and Their Applications,* volume 735 of *Lecture Notes in Computer Science,* pages 256–266. Springer-Verlag, 1993. Extended abstract.

# Polytypic Downwards Accumulations

Jeremy Gibbons

School of Computing and Mathematical Sciences,
Gipsy Lane, Headington,
Oxford Brookes University,
Oxford OX3 0BP, UK.
Email jgibbons@brookes.ac.uk.

**Abstract.** A *downwards accumulation* is a higher-order operation that distributes information downwards through a data structure, from the root towards the leaves. The concept was originally introduced in an ad hoc way for just a couple of kinds of tree. We generalize the concept to an arbitrary polynomial datatype; our generalization proceeds via the notion of a *path* in such a datatype.

## 1 Introduction

The notion of *scans* or *accumulations* on lists is well known, and has proved very fruitful for expressing and manipulating programs involving lists [5]. Gibbons [8, 9] generalized the notion of accumulation to various kinds of tree; that generalization too has proved fruitful, underlying the derivations of a number of tree algorithms, such as the parallel prefix algorithm for prefix sums [9], Reingold and Tilford's algorithm for drawing trees tidily [11], and algorithms for query evaluation in structured text [18].

There are two varieties of accumulation on lists, leftwards and rightwards. Leftwards accumulation labels every node of the list with some function of its *successors*—the tail segment starting at that node—thereby passing information from right to left along the list; rightwards accumulation labels every node with some function of its *predecessors*—the initial segment ending at that node—passing information from left to right. Similarly, there are two varieties of accumulation on trees, upwards and downwards. Upwards accumulation labels every node with some function of its *descendants*—the subtree rooted at that node—thereby passing information up the tree; downwards accumulation labels every node with some function of its *ancestors*—the path from the root to that node—passing information down the tree.

A flaw in the definitions of accumulations on trees from [8, 9] is that they were rather ad hoc. There is no formal relationship between accumulations on different kinds of tree, so each new kind of tree has to be considered from scratch. A recent trend in constructive algorithmics has been the development of theories of *generic* [1, 14] or *polytypic* [15] operations, parameterized by a datatype. (Another name for this kind of abstraction is *higher-order polymorphism.*) A generic program in this sense eliminates the unwanted ad-hockery. The categorical approach to datatypes popularized by Malcolm [16] is an early example of generic programming: it allows a single unified definition of operations such as map and fold, parameterized by the datatype concerned.

Bird *et al* [2] generalize upwards accumulation to an arbitrary polynomial datatype, unifying the previous ad hoc definitions. In this paper, we generalize downwards accumulation to an arbitrary polynomial datatype too. This is a more difficult problem: whereas the descendants of a node in a data structure (some kind of tree) form another data structure of the same type (another tree), the ancestors of a node are in general of a completely different type (a 'path').

Actually, Bird *et al* give a ***generic*** or ***parametric higher-order polymorphic*** definition of upwards accumulation, in the style of Hoogendijk and Backhouse, in the sense that their construction is based on ***semantic*** operations on the type functors involved. In contrast, the definition of downwards accumulation presented here is ***polytypic*** or ***ad-hoc higher-order polymorphic***, in the style of Jeuring, based on ***syntactic*** properties of the type functor inducing the datatype. This is a problem with our approach: a generic definition would arguably be more elegant, but it is an open question whether a generic definition of downwards accumulation is possible.

We conclude this introductory section with a summary of notation. The remainder of the paper is structured as follows. In Section 2 we recall the monotypic definitions of upwards and downwards accumulations on trees from [8, 9]. We briefly summarize the theory of datatypes in Section 3. In Section 4 we discuss Bird *et al*'s [2] generic definition of upwards accumulations. In Section 5 we develop a polytypic definition of paths in a datatype, which we use in Section 6 to give a polytypic definition of downwards accumulations. This simple definition is inefficient; in Section 7 we show how to make it efficient. Section 8 concludes.

### 1.1 Functions

The type judgement '$a :: A$' declares that value $a$ is of type $A$; the type $A \to B$ denotes the type of functions from $A$ to $B$. Function application is denoted by juxtaposition; the identity function is written $\mathsf{id}$, so that $\mathsf{id}\, a = a$ for every $a$. The unit type 1 has just one element; there is a unique total function $\mathsf{one} :: A \to 1$ for every type $A$.

### 1.2 The Pair Calculus

The functors $+$ and $\times$ denote disjoint sum and cartesian product respectively; $\times$ binds tighter than $+$. The product projections are fst and snd, and the product morphism $f \vartriangle g$ has type $A \to B \times C$ when $f :: A \to B$ and $g :: A \to C$; the sum morphism $f \triangledown g$ has type $A + B \to C$ when $f :: A \to C$ and $g :: B \to C$. We write '$\sum_{i=1}^{n} A_i$' and '$\prod_{i=1}^{n} A_i$' for generalized sum and product; the generalized sum injections are $\mathsf{inj}_i$ and the generalized sum morphism is $\triangledown_{i=1}^{n} f_i$.

# 2 Accumulations on Binary Trees

To provide motivation and intuition for what follows, we review here the 'monotypic' definitions of upwards and downwards accumulations on binary trees, as presented in [8, 9]. Bird *et al*'s generalization of upwards accumulation and our generalization of downwards accumulation, when specialized to the same kind of tree, reduce essentially to these monotypic definitions.

## 2.1 Homogeneous Binary Trees

We will use as an example the datatype of *homogeneous binary trees*, that is, trees with internal and external labels of the same type. In Haskell, these can be modelled by the type definition

```
data Tree a = Leaf a | Bin a (Tree a) (Tree a)
```

Thus, a tree is either a leaf with a label, or a node with a label and two subtrees.

Two higher-order operations on trees that we shall need in the following are a map and a fold. Again in Haskell, these are defined by

```
mapTree :: (a->b) -> Tree a -> Tree b
mapTree f (Leaf a) = Leaf (f a)
mapTree f (Bin a t u) = Bin (f a) (mapTree f t) (mapTree f u)

foldTree :: (a->b, a->b->b->b) -> Tree a -> b
foldTree (g,h) (Leaf a) = g a
foldTree (g,h) (Bin a t u) = h a (foldTree (g,h) t)
                                 (foldTree (g,h) u)
```

In fact, `mapTree` can be written as a fold:

```
mapTree f = foldTree (g,h) where
            g a = Leaf (f a)
            h a t u = Bin (f a) t u
```

or, shorter but more cryptically,

```
mapTree f = foldTree (Leaf . f, Bin . f)
```

A simpler example of a fold is the function `size`, which returns the size of (that is, the number of elements in) a tree:

```
size :: Tree a -> Int
size = foldTree (g,h) where g a = 1
                            h a m n = 1+m+n
```

## 2.2 Monotypic Upwards Accumulations

Upwards accumulations are defined in terms of the function `subtrees`, which labels every node with the subtree rooted at that node.

```
subtrees :: Tree a -> Tree (Tree a)
subtrees (Leaf a) = Leaf (Leaf a)
subtrees (Bin a t u) = Bin (Bin a t u) (subtrees t) (subtrees u)
```

Now upwards accumulation is simple to define: it is merely a fold mapped over the subtrees.

```
upTree :: (a->b, a->b->b->b) -> Tree a -> Tree b
upTree (g,h) = mapTree (foldTree (g,h)) . subtrees
```

For example, the function `sizes`, which labels every node with the number of descendants it has, is given by

```
sizes :: Tree a -> Tree Int
sizes = upTree (g,h) where g a = 1
                           h a m n = 1+m+n
```

Of course, this is a very inefficient definition: it does not capitalize on the fact that the folds of the children of a node can be used in computing the fold of the node itself. However, a simple application of *deforestation* [19], together with a little manipulation using the observation that

```
foldTree (g,h) = root . upTree (g,h)
```

where the function `root` returns the root label of a tree:

```
root :: Tree a -> a
root (Leaf a) = a
root (Bin a t u) = a
```

removes this inefficiency:

```
upTree (g,h) (Leaf a) = Leaf (g a)
upTree (g,h) (Bin a t u) = Bin (h a (root t') (root u')) t' u'
                           where t' = upTree (g,h) t
                                 u' = upTree (g,h) u
```

With this improved definition, computing `upTree (g,h)` takes essentially no longer than computing `foldTree (g,h)`.

## 2.3 Monotypic Downwards Accumulations

As noted earlier, downwards accumulations are more complicated than upwards accumulations because they involve another datatype. Consider the tree

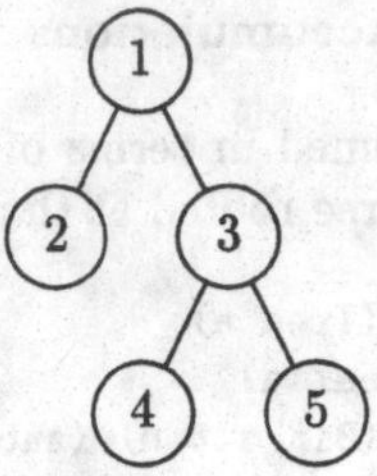

which is represented by the expression

```
Bin 1 (Leaf 2) (Bin 3 (Leaf 4) (Leaf 5))
```

Intuitively, the path from the root to a node of this tree is either a singleton, or consists of a label followed by a left or a right turn to another path. We therefore model paths by the datatype

```
data Path a = Single a | TurnL a (Path a) | TurnR a (Path a)
```

For example, the path to the node labelled 2 is `TurnL 1 (Single 2)`, and the path to the node labelled 4 is `TurnR 1 (TurnL 3 (Single 4))`.

Now, the function `paths` labels every node of the tree with the path from the root to that node. We have

```
paths :: Tree a -> Tree (Path a)
paths (Leaf a) = Leaf (Single a)
paths (Bin a t u) = Bin (Single a) (mapTree (TurnL a) (paths t))
                                   (mapTree (TurnR a) (paths u))
```

Downwards accumulation is a fold mapped over the paths, but this fold has to be a path fold. We therefore define the function `foldPath` by

```
foldPath :: (a->b, a->b->b, a->b->b) -> Path a -> b
foldPath (f,g,h) (Single a) = f a
foldPath (f,g,h) (TurnL a p) = g a (foldPath (f,g,h) p)
foldPath (f,g,h) (TurnR a p) = h a (foldPath (f,g,h) p)
```

For example, the function `pLength`, which returns the length of a path, is given by

```
pLength :: Path a -> Int
pLength = foldPath (f,g,g) where f a = 1
                                 g a n = 1+n
```

Now downwards accumulation can be defined simply by

```
daTree :: (a->b, a->b->b, a->b->b) -> Tree a -> Tree b
daTree (f,g,h) = mapTree (foldPath (f,g,h)) . paths
```

For example, the function `depths`, which labels every node of a tree with its depth, is simply

```
depths :: Tree a -> Tree Int
depths = daTree (f,g,g) where f a = 1
                              g a n = 1+n
```

### 2.4 Complications

The monotypic example given above is simplistic in three ways, apart from the very fact that it is monotypic and not polytypic.

The first simplification we made was to choose the datatype of homogeneous trees carefully, so that every node has a label at which to store the value computed by the accumulations. In general, not all nodes of a data structure possess such a label, so an accumulation will in general not return a data structure of the same type as its argument. Rather, Bird *et al* show how to define a *labelled variant* of a datatype, adding labels in all the right places, in a generic way. This construction is discussed in Section 4.2.

The second simplification is that we did not distinguish between the path to the node labelled 1 in the tree given above, and the path to the node labelled 1 in the singleton tree `Leaf 1`: the former path ends at an internal node of the original data structure, whereas the latter ends at an external node, although both contain the same 'data'. In fact, the datatype of paths that we construct in Section 5.1 will have two singleton constructors, one for paths ending at internal nodes and one for paths ending at external nodes:

```
data Path a = SingleI a | SingleE a | TurnL a (Path a) | TurnR a (Path a)
```

The third problem is that the function `paths` and downwards accumulation as defined above are inefficient, for the same reason that the first attempt at upwards accumulation was inefficient: we cannot afford the two maps over the children, but we can (sometimes) reuse the value computed at a parent in computing the values at the children. We address this problem in Section 7.

## 3 Datatypes

In this section, we briefly review the construction of polynomial datatypes, in the style of Malcolm [16]. Given a bifunctor $F$, the datatype $T$ is the type functor such that the type $T(A)$ is isomorphic to $F(A, T(A))$; the isomorphism is provided by the constructor $\mathsf{in}_F :: F(A, T(A)) \to T(A)$ and the destructor $\mathsf{out}_F :: T(A) \to F(A, T(A))$. We call $T(A)$ the *canonical fixpoint* of the functor $F(A, \_)$. A strict function $\phi :: F(A, B) \to B$ induces a fold $\mathsf{fold}_F\,\phi :: T(A) \to B$, and a function $\psi :: B \to F(A, B)$ induces an unfold $\mathsf{unfold}_F\,\psi :: B \to T(A)$.

**Example 1.** We will use the following datatypes as running examples throughout the paper.

1. Leaf-labelled binary trees are built from the functor $F(A, X) = A + X \times X$.

   ```
   data Ltree a  =  LeafT a | BinT (Ltree a) (Ltree a)
   ```

   The corresponding fold is

   ```
   foldT :: (Either a (b,b) -> b) -> Ltree a -> b
   foldT phi (LeafT a) = phi (Left a)
   foldT phi (BinT t u) = phi (Right (foldT phi t, foldT phi u))
   ```

For example, the function **sizeT**, which returns the size of a leaf-labelled binary tree, is a fold:

```
sizeT :: Ltree a -> Int
sizeT = foldT phiSizeT
phiSizeT (Left a) = 1
phiSizeT (Right (m,n)) = m+n
```

(We will use **phiSizeT** later.)

2. Branch-labelled binary trees are constructed from the functor $F(A, X) = 1 + A \times X \times X$:

```
data Btree a  =  Empty | BinB a (Btree a) (Btree a)
```

The corresponding fold is

```
foldB :: (Either () (a,b,b) -> b) -> Btree a -> b
foldB phi Empty = phi (Left ())
foldB phi (BinB a t u) =
  phi (Right (a, foldB phi t, foldB phi u))
```

The function **sizeB** is defined as follows:

```
sizeB :: Btree a -> Int
sizeB = foldB phiSizeB
phiSizeB (Left ()) = 0
phiSizeB (Right (a,m,n)) = 1+m+n
```

3. A funny kind of tree can be constructed from the functor $F(A, X) = \mathsf{Int} + A \times X + \mathsf{Bool} \times X \times X$:

```
data Ftree a = TipF Int | MonF a (Ftree a) |
               BinF Bool (Ftree a) (Ftree a)
```

A tree of type **Ftree a** is either a terminal node **TipF** with an integer label, a parent with a label of type **a** and a single child, or a parent with a boolean label and two children. The corresponding fold is

```
foldF :: (Either3 Int (a,b) (Bool,b,b) -> b) -> Ftree a -> b
foldF phi (TipF n) = phi (In1 n)
foldF phi (MonF a x) = phi (In2 (a, foldF phi x))
foldF phi (BinF b x y) = phi (In3 (b, foldF phi x, foldF phi y))
```

where

```
data Either3 a b c = In1 a | In2 b | In3 c
```

The function **sizeF** is defined as follows:

```
sizeF :: Ftree a -> Int
sizeF = foldF phiSizeF
phiSizeF :: Either3 Int (a,Int) (Bool,Int,Int) -> Int
phiSizeF (In1 n) = 0
phiSizeF (In2 (a,n)) = 1+n
phiSizeF (In3 (b,m,n)) = m+n
```

(It is not so obvious what the 'size' of such a bizarre species of tree should be. This definition simply counts the number of occurrences of the type parameter a, so that for example the rather large tree

```
BinF True (TipF 5) (BinF False (TipF 6) (TipF 7))
```

still has size 0. There are other reasonable definitions.)

□

# 4 Polytypic Upwards Accumulations

Bird *et al* [2] generalized upwards accumulations to an arbitrary polynomial datatype, giving ***polytypic upwards accumulations***. We summarize their construction here. It is related to, but not the same as, Meertens' generic definition of the 'predecessors' of a data structure [17]. This section serves partly as motivation and 'intuitive support', as upwards accumulations are simpler than downwards accumulations. More importantly, however, we will use part of their construction ourselves in Section 6.

## 4.1 The Essential Idea

As suggested in Section 2, an upwards accumulations on a tree is related to the subtrees of that tree; in general, an upwards accumulation on a data structure is related to the substructures of that data structure. A substructure of a structure is a subterm of the term representing that structure. We will define a function $\mathsf{subs}_F$, which generates a structure of substructures from a structure: a list of sublists from a list, a tree of subtrees from a tree, and so on.

Upwards accumulations are defined in terms of substructures. The upwards accumulation of a data structure consists of folding every substructure of that structure; in other words, an upwards accumulation is a fold mapped over the substructures.

The definitions in this section generalize those of Section 2.2.

## 4.2 Labelled Types

The function $\mathsf{subs}_F$ takes a data structure and returns another data structure, with every node 'labelled' with the corresponding substructure of the original data structure rooted at that node. Therefore, in general, the source and target types of $\mathsf{subs}_F$ will not be the same: the target type must have labels at every node, whereas the source type may not. For example, $\mathsf{subs}_F$ should take a leaf-labelled binary tree to a homogeneous binary tree of leaf-labelled binary trees. In particular, we want $\mathsf{subs}_F$ to take the leaf-labelled tree

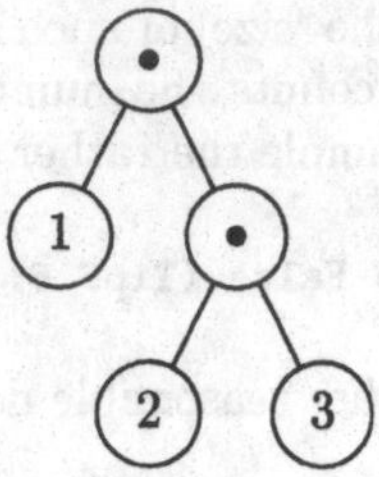

to the homogeneous binary tree of leaf-labelled binary trees

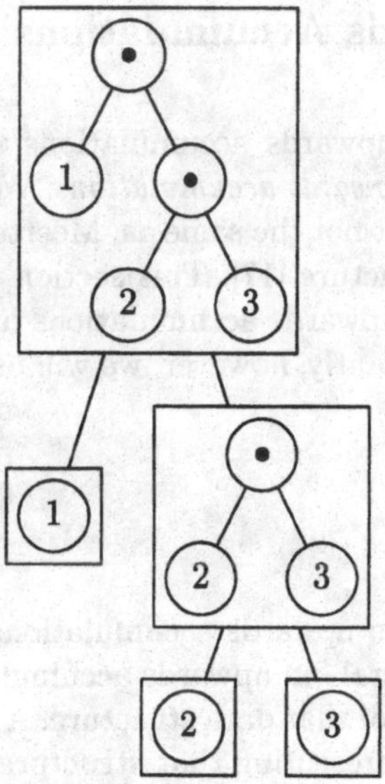

Bird *et al* call the datatype of homogeneous binary trees the *labelled variant* of the type of leaf-labelled binary trees, and give a general construction for it, as follows.

**Definition 2.** Given a datatype $T(A)$, the canonical fixpoint of a functor $F(A, \_)$, the corresponding labelled type $L(A)$ is the canonical fixpoint of the functor $G(A, \_)$, where $G$ is defined by $G(A, X) = A \times F(1, X)$. □

Informally, $F(1, X)$ is like $F(A, X)$, but with all the labels (of type $A$) removed; thus, using $A \times F(1, X)$ ensures that every node carries precisely one label.

**Example 3.**

1. The datatype of leaf-labelled binary trees is constructed from the functor $F(A, X) = A + X \times X$, so the functor $G$ is given by

$$\begin{aligned} G(A, X) &= A \times F(1, X) \\ &= A \times (1 + X \times X) \end{aligned}$$

This induces the labelled type of homogeneous binary trees, as desired:

```
data Htree a  =  ConsH a (Either () (Htree a,Htree a))
```

(This is isomorphic to the type Tree of Section 2.) The unfold for Htree is

```
unfoldH :: (b -> (a, Either () (b,b))) -> b -> Htree a
unfoldH phi b = f (phi b)
  where
    f (a, Left ()) = ConsH a (Left ())
    f (a, Right (b',b'')) = ConsH a (Right (unfoldH phi b',
                                            unfoldH phi b''))
```

2. The datatype of branch-labelled binary trees is constructed from the functor $F(A,X) = 1 + A \times X \times X$, so the functor $G$ is given by

$$\begin{aligned} G(A,X) &= A \times F(1,X) \\ &= A \times (1 + 1 \times X \times X) \\ &\approx A \times (1 + X \times X) \end{aligned}$$

and induces the labelled type of homogeneous binary trees, just as for leaf-labelled binary trees.

3. The datatype of homogeneous binary trees is constructed from the functor $F(A,X) = A \times (1 + X \times X)$, so the functor $G$ is given by

$$\begin{aligned} G(A,X) &= A \times F(1,X) \\ &= A \times (1 \times (1 + X \times X)) \\ &\approx A \times (1 + X \times X) \end{aligned}$$

and so homogeneous binary trees are their own labelled type. In general, if $G(A,X) = A \times F(1,X)$ then $A \times G(1,X) \approx G(A,X)$, that is, 'constructing the labelled variant' is an idempotent operation.

4. The datatype of funny trees is constructed from the functor $F(A,X) = \mathsf{Int} + A \times X + \mathsf{Bool} \times X \times X$, so the functor $G$ is given by

$$\begin{aligned} G(A,X) &= A \times F(1,X) \\ &= A \times (\mathsf{Int} + 1 \times X + \mathsf{Bool} \times X \times X) \\ &\approx A \times (\mathsf{Int} + X + \mathsf{Bool} \times X \times X) \end{aligned}$$

For want of a better name, we call the labelled variant so induced 'odd trees':

```
data Otree a =
  ConsO a (Either3 Int (Otree a) (Bool,Otree a,Otree a))
```

The corresponding unfold is

```
unfoldO :: (b -> (a, Either3 Int b (Bool,b,b))) -> b -> Otree a
unfoldO phi b = f (phi b)
  where
    f (a, In1 n)  = ConsO a (In1 n)
    f (a, In2 b') = ConsO a (In2 (unfoldO phi b'))
    f (a, In3 (bool,b',b''))
                  = ConsO a (In3 (bool, unfoldO phi b',
                                        unfoldO phi b''))
```

□

We define the functions root and kids on labelled types only, as follows.

**Definition 4.** The functions root :: $L(A) \to A$ and kids :: $L(A) \to F(1, L(A))$ are defined by

$$\mathsf{root} = \mathsf{fst} \circ \mathsf{out}_G$$
$$\mathsf{kids} = \mathsf{snd} \circ \mathsf{out}_G$$

(Remember that $G(A, X) = A \times F(1, X)$, so that $\mathsf{out}_G$ returns a pair of type $A \times F(1, L(A))$.) □

**Example 5.**

1. For homogeneous binary trees, we have

```
rootH :: Htree a -> a
rootH (ConsH a x) = a
```

2. For odd trees, we have

```
rootO :: Otree a -> a
rootO (ConsO a x) = a
```

□

### 4.3 Substructures

The function $\mathsf{subs}_F$ has type $T(A) \to L(T(A))$, where $T$ and $L$ are the original and labelled types, as defined above.

**Definition 6.** The function $\mathsf{subs}_F :: T(A) \to L(T(A))$ is given by

$$\mathsf{subs}_F = \mathsf{unfold}_G\,(\mathsf{id} \vartriangle (F(\mathsf{one}, \mathsf{id}) \circ \mathsf{out}_F))$$

□

Thus, the root of the substructures of a data structure $x$ is $x$ itself:

**Theorem 7.**

$$\mathsf{root} \circ \mathsf{subs}_F = \mathsf{id}$$

□

*Proof.* We have

$$
\begin{array}{ll}
 & \mathsf{root} \circ \mathsf{subs}_F \\
= & \quad \{ \mathsf{root};\ \mathsf{subs}_F \} \\
 & \mathsf{fst} \circ \mathsf{out}_G \circ \mathsf{unfold}_G\,(\mathsf{id} \vartriangle (F(\mathsf{one}, \mathsf{id}) \circ \mathsf{out}_F)) \\
= & \quad \{ \text{unfold} \} \\
 & \mathsf{fst} \circ G\,(\mathsf{id}, \mathsf{subs}_F) \circ (\mathsf{id} \vartriangle (F(\mathsf{one}, \mathsf{id}) \circ \mathsf{out}_F)) \\
= & \quad \{ \mathsf{fst} \circ G\,(f, g) = \mathsf{fst} \circ (f \times F(\mathsf{id}, g)) = f \circ \mathsf{fst} \} \\
 & \mathsf{fst} \circ (\mathsf{id} \vartriangle (F(\mathsf{one}, \mathsf{id}) \circ \mathsf{out}_F)) \\
= & \quad \{ \text{pairs} \} \\
 & \mathsf{id}
\end{array}
$$

□

Actually, Bird *et al* give an alternative definition of $\mathsf{subs}_F$ as a fold:

$$\mathsf{subs}_F = \mathsf{fold}_F\,(\mathsf{in}_G \circ (\mathsf{in}_F \circ F(\mathsf{id}, \mathsf{root})) \vartriangle F(\mathsf{one}, \mathsf{id}))$$

We claim that the definition in terms of an unfold is simpler and more natural. As a general observation, we believe that unfolds are under-appreciated, even amongst functional programming experts, who should be aficionados of higher-order operators [13]. On the other hand, it turns out that our definition as an unfold leads to an inefficient characterization of upwards accumulations, as we shall see shortly; in removing the inefficiency, we end up with exactly Bird *et al*'s definition. Nevertheless, it is better to start from the natural but inefficient characterization and derive from it the less natural but more efficient characterization.

**Example 8.**

1. For leaf-labelled binary trees, the corresponding labelled type is homogeneous binary trees, so `subsT` is defined in terms of `unfoldH`:

```
subsT :: Ltree a -> Htree (Ltree a)
subsT = unfoldH phi
  where phi (LeafT a) = (LeafT a, Left ())
        phi (BinT t u) = (BinT t u, Right (t, u))
```

2. For branch-labelled binary trees too, the labelled variant is homogeneous binary trees:

```
subsB :: Btree a -> Htree (Btree a)
subsB = unfoldH phi
  where phi Empty = (Empty, Left ())
        phi (BinB a t u) = (BinB a t u, Right (t, u))
```

3. For funny trees, the corresponding labelled type is odd trees, so we use `unfoldO`:

```
subsF :: Ftree a -> Otree (Ftree a)
subsF = unfoldO phi
  where phi (TipF n) = (TipF n, In1 n)
        phi (MonF a x) = (MonF a x, In2 x)
        phi (BinF b x y) = (BinF b x y, In3 (b, x, y))
```

□

## 4.4 Upwards Accumulations

Given $\mathsf{subs}_F$, upwards accumulation is easy to define: it is simply a fold mapped over the substructures.

**Definition 9.** Upwards accumulation $\mathsf{ua}_F :: (F(A, B) \to B) \to T(A) \to L(B)$ is defined by

$$\mathsf{ua}_F\,\phi = L\,(\mathsf{fold}_F\,\phi) \circ \mathsf{subs}_F$$

□

**Corollary 10.**

$$\mathsf{root} \circ \mathsf{ua}_F\, \phi = \mathsf{fold}_F\, \phi$$

*Proof.* Immediate from Theorem 7 and naturality of root:

$$\mathsf{root} \circ L\, f = f \circ \mathsf{root}$$

□

Of course, taken literally, Definition 9 makes rather an inefficient program: it does not exploit the fact that the results of folding the children of a node can be reused in folding the substructure rooted at the node itself. This efficiency can be removed by *deforestation* [19], one corollary of which states that an unfold followed by a fold can be fused into a single recursion:

**Lemma 11 (Deforestation).** *Suppose* $h = \mathsf{fold}_F\, \psi \circ \mathsf{unfold}_F\, \phi$. *Then*

$$h = \psi \circ F\,(\mathsf{id}, h) \circ \phi$$

□

*Proof.* We have

$$\begin{array}{ll} & h \\ = & \{\ \text{hypothesis}\ \} \\ & \mathsf{fold}_F\, \psi \circ \mathsf{unfold}_F\, \phi \\ = & \{\ \mathsf{in}_F \circ \mathsf{out}_F = \mathsf{id}\ \} \\ & \mathsf{fold}_F\, \psi \circ \mathsf{in}_F \circ \mathsf{out}_F \circ \mathsf{unfold}_F\, \phi \\ = & \{\ \text{folds, unfolds}\ \} \\ & \psi \circ F\,(\mathsf{id}, \mathsf{fold}_F\, \psi) \circ F\,(\mathsf{id}, \mathsf{unfold}_F\, \phi) \circ \phi \\ = & \{\ \text{functors}\ \} \\ & \psi \circ F\,(\mathsf{id}, \mathsf{fold}_F\, \psi \circ \mathsf{unfold}_F\, \phi) \circ \phi \\ = & \{\ \text{hypothesis}\ \} \\ & \psi \circ F\,(\mathsf{id}, h) \circ \phi \end{array}$$

□

Now we can write $\mathsf{ua}_F\, \phi$ as a fold:

**Theorem 12.**

$$\mathsf{ua}_F\, \phi = \mathsf{fold}_F\, (\mathsf{in}_G \circ (\phi \circ F(\mathsf{id}, \mathsf{root})) \vartriangle F(\mathsf{one}, \mathsf{id}))$$

□

*Proof.* To write $\mathsf{ua}_F\, \phi$ as a fold $\mathsf{fold}_F\, \psi$, we have to construct a $\psi$ for which

$$\mathsf{ua}_F\, \phi \circ \mathsf{in}_F = \psi \circ F(\mathsf{id}, \mathsf{ua}_F\, \phi)$$

We have

$$
\begin{aligned}
& \mathsf{ua}_F\,\phi \circ \mathsf{in}_F \\
= \quad & \{\ \mathsf{ua}\ \} \\
& L\,(\mathsf{fold}_F\,\phi) \circ \mathsf{subs}_F \circ \mathsf{in}_F \\
= \quad & \{\ L \text{ as a fold; } \mathsf{subs}_F\ \} \\
& \mathsf{fold}_G\,(\mathsf{in}_G \circ G\,(\mathsf{fold}_F\,\phi, \mathsf{id})) \circ \mathsf{unfold}_G\,(\mathsf{id} \vartriangle (F(\mathsf{one}, \mathsf{id}) \circ \mathsf{out}_F)) \circ \mathsf{in}_F \\
= \quad & \{\ \text{Lemma 11}\ \} \\
& \mathsf{in}_G \circ G\,(\mathsf{fold}_F\,\phi, \mathsf{id}) \circ G\,(\mathsf{id}, \mathsf{ua}_F\,\phi) \circ (\mathsf{id} \vartriangle (F\,(\mathsf{one}, \mathsf{id}) \circ \mathsf{out}_F)) \circ \mathsf{in}_F \\
= \quad & \{\ \text{functors}\ \} \\
& \mathsf{in}_G \circ G\,(\mathsf{fold}_F\,\phi, \mathsf{ua}_F\,\phi) \circ (\mathsf{id} \vartriangle (F\,(\mathsf{one}, \mathsf{id}) \circ \mathsf{out}_F)) \circ \mathsf{in}_F \\
= \quad & \{\ \text{pairs; } \mathsf{out}_F \circ \mathsf{in}_F = \mathsf{id}\ \} \\
& \mathsf{in}_G \circ G\,(\mathsf{fold}_F\,\phi, \mathsf{ua}_F\,\phi) \circ (\mathsf{in}_F \vartriangle F\,(\mathsf{one}, \mathsf{id})) \\
= \quad & \{\ G\ \} \\
& \mathsf{in}_G \circ (\mathsf{fold}_F\,\phi \times F\,(\mathsf{id}, \mathsf{ua}_F\,\phi)) \circ (\mathsf{in}_F \vartriangle F\,(\mathsf{one}, \mathsf{id})) \\
= \quad & \{\ \text{pairs}\ \} \\
& \mathsf{in}_G \circ ((\mathsf{fold}_F\,\phi \circ \mathsf{in}_F) \vartriangle (F\,(\mathsf{id}, \mathsf{ua}_F\,\phi) \circ F\,(\mathsf{one}, \mathsf{id}))) \\
= \quad & \{\ \text{fold; functors}\ \} \\
& \mathsf{in}_G \circ ((\phi \circ F\,(\mathsf{id}, \mathsf{fold}_F\,\phi)) \vartriangle F\,(\mathsf{one}, \mathsf{ua}_F\,\phi)) \\
= \quad & \{\ \text{Corollary 10; pairs}\ \} \\
& \mathsf{in}_G \circ ((\phi \circ F\,(\mathsf{id}, \mathsf{root})) \vartriangle F\,(\mathsf{one}, \mathsf{id})) \circ F\,(\mathsf{id}, \mathsf{ua}_F\,\phi)
\end{aligned}
$$

and so

$$\psi = \mathsf{in}_G \circ ((\phi \circ F\,(\mathsf{id}, \mathsf{root})) \vartriangle F\,(\mathsf{one}, \mathsf{id}))$$

□

With this improved characterization, the upwards accumulation $\mathsf{ua}_F\,\phi$ takes asymptotically no longer to compute than the ordinary fold $\mathsf{fold}_F\,\phi$.

**Example 13.**

1. For leaf-labelled binary trees, we have

```
uaT :: (Either a (b,b) -> b) -> Ltree a -> Htree b
uaT phi = foldT psi
  where
    psi (Left a) = ConsH (phi (Left a)) (Left ())
    psi (Right (t,u))
       = ConsH (phi (Right (rootH t, rootH u))) (Right (t,u))
```

For example, the function `sizesT` labels every node of a leaf-labelled binary tree with the size of the subtree rooted there:

```
sizesT :: Ltree a -> Htree Int
sizesT = uaT phiSizeT
```

where `phiSizeT` is as defined in Example 1.

2. For branch-labelled binary trees, we have

```
uaB :: (Either () (a,b,b) -> b) -> Btree a -> Htree b
uaB phi = foldB psi
  where
    psi (Left ()) = ConsH (phi (Left ())) (Left ())
    psi (Right (a,t,u))
      = ConsH (phi (Right (a, rootH t, rootH u))) (Right (t,u))
```

The corresponding 'sizes' function on these trees is

```
sizesB :: Btree a -> Htree Int
sizesB = uaB phiSizeB
```

3. For funny trees we have

```
uaF :: (Either3 Int (a,b) (Bool,b,b) -> b) -> Ftree a -> Otree b
uaF phi = foldF psi
  where
    psi (In1 n) = ConsO (phi (In1 n)) (In1 n)
    psi (In2 (a,x)) = ConsO (phi (In2 (a, rootO x))) (In2 x)
    psi (In3 (b,x,y))
      = ConsO (phi (In3 (b, rootO x, rootO y))) (In3 (b,x,y))
```

The corresponding 'sizes' function is

```
sizesF :: Ftree a -> Otree Int
sizesF = uaF phiSizeF
```

□

# 5 Polytypic Paths

As described in the previous section, an *upwards* accumulation on a data structure is a fold mapped over the substructures of that structure; for example, upwards accumulation on a binary tree is a tree fold mapped over the subtrees of that tree. A substructure of a data structure of type $T(A)$ is itself of type $T(A)$. Thus, an upwards accumulation replaces every node of a data structure with some function of the descendants of that node. In contrast, a *downwards* accumulation replaces every node of a data structure with some function of the *ancestors* of that node; a downwards accumulation is a fold mapped over the *paths*, where the path to a node in a data structure represents the ancestors of that node. A path in a data structure is in general of a completely different type from the data structure itself; in particular, a path is necessarily a linear structure, each parent having a single child, whereas the data structure itself may be non-linear. So the first thing we need in developing a polytypic definition of downwards accumulations is a polytypic notion of paths.

## 5.1 Linearization

Recall that a datatype $T(A)$ is built as the canonical fixpoint of the functor $F(A, \_)$ for some bifunctor $F$. For example, leaf-labelled binary trees are built from the functor $F$ given by

$$F(A,X) = A + X \times X$$

The first step in constructing the appropriate notion of paths is to partition $F$ into a sum of products; that is, we suppose that

$$F(A,X) = \sum_{i=1}^{n} F_i(A,X)$$

where each $F_i$ is a product of literals:

$$F_i(A,X) = \prod_{j=1}^{m_i} F_{i,j}(A,X)$$

where each $F_{i,j}(A,X)$ is either $A$, $X$ or some constant type such as *Int* or *Bool*. For example, for leaf-labelled binary trees, $n = 2$, $m_1 = 1$ and $m_2 = 2$, and we have

$$\begin{aligned}
F(A,X) &= F_1(A,X) + F_2(A,X)\\
F_1(A,X) &= F_{1,1}(A,X)\\
F_{1,1}(A,X) &= A\\
F_2(A,X) &= F_{2,1}(A,X) \times F_{2,2}(A,X)\\
F_{2,1}(A,X) &= X\\
F_{2,2}(A,X) &= X
\end{aligned}$$

Now, the $F_i(A,X)$ will in general be 'non-linear', in the sense that they may contain no $X$ or more than one $X$. Paths, on the other hand, are inherently linear. Therefore, for each bifunctor $F_i$ we construct a multi-functor $F_i'$, linear in each argument except perhaps the first; informally, this multi-functor will be a $(k_i + 1)$-functor where $F_i(A,X)$ contains $k_i$ occurrences of $X$. For example, for leaf-labelled binary trees we have $k_1 = 0$ (because $F_1(A,X) = A$ contains no occurrences of $X$) and $k_2 = 2$ (because $F_2(A,X) = X \times X$ contains two occurrences of $X$), and so we define

$$\begin{aligned}
F_1'(A) &= A\\
F_2'(A,X_1,X_2) &= X_1 \times X_2
\end{aligned}$$

Notice that $F_1'(A) = F_1(A,X)$ and $F_2'(A,X,X) = F_2(A,X)$.

We formalize the above as follows.

**Definition 14.** A functor $H$ is ***linear*** if it distributes over sum:

$$H(X+Y) \approx H(X) + H(Y)$$

□

In particular, a functor constructing a product of literals is linear when its argument is used precisely once, and so neither $H(X) = A$ nor $H(X) = X \times X$ are linear.

For each bifunctor $F_i$, we construct the linearization (a $(k_i + 1)$-functor $F_i'$) of the functor $F_i(A, \_)$, as follows. Abusing the term, we call $F_i'$ 'the linearization of $F_i$' instead of 'the linearization of $F_i(A, \_)$'.

**Definition 15.** Suppose bifunctor $H$ is a product of literals. A ***linearization*** of $H$ is a $(k + 1)$-functor $H'$ such that:

- $H'$ is a generalization of $H$:

$$H'(A, \underbrace{X, \ldots, X}_{k \text{ times}}) = H(A, X)$$

- $H'$ is linear in all arguments, except perhaps the first:

$$\begin{aligned} & H'(A, X_1, \ldots, X_{j-1}, Y + Z, X_{j+1}, \ldots, X_k) \\ & \qquad \approx H'(A, X_1, \ldots, X_{j-1}, Y, X_{j+1}, \ldots, X_k) + \\ & \qquad\quad\; H'(A, X_1, \ldots, X_{j-1}, Z, X_{j+1}, \ldots, X_k) \end{aligned}$$

  for $1 \leq j \leq k$.

□

Note that the linearization is unique up to isomorphism: for $H(A, X) = X \times X$, for example, there are just the two isomorphic linearizations

$$H'(A, X_1, X_2) = X_1 \times X_2 \approx X_2 \times X_1$$

In particular, all linearizations of a functor have the same number of arguments.

To define downwards accumulations in Section 6 we must choose a linearization $F_i'$ of each $F_i$, but to construct the path type in Section 5.2 we need only the $k_i$. We call the number $k_i$ the 'degree of branching' of the bifunctor $F_i$:

**Definition 16.** Suppose bifunctor $H$ is a product of literals. Then the ***degree of branching*** of $H$ is the natural number $k$ such that linearizations of $H$ are $(k + 1)$-functors. □

### 5.2 The Path Type

Consider the leaf-labelled binary tree illustrated on page 9:

```
BinT (LeafT 1) (BinT (LeafT 2) (LeafT 3))
```

This data structure has five nodes, the paths to each being as follows:

- the path to the root node is just 'empty';
- the path to the other internal node is 'right, then empty';
- the path to the node labelled 1 is 'left, then the label 1';
- the path to the node labelled 2 is 'right, then left, then the label 2';
- the path to the node labelled 3 is 'right, then right, then the label 3'.

Thus, a path is essentially a kind of cons list, and that is how we define the type of paths below.

The last element of a path is the label at some node of the data structure. That is, the last element of a path is constructed from information of type $F(A,1)$. For example, for leaf-labelled binary trees $F(A,1) = A+1$; the last element of the path to the root node of our example tree is 'nothing', and the last element of the path to the node labelled 1 is 'the label 1'.

Every other element of a path corresponds to an internal node of some variant $i$ of the data structure, and is constructed from the label at that node together with a record of which direction to go next. That is, internal elements of a path are constructed from information of type $\sum_{i=1}^{n}(F_i(A,1) \times \{1,\ldots,k_i\})$ (or equivalently, $\sum_{i=1}^{n}\sum_{j=1}^{k_i} F_i(A,1)$) and another path. For example, for leaf-labelled binary trees,

$$\sum_{i=1}^{n}\sum_{j=1}^{k_i} F_i(A,1) = F_2(A,1) + F_2(A,1) \approx 1+1$$

and the internal elements of paths are all either 'left turn' or 'right turn', followed by another path.

We therefore construct the path type as follows.

**Definition 17.** The path type $P(A)$ is the canonical fixpoint of the bifunctor $H$ defined by

$$H(A,X) = F(A,1) + \sum_{i=1}^{n}\sum_{j=1}^{k_i}(F_i(A,1) \times X)$$

We will use a constructor **endp** for the last element of a path, and a family of constructors $\mathsf{consp}_{i,j}$ for $1 \le i \le n$ and $1 \le j \le k_i$ for the other elements:

$$\begin{aligned} \mathsf{endp} &:: F(A,1) \to P(A) \\ \mathsf{consp}_{i,j} &:: F_i(A,1) \times P(A) \to P(A) \end{aligned}$$

(Note that the path constructed by **endp** need not be 'empty'; it could be a 'singleton'.) □

**Example 18.**

1. For leaf-labelled binary trees we have

$$\begin{aligned} H(A,X) &= (A + 1 \times 1) + (1 \times 1 \times X + 1 \times 1 \times X) \\ &\approx (1+A) + X + X \end{aligned}$$

Therefore paths for leaf-labelled binary trees could be modelled in Haskell by

```
data PathT a = EndpT (Either () a) |
               ConspT1 (PathT a) | ConspT2 (PathT a)
```

The fold operator for this type is

```
foldPT :: (Either () a -> b, b -> b, b -> b) -> PathT a -> b
foldPT (f,g,h) (EndpT a) = f a
foldPT (f,g,h) (ConspT1 x) = g (foldPT (f,g,h) x)
foldPT (f,g,h) (ConspT2 x) = h (foldPT (f,g,h) x)
```

For example, the 'length' function on this kind of path is

```
lengthT = foldPT phiLengthT
phiLengthT = (const 1, (1+), (1+))
```

2. For branch-labelled binary trees, we have

$$
\begin{aligned}
F(A,X) &= 1 + A \times X \times X \\
F_1(A,X) &= 1 \\
F_2(A,X) &= A \times X \times X \\
k_1 &= 0 \\
k_2 &= 2 \\
H(A,X) &= (1 + A \times 1 \times 1) + (A \times 1 \times 1 \times X + A \times 1 \times 1 \times X) \\
&\approx (1 + A) + A \times X + A \times X
\end{aligned}
$$

This could be modelled in Haskell by

```
data PathB a = EndpB (Either () a) |
               ConspB1 a (PathB a) | ConspB2 a (PathB a)
```

with a fold operator

```
foldPB :: (Either () a -> b, a->b->b, a->b->b) ->
          PathB a -> b
foldPB (f,g,h) (EndpB a) = f a
foldPB (f,g,h) (ConspB1 a x) = g a (foldPB (f,g,h) x)
foldPB (f,g,h) (ConspB2 a x) = h a (foldPB (f,g,h) x)
```

The corresponding length function is

```
lengthB = foldPB phiLengthB
phiLengthB = (const 1, inc, inc) where inc a n = 1+n
```

3. For funny trees, we have

$$
\begin{aligned}
F(A,X) &= \mathsf{Int} + A \times X + \mathsf{Bool} \times X \times X \\
F_1(A,X) &= \mathsf{Int} \\
F_2(A,X) &= A \times X \\
F_3(A,X) &= \mathsf{Bool} \times X \times X \\
k_1 &= 0 \\
k_2 &= 1 \\
k_3 &= 2 \\
H(A,X) &= (\mathsf{Int} + A \times 1 + \mathsf{Bool} \times 1 \times 1) + A \times 1 \times X + \\
&\qquad \mathsf{Bool} \times 1 \times 1 \times X + \mathsf{Bool} \times 1 \times 1 \times X \\
&\approx (\mathsf{Int} + A + \mathsf{Bool}) + A \times X + \mathsf{Bool} \times X + \mathsf{Bool} \times X
\end{aligned}
$$

This could be modelled in Haskell by

```
data PathF a = EndpF (Either3 Int a Bool) |
               ConspF1 a (PathF a) |
               ConspF2 Bool (PathF a) | ConspF3 Bool (PathF a)
```

with a fold operator

```
foldPF :: (Either3 Int a Bool -> b, a->b->b, Bool->b->b, Bool->b->b) ->
          PathF a -> b
foldPF (f,g,h,j) (EndpF a) = f a
foldPF (f,g,h,j) (ConspF1 a x) = g a (foldPF (f,g,h,j) x)
foldPF (f,g,h,j) (ConspF2 b x) = h b (foldPF (f,g,h,j) x)
foldPF (f,g,h,j) (ConspF3 b x) = j b (foldPF (f,g,h,j) x)
```

The corresponding length function is

```
lengthF = foldPF phiLengthF
phiLengthF = (const 1, inc, inc, inc) where inc a n = 1+n
```

(As with `sizeF`, what constitutes the 'right' definition of `lengthF` is a moot point. This definition counts the number of nodes in a path, regardless of whether or not those nodes carry a label of the type parameter a.)

□

## 6 Polytypic Downwards Accumulations

Having a polytypic notion of paths, we are now able to make a polytypic definition of downwards accumulations. The essential ingredient is a polytypic function $\mathsf{paths}_F$, analogous to the function $\mathsf{subs}_F$ from Section 4; the difference is that $\mathsf{paths}_F$ labels every node of a data structure with its *ancestors*, a path, whereas $\mathsf{subs}_F$ labels every node with its *descendants*, another instance of the same datatype. Thus, the function $\mathsf{paths}_F$ has type $T(A) \to L(P(A))$.

The simplest characterization of $\mathsf{paths}_F$ is as a fold. The root of $\mathsf{paths}_F\, t$ is a trivial path to the root node of $t$. This is constructed by applying $\mathsf{endp}$ to something of type $F(A, 1)$; the latter can be obtained by discarding the children after deconstructing $t$:

$$\mathsf{root}\,(\mathsf{paths}_F\, t) = \mathsf{endp}\,(F(\mathsf{id}, \mathsf{one})\,(\mathsf{out}_F\, t))$$

The children of $\mathsf{paths}_F\, t$ are a little more tricky. We need to construct a value of type $F(1, L(P(A)))$. Suppose that $t$ is of variant $i$, that is, $t = \mathsf{in}_i\, x$ where $x :: F_i(A, T(A))$. Now, $x$ will contain $k_i$ children, where $k_i$ is the degree of branching of $F_i$. In order for $\mathsf{paths}_F$ to be a fold, the answer has to be composed from $F_i(\mathsf{id}, \mathsf{paths}_F)\, x$ somehow. However, each path in child $j$ (where $1 \le j \le k_i$) must be prefixed with the root label of $t$ and a record that from the root one must choose child $j$ first; in other words, each path in child $j$ should be subjected to $\mathsf{consp}_{i,j}\,a$ where $a = F_i(\mathsf{id},\mathsf{one})\,x$. Therefore, we have, with $F_i'$ the chosen linearization of $F_i$,

$$\begin{aligned}&\mathsf{kids}\,(\mathsf{paths}_F\,(\mathsf{in}_i\,x))\\ &\quad = \mathsf{inj}_i\,(F_i'(\mathsf{one}, L\,(\mathsf{consp}_{i,1}\,a), \ldots, L\,(\mathsf{consp}_{i,k_i}\,a))\,(F_i(\mathsf{id},\mathsf{paths}_F)\,x))\end{aligned}$$

where $a = F_i(\mathsf{id},\mathsf{one})\,x$. We therefore define $\mathsf{paths}_F$ as follows.

**Definition 19.**

$$\mathsf{paths}_F = \mathsf{fold}_F\,\phi$$

where

$$\begin{aligned}\phi\,(\mathsf{in}_i\,x) = \mathsf{in}_G\,(&\mathsf{endp}\,(F(\mathsf{id},\mathsf{one})\,(\mathsf{in}_i\,x)),\\ &\mathsf{inj}_i\,(F_i'(\mathsf{one}, L\,(\mathsf{consp}_{i,1}\,a), \ldots, L\,(\mathsf{consp}_{i,k_i}\,a))\,x))\\ &\text{where } a = F_i(\mathsf{id},\mathsf{one})\,x\end{aligned}$$

□

Unfortunately, the maps $L$ in this characterization make it very inefficient. To get around this problem, we must define $\mathsf{paths}_F$ using $\mathsf{unfold}$. However, we cannot simply define

$$\mathsf{paths}_F = \mathsf{unfold}_G\,\theta$$

for some suitable $\theta$. Consider a substructure $y$ of a data structure $x$. The substructure of $\mathsf{paths}_F\,x$ that corresponds to $y$ is not constructed from $y$ alone; it depends also on the ancestors of $y$ in $x$. Therefore, we have to use an extra *accumulating parameter* [3] to carry this contextual information about the ancestors. In fact, we will define

$$\mathsf{paths}_F\,t = \mathsf{unfold}_G\,\theta\,(t,\mathsf{id})$$

where the extra accumulating parameter is a function of type $P(A) \to P(A)$. Intuitively, this accumulating parameter is mapped over the paths:

$$\mathsf{unfold}_G\,\theta\,(t,f) = L\,f\,(\mathsf{paths}_F\,t)$$

From this characterization it is possible to calculate the appropriate definition of $\theta$.

**Theorem 20.**

$$\mathsf{paths}_F\,t = \mathsf{unfold}_G\,\theta\,(t,\mathsf{id})$$

where

$$\begin{aligned}\theta\,(\mathsf{in}_i\,x, f) &= (f\,(\mathsf{endp}\,(\mathsf{inj}_i\,a)), \mathsf{inj}_i\,(F_i'(\mathsf{one}, g_1, \ldots, g_{k_i})\,x))\\ &\qquad\text{where } a = F_i\,(\mathsf{id},\mathsf{one})\,x\\ &\qquad\phantom{\text{where }} g_j\,y = (y, f \circ \mathsf{consp}_{i,j}\,a)\end{aligned}$$

where $k_i$ is the degree of branching of $F_i$. □

**Example 21.**

1. For leaf-labelled binary trees, we have

```
pathsT :: Ltree a -> Htree (PathT a)
pathsT t = unfoldH theta (t,id)
  where
    theta (LeafT a, f) = (f (EndpT (Right a)), Left ())
    theta (BinT t u, f) =
      (f (EndpT (Left ())), Right ((t,f.ConspT1), (u,f.ConspT2)))
```

2. For branch-labelled binary trees, we have

```
pathsB :: Btree a -> Htree (PathB a)
pathsB t = unfoldH theta (t,id)
  where
    theta (Empty, f) = (f (EndpB (Left ())), Left ())
    theta (BinB a t u, f) =
      (f (EndpB (Right a)), Right ((t,f.ConspB1 a),
                                   (u,f.ConspB2 a)))
```

3. For funny trees, we have

```
pathsF :: Ftree a -> Otree (PathF a)
pathsF t = unfoldO theta (t,id)
  where
    theta (TipF n, f) = (f (EndpF (In1 n)), In1 n)
    theta (MonF a x, f) =
      (f (EndpF (In2 a)), In2 (x,f.ConspF1 a))
    theta (BinF b x y, f) =
      (f (EndpF (In3 b)), In3 (b, (x,f.ConspF2 b),
                                  (y,f.ConspF3 b)))
```

□

Given $\mathsf{paths}_F$, the downwards accumulation is straightforward to define: it is simply a path fold mapped over the paths:

$$\mathsf{da}_F\,\phi = L\,(\mathsf{fold}_H\,\phi) \circ \mathsf{paths}_F$$

In the next section we shall see that this definition is inefficient, and show how to make it efficient.

# 7 Polytypic Downwards Accumulations, Quickly

Consider the characterization of downwards accumulations from the previous section:

$$\mathsf{da}_F\,\phi = L\,(\mathsf{fold}_H\,\phi) \circ \mathsf{paths}_F$$

From type information we know that the $\phi$ here is of the form

$$f \triangledown \mathop{\triangledown}_{i=1}^{n} \mathop{\triangledown}_{j=1}^{k_i} \oplus_{i,j}$$

where $f :: F(A,1) \to B$ and $\oplus_{i,j} :: F_i(A,1) \times B \to B$; we introduce the shorthand $\langle f, \oplus \rangle$ for such a function.

This characterization is inefficient, because it takes no account of the fact that the paths to the children of a node $x$ are closely related to the path to $x$ itself. Rather, it computes the labels of a node and its children independently.

Recall that

$$\mathsf{unfold}_G\,\theta\,(t, f) = L\,f\,(\mathsf{paths}_F\,t)$$

Therefore we have

$$\begin{array}{ll} & \mathsf{da}_F\,\langle f, \oplus \rangle\,t \\ = & \quad \{\,\mathsf{da}\,\} \\ & L\,(\mathsf{fold}_H\,\langle f, \oplus \rangle)\,(\mathsf{paths}_F\,t) \\ = & \quad \{\text{ equation above }\} \\ & \mathsf{unfold}_G\,\theta\,(t, \mathsf{fold}_H\,\langle f, \oplus \rangle) \end{array}$$

But this is no direct help, because the accumulating parameter in the unfold just builds up into a function of the form

$$\mathsf{fold}_H\,\langle f, \oplus \rangle \circ \mathsf{consp}_{i_1,j_1}\,a_1 \circ \cdots \circ \mathsf{consp}_{i_r,j_r}\,a_r$$

We do have

$$\begin{array}{ll} \mathsf{fold}_H\,\langle f, \oplus \rangle \circ \mathsf{endp} & = f \\ \mathsf{fold}_H\,\langle f, \oplus \rangle \circ \mathsf{consp}_{i,j}\,a & = (a \oplus_{i,j}) \circ \mathsf{fold}_H\,\langle f, \oplus \rangle \end{array}$$

so this big accumulating parameter can be simplified to

$$(a_1 \oplus_{i_1,j_1}) \circ \cdots \circ (a_r \oplus_{i_r,j_r}) \circ \mathsf{fold}_H\,\langle f, \oplus \rangle$$

However, in general, it simplifies no further. Thus, applying the accumulating parameter at a node at depth $r$ takes at least $r$ steps, and so the whole downwards accumulation is super-linear. (This is inherent in the definition of downwards accumulation, not an unfortunate artifact of our algorithm for computing it. For example, the function $\mathsf{paths}_F$ itself is a downwards accumulation, with $f = \mathsf{endp}$ and $\oplus = \mathsf{consp}$, and $\mathsf{paths}_F$ necessarily takes super-linear time to compute because it returns a tree with super-linearly many different subexpressions in it.)

The way around this problem is to assume an efficient representation of functions of the form $(a \oplus_{i,j})$ and of compositions of such functions.

**Definition 22.** The function $\langle f, \oplus \rangle$ is *efficiently representable* if there is a type $C$, a function $\mathsf{rep} :: (B \to B) \to C$, a function $\mathsf{abs} :: C \to (B \to B)$ such that

$$\mathsf{abs}\,(\mathsf{rep}\,(a \oplus_{i,j})) = (a \oplus_{i,j})$$

and a $\mathsf{zero} :: C$ and $\otimes :: C \to C \to C$ such that

$$\begin{array}{ll} \mathsf{abs}\,\mathsf{zero} & = \mathsf{id} \\ \mathsf{abs}\,(p \otimes q) & = \mathsf{abs}\,p \circ \mathsf{abs}\,q \end{array}$$

for which $\mathsf{rep}$, $\mathsf{abs}$ and $\otimes$ can all be computed in constant time. □

**Example 23.** For example, if $a \oplus_{i,j} n = g_{i,j}\, a + n$ for every $i, j$, and the $g_{i,j}$s can be computed in constant time, then $\langle f, \oplus \rangle$ is efficiently representable. The functions $(a\oplus_{i,j})$ and compositions of such functions are all of the form $(m+)$ for some $m$, and can be represented by the value $m$ itself. Thus, $\mathsf{rep}\, g = g\, 0$, $\mathsf{abs}\, m = (m+)$, $\mathsf{zero} = 0$ and $\otimes = +$.

Downwards accumulations with efficiently representable parameters can be computed efficiently [20].

**Theorem 24.** Suppose $\langle f, \oplus \rangle$ is efficiently representable. Then

$$\mathsf{da}\,\langle f, \oplus \rangle\, t = \mathsf{unfold}_G\, \theta'\,(t, \mathsf{zero})$$

where

$$\begin{aligned} \theta'\,(\mathsf{in}_i\, x, p) = (\mathsf{abs}\, p\, (f\,(\mathsf{inj}_i\, a)), \mathsf{inj}_i\,(F_i'(\mathsf{one}, g_1, \ldots, g_k)\, x)) \\ \text{where } a = F_i\,(\mathsf{id}, \mathsf{one})\, x \\ g_j\, y = (y, p \otimes \mathsf{rep}\,(a\oplus_{i,j})) \end{aligned}$$

This takes linear time, assuming $f$ and $\oplus$ both take constant time. □

*Proof.* It is straightforward but tedious to calculate the above definition of $\theta'$ from the specification

$$\mathsf{unfold}_G\, \theta'\,(t, p) = \mathsf{unfold}_G\, \theta\,(t, \mathsf{abs}\, p \circ \mathsf{fold}_H\,\langle f, \oplus \rangle)$$

□

**Example 25.** We assume throughout these examples that `rep :: (b->b)->c`, `abs :: c->(b->b)` and `zero :: c`. To represent the operator $\otimes$ we use the Haskell identifier '`.:. :: c -> c -> c`'.

1. For leaf-labelled binary trees, we have

```
daT :: (Either () a -> b, b->b, b->b) -> Ltree a -> Htree b
daT (f,g,h) t = unfoldH theta' (t,zero)
  where
    theta' (LeafT a, p) = (abs p (f (Right a)), Left ())
    theta' (BinT t u, p)
      = (abs p (f (Left ())),
         Right ((t,p .:. rep g), (u,p .:. rep h)))
```

For example, the function `depthsT`, which labels every node in the tree with its depth, is a downwards accumulation:

```
depthsT :: Ltree a -> Htree Int
depthsT = daT phiLengthT
```

where `phiLengthT` is as defined in Example 18.

2. For branch-labelled binary trees, we have

```
daB :: (Either () a -> b, a->b->b, a->b->b) -> Btree a -> Htree b
daB (f,g,h) t = unfoldH theta' (t,zero)
  where
    theta' (Empty, p) = (abs p (f (Left ())), Left ())
    theta' (BinB a t u, p)
      = (abs p (f (Right a)),
           Right ((t,p .:. rep (g a)), (u,p .:. rep (h a))))
```

The corresponding depths function is

```
depthsB :: Btree a -> Htree Int
depthsB = daB phiLengthB
```

3. For funny trees, we have

```
daF :: (Either3 Int a Bool -> b, a->b->b, Bool->b->b, Bool->b->b) ->
         Ftree a -> Otree b
daF (f,g,h,j) t = unfoldO theta' (t,zero)
  where
    theta' (TipF n, p) = (abs p (f (In1 n)), In1 n)
    theta' (MonF a x, p) =
      (abs p (f (In2 a)), In2 (x,p .:. rep (g a)))
    theta' (BinF b x y, p) =
      (abs p (f (In3 b)), In3 (b, (x,p .:. rep (h b)),
                                  (y,p .:. rep (j b))))
```

The corresponding depths function is

```
depthsF :: Ftree a -> Otree Int
depthsF = daF phiLengthF
```

□

# 8 Conclusion

We have shown how to generalize the notion of *downwards accumulation* [8,9] to an arbitrary polynomial datatype, building on Bird *et al*'s [2] generalization of upwards accumulation.

Downwards accumulations are much harder to handle than upwards accumulations, because the *ancestors* of a node in a datatype (on which the downwards accumulation depends) form an instance of a completely different datatype, whereas the *descendants* of a node (on which the upwards accumulation depends) form an instance of the same datatype.

On the other hand, Bird *et al*'s construction is ***parametric higher-order polymorphic***, whereas ours is merely ***ad-hoc higher-order polymorphic***, because our definition is based on the syntactic presentation of the type functors involved; it is an open question whether one can construct a parametric higher-order polymorphic definition of downwards accumulations. In fact, our construction is not even fully polytypic in the sense of Jeuring, in that we deal only with *polynomial* datatypes, whereas Jeuring deals with the more general *regular* datatypes. Another open question is whether our construction can be extended to regular but non-polynomial datatypes.

We have addressed the question of efficiency in computing downwards accumulations by assuming a particular data refinement of the operations concerned. This data refinement allows the order of evaluation of a path fold to be inverted [6, 20], so that it is computed from top to bottom instead of from bottom to top. This is a different approach to the one taken in the original definition of downwards accumulation [8, 9]. There, the order of evaluation is reversed by switching to a dual path datatype—informally, if the path datatypes we construct here are variations on cons lists, then the switch is to variations on snoc lists. This works neatly for the simple monotypic cases considered in the original definitions, but it is rather more complicated in the general case. The reason is that a snoc-style path ending at a node of variant $i$ can be extended downwards only by a 'direction' corresponding to variant $i$ (for example, a path ending at an external node of the data structure clearly cannot be extended at all). In contrast, a cons-style path can be extended upwards in any direction.

Nevertheless, we intend to explore the idea of snoc-style paths further. One motivation for doing so is to see whether they yield a simpler definition of downwards accumulations. A more important reason, however, is the hope of generalizing the *Third Homomorphism Theorem* [12] to our polytypic paths. The Third Homomorphism Theorem, first stated by Bird and proved by Meertens, says that any list function that can be computed both from left to right and from right to left can also be computed as an associative fold; this is much better suited to parallel computation. We have shown [10] that this leads to a very fast parallel algorithm for computing (the original kind of) downwards accumulations. We hope that it will also lead to a fast parallel algorithm for computing polytypic downwards accumulations.

## Acknowledgements

I would like to thank the members of the Oxford University Computing Laboratory, especially Richard Bird, Jesús Ravelo and Pedro Borges, for their many helpful suggestions and comments; the MPC referees have also suggested many improvements.

## References

1. Roland Backhouse, Henk Doornbos, and Paul Hoogendijk. A class of commuting relators. In *STOP 1992 Summerschool on Constructive Algorithmics*. STOP project, 1992.
2. Richard Bird, Oege de Moor, and Paul Hoogendijk. Generic functional programming with types and relations. *Journal of Functional Programming*, 6(1):1–28, 1996.

3. Richard S. Bird. The promotion and accumulation strategies in transformational programming. *ACM Transactions on Programming Languages and Systems*, 6(4):487–504, October 1984. See also [4].
4. Richard S. Bird. Addendum to "The promotion and accumulation strategies in transformational programming". *ACM Transactions on Programming Languages and Systems*, 7(3):490–492, July 1985.
5. Richard S. Bird. An introduction to the theory of lists. In M. Broy, editor, *Logic of Programming and Calculi of Discrete Design*, pages 3–42. Springer-Verlag, 1987. Also available as Technical Monograph PRG-56, from the Programming Research Group, Oxford University.
6. E. A. Boiten. Improving recursive functions by inverting the order of evaluation. *Science of Computer Programming*, 18:139–179, January 1992. Also in [7].
7. Eerke Boiten. *Views of Formal Program Development.* PhD thesis, Department of Informatics, University of Nijmegen, 1992.
8. Jeremy Gibbons. *Algebras for Tree Algorithms.* D. Phil. thesis, Programming Research Group, Oxford University, 1991. Available as Technical Monograph PRG-94.
9. Jeremy Gibbons. Upwards and downwards accumulations on trees. In R. S. Bird, C. C. Morgan, and J. C. P. Woodcock, editors, *LNCS 669: Mathematics of Program Construction*, pages 122–138. Springer-Verlag, 1993. A revised version appears in the Proceedings of the Massey Functional Programming Workshop, 1992.
10. Jeremy Gibbons. Computing downwards accumulations on trees quickly. *Theoretical Computer Science*, 169(1):67–80, 1996. Earlier version appeared in Proceedings of the 16th Australian Computer Science Conference, Brisbane, 1993.
11. Jeremy Gibbons. Deriving tidy drawings of trees. *Journal of Functional Programming*, 6(3):535–562, 1996. Earlier version appears as Technical Report No. 82, Department of Computer Science, University of Auckland.
12. Jeremy Gibbons. The Third Homomorphism Theorem. *Journal of Functional Programming*, 6(4):657–665, 1996. Earlier version appeared in C. B. Jay, editor, *Computing: The Australian Theory Seminar*, Sydney, December 1994, p. 62–69.
13. Jeremy Gibbons and Geraint Jones. Against the grain: Linear-time breadth-first tree algorithms. Oxford Brookes University and Oxford University Computing Laboratory, 1998.
14. Paul Hoogendijk. *A Generic Theory of Datatypes.* PhD thesis, TU Eindhoven, 1997.
15. Johan Jeuring and Patrick Jansson. Polytypic programming. In John Launchbury, Erik Meijer, and Tim Sheard, editors, *LNCS 1129: Advanced Functional Programming*. Springer-Verlag, 1996.
16. Grant Malcolm. Data structures and program transformation. *Science of Computer Programming*, 14:255–279, 1990.
17. Lambert Meertens. Paramorphisms. *Formal Aspects of Computing*, 4(5):413–424, 1992. Also available as Technical Report CS-R9005, CWI, Amsterdam.
18. David B. Skillicorn. Structured parallel computation in structured documents. *Journal of Universal Computer Science*, 3(1), 1997.
19. Philip Wadler. Deforestation: Transforming programs to eliminate trees. *Theoretical Computer Science*, 73:231–248, 1990.
20. Mitchell Wand. Continuation-based program transformation strategies. *Journal of the ACM*, 27(1):164–180, January 1980.

# Formal Derivation of a Loadable Asynchronous Counter *

Mark B. Josephs

Centre for Concurrent Systems and VLSI, South Bank University,
School of Computing, Information Systems and Mathematics,
103 Borough Road, London SE1 0AA, U.K. Mark.Josephs@sbu.ac.uk

**Abstract.** A loadable asynchronous counter is designed in a disciplined and formal manner. First, the behaviour of the counter is specified in terms of the way in which it *handshakes* with its environment. Next, the counter is decomposed into a linear array of cells, in which only adjacent cells can communicate, again by handshaking. Finally, the individual cells are decomposed into standard components that communicate by following a *delay-insensitive* signalling scheme.
In exploring the design space, "lazy cells" versus "eager cells" and "two-phase handshaking" versus "four-phase handshaking" are considered. Simplified designs are also provided for cells known to be always "even" and always "odd".
This example demonstrates how formal specification and verification can be carried out *at appropriate levels of abstraction* by using Handshake Algebra and Delay-Insensitive Algebra.

## 1 Introduction

This paper develops a solution to an asynchronous circuit design problem in a disciplined and formal way, using Handshake Algebra (HS-Algebra) [8,5] and Delay-Insensitive Algebra (DI-Algebra) [6,7]. It demonstrates how formal specification and verification can be carried out at the highest level of abstraction appropriate to each stage of design. In fact, this must be done if one is to keep the complexity of specification and proof under control.

Handshaking imposes a port structure on systems (asynchronous circuits in this case) and requires that the direction of communication on each port must alternate between input and output, something that is built into the semantics of HS-Algebra. We shall see how to define processes in HS-Algebra that specify the behaviour of components in terms of the way in which they handshake with their environment. Both two-phase handshakes and four-phase handshakes are shown to be representable within the formalism. The composition of components that handshake with each other will be calculated by symbolic manipulation.

Because handshaking is a restricted form of delay-insensitive signalling, processes in HS-Algebra can always be *refined* into DI-Algebra. This should be

* This work has been supported by the European Commission under Working Group ACiD-WG (Esprit Nr. 21949) as part of the Fourth Framework.

done when a component has been decomposed into parts as far as is practical at the handshaking level of abstraction; decomposition can then continue at a lower level of abstraction (top-down design). Conversely, processes in DI-Algebra can be *abstracted* into HS-Algebra by associating inputs and outputs with ports — this allows one to design bottom-up. Both refinement and abstraction will be illustrated in this paper. (As we shall also see, speed-independent or quasi-delay-insensitive signalling represents a still lower level of abstraction.)

In the remainder of this section, we overview the process algebras and provide the background to the design problem. The problem is concerned with systolic counters. Section 2 specifies a counter using HS-Algebra. Section 3 uses HS-Algebra to show how a $k$-bit counter can be decomposed into an array $k$ of cells. Section 4 shows how, with DI-Algebra, we are able to design the counter cells out of standard asynchronous elements. The tradeoffs between "lazy" versus "eager" cells and between two-phase versus four-phase handshaking are indicated. Conclusions are drawn in Section 5.

## HS-Algebra and DI-Algebra

HS-Algebra and DI-Algebra are formalisms that allow one to specify the way in which a system is required to communicate with its environment and to prove that a network of subsystems satisfies that specification. Specification involves the (recursive) definition of processes. Algebraic laws support reasoning about the equivalence and refinement of processes. Recursion-induction is available as a proof technique.

A complete set of laws for each algebra can be given (e.g. [1,8,12]), in the usual sense (cf. [16]) that every (non-recursive) process can be transformed into a normal form. Receptive process theory [3] provides a semantic model based on which the soundness of the laws can be demonstrated (e.g. [11]). Actually, much of the theory of Communicating Sequential Processes [2,16] carries over to HS-Algebra and DI-Algebra, including the notion of guardedness/constructiveness that is pertinent to proofs that involve recursion [13].

When defining a process $P$ in HS-Algebra, we shall state its port alphabet $\mathbf{p}P$. Suppose $c \in \mathbf{p}P$. Then $c?$ will denote an input signal, $c!$ an output signal, $c?!$ a passive (two-phase) handshake and $c!?$ an active handshake. It is remarkable that, while we can freely separate handshakes into their constituent signals, we can also express and manipulate handshakes as atomic operations within HS-Algebra.

On the other hand, a process $P$ in DI-Algebra has both an input alphabet $\mathbf{i}P$ and an output alphabet $\mathbf{o}P$. These alphabets must be disjoint. As before $c?$ will denote an input signal (but this time for $c \in \mathbf{i}P$) and $c!$ an output signal (for $c \in \mathbf{o}P$).

More generally, signals and handshakes can involve communication of data. That is, $c?x$ denotes a communication in which variable $x$ is bound to the actual value input, and $c!e$ denotes an output communication of the value of expression $e$. Indeed, in the handshake $c?x!e$ the variable $x$ may occur in $e$.

We now describe the operators out of which processes are constructed and point out some of their algebraic properties.

- Chaos. The process $\perp$ models a system in an unsafe or undesirable state, a system with undefined behavior. Anything is better than $\perp$.
- Nondeterministic Choice. The process $P \sqcap Q$ can behave in any way that $P$ or $Q$ can behave. $P$ refines $Q$ ($P \sqsupseteq Q$) if and only if $P \sqcap Q = Q$.
- Conditional. The process **if** *bool* **then** $P$ **else** $Q$ behaves like $P$ if *bool* is true, and like $Q$ if it is false.
- Prefixing. The process $c?; P$ models a system that must receive signal $c?$ before it can behave like $P$. Similarly, the process $c!; P$ models a system that will eventually send signal $c!$ and then behave like $P$. Prefixing has several interesting algebraic properties:
  The possibility of transmission intereference means that $c?; c?; P = c?; c?; \perp$ and that $c!; c!; P = \perp$. N.B. An input-prefixed process cannot be chaos, i.e., $c?; P \neq \perp$, but we have no such guarantee for an output-prefixed process.
  The insensitivity of a system to wire delays means that $c?; d?; P = d?; c?; P$ and that $c!; d!; P = d!; c!; P$. Thus we can generalize from prefixing with an input (output) signal to prefixing with a set of input (output) signals should we wish to make the concurrency of signals more obvious.
  In HS-Algebra, we can define handshake-prefixing by $c?!; P = c?; c!; P$ and $c!?; P = c!; c?; P$.
- Guarded Choice. The guarded choice $[L]$, where $L$ is a finite family of alternatives, is a generalization of prefixing. Each alternative consists of a guard and a process. The system must eventually choose one alternative, unless all its guards are input signals, all of which the environment refrains from supplying.
  The selection of an alternative $(c! \rightarrow P)$ involves the system sending signal $c!$ and then behaving like $P$. The selection of an alternative $(c? \rightarrow P)$ can only take place if signal $c?$ has been supplied by the environment, after which the system behaves like $P$. Thus $c?; P = [(c? \rightarrow P)]$ and $c!; P = [(c! \rightarrow P)]$.
  We list the alternatives in $L$ separating them with the symbol $\Box$.
  In HS-Algebra, we can define handshake-guards by

$$[(c?! \rightarrow P)\Box L] = [(c? \rightarrow c!; P)\Box L] \text{ and } [(c!? \rightarrow P)\Box L] = [(c! \rightarrow c?; P)\Box L] .$$

- After-input. The process $P/c?$ behaves like $P$ after the environment has supplied signal $c?$. In particular, if $P$ is a guarded choice with an alternative $(c? \rightarrow P')$, $P/c?$ can behave like $P'$.
- Port-status. In HS-Algebra, the $c$-active process $< c! > P$ and $c$-passive process $<c?> P$ both behave like $P$. However, the former requires that the next signal on port $c$ is an output and the latter requires that the next signal on $c$ is an input. Violation of this protocol, by the environment or by the system, will result in chaos. That is, $(<c!> P)/c? = \perp$ and $<c?> c!; P = \perp$.
  The laws of HS-Algebra enable us to eliminate the port-status operators from expressions, at the expense of having to indicate undefined behaviour ($\perp$) explicitly.

– Renaming. Signals and ports can be renamed, e.g., $s.P$ behaves like handshake process $P$ except that every port $c$ of $P$ is renamed $s.c$ .
– Parallel composition. The parallel composition of processes $P$ and $Q$ is denoted by $P\backslash\backslash Q$. It models a system built out of subsystems. Signals/ports that $P$ and $Q$ have in common are used for (internal) communication between the two subsystems. The remainder are used for communication with the environment.
  An algebraic property that eases the expansion of parallel composition is that $(c!; P)\backslash\backslash Q$ is equivalent to $P\backslash\backslash(Q/c?)$, if $c?$ is an input to $Q$, and is equivalent to $c!; (P\backslash\backslash Q)$, otherwise. Furthermore, in HS-Algebra,

$$(c!?; P)\backslash\backslash(c?!; Q) = (<c!> P)\backslash\backslash Q \ .$$

A final remark concerns data communication. We allow $c?v$ to be used as a prefix or guard, where $v$ is a constant rather than a variable. By convention, it is unsafe for the environment to supply any value other than $v$ at that point. Thus, $c?v; P = c?x; \textbf{if } x = v \textbf{ then } P \textbf{ else } \bot$, if $x$ is not free in $P$. Our treatment of input constants and variables extends in the natural way to patterns in which constructor functions are applied to variables, i.e., $c?f(x)$ .

## Systolic Counters

Van Berkel has previously published a systolic implementation of a modulo-$N$ counter [18, 19]. The $N$-fold repetition of a statement in the Tangram VLSI programming language is apparently translated into such a circuit. This requires the value of $N$ to be known at compile time.

Participants in the ACiD-WG Workshop in September 1996 were invited to tackle the problem of how to implement a "loadable counter". A number $n$ is input; a one is then output (and acknowledged) $n$ times; finally a zero is output. Again the solution may be useful in silicon compilation, viz., for $n$-fold repetition where the value of $n$ is computed during program execution. Indeed the concluding remark in [10] is that a power-efficient circuit for such a loadable counter would have enabled further reduction of the power dissipation of the standby circuitry for a radio-pager.

We shall follow the strategy [9, 18] of decomposing a counter (which handshakes with its environment) into a linear array of $k$ cells, where $n$ is a $k$-bit binary number; only adjacent cells can communicate (again by handshaking). This strategy has been applied to the loadable counter problem by others [21, 10]. (An alternative decomposition strategy gives rise to a systolic array of $2^k - 1$ cells [4].)

Even with this decomposition strategy, we discover that there is a choice as to whether a cell is to be "lazy" or "eager". At one extreme all the cells are lazy and the flow of control through the array is entirely sequential. Its attractions are minimal power and area. The other extreme, in which all the cells are eager, enables computation to proceed in a systolic fashion. It offers higher throughput at the cost of increased power and area. Both kinds of cell are designed out of standard asynchronous control components. No processing or latching is required on the datapath! Actually, when lazy cells are replaced by eager ones, using our designs, the cost in terms of circuit area and total energy consumption would appear to be marginal, so this should probably be done in practice.

Assuming two-phase handshaking, we shall see how to implement a cell as a delay-insensitive composition of standard components, such as Select, Merge and Call elements [17]. Our designs will also be adapted to four-phase handshaking by insertion of Martin's Q element [14] (also known as an S element [18] and as a "multiple use circuit" [20]) where appropriate. This adaptation enables us to use smaller and faster implementations of the standard components.

We shall also consider how to modify the cells to implement a counter in which all or some of the bits that make up the binary representation of $n$ are fixed. The result turns out to be an improvement on Van Berkel's cells for odd and even $N$ [18, 19].

## 2 Specification of the Loadable Counter

The behaviour of a counter will be specified in HS-Algebra by the process $C_k$. The counter has a single port $a$, so we define the port alphabet $\mathbf{p}C_k$ of the process to be $\{a\}$. Port $a$ is is initially passive: a request is expected to arrive on it to count up to a $k$-bit binary number.

$a?\text{count}(n)$ denotes a request to count $n$ times. We implicitly assume that $n$ is in the range $0 \leq n < 2^k$. We have in mind a bundled-data implementation [17] consisting of $k$ data wires and a control wire, i.e., a signal on the count control wire indicates that valid data has arrived.

$a!1?\text{ack}$ denotes a handshake in which the counter outputs a one and receives an acknowledgement signal. (In response to $a?\text{count}(n)$ the counter engages in $n$ such handshakes.) $a!0$ denotes the output of a zero by the counter; we assume that data must remain valid until this occurs. Thus $a!0$ signals completion of counting and readiness to deal with another count request. (Signalling zeros on one wire and ones on another is known as "dual-rail".)

In total, therefore, port $a$ consists of $k+4$ wires, the four control wires being count, ack, 0 and 1.

Formally, $C_k$ is defined as follows:

$$\begin{aligned} C_k &= a?\text{count}(n); C'_{k,n} \text{ , where} \\ C'_{k,m} &= \textbf{if } m = 0 \textbf{ then } a!0; C_k \textbf{ else } a!1?\text{ack}; C'_{k,m-1} \text{ ,} \end{aligned}$$

for $0 \leq m < 2^k$.

Note that $C_k$ is $a$-passive:

$$\begin{aligned} & C_k \\ = & \{ \text{ definition of } C_k \} \\ & a?\text{count}(n); C'_{k,n} \\ = & \{ \text{ law } c?f(x); P = <c?> c?f(x); P \} \end{aligned}$$

$<a?> a?n; C'_{k,n}$ .

Note also that $C'_{k,m}$ is $a$-active:

$$
\begin{aligned}
& C'_{k,m} \\
= \quad & \{ \text{ definition of } C'_{k,m} \} \\
& \textbf{if } m = 0 \textbf{ then } a!0; C_k \textbf{ else } a!1?\text{ack}; C'_{k,m-1} \\
= \quad & \{ \text{ laws } c!e; P = <c!> c!e; P \text{ and} \\
& \quad \textbf{if } \mathit{bool} \textbf{ then } <c!> Q \textbf{ else } <c!> R = <c!> \textbf{if } \mathit{bool} \textbf{ then } Q \textbf{ else } R \} \\
& <a!> \textbf{if } m = 0 \textbf{ then } a!0; C_k \textbf{ else } a!1?\text{ack}; C'_{k,m-1} .
\end{aligned}
$$

It follows that $C_k/a?\text{count}(m) = C'_{k,m}$:

$$
\begin{aligned}
& C_k/a?\text{count}(m) \\
= \quad & \{ \text{ definition of } C_k \} \\
& (a?\text{count}(n); C'_{k,n})/a?\text{count}(m) \\
= \quad & \{ \text{ law } (c?f(x); P_x)/c?f(v) = P_v \text{ if } P_v \text{ is } c\text{-active} \} \\
& C'_{k,m} .
\end{aligned}
$$

If one interprets an input signal or an output signal as a change in logic level of a wire, either from 0 to 1 or from 1 to 0, one can appreciate that the levels of the control wires participating in a simple exchange of signals (a two-phase handshake) are changed. To implement "return-to-zero" signalling, four-phase handshaking can be adopted.

To conclude this section, we specify a counter $C^*_k$ that engages in four-phase handshakes instead of two-phase handshakes. We assume that the number input at the beginning of each count cycle remains valid until the control wire that implements $a!0$ has returned to zero.

$$
\begin{aligned}
C^*_k &= a?\text{count}(n); C^{*'}_{k,n,n} \text{ , where} \\
C^{*'}_{k,l,m} &= \textbf{if } l = 0 \textbf{ then } a!0?\text{count}(m); a!0; C^*_k \\
& \qquad \textbf{else } a!1?\text{ack}; a!1?\text{ack}; C^{*'}_{k,l-1,m} ,
\end{aligned}
$$

for $0 \le l \le m < 2^k$.

## 3 Decomposition of a $k$-bit Counter into an Array

Our decomposition strategy for $C_k$, $k > 1$, is encapsulated in the following design equation, which we have to solve for HS-process $X$:

$$
C_k \; = \; s.C_{k-1} \backslash\backslash X \tag{1}
$$

The idea is that, if we know how to construct a subcounter for $(k-1)$-bit numbers and we can design the cell specified by $X$, then composing the two yields a counter for $k$-bit numbers. In other words, $C_k$ can be implemented by a linear array of $k$ cells, $C_1$ being the leftmost cell (handling the most significant bit) and each of the remaining cells being an implementation of $X$.

Analysing the structure of the components, $\mathbf{p}X$ must be $\{s.a, a\}$ since $\mathbf{p}s.C_{k-1} = \{s.a\}$. Also keep in mind a count $n$ communicated on $s.a$ must be in the range $0 \le n < 2^{k-1}$. Now $C_k$ is $a$-passive. Likewise, $s.C_{k-1}$ is $s.a$-passive. Therefore $X$ must be $a$-passive (since this is the case for $C_k$), and it must be $s.a$-active (since it has to communicate with $s.C_{k-1}$ on this port).

To solve (1) for $X$, we start from its LHS and calculate as follows:

$$\begin{array}{ll}
& C_k \\
= & \{ \text{ definition of } C_k \ \} \\
& a?\mathrm{count}(n); C'_{k,n} \\
= & \{ \text{ separating case } n \text{ even from case } n \text{ odd } \} \\
& a?\mathrm{count}(n); \mathbf{if}\ n \bmod 2 = 0\ \mathbf{then}\ C'_{k,2\times(n\,\mathrm{div}\,2)} \\
& \qquad\qquad\qquad \mathbf{else}\ C'_{k,1+2\times(n\,\mathrm{div}\,2)} \\
= & \{ \text{ definition of } C'_{k,m} \text{ for } m > 0 \ \} \\
& a?\mathrm{count}(n); \mathbf{if}\ n \bmod 2 = 0\ \mathbf{then}\ C'_{k,2\times(n\,\mathrm{div}\,2)} \qquad\qquad (*) \\
& \qquad\qquad\qquad \mathbf{else}\ a!1?\mathrm{ack}; C'_{k,2\times(n\,\mathrm{div}\,2)} \ .
\end{array}$$

At this stage, we might try putting

$$\begin{array}{l}
X = \ <s.a!>\ a?\mathrm{count}(n); \\
\quad \mathbf{if}\ n \bmod 2 = 0\ \mathbf{then}\ s.a!\mathrm{count}(n\,\mathrm{div}\,2); X' \\
\quad \mathbf{else}\ (a!1?\mathrm{ack}; s.a!\mathrm{count}(n\,\mathrm{div}\,2); X') \sqcap (s.a!\mathrm{count}(n\,\mathrm{div}\,2); a!1?\mathrm{ack}; X') \ ,
\end{array}$$

where $X'$ is a new unknown. The nondeterministic choice keeps our options open as to whether communication $s.a!\mathrm{count}(n\,\mathrm{div}\,2)$ with the subcounter should take place after, or concurrently with, a handshake $a!1?\mathrm{ack}$.

To check that this definition of $X$ is reasonable and to determine an auxiliary design equation for $X'$, we continue our calculation, this time from the RHS of (1):

$$\begin{array}{ll}
& s.C_{k-1}\backslash\backslash X \\
= & \{ \text{ definition of } X \ \} \\
& s.C_{k-1}\backslash\backslash(<s.a!>\ a?\mathrm{count}(n); \\
& \qquad \mathbf{if}\ n \bmod 2 = 0\ \mathbf{then}\ s.a!\mathrm{count}(n\,\mathrm{div}\,2); X' \\
& \qquad \mathbf{else}\ \ (a!1?\mathrm{ack}; s.a!\mathrm{count}(n\,\mathrm{div}\,2); X') \\
& \qquad\qquad \sqcap(s.a!\mathrm{count}(n\,\mathrm{div}\,2); a!1?\mathrm{ack}; X')) \\
= & \{ \text{ laws } P\backslash\backslash(<c!>\ Q) = P\backslash\backslash Q \text{ if } c\text{-passive } P, \\
& \quad P\backslash\backslash(c?f(x); Q) = c?f(x); (P\backslash\backslash Q) \\
& \quad \text{if } c \notin \mathbf{p}P,\ P \ne \perp,\ \mathbf{p}P \subset \mathbf{p}Q \text{ and } x \text{ not free in } P, \\
& \quad \text{and } P\backslash\backslash(\mathbf{if}\ \mathit{bool}\ \mathbf{then}\ Q\ \mathbf{else}\ R) = \mathbf{if}\ \mathit{bool}\ \mathbf{then}\ P\backslash\backslash Q\ \mathbf{else}\ P\backslash\backslash R \ \} \\
& a?\mathrm{count}(n); \mathbf{if}\ n \bmod 2 = 0\ \mathbf{then}\ s.C_{k-1}\backslash\backslash(s.a!\mathrm{count}(n\,\mathrm{div}\,2); X') \\
& \qquad \mathbf{else}\ s.C_{k-1}\backslash\backslash(\,(a!1?\mathrm{ack}; s.a!\mathrm{count}(n\,\mathrm{div}\,2); X') \\
& \qquad\qquad\qquad \sqcap(s.a!\mathrm{count}(n\,\mathrm{div}\,2); a!1?\mathrm{ack}; X'))
\end{array}$$

$$
\begin{aligned}
= \;& \{ \text{ laws } P\backslash\backslash(c!e;Q) = (P/c?e)\backslash\backslash Q \text{ if } c \in \mathbf{p}P, \\
& \quad P\backslash\backslash(Q \sqcap R) = (P\backslash\backslash Q) \sqcap (P\backslash\backslash R), \\
& \quad P\backslash\backslash(c!e?x;Q) = c!e?x;(P\backslash\backslash Q) \\
& \quad \text{if } c \notin \mathbf{p}P,\ P \neq \perp,\ \mathbf{p}P \subset \mathbf{p}Q \text{ and } x \text{ not free in } P, \\
& \quad \text{and } P \sqcap P = P \ \} \\
& a?\mathrm{count}(n);\ \mathbf{if}\ n \bmod 2 = 0\ \mathbf{then}\ (s.C_{k-1}/s.a?\mathrm{count}(n \operatorname{div} 2))\backslash\backslash X' \\
& \qquad\qquad \mathbf{else}\ a!1?\mathrm{ack};\ ((s.C_{k-1}/s.a?\mathrm{count}(n \operatorname{div} 2))\backslash\backslash X') \\
= \;& \{ \text{ property } C_k/a?\mathrm{count}(m) = C'_{k,m} \ \} \\
& a?\mathrm{count}(n);\ \mathbf{if}\ n \bmod 2 = 0\ \mathbf{then}\ s.C'_{k-1,n \operatorname{div} 2}\backslash\backslash X' \\
& \qquad\qquad \mathbf{else}\ a!1?\mathrm{ack};\ (s.C'_{k-1,n \operatorname{div} 2}\backslash\backslash X') \ .
\end{aligned}
$$

Comparing this expression with (*) suggests the following design equation:

$$
C'_{k,2\times n} \;=\; s.C'_{k-1,n}\backslash\backslash X' \ . \tag{2}
$$

To solve (2) for $X'$, we start from its LHS and calculate as follows:

$$
\begin{aligned}
& C'_{k,2\times n} \\
= \;& \{ \text{ definition of } C'_{k,m} \ \} \\
& \mathbf{if}\ 2 \times n = 0\ \mathbf{then}\ a!0; C_k\ \mathbf{else}\ a!1?\mathrm{ack}; C'_{k,2\times n-1} \\
= \;& \{ \text{ arithmetic } \} \\
& \mathbf{if}\ n = 0\ \mathbf{then}\ a!0; C_k\ \mathbf{else}\ a!1?\mathrm{ack}; C'_{k,1+2\times(n-1)} \\
= \;& \{ \text{ definition of } C'_{k,m} \text{ for } m > 0 \ \} \\
& \mathbf{if}\ n = 0\ \mathbf{then}\ a!0; C_k\ \mathbf{else}\ a!1?\mathrm{ack}; a!1?\mathrm{ack}; C'_{k,2\times(n-1)} \ . \qquad (**)
\end{aligned}
$$

At this stage, we might try putting

$$
\begin{aligned}
X' = s.a?x; \mathbf{if}\ x = 0\ \mathbf{then}\ a!0; X\ \mathbf{else}\ & (a!1?\mathrm{ack}; a!1?\mathrm{ack}; s.a!\mathrm{ack}; X') \\
& \sqcap(s.a!\mathrm{ack}; a!1?\mathrm{ack}; a!1?\mathrm{ack}; X') \ .
\end{aligned}
$$

The nondeterministic choice keeps our options open as to whether communication $s.a!\mathrm{ack}$ with the subcounter should take place after, or concurrently with, a pair of handshakes $a!1?\mathrm{ack}$.

Note that

$$
\begin{aligned}
X'/s.a?v = \;& \mathbf{if}\ v = 0\ \mathbf{then}\ a!0; X \\
& \mathbf{else}\ (a!1?\mathrm{ack}; a!1?\mathrm{ack}; s.a!\mathrm{ack}; X') \\
& \qquad \sqcap(s.a!\mathrm{ack}; a!1?\mathrm{ack}; a!1?\mathrm{ack}; X') \ :
\end{aligned}
$$

$$
\begin{aligned}
& X'/s.a?v \\
= \;& \{ \text{ definition of } X' \ \} \\
& (s.a?x; \mathbf{if}\ x = 0\ \mathbf{then}\ a!0; X\ \mathbf{else}\ (a!1?\mathrm{ack}; a!1?\mathrm{ack}; s.a!\mathrm{ack}; X') \\
& \qquad\qquad \sqcap(s.a!\mathrm{ack}; a!1?\mathrm{ack}; a!1?\mathrm{ack}; X'))/s.a?v \\
= \;& \{ \text{ laws } (c?x; P_x)/c?e = \langle c! \rangle P_e \text{ and} \\
& \quad \langle c! \rangle\, \mathbf{if}\ \mathit{bool}\ \mathbf{then}\ P\ \mathbf{else}\ Q = \mathbf{if}\ \mathit{bool}\ \mathbf{then}\ \langle c! \rangle P\ \mathbf{else}\ \langle c! \rangle Q \ \} \\
& \mathbf{if}\ v = 0\ \mathbf{then}\ \langle s.a! \rangle\, a!0; X\ \mathbf{else}\ \langle s.a! \rangle\, ((a!1?\mathrm{ack}; a!1?\mathrm{ack}; s.a!\mathrm{ack}; X') \\
& \qquad\qquad \sqcap(s.a!\mathrm{ack}; a!1?\mathrm{ack}; a!1?\mathrm{ack}; X'))
\end{aligned}
$$

$$
\begin{aligned}
= \quad & \{ \text{ laws } <c!> d!e; P = d!e; <c!> P \text{ if } c \neq d, \\
& \quad <c!> P = P \text{ if } c\text{-active } P, \text{ and} \\
& \quad <c!> (Q \sqcap R) = Q \sqcap R \text{ if } c\text{-active } Q \text{ or } c\text{-active } R \,\} \\
& \textbf{if } v = 0 \textbf{ then } a!0; X \textbf{ else } \ (a!1?\text{ack}; a!1?\text{ack}; s.a!\text{ack}; X') \\
& \qquad\qquad\qquad\qquad\qquad\qquad \sqcap (s.a!\text{ack}; a!1?\text{ack}; a!1?\text{ack}; X') \ .
\end{aligned}
$$

To check that our definition of $X'$ is reasonable, we continue our calculation, this time from the RHS of (2):

$$
\begin{aligned}
& s.C'_{k-1,n} \backslash\backslash X' \\
= \quad & \{ \text{ definition of } C'_{k,m} \text{ and renaming ports } \} \\
& (\textbf{if } n = 0 \textbf{ then } s.a!0; s.C_{k-1} \textbf{ else } s.a!1?\text{ack}; s.C'_{k-1,n-1}) \backslash\backslash X' \\
= \quad & \{ \text{ laws } (\textbf{if } \mathit{bool} \textbf{ then } P \textbf{ else } Q) \backslash\backslash R = \textbf{if } \mathit{bool} \textbf{ then } P \backslash\backslash R \textbf{ else } Q \backslash\backslash R, \\
& \quad \text{and } (c!e; P) \backslash\backslash Q = P \backslash\backslash (Q/c?e) \text{ if } c \in \mathbf{p}Q \,\} \\
& \textbf{if } n = 0 \textbf{ then } s.C_{k-1} \backslash\backslash (X'/s.a?0) \textbf{ else } (s.a?\text{ack}; s.C'_{k-1,n-1}) \backslash\backslash (X'/s.a?1) \\
= \quad & \{ \text{ substituting for } X'/s.a?v, \ v = 0, 1 \ \} \\
& \textbf{if } n = 0 \textbf{ then } s.C_{k-1} \backslash\backslash (a!0; X) \\
& \textbf{else } (s.a?\text{ack}; s.C'_{k-1,n-1}) \backslash\backslash (\,(a!1?\text{ack}; a!1?\text{ack}; s.a!\text{ack}; X') \\
& \qquad\qquad\qquad\qquad\qquad\qquad \sqcap (s.a!\text{ack}; a!1?\text{ack}; a!1?\text{ack}; X')) \\
= \quad & \{ \text{ laws } P \backslash\backslash (c!e; Q) = c!e; (P \backslash\backslash Q) \text{ if } c \notin \mathbf{p}P, \\
& \quad P \backslash\backslash (Q \sqcap R) = (P \backslash\backslash Q) \sqcap (P \backslash\backslash R), \\
& \quad P \backslash\backslash (c!e?x; Q) = c!e?x; (P \backslash\backslash Q) \\
& \quad \text{if } c \notin \mathbf{p}P, \ P \neq \perp, \ \mathbf{p}P \subset \mathbf{p}Q \text{ and } x \text{ not free in } P \\
& \quad (c?v; P) \backslash\backslash (c!v; Q) = P \backslash\backslash Q \text{ if } c\text{-active } P, \text{ and } P \sqcap P = P \,\} \\
& \textbf{if } n = 0 \textbf{ then } a!0; (s.C_{k-1} \backslash\backslash X) \textbf{ else } a!1?\text{ack}; a!1?\text{ack}; (s.C'_{k-1,n-1} \backslash\backslash X') \ .
\end{aligned}
$$

By recursion-induction, using (1) and (2), this expression is equivalent to (**).

Thus, $X$ satisfies a request for $n$ ones on $a$ by outputting $(n \bmod 2)$ ones on $a$, requesting $s.C_{k-1}$ to output $(n \operatorname{div} 2)$ ones on $s.a$, and outputting two ones on $a$ for every one that it receives on $s.a$ .

The nondeterminism in $X$ and $X'$ can be refined away to yield the following two extreme solutions:

*Lazy cell.*

$$
\begin{aligned}
X = <s.a!> a?\text{count}(n); \textbf{ if } n \bmod 2 = 0 \textbf{ then } & s.a!\text{count}(n \operatorname{div} 2); X' \\
\textbf{else } & a!1?\text{ack}; s.a!\text{count}(n \operatorname{div} 2); X' \ ,
\end{aligned}
$$

where $X' = s.a?x; \textbf{if } x = 0 \textbf{ then } a!0; X \textbf{ else } a!1?\text{ack}; a!1?\text{ack}; s.a!\text{ack}; X'$.

*Eager cell.*

$$
\begin{aligned}
X = <s.a!> a?\text{count}(n); s.a!\text{count}(n \operatorname{div} 2); \textbf{ if } n \bmod 2 = 0 \textbf{ then } & X' \\
\textbf{else } & a!1?\text{ack}; X' \ ,
\end{aligned}
$$

where $X' = s.a?x; \textbf{if } x = 0 \textbf{ then } a!0, X \textbf{ else } s.a!\text{ack}; a!1?\text{ack}; a!1?\text{ack}; X'$.

Solutions to the design equation for four-phase handshaking, i.e., $C^*_k = s.C^*_{k-1} \backslash\backslash X$, can be obtained in a similar fashion. The most general solution exhibits even more nondeterminism. As we shall see in the next section, it turns out that compact implementations exist for the following specifications of a lazy cell and an eager cell.

*Lazy cell (four-phase).*

$$X =\langle s.a! \rangle\ a?\text{count}(n);\ \textbf{if}\ n \bmod 2 = 0\ \textbf{then}\ s.a!\text{count}(n\,\text{div}\,2); X'_n$$
$$\textbf{else}\ a!1?\text{ack}; a!1?\text{ack}; s.a!\text{count}(n\,\text{div}\,2); X'_n\ ,$$

where $X'_m = s.a?x;\ \textbf{if}\ x = 0\ \textbf{then}\ a!0?\text{count}(m); s.a!\text{count}(m\,\text{div}\,2)?0; a!0; X$
$\textbf{else}\ a!1?\text{ack}; a!1?\text{ack}; a!1?\text{ack}; s.a!\text{ack}?1; a!1?\text{ack}; s.a!\text{ack}; X'_m\ .$

*Eager cell (four-phase).*

$$X =\langle s.a! \rangle\ a?\text{count}(n); s.a!\text{count}(n\,\text{div}\,2);\ \textbf{if}\ n \bmod 2 = 0\ \textbf{then}\ X'_n$$
$$\textbf{else}\ a!1?\text{ack}; a!1?\text{ack}; X''_n\ ,$$

where $X'_m = s.a?x;\ \textbf{if}\ x = 0\ \textbf{then}\ a!0?\text{count}(m); s.a!\text{count}(m\,\text{div}\,2)?0; a!0; X$
$\textbf{else}\ s.a!\text{ack}; a!1?\text{ack}; a!1?\text{ack}; a!1?\text{ack}; a!1?\text{ack}; s.a?1!\text{ack}; X'_m$
and $X''_m = s.a?x;\ \textbf{if}\ x = 0\ \textbf{then}\ a!0?\text{count}(m); s.a!\text{count}(m\,\text{div}\,2)?0; a!0; X$
$\textbf{else}\ s.a!\text{ack}; a!1?\text{ack}; a!1?\text{ack}; s.a?1!\text{ack}; a!1?\text{ack}; a!1?\text{ack}; X''_m\ .$

# 4 Decomposition of the Cells of the Array

## 4.1 The One-bit Counter

The special case $k = 1$ (so that $n$ can be either 0 or 1) of $C_k$ is of particular interest because larger counters can be constructed out of it, as we saw in the last section.

$C_1$
$=$ { definitions of $C_k$ and $C'_{k,m}$ }
$a?\text{count}(n);\ \textbf{if}\ n = 0\ \textbf{then}\ a!0; C_1\ \textbf{else}\ a!1?\text{ack}; a!0; C_1\ .$

Then it follows by recursion-induction that the design equation

$$C_1 \sqsubseteq Y \tag{3}$$

and the auxiliary equation

$$a?\text{ack}; a!0; C_1 \sqsubseteq Y \tag{4}$$

are solved by putting $Y = a?x;\ \textbf{if}\ x = \mathit{count}(1)\ \textbf{then}\ a!1; Y\ \textbf{else}\ a!0; Y$.

We are now ready to decompose the one-bit counter delay-insensitively into parts. In order to do this formally, we must work within DI-Algebra. There is no concept of "handshake port" in DI-Algebra and so port-status and handshake prefixes and guards should not appear in expressions. Our definition of $Y$ satisfies these criteria. To achieve disjointness of input alphabet and output alphabet, we strip the port name from each communication, renaming $a?\text{count}(n)$ to count?$n$, $a?$ack to ack?, $a!0$ to 0! and $a!1$ to 1! .

Thus, we define process $Y'$ (equivalent to $Y$) in DI-Algebra, with input alphabet $\mathbf{i}Y' = \{\mathrm{count}, \mathrm{ack}\}$ and output alphabet $\mathbf{o}Y' = \{0, 1\}$, as follows:

$$\begin{aligned} Y' \ &= [(\mathrm{count}?n \to \mathbf{if}\ n = 0\ \mathbf{then}\ 0!; Y'\ \mathbf{else}\ 1!; Y') \\ &\quad \Box\ (\mathrm{ack}? \to 0!; Y')]\ . \end{aligned}$$

The specification of the one-bit counter is now in a form similar to those of the following building blocks:

- Select element. This converts a bundled-bit into dual-rail, viz.,

$$SEL \ = \ \mathrm{count}?n; \mathbf{if}\ n = 0\ \mathbf{then}\ 0'!; SEL\ \mathbf{else}\ 1!; SEL\ ,$$

  where $\mathbf{i}SEL = \{\mathrm{count}\}$ and $\mathbf{o}SEL = \{0', 1\}$.
- Merge element. $M \ = \ [(0'? \to 0!; M)\ \Box\ (\mathrm{ack}? \to 0!; M)]$, where $\mathbf{i}M = \{0', \mathrm{ack}\}$ and $\mathbf{o}M = \{0\}$.

Indeed $Y' = SEL\backslash\backslash M$: we note that $\mathbf{i}Y' = \mathbf{i}(SEL\backslash\backslash M)$ and $\mathbf{o}Y' = \mathbf{o}(SEL\backslash\backslash M)$ (Fig. 1) and, starting from the RHS, calculate

$$\begin{aligned}
& SEL\backslash\backslash M \\
= \ & \{\ \text{definitions of } SEL \text{ and } M\ \} \\
& (\mathrm{count}?n; \mathbf{if}\ n = 0\ \mathbf{then}\ 0'!; SEL\ \mathbf{else}\ 1!; SEL) \\
& \backslash\backslash[(0'? \to 0!; M)\ \Box\ (\mathrm{ack}? \to 0!; M)] \\
= \ & \{\ \text{expansion theorem}\ \} \\
& [(\mathrm{count}?n \to (\mathbf{if}\ n = 0\ \mathbf{then}\ 0'!; SEL\ \mathbf{else}\ 1!; SEL)\backslash\backslash M) \\
& \Box\ (\mathrm{ack}? \to SEL\backslash\backslash(0!; M))] \\
= \ & \{\ \text{laws } (\mathbf{if}\ bool\ \mathbf{then}\ P\ \mathbf{else}\ Q)\backslash\backslash R = \mathbf{if}\ bool\ \mathbf{then}\ P\backslash\backslash R\ \mathbf{else}\ Q\backslash\backslash R, \\
& \quad (c!; P)\backslash\backslash Q = P\backslash\backslash(Q/c?) \text{ if } c \in \mathbf{i}Q, \text{ and } c!; (P\backslash\backslash Q) \text{ otherwise}\ \} \\
& [(\mathrm{count}?n \to \mathbf{if}\ n = 0\ \mathbf{then}\ SEL\backslash\backslash(M/0'?)\ \mathbf{else}\ 1!; (SEL\backslash\backslash M)) \\
& \Box\ (\mathrm{ack}? \to 0!; (SEL\backslash\backslash M))] \\
= \ & \{\ \text{property } M/0'? = 0!; M \text{ and} \\
& \quad \text{law } P\backslash\backslash(c!; Q) = c!; (P\backslash\backslash Q) \text{ if } c \notin \mathbf{i}P\ \} \\
& [(\mathrm{count}?n \to \mathbf{if}\ n = 0\ \mathbf{then}\ 0!; (SEL\backslash\backslash M)\ \mathbf{else}\ 1!; (SEL\backslash\backslash M)) \\
& \Box\ (\mathrm{ack}? \to 0!; (SEL\backslash\backslash M))]\ .
\end{aligned}$$

The result follows by the uniqueness of fixed points for guarded recursions.

Unfortunately the Merge and Select elements are unattractive to implement in general: the Merge element requires an XOR gate and the Select element two latches and two XOR gates. It turns out, however, that in the design of the four-phase counter $C_1^*$ the elements will be used in a restricted way. The restriction on the use of the Merge element amounts to $0'$ and ack being mutually exclusive, in the sense that at most one can be high at any time, and so the element can be implemented with an OR gate. The restriction on the use of the Select element is that the number input on port $a$ when count goes high remains valid until count goes low; the element can be implemented by two AND gates (composed speed-independently), cf. the read circuitry of a Variable element (a boolean

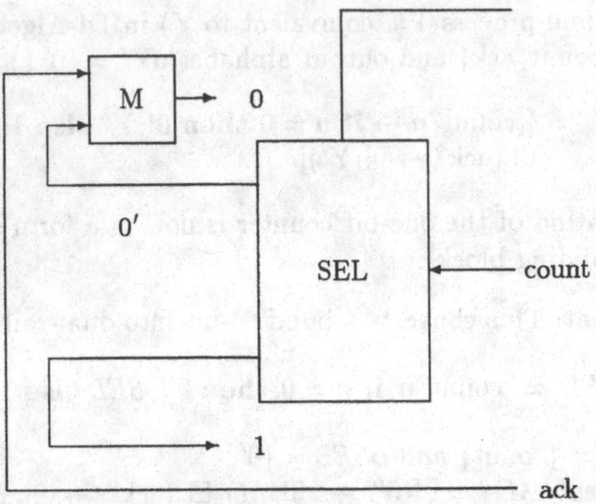


**Fig. 1.** Delay-insensitive decomposition of $C_1$.

register) [14]. In the revised specifications, $SEL^*$ and $M^*$, these restrictions are captured by the appearance of constants in input-prefixes and of $\perp$ in input-guarded alternatives:

$$SEL^* = \text{count?}n; \textbf{if } n = 0 \textbf{ then } 0'!; \text{count?}0; 0'!; SEL^* \textbf{ else } 1'!; \text{count?}1; 1'!; SEL^*$$

$$M^* = [(0'? \to 0!; M_0^{*'}) \,\Box\, (\text{ack}'? \to 0!; M_1^{*'})]$$

$$M_0^{*'} = [(0'? \to 0!; M^*) \,\Box\, (\text{ack}'? \to \perp)]$$

$$M_1^{*'} = [(0'? \to \perp) \,\Box\, (\text{ack}'? \to 0!; M^*)]$$

where $\mathbf{i}SEL^* = \{\text{count}\}$, $\mathbf{o}SEL^* = \{0', 1'\}$, $\mathbf{i}M^* = \{0', \text{ack}'\}$ and $\mathbf{o}M^* = \{0\}$.

We can now expand out the composition of $SEL^*$ and $M^*$:

$$\begin{aligned} SEL^* \backslash\backslash M^* = [&(\text{count?}n \to \textbf{if } n = 0 \textbf{ then } 0!; ((\text{count?}0; 0'!; SEL^*) \backslash\backslash M_0^{*'}) \\ &\qquad\qquad\qquad \textbf{else } 1'!; ((\text{count?}1; 1'!; SEL^*) \backslash\backslash M^*)) \\ &\Box\, (\text{ack}'? \to \ldots)] \end{aligned}$$

$$\begin{aligned} (\text{count?}0; 0'!; SEL^*) \backslash\backslash M_0^{*'} &= [(\text{count?}0 \to 0!; (SEL^* \backslash\backslash M^*)) \\ &\quad\ \Box\, (\text{ack}'? \to \ldots)] \\ (\text{count?}1; 1'!; SEL^*) \backslash\backslash M^* &= [(\text{count?}1 \to \ldots) \\ &\quad\ \Box\, (\text{ack}'? \to 0!; (\text{count?}1; 1'!; SEL^*) \backslash\backslash M_1^*))] \\ (\text{count?}1; 1'!; SEL^*) \backslash\backslash M_1^* &= [(\text{count?}1 \to 1'!; (SEL^* \backslash\backslash M_1^*)) \\ &\quad\ \Box\, (\text{ack}'? \to \ldots)] \\ SEL^* \backslash\backslash M_1^* &= [(\text{count?}n \to \ldots) \\ &\quad\ \Box\, (\text{ack}'? \to 0!; (SEL^* \backslash\backslash M^*))] \,. \end{aligned}$$

Abstraction into HS-Algebra is now possible and yields the process $SM^*$, defined by

$$SM^* = a?\mathrm{count}(n); \textbf{ if } n = 0 \textbf{ then } a!0?\mathrm{count}(0); a!0; SM^* \\ \textbf{else } a!1'?\mathrm{ack}'; a!0?\mathrm{count}(1); a!1'?\mathrm{ack}'; a!0; SM^* \ .$$

This is essentially a reshuffling [14] of $C_1^*$ and, indeed, by inserting Martin's Q element into the circuit, Fig. 2, we finally obtain a four-phase one-bit counter.

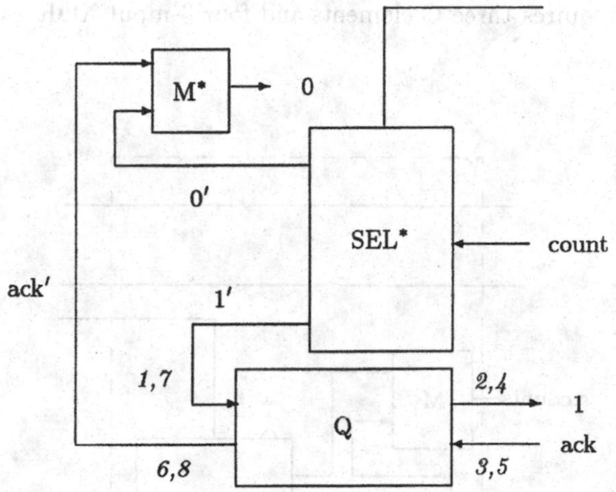


**Fig. 2.** DI-decomposition of four-phase counter $C_1^*$ (with order of signals at Q indicated).

In summary:

1. It was easy to see how to decompose $C_1$ into $SEL$ and $M$, but the resulting circuit was unattractive.
2. We arrived at a decomposition of $C_1^*$ by adapting our decomposition of $C_1$. Additional sequencing circuitry was required, but this enabled selection and merging to be performed more efficiently.

Finally, we conclude this subsection by considering what happens if $n$ does not have to be input, but instead takes a known, fixed value, 0 or 1. The two-phase version of the counter can be implemented simply with wires, as can the four-phase version when $n = 0$; the four-phase version when $n = 1$ requires a Q element.

## 4.2 A Lazy Cell

As defined in Sect. 3, a lazy cell only communicates with the subcounter when it cannot otherwise determine whether to signal 0 or 1 on $a$; in the meantime the subcounter is suspended. In this case, the response time of the counter is the sum of the delay before the cell communicates with the subcounter, the response time of the subcounter and the delay before the cell communicates on $a$.

The cell can itself be decomposed into subcells $Y$ and $Z$; $Y$ and $Z$ can then be decomposed delay-insensitively into parts, Fig. 3. $Y$ decomposes into Select and Merge elements, like $C_1$, and a Buffer element (implementable as a wire) which propagates signals from $s.a?0$ to $a!0$. $Z$ decomposes into a 3-way Call element and a Buffer element. Unfortunately, in general, implementing a 3-way Call element requires three C elements and four 3-input XOR gates.

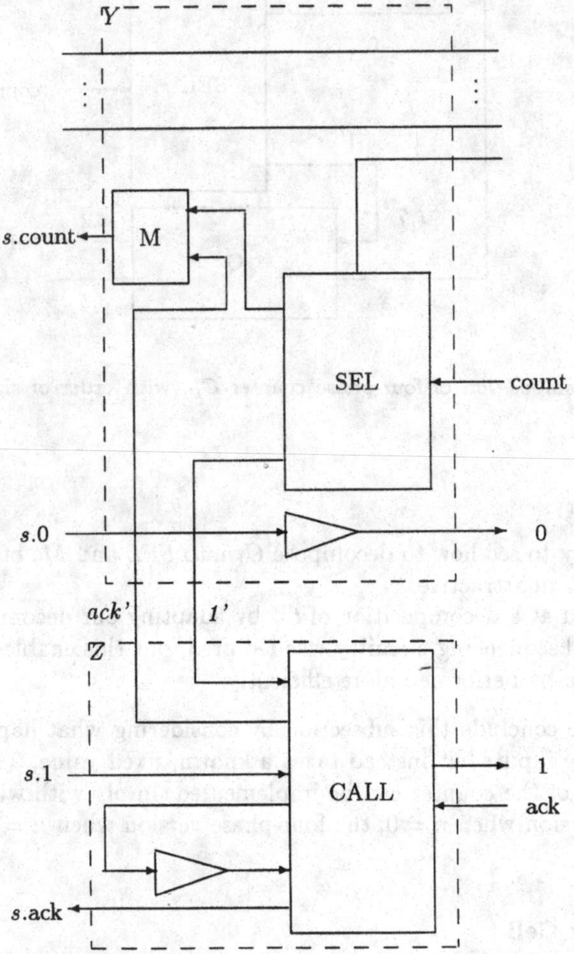


**Fig. 3.** DI-decomposition of lazy cell.

Adapting $Y$ and $Z$ to four-phase handshaking can be achieved, as before, with Q elements, Fig. 4. It enables us to speed-independently decompose the 3-way Call element into three asymmetric C elements and a 3-input OR gate [15].

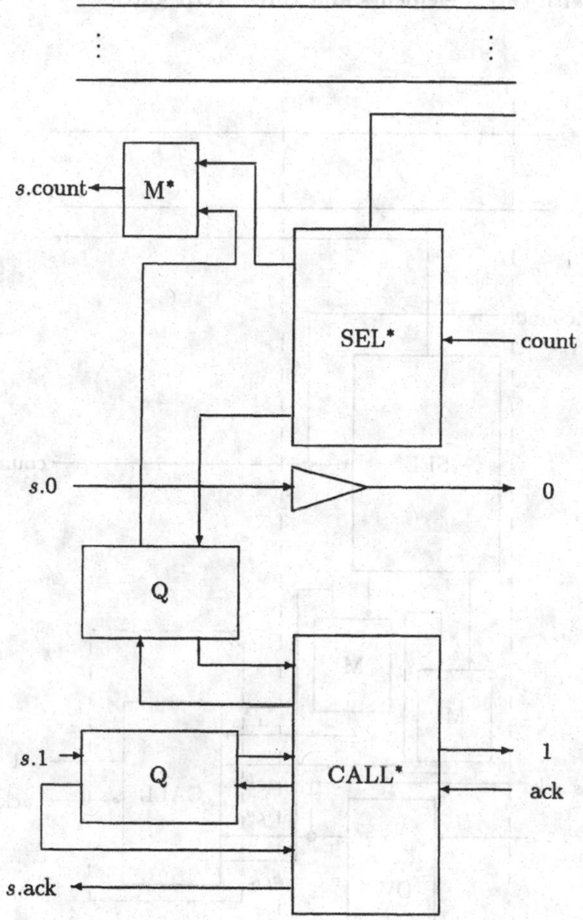


**Fig. 4.** DI-decomposition of four-phase lazy cell.

### 4.3 An Eager Cell

An eager cell activates the subcounter early, so as to overlap as much as possible of its own response time with that of the subcounter. This speeds up the overall rate of counting.

Again, the cell can be decomposed into subcells $Y$ and $Z$, though with a different interface. We propose (again without proof) a delay-insensitive decomposition of $Y$ into Select, 2-by-1 Decision-Wait, two Fork and two Merge elements, Fig. 5. ($Z$ is simply a 2-way Call element.) The Decision-Wait element can be implemented with two C elements and two XOR gates, and the 2-way Call element with two C elements and three XOR gates.

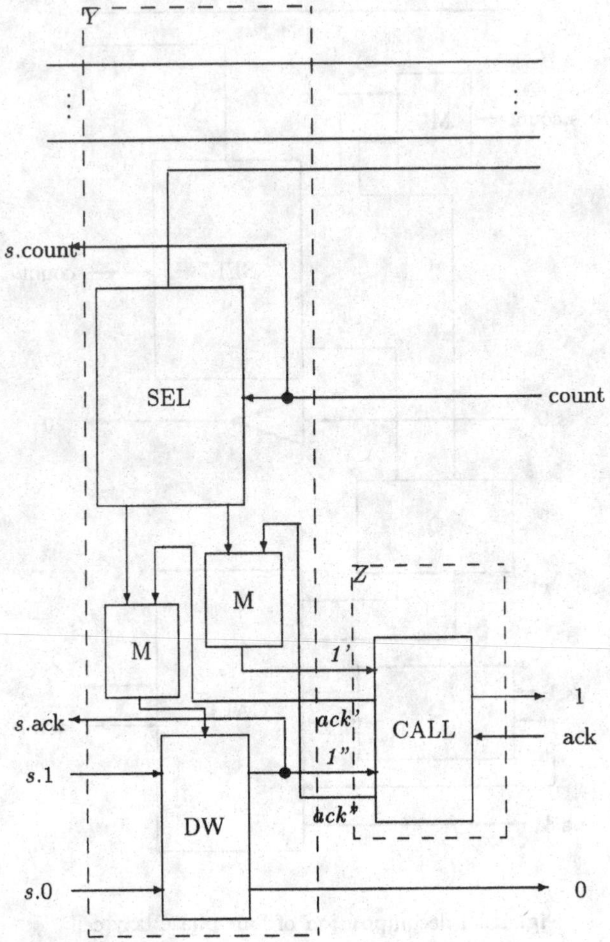


**Fig. 5.** DI-decomposition of eager cell.

Adapting the cell to four-phase handshaking involves inserting two Q elements, Fig. 6. The Select element simplifies as before, whilst the Decision-Wait element and the Call element can be speed-independently decomposed, respectively, into two C elements and into two asymmetric C elements and an OR gate. Note that the Merge elements would still need to be implemented by XOR gates.

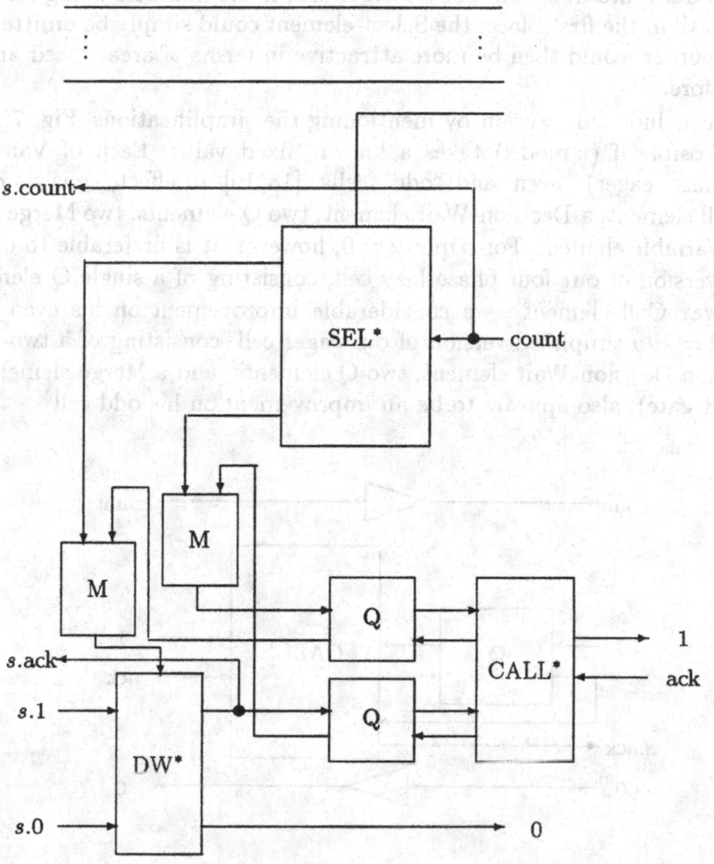


**Fig. 6.** DI-decomposition of four-phase eager cell.

### 4.4 Comparison

For both two-phase and four-phase handshaking, eager cells introduce parallelism and so may be more suitable for building fast counters than lazy cells. Less obviously, this parallelism comes with little to no area overhead: the reduction in the size of the Call element from 3-way to 2-way compensates for the inclusion of the Decision-Wait element to buffer signals.

The advantage of four-phase over two-phase seems to be one of area improvement rather than of speed improvement. The reduced area comes about from the simplified implementation of Select and Call elements (and, in the case of eager cells, Decision-Wait elements) which outweighs the cost of the additional sequencing circuitry. Recall that the purpose of the Select elements is to turn bundled-data into dual-rail. For an eager cell, if the numbers being loaded were in dual-rail in the first place, the Select element could simply be omitted; a two-phase counter would then be more attractive in terms of area, speed and power than before.

We conclude this section by mentioning the simplifications, Fig. 7, that become possible if $(n \bmod 2)$ takes a known, fixed value. Each of Van Berkel's (four-phase, eager) "even' and "odd" cells [18, 19], in effect, consists of a two-way Call element, a Decision-Wait element, two Q elements, two Merge elements and a Variable element. For $n \bmod 2 = 0$, however, it is preferable to use a simplified version of our four-phase lazy cell, consisting of a single Q element and a two-way Call element — a considerable improvement on his even cell. For $n \bmod 2 = 1$, a simplified version of our eager cell, consisting of a two-way Call element, a Decision-Wait element, two Q elements, and a Merge element (albeit an XOR gate), also appears to be an improvement on his odd cell.

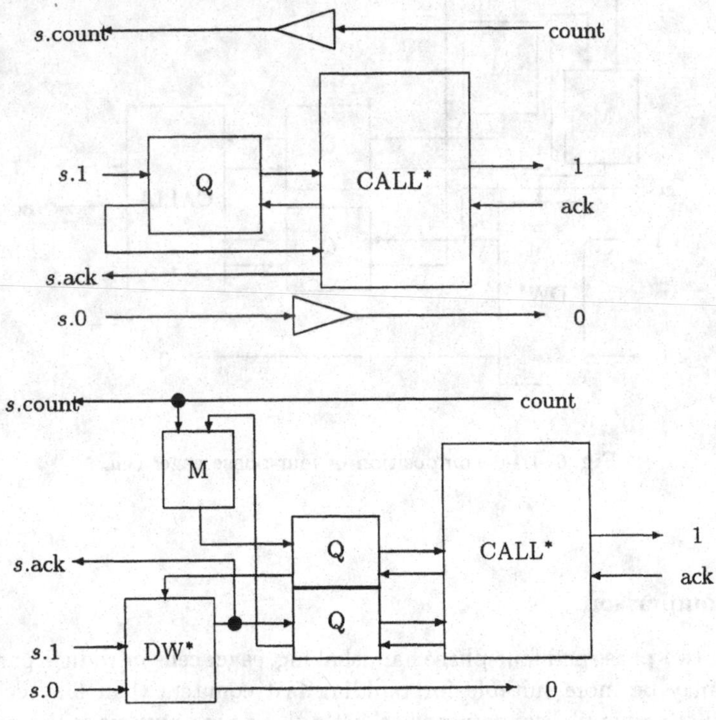


**Fig. 7.** Lazy even cell and eager odd cell (assuming four-phase handshaking).

## 5 Conclusion

We have tackled a small, but nontrivial, design problem in a disciplined and formal manner. In this approach we first follow the handshaking discipline, decomposing a subsystem into components that handshake with each other. We then follow the less restrictive delay-insensitive discipline for decomposing those components into standard parts. Working with two-phase handshakes makes the decomposition task that much easier, and adaptation to four-phase handshaking (and so efficient building blocks) can be carried out at a late stage in design. Constructing formal specifications and proofs should help us to gain insight into the design problem and to avoid errors.

The solution that we have obtained to the loadable counter problem seems to be quite practical. Furthermore, it has suggested to us possible improvements to the modulo-$N$ counter implementation previously published by Van Berkel.

*Acknowledgements. I am grateful to Joep Kessels, Ad Peeters and Alex Yakovlev for their presentations and discussions concerning this problem at the ACiD-WG Workshop in Groningen. I also wish to thank the anonymous referees of MPC'98, whose desire for more formality and a more calculational approach encouraged me to make significant improvements to this paper.*

## References

1. R. Groenboom, M.B. Josephs, P.G. Lucassen, J.T. Udding. Normal form in a delay-insensitive algebra. In: S. Furber, M. Edwards (eds.) Asynchronous Design Methodologies (A-28), pp. 57–70, IFIP North-Holland, 1993.
2. C.A.R. Hoare. Communicating Sequential Processes. Prentice Hall, 1985.
3. M.B. Josephs. Receptive process theory. Acta Informatica 29:17-31, Springer-Verlag, 1992.
4. M.B. Josephs. Using Handshake Algebra to help solve the loadable counter problem. In: ACiD-WG Workshop, University of Groningen Technical Report CSN 9602, 1996.
5. M.B. Josephs, P.G. Lucassen, J.T. Udding, T. Verhoeff. Formal design of an asynchronous DSP counterflow pipeline: a case study in Handshake Algebra. In: Proc. Int. Sym. on Advanced Research in Asynchronous Circuits and Systems, pp. 206-215, IEEE CS Press, 1994.
6. M.B. Josephs, J.T. Udding. Delay-insensitive circuits: an algebraic approach to their design. In: J. Baeten, J. Klop (eds.) CONCUR'90. Lecture Notes in Computer Science 458, pp. 342-366, Springer-Verlag, 1990.
7. M. B. Josephs, J. T. Udding. An Overview of DI Algebra. In: T.N. Mudge, V. Milutinovic, L. Hunter (eds.) Proc. 26th Annual Hawaii Int. Conf. on System Sciences, Vol. 1, pp. 329–338, IEEE Computer Society Press, 1993.
8. M.B. Josephs, J.T. Udding, J.T. Yantchev. Handshake Algebra. South Bank University Technical Report SBU-CISM-93-1, 1993.
9. J.L.W. Kessels. Calculational derivation of a counter with bounded response time and bounded power dissipation. Distributed Computing 8:143-149, Springer-Verlag, 1995.

10. J.L.W. Kessels, P. Marston. Designing Asynchronous Standby Circuits for a Low-Power Pager. In: Proc. Int. Sym. on Advanced Research in Asynchronous Circuits and Systems, pp. 268-278, IEEE Computer Society Press, 1997.
11. P.G. Lucassen. A denotational model and composition theorems for a calculus of delay-insensitive specifications. Ph.D. Thesis, Groningen University, 1994.
12. P.G. Lucassen, I. Polak, J.T. Udding. Normal Form in DI-Algebra with Recursion. In: Proc. Int. Sym. on Advanced Research in Asynchronous Circuits and Systems, pp. 167-174, IEEE Computer Society Press, 1997.
13. W.C. Mallon, J.T. Udding. Using Metrics for Proof Rules for Recursively Defined Delay-insensitive Specifications. In: Proc. Int. Sym. on Advanced Research in Asynchronous Circuits and Systems, pp. 175-183, IEEE Computer Society Press, 1997.
14. A.J. Martin. Programming in VLSI: from communicating processes to delay-insensitive circuits. In: C.A.R. Hoare (ed.) Developments in Concurrency and Communication. Addison-Wesley, 1990.
15. A.M.G. Peeters. Single-Rail Handshake Circuits. Ph.D. Thesis, Eindhoven University of Technology, 1996.
16. A.W. Roscoe. The Theory and Practice of Concurrency. Prentice Hall, 1998.
17. I.E. Sutherland. Micropipelines. Communications of the ACM 32(6):720-738, 1989.
18. K. van Berkel. Handshake Circuits: an Asynchronous Architecture for VLSI Programming. Cambridge University Press, 1993.
19. K. van Berkel. VLSI programming of a modulo-$N$ counter with constant response time and constant power. In: S. Furber, M. Edwards (eds.) Asynchronous Design Methodologies (A-28), pp. 1-11, IFIP North-Holland, 1993.
20. V.I. Varshavsky (ed.) Self-Timed Control of Concurrent Processes. Kluwer Academic Publishers, 1990.
21. A.V. Yakovlev. Solving ACiD-WG Design Problems with Petri Net Based Methods. In: ACiD-WG Workshop, University of Groningen Technical Report CSN 9602, 1996.

# A Semantic Approach to Secure Information Flow

K. Rustan M. Leino[1] and Rajeev Joshi[2]

[1] DEC SRC, Palo Alto, CA 94301, USA
rustan@pa.dec.com
[2] University of Texas, Austin, TX 78712, USA
joshi@cs.utexas.edu

**Abstract.** A classic problem in security is to determine whether a program has *secure information flow*. Informally, this problem is described as follows: Given a program with variables partitioned into two disjoint sets of "high-security" and "low-security" variables, check whether observations of the low-security variables reveal any information about the initial values of the high-security variables. Although the problem has been studied for several decades, most previous approaches have been syntactic in nature, often using type systems and compiler data flow analysis techniques to analyze program texts. This paper presents a considerably different approach to checking secure information flow, based on a semantic characterization. A semantic approach has several desirable features. Firstly, it gives a more precise characterization of security than that provided by most previous approaches. Secondly, it applies to any programming constructs whose semantics are definable; for instance, the introduction of nondeterminism and exceptions poses no additional problems. Thirdly, it can be used for reasoning about indirect leaking of information through variations in program behavior (*e.g.*, whether or not the program terminates).

## 0 Introduction

A classic problem in security is that of determining whether a given program has *secure information flow* [BLP73,Den76]. In its simplest form, this problem may be described informally as follows: Given a program whose variables are partitioned into two disjoint sets of "high-security" and "low-security" variables, check whether observations of the low-security variables reveal anything about the initial values of the high-security variables. A related problem is that of detecting *covert flows*, where information is leaked indirectly, through variations in program behavior [Lam73]. For instance, it may be possible to deduce something about the initial values of the high-security variables by examining the resource usage of the program (*e.g.*, by counting the number of times it accesses the disk head).

Although this problem has been studied for several decades, most of the previous approaches have been syntactic in nature, often using type systems and compiler data flow analysis techniques to analyze program texts. In this paper, we present a considerably different approach to secure information flow, based on a semantic notion of program equality. A definition based on program semantics has several desirable features. Firstly, it provides a more precise characterization of secure information flow than that provided by most previous approaches. Secondly, it is applicable to any programming construct whose semantics are defined; for instance, nondeterminism and exceptions pose no additional problems. Thirdly, it can be applied to reasoning about a variety of covert flows, including termination behavior and timing dependent flows.

The outline of the rest of the paper is as follows. We start in section 1 by informally describing the problem and discussing several small examples. We present our formal characterization of security in section 2. In section 3, we relate our definition to the notion used elsewhere in the literature. In sections 4 and 5, we show how to rewrite our definition in the weakest precondition calculus so that it is amenable for use with tools for mechanical verification. We discuss related work in section 6 and end with a short summary in section 7.

# 1 Informal description of the problem

Throughout the rest of the paper, we assume that in each program considered, the variables are partitioned into two disjoint tuples $h$ (denoting "high-security" variables) and $k$ (denoting "low-security" variables). Informally, we say that a program is *secure* if:

> Observations of the initial and final values of $k$ do not provide any information about the initial value of $h$.

(Notice that it is only the *initial* value of $h$ that we care about.) We illustrate this informal description of the problem with a few examples. Throughout our discussion, we refer to an "adversary" who is trying to glean some information about the initial value of $h$. We assume that this adversary has knowledge of the program text and of the initial and final values of $k$.

The program

$$k := h$$

is not secure, since the initial value of $h$ can be observed as the final value of $k$. However, the program

$$h := k$$

*is* secure, since $k$, whose value is not changed, is independent of the initial value of $h$. Similarly, the program

$$k := 6$$

is secure, because the final value of $k$ is always $6$, regardless of the initial value of $h$.

It is possible for an insecure program to occur as a subprogram of a secure program. For example, in each of the four programs

$$k := h \,;\, k := 6 \qquad (0)$$
$$h := k \,;\, k := h \qquad (1)$$
$$k := h \,;\, k := k - h \qquad (2)$$
$$\textbf{if } \mathit{false} \textbf{ then } k := h \textbf{ end} \qquad (3)$$

the insecure program $k := h$ occurs as a subprogram; nevertheless, the four programs are all secure.

There are more subtle ways in which a program can be insecure. For example, with $h, k$ of type boolean, the program

**if** $h$ **then** $k := \mathit{true}$ **else** $k := \mathit{false}$ **end**

is insecure, despite the fact that each branch of the conditional is secure. This program has the same effect as $k := h$, and the flow of information from $h$ to $k$ is called *implicit* [Den76].

In the insecure programs shown so far, the exact value of $h$ is leaked into $k$. This need not always be the case: a program is considered insecure if it reveals *any* information about the initial value of $h$. For example, if $h$ and $k$ are of type integer, neither of the two programs shown below,

$k := h * h$
**if** $0 \leq h$ **then** $k := 1$ **else** $k := 0$ **end**

transmits the entire value of $h$, but both programs are insecure because the final value of $k$ does reveal something about the initial value of $h$.

A nondeterministic program can be insecure even if the adversary has no knowledge of how the nondeterminism is resolved. For example, the following program is insecure, because the final value of $k$ is always very close to the initial value of $h$:

$k := h - 1 \;\square\; k := h + 1$

(The operator $\square$ denotes demonic choice: execution of $S \;\square\; T$ consists of choosing any one of $S$ or $T$ and executing it.) The program

$\mathit{skip} \;\square\; k := h$

is also considered insecure, because if the initial and final values of $k$ are observed to be different, then the initial value of $h$ is revealed.

Finally, we give some examples of programs that transmit information about $h$ via their termination behavior. The nicest way to present these examples is by using Dijkstra's **if fi** construct [Dij76]. The operational interpretation of the program

**if** $B0 \longrightarrow S0 \;\square\; B1 \longrightarrow S1$ **fi**

is as follows. From states in which neither $B0$ nor $B1$ is true, the program loops forever; from all other states it executes either $S0$ (if $B0$ is true) or $S1$ (if $B1$ is true). If both $B0$ and $B1$ are true, the choice between $S0$ and $S1$ is made arbitrarily. Now, the deterministic program

**if** $h = 0 \longrightarrow \mathit{loop} \;\square\; h \neq 0 \longrightarrow \mathit{skip}$ **fi** (4)

(where *loop* is the program that never terminates) is insecure, because whether or not the program terminates depends on the initial value of $h$. Next, consider the following two nondeterministic programs:

**if** $h = 0 \longrightarrow \mathit{skip} \;\square\; \mathit{true} \longrightarrow \mathit{loop}$ **fi** (5)
**if** $h = 0 \longrightarrow \mathit{loop} \;\square\; \mathit{true} \longrightarrow \mathit{skip}$ **fi** (6)

Note that program (5) terminates only if the initial value of $h$ is $0$. Although there is always a possibility that the program will loop forever, if the program is observed to terminate, the initial value of $h$ is revealed; thus the program is considered insecure. Program (6) is more interesting. If we take the view that nontermination is indistinguishable from slow execution, then the program is secure. However, if we take the view that an adversary is able to detect infinite looping, then it can deduce that the initial value of $h$ is $0$, and the program should be considered insecure.

**Remark.** Readers may be wondering just how much time an adversary would have to spend in order to "detect infinite looping", so the second viewpoint above requires a little explanation. One way to address the issue of nontermination is to require that machine-specific timing information (which the adversary may exploit to detect nontermination) be made explicit in the programming model (*e.g.*, by adding a low-security timer variable, which is updated by each instruction). Another way, which we adopt in this paper, is to strengthen the definition of security by considering powerful adversaries who can detect nontermination. As we will see later, these two approaches yield the same definition for deterministic programs; it is only in the presence of nondeterminism that differences arise. Even then, our definition is at worst a little conservative, in that it classifies a program such as (6) as insecure. *(End of Remark.)*

We hope that these examples, based on our informal description of secure information flow, have helped give the reader an operational understanding of the problem. From now on, we will adopt a more rigorous approach. We start in the next section by formally defining security in terms of program semantics.

## 2 Formal characterization

Our formal characterization of secure information flow is expressed as an equality between two programs. We use the symbol $\doteq$ to denote program equality based on total correctness and write " $S$ is secure" to mean that program $S$ has secure information flow.

A key ingredient in our characterization is the program

"assign to $h$ an arbitrary value"

which we denote by $HH$ ("havoc on $h$"). Program $HH$ may be used to express some useful properties. Firstly, observe that the difference between a program $S$ and the program " $HH$ ; $S$ " is that the latter executes $S$ after setting $h$ to an arbitrary value. Secondly, observe that the program " $S$ ; $HH$ " 'discards' the final value of $h$ resulting from the execution of $S$. We use these observations below in giving an informal understanding of the following definition of security.

**Definition (Secure Information Flow)**

$$S \text{ is secure} \equiv (HH\;;\;S\;;\;HH \;\doteq\; S\;;\;HH) \tag{7}$$

Using the two observations above, this characterization may be understood as follows. First, note that the final occurrence of $HH$ on each side means that only the final value of $k$ (but not of $h$) is retained. Next, observe that the prefix " $HH$ ; " in the first program means that the two programs are equal provided that the final value of $k$ produced by $S$ does not depend on the initial value of $h$. In section 3, we provide a more rigorous justification for this definition, by relating it to a notion of secure information flow that has been used elsewhere in the literature, but for now, we hope that this informal argument gives the reader some operational understanding of our definition. In the rest of this section, we discuss some of the features of our approach.

Firstly, note that we have not stated the definition in terms of a particular style of program semantics (*e.g.*, axiomatic, denotational, or operational). Sequential program equality can be expressed in any of these styles and different choices are suitable for different purposes. For instance, in this paper, we will use a relational semantics to justify our characterization, but we will use weakest precondition semantics to obtain a condition that is more amenable for use in mechanical verification. Secondly, observe that our definition is given purely in terms of program semantics; thus it can be used to reason about any programming construct whose semantics are defined. For instance, nondeterminism and exceptions pose no additional problems in this approach, nor do data structures such as arrays, records, or objects. (In contrast, definitions based on type systems often need to be extended with the introduction of new constructs.) Finally, note that our definition leaves open the decision of which variables are deemed to be low-security (*i.e.*, observable by an adversary). Different choices may be used to reason about different kinds of covert flows, by introducing appropriate special variables (such as those used by Hehner [Heh84]) and including them in the low-security variables $k$. For example, one can reason about covert flows involving timing considerations by including in $k$ a program variable that records execution time.

## 3 Security in the relational calculus

In this section, we formally justify definition (7) by showing that it is equivalent to the notion used elsewhere in the literature. Since that notion was given in operational terms, we find it convenient to use a relational semantics for total correctness. Thus, for the purposes of this section, a program is a relation over the space formed by extending the state space defined by $h$ and $k$ with the special "looping state" $\infty$ [RMD92]. We use the following notational conventions: Identifiers $w, x, y, z$ denote program states; we write $x.k$ and $x.h$ to denote the values of $k$ and $h$ in state $x$. For any relation $S$ and states $x$ and $y$, we write $x\langle S\rangle y$ to denote that $S$ relates $x$ to $y$; this means that there is an execution of program $S$ from the initial state $x$ to final state $y$. We assume that every program $S$ satisfies $x\langle S\rangle\infty \;\equiv\; x=\infty$ for all $x$ and that $\infty.k$ differs from $x.k$ for all $x$ that differ from $\infty$. The identity relation is denoted by " $Id$ " ; it satisfies $x\langle Id\rangle y \;\equiv\; x = y$ for all $x$ and $y$. The symbol $\subseteq$ denotes relational containment and the operator ; denotes relational composition. We will use the facts that $Id$ is a left- and a right-identity of composition and that ; is monotonic with respect to $\subseteq$ in both arguments.

We use the following format for writing quantified expressions [DS90]: For $\mathcal{Q}$ denoting either $\forall$ or $\exists$, we write

$$(\mathcal{Q}j : r.j : t.j)$$

to denote the quantification over all $j$ satisfying $r.j$. Identifier $j$ is called the *dummy*, $r.j$ is called the *range*, and $t.j$ is called the *term* of the quantification. When the range is *true* or is understood from context, it is sometimes omitted. We use a similar convention to define sets, and write

$$\{j : r.j : t.j\}$$

to mean the set of all elements of the form $t.j$ for $j$ satisfying $r.j$.

The relational semantics of program $HH$ are given as follows.

$$(\forall x, y :: x\langle HH\rangle y \equiv x.k = y.k)$$

Note that the relation $HH$ is both reflexive and transitive:

$$Id \subseteq HH \tag{8}$$

$$HH ; HH \subseteq HH \tag{9}$$

Using these properties, condition (7) may be rewritten in relational terms as follows.

$$
\begin{array}{ll}
 & S \text{ is secure} \\
= & \quad \{ \text{ Definition (7), program equality } \doteq \text{ is relational equality } = \ \} \\
 & HH ; S ; HH = S ; HH \\
\Rightarrow & \quad \{ \text{ (8) and } ; \text{ monotonic, hence } HH ; S ; Id \subseteq HH ; S ; HH \ \} \\
 & HH ; S \subseteq S ; HH \\
\Rightarrow & \quad \{ \text{ Applying " } ; HH \text{ " to both sides, using } ; \text{ monotonic } \} \\
 & HH ; S ; HH \subseteq S ; HH ; HH \\
\Rightarrow & \quad \{ \text{ (9) and } ; \text{ monotonic, hence } S ; HH ; HH \subseteq S ; HH \ \} \\
 & HH ; S ; HH \subseteq S ; HH \\
\Rightarrow & \quad \{ \text{ (8) and } ; \text{ monotonic, hence } Id ; S ; HH \subseteq HH ; S ; HH \ \} \\
 & HH ; S ; HH = S ; HH
\end{array}
$$

Since the second expression equals the final one, we have equivalence throughout, and we have:

$$S \text{ is secure} \equiv (HH ; S \subseteq S ; HH) \tag{10}$$

This result is useful because it facilitates the following derivation, which expresses security in terms of the values of program variables.

$$
\begin{array}{ll}
 & HH ; S \subseteq S ; HH \\
= & \quad \{ \text{ Definition of relational containment } \} \\
 & (\forall y, w :: y\langle HH;S\rangle w \Rightarrow y\langle S;HH\rangle w) \\
= & \quad \{ \text{ Definition of relational composition, twice } \}
\end{array}
$$

$$
\begin{array}{ll}
& (\forall\, y, w :: (\exists\, x :: y\langle HH\rangle x \ \wedge\ x\langle S\rangle w\,) \\
& \qquad \Rightarrow\ (\exists\, z :: y\langle S\rangle z \ \wedge\ z\langle HH\rangle w\,)) \\
= & \qquad \{\ \text{Relational semantics of } HH \text{ , shunting between range and term }\ \} \\
& (\forall\, y, w :: (\exists\, x :: y.k = x.k \ \wedge\ x\langle S\rangle w\,) \\
& \qquad \Rightarrow (\exists\, z : y\langle S\rangle z : z.k = w.k\,)) \\
= & \quad \{\ \text{Predicate calculus}\ \} \\
& (\forall\, y, w :: (\forall\, x :: y.k = x.k \ \wedge\ x\langle S\rangle w \\
& \qquad \Rightarrow (\exists\, z : y\langle S\rangle z : z.k = w.k\,))) \\
= & \quad \{\ \text{Unnesting of quantifiers}\ \} \\
& (\forall\, x, y, w :: y.k = x.k \ \wedge\ x\langle S\rangle w \\
& \qquad \Rightarrow\ (\exists\, z : y\langle S\rangle z : z.k = w.k\,)) \\
= & \qquad \{\ \text{Nesting, shunting}\ \} \\
& (\forall\, x, y : y.k = x.k : (\forall\, w :: x\langle S\rangle w \\
& \qquad\qquad \Rightarrow\ (\exists\, z : y\langle S\rangle z : z.k = w.k\,))) \\
= & \qquad \{\ \text{Set calculus}\ \} \\
& (\forall\, x, y : y.k = x.k : \{\, w : x\langle S\rangle w : w.k\,\} \subseteq \{\, z : y\langle S\rangle z : z.k\,\}) \\
= & \qquad \{\ \text{Expression is symmetric in } x \text{ and } y\ \} \\
& (\forall\, x, y : y.k = x.k : \{\, w : x\langle S\rangle w : w.k\,\} \ = \ \{\, z : y\langle S\rangle z : z.k\,\})
\end{array}
$$

Thus, we have established that, for any $S$ ,

$$
S \text{ is secure } \equiv \ (\forall\, x, y : x.k = y.k : \ \ \{\, w : x\langle S\rangle w : w.k\,\} = \{\, z : y\langle S\rangle z : z.k\,\}\ ) \qquad (11)
$$

This condition says that the set of possible final values of $k$ is independent of the initial value of $h$ . It has appeared in the literature [BBLM94] as the definition of secure information flow. (Similar definitions, restricted to the deterministic case, have appeared elsewhere [VSI96,VS97b].) Thus, one may view the derivation above as a proof of the equivalence of (7) with respect to the notion used by others.

## 4 Security in the weakest precondition calculus

In this section and the next, we show how our definition of secure information flow may be expressed in the weakest precondition calculus [Dij76]. Our first formulation, presented in this section, involves a quantification over predicates; it is therefore somewhat inconvenient to use. In the next section, we show how this formulation can be written more simply as a condition involving quantification over the domain of $k$ .

Recall that for any program $S$ , the predicate transformers $wlp.S$ ("weakest liberal precondition") and $wp.S$ ("weakest precondition") are informally defined as follows: For any predicate $p$ ,

> $wlp.S.p$ holds in exactly those initial states from which every terminating computation of $S$ ends in a state satisfying $p$ , and $wp.S.p$ holds in exactly those initial states from which every computation of $S$ terminates in a state satisfying $p$ .

The two predicate transformers are related by the following pairing property: For any program $S$ ,

$$(\forall p :: wp.S.p \;=\; wlp.S.p \land wp.S.true) \qquad (12)$$

We assume that for all statements $S$ considered here, the predicate transformer $wlp.S$ is *universally conjunctive* (i.e., it distributes over arbitrary conjunctions), and (hence) monotonic [DS90].

We start by introducing some notation. For any program with a variable named $v$ , we define the unary predicate transformer $[v : \_]$ (read " $v$ -everywhere") as follows: For any predicate $p$ ,

$$[v : p] \;=\; (\forall M :: wlp.\text{“}v := M\text{”}.p)$$

where $M$ ranges over the domain of $v$ . This unary predicate transformer has all the properties of universal quantification; in particular, it is universally conjunctive. Furthermore, for any variables $v, w$ and any predicate $p$ , we have

$$[v : [w : p]] \;=\; [w : [v : p]]$$

Recall that we are interested in programs whose variables are partitioned into $k$ and $h$ . For any such program, we write $[p]$ (read "everywhere $p$ ") as shorthand for $[h : [k : p]]$ . The $wlp$ and $wp$ semantics of the program $HH$ are:

$$(\forall p :: [wlp.HH.p \;\equiv\; [h : p]])$$
$$[wp.HH.true \;\equiv\; true]$$

Program equality in the weakest precondition calculus is given by equality of $wp$ and $wlp$ :

$$S \doteq T \;\equiv\; (\forall p :: [wlp.S.p \equiv wlp.T.p] \;\land\; [wp.S.p \equiv wp.T.p])$$

which, on account of the pairing property, can be simplified to

$$S \doteq T \;\equiv\; (\forall p :: [wlp.S.p \equiv wlp.T.p]) \;\land\; [wp.S.true \equiv wp.T.true]$$

Using this definition of program equality, we now rewrite security condition (7) in the weakest precondition calculus as follows.

$$\begin{array}{ll}
 & HH \,;\, S \,;\, HH \;\doteq\; S \,;\, HH \\
= & \quad \{ \text{ Program equality in terms of } wlp \text{ and } wp \;\} \\
 & (\forall p :: [wlp.(HH \,;\, S \,;\, HH).p \;\equiv\; wlp.(S \,;\, HH).p]) \\
 & \land\, [wp.(HH \,;\, S \,;\, HH).true \;\equiv\; wp.(S \,;\, HH).true] \\
= & \quad \{ \;\; wlp \text{ and } wp \text{ of } HH \text{ and } ; \;\; \} \\
 & (\forall p :: [[h : wlp.S.[h : p]] \;\equiv\; wlp.S.[h : p]]) \qquad (13) \\
 & \land\, [[h : wp.S.true] \;\equiv\; wp.S.true] \qquad (14)
\end{array}$$

The last formula above contains expressions in which a predicate $q$ satisfies

$$[[h : q] \equiv q] \;.$$

Predicates with this property occur often in our calculations, so it is convenient to introduce a special notation for them and identify some of their properties. This is the topic of the following subsection.

### 4.0 Cylinders

Informally speaking, a predicate $q$ that satisfies $[q \equiv [h : q]]$ has the property that its value is independent of the variable $h$. We refer to such predicates as "$h$-cylinders", or simply as "cylinders" as $h$ is understood from context. For notational convenience, we define the set $Cyl$ of all $h$-cylinders:

**Definition (Cylinders)** *For any predicate* $q$,

$$q \in Cyl \;\equiv\; [q \equiv [h : q]] \tag{15}$$

The following lemma provides several equivalent ways of expressing that a predicate is a cylinder.

**Lemma 0** *For any predicate* $q$, *the following are all equivalent to* $q \in Cyl$.

*i.* $[q \equiv [h : q]]$
*ii.* $[q \Rightarrow [h : q]]$
*iii.* $(\exists p :: [q \equiv [h : p]])$
*iv.* $\neg q \in Cyl$

**Proof.** Follows from predicate calculus. *(End of Proof.)*

### 4.1 Security in terms of cylinders

We now use the results in the preceding subsection to simplify the formulation of security in the weakest precondition calculus. We begin by rewriting (13) as follows.

$$
\begin{array}{ll}
 & (\forall p :: [[h : wlp.S.[h : p]] \equiv wlp.S.[h : p]]) \\
= & \quad \{ \text{ Definition of } Cyl \text{ (15) } \} \\
 & (\forall p :: wlp.S.[h : p] \in Cyl) \\
= & \quad \{ \text{ One-point rule } \} \\
 & (\forall p, q : [q \equiv [h : p]] : wlp.S.q \in Cyl) \\
= & \quad \{ \text{ Nesting and trading } \} \\
 & (\forall q :: (\forall p :: [q \equiv [h : p]] \Rightarrow wlp.S.q \in Cyl)) \\
= & \quad \{ \text{ Predicate calculus } \} \\
 & (\forall q :: (\exists p :: [q \equiv [h : p]]) \Rightarrow wlp.S.q \in Cyl) \\
= & \quad \{ \text{ Lemma 0.iii, and trading } \} \\
 & (\forall q : q \in Cyl : wlp.S.q \in Cyl)
\end{array}
$$

Similarly, we rewrite the expression (14) as follows.

$$
\begin{array}{ll}
 & [[h : wp.S.true] \equiv wp.S.true] \\
= & \quad \{ \text{ Definition of } Cyl \text{ (15) } \} \\
 & wp.S.true \in Cyl
\end{array}
$$

Putting it all together, we get the following condition for security: For any program $S$,

$$S \text{ is secure} \equiv (\forall p : p \in Cyl : wlp.S.p \in Cyl) \wedge wp.S.true \in Cyl \tag{16}$$

# 5 A simpler characterization

Using (16) to check whether a given program $S$ is secure requires evaluation of the following term:

$$(\forall p : p \in Cyl : wlp.S.p \in Cyl) \qquad (17)$$

Since this term involves a quantification over all cylinders, it is somewhat inconvenient to use. In this section, we show how this quantification over predicates $p$ can be reduced to a simpler quantification over the domain of $k$ .

To explain how this simplification is brought about, we introduce the notions of *conjunctive* and *disjunctive spans*. These notions are defined formally below, but, informally speaking, for any set $X$ of predicates, the conjunctive span $\mathcal{A}.X$ is the set of predicates obtained by taking conjunctions over the subsets of $X$ . Similarly, the disjunctive span $\mathcal{E}.X$ is the set of predicates obtained by taking disjunctions over the subsets of $X$ . The main theorem of this section asserts that the range of $p$ in (17) may be replaced by any set of predicates whose conjunctive span is the set $Cyl$ . The usefulness of the theorem is demonstrated in subsection 5.1, where we show that there is a simple set of predicates whose conjunctive span is $Cyl$ .

We use the following notational conventions in this section. For any set $X$ of predicates, we write $\neg X$ to mean the set $\{ q : q \in X : \neg q \}$ . We also write $\forall.X$ to mean the conjunction of all the predicates in $X$ , and $\exists.X$ to mean the disjunction of all the predicates in $X$ . Note that as a result of these conventions, we have $[\neg(\forall.X) \equiv \exists.(\neg X)]$ .

## 5.0 Spans

For any set $X$ of predicates, define the sets $\mathcal{A}.X$ and $\mathcal{E}.X$ as follows.

**Definition (Spans)**

$$\mathcal{A}.X = \{ XS : XS \subseteq X : \forall.XS \}$$
$$\mathcal{E}.X = \{ XS : XS \subseteq X : \exists.XS \}$$

The two notions are related by the following lemma.

**Lemma 1** *For any set $X$ of predicates,*

$$\neg\, \mathcal{E}.X = \mathcal{A}.(\neg X)$$

**Proof.** Follows from predicate calculus. *(End of Proof.)*

We are now ready to present the main theorem of this section.

**Theorem 0** *Let $f$ be a universally conjunctive predicate transformer and let $X$ be any set of predicates. Then*

$$(\forall p : p \in X : f.p \in Cyl) \equiv (\forall q : q \in \mathcal{A}.X : f.q \in Cyl)$$

**Proof.** Note that the left-hand side follows from the right-hand side since $X \subseteq \mathcal{A}.X$; thus, it remains to prove the implication

$$(\forall p : p \in X : f.p \in Cyl) \Rightarrow (\forall q : q \in \mathcal{A}.X : f.q \in Cyl)$$

We prove this implication by showing that for any predicate $q$ in $\mathcal{A}.X$, the antecedent implies that $f.q$ is a cylinder. By the definition of a conjunctive span, there is a subset $XS$ of $X$ such that $[q \equiv \forall.XS]$. From the definition of cylinders (15), $XS \subseteq X$, and the antecedent, we have:

$$(\forall p : p \in XS : [f.p \equiv [h : f.p]]) \tag{18}$$

Now, we observe:

$$
\begin{array}{ll}
 & f.q \in Cyl \\
= & \{ \text{ Choice of } XS \ \} \\
 & f.(\forall p : p \in XS : p) \in Cyl \\
= & \{ \ f \text{ is universally conjunctive } \} \\
 & (\forall p : p \in XS : f.p) \in Cyl \\
= & \{ \text{ Definition of cylinders (15) } \} \\
 & [(\forall p : p \in XS : f.p) \equiv [h : (\forall p : p \in XS : f.p)]] \\
= & \{ \ [h : \_] \text{ is universally conjunctive } \} \\
 & [(\forall p : p \in XS : f.p) \equiv (\forall p : p \in XS : [h : f.p])] \\
= & \{ \ (18) \ \} \\
 & [(\forall p : p \in XS : f.p) \equiv (\forall p : p \in XS : f.p)] \\
= & \{ \text{ Predicate Calculus } \} \\
 & true
\end{array}
$$

*(End of Proof.)*

From the standpoint of mechanical verification, the usefulness of the result above is due to the fact that there is a simple set of predicates whose conjunctive span is $Cyl$.

## 5.1 A simpler quantification

Consider the following two sets of predicates, where $M$ ranges over the domain of $k$.

$$PP = \{ M :: \text{“}k = M\text{”} \} \tag{19}$$

$$NN = \{ M :: \text{“}k \neq M\text{”} \} \tag{20}$$

It follows directly from these definitions that

$$PP = \neg NN \tag{21}$$

The relationship of these sets to $Cyl$ is given by the following lemma.

**Lemma 2** *With $PP$ and $NN$ as defined above, we have*

*i.* $\mathcal{E}.PP = Cyl$
*ii.* $\mathcal{A}.NN = Cyl$

**Proof.** We give an informal sketch of the proof here; details are left to the reader. By definition, $Cyl$ consists of exactly those predicates that are independent of $h$, that is, they depend on the variable $k$ only. But every predicate on $k$ may be written as a disjunction of predicates, one for each value in the domain of $k$ for which the predicate holds; thus part (i) follows. Part (ii) follows directly from part (i), observation (21), Lemma 1, and Lemma 0.iv. *(End of Proof.)*

Using the fact that $wlp.S$ is universally conjunctive for any statement $S$, and Lemma 2.ii, we apply Theorem 0 with $f, X := wlp.S, NN$ to obtain the following reformulation of (16):

$$S \text{ is secure} \;\equiv\; (\forall q : q \in NN : wlp.S.q \in Cyl) \;\wedge\; wp.S.true \in Cyl.$$

Applying the definition of $NN$ (20), this yields the following condition:

$$S \text{ is secure} \;\equiv\; (\forall M :: wlp.S.(k \neq M) \in Cyl) \;\wedge\; wp.S.true \in Cyl \qquad (22)$$

Note that this is simpler than (16) since the quantification ranges over the domain of $k$.

## 5.2 Deterministic programs

In the case that $S$ is also known to be deterministic and non-miraculous, we can further simplify the security condition (22). Recall that a deterministic, non-miraculous program $S$ satisfies the following properties [DS90]:

$$(\forall p :: [wp.S.p \equiv \neg wlp.S.(\neg p)]) \qquad (23)$$
$$wp.S \text{ is universally disjunctive} \qquad (24)$$

Consequently, the term involving $wp$ in (22) is subsumed by the term involving $wlp$:

$$\begin{array}{ll} & wp.S.true \in Cyl \\ = & \quad \{ \text{(23), with } p := true \} \\ & \neg wlp.S.false \in Cyl \\ = & \quad \{ \text{Lemma 0.iv} \} \\ & wlp.S.false \in Cyl \\ \Leftarrow & \quad \{ false \in Cyl \} \\ & (\forall q : q \in Cyl : wlp.S.q \in Cyl) \end{array}$$

Thus, the security condition for deterministic $S$ is given by

$$S \text{ is secure} \;\equiv\; (\forall M :: wlp.S.(k \neq M) \in Cyl) \qquad (25)$$

Next, we show that condition (25) may also be expressed in terms of $wp$ and $PP$ instead of $wlp$ and $NN$.

$$
\begin{array}{ll}
 & (\forall q : q \in Cyl : wlp.S.q \in Cyl) \\
= & \quad \{ \text{ Theorem 0 } \} \\
 & (\forall q : q \in NN : wlp.S.q \in Cyl) \\
= & \quad \{ \text{ Negation is its own inverse, so rename dummy } q \text{ to } \neg p \ \} \\
 & (\forall p : \neg p \in NN : wlp.S.(\neg p) \in Cyl) \\
= & \quad \{ \text{ Observation (21), and (23) } \} \\
 & (\forall p : p \in PP : \neg wp.S.p \in Cyl) \\
= & \quad \{ \text{ Lemma 0.iv } \} \\
 & (\forall p : p \in PP : wp.S.p \in Cyl)
\end{array}
$$

Thus we have another way of expressing the condition for security of deterministic programs, namely,

$$
S \text{ is secure } \equiv (\forall M :: wp.S.(k = M) \in Cyl) \qquad (26)
$$

### 5.3 Examples

We give some examples to show our formulae at work.

Firstly, consider the secure program (2). We calculate,

$$
\begin{array}{ll}
 & (k := h\,;\, k := k - h) \text{ is secure} \\
= & \quad \{ \text{ Security condition (22) } \} \\
 & \quad (\forall M :: wlp.(k := h\,;\, k := k - h).(k \neq M) \in Cyl) \\
 & \wedge\ wp.(k := h\,;\, k := k - h).true \in Cyl \\
= & \quad \{ \ wlp \text{ and } wp \text{ of } := \text{ and } ; \ \} \\
 & (\forall M :: (h - h \neq M) \in Cyl) \wedge true \in Cyl \\
= & \quad \{ \text{ Lemma 0.i, and } true \in Cyl \ \} \\
 & (\forall M :: [h - h \neq M \ \equiv \ [h : h - h \neq M]]) \\
= & \quad \{ \text{ Arithmetic } \} \\
 & (\forall M :: [0 \neq M \ \equiv \ [h : 0 \neq M]]) \\
= & \quad \{ \text{ Definition of } [h : \_] \text{, predicate calculus } \} \\
 & true
\end{array}
$$

This shows that our method does indeed establish that program (2) is secure.

Secondly, we apply the security condition to program (5), which is insecure because of its termination behavior. Letting $N$ range over the domains of $h$, we have:

$$
\begin{array}{ll}
 & (\textbf{if } h = 0 \longrightarrow skip \ \square \ true \longrightarrow loop \ \textbf{fi}) \text{ is secure} \\
= & \quad \{ \text{ Security condition (22) } \} \\
 & \quad (\forall M :: wlp.(\textbf{if } h = 0 \longrightarrow skip \ \square \ true \longrightarrow loop \ \textbf{fi}).(k \neq M) \in Cyl) \\
 & \wedge\ wp.(\textbf{if } h = 0 \longrightarrow skip \ \square \ true \longrightarrow loop \ \textbf{fi}).true \in Cyl \\
= & \quad \{ \ wlp \text{ and } wp \text{, using } (\forall p :: [wlp.loop.p \equiv true]) \\
 & \qquad \qquad \qquad \text{and } [wp.loop.true \equiv false] \ \} \\
 & \quad (\forall M :: ((h = 0 \Rightarrow k \neq M) \wedge (true \Rightarrow true)) \in Cyl) \\
 & \wedge\ ((h = 0 \vee true) \wedge (h = 0 \Rightarrow true) \wedge (true \Rightarrow false)) \in Cyl \\
= & \quad \{ \text{ Predicate Calculus } \} \\
 & (\forall M :: (h = 0 \Rightarrow k \neq M) \in Cyl) \wedge false \in Cyl \\
= & \quad \{ \text{ Lemma 0.i, and } false \in Cyl \ \}
\end{array}
$$

$$
\begin{array}{ll}
 & (\forall M :: [h = 0 \Rightarrow k \neq M \;\equiv\; [h : h = 0 \Rightarrow k \neq M]]) \\
\Rightarrow & \quad \{ \text{ Instantiate with } M := 2 \; \} \\
 & [h = 0 \Rightarrow k \neq 2 \;\equiv\; [h : h = 0 \Rightarrow k \neq 2]] \\
= & \quad \{ \; [p] \text{ is shorthand for } [h : [k : p]] \; \} \\
 & [h : [k : h = 0 \Rightarrow k \neq 2 \;\equiv\; [h : h = 0 \Rightarrow k \neq 2]]] \\
= & \quad \{ \text{ Definition of } [v : \_] \text{, twice; } wlp \text{ of } := \; \} \\
 & (\forall M, N :: wlp.(k, h := M, N).( \quad h = 0 \Rightarrow k \neq 2 \\
 & \qquad\qquad\qquad\qquad\qquad\qquad \equiv \; [h : h = 0 \Rightarrow k \neq 2])) \\
\Rightarrow & \quad \{ \text{ Instantiate with } M, N := 2, 2 \; \} \\
 & 2 = 0 \Rightarrow 2 \neq 2 \;\equiv\; [h : h = 0 \Rightarrow 2 \neq 2] \\
= & \quad \{ \text{ Predicate Calculus, identity of } \equiv \; \} \\
 & [h : h \neq 0] \\
= & \quad \{ \text{ Definition of } [h : \_] \; \} \\
 & (\forall N :: wlp.(h := N).(h \neq 0)) \\
\Rightarrow & \quad \{ \text{ Instantiate } N := 0 \; \} \\
 & 0 \neq 0 \\
= & \quad \{ \text{ Predicate Calculus } \} \\
 & false
\end{array}
$$

Finally, using program (4), we illustrate how one can reason about secure termination behavior of deterministic programs using $wlp$.

$$
\begin{array}{ll}
 & (\textbf{if } h = 0 \longrightarrow loop \;\square\; h \neq 0 \longrightarrow skip \textbf{ fi}) \text{ is secure} \\
= & \quad \{ \text{ Security condition for deterministic programs (25) } \} \\
 & (\forall M :: wlp.(\textbf{if } h = 0 \longrightarrow loop \;\square\; h \neq 0 \longrightarrow skip \textbf{ fi}).(k \neq M) \in Cyl) \\
= & \quad \{ \; wlp \; \} \\
 & (\forall M :: ((h = 0 \Rightarrow true) \wedge (h \neq 0 \Rightarrow k \neq M)) \in Cyl) \\
= & \quad \{ \text{ Definition of } Cyl \text{ : note } h \neq 0 \Rightarrow k \neq M \text{ depends on } h \; \} \\
 & false
\end{array}
$$

# 6 Related work

The problem of secure information flow has been studied for several decades. A commonly used mathematical model for secure information flow is Denning's lattice model [Den76], which is based on the Bell and La Padula security model [BLP73]. Most approaches to static certification of secure information flow (an area pioneered by Denning and Denning [Den76,DD77]) seem to fall into one of two general categories: type systems and data flow analysis techniques. In this section, we discuss these approaches and compare them to our work. A historical perspective of secure information flow appears in a book by Gasser [Gas88].

## 6.0 Approaches based on type systems

The static certification mechanism proposed by Denning and Denning [DD77] is essentially a type checker for secure information flow. Each variable $x$ occurring in a program is declared with a particular *security class*, denoted by $class.x$ . These security classes are assumed to form a lattice, ordered by $\leq$ , with meet (greatest lower bound) denoted by $\downarrow$ and join (least upper bound) denoted by $\uparrow$ . The type checker computes the class of an expression as the join of the classes of its subexpressions. For example, for an expression involving addition, we have

$$class.(E+F) \;=\; class.E \uparrow class.F$$

A security class is also assigned to each statement, and is computed as the meet of the security classes of the variables assigned to by that statement. For instance,

$$class.(x := E) \;=\; class.x$$
$$class.(\textbf{if } E \textbf{ then } S \textbf{ else } T \textbf{ end}) \;=\; class.S \downarrow class.T$$

The type checker certifies a program $S$ as being secure provided the following two conditions hold:

0. For every assignment statement $x := E$ in $S$, $class.E \leq class.x$
1. For every conditional statement **if** $E$ **then** $T$ **else** $U$ **end** in $S$ , $class.E \leq class.T$ and $class.E \leq class.U$ .

Other programming constructs, such as loops, give rise to similar requirements.

Denning and Denning gave an informal argument for the soundness of their certification mechanism (*i.e.*, a proof that the mechanism certifies only secure programs). Recently, Volpano *et al.* have given a more rigorous proof [VSI96,VS97b].

The advantage of using a type system as the basis of a certification mechanism is that it is simple to implement. However, most certification mechanisms based on types reject any program that contains an insecure subprogram. As we saw in examples (0)–(3) of section 1, a secure program may contain an insecure subprogram. In contrast, with a semantic approach like ours, it is possible to identify such programs as being secure. Another problem with such approaches is that they are difficult to use for reasoning about programs that leak information via termination behaviour. (Volpano and Smith [VS97a] have attempted to extend their type-based approach to handle termination behaviour. However, their type system rejects any program that mentions $h$ in a loop guard. Such an approach seems terribly restrictive.)

## 6.1 Approaches based on data flow analyses

The key idea behind approaches based on data flow analyses is to transform a given program $S$ into a program $S'$ that provides a simpler representation of the possible data flows in program $S$ . This is done as follows. (We assume, as in the previous section, that we are given a lattice of security classes.) For every variable $x$ in program $S$ , program $S'$ contains a variable $x'$ , representing the highest security class of the values used in computing the current value for $x$ . To deal with implicit flows, $S'$ also contains a special variable *local'* , representing the lowest security class of the values used to compute the guards that led to execution of the current instruction.For example, for every assignment statement in $S$ of the form $x := y + z$, $S'$ contains a corresponding statement

$$x' := y' \uparrow z' \uparrow local'$$

For a conditional statement in $S$ such as

$$\textbf{if } x = y \longrightarrow S0 \;\square\; z < 0 \longrightarrow S1 \textbf{ fi}$$

$S'$ contains a corresponding statement

**var** *old* := *local'* **in**
  *local'* := *local'* ↑ *x'* ↑ *y'* ↑ *z'*
  ; **if** *true* ⟶ *S0'* □ *true* ⟶ *S1'* **fi**
  ; *local'* := *old*
**end**

where $S0'$ and $S1'$ are the statements in $S'$ that correspond to $S0$ and $S1$. If a program $S$ has the variables $k$ and $h$ belonging to the security classes low and high (denoted $\bot$ and $\top$, respectively, where $\bot \leq \top$), then " $S$ is secure" can be expressed as the following Hoare triple on $S'$:

$$\{\, k' \leq \bot \;\wedge\; h' \leq \top \;\wedge\; local' \leq \bot \,\} \quad S' \quad \{\, k' \leq \bot \,\} \tag{27}$$

The first data flow analysis approach of this kind was given by Andrews and Reitman [AR80], whose treatment also dealt with communicating sequential processes. Banâtre *et al.* [BBLM94] used a variation of the method described above that attempts to keep track of the set of initial variables used to produce a value rather than only the security class of the value. They also developed an efficient algorithm for their approach, similar to data flow analysis algorithms used in compilers, and attempted a proof of soundness. (Unlike our description above, Andrews and Reitman used the deterministic **if then else** construct rather than Dijkstra's **if fi** construct. Banâtre *et al.* used the **if fi** construct, but, as Volpano *et al.* point out, their soundness theorem is actually false for nondeterministic programs [VSI96].)

The data flow analysis approach can provide more precision than the type system approach. For example, the approach certifies programs (0) and (1). However, the approach still rejects some secure programs that our approach will certify. This comes about because of two reasons. The first reason is that the semantics of operators like $+$ and $-$ are lost in the rewriting of $S$ into $S'$. Thus a program like (2), which is secure on account of that $h - h = 0$, is rejected by the data flow analysis approach. The second reason is that guards are replaced by *true* in the rewriting of $S$ into $S'$. Thus, a program like (3), whose security depends on when control can reach a certain statement, is rejected.

One way to improve on this approach is to augment it with a logic, as suggested by Andrews and Reitman [AR80]. Instead of rewriting program $S$ into $S'$, one superimposes new variables ( $k'$, $h'$, $local'$ ) and their updates onto program $S$, and then reasons about $S$ using the Hoare triple (27) but with $S$ instead of $S'$. A consequence of this approach is that one can rule out some impossible control paths, such as the one in program (3).

### 6.2 The use of determinism

It has been noted elsewhere that "semantic models always make implicit assumptions about what sort of things are interesting about a process' behaviour" [Ros95]. In the context of security, these assumptions specify what we consider observable by the adversary. We argued in section 2 that our definition can be used to model adversaries that exploit covert flows (*e.g.*, adversaries monitoring resource usage) by appropriately choosing the low-security variables. There is, however, one subtle issue that arises in the context of nondeterminism: security is not preserved by refinement. For example, the secure program "assign to $k$ an arbitrary value" is refined by the insecure program "$k := h$". Since sequential programs are often implemented by refining their nondeterminism, this leads to the undesirable situation in which a secure program is rendered insecure by its implementation.

There are two ways of addressing this issue. The first is by recognizing that refinements are a concern only if the adversary is aware of how they are made. If we take the position that the adversary has absolutely no knowledge of how a program is refined during implementation (or how nondeterministic choices are resolved during execution), we can assert that its observations reveal no information about the initial value of $h$. The second way of addressing the issue is by noting that the problem does not arise for deterministic programs, since the latter are maximal in the refinement ordering. Thus we can avoid the difficulty by requiring that secure programs be deterministic. [1] This latter approach is similar to the one advocated by Roscoe, who gives several characterizations (corresponding to different observational models) for the secure information flow property for CSP processes. He makes a persuasive argument for requiring determinism by showing that these characterizations are all equivalent for deterministic processes.

## 7 Summary

We have presented a simple and new mathematical characterization of what it means for a program to have secure information flow. The characterization is general enough to accommodate reasoning about a variety of covert flows, including nontermination. Unlike previous methods, which were based on type systems and compiler data flow analysis techniques, our characterization is in terms of program semantics, thus it is more precise than these syntactic approaches. We are currently investigating ways of using our characterization as a basis for developing a mechanically-assisted technique for verifying secure flow.

*Acknowledgments.* We are grateful to the following colleagues for sharing their insights and comments on our work: Martín Abadi, Ernie Cohen, Rutger M. Dijkstra, Mark Lillibridge, Jayadev Misra, Greg Nelson, Raymie Stata, the members of the Austin Tuesday Afternoon Club, the participants at the September 1997 session of the IFIP WG 2.3 meeting in Alsace, France, and the four anonymous referees.

[1] Actually, it suffices to place the weaker requirement that programs be deterministic with respect to the low-security variables in the following sense: the initial state determines the final value of $k$.

## References


[AR80] Gregory R. Andrews and Richard P. Reitman. An axiomatic approach to information flow in programs. *ACM Transactions on Programming Languages and Systems*, 2(1):56–76, January 1980.

[BBLM94] Jean-Pierre Banâtre, Ciarán Bryce, and Daniel Le Métayer. Compile-time detection of information flow in sequential programs. In *Proceedings of the European Symposium on Research in Computer Security*, pages 55–73. Lecture Notes in Computer Science 875, Sprinter Verlag, 1994.

[BLP73] D. E. Bell and L. J. La Padula. Secure computer systems: Mathematical foundations and model. Technical Report M74-244, MITRE Corporation, Bedford, Massachusetts, 1973.

[DD77] Dorothy E. Denning and Peter J. Denning. Certification of programs for secure information flow. *Communications of the ACM*, 20(7):504–513, July 1977.

[Den76] Dorothy E. Denning. A lattice model of secure information flow. *Communications of the ACM*, 19(5):236–243, May 1976.

[Dij76] Edsger W. Dijkstra. *A Discipline of Programming*. Prentice-Hall, Englewood Cliffs, NJ, 1976.

[DS90] Edsger W. Dijkstra and Carel S. Scholten. *Predicate Calculus and Program Semantics*. Texts and Monographs in Computer Science. Springer-Verlag, 1990.

[Gas88] Morrie Gasser. *Building a secure computer system*. Van Nostrand Reinhold Company, New York, 1988.

[Heh84] Eric C. R. Hehner. Predicative programming Part I. *Communications of the ACM*, 27(2):134–143, February 1984.

[Lam73] Butler W. Lampson. A note on the confinement problem. *Communications of the ACM*, 16(10):613–615, October 1973.

[RMD92] R.M. Dijkstra. Relational calculus and relational program semantics. Eindhoven Institute of Technology, 1992.

[Ros95] A. W. Roscoe. CSP and determinism in security modelling. In *Security and Privacy*. IEEE, 1995.

[VS97a] Dennis Volpano and Geoffrey Smith. Eliminating covert flows with minimum typings. In *Proceedings of the 10th IEEE Computer Security Foundations Workshop*, pages 156–168, June 1997.

[VS97b] Dennis Volpano and Geoffrey Smith. A type-based approach to program security. In *Theory and Practice of Software Development: Proceedings / TAPSOFT '97, 7th International Joint Conference CAAP/FASE*, volume 1214 of *Lecture Notes in Computer Science*, pages 607–621. Springer, April 1997.

[VSI96] Dennis Volpano, Geoffrey Smith, and Cynthia Irvine. A sound type system for secure flow analysis. *Journal of Computer Security*, 4(3):1–21, 1996.

# Slack Elasticity in Concurrent Computing

Rajit Manohar and Alain J. Martin

California Institute of Technology, Pasadena CA 91125, USA

**Abstract.** We present conditions under which we can modify the slack of a channel in a distributed computation without changing its behavior. These results can be used to modify the degree of pipelining in an asynchronous system. The generality of the result shows the wide variety of pipelining alternatives presented to the designer of a concurrent system. We give examples of program transformations which can be used in the design of concurrent systems whose correctness depends on the conditions presented.

## 1 Introduction

In the design of an asynchronous clone of a MIPS R3000 microprocessor, we were faced with the problem of reasoning about a number of new program transformations that were introduced for performance reasons. The majority of the transformations corresponded to the introduction of pipelining in the processor [6]. In this paper, we provide general conditions under which we can pipeline a distributed computation.

We specify a distributed computation using CHP, a variant of CSP [2] (a brief description is contained in the appendix), and restrict our attention to systems that do not share variables among concurrent processes. The processes in the computation interact by exchanging messages over first-in first-out channels. Each channel in the computation has a fixed amount of *slack*, or buffering, which specifies the maximum number of outstanding messages on a channel.

The CHP specification of a process completely characterizes both the computation it performs as well as its synchronization behavior. For instance, we can specify a process that performs addition with the following CHP:

$$*[\ (A?x \| B?y);\ \ C!(x+y)\ ]$$

Unfortunately, for performance reasons, this specification can be very restrictive in practice. If $\mathbf{c}X$ is the number of completed actions on channel $X$, the specification includes the property that

$$0 \le \mathbf{c}A - \mathbf{c}C \le 1$$

In other words, the specification includes the fact that an implementation cannot accept its next set of inputs on channel $A$ without producing an output on channel $C$. This restriction causes the throughput of an asynchronous delay-insensitive circuit that implements the computation to degrade as $1/\log N$, where $N$ is the number of bits used to represent $x$. However, it is possible that this property of the specification is not critical—namely, modifying it to the weaker

$0 \leq \mathbf{c}A - \mathbf{c}C \leq \log N$

does not affect the correctness of the computation. In that case, we can prevent the throughput degradation by pipelining the computation—a significant performance improvement.

It is often necessary to adjust the amount of pipelining in an asynchronous computation to optimize its performance based on the timing behavior of components of the system [9]. Ideally this should be a transformation applied after the high-level design is completed, since we may not have the necessary timing information until the physical design of the system has been simulated. Such transformations, in general, involve examining the entire asynchronous system instead of just a single process.

In this paper, we address the issues raised above by examining the following question: when can we change the slack of communication channels that are part of a system without modifying the behavior of the system? This single transformation can be used to show the correctness (or lack thereof) of a number of different program transformation techniques. Changing the slack of a synchronization channel is a non-trivial operation. Consider the following example in which channels $A$, $X$, and $Y$ are slack-zero channels.

$$X; A \parallel A; Y \parallel [\ \overline{X} \longrightarrow X; Y;\ \text{"}\textit{good}\text{"} \ \square\ \overline{Y} \longrightarrow Y; X;\ \text{"}\textit{bad}\text{"}\ ]$$

The only possible computation is the sequence $X; A; Y;$ "*good*". However, if we introduce slack on channel $A$, we now have the possibility $A; Y; X;$ "*bad*".

When we are permitted to add slack to a channel in the system, we say that the particular channel is ***slack elastic***. If every channel in the system is slack elastic, the system is said to be slack elastic.

# 2 Model

We assume that the computation of interest is described by a collection of CHP programs communicating via first-in first-out channels. The programs do not share any variables; all interaction is via message-passing using single-sender single-receiver channels. Let $X$ be a command causing an "$X$-action" when executed. We define $\mathbf{c}X$ to be the number of ***completed*** $X$-actions since the beginning of a computation.

## 2.1 Synchronization

$(X,Y)$ form a pair of synchronization primitives if the difference $|\mathbf{c}X - \mathbf{c}Y|$ is bounded [4]. Formally, there exist two integer constants $\mathbf{k}X$ and $\mathbf{k}Y$ such that at least one of the two constants is finite, and:

$-\mathbf{k}Y \leq \mathbf{c}X - \mathbf{c}Y \leq \mathbf{k}X$ (SAFETY REQUIREMENT)

The quantity $K = \mathbf{k}X + \mathbf{k}Y$ is called the ***synchronization slack*** [4].

The probe of a synchronization primitive can be used to determine if the action can complete [5]. Formally,

$$\overline{X} \Rightarrow (\mathbf{c}X - \mathbf{c}Y < \mathbf{k}X) \quad \wedge \quad (\mathbf{c}X - \mathbf{c}Y < \mathbf{k}X) \Rightarrow \Diamond\overline{X}$$

$$\overline{Y} \Rightarrow (-\mathbf{k}Y < \mathbf{c}X - \mathbf{c}Y) \quad \wedge \quad (-\mathbf{k}Y < \mathbf{c}X - \mathbf{c}Y) \Rightarrow \Diamond\overline{Y}$$

where $\Diamond E$ means that expression $E$ becomes true eventually. Probes can only occur in the guards of selection statements.

The value $\mathbf{q}X$ is defined as the number of $X$-actions currently *suspended*. The progress requirement on synchronization primitives states that the set of suspended actions is minimal, i.e., the completion of any non-empty subset of suspended actions would violate the safety requirement [4]. Formally, if $(X, Y)$ form a pair of synchronization primitives,

$$\mathbf{q}X = 0 \vee \mathbf{q}Y = 0 \qquad \text{(PROGRESS REQUIREMENT)}$$

CHP communication channels that carry data can be described using this framework. A CHP channel $C$ has two *ports* associated with it: a sender $C!$, and a receiver $C?$. $(C!, C?)$ form a pair of synchronization primitives. We define $\mathbf{s}C!$ to be the sequence of data values that have been sent on the sender port, and $\mathbf{s}C?$ the sequence of received values. Let $|s|$ be the length of sequence $s$. Then, $|\mathbf{s}C!| = \mathbf{c}C!$ and $|\mathbf{s}C?| = \mathbf{c}C?$.

## 2.2 Computations and Behaviors

We restrict our attention to systems that satisfy the four properties listed below; their need will become evident in the sections that follow.

- the system is closed, i.e., we have specified the CHP processes of interest and their environment;
- the system is deadlock-free;
- negated probes of the sender port of channels are not used in the computation;
- if a sender port is probed, the probe will be true infinitely often.

An execution *trace* is a particular interleaving of atomic actions that can occur during execution of the system. The system is completely characterized by the set of possible traces that can occur [8]. We only consider the *complete* traces of the system [3]. The execution of processes is assumed to be weakly fair, and the selection statement is assumed to be unfair. (The appendix contains a more detailed description of the model.)

Given a concurrent system, we are not interested in the possible interleavings of actions that occur in a trace. Rather, we are interested in the sequence of data values that are sent on certain channels of the system, given the sequence of values being sent on other channels. For instance, in the example above, we might only be interested in the fact that the data values sent on channel $C$ correspond to the sum of the values received on channels $A$ and $B$. To this end, we define a *behavior* of a system in terms of the possible traces that can occur.

A behavior in our model is primarily characterized by the sequence of values that are sent and received on the channels of the system. Since processes in the system can only interact using communication channels, behaviors capture the data values that are exchanged by interacting processes. Therefore behaviors can be used to describe the input/output characteristics of processes in the system. In addition, we would like to specify a computation without specifying the synchronization behavior as far as possible. In our model, the only ordering between values that have been sent on various channels that can be inferred from the behavior itself is the ordering preserved by the FIFO nature of the individual channels.

Since the sequences of values sent and received on channels can be infinite, behaviors capture the notion of weakly fair execution. The notion of weak fairness in traces corresponds to enabled actions in a process being executed eventually; the notion of weak fairness in behaviors corresponds to the next value (if any) that can be sent/received on a channel being sent/received eventually.

The other component of a behavior is the sequence of non-deterministic choices made by processes in the system, since these choices can affect the data values being sent on channels. The only construct in CHP that introduces such choices is the selection statement.

We assume that all the channels in the system are initialized empty, i.e., for all channels $c$, $\mathbf{k}c? = 0$. The assignment of initial values to variables and the initialization of channels is assumed to be part of the CHP program for each process. Therefore, the actual initial values of variables do not affect the behavior, because every variable is assigned a value initially (or the value the variable has initially is not used).

Given the sequence of choices made by a process and the sequence of values that have been received by the process, we can completely determine the local state of a process. Therefore, our model does not include the local state of the process as part of a behavior.

**Definition 1 (decision point).** *Given a trace, a decision point for a process $p$ is a point between two actions in the trace where $p$ has selected a guard of a selection statement for execution and several guards of the selection are true.*

*A decision point is characterized by a tuple $(n, sel, gset, alt)$, where $n$ is the occurrence index of the selection statement in the execution of $p$, $sel$ denotes the selection statement, $gset$ is the set of guards of the selection statement that are true, and $alt$ is the alternative chosen by $p$.*

Decision points of the system correspond to places where a non-deterministic choice is made. We assume we have no control over the mechanism used to implement this choice; therefore, the choice made by the computation is assumed to be unfair.

**Definition 2 (behavior).** *Given a trace, the corresponding behavior $\mathcal{B}$ of a system is a function that maps each channel $c$ in the system to pairs of sequences of values $(\mathbf{s}c?, \mathbf{s}c!)$ that occurred in the trace, and processes to their set of decision points in the trace.*

Given a channel $c$ and process $p$, we denote $(\mathbf{s}c?, \mathbf{s}c!)$ by $\mathcal{B}.c$, and the set of decision points corresponding to $p$ by $\mathcal{B}.p$. The behavior corresponding to a trace is unique. However, multiple traces can map onto the same behavior, since different interleavings of actions that do not interact will be reduced to the same behavior if they do not affect the sequence of values sent on the channels in the system.

**Definition 3 (system).** *A system is a closed, deadlock-free collection of CHP processes and is defined by the set of behaviors that can occur during execution.*

Note that a system will be the empty set just when it does not contain any processes.

*Example 1.* The system

$$
\begin{array}{l}
\quad *[\ X!0\ ]\ \|\ *[\ Y!1\ ]\ \|\ *[\ Z?w\ ] \\
\|\ *[[\overline{X} \longrightarrow X?x;\ Z!x;\ [\overline{Y} \longrightarrow Y?x; Z!x\ \mid\ \neg\overline{Y} \longrightarrow \textbf{skip}] \\
\quad\quad \mid \overline{Y} \longrightarrow Y?y;\ Z!y;\ [\overline{X} \longrightarrow X?y; Z!y\ \mid\ \neg\overline{X} \longrightarrow \textbf{skip}] \\
\quad\quad ]]
\end{array}
$$

has an execution that corresponds to the sequence $(X!0\|X?x)$; $(Z!0\|Z?w)$; $(Y!1\|Y?x)$; $(Z!1\|Z?w)\ldots$ where the first guard $\overline{X} \rightarrow ...$ is chosen for execution with $\overline{Y}$ being true in the outer selection statement, and $\overline{Y} \rightarrow ...$ is chosen in the inner selection statement. The behavior corresponding to this trace maps $Y$ to the pair of infinite sequences $([1,1,\ldots],[1,1,\ldots])$, $X$ to $([0,0,\ldots],[0,0,\ldots])$, $Z$ to $([0,1,0,1,\ldots],[0,1,0,1,\ldots])$, and the process with the selection statements to the set $\{(0, \mathit{selout}, \{\overline{X},\overline{Y}\}, \overline{X}), (1, \mathit{selout}, \{\overline{X},\overline{Y}\}, \overline{X}), \ldots\}$, where *selout* is the outer selection statement that selects between $\overline{X}$ and $\overline{Y}$, and the labels $\overline{X}$ and $\overline{Y}$ refer to the alternatives in the selection statement.

### 2.3 Specifications and Observability

The specification of a closed CHP program is a set of behaviors. Usually a specification does not completely specify the sequence of values sent and received on all channels of the system. Accordingly, we classify the channels of the system into *internal* and *external* channels, depending on whether or not the data values sent on those channels are part of the specification. All properties of interest must be specified only using the quantities $\mathbf{s}E!$ and $\mathbf{s}E?$, where $E$ is an external channel.

*Example 2.* It is possible that we may not be able to observe certain properties of a computation, since behaviors do not contain as much information as the sequence of actions in the computation. For example, consider the following two processes:

$$
\begin{array}{l}
\quad *[\ \mathit{NCS}_1;\ \ \mathit{CS}_1\ ] \\
\|\ *[\ \mathit{NCS}_2;\ \mathit{CS}_2\ ]
\end{array}
$$

We cannot directly observe the property that two processes access their critical sections $CS_i$ in an exclusive manner since we can only observe the sequence of values on channels. However, we can make the mutual exclusion property visible by the introduction of a third process and an external channel $C$ as follows:

$$
\begin{array}{l}
*[\ NCS_1;\ \ A!1; A!1; CS_1\ ] \\
\|\ *[\ NCS_2;\ \ B!2; B!2; CS_2\ ] \\
\|\ *[[\overline{A} \longrightarrow A?x\ \square\ \overline{B} \longrightarrow B?x];\ \ C!x\ ]
\end{array}
$$

By observing the sequence of values on channel $C$, we can determine if mutual exclusion is maintained. For instance, if sequence $1, 2, 1, 2, \ldots$ is possible, we have violated the mutual exclusion requirement.

**Definition 4.** *Given two sets of decision points $D_1$ and $D_2$ for a process p, we say that $D_1 \sqsubseteq D_2$ iff for every decision point $(n_1, sel_1, gset_1, alt_1) \in D_1$, there exists $(n_2, sel_2, gset_2, alt_2) \in D_2$ such that $n_1 = n_2$, $sel_1 = sel_2$, $gset_1 \subseteq gset_2$, and $alt_1 = alt_2$.*

The relation "$\sqsubseteq$" on sets of decision points orders them in terms of the number of non-deterministic choices that were possible.

**Definition 5 (implementation).** *We say that a system implements a specification if for each behavior $\mathcal{B}_{sys}$ of the system, there exists a behavior $\mathcal{B}_{spec}$ in the specification such that the sequence of values on all external channels in $\mathcal{B}_{spec}$ is the same as in $\mathcal{B}_{sys}$, and $(\forall p :: \mathcal{B}_{sys}.p \sqsubseteq \mathcal{B}_{spec}.p)$.*

This implementation relation is different from the traditional implementation relations used in trace theory and other models of concurrent programming because it does not include the synchronization behavior of the computation.

*Example 3.* Consider the following two systems:

$$
\begin{array}{l}
S_0 \equiv\ *[\ X!0\ ]\ \|\ *[\ Y!0\ ]\ \|\ *[\ X?x\ ]\ \|\ *[\ Y?y\ ] \\
S_1 \equiv\ *[\ X!0;\ \ Y!0\ ]\ \|\ \textbf{skip}\ \|\ *[\ X?x\ ]\ \|\ *[\ Y?y\ ]
\end{array}
$$

The computations specified by $S_0$ and $S_1$ are indistinguishable under our model because the sequence of values sent and received on channels $X$ and $Y$ remain unchanged, and both systems have no decision points. Standard concurrency models will differentiate them because the communication on $X$ and $Y$ cannot be executed in parallel, and because of the additional bound $0 \leq \mathbf{c}X - \mathbf{c}Y \leq 1$ in system $S_1$.

We now present the theorems that enable a large number of transformations, including the introduction and elimination of pipelining, data-flow style process decomposition, and pipelined completion detection.

## 3 Main Theorems

Throughout this section we will use $\mathcal{S}$ to denote the set of possible behaviors of the system of interest, $p$ to denote a process in the system, and $c$ to denote a channel in the system.

**Lemma 1 (monotonicity).** *Let $\mathcal{S}^+$ be the system obtained from $\mathcal{S}$ by increasing the slack on a particular channel. Then $\mathcal{S} \subseteq \mathcal{S}^+$*

*Proof:* Consider any behavior of $\mathcal{S}$. This behavior corresponds to some execution of system $\mathcal{S}$. It suffices to show that this execution is possible in $\mathcal{S}^+$. Let $c$ be the channel whose slack was increased from $\mathbf{k}c!$ to $\mathbf{k}c! + n$. By definition, computations from $\mathcal{S}$ satisfy $\mathbf{c}c! - \mathbf{c}c? \leq \mathbf{k}c!$. These computations still exist in $\mathcal{S}^+$ because we can postpone any attempted send action on $c$ so that this condition is satisfied, since $\mathcal{S}$ is deadlock-free. We now show that the communication actions that were attempted in $\mathcal{S}$ can also occur in $\mathcal{S}^+$.

The only construct in CHP which can affect control flow behavior is the selection statement. Increasing slack does not change the probe of the receiver end of the channel (by definition). The probe of a sender is monotonic with slack (by definition). Since we disallow negated probes of sender ports, this implies that all guards of selection statements are monotonic with slack. Also, a true probe on a sender port can be postponed (since probes only become true eventually) in $\mathcal{S}^+$ until the point when it becomes true in $\mathcal{S}$. Therefore, the guards true in $\mathcal{S}$ will eventually become true in $\mathcal{S}^+$, and so any behavior from $\mathcal{S}$ could occur in $\mathcal{S}^+$. □

Lemma 1 shows that the set of behaviors is monotonic with the slack on the channels. We now show that the only way in which increasing the slack on a channel can affect the computation is by increasing non-determinism. Note that both restrictions on computations that were mentioned in the previous section are needed for this proof.

**Theorem 1 (decreasing slack).** *Decreasing the slack of a channel does not affect the correctness of computations if and only if it does not introduce deadlock.*

*Proof:* Let $\mathcal{S}^-$ be the system obtained from $\mathcal{S}$ by decreasing the slack of a channel. If $\mathcal{S}^-$ is deadlock-free, $\mathcal{S}^- \subseteq \mathcal{S}$ by lemma 1. By definition 5, $\mathcal{S}^-$ implements $\mathcal{S}$. □

**Definition 6 (extension).** *A behavior $\mathcal{B}'$ is said to be the extension of behavior $\mathcal{B}$ iff:*

$$(\forall c :: \mathcal{B}.c = \mathcal{B}'.c) \wedge$$
$$(\exists p_0 :: (\forall p : p \neq p_0 : \mathcal{B}.p = \mathcal{B}'.p) \wedge \mathcal{B}.p_0 \neq \mathcal{B}'.p_0 \wedge \mathcal{B}.p_0 \sqsubseteq \mathcal{B}'.p_0)$$

Intuitively, the extension of a behavior corresponds to the same data behavior but with at least one additional choice which did not exist in the original behavior.

**Theorem 2 (increasing slack).** *Let $\mathcal{S}^+$ be the system obtained from $\mathcal{S}$ by increasing the slack of a channel. Then either $\mathcal{S} = \mathcal{S}^+$, or there exists a behavior $\mathcal{B}^+ \in (\mathcal{S}^+ - \mathcal{S})$ that is the extension of a behavior in $\mathcal{S}$.*

*Proof:* By lemma 1, $\mathcal{S} \subseteq \mathcal{S}^+$. Therefore either $\mathcal{S} = \mathcal{S}^+$, or there exists $\mathcal{B}_0 \in \mathcal{S}^+ - \mathcal{S}$. Assume such a $\mathcal{B}_0$ exists. Now $\mathcal{B}_0$ differs from every behavior in $\mathcal{S}$ in either the sequence of values sent on some channel or in the set of decision points for some process in $S$. This implies that the local state of some process from $S^+$ differs from the the local state that could occur in $S$. Consider the first point in execution when this occurs. The only non-deterministic construct in CHP is the selection statement, and therefore the only way a new local state could occur is because of a new true guard in a selection statement. By the same argument as in lemma 1, the guards true in $S$ will eventually become true in $S^+$. Therefore, we can pick an alternative of the selection statement that is possible in $S$, and continue execution as in the original system $S$. This new behavior is the required extension. □

The strength of Theorem 2 lies in the fact that if we can show that we cannot possibly introduce new decision points, this implies that adding slack does not change the behavior of a computation.

We now present some corollaries of the results of the previous section that can be used to reason about a large class of CHP programs.

## 4 Subsidiary Results

The monotonicity lemma coupled with Theorem 2 permits us to make the following statement that is very useful in practice.

**Corollary 1 (sandwich theorem).** *If a system satisfies its specification when the slack on channel c is k and when the slack on channel c is l (> k), it satisfies its specification when the slack on c is s, for all s satisfying $k \leq s \leq l$.*

*Proof:* The set of behaviors (and therefore the implementation relation) is monotonic with slack. Therefore, if the system is correct with $c$ having slack $k$ and slack $l$, the set of decision points is included on the set of those at slack $l$ for all slack $s$ satisfying $k \leq s \leq l$, concluding the proof. □

When computations are entirely deterministic, we can introduce slack on any channel without affecting correctness.

**Corollary 2 (deterministic computations).** *If the guards in selection statements are syntactically mutually exclusive and there are no probed channels, the system has only one behavior.*

*Proof:* Since the computation is deterministic, the sequence of values sent on channels is always the same and there are no decision points. □

A selection statement with probed channels in its guards is said to exhibit *maximal non-determinism* if all the guards can be true whenever the selection statement is executed.

**Corollary 3 (maximal non-determinism).** *If all selection statements with probes have maximal non-determinism, the system is slack elastic.*

*Proof:* The set of decision points of the system cannot be increased, so by Theorem 2 we can increase the slack on any channel without changing the behavior of the system. □

Corollary 3 is extremely useful in practice. The design of the MIPS R3000 processor undertaken by our group satisfies its requirements.

Consider the problem of measuring the slack of a channel $c$. To be able to measure the slack of $c$, we must be provided with a collection of processes to which $c$ is connected, and a single channel which produces one output on channel *result*: *true*, if the slack of $c$ is equal to a specified value, say $k$, or *false* otherwise. We claim that this task is impossible under the assumptions of the model.

**Corollary 4 (impossibility of measuring slack).** *It is not possible to measure the slack of a communication channel.*

*Proof:* Assume that a collection of deadlock-free processes can be used to answer the question "is the slack of channel $c$ equal to $k$?" Consider the closed system $S$ where we observe channel *result*, and where $c$ has slack $k$. The only possible output on *result* is *true*, by our assumption. Let $S^+$ be the system, where we add slack 1 to channel $c$. By Theorem 1, $S$ implements $S^+$. Therefore, *result* can produce the value *true* in $S^+$—a contradiction. □

More generally, if a system can be used to compute any relationship among the slacks of a set of channels, then the relation must be trivial—i.e., the system always outputs *true* or always outputs *false*.

# 5 Applications

When designing concurrent systems, we can increase the slack on a particular channel under the conditions outlined above. We now present some important transformations that can be shown to be semantics-preserving using the results derived above.

## 5.1 Pipelining

Pipelining is a technique whereby the computation of a function is distributed over a number of stages so as to reduce the cycle time of the system—increasing the throughput—at the cost of increasing the latency of the computation. A simple two-stage linear pipeline can be described by the following program:

$$*[\ L?x;\ \ I!f(x)\ ]\ \|\ *[\ I?y;\ \ R!g(y)\ ]$$

We introduce pipelining when we transform program:

$$*[\ L?x;\ \ R!g(f(x))\ ]$$

into the program shown above. It should be clear that we can apply this transformation if and only if we are permitted to increase the slack on channels $L$ or $R$. Under those conditions, we can formally pipeline a computation as follows:

$$
\begin{array}{ll}
& *[L?x; R!g(f(x))] \\
= & \{ \text{ add slack 1 to channel } R\text{, introducing internal channel } I \} \\
& *[L?x; I!g(f(x))] \parallel *[I?y; R!y] \\
= & \{ \text{ distribute computation—} I \text{ is internal } \} \\
& *[L?x; I!f(x)] \parallel *[I?t; R!g(t)]
\end{array}
$$

## 5.2 Eliminating Synchronization Among Actions

When designing a delay-insensitive system, we face a problem when attempting to design datapaths where the quantities being manipulated are constituted of a large number of bits. The problem is illustrated by examining the circuit implementation of the following program:

$$*[\ L?x;\ \ R!x\ ]$$

Before we send value $x$ on channel $R$, we must be sure that all the bits used to represent $x$ have been received on channel $L$. The circuit that waits for all the bits to have been received has a throughput that degrades as $1/\log N$, where $N$ is the number of bits. As a result, as we increase the number of bits in $x$, the system throughput will decrease.

Instead, we examine an alternative implementation strategy. We implement channel $L$ using an array of $\Theta(N)$ channels, where the individual channels use a fixed number of bits. As a result, we transform the program shown above into:

$$*[\ (\|i :: L[i]?x[i]);\ \ (\|i :: R[i]!x[i])\ ]$$

We have moved the performance problem from the implementation of the communication action on a channel to the implementation of the semicolon that separates the $L$ and $R$ actions. However, we observe that there is no data-dependency between channels $L[i]$ and $R[j]$ when $i \neq j$. We will attempt to remove the synchronization between the parts of the program that are not data-dependent.

We introduce a dummy process that enforces the sequencing specified by the program above. The original program is equivalent to:

$$
\begin{array}{l}
(\|i :: *[\ S[i] \bullet L[i]?x[i];\ \ S[i] \bullet R[i]!x[i]\ ]) \\
\| *[\ (\|i :: S[i])\ ]
\end{array}
$$

since the slack zero $S[i]$-actions ensure that the actions on channels $L$ and $R$ are properly sequenced. (The bullet operator "$\bullet$" ensures that actions on $S[i]$ and $L[i]$ (or $R[i]$) are tightly synchronized.)

Now, we increase the slack on channels $S[i]$. If we let the slack on channels $S[i]$ go to infinity, the program shown above is equivalent to:

$$(\|i :: *[\ L[i]?x[i];\ \ R[i]!x[i]\ ])$$

Therefore, we can transform the original program into this one if and only if we can add slack on channels $S[i]$. Observe that we now have $\Theta(N)$ *independent* processes, and increasing $N$ will not affect the throughput of the system. This transformation can be generalized to a technique which permits the distribution of a control value in a loosely synchronized manner [7].

### 5.3 General Function Decomposition

In general, if we have a computation graph which is supposed to implement a function that has a simple sequential specification, we can show its correctness by introducing "ghost channels" which sequence all the actions in the computation graph. A single process that sequences all the actions in the computation is introduced, so that the resulting system mimics the behavior of the sequential program. Adding slack to the ghost channels introduced for sequencing permits the processes in the computation graph to proceed in parallel; when we add infinite slack to the sequencing channels, we have a computation that behaves exactly like the original computation without the sequencer process, and the ghost channels can be deleted without modifying the behavior of the computation. Therefore, showing the correctness of the original computation can be reduced to showing whether adding slack on the ghost channels modifies the behavior of the system.

*Example 4.* Suppose we would like to demonstrate that the following CHP program implements a first-in first-out buffer:

$$*[\ L?x;\ \ U!x;\ \ L?x;\ \ D!x\ ]\ \|\ *[\ U?y;\ \ R!y;\ \ D?y;\ \ R!y\ ]$$

We begin by closing the system with the introduction of two processes which send data on channel $L$ and receive data from channel $R$. Next, we introduce a sequencer process which sequences the actions in the computation. The resulting system is shown below.

$$\begin{array}{l} i := 0; *[\ L!i;\ \ i := i+1\ ]\ \|\ *[\ R?w\ ] \\ \|\ *[\ L?x \bullet S_1;\ \ U!x \bullet S_2;\ \ L?x \bullet S_4;\ \ D!x \bullet S_5\ ] \\ \|\ *[\ U?y;\ \ R!y \bullet S_3;\ \ D?y;\ \ R!y \bullet S_6\ ] \\ \|\ *[\ S_1;\ \ S_2;\ \ S_3;\ \ S_4;\ \ S_5;\ \ S_6\ ] \end{array}$$

The sequencer process restricts the computation so that only one interleaving is possible, namely the sequence

$$(L!0\|L?x); (U!x\|U?y); (R!y\|R?w); (L!1\|L?x); (D!x\|D?y); (R!y\|R?w);$$
$$(L!2\|L?x);\ \ldots$$

which clearly implements a first-in first-out buffer, since the sequence of values sent on $R$ is the same as the sequence of values received on $L$. We can increase the slack on channels $S_i$ without modifying its behavior because the computation is deterministic. In the limit of infinite slack on the channels $S_i$ for all $i$, the sequencer process does not enforce any synchronization between the actions, and we can eliminate the sequencer process entirely leaving us with the original computation. Therefore, the original computation implements a first-in first-out buffer.

### 5.4 A Recipe for Slack Elastic Programs

Corollary 3 can be used as a guideline for the design of programs that are guaranteed to be slack elastic. Ensuring slack elasticity of the design is important in order to be able to postpone decisions related to the amount of pipelining to be used in an implementation. In the design of an asynchronous MIPS processor, we found it necessary to adjust the slack on communication channels after most of the physical layout was complete because we did not have accurate estimates of the timing behavior of the processes we used until analog simulations were performed.

There are two selection statements in CHP. Selection statements that are described using the thick bar "▯" indicate that the guards are mutually exclusive. If such selection statements do not use any probes in their guards, they cannot be the cause of the introduction of new decision points. Selection statements that use the thin bar "|" indicate that their guards might not be mutually exclusive. If such selection statements are maximally non-deterministic—i.e., if the computation meets its specification irrespective of the alternative chosen when the selection is encountered, then they will not be the cause of erroneous computations. If we follow these two guidelines, we will be guaranteed that the computation is slack elastic. Every process in the high-level description of the asynchronous MIPS processor we designed satisfied these criteria.

## 6 Conclusion

We have presented a new technique for reasoning about the correctness of a concurrent system based on the concept of synchronization slack, and presented conditions under which the slack of a channel in a distributed computation can be modified without affecting its behavior.

We showed how a number of program transformations can be analyzed by considering the effect of changing the slack of a communication channel, demonstrating that slack elasticity is an important property for a computation to have.

We presented sufficient conditions under which a distributed computation is slack elastic. The conditions were strong enough to be satisfied by the complete high-level design of an asynchronous processor. Slack elasticity was an important tool that enabled us to reason about a number of complex transformations in the design of the processor.

## References

1. van der Goot, M.: The Semantics of VLSI Synthesis. Ph.D. thesis, California Institute of Technology (1996)

2. Hoare, C.A.R.: Communicating Sequential Processes. *Communications of the ACM*, **21**(8) (1978) 666–677
3. van Horn, K.S.: *An Approach to Concurrent Semantics Using Complete Traces*. M.S. thesis, California Institute of Technology (1986)
4. Martin, A.J.: An Axiomatic definition of synchronization primitives. *Acta Informatica*, **16** (1981) 219–235
5. Martin, A.J.: The Probe: An addition to communication primitives. *Information Processing Letters*, **20** (1985) 125–130
6. Martin, A.J., Lines A., Manohar R., Nyström, M., Penzes, P., Southworth, R., Cummings, U.V., and Lee, T.K.: The design of an asynchronous MIPS R3000. *Proceedings of the 17th Conference on Advanced Research in VLSI* (1997)
7. Manohar, R.: The Impact of Asynchrony on Computer Architecture. Ph.D. thesis, California Institute of Technology (1998)
8. van de Snepscheut, J.L.A.: Trace theory and VLSI design. Lecture Notes in Computer Science 200, Springer-Verlag (1985)
9. Williams, T.E.: Self-timed Rings and their Application to Division. Ph.D. thesis, Computer Systems Laboratory, Stanford University (1991)

# A Notation

The notation we use is based on Hoare's CSP [2]. What follows is a short and informal description of the notation we use. A formal semantics can be found in [1].

**Simple statements and expressions.**

- Skip: **skip**. This statement does nothing.
- Assignment: $x := E$. This statement means "assign the value of $E$ to $x$."
- Communication: $X!e$ means send the value of $e$ over channel $X$; $Y?x$ means receive a value over channel $Y$ and store it in variable $x$. When we are not communicating data values over a channel, the directionality of the channel is unimportant. In this case, the statement $X$ denotes a synchronization action on port $X$.
- Probe: The boolean $\overline{X}$ is true if and only if a communication over port $X$ can complete without suspending.

**Compound statements.**

- Selection: $[G_1 \rightarrow S_1 \; ▯ \; ... \; ▯ \; G_n \rightarrow S_n]$, where $G_i$'s are boolean expressions (guards) and $S_i$'s are program parts. The execution of this command corresponds to waiting until one of the guards is true, and then executing one of the statements with a true guard. The notation $[G]$ is short-hand for $[G \rightarrow$ **skip**$]$, and denotes waiting for the predicate $G$ to become true. If the guards are not mutually exclusive, we use the vertical bar "|" instead of "▯."

- Repetition: $*[G_1 \rightarrow S_1 \; [] \; ... \; [] \; G_n \rightarrow S_n]$. The execution of this command corresponds to choosing one of the true guards and executing the corresponding statement, repeating this until all guards evaluate to false. The notation $*[S]$ is short-hand for $*[\mathbf{true} \rightarrow S]$. If the guards are not mutually exclusive, we use the vertical bar "|" instead of "[]."
- Sequential Composition: $S; T$. The semicolon binds tighter than the parallel composition operator $\|$, but weaker than the comma or bullet.
- Parallel Composition: $S \parallel T$ or $S, T$. The $\|$ operator binds weaker than the bullet or semicolon. The comma binds tighter than the semicolon but weaker than the bullet.
- Simultaneous Composition: $S \bullet T$ (read "$S$ bullet $T$") means that the actions $S$ and $T$ complete simultaneously. The bullet synchronizes the two actions by enforcing $\mathbf{c}S = \mathbf{c}T$. Action $S \bullet T$ is implemented by decomposing actions $S$ and $T$ into smaller actions and interleaving them. The operator binds tighter than the semicolon and parallel composition.

The concurrent execution of a collection of CHP processes is assumed to be *weakly fair*—every continuously enabled action will be given a chance to execute eventually. The selection statement is assumed to be demonic, and it therefore *not* fair. Consider the following four processes:

$$
\begin{array}{l}
*[\; X!0 \;] \parallel *[\; Y!1 \;] \\
\parallel *[[\overline{X} \longrightarrow X?x \; [] \; \overline{Y} \longrightarrow Y?x \;]; \; Z!x \;] \\
\parallel *[\; W!2 \;]
\end{array}
$$

Since the selection statement is not fair, $Z$ is permitted to output an infinite sequence of zeros. However, both $Z!x$ and $W!2$ will execute eventually, since parallel composition is assumed to be weakly fair.

# Beyond Fun: Order and Membership in Polytypic Imperative Programming

David A. Naumann

Stevens Institute of Technology, Hoboken NJ 07030, USA
naumann@cs.stevens-tech.edu

**Abstract.** We argue that the category of transformers of monotonic predicates on posets is superior to the category of transformers on powersets, as the basis for a calculus of higher order imperative programming. We show by an example polytypic program derivation that such transformers (and the underlying categories of order-compatible relations and monotonic functions) model a calculus quite similar to the more familiar calculus of functional programs and relations. The derived program uses as a data type an exponent of transformers; unlike function-space, this transformer-space is adequate for semantics of higher order imperative programs.

## 1 Introduction

Programs are arrows of a category whose objects are data types — but what category? what objects? what arrows? The primordial, if fanciful, answer is **Fun**, the category of "all" sets and functions (often called **Set**). If we choose a few objects as primitives, say integers and booleans, we get a rich collection of types by application of constructs like $\mathcal{P}, \times, +, \rightarrow$, and fixpoints of polynomial functors. These types have beautifully simple algebraic characterizations that are useful in program derivation. Other categories (topoi) of functions, say computable ones, are almost as fun. But computational phenomena like demonic nondeterminacy and divergence force us to use still other categories to model programs, e.g., predicate transformers or Kleisli categories for monads of computational effects. And to model *programming* we need other categories because not every specification can be expressed as a program. A good category of specifications has programs as a subcategory, so that programs can be derived using constructs and properties not available in the category of programs alone (e.g., everywhere-defined relative converse). The purpose of this paper is to make a case for going slightly beyond **Fun** to the category **Mofun** of monotonic functions between posets, and far beyond to a category of transformers based on **Mofun**. (**Mofun** is often called **Poset**.) The case has three parts: we explain why **Fun** and its associated predicate transfomers are unsatisfactory as a basis for higher order imperative programming, we show how the proposed alternative is familiar and unsurprising, and we apply the results to a modest but nontrivial example.

The textbook of Bird and de Moor summarizes work in the Squiggol community (Backhouse, Meertens, and many others) on a categorical approach to program construction which we seek to extend [1]. Our proposal is familiar and unsurprising in that the notions and laws used in that book carry over with little change to **Mofun** and its associated category **Idl** of what we will call ideal relations.[1] More importantly, those notions can be lifted to a predicate-transformer model of imperative programs and their specifications. It is for this lifting that **Fun** is unsatisfactory. In order for there to be an exponent of transformers that is both calculationally well-behaved and operationally adequate to model higher-order procedures, it turns out that predicates must be monotonic with respect to refinement. Making this idea precise means moving from **Fun** to **Mofun**.

The algebra of transformers is applied here to the *repmin* problem: In a single pass over a tree, replace every value with the minimum value in the original tree. Our purpose is to expose the relevant mathematics for readers familiar with Squiggol, categories, and predicate transformers, say at the level of [1] and [13]. We do not provide a tutorial for ideas already well-explained elsewhere, nor do we propose notations for practical use. The point is to explore the possibility of a tractable calculus of imperative programs much like the calculus of functional programs. Three features of the Squiggol are salient:

**Embedding:** The category of programs is embedded in a category of specifications that has convenient structure. Computable functions on countable sets are embedded in the category **Fun** of all (small) sets and functions. More to the point, **Fun** is embedded in the category **Rel** of binary relations, which has convenient structure such as everywhere-defined relative converse. Functions can be specified by relations, and a total function $f$ meeting specification $R$ is obtained by a constructive proof of $R \supseteq f$.

**Lifting:** The structure of data types in the category of specifications is obtained from the type structure of the base category, in such a way that generic results can be expressed and proved —e.g., functors on **Fun** are lifted to monotonic functors on **Rel**.

**Polytypism and membership:** For higher-order polymorphism, i.e., programs parameterized by type-constructor, an important recent development is the notion of membership [8] which refines earlier characterizations of functors that represent data types. Membership facilitates proofs of generic results without recourse to induction on type contructors.

Type-constructors like products and exponents are well-known and useful. Their categorical properties have been widely exploited in program construction and language design, where simple forms of genericity are embodied in natural transformations and Hindley-Milner polymorphism. Not surprisingly, well-behaved products and exponents of transformers are needed for our *repmin* derivation. In addition to basic constructs like $\times$ and $\rightarrow$, type-constructors can be defined as fixpoints. For example, consider the constructor *Ltree* of non-empty

[1] We restrict attention to posets rather than preorders because it is slightly simpler to work in a setting where equivalent objects are isomorphic and adjoint arrows are unique up to identity. We can accurately say "isomorphic" instead of having to define "biëquivalent". Essentially the same results go through for preorders [17].

leaf trees specified by

$$Ltree\,B = Leaf\,B \mid Bin(Ltree\,B, Ltree\,B)\ .$$

For each type $B$, the type $Ltree\,B$ is the least fixpoint of the functor $F(B, -)$ with $F$ defined by $F(B,Y) = B+(Y\times Y)$. Such type constructors are themselves functorial. For example, if $f$ is a function $f : B \to C$ then $Ltree\,f : Ltree\,B \to Ltree\,C$ is the function that maps $f$ over a tree. Our generic name for such type-constructors is $fix$, and we implicitly associate $fix$ with a base functor named $F$ throughout the paper.

One might like to write a single map program $fix$ that works for all inductive data types, thus parameterized by type-construct. Recently, such higher-order polymorphism has been explored fruitfully, under the rubric *polytypic programming*. Jansson and Jeuring [9] extended Haskell with means to define polytypic functions by induction on the definition of the type-constructor (more properly, on the definition of the polynomial basis, our $F$). Others have explored languages with certain polytypic operators like map as primitive [2].

For program construction, the Squiggol community has developed notations and results on *catamorphisms* and their ilk — abstracting common properties of all inductive data types and in particular providing algebraic alternatives to explicit induction proofs. De Moor [4] derives a polytypic program for the *repmin* problem for arbitrary inductive type (subject to the proviso that elements of the type are non-empty, like *Ltree*, so that every structure has a minimum). The resulting program is polymorphic in the type-constructor $fix$ —parametrically, i.e., it is not defined inductively on the definition of $F$. The derivation uses that $F$ has *membership*, a notion discussed later. Our main result is that a similar derivation can be used with predicate transformers, yielding a higher-order imperative program solving the problem.

The notions above have been developed primarily for functional programs, and modeled by **Fun**, explicitly or not, with **Rel** as the ambient category of specifications. Variants like partial functions and CPO have also been used. The paradigm is a structure $\mathbf{C} \hookrightarrow \mathbf{D}$ where $\mathbf{C}$ is some category of programs which is embedded in a richer category $\mathbf{D}$ of specifications. The structure $\mathbf{C} \hookrightarrow \mathbf{D}$ also appears in domain-theoretic semantics, where recursive domain equations are solved in a category $\mathbf{C}$ of embedding-projection pairs embedded in a category $\mathbf{D}$ of continuous functions between CPOs. Moggi [12] initiated the use of monads to treat programs exhibiting imperative phenomena; Power and Robinson [19] have reinterpreted this as another situation of the form $\mathbf{C} \hookrightarrow \mathbf{D}$. In each case, $\mathbf{C}$ has the same objects as $\mathbf{D}$, and $\mathbf{C}$ consists of the well-behaved arrows, e.g., total deterministic programs, in terms of which the type-structure is characterized by adjunctions.

For the algebra of imperative programs and their specifications, previous investigations sought to replace $\mathbf{Fun} \hookrightarrow \mathbf{Rel}$ with $\mathbf{Fun} \hookrightarrow \mathbf{Tran}$ where **Tran** is the category of monotonic predicate transformers between powersets [6, 3, 10, 15, 5]. It is convenient to factor through **Rel**, that is, $\mathbf{Fun} \hookrightarrow \mathbf{Rel} \hookrightarrow \mathbf{Tran}$. But **Tran** is unsatisfactory from a calculational point of view: by contrast with products, the exponent's laws are too weak for it to be axiomatized as a lax exponent, and it does not preserve data refinement. As the *repmin* example shows, exponents are useful even for first-order problems. We derive the *repmin* program using the better-behaved exponent in a category **Spec** of transformers based on **Mofun**.

To avoid cluttering the paper with citations, we give an outline that includes references for previous results used but not proved in the sequel. Section 2 elaborates on the shortcomings of **Tran**, based on [6,16]. After Section 2, the reader may care to skim the specification of *repmin* in Section 6 and its derivation which comprises Section 9. The other sections are as follows. Section 3 describes the category **Idl** of ideal relations and the embedding **Mofun** $\hookrightarrow$ **Idl**. Section 4 describes predicates and transformers in terms of **Idl**, in the structure **Mofun** $\hookrightarrow$ **Idl** $\hookrightarrow$ **Spec** that we advocate in place of **Fun** $\hookrightarrow$ **Rel** $\hookrightarrow$ **Tran**. Section 4 also introduces membership, based on [7,8]. Section 5 describes type-constructs like $\times, +, \rightarrow$ for **Idl**, as background for Section 7 which does the same for transformers, including a complete axiomatization for the exponent in **Spec**. Sections 3, 4, 5 and 7 are based on [17], except for new results on membership. Section 8 deals with transformers on inductive data types, based on [18,3]. Section 11 assesses the case for going beyond **Fun**.

## 2 Inadequacy of Tran

Predicate transformers can model temporal properties of concurrent programs, but the two imperative phenomena of nondeterminacy and divergence already force us beyond **Fun** and **Rel**. An imperative program of type $A \rightarrow B$ can be modeled by a termination set $\alpha \subseteq A$ and an input-output relation $R$ in **Rel**$(A, B)$. Pre-post specifications can involve auxiliary variables of some type $X$, so they can be modeled by a so-called *span*

$$A \xleftarrow{\;S\;} X \xrightarrow{\;T\;} B \qquad (1)$$

i.e., an ordered pair $(S, T)$ of relations with common source object. Spans can be made into a category, using a lax kind of pullback so that $\swarrow\searrow\swarrow\searrow$ can be composed as $\begin{array}{c}\swarrow\;\searrow\\ \swarrow\searrow\swarrow\searrow\end{array}$. This suggests embedding a category **C** of pairs $(\alpha, R)$ in a category **D** of spans. Some summarizing propositions below make reference to the span construction, but full definitions are not needed in the sequel (see [6]).

Transformers are a simpler model of imperative programming. The category of monotonic transformers between powersets is isomorphic to the category of spans over **Rel** [6], and it is well known that so-called healthy transformers model imperative programs [13]. The first simplification, as compared with spans and other models, is that sequential composition is just composition of functions. Of course composition is key to all the categorical descriptions of data types.[2] The second simplification is that program refinement (and satisfaction of specifications) is just the pointwise order $\sqsubseteq$ on transformers.

That second simplification facilitated development by Back, Morris, and Morgan of the refinement calculus of first-order imperative programming [13]. Derivations in refinement calculus typically involve explicit, monomorphically-typed state variables as well as manipulations of predicates on such variables. Our aim is to augment refinement calculus with tools for calculating at the program level and calculating polytypically. Our approach is to lift type-structure from functions to transformers.

To explain lifting we need some notation: $S^o$ denotes the *reciprocal* (converse) of any relation $S$, and (;) the composition of relations: $(f\,;g)a = g(f\,a)$ in the case of functions $f : A \to B$ and $g : B \to C$. Application binds more tightly than (;) and less so than reciprocation. Operators introduced later, like $\Delta, \otimes, \hat{\Delta}, \to$, bind less tightly than compositions (both (;) and later ($\hat{;}$)).

Consider first the lifting of type-structure to relations. Every relation $R$ has a factorization $R = f^o\,; h$ where $f, h$ are functions (to wit, the projection functions from the set of ordered pairs comprising $R$). Given a functorial type-construct $G : \mathbf{Fun} \to \mathbf{Fun}$, we can lift $G$ to relations by using factorization in the definition

$$GR = (Gf)^o\,; Gh \quad \text{where } R \text{ factors as } R = f^o\,; h\ .$$

Factorization is only unique up to a suitable equivalence, so it takes some work to verify these claims and those we quote below. Each transformer factors as a composite $[R]\,;\langle S\rangle$ where $[R]$ is the inverse-image function of relation $R$ and $\langle S\rangle$ is the direct-image of $S$. A functorial type-construct $G : \mathbf{Rel} \to \mathbf{Rel}$ can be extended to $\widehat{G}$ on transformers $h$ by the definition

$$\widehat{G}h = [GR]\,;\langle GS\rangle \quad \text{where } h \text{ factors as } h = ([R]\,;\langle S\rangle)\ .$$

This works quite nicely for the coproduct $+$, as $\hat{+}$ is a categorical coproduct of transformers, and —like all such liftings— it is monotonic with respect to refinement. The lifted product is somewhat weaker.

Consider an imperative program $A \xrightarrow{f \Delta g} B \times C \xrightarrow{\pi} B$ which forms a pair by executing programs $f : A \to B$ and $g : A \to C$ and then projects out just the first component of the pair. It is not necessarily equal to $f$, if $g$ could diverge. The refinement $(f \Delta g)\,; \pi \sqsubseteq f$ does hold, but only if $g$ obeys the law of the 'excluded miracle'. Deterministic programs $h$ satisfy the other fundamental law of categorical products, $h; \pi_0 \Delta h; \pi_1 = h$, which says that for pair-producing $h$ the components of an output pair can be constructed separately and combined to yield the same pair. But this weakens to an inequality if $h$ is nondeterministic, because two independent executions of $h$ may have different outcomes. A complete axiomatization for the weak product of transformers is obtained by

[2] Simplicity of composition is one of the main advantages of Power and Robinson's notion [19] over Moggi's use of Kleisli categories.

combining such inequalities with implications giving the usual equations for well-behaved programs. This is typical of how the paradigm $\mathbf{C} \hookrightarrow \mathbf{D}$ is used, e.g., see Propositions 6 and 8, and the similar laws for products in **Rel** [1]. Fortunately, coproduct is not the only structure that lifts without weakening: inductive data types do as well [3].

Higher-order functions give much of the expressiveness of functional programming, so for imperative programming one naturally looks to higher-order procedures. Here there is a gap: lifting as described above extends the construct to new arrows but does not yield new objects. Lifting the exponential constructor $\rightarrow$ to relations and to transformers gives the function space as a data type, but it does not give the 'internal hom' and it does not model programs as a data type. Besides being called an exponent, the function space $A \rightarrow B$ is called an *internal hom* of **Fun** because $A \rightarrow B$ is a homset $\mathbf{Fun}(A, B)$ taken as an object of **Fun**. In general, the paradigm $\mathbf{C} \hookrightarrow \mathbf{D}$ is used where $\mathbf{C}$ is a category of data types to be used in $\mathbf{D}$, and most work has dealt with types that are intrinsic to $\mathbf{C}$, like its internal hom. But the internal hom of $\mathbf{D}$ may exist as a less-familiar data type in $\mathbf{C}$. Section 5.2 considers the homset $\mathbf{Rel}(A, B)$ as a relation-space $A \leftrightarrow B$ in **Fun**, and Section 7.2 treats the transformer-space as an object of **Mofun**.

The *repmin* problem starts with a simple problem-specification: a program to find the minimum of a tree, composed with a program that replaces every value in a tree by a given element. Both finding the minimum and replacing every value can be described as tree traversals; the problem is to derive a program that traverses the tree only once. In a functional language, this can be done using a higher order function. De Moor derives a *repmin* program using just properties of exponents, and makes the beautiful observation that the result can be interpreted in **Fun** as a higher-order function, but also in **Rel**, essentially as a first-order logic program (because, in **Rel**, $\times$ has the formal properties of an exponent). One would hope that any function can be programmed in a higher-order imperative language, but imperative languages in wide use have somewhat stunted forms of higher-order functions. Some do have higher-order procedures, however, and the exponent of transformers models such languages adequately [14]. Although it should be possible to interpret the *repmin* derivation using a function-space lifted to transformers, we need to use the internal hom of transformers if we are to interpret the resulting program as a conventional imperative one.

Unfortunately, the transformer-space is not a categorical exponent, so de Moor's derivation is not, on the face of it, sound for this imperative interpretation. Worse yet, in **Tran** the internal hom does not have a simple complete axiomatization, and it does not preserve data refinement; the laws are a little too weak. The root of the problem is that too many distinctions can be made if arbitrary subsets are allowed as predicates at higher types. But in the category **Spec** of transformers based on **Mofun**, predicates are monotonic and the internal hom is completely axiomatized as a weak exponent. Those laws suffice for a derivation of *repmin* much like de Moor's.

The internal hom $A \leadsto B$ consists of all transformers (from $A$ to $B$), which means that even specifications count as data values. Elsewhere [18], we justify the use of $A \leadsto B$ in derivations by giving a (polytypic) data-refinement to a type $A \leadsto' B$ of concrete programs — which can be any class specified by healthiness conditions.

The poset $A \leadsto B$ can be taken as an object in the base category **Mofun**, and this extends to a functor for which we can consider membership. We also consider membership for the relation-space $A \leftrightarrow B$, i.e., the internal hom for relations. This investigation helps justify our choice of turning relations right-side-up: unafraid to reverse the familiar, in the Squiggol spirit, we order them by $\supseteq$ rather than the usual $\subseteq$. This may be rather trivial, but it simplifies some notations and reduces the number of dualities we have to contend with — still rather many, an unavoidable aspect of transformers.

## 3 Ideal relations

Because new categories are proposed, an embarassement of background material is needed. This section covers monotonic functions and ideals.

A *pocat* is a category with homsets partially ordered and composition monotonic. A *map* in a pocat is an arrow $g$ with a right adjoint $g^*$ called its *comap*; i.e., $g$ and $g^*$ satisfy $\mathsf{id} \sqsubseteq g ; g^*$ and $g^* ; g \sqsubseteq \mathsf{id}$. We assume the reader knows that **Fun** is the subcategory of maps of **Rel** (ordered by $\subseteq$) and that the comap of a function $f$ is its *reciprocal* $f^o$ (i.e., its converse). Maps in a pocat **C** are the comaps of the arrow-dual $\mathbf{C}^{op}$ and they are also comaps in the order-dual $\mathbf{C}^{co}$ obtained by reversing the order on homsets. Due to dualizations, comaps appear later where some readers may expect maps. A *bimap* is both a map and a comap.

In the sequel, the symbols $\subseteq$ and $\supseteq$ always have their usual set-theoretic meaning, and $\sqsubseteq$ is always the pointwise order on functions between posets. For poset $A$ we write $\preceq_A$ or just $\preceq$ for the order and $A$ for the set of values.

**Definition 1.** *If $R : A \to B$ is a relation between posets, it is an* ideal *if*

$$\preceq_A ; R ; \preceq_B \ \subseteq \ R .$$

*Ideals are the arrows of the pocat* **Idl** *whose objects are all (small) posets. Composition in* **Idl** *is the same as in* **Rel**, *but the identity on $A$ is $\preceq_A$. Homsets are ordered by $\supseteq$. The* graph functor $\mathsf{Gr} : \mathbf{Mofun} \to \mathbf{Idl}$ *is defined by* $\mathsf{Gr} f = (f ; \preceq)$ *and* $\mathsf{Gr} A = A$.

For us, **Idl** is a stepping-stone between **Mofun** and **Spec**; the ideal property is not suitable for input-output relations. But note that if $S, T$ in (1) are a pre-post specification then the ideal property says that they are monotonic as predicates on $A$ and $B$ (the index set $X$ can be ordered discretely for this purpose).

We write *id* only for an identity function, and usually we write $\preceq$ for an identity in **Idl**; but sometimes we write id *sans serif* for the identity arrow in a category. If $A, B$ are discretely ordered then $\preceq_A$ is just $id_A$ and any relation $A \rightarrow B$ is an ideal. Thus $\mathbf{Rel}^{co}$ is a full subpocat of **Idl**.

The reader may enjoy checking the properties of Gr. To show that it preserves composition, use the fact that monotonicity of a function $f : A \rightarrow B$ on posets is equivalent to $(\preceq ; f) \subseteq (f ; \preceq)$. For monotonicity of Gr, show that $f \sqsubseteq g \equiv (g ; \preceq) \subseteq (f ; \preceq)$ for $f, g$ in **Mofun**. To show that $\mathrm{Gr}f$ is an ideal, and that Gr preserves identities, use the fact that if $f$ is in $\mathbf{Mofun}(A, B)$ and $R$ is in $\mathbf{Idl}(B, C)$ then $(f ; R)$ is in $\mathbf{Idl}(A, C)$.

Usually **Rel** is ordered by $\subseteq$,[3] but for **Idl** that would make the graph functor order-contravariant. In the case of **Fun** and **Rel**, the graph functor is order-covariant because **Fun** is discretely ordered; but, by the same token, the reverse embedding $\mathbf{Rel} \hookrightarrow \mathbf{Fun}$ is not even monotonic (compare Proposition 2).

**Lemma 1.** *If $f$ is in **Mofun** then $\mathrm{Gr}f$ is a comap in **Idl**, with map $(\preceq ; f^{o})$. All comaps in **Idl** have the form $\mathrm{Gr}f$ for monotonic $f$, and all maps have the form $\preceq ; f^{o}$ (this depends on the axiom of choice).*

The order dual of poset $A$ is written $\widetilde{A}$, so $\preceq_{\widetilde{A}}$ is $(\preceq_A)^{o}$. For $f$ in $\mathbf{Mofun}(A, B)$, let $\widetilde{f}$ denote the same mapping considered as a function from $\widetilde{A}$ to $\widetilde{B}$. Order-duals are needed primarily for predicates (Section 4): For the axiomatization of powersets, subsets must be ordered by $\supseteq$, but to get the refinement order on transformers they must be ordered by $\subseteq$.

**Lemma 2.** *For $f$ and $g$ in $\mathbf{Mofun}(A, B)$, $\widetilde{f}$ is in $\mathbf{Mofun}(\widetilde{A}, \widetilde{B})$ and $f \sqsubseteq g \equiv \widetilde{g} \sqsubseteq \widetilde{f}$.*

We say a functor $G : \mathbf{C} \rightarrow \mathbf{D}$ is an *embedding* if (i) it is an order embedding on homsets, i.e., $f \leq h \equiv Gf \leq Gh$ for all $f, h$, and (ii) it is the identity on objects. Condition (ii) is unusually strong but adequate for our purposes. Gr is an embedding of **Mofun** onto the comaps of **Idl**. That is, **Mofun** is isomorphic to the comaps of **Idl**, just as **Fun** is isomorphic to —indeed, identical to— the maps of **Rel**.

Every $R : A \rightarrow B$ in **Idl** factors as $R = (\preceq ; f^{o}) ; (g ; \preceq)$ for some $f, g$ in **Mofun**. Assuming the axiom of choice, this factorization is unique up to equivalence. Equivalence of spans is with respect to the preorder $\leq$ on spans defined by

$$(f, g) \leq (f', g') \equiv (\exists h : h ; f' \sqsubseteq f : g \sqsubseteq h ; g') \quad (2)$$

Uniqueness of factorization yields the following.

**Proposition 1.** ***Idl** is isomorphic to the pocat of spans over **Mofun**.*

Each homset $\mathbf{Idl}(A, B)$ is a complete lattice: the supremum of a family of ideals is its intersection, and the infimum is its union. Composition (;) in **Idl**

[3] And for that reason $\mathbf{Idl}^{co}$ is used in [17, 18], where it is called **IRel**.

distributes over infima in both arguments. Thus for ideals $R, S$ with common target there is *quotient* $S/R$ such that, for all $Q$ of appropriate type,

$$S/R \supseteq Q \equiv S \supseteq Q \,;\, R$$

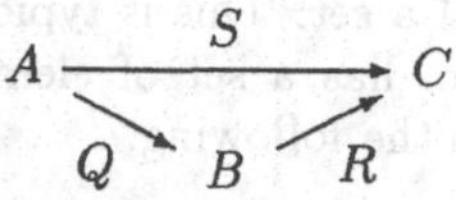


In fact $S/R$ is the quotient in **Rel**; in terms of points:

$$a(S/R)b \equiv (\,\forall c \,:\, bRc \,:\, aSc\,)\ . \tag{3}$$

We let $(/)$ bind more tightly than $(;)$ but less tightly than application.

## 4 Predicates, membership, and transformers

Our first type-constructor in **Idl** generalizes powersets. It serves both as an introduction to membership and as the basis for defining transformers.

We shall take predicates on poset $A$ to be *updeals*, i.e., subsets closed upward under $\preceq_A$. (They can be described as monotonic functions $A \to \{\top, \bot\}$ into the two-point chain, hence the term 'monotonic predicate' in Section 2.) The poset $\mathcal{U}A$ is defined to be the set of updeals on $A$, ordered by $\subseteq$. For the reciprocal $\ni$ of the membership relation on a poset to be an arrow in **Idl** we need $(\ni ; \preceq) \subseteq \ni$, which says exactly that the source of $\ni$ contains only updeals. For $(\preceq ; \ni) \subseteq \ni$ to hold, however, that set of updeals should be ordered by $\supseteq$ or $=$. We order it by $\supseteq$ so the upward closure function up is monotonic. Writing $\widetilde{\mathcal{U}}A$ for the order dual $\widetilde{\mathcal{U}A}$ of $\mathcal{U}A$, we thus have $\ni$ in $\mathbf{Idl}(\widetilde{\mathcal{U}}A, A)$ and up in $\mathbf{Mofun}(A, \widetilde{\mathcal{U}}A)$.

For $R$ in $\mathbf{Idl}(A, B)$, the function $\Lambda R : A \to \widetilde{\mathcal{U}}B$ sends $a$ to its direct image through $R$. The direct and inverse image functions can be defined in these terms:

$$\langle R \rangle = \Lambda(\ni ; R) \quad \text{and} \quad [R] = \Lambda(\ni / R)\ .$$

This gives monotonic functions $\langle R \rangle : \widetilde{\mathcal{U}}A \to \widetilde{\mathcal{U}}B$ and $[R] : \widetilde{\mathcal{U}}B \to \widetilde{\mathcal{U}}A$ to which we shall later (implicitly) apply $\widetilde{()}$ to obtain transformers. The monotonic functor $\mathsf{E}$ : **Idl** $\to$ **Mofun** is defined by $\mathsf{E}A = \widetilde{\mathcal{U}}A$ and $\mathsf{E}R = \langle R \rangle$. A single law characterizes $\widetilde{\mathcal{U}}, \Lambda$ and $\ni$:

$$f = \Lambda R \equiv f \,;\, \ni = R \quad \text{for all } R, S \text{ in } \mathbf{Idl} \text{ and } f \text{ in } \mathbf{Mofun}.$$

A key fact is

$$R \supseteq S \equiv \Lambda R \sqsubseteq_{\widetilde{\mathcal{U}}B} \Lambda S \quad \text{for } R, S \text{ in } \mathbf{Idl}(A, B). \tag{4}$$

Thanks to ordering **Idl** properly, the power adjunction is covariant (by contrast with [17]) and is order-enriched (by contrast with [1]).

**Proposition 2.** $\mathsf{E}$ *is an embedding of* **Idl** *in* **Mofun**, *and* $\mathsf{Gr}$ *is left adjoint to* $\mathsf{E}$ *with counit* $\ni$ *and unit* up.

### 4.1 Membership

Objects of a category —sets— model data types. In the case of $\widetilde{\mathcal{U}}A$, each element of $\widetilde{\mathcal{U}}A$ is itself a set. This is typical of types used as data structures: each list, tree, pair, etc. has a set of elements. Hoogendijk and de Moor's very useful abstraction is the following.

**Definition 2.** *For monotonic functor $F$ : **Idl** $\to$ **Idl** to have* membership $\delta$ *means that $\delta$ is a family of ideals $\delta_B : FB \to B$ such that*

$$R/\delta = \preceq/\delta\,; FR \qquad \textit{for all ideals } R : B \to C\ . \tag{5}$$

*The ideal $\preceq/\delta$ has type $B \to FB$ and is called the* fan *for $F$.*

Types in the rather opaque property (5) can be depicted as follows:

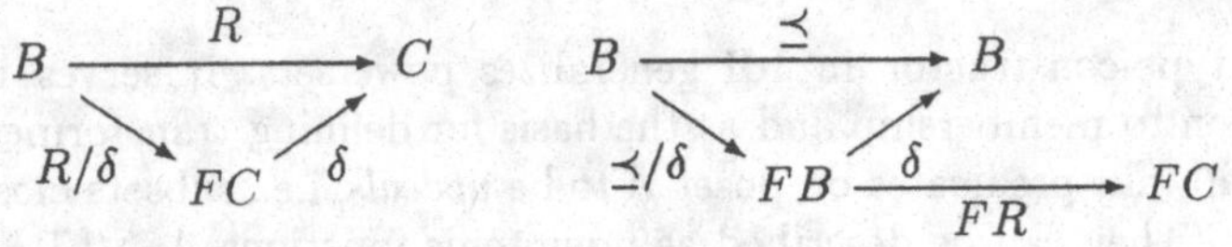


The idea is that if $\beta$ is in $FB$ then $\beta\delta b$ means that $b$ is an element of $\beta$, and $b(\preceq/\delta)\beta$ means that $\beta$ is a structure made entirely of copies of $b$. Later we refine this interpretation of fans.

A *lax transformation* from functor $F$ to functor $G$ is a family of ideals $S_A$ : $FA \to GA$ such that

$$S\,; GR \supseteq FR; S \quad \text{for all } R.$$

It can be shown that $\delta$ is the largest lax transformation from $F$ to the identity, and also that $\preceq/\delta$ is a lax transformation from the identity to $F$. More precisely, this and subsequent results about membership are shown for **Rel** by Hoogendijk and de Moor [8,7], and that suffices for our limited purposes later. It seems likely that their results extend to **Idl**, which satisfies the following so-called identification axiom used in their proofs.

**Proposition 3.** *The identity transformation is the largest lax transformation from and to id* : **Idl** $\to$ **Idl**.

*Proof.* By contradiction. Suppose $S$ is a lax transformation from and to *id*, but for some $A$ we do not have $S_A \subseteq (\preceq_A)$. Let $a, b$ witness the failure, i.e., $aSb$ but not $a \preceq b$. Define $R$ to be the ideal $\mathsf{Gr}(\lambda x :: a)$, i.e., $xRy \equiv a \preceq y$. Now $a(R\,;S)b$ but not $a(S\,;R)b$, contradicting the lax transformation property $S;R \supseteq R;S$. □

Our first example is the membership relation $\ni\, : \widetilde{\mathcal{U}}B \to B$. We define $\widetilde{\mathcal{U}}$ as a functor on **Mofun** which extends to a functor on **Idl**. For $f$ in **Mofun**$(A, B)$ we define $\widetilde{\mathcal{U}}f$ to be the function $\mathsf{E}(\mathsf{Gr}f)$ in **Mofun**$(\widetilde{\mathcal{U}}A, \widetilde{\mathcal{U}}B)$. Thus $\widetilde{\mathcal{U}}f\alpha$ is the upward closure of the direct image of $f$ on $\alpha$, for $\alpha$ in $\widetilde{\mathcal{U}}A$.

Just as the functor $\widetilde{\mathcal{U}}$ on **Mofun** is the composite $\mathsf{Gr}\,;\mathsf{E}$, so too the composite $\mathsf{E}\,;\mathsf{Gr}$ gives a monotonic functor on **Idl** that we also denote by $\widetilde{\mathcal{U}}$. It satisfies

$\alpha(\widetilde{\mathcal{U}}R)\beta \equiv \langle R\rangle\alpha \supseteq \beta$ for $R \in \mathbf{Idl}(A,B)$ and updeals $\alpha, \beta$. Say a functor $G$ on **Idl** *extends* $F$ on **Mofun** if it commutes with Gr, i.e., $G(\mathsf{Gr}h) = \mathsf{Gr}(Fh)$. Clearly $\widetilde{\mathcal{U}}$ on **Idl** extends the functor of the same name on **Mofun**.

The fan $\preceq/\ni$ for $\ni$ satisfies $a(\preceq/\ni)\alpha \equiv (\,\forall a' : \alpha \ni a' : a \preceq a'\,)$, and the latter in turn is equivalent to $\alpha \subseteq (\mathsf{up}\,a)$. Thus $\preceq/\ni = \mathsf{Gr\,up}$, i.e., $\preceq/\ni = (\mathsf{up}\,;\supseteq)$.

**Proposition 4.** $\widetilde{\mathcal{U}} : \mathbf{Idl} \to \mathbf{Idl}$ *has membership* $\ni$.

*Proof.* We need to show $R/\ni = \preceq/\ni\,; \widetilde{\mathcal{U}}R$ for all $A, B$ and $R \in \mathbf{Idl}(A,B)$. Here is the picture:

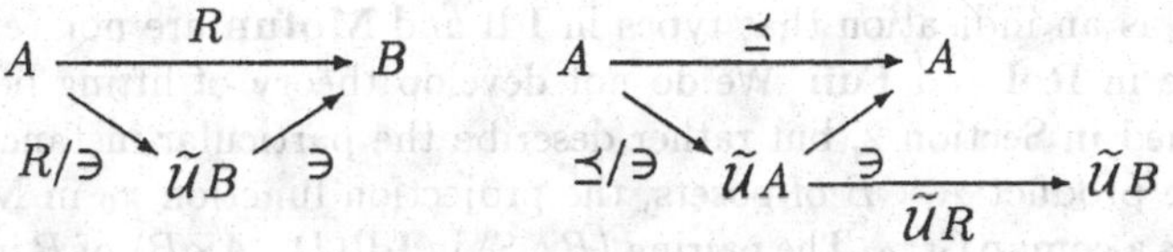


Observe for any $a, \beta$

$$
\begin{array}{ll}
 & a(R/\ni)\beta \\
\equiv & \quad \text{quotient (3)} \\
 & (\,\forall b : \beta \ni b : aRb\,) \\
\equiv & \quad \text{definitions} \\
 & \langle R\rangle(\mathsf{up}\,a) \supseteq \beta \\
\equiv & \quad \text{monotonicity of } \langle R\rangle \\
 & (\,\exists \alpha : \mathsf{up}\,a \supseteq \alpha : \langle R\rangle\alpha \supseteq \beta\,) \\
\equiv & \quad \text{definition of } \widetilde{\mathcal{U}} \\
 & (\,\exists \alpha : \mathsf{up}\,a \supseteq \alpha : \alpha(\widetilde{\mathcal{U}}R)\beta\,) \\
\equiv & \quad \preceq/\ni = \mathsf{Gr\,up} \\
 & (\,\exists \alpha : a(\preceq/\ni)\alpha : \alpha(\widetilde{\mathcal{U}}R)\beta\,) \\
\equiv & \\
 & a(\preceq/\ni\,; \widetilde{\mathcal{U}}R)\beta
\end{array}
$$

## 4.2 Transformers

A *transformer* is a monotonic function between updeal lattices. For perspicuity, the category of transformers will be defined so that arrows from $A$ to $B$ correspond to programs with inputs in $A$. The category **Spec** is defined to have all posets as objects, and $\mathbf{Spec}(A,B)$ is just $\mathbf{Mofun}(\mathcal{U}B, \mathcal{U}A)$. In particular, $\mathbf{Spec}(A,B)$ is ordered pointwise. Note that predicates are ordered by $\subseteq$, i.e., transformers are defined in terms of $\mathcal{U}$, not $\widetilde{\mathcal{U}}$, so that the pointwise order $\sqsubseteq$ on transformers is the usual refinement order. Composition in **Spec** is just functional composition, for which we write $\fatsemi$ so that for $f$ in $\mathbf{Spec}(A,B)$ and $g$ in $\mathbf{Spec}(B,C)$ we have $f \fatsemi g = g\,; f$. The identity on $A$ is the identity function $id_{\mathcal{U}A}$. The full subpocat determined by the discrete posets is just $\mathbf{Tran}^{op}$.

There are two mappings that embed **Fun** in **Rel** ($f \mapsto f$ and $f \mapsto f^{o}$), and **Mofun** is embedded onto the comaps of **Idl** by Gr and onto the maps by $f \mapsto (\preceq; f^{o})$. So too we have two embeddings of **Idl** into **Spec**. Using (4) and Lemma 2, we get that $[-]$ preserves order and is arrow-covariant, whereas $\langle - \rangle$ is both arrow- and order-contravariant.

**Lemma 3.** *For $R$ in* **Idl**$(A, B)$, $[R]$ *is a map in* **Spec**$(A, B)$, *with comap* $\langle R \rangle$. *Moreover* $\langle - \rangle$ *is an embedding* $\mathbf{Idl}^{co\ op} \to$ **Spec** *onto the comaps, and* $[-]$ *is an embedding* **Idl** $\to$ **Spec** *onto maps. For $f$ in* **Mofun**, $[\mathsf{Gr}\, f]$ *is a bimap.*

**Proposition 5.** *Every $f$ in* **Spec**$(A, B)$ *factors as* $\langle R \rangle \,;\, [S]$ *for some ideals $R, S$, and this factorization is unique up to equivalence of spans. Hence* **Spec** *is isomorphic to the pocat of spans of ideals.*

## 5 Types and membership for ideals

This section reviews some type-constructs in **Idl**, as a basis for their lifting to **Spec** and as an indication that types in **Idl** and **Mofun** are not very different from those in **Rel** and **Fun**. We do not develop theory of lifting beyond what was sketched in Section 2, but rather describe the particular instances.

For the product $A \times B$ of posets, the projection function $\pi_0$ in **Mofun**$(A \times B, A)$ gives a comap $\mathsf{Gr}\pi_0$. The pairing $(R \Delta S)$ in **Idl**$(D\,,\, A \times B)$ of $R$ in **Idl**$(D, A)$ and $S$ in **Idl**$(D, B)$ is defined by $d(R \vartriangle S)(a, b) \equiv dRa \wedge dSb$ just as in **Rel**. Clearly $\mathsf{Gr} f \vartriangle \mathsf{Gr} g = \mathsf{Gr}(f \vartriangle g)$ where the second pairing $\vartriangle$ is that of **Mofun**. Defining $Q \times R$ as usual makes it an extension of the product functor on **Mofun**. It is a monotonic functor $\times : \mathbf{Idl}^2 \to \mathbf{Idl}$, and moreover

$$R \supseteq (R \vartriangle S) \,;\, \mathsf{Gr}\pi_0 \quad (=, \text{ if } S \text{ is a comap})$$
$$R \,;\, \mathsf{Gr}\pi_0 \vartriangle R \,;\, \mathsf{Gr}\pi_1 \supseteq R \quad (=, \text{ if } R \text{ is a comap})$$

In categorical lingo, completeness of the laws is formulated in the following way which is typical of the $\mathbf{C} \hookrightarrow \mathbf{D}$ embedding approach to types discussed in Section 1. An adequate theory of weak adjunctions is [11].

**Proposition 6.** *The monotonic functor $\times$ is locally right adjoint to the diagonal* $\Delta : \mathbf{Idl} \to \mathbf{Idl}^2$. *It is an adjunction on comaps and up to natural isomorphism it is the unique local right adjoint to the diagonal that is an adjunction on comaps.*

For fixed $A$, membership $\delta$ for $(A\times)$ is given by the projection $\mathsf{Gr}\pi_1 : A \times B \to B$ (see [7] for membership of bifunctors). The associated fan $\preceq/\pi_1$ satisfies $b'(\preceq/\pi_1)(a, b) \equiv b' \preceq b$ for all $a, b', b$, so $\preceq/\pi_1$ is the map $\preceq \,;\, \pi_1^{\circ}$. For posets not discretely ordered, fans create structures not with copies of a given value, but rather with refinements of a given value.

Coproducts lift more simply than products, yielding a monotonic functor on **Idl** that delivers categorical coproducts. Coproducts in **Idl**, and even in **Spec**, are just like in **Fun** and **Mofun**.

### 5.1 Function space

The exponent also lifts from **Mofun**. The exponent in **Mofun** is the hom-poset **Mofun**$(A, B)$ taken to be an object $A \to B$. For $R$ in **Idl**$(B \times A, C)$, define $\widehat{\mathsf{curry}}\, R$ in **Idl**$(B, A \to C)$ by

$$b(\widehat{\mathsf{curry}}\, R)f \equiv (\,\forall a \,:\, a \in A \,:\, (b, a)R(fa)\,)\ .$$

Clearly $\hat{\mathsf{curry}}\, R$ is an ideal and $\hat{\mathsf{curry}}$ is monotonic. If $R$ is a comap then so is $\hat{\mathsf{curry}}\, R$, which follows from the fact that $\hat{\mathsf{curry}}$ extends $\mathsf{curry}$, i.e., $\hat{\mathsf{curry}}\,(\mathsf{Gr} h) = \mathsf{Gr}(\mathsf{curry}\, h)$ for all $h$ in $\mathbf{Mofun}(B \times A, C)$.

Application in **Idl** is simply $\mathsf{Gr\,apply}$ for the usual application function $\mathsf{apply}_{B,C}$ in $\mathbf{Mofun}((A \to B) \times A, B)$. The covariant hom functor is defined by $A \hat{\to} S = \hat{\mathsf{curry}}\,(\mathsf{Gr\,apply}\,; S)$. Thus $f(A \hat{\to} R)g \equiv f\,; R \supseteq g$, which at the level of points says $(\forall b\ ::\ (fb)R(gb)\,)$. For all $R, S$ of suitable types we have:

$$R \supseteq (\hat{\mathsf{curry}}\, R \times \preceq)\,; \mathsf{Gr\,apply} \quad (=, \text{ if } R \text{ is a comap})$$

$$\hat{\mathsf{curry}}\,((R \times \preceq)\,; \mathsf{Gr\,apply}) \supseteq R \quad (=, \text{ if } R \text{ is a comap})$$

We refrain from stating the uniqueness result here and subsequently.

Define the membership $\delta$ in $\mathbf{Idl}((A \to B), B)$ by

$$f \delta b \equiv (\,\exists a\ :\ a \in A\ :\ fa \preceq b\,) \quad \text{i.e.,} \quad b \in \langle \mathsf{Gr} f \rangle A \quad \text{or} \quad \langle \mathsf{Gr} f \rangle A \supseteq \mathsf{up}\, b\ .$$

The reader is encouraged to show that $\delta$ does have the membership property $R/\delta = \preceq/\delta\,; (A \hat{\to} R)$.

The fan $(\preceq/\delta)$ satisfies $b(\preceq/\delta)f \equiv \langle \mathsf{Gr} f \rangle A \subseteq \mathsf{up}\, b$ for all $b, f$. This fan nondeterministically chooses any monotonic function with values all above $b$.

## 5.2 Relation space

Having considered the liftings of $\times, +, \to$ from **Mofun**, we turn to a less common construct. Just as $A \to B$ internalizes the homset $\mathbf{Mofun}(A, B)$ as an object, the *relation space* $A \leftrightarrow B$ internalizes the homset of ideals. We define poset $A \leftrightarrow B = \mathbf{Idl}(A, B)$ and define $\mathsf{rap}$ in $\mathbf{Idl}((A \leftrightarrow B) \times A\,,\ B)$ by $(S, a)\,\mathsf{rap}\, b \equiv aSb$. This extends $\mathsf{apply}$ because

$$(\mathsf{Gr} f, a)\mathsf{rap}\, b \equiv fa \preceq b \quad \text{i.e.,} \quad (\mathsf{Gr} f, a)\mathsf{rap}\, b \equiv (f, a)(\mathsf{Gr\,apply})b\ .$$

Because each $S$ in $A \leftrightarrow B$ is an ideal, $(\mathsf{rap}\,;\preceq) = \mathsf{rap}$. We also have $(\supseteq;\mathsf{rap}) \subseteq \mathsf{rap}$, so $\mathsf{rap}$ is an ideal thanks to our choice of order on **Idl**. If $A \leftrightarrow B$ were to be ordered by $\subseteq$, $\mathsf{rap}$ would not be an ideal.

For $R$ in $\mathbf{Idl}(C \times A\,,\ B)$, define relation $\mathit{cur}\, R$ by $c(\mathit{cur}\, R)S \equiv (\,\forall a, b\ ::\ aSb \equiv (c, a)Rb\,)$. Note that $\mathit{cur}\, R$ is not monotonic in $R$, but it is a monotonic function from $C$ to $A \leftrightarrow B$. So we take $\mathsf{rcur}\, R$ in $\mathbf{Idl}(C\,,\ A \leftrightarrow B)$ to be the comap $\mathsf{Gr}(\mathit{cur}\, R)$. Fixing one argument, define $(A \leftrightarrow)$ by $(A \leftrightarrow R) = \mathsf{rcur}\,(\mathsf{rap}\,; R)$ so that

$$S(A \leftrightarrow R)T \equiv S\,; R \supseteq T\ . \tag{6}$$

It can be shown that $(A \leftrightarrow)$ is a monotonic functor that is locally right adjoint to $(\times A)$. It satisfies the following laws:

$$(\mathsf{rcur}\, R \times \preceq)\,; \mathsf{rap} = R$$

$$\mathsf{rcur}\,((S \times \preceq)\,; \mathsf{rap}) \supseteq S \quad (=, \text{ if } S \text{ is a comap})$$

$$\mathsf{rcur}\,(R\,; S) = \mathsf{rcur}\, R\,; (A \leftrightarrow S)$$

$$\mathsf{rcur}\,((R \times \preceq)\,; S) \supseteq R\,; \mathsf{rcur}\, S \quad (= \text{ if } R, S \text{ are comaps})$$

This does not cut down to an adjunction in the subcategory of comaps, because $\mathsf{rap}$ is not a comap, although $(A\leftrightarrow)$ extends $(A\hat{\rightarrow})$, i.e., $(\mathsf{Gr}f)(A\leftrightarrow R)(\mathsf{Gr}g) \equiv f(A\hat{\rightarrow}R)g$.

The reader may have noticed that $\mathsf{rap}$ would be an ideal if $A \leftrightarrow B$ were to be ordered discretely. But then $(A\leftrightarrow)$ would not preserve identities; the above definitions, interpreted in **Rel**, give only $A \leftrightarrow id \supseteq id$. An alternative in **Rel** is to define $(A \leftrightarrow R)$ to be the function sending $S$ to $S\,;R$. This is functorial, but not monotonic: if $R \subseteq R'$ is a proper inclusion, then $(A \leftrightarrow R)$ and $(A \leftrightarrow R')$ would be incomparable (being functions).

The functor $(A\leftrightarrow)$ has membership $\delta$ in $\mathbf{Idl}((A \leftrightarrow B), B)$. The extension requirement $f\delta^{\rightarrow}c \equiv (\mathsf{Gr}f)\delta c$ leads to the definition:

$$S\delta b \equiv (\,\exists a \,:\, a \in A \,:\, aSb\,) \quad \text{i.e.,} \quad \langle S\rangle A \supseteq \mathsf{up}\,b\ . \tag{7}$$

The associated fan satisfies

$$b(\preceq/\delta)S \equiv \langle S\rangle A \subseteq \mathsf{up}\,b\ . \tag{8}$$

Thus $b$ fans to any ideal $S$ with range all above $b$ — for example, the empty relation.

**Proposition 7.** $(A\leftrightarrow) : \mathbf{Idl} \rightarrow \mathbf{Idl}$ *has membership* $\delta$.

*Proof.* We need to show $R/\delta = \preceq/\delta\,; (A \leftrightarrow R)$ for all $B, C$ and $R$ in $\mathbf{Idl}(B,C)$. Here is the picture:

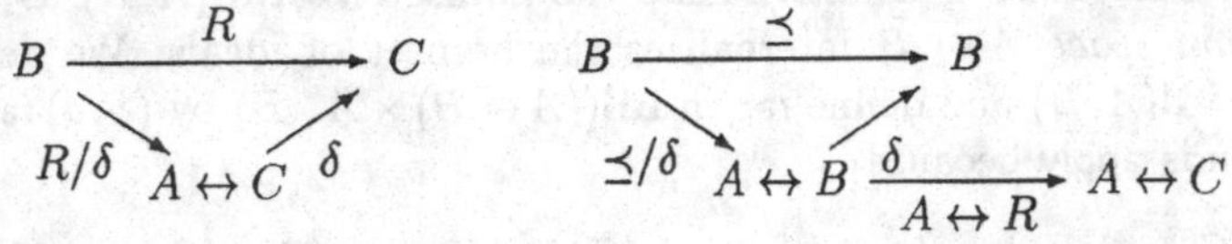


(Verifications of the membership property are not always easy, and the reader may prefer try her hand at it rather than reading the following messy point-level calculations.) Observe for any $b, S$

$$\begin{array}{ll}
 & b(R/\delta)S \\
\equiv & \qquad \text{quotient (3)} \\
 & (\,\forall c \,:\, S\delta c \,:\, bRc\,) \\
\equiv & \qquad \text{posets and ideals} \\
 & (\,\forall c \,:\, S\delta c \,:\, \langle R\rangle(\mathsf{up}\,b) \supseteq \mathsf{up}\,c\,) \\
\equiv & \qquad \text{definition (7)} \\
 & (\,\forall c \,:\, \langle S\rangle A \supseteq \mathsf{up}\,c \,:\, \langle R\rangle(\mathsf{up}\,b) \supseteq \mathsf{up}\,c\,) \\
\equiv & \qquad \text{posets} \\
 & \langle S\rangle A \subseteq \langle R\rangle(\mathsf{up}\,b) \\
\equiv & \qquad \text{see below} \\
 & (\,\exists T \,:\, \langle T\rangle A \subseteq \mathsf{up}\,b \,:\, T\,;R \supseteq S\,) \\
\equiv & \qquad \text{(8) and (6)} \\
 & (\,\exists T \,:\, b(\preceq/\delta)T \,:\, T(A \leftrightarrow R)S\,) \\
\equiv & \\
 & b(\preceq/\delta\,; (A \leftrightarrow R))S
\end{array}$$

The fifth step is by ping-pong. For $(\Leftarrow)$, we calculate in a line

$$\langle S\rangle A \subseteq \langle T\,; R\rangle A = \langle R\rangle(\langle T\rangle A) \subseteq \langle R\rangle(\mathsf{up}\,b)$$

using monotonicity and functoriality of $\langle R\rangle$. For $(\Rightarrow)$, define $T$ by $aTb' \equiv b' \succeq b$ so that $\langle T\rangle A \subseteq \mathsf{up}\, b$. Then we have

$$T\,;R \supseteq S \;\Leftarrow\; \langle S\rangle A \subseteq \langle T\,;R\rangle A \;\equiv\; \langle S\rangle A \subseteq \langle R\rangle(\langle T\rangle A) \;\Leftarrow\; \langle S\rangle A \subseteq \langle R\rangle(\mathsf{up}\, b)$$

using in the last step $\langle T\rangle A \subseteq \mathsf{up}\, b$ and monotonicity of $\langle R\rangle$.

### 5.3 Inductive data types

A functor $F : \mathbf{C}^2 \to \mathbf{C}$ on pocat $\mathbf{C}$ *has fixpoints* if for each object $B$ there is an object $fix B$ and arrow

$$inB : F(B, fixB) \to fixB$$

that is *initial* for $B$ in the following sense. For each $A$ and each $R : F(B,A) \to A$ there is a *catamorphism* $([R]) : fixB \to A$ such that for all $S$

$$S = ([R]) \;\equiv\; inB\,;S = F(\mathsf{id}, S)\,;R \qquad \begin{array}{ccc} F(B, fixB) & \xrightarrow{inB} & fixB \\ {\scriptstyle F(\mathsf{id},S)}\downarrow & & \downarrow{\scriptstyle S} \\ F(B,A) & \xrightarrow[R]{} & A \end{array} \qquad (9)$$

Dependence on $F$ is suppressed in the notation: $fixB$ is not the fixed point of $B$ but rather of the functor $F(B,-)$ of one argument. Polynomial functors on **Mofun** (those defined using $\times, +, id$, projection, and constants) have fixpoints, just as in **Fun**. We sometimes call elements of $fix B$ *structures*.

If $F$ is a monotonic functor on **Rel** and its restriction to **Fun** has an initial algebra then that algebra is initial in **Rel**. This can be proved using power adjunction without reciprocation [1]. The same proof shows that fixpoints lift from **Mofun** to **Idl**, which we state as follows.

**Lemma 4.** *If $F$ is a monotonic functor* $\mathbf{Idl}^2 \to \mathbf{Idl}$, *and it has fixpoints in the subcategory of comaps, then it has fixpoints in* **Idl**.

The definition of $fix$ on arrows works for fixpoints in any category (although $fix$ need not be a functor if $F$ is not). For $h$ of type $B \to C$, define $fix\, h$ of type $fix\, B \to fix\, C$ by

$$fix\, h = ([F(h, \mathsf{id})\,; in\, C]) \;, \tag{10}$$

where the types are indicated by $F(B, fix\, C) \xrightarrow{F(h,\mathsf{id})} fixB \xrightarrow{in\, C} fix\, C$. At least in **Rel**, $fix$ has membership provided that $F$ does [7].

## 6 The *repmin* problem

This section specifies the repmin problem. In so doing, we introduce distributors, which are needed to solve the problem and which can be derived from membership. The problem and solution are polymorphic in the type-constructor $fix$ which delivers fixpoints for a polynomial base functor $F : \mathbf{Mofun}^2 \to \mathbf{Mofun}$.

The problem is specified in terms of a given poset $N$ and monotonic function

$$m : F(N,N) \to N \ .$$

With $F$ the base for *Ltree*, the given has type $m : N + (N \times N) \to N$. If $N$ is the set of natural numbers, ordered discretely, then $m$ could be the copairing of the identity (for the left summand) and the numerical minimum of a pair (for the right). Define $min : fix N \to N$ as a catamorphism in **Mofun**:

$$min = (\!|m|\!) \ . \tag{11}$$

If $m$ gives minimum values —with respect to some magnitude order, not the approximation order $\preceq_N$— then $min$ gives the minimum value for each structure in $fix N$. Of course $min$ is parameterized by $F$ and $m$ but we do not make that explicit.[4]

One last ingredient: A *distributor* (sometimes called strength) for upfunctor $G$ is a family

$$dist\, G : GA \times B \to G(A \times B)$$

of arrows, with the naturality property

$$dist\, G \,;\, G(f \times id) = (Gf \times id) \,;\, dist\, G \quad \text{for all } f.$$

For example, $dist\ Ltree\ (t, b)$ is a tree shaped like $t$ but with each leaf $a$ replaced by the pair $(a, b)$. Given a distributor, we can define a family of functions $rep\, G : GA \times B \to GB$ which take a structure and an element, returning a structure of the same shape populated just by that element (or refinements thereof):

$$rep\, G = dist\, G \,;\, G\pi_1 \tag{12}$$

where $\pi_1$ is the right projection. Note that $rep\, G$ and $dist\, G$ are parametric in $A, B$, and $dist$ and $rep$ are parametric in type-constructor $G$.

The "obviously correct" definition for *repmin* says that replacing every element of a tree by the minimum element can be done by constructing the pair consisting of the tree and its minimum, and then replacing all elements with that value:

$$repmin = (id \vartriangle min) \,;\, rep\, fix \quad . \tag{13}$$

Both $min$ and $rep\, fix$ involve catamorphisms: for $min$ this is (11), and for $rep\, fix$ this can be shown in **Mofun** but later we show it in **Spec**, see (28). Executing *repmin* as defined would result in two traversals of the structure, one to find the minimum and one to replace each node by that value. The problem solved in Section 9 is to derive a program making a single traversal.

The derivation in Section 9 depends on $m$ being a function, but not on its yielding minima. The program and its derivation are parametric in the data type $N$ and function $m$. But they are also parameteric in the type-constructor

[4] If we assume that that $F(\emptyset, \emptyset) = \emptyset$ —so that every structure in $fix A$ has at least one member— then any well-order on a set $N$ gives rise to a minimum-function $m$.

$fix$ and its associated $F$, requiring only that $F$ and $fix$ be equipped with a distributor. It can be shown that a distributor for $F$ determines one for $fix$; for **Spec** this is (30) in Section 9.

In fact, in **Fun** and **Rel** any functor that has membership has a distributor. The proofs in [8, 7] use reciprocation, so it will take some work to extend the result to **Idl**. For our purposes the known results are adequate, as we now outline. We assume that any constants in the definition of $F$ are discretely ordered. As a consequence, if $B, A$ are discretely ordered then so are $F(B, A)$ and $fixB$. This allows us to use known results on membership in **Rel**, thanks to the following Lemma which can be shown using initiality.

**Lemma 5.** *Let* $F : \mathbf{Mofun}^2 \to \mathbf{Mofun}$ *be a functor such that* $F(A, B)$ *is discretely ordered for any discretely ordered* $A, B$. *Suppose the restriction of* $F$ *to* **Fun** *has fixpoints. Then for discretely ordered* $B$ *the initial algebra* $inB : F(B, fixB) \to B$ *for* $F$ *in* **Fun** *is initial in* **Mofun**, *with* $fixB$ *taken to be discretely ordered.*

In summary, we can either assume that *dist* $F$ is given, or we can assume $F$ has membership and that the sets involved are discretely ordered. With the latter assumption, order still plays an important role: the exponent of transformers is ordered by program refinement.

## 7 Product and exponent for transformers

This section gives the laws for the weak product and weak exponent in **Spec**. The product can be obtained by lifting, and as indicated in Section 2 its properties are rather weak. The exponent given by the internal hom of **Spec** is not the lift of the function space or relation space, but it does extend these constructs appropriately. After recounting known results on axiomatization, we show that the exponent restricts to a functor on **Mofun** and on **Idl**, for which we explore membership. Coproducts in **Idl** lift to categorical coproducts in **Spec**, and the other functors $\widetilde{\mathcal{U}}, \to, \leftrightarrow$ also lift, but none of these are needed for the *repmin* derivation.

An *upfunctor* $F$ on **Spec** is a monotonic graph morphism that preserves identities and satisfies the inequation $F(g \,;\, h) \sqsubseteq Fg \,;\, Fh$. A *strict upfunctor* is one that preserves maps and comaps. Let $F : \mathbf{Idl} \to \mathbf{Idl}$ be a monotonic functor, and define $\widehat{F}A = FA$ and $\widehat{F}g = [FR] \,;\, \langle FS \rangle$, where $g$ factors as $g = [R] \,;\, \langle S \rangle$. Then $\widehat{F}$ is a strict upfunctor on **Spec**, and it is the minimum upfunctor that *extends* $F$ in the sense that $\widehat{F}[R] = [FR]$. As a consequence of being a strict upfunctor, $\widehat{F}$ satisfies

$$\widehat{F}(f \,;\, g \,;\, h) = \widehat{F}f \,;\, \widehat{F}g \,;\, \widehat{F}h \quad \text{if } f \text{ is a comap and } h \text{ a map.} \qquad (14)$$

Bifunctors lift in the evident way. The lifted coproduct $\widehat{+}$ is monotonic and is a categorical coproduct, but the lifted product —which we write as $\otimes$— weakens.

Define $A \otimes B$ to be the product $A \times B$ of posets. The left projection $\widehat{\pi}_0$ in $\mathbf{Spec}(A \otimes B, A)$ is defined to be $[\mathsf{Gr}\pi_0]$. For $f \in \mathbf{Spec}(D, A)$ and $g \in \mathbf{Spec}(D, B)$, the lifted pairing[5] $(f \mathbin{\widehat{\triangle}} g)$ is in $\mathbf{Spec}(D, A \otimes B)$. We define the usual $f \otimes g = \widehat{\pi}_0 \mathbin{⨾} f \mathbin{\widehat{\triangle}} \widehat{\pi}_1 \mathbin{⨾} g$.

Conventional semantics of imperative languages uses only transformers with the same initial as final state space. In the case of a procedure with value parameter $x : A$ and result $y : B$, the procedure body is a transformer in $\mathbf{Spec}(A \otimes B, A \otimes B)$ (abstracting from parameter and coordinate names). The meaning of a procedure call in some other state space is defined in terms of substitutions for parameter passing. For our purposes it may be helpful to imagine a semantics in which the procedure body is interpreted in $\mathbf{Spec}(A, B)$. A formal language and semantics are beyond the scope of this paper; we rely on the reader's good will to make sense of the informal interpretations sketched in the sequel.

Interpreting components of a product as coordinates of state space, a command $f : A \otimes B \to A \otimes B$ can be made to act in state space $B$ by treating $A$ as a local variable with initialization $i : B \to A$ in the command $(i \mathbin{\triangle} id_B) ; f ; \widehat{\pi}_1$. In some refinement calculi, $\langle \pi_1 \rangle$ and $\widehat{\pi}_1$ are used as separate constructs, with the former introducing an uninitialized variable.

In the laws to follow, we say $f$ in $\mathbf{Spec}(A, B)$ is *strict* if $\emptyset = \emptyset$ (excluded miracle) and *costrict* (total) if $fB = A$. Comaps are strict and maps costrict.

**Proposition 8.** *For all transformers $d, e, f, g, h$ of suitable types we have*

$$(f \mathbin{\widehat{\triangle}} g) \mathbin{⨾} \widehat{\pi}_0 \sqsubseteq f \quad \text{if } g \text{ strict} \tag{15}$$

$$(f \mathbin{\widehat{\triangle}} g) \mathbin{⨾} \widehat{\pi}_0 \sqsupseteq f \quad \text{if } g \text{ costrict} \tag{16}$$

$$h \mathbin{⨾} \widehat{\pi}_0 \mathbin{\widehat{\triangle}} h \mathbin{⨾} \widehat{\pi}_1 \sqsupseteq h \quad \text{if } h \text{ is a comap (and } \sqsubseteq \text{ if } h \text{ is a map)}$$

$$h \mathbin{⨾} f \mathbin{\widehat{\triangle}} h \mathbin{⨾} g \sqsupseteq h \mathbin{⨾} (f \mathbin{\widehat{\triangle}} g) \quad \text{if } h \text{ is a comap} \tag{17}$$

$$h \mathbin{⨾} f \mathbin{\widehat{\triangle}} h \mathbin{⨾} g \sqsubseteq h \mathbin{⨾} (f \mathbin{\widehat{\triangle}} g) \quad \text{if } h \text{ is a map} \tag{18}$$

$$d \mathbin{⨾} f \mathbin{\widehat{\triangle}} e \mathbin{⨾} g \sqsubseteq (d \mathbin{\widehat{\triangle}} e) \mathbin{⨾} (f \otimes g)$$

$$d \mathbin{⨾} f \mathbin{\widehat{\triangle}} e \mathbin{⨾} g = (d \mathbin{\widehat{\triangle}} e) \mathbin{⨾} (f \otimes g) \quad \text{if } f, g \text{ maps or all are comaps} \tag{19}$$

*Moreover, $\widehat{\triangle}$, $\otimes$ preserve maps and comaps. Such a structure is is unique up to natural isomorphism.*

Law (15) says that unless $g$ is magic, running it in parallel with $f$ and then discarding its result can only be worse than $f$ alone (because $g$ may diverge); law (16) strengthens this to an equality if $g$ always terminates. Transformers that are maps correspond to programs without angelic nondeterminacy. Law (18), which holds for even positively conjunctive $h$, says that it is better to run a single copy of demonically nondeterministic $h$, unless $h$ is in fact deterministic so that (17) applies as well.

---

[5] Circled symbols have hats seen from above, as opposed to the side view in $\widehat{F}$.

## 7.1 Transformer space as exponent

For the exponent, define the poset $B \rightsquigarrow C$ to be **Spec**$(B, C)$ ordered by $\sqsubseteq$. In effect, this is used in [14] for semantics of the data type of procedures with value parameter $B$ and result parameter of type $C$.[6] The generalized application $\mathsf{ap}_{B,C}$ is in **Spec**$((B \rightsquigarrow C) \otimes B\,, C)$, and is defined by $(b, g) \in \mathsf{ap}\gamma \equiv b \in g\gamma$ for all $\gamma \in \mathcal{U}C$, $b \in B$, and $g \in B \rightsquigarrow C$. This models the call of a procedure variable: in a state where the variable's value is $g$ and the rest of the state is $b$, the call executes $g$ in initial state $b$.

For $f$ in **Spec**$(A \otimes B, C)$, generalized currying gives $\mathsf{cur}f$ in **Spec**$(A, B \rightsquigarrow C)$. The definition extends currying of functions $h$ in **Mofun**$(A \times B, C$ in that $\mathsf{cur}[\mathsf{Gr}h] = [\mathsf{Gr}(curry\,h)]$ —despite the fact that $\rightsquigarrow$ is not obtained by lifting $\rightarrow$. The types are sufficiently confusing to merit a picture; here are depictions in **Spec** and **Mofun** for law (20) given later:

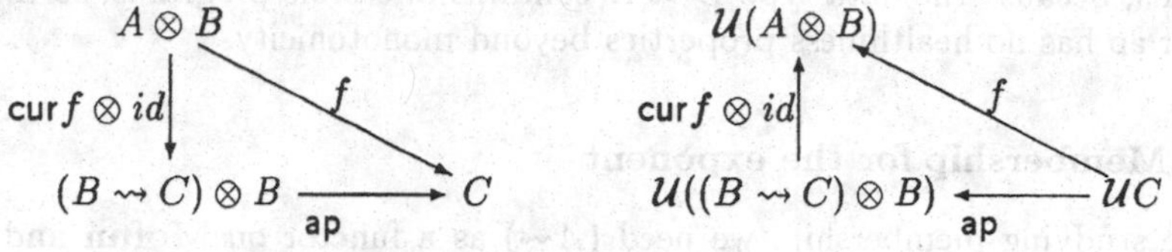


We do not need the definition of cur in the sequel, but for completeness here it is: $a \in \mathsf{cur}f\phi \equiv \mathsf{cu}fa \in \phi$ for all $a \in A$ and $\phi \in \mathcal{U}(B \rightsquigarrow C)$, where $\mathsf{cu}fa \in$ **Spec**$(B, C)$ is defined by $b \in \mathsf{cu}fa\gamma \equiv (a, b) \in f\gamma$.

In the special case that $A$ is a one-point set, $\mathsf{cur}f$ is essentially an element of $B \rightsquigarrow C$. So cur turns a command into a procedure value (an abstract closure) that can be stored in a variable. (This is akin to lambda abstraction, although it is obscured in imperative languages where procedures can only be manipulated via their names.) Note that this is a deterministic and terminating process even when $f$ is divergent and nondeterministic. Indeed, $\mathsf{cur}f$ is a bimap for any $f$, and this proves to be crucial in the *repmin* derivation and its supporting results.

The next construct does not correspond nicely to a usual feature of imperative languages. For $h$ in **Spec**$(C, A)$, define $B \rightsquigarrow h = \mathsf{cur}(\mathsf{ap}\,;\,h)$, so that $B \rightsquigarrow h$ is in **Spec**$((B \rightsquigarrow C), (B \rightsquigarrow A))$.

**Proposition 9.** *For any $B$, $(B\rightsquigarrow)$ :* **Mtran** $\rightarrow$ **Mtran** *is a monotonic functor, and for all $f, g$ of suitable types we have*

$$(\mathsf{cur}f \otimes id)\,;\,\mathsf{ap} = f \tag{20}$$

$$\mathsf{cur}((f \otimes id)\,;\,\mathsf{ap}) \sqsubseteq f \quad \text{if } f \text{ is a map} \tag{21}$$

$$\mathsf{cur}((f \otimes id)\,;\,\mathsf{ap}) = f \quad \text{if } f \text{ is a bimap} \tag{22}$$

$$\mathsf{cur}(g\,;\,f) = g\,;\,(B \rightsquigarrow f)$$

$$\mathsf{cur}((f \otimes id)\,;\,g) \sqsubseteq f\,;\,\mathsf{cur}\,g \quad \text{if } f \text{ is a map}$$

$$\mathsf{cur}((f \otimes id)\,;\,g) = f\,;\,\mathsf{cur}\,g \quad \text{if } f \text{ is a bimap} \tag{23}$$

[6] As indicated earlier in this section, a procedure with value parameter of type $B$ and result of type $C$ is actually treated as having type $B \otimes C \rightsquigarrow B \otimes C$ in [14].

*Such a structure is unique up to natural isomorphism.*

Law (20) says that storing a command $f$ and then calling the stored closure is the same as just executing $f$. In an imperative notation one might write

$$f \;=\; \|[\,\mathbf{var}\,p;\, p := \ulcorner f \urcorner;\, p\,]\|$$

where $\ulcorner f \urcorner$ denotes the closure encapsulating $f$ as a value. Law (21) says that for terminating and non-angelic $f$ in $\mathbf{Spec}(A, B \rightsquigarrow C)$ that produces a closure, $f$ can be approximated by producing the closure of a procedure that executes $f$ and then executes the value produced by $f$. One might write $(p := \ulcorner f; p \urcorner) \sqsubseteq f$ where $p$ is the variable of type $B \rightsquigarrow C$ into which $f$ stores. This is only an approximation because $f$ could be magic; that is ruled out in (22).

We should not expect these laws to be entirely justifiable on operational grounds, because the data type $B \rightsquigarrow C$ contains infeasible programs, so in particular ap has no healthiness properties beyond monotonicity.

## 7.2 Membership for the exponent

Before studying membership, we need $(A\rightsquigarrow)$ as a functor on **Mofun** and **Idl**. For $f \in \mathbf{Mofun}(B, C)$, let $(A \rightsquigarrow f)$ in $\mathbf{Mofun}((A \rightsquigarrow B), (A \rightsquigarrow C))$ be defined by

$$(A \rightsquigarrow f)g = [\mathsf{Gr} f]\,;g \quad \text{with types} \quad \mathcal{U}C \xrightarrow{[\mathsf{Gr} f]} \mathcal{U}B \xrightarrow{\;g\;} \mathcal{U}A\ .$$

If $f \sqsubseteq f'$ in **Mofun** then $[\mathsf{Gr} f]\,;g \sqsubseteq [\mathsf{Gr} f']\,;g$ because both Gr and $[-]$ are monotonic. This is another indication that $\sqsubseteq$ (the pointwise order based on $\subseteq$, not $\supseteq$) is the most suitable order for transformers. The reader may care to check that $(A\rightsquigarrow)$ is indeed a monotonic functor in **Mofun**.

To define $(A\rightsquigarrow)$ as a functor on **Idl** we cannot simply extend the definition to

$$g(A \rightsquigarrow R)h \equiv [R]\,;g = h$$

because that defines a monotonic function $(A \rightsquigarrow B) \to (A \rightsquigarrow C)$, and we need an ideal of that type. Applying Gr gives the desired result:

$$g(A \rightsquigarrow R)h = [R]\,;g \sqsubseteq h \quad \text{i.e.,} \quad (A \rightsquigarrow R) = \mathsf{Gr}(\lambda g \in A \rightsquigarrow B :: [R]\,;g)\ .$$

The reader may verify that this gives a monotonic functor $(A\rightsquigarrow)$ on **Idl**. Moreover, this is extended by the functor $(A\rightsquigarrow)$ on **Spec** because the latter satisfies $(A \rightsquigarrow f) = [\mathsf{Gr}(\lambda g \in A \rightsquigarrow B :: f\,;g)]$ for $f$ in $\mathbf{Spec}(B, C)$.

The challenge is to define membership $\delta$ in $\mathbf{Idl}(A \rightsquigarrow B, B)$. Although $A \rightsquigarrow B$, being $\mathbf{Mofun}(\mathcal{U}B, \mathcal{U}A)$, is an exponent object in **Mofun**, it is more closely connected to $A \to B$, as the facts about extension indicate. Yet membership for $\to$ does not seem to help define membership for $\rightsquigarrow$.

In the cases of $\to$ and $\leftrightarrow$, membership is compatible with the embedding of $A \to B$ in $A \leftrightarrow B$ given by the graph functor. Writing $\delta^{\to}$ and $\delta^{\leftrightarrow}$ for those two memberships, we have $f\delta^{\to}b \equiv (\mathsf{Gr} f)\delta^{\leftrightarrow}b$ for all $b \in B$ and $f \in \mathbf{Mofun}(A, B)$, as in the discussion preceding (7). By the same token, one would expect membership $\delta$ on $(A\rightsquigarrow)$ to be compatible with the embedding of $A\leftrightarrow B$ in $A\rightsquigarrow B$ given by $[-]$; thus:

$$R\delta^{\leftrightarrow}b \equiv [R]\delta b \quad \text{for all } c \in C \text{ and } R \in \mathbf{Idl}(B,C)\ .$$

But to define $f\delta\, b$ for arbitrary $f$ in $A\rightsquigarrow B$, we have to connect an element $b$ with an element $\beta \in \mathcal{U}B$ of the domain of $f$ (it being a function in $\mathbf{Mofun}(\mathcal{U}B,\mathcal{U}A)$).

There are two extremal ways to turn transformers into relations, the disjunctive and conjunctive, and both are plausible candidates for extending the definition of membership from **Idl**. But neither seems to work.[7]

Perhaps existence of membership for function-spaces is misleading. Although certain functions model data structures like arrays, it is not reasonable to treat an arbitrary program as a data structure. Although $(A\rightsquigarrow B)$ is a data type [14], it is not a type of data structures.

# 8 Transformers on inductive data types

This section shows that inductive data types are the same in **Spec** as in **Fun**, in terms of initiality and the recursion theorem.

It is well known that initial algebras for relations are final coalgebras, by reciprocation. Final coalgebras are needed to lift initial algebras from **Idl** to **Spec**, and to state the result we need something akin to reciprocation. If $R$ is in $\mathbf{Idl}(A,B)$, the reciprocal $R^o$ does not have the ideal property in general; rather, it is an ideal with respect to the order-dual prosets. We define the *op-reciprocal* $R^{\ominus}$ to be $R^o$ construed as an element of $\mathbf{Idl}(\widetilde{B},\widetilde{A})$. For a functor $F$ on **Idl** to *commute with op-reciprocation* means $F\widetilde{B} = (FB)^{\sim}$ and $FR^{\ominus} = (FR)^{\ominus}$.

**Lemma 6.** *The following functors on* **Idl** *commute with op-reciprocation:* $+$, $\times$, *id, the projections* $\mathbf{Idl}^2 \to \mathbf{Idl}$, *and those constant-valued functors whose valuc is discretely ordered. If $F$ commutes with op-reciprocation then so does fix.*

**Proposition 10.** *If* $F : \mathbf{Idl}^2 \to \mathbf{Idl}$ *is a monotonic functor that has fixpoints and commutes with op-reciprocation, then the upfunctor* $\widehat{F} : \mathbf{Spec}^2 \to \mathbf{Spec}$ *has fixpoints.*

The initial algebra for $B$, written $\widehat{inB}$, is the inverse image $[in\widetilde{B}]$ of the initial algebra for $\widetilde{B}$ in **Idl**. For $g$ in $\mathbf{Spec}(F(B,A),A)$, we write $(\!|g|\!)$ for the catamorphism in **Spec**.

Let $F$ be the base functor for *Ltree* and $N$ be the naturals. Consider $f$ in $\mathbf{Spec}(F(N,N),N)$ that models a command acting as follows. For any element

[7] Here is a quick sketch of the candidate definitions. For any $f \in \mathbf{Spec}(A,B)$ there is $\mathrm{rc}\, f$ in $\mathbf{Idl}(A,B)$, which satisfies $f = [\mathrm{rc}\, f]$ for any map $f$. This suggests the definition $f\delta b \equiv (\, \exists a \;::\; a(\mathrm{rc}\, f)b\,)$, i.e., $(\,\exists a \;::\; (\,\forall \alpha \in \mathcal{U}A \;:\; b \in f\alpha \;:\; a \in \alpha\,)\,)$. Attempts at proving the membership property with this definition indicate that it does not work, but I have not found a counter-example. Because $R = \mathrm{rc}\,[R]$ for any ideal $R$, a counter-example cannot be based on a relation. The other candidate is compatible with $\langle - \rangle$. It boils down to $f\delta b \equiv f(\mathrm{up}\, b) \neq \emptyset$, which does not work.

in the left summand of $N + (N \times N)$, it returns that element, but aborts if it exceeds 100. For any pair $(x, y)$ in the right summand, it nondeterministically chooses between returning $x$ and returning $y$. Then $(\![f]\!)$ chooses any element of its input tree, except that it aborts if the tree has some value exceeding 100.

**Lemma 7.** *For $f$ in* **Mofun** *we have* $[\mathsf{Gr}(\![f]\!)] = (\![\,[\mathsf{Gr} f]\,]\!)$. *Hence if transformer $g$ is a bimap then so is the catamorphism $(\![g]\!)$ in* **Spec**.

On the face of it, catamorphisms embody only a very simple form of structural recursion. In combination with exponents, however, catamorphisms give a more general form of recursion with an extra parameter. For *repmin*, we shall need a recursion theorem a bit more general than the one in [1]. To state the theorem, we need a strict upfunctor $\hat{F} : \mathbf{Spec}^2 \to \mathbf{Spec}$ with fixpoints, and an upfunctor $G : \mathbf{Spec}^3 \to \mathbf{Spec}$ such that

$$G(id, id, (f \,;\, h)) = G(id, id, f) \,;\, G(id, id, h) \quad \text{for all } h \text{ and all bimaps } f. \quad (24)$$

We also need a family $\psi$ of arrows

$$\psi_{A,B,C} : (F(A, B) \otimes C) \to G(A, C, B \otimes C)$$

with the following naturality property:

$$\psi \,;\, G(id, id, f \otimes id) = (F(id, f) \otimes id) \,;\, \psi \quad \text{for all bimaps } f. \quad (25)$$

Our main applications will have $G(A, B, C) = F(A \otimes B, C)$ in one case and $G(A, B, C) = F(B, C)$ in the other; in both cases, $\psi$ will be derived from *dist* $F$ of Section 6. The theorem gives a unique $x$ making the following diagram commute:

$$\begin{array}{ccc}
\hat{F}(A, fixA) \otimes B & \xrightarrow{\widehat{inA} \otimes id} & fixA \otimes B \\
\downarrow \psi & & \\
G(A, B, fixA \otimes B) & & \downarrow x \\
\downarrow G(id, id, x) & & \\
G(A, B, C) & \xrightarrow[h]{} & C
\end{array}$$

The types indicate how the result gives a parameterized form of the catamorphism recursion, and why $\psi$ is needed.

The proof is included here both because it is more general than usual and because it goes through entirely within the calculus of **Spec** —even though the standard proof does not— so it shows the calculus at play. The basic idea is the usual one, however: curry the above diagram and massage it into the catamorphism form.

**Theorem 1.** *Suppose $F, G, \psi$ are given as above. Then for any $A, B, C$, any $h$ in* $\mathbf{Spec}(G(A, B, C), C)$, *and any $x$ in* $\mathbf{Spec}(fixA \otimes B, C)$, *we have*

$$(\widehat{inA} \otimes id) \,;\, x = \psi \,;\, G(id, id, x) \,;\, h \;\equiv\; x = ((\![\mathsf{cur}(\psi \,;\, G(id, id, \mathsf{ap}) \,;\, h)]\!) \otimes id) \,;\, \mathsf{ap}$$

*Proof.* We calculate in **Spec**:

$$
\begin{array}{ll}
& (\widehat{inA} \otimes id) \mathbin{;} x = \psi \mathbin{;} G(id, id, x) \mathbin{;} h \\
\equiv & \qquad \text{cur injective (by (20))} \\
& \mathsf{cur}((\widehat{inA} \otimes id) \mathbin{;} x) = \mathsf{cur}(\psi \mathbin{;} G(id, id, x) \mathbin{;} h) \\
\equiv & \qquad \widehat{inA} \text{ bimap, exponent (23)} \\
& \widehat{inA} \mathbin{;} \mathsf{cur}\, x = \mathsf{cur}(\psi \mathbin{;} G(id, id, x) \mathbin{;} h) \\
\equiv & \qquad \text{(26) below introduces } k \\
& \widehat{inA} \mathbin{;} \mathsf{cur}\, x = \widehat{F}(id, \mathsf{cur}\, x) \mathbin{;} k \\
\equiv & \qquad \text{catamorphism (9)} \\
& \mathsf{cur}\, x = (\!|k|\!) \\
\Rightarrow & \qquad \text{exponent (20)} \\
& x = ((\!|k|\!) \otimes id) \mathbin{;} \mathsf{ap}
\end{array}
$$

The third step assumes there is $k : \widehat{F}(A, B \rightsquigarrow C) \to B \rightsquigarrow C$ such that

$$\mathsf{cur}(\psi \mathbin{;} G(id, id, x) \mathbin{;} h) = \widehat{F}(id, \mathsf{cur}\, x) \mathbin{;} k \ . \tag{26}$$

It remains to discharge this assumption and to show the reverse of the last step. We derive $k$ as follows, using that $\mathsf{cur}\, x \otimes id$ is a bimap because $\mathsf{cur}\, x$ is.

$$
\begin{array}{ll}
& \mathsf{cur}(\psi \mathbin{;} G(id, id, x) \mathbin{;} h) \\
= & \qquad \text{exponent (20)} \\
& \mathsf{cur}(\psi \mathbin{;} G(id, id, (\mathsf{cur}\, x \otimes id) \mathbin{;} \mathsf{ap}) \mathbin{;} h) \\
= & \qquad \text{hyp. (24), } \mathsf{cur}\, x \otimes id \text{ bimap} \\
& \mathsf{cur}(\psi \mathbin{;} G(id, id, \mathsf{cur}\, x \otimes id) \mathbin{;} G(id, id, \mathsf{ap})) \mathbin{;} h) \\
= & \qquad \mathsf{cur}\, x \text{ bimap, } \psi \text{ natural (25)} \\
& \mathsf{cur}((\widehat{F}(id, \mathsf{cur}\, x) \otimes id) \mathbin{;} \psi \mathbin{;} G(id, id, \mathsf{ap}) \mathbin{;} h) \\
= & \qquad \text{exponent (23), } \mathsf{cur}\, x \text{ bimap} \\
& \widehat{F}(id, \mathsf{cur}\, x) \mathbin{;} \mathsf{cur}(\psi \mathbin{;} G(id, id, \mathsf{ap}) \mathbin{;} h)
\end{array}
$$

We have derived $k = \mathsf{cur}(\psi \mathbin{;} G(id, id, \mathsf{ap}) \mathbin{;} h)$ (here $\psi$ is $\psi_{A, B \rightsquigarrow C, B}$). Because $k$ is in the range of cur, it is a bimap, hence so is $(\!|k|\!)$ (Lemma 7), which we use to show the reverse of the implication step in the first calculation.

$$
\begin{array}{ll}
& x = ((\!|\mathsf{cur}(\psi \mathbin{;} G(id, id, \mathsf{ap}) \mathbin{;} h)|\!) \otimes id) \mathbin{;} \mathsf{ap} \\
\Rightarrow & \qquad \text{Leibniz, definition of } k \\
& \mathsf{cur}\, x = \mathsf{cur}(((\!|k|\!) \otimes id) \mathbin{;} \mathsf{ap}) \\
\Rightarrow & \qquad \text{exponent (22), } (\!|k|\!) \text{ bimap} \\
& \mathsf{cur}\, x = (\!|k|\!)
\end{array}
$$

□

A crucial step in the repmin derivation is to express the tupling of two catamorphisms as a single catamorphism. This is known as *loop fusion* or *banana split*.

**Lemma 8.** *If* $(\!|h|\!)$ *and* $(\!|k|\!)$ *in* **Spec** *are bimaps with* $h : F(B, A) \to A$ *and* $k : F(B, C) \to C$ *then*

$$(\!|h|\!) \mathbin{\triangle} (\!|k|\!) = (\!|\widehat{F}(id, \widehat{\pi}_0) \mathbin{;} h \mathbin{\triangle} \widehat{F}(id, \widehat{\pi}_1) \mathbin{;} k|\!)$$

*Proof.* Aiming to use the catamorphism property, we calculate

$$
\begin{array}{ll}
& \widehat{inB} \mathbin{;} ((\![h]\!) \mathbin{\blacktriangle} (\![k]\!)) \\
= & \quad \text{product (17), (18), } \widehat{inB} \text{ bimap} \\
& \widehat{inB} \mathbin{;} (\![h]\!) \mathbin{\blacktriangle} \widehat{inB} \mathbin{;} (\![k]\!) \\
= & \quad \text{catamorphism (9) twice} \\
& \widehat{F}(id, (\![h]\!)) \mathbin{;} h \mathbin{\blacktriangle} \widehat{F}(id, (\![k]\!)) \mathbin{;} k \\
= & \quad \text{product (15), (16), } (\![k]\!) \text{ and } (\![k]\!) \text{ are bimaps} \\
& \widehat{F}(id\,, ((\![h]\!) \mathbin{\blacktriangle} (\![k]\!)) \mathbin{;} \widehat{\pi}_0) \mathbin{;} h \mathbin{\blacktriangle} \widehat{F}(id\,, ((\![h]\!) \mathbin{\blacktriangle} (\![k]\!)) \mathbin{;} \widehat{\pi}_1) \mathbin{;} k \\
= & \quad \widehat{F} \text{ strict upfunctor (14), } \widehat{\pi} \text{ bimap} \\
& \widehat{F}(id\,, (\![h]\!) \mathbin{\blacktriangle} (\![k]\!)) \mathbin{;} \widehat{F}(id, \widehat{\pi}_0) \mathbin{;} h \mathbin{\blacktriangle} \widehat{F}(id\,, (\![h]\!) \mathbin{\blacktriangle} (\![k]\!)) \mathbin{;} \widehat{F}(id, \widehat{\pi}_1) \mathbin{;} k \\
= & \quad \text{products (17) and (18), } \widehat{F} \text{ and } \mathbin{\blacktriangle} \text{ preserve bimaps} \\
& \widehat{F}(id\,, (\![h]\!) \mathbin{\blacktriangle} (\![k]\!)) \mathbin{;} (\widehat{F}(id, \widehat{\pi}_0) \mathbin{;} h \mathbin{\blacktriangle} \widehat{F}(id, \widehat{\pi}_1) \mathbin{;} k)
\end{array}
$$

## 9 Repmin derived in the algebra of transformers

Having assembled the basic theory, we proceed to derive a single catamorphism equal to [Gr *repmin*] as defined by (13). This leads to two additional lemmas about polytypic structural arrows like *dist*.

We shall elide the graph functor in the context of [−], writing for example [*min*] for [Gr *min*]. We aim to use loop fusion to combine two catamorphisms into one. The main calculation is as follows.

$$
\begin{array}{lll}
& [\mathsf{Gr}\, repmin] & \\
= & & \text{def. Gr, def. } repmin \text{ (13), } [-] \text{ functor} \\
& [\preceq \vartriangle min] \mathbin{;} [rep] & \\
= & & \mathbin{\blacktriangle} \text{ extends } \vartriangle, [\preceq] = id \\
& (id \mathbin{\blacktriangle} [min]) \mathbin{;} [rep] & \\
= & & \text{exponent (20)} \\
& (id \mathbin{\blacktriangle} [min]) \mathbin{;} (\mathsf{cur}[rep] \otimes id) \mathbin{;} \mathsf{ap} & \\
= & & \text{product (19), all bimaps} \\
& (\mathsf{cur}[rep] \mathbin{\blacktriangle} [min]) \mathbin{;} \mathsf{ap} & \\
= & & \text{definition (11) and Lemma 7} \\
& (\mathsf{cur}[rep] \mathbin{\blacktriangle} (\![\,[m]\,]\!)) \mathbin{;} \mathsf{ap} & \\
= & & \text{(27) below introduces } f \\
& ((\![f]\!) \mathbin{\blacktriangle} (\![\,[m]\,]\!)) \mathbin{;} \mathsf{ap} & \\
= & & \text{banana split Lemma 8} \\
& (\![\widehat{F}(id, \widehat{\pi}_0) \mathbin{;} f \mathbin{\blacktriangle} \widehat{F}(id, \widehat{\pi}_1) \mathbin{;} [m]]\!) \mathbin{;} \mathsf{ap} &
\end{array}
$$

To use Lemma 8 in the last step, $f$ needs to be a bimap; we also use that $(\![\,[m]\,]\!)$ is a bimap (by Lemma 7). It remains to derive bimap $f$ such that

$$
\mathsf{cur}\,[rep] = (\![f]\!) \ . \tag{27}
$$

This can be done as a general result with the typing

$$
fix A \times B \xrightarrow{dist\, fix} fix(A \times B) \xrightarrow{fix\ \pi_1} fix B
$$

of *rep* as in (12), not just for the instance $A, B := N, N$. Thus $\mathsf{cur}[rep]$ is in $\mathbf{Spec}(fix A, (B \rightsquigarrow fix B))$. Observe that

$$
\begin{array}{ll}
& \mathsf{cur}[\mathit{rep}] \\
= & \quad \text{(28) below introduces } g \\
& \mathsf{cur}((\llbracket \mathsf{cur}\, g \rrbracket \otimes \mathit{id}) \,\text{;}\, \mathsf{ap}) \\
= & \quad \text{exponent (22), cur } g \text{ bimap, Lemma 7} \\
& \llbracket \mathsf{cur}\, g \rrbracket
\end{array}
$$

Thus, by (20), finding $f$ in (27) is reduced to finding $g$ with

$$[\mathit{rep}] = (\llbracket \mathsf{cur}\, g \rrbracket \otimes \mathit{id}) \,\text{;}\, \mathsf{ap} \tag{28}$$

which can also be done for any $A, B$. (Taking $f = \mathsf{cur}\, g$ makes $f$ a bimap as required for (27).) Instantiate the recursion Theorem 1 with $C := \mathit{fix}\, B$, $h := \widehat{\mathit{in}} B$, $x := [\mathit{rep}]$, $\psi := ([\mathit{dist}\, F] \,\text{;}\, \widehat{F}(\widehat{\pi}_1, \mathit{id}))$, and $G(X, Y, Z) := \widehat{F}(Y, Z)$ for all $X, Y, Z$. By definition (12) of $\mathit{rep}$, we have $[\mathit{rep}] = [\mathit{dist}\, \mathit{fix}] \,\text{;}\, \widehat{\mathit{fix}} \widehat{\pi}_1$ using that $[-]$ is a functor (and $\mathit{fix}, \pi$ extend). The diagram is as follows:

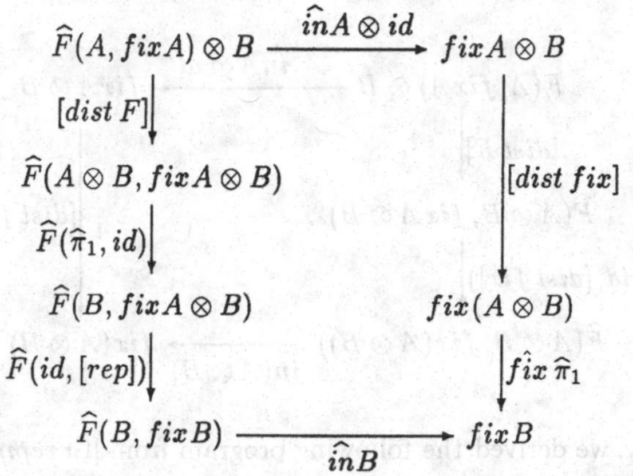


It commutes because

$$
\begin{array}{ll}
& \psi \,\text{;}\, \widehat{F}(\mathit{id}, [\mathit{rep}]) \,\text{;}\, \widehat{\mathit{in}}B \\
= & \quad \text{definitions } \psi,\ \mathit{rep}\ (12),\ \widehat{F} \text{ strict upfunctor (14)} \\
& [\mathit{dist}\, F] \,\text{;}\, \widehat{F}(\widehat{\pi}_1, \mathit{id}) \,\text{;}\, \widehat{F}(\mathit{id}, [\mathit{dist}\, \mathit{fix}]) \,\text{;}\, \widehat{F}(\mathit{id}, \widehat{\mathit{fix}}\, \widehat{\pi}_1) \,\text{;}\, \widehat{\mathit{in}}B \\
= & \quad \text{definition (10) for } \widehat{\mathit{fix}} \\
& [\mathit{dist}\, F] \,\text{;}\, \widehat{F}(\widehat{\pi}_1, \mathit{id}) \,\text{;}\, \widehat{F}(\mathit{id}, [\mathit{dist}\, \mathit{fix}]) \,\text{;}\, \widehat{F}(\mathit{id}, \llbracket \widehat{F}(\widehat{\pi}_1, \mathit{id}) \,\text{;}\, \widehat{\mathit{in}}B \rrbracket) \,\text{;}\, \widehat{\mathit{in}}B \\
= & \quad \widehat{F} \text{ strict upfunctor} \\
& [\mathit{dist}\, F] \,\text{;}\, \widehat{F}(\mathit{id}, [\mathit{dist}\, \mathit{fix}]) \,\text{;}\, \widehat{F}(\mathit{id}, \llbracket \widehat{F}(\widehat{\pi}_1, \mathit{id}) \,\text{;}\, \widehat{\mathit{in}}B \rrbracket) \,\text{;}\, \widehat{F}(\widehat{\pi}_1, \mathit{id}) \,\text{;}\, \widehat{\mathit{in}}B \\
= & \quad \text{catamorphism (9)} \\
& [\mathit{dist}\, F] \,\text{;}\, \widehat{F}(\mathit{id}, [\mathit{dist}\, \mathit{fix}]) \,\text{;}\, \widehat{\mathit{in}}(A \otimes B) \,\text{;}\, \llbracket \widehat{F}(\widehat{\pi}_1, \mathit{id}) \,\text{;}\, \widehat{\mathit{in}}B \rrbracket \\
= & \quad \text{definition (10) for } \widehat{\mathit{fix}} \\
& [\mathit{dist}\, F] \,\text{;}\, \widehat{F}(\mathit{id}, [\mathit{dist}\, \mathit{fix}]) \,\text{;}\, \widehat{\mathit{in}}(A \otimes B) \,\text{;}\, \widehat{\mathit{fix}}\, \widehat{\pi}_1 \\
= & \quad \text{see (29) below} \\
& (\widehat{\mathit{in}}A \otimes \mathit{id}) \,\text{;}\, [\mathit{dist}\, \mathit{fix}] \,\text{;}\, \widehat{\mathit{fix}}\, \widehat{\pi}_1 \\
= & \quad \text{definition } \mathit{rep}\ (13),\ [-] \text{ functor} \\
& (\widehat{\mathit{in}}A \otimes \mathit{id}) \,\text{;}\, [\mathit{rep}]
\end{array}
$$

Thus we have (28) by the recursion theorem, and hence (27). It remains to justify the penultimate step in this last calculation; this is another general lemma:

$$[\mathit{dist}\,F] \mathbin{;} \widehat{F}(id, [\mathit{dist}\,\mathit{fix}]) \mathbin{;} \widehat{in}(A \otimes B) = (\widehat{in}A \otimes id) \mathbin{;} [\mathit{dist}\,\mathit{fix}] \ . \qquad (29)$$

This is proved by instantiating the recursion theorem with $C := \mathit{fix}(A \otimes B)$, $x := [\mathit{dist}\,\mathit{fix}]$, $h := \widehat{in}(A \otimes B)$, $\psi := [\mathit{dist}\,F]$, and $G(X, Y, Z) := \widehat{F}(X \otimes Y, Z)$. We also need the definition of $[\mathit{dist}\,\mathit{fix}]$ in terms of $[\mathit{dist}\,F]$:

$$[\mathit{dist}\,\mathit{fix}] = ((\!|\mathsf{cur}([\mathit{dist}\,F] \mathbin{;} \widehat{F}(id, \mathsf{ap}) \mathbin{;} \widehat{in}(A \otimes B))|\!) \otimes id) \mathbin{;} \mathsf{ap} \ . \qquad (30)$$

Now the theorem says that (29) holds. Here is the picture:

$$\begin{array}{ccc}
\widehat{F}(A, \mathit{fix}A) \otimes B & \xrightarrow{\widehat{in}A \otimes id} & \mathit{fix}A \otimes B \\
\downarrow{\scriptstyle [\mathit{dist}\,F]} & & \\
\widehat{F}(A \otimes B, \mathit{fix}A \otimes B) & & \downarrow{\scriptstyle [\mathit{dist}\,\mathit{fix}]} \\
\downarrow{\scriptstyle \widehat{F}(id, [\mathit{dist}\,\mathit{fix}])} & & \\
\widehat{F}(A \otimes B, \mathit{fix}(A \otimes B)) & \xrightarrow[\widehat{in}(A \otimes B)]{} & \mathit{fix}(A \otimes B)
\end{array}$$

In summary, we derived the following program from [Gr *repmin*]:

$$\mathit{fix}\,N \xrightarrow{(\!|\widehat{F}(id, \widehat{\pi}_0) \,;\, f \,\triangle\, \widehat{F}(id, \widehat{\pi}_1) \,;\, [m]|\!)} (N \rightsquigarrow \mathit{fix}\,N) \otimes N \xrightarrow{\mathsf{ap}} \mathit{fix}\,N \quad (31)$$

where $f = \mathsf{cur}([\mathit{dist}\,F] \mathbin{;} \widehat{F}(\widehat{\pi}_1, id) \mathbin{;} \widehat{F}(id, \mathsf{ap}) \mathbin{;} \widehat{in}N)$. Because $\widehat{F}$ is a strict upfunctor and $\widehat{\pi}_1$ is a bimap, $f$ can be simplified to $\mathsf{cur}([\mathit{dist}\,F] \mathbin{;} \widehat{F}(\widehat{\pi}_1, \mathsf{ap}) \mathbin{;} \widehat{in}N)$ thanks to (14).

## 10 Interpreting the result

It is hardly obvious how to interpret in an imperative language the expression derived for *repmin*. One reason is that commands in conventional languages have the same final as initial state space, unlike the transformers in (31). Another reason is that cur is not found in full generality in most imperative languages, although special cases of cur and ap do model procedures, as mentioned in Section 7. That being so, we claim the derived transformer models a higher order a program like the following program in Standard ML (with polytypism eliminated by instantiating $F$ to the base for type *Ltree*).

```
datatype 'b tree = Leaf of 'b | Bin of ('b tree) * ('b tree);
fun repm (Leaf x)     = (x, Leaf)
 | repm (Bin(u,v)) = let val (x,f) = repm u
                         val (y,g) = repm v
                     in ( min(x,y), fn w => Bin (f w, g w) )
                    end;
fun repmin t = let val (n,p) = repm t in p(n) end;
```

Function `repmin` works by constructing a pair consisting of the minimum `n` of the tree and a closure `p` which is then applied to `n`.

It is rather anti-climactic for the end result to be essentially functional, when the point was to carry out the derivation in a setting that supports imperative constructs. It would be more interesting to derive code that is essentially imperative. A possibility using pointers is discussed inconclusively in [18]. Another possibility is the following, which treats `n` as a global variable: this version of `repm` has the side effect of maintaining that `n` is the minimum of the leaves 'traversed so far'.

```
val n = ref 0;
fun repm (Leaf x)     = ( n := min(x,!n); Leaf )
 |  repm (Bin(u,v)) = let val f = repm u
                          val g = repm v
                      in  fn w => Bin (f w, g w)
                     end;
fun repmin t = ( n := maxint; let val p = repm t in p(!n) end );
```

To derive such a program, we first replace $m : F(N,N) \to N$ (of Section 6) by function $m' : F(N,N) \times N \to N$ that gives the minimum of all its arguments. Then, leaving aside the initialization of `n`, definition (13) of *repmin* is replaced by

$$(\pi_0 \vartriangle min')\,;rep\,fix \;:\; fix N \times N \to fix N \times N$$

which yields the minimum value along with the tree. The recursion theorem is needed to define *min'* from $m'$ because $(\![-]\!)$ is not defined on $m'$. All but the last step of the original derivation can be recapitulated, using lemma (29) without change. Unfortunately, Lemma 8 no longer applies in that last step because *min'* is not a catamorphism. Generalization of the Lemma is left as future work.

## 11 Discussion

We derived in **Spec** a single-pass *repmin* program by a calculation almost the same as de Moor's in **Fun** and **Rel**. The derivation is remarkable because the constructs —especially products and exponents— satisfy much weaker laws than in **Fun** and **Rel**. We proved subsidiary results about catamorphisms on transformers, e.g., (30), (29) and the recursion Theorem 1. These are promising in that they are no weaker than their correlates in **Fun**. Theorem 1 is notable both because it allows arbitrary transformers as the basis of a recursive definition and because it can be proved using only the algebra of **Spec**. By contrast, the banana split Lemma 8 can be proved in **Spec** but it applies only to bimaps: in effect, it only pertains to **Mofun**, and the result might as well be lifted from **Mofun**.

The derived program is interesting in that it uses the transformer space $A \rightsquigarrow B$ which is not a data type in conventional functional languages. Because only exponent properties are needed, the derivation may well go through for the function-space or relation-space lifted to transformers (just as de Moor's derivation is valid for two different exponent structures, both interesting). But it is $A \rightsquigarrow B$ that models imperative procedures as a data type.

The *repmin* example does not fully exploit the power of imperative specifications and transformers: the derived program is essentially functional. We sketched a variation that can be interpreted as a program that makes modest use of imperative variables, but more convincing examples will be welcome, especially ones where the specification is not functional. The case for **Mofun** over **Fun** is strong, but a functional example cannot make the case that Squiggol extends to imperative programming.

Many specifications involve sets represented by data structures, so membership is ubiquitous. Hoogendijk and De Moor's notion of membership seems robust in that the constructors on **Idl** have membership, but it remains to be seen whether their general theory can be extended to categories like **Idl** that lack reciprocation. That lack is the most prominent loss in the move from **Fun** to **Mofun**. The simple view of basic data types as sets (i.e., discrete posets, not necessarily CPOs) is retained. Gained are some equations for transformers.

## Acknowledgements

Thanks to Oege de Moor for warnings and encouragement, and to Steve Bloom for discussions about inductive data types in **Mofun**. Augusto Sampaio and his colleagues at Universidade Federal de Pernambuco provided an engaging environment in which to complete the writing.

## References

1. R. Bird and O. de Moor. *Algebra of Programming.* Prentice-Hall, 1996.
2. R. Cockett and D. Spencer. Strong categorical datatypes I. In R. A. G. Seely, editor, *International Meeting on Category Theory 1991*, Canadian Mathematical Society Proceedings. AMS, 1992.
3. O. de Moor. Inductive data types for predicate transformers. *Inf. Process. Lett.*, 43(3):113–118, 1992.
4. O. de Moor. An exercise in polytypic programming: repmin. Typescript, www.comlab.ox.ac.uk/oucl/publications/books/algebra/papers/repmin.ps.gz,, Sept. 1996.
5. P. Gardiner. Algebraic proofs of consistency and completeness. *Theoretical Comput. Sci.*, 150:161–191, 1995.

6. P. H. Gardiner, C. E. Martin, and O. de Moor. An algebraic construction of predicate transformers. *Science of Computer Programming*, 22:21–44, 1994.
7. P. Hoogendijk. A generic theory of data types. Dissertation, Technische Universiteit Eindhoven, 1997.
8. P. Hoogendijk and O. de Moor. What is a data type? Technical Report 96/16, Eindhoven University of Technology, 1996. www.win.tue.nl/win/cs/wp/papers.
9. P. Jansson and J. Jeuring. PolyP — a polytypic programming language extension. In *Proceedings, Principles of Programming Languages*, pages 470–82. ACM Press, 1997.
10. C. Martin. Towards a calculus of predicate transformers. In *Proceedings, Mathematical Foundations of Computer Science*, volume 969 of *Springer LNCS*, pages 489–49, 1995.
11. C. Martin, C. Hoare, and J. He. Pre-adjunctions in order enriched categories. *Mathematical Structures in Computer Science*, 1:141–158, 1991.
12. E. Moggi. Notions of computation and monads. *Information and Computation*, 93:55–92, 1991.
13. C. Morgan. *Programming from Specifications, second edition*. Prentice Hall, 1994.
14. D. A. Naumann. Predicate transformer semantics of an Oberon-like language. In E.-R. Olderog, editor, *Programming Concepts, Methods and Calculi*, IFIP Transactions A-56. Elsevier, 1994.
15. D. A. Naumann. A recursion theorem for predicate transformers on inductive data types. *Inf. Process. Lett.*, 50:329–336, 1994.
16. D. A. Naumann. Predicate transformers and higher order programs. *Theoretical Comput. Sci.*, 150:111–159, 1995.
17. D. A. Naumann. A categorical model for higher order imperative programming. *Mathematical Structures in Computer Science*, 1996. To appear.
18. D. A. Naumann. Towards squiggly refinement algebra. In W.-P. de Roever and D. Gries, eds., *IFIP Working Conference on Programming Concepts and Methods*. Chapman and Hall, 1998.
19. J. Power and E. Robinson. Premonoidal categories and notions of computation. *Mathematical Structures in Computer Science*, 7:453–468, 1997.

# Convergence of Program Transformers in the Metric Space of Trees

Morten Heine B. Sørensen

Department of Computer Science, University of Copenhagen (DIKU)
Universitetsparken 1, DK-2100 Copenhagen Ø, Denmark
E-mail: rambo@diku.dk

**Abstract.** In recent years increasing consensus has emerged that program transformers, e.g., partial evaluation and unfold/fold transformations, should terminate; a compiler should stop even if it performs fancy optimizations! A number of techniques to ensure termination of program transformers have been invented, but their correctness proofs are sometimes long and involved.

We present a framework for proving termination of program transformers, cast in the *metric space of trees*. We first introduce the notion of an *abstract program transformer;* a number of well-known program transformers can be viewed as instances of this notion. We then formalize what it means that an abstract program transformer *terminates* and give a general *sufficient condition* for an abstract program transformer to terminate. We also consider some *specific techniques* for satisfying the condition. As *applications* we show that termination of some well-known program transformers either follows directly from the specific techniques or is easy to establish using the general condition.

Our framework facilitates simple termination proofs for program transformers. Also, since our framework is independent of the language being transformed, a single correctness proof can be given in our framework for program transformers using essentially the same technique in the context of different languages. Moreover, it is easy to extend termination proofs for program transformers to accommodate changes to these transformers. Finally, the framework may prove useful for designing new termination techniques for program transformers.

## 1 Introduction

Numerous program transformation techniques have been studied in the areas of functional and logic languages, e.g., partial evaluation and unfold/fold transformations. Pettorossi and Proietti [30] show that many of these techniques can be viewed as consisting of three conceptual phases which may be interleaved: *symbolic computation, search for regularities,* and *program extraction.*

Given a program, the first phase constructs a possibly infinite tree in which each node is labeled with an expression; children are added to the tree by *unfolding* steps. The second phase employs *generalization* steps to ensure that one constructs a finite tree. The third phase constructs from this finite tree a new program.

The most difficult problem for most program transformers is to formulate the second phase in such a way that the transformer both performs interesting optimizations and always terminates. Solutions to this problem now exist for most transformers.

The proofs that these transformers indeed terminate—including some proofs by the author—are sometimes long, involved, and read by very few people. One reason for this is that such a proof needs to formalize what it means that the transformer terminates, and significant parts of the proof involve abstract properties about the formalization.

In this paper we present a framework for proving termination of program transformers. We first introduce the notion of an *abstract program transformer*, which is a map from trees to trees expressing one step of transformation. A number of well-known program transformers can be viewed as instances of this notion. Indeed, using the notion of an abstract program transformer and associated general operations on trees, it is easy to specify and compare various transformers, as we shall see.

We then formalize what it means that that an abstract program transformer *terminates* and give a *sufficient condition* for an abstract program transformer to terminate. A number of well-known transformers satisfy the condition. In fact, termination proofs for some of these transformers implicitly contain the correctness proof of the condition. Developing the condition once and for all factors out this common part; a termination proof within our framework for a program transformer only needs to prove properties that are specific to the transformer. This yields shorter, less error-prone, and more transparent proofs, and means that proofs can easily be extended to accommodate changes in the transformer. Also, our framework isolates exactly those parts of a program transformer relevant for ensuring termination, and this makes our framework useful for designing new termination techniques for existing program transformers.

The insight that various transformers are very similar has led to the exchange of many ideas between researchers working on different transformers, especially techniques to ensure termination. Variations of one technique, used to ensure termination of positive supercompilation [35], have been adopted in partial deduction [23], conjunctive partial deduction [16], Turchin's supercompiler [41], and partial evaluation of functional-logic programs [1]. While the technique is fairly easily transported between different settings, a separate correctness proof has been given in each setting.

It would be better if one could give a single proof of correctness for this technique in a setting which abstracts away irrelevant details of the transformers. Therefore, we consider *specific techniques*, based on well-known transformers, for satisfying the condition in our framework. The description of these techniques is *specific* enough to imply termination of well-known transformers, and *general* enough to establish termination of different program transformers using essentially the same technique in the context of different languages. As *applications* we demonstrate that this is true for positive supercompilation and partial deduction (in the latter case by a brief sketch).

The set of trees forms a metric space, and our framework can be elegantly presented using such notions as convergence and continuity in this metric space. We also use a few well-known results about the metric space of trees, e.g., completeness. However, we do not mean to suggest that the merits of our approach stem from the supposed depth of any of these results; rather, the metric space of trees offers concepts and terminology useful for analyzing termination of abstract program transformers.

Section 2 introduces program transformers as maps from trees to trees. This is then formalized in the notion of an abstract program transformer in Section 3. Section 4 presents positive supercompilation as an abstract program transformer. Section 5 presents the metric space of trees, and Section 6 uses this to present our sufficient condition for termination, as well as the specific techniques to satisfy the condition. Section 7 shows that positive supercompilation terminates. It also sketches Martens and Gallagher's [26] generic algorithm for partial deduction as an abstract program transformer and sketches a proofs that it terminates.

We stress that it is not the intention of this paper to advocate any particular technique that ensures termination of program transformers; rather, we are concerned with a general method to prove that such techniques are correct.

This work is part of a larger effort to understand the relation between deforestation, supercompilation, partial deduction, and other program transformers better [17, 18, 20, 36, 37] and to develop a unifying theory for such transformers.

## 2 Trees in Transformation

We now proceed to show how program transformers may be viewed as maps that manipulate certain trees, following Pettorossi and Proietti [30].

*Example 1.* Consider a functional program appending two lists.

$$\begin{aligned} a([], vs) &= vs \\ a(u : us, vs) &= u : a(us, vs) \end{aligned}$$

A simple and elegant way to append *three* lists is to use the expression $a(a(xs, ys), zs)$. However, this expression is inefficient since it traverses $xs$ twice. We now illustrate a standard transformation obtaining a more efficient method.

We begin with a tree whose single node is labeled with $a(a(xs, ys), zs)$:

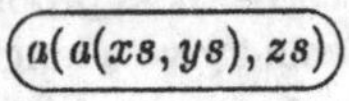


By an *unfolding* step which replaces the inner call to append according to the different patterns in the definition of $a$, two new expressions are added as labels on children:

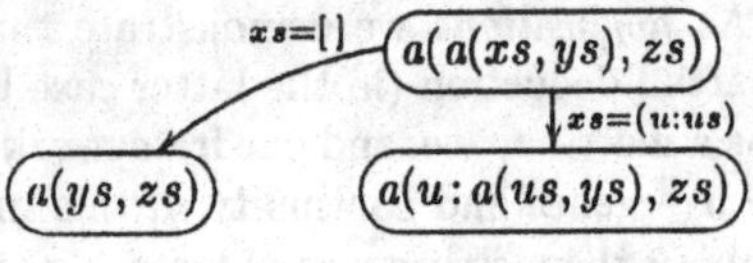


In the rightmost child we can perform an unfolding step which replaces the outer call to append:

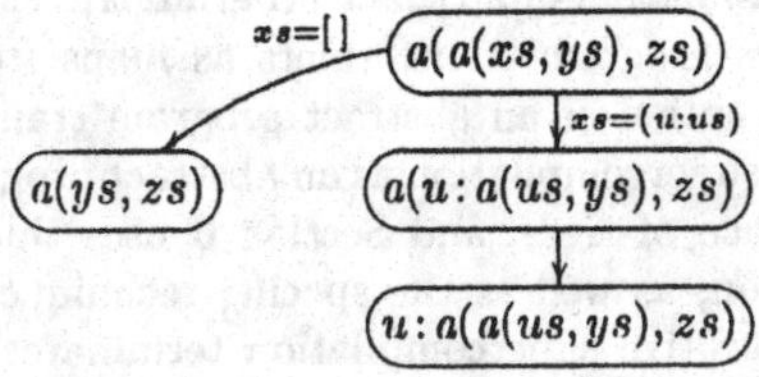

The label of the new child contains an outermost constructor. For transformation to propagate to the subexpression of the constructor we again add children:

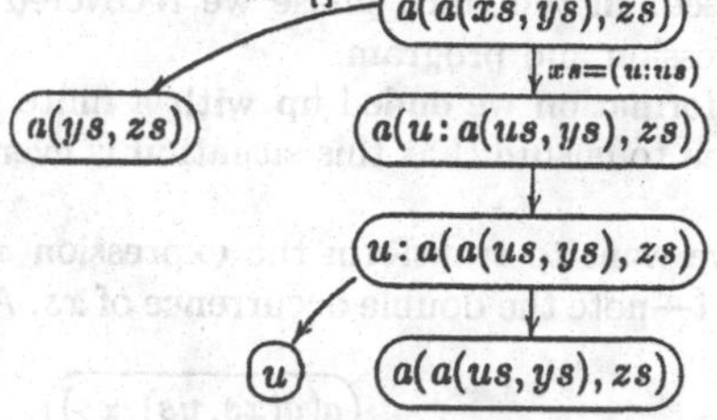


The expression in the rightmost child is a renaming of the expression in the root; that is, the two expressions are identical up to choice of variable names. As we shall see below, no further processing of such a node is required. Unfolding the child with label $a(ys, zs)$ two steps leads to:

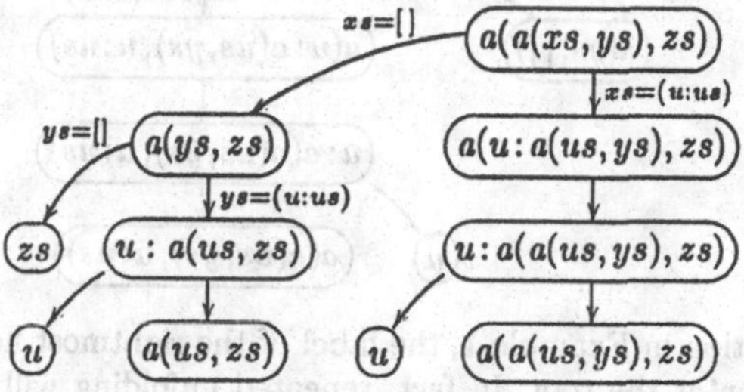


The tree is now *closed* in the sense that each leaf expression either is a renaming of an ancestor's expression, or contains a variable or a 0-ary constructor. Informally, a closed tree is a representation of all possible computations with the expression $e$ in the root, where branchings in the tree correspond to different run-time values for the free variables of $e$.

To construct a new program from a closed tree, we introduce, roughly, for each node $\alpha$ with child $\beta$ a definition where the left and right hand side of the definition are derived from $\alpha$ and $\beta$, respectively. More specifically, in the above example we rename expressions of form $a(a(xs, ys), zs)$ as $aa(xs, ys, zs)$, and derive from the tree the following new program:

$$\begin{aligned} aa([\,], ys, zs) &= a(ys, zs) \\ aa(u\!:\!us, ys, zs) &= u : aa(us, ys, zs) \\ \\ a([\,], zs) &= zs \\ a(u\!:\!us, zs) &= u : a(us, zs) \end{aligned}$$

The expression $aa(\ xs,\ ys,\ zs)$ in this program is more efficient than $a(a(xs, ys), zs)$ in the original program, since the new expression traverses $xs$ only once.

The transformation in Example 1 proceeded in three phases—symbolic computation, search for regularities, and program extraction—the first two of which were interleaved. In the first phase we performed unfolding steps that added children to the tree. In the second phase we made sure that no node with an expression which was a renaming of ancestor's expression was unfolded, and we continued the overall process until the tree was closed. In the third phase we recovered from the resulting finite, closed tree a new expression and program.

In the above transformation we ended up with a finite closed tree. Often, special measures must be taken to ensure that this situation is eventually encountered.

*Example 2.* Suppose we want to transform the expression $a(a(xs, ys), xs)$, where $a$ is defined as in Example 1—note the double occurrence of $xs$. As above we start out with:

$$a(a(xs, ys), xs)$$

After the first few steps we have:

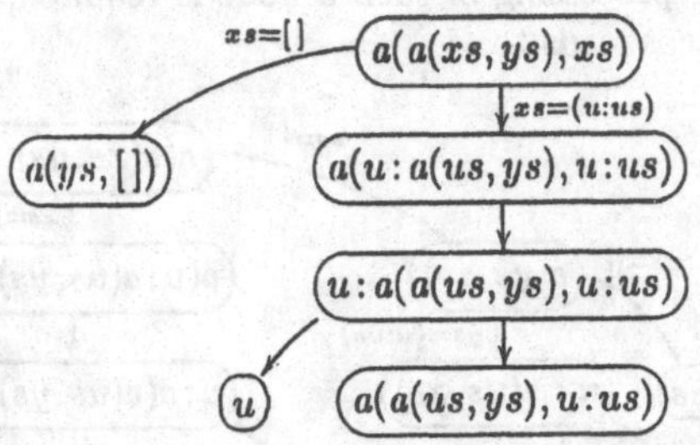


Unlike the situation in Example 1, the label of the rightmost node is not a renaming of the expression at the root. In fact, repeated unfolding will *never* lead to that situation; special measures must be taken.

One solution is to ignore the information that the argument $xs$ to the inner call and the argument $xs$ to the outer call are the same. This is achieved by a *generalization* step that replaces the whole tree by a single new node:

$$\textbf{let } zs{=}xs \textbf{ in } a(a(xs, ys), zs)$$

When dealing with nodes of the new form **let** $zs{=}e$ **in** $e'$ we then transform $e$ and $e'$ independently. Thus we arrive at:

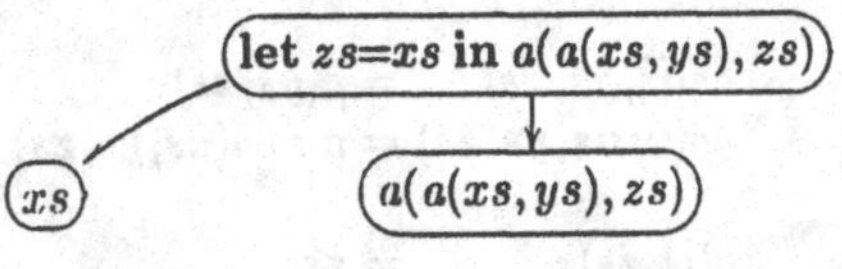


Unfolding of the node labeled $a(a(xs, ys), zs)$ leads to the same tree as in Example 1.

When generating a new term and program from such a tree, we can eliminate all let-expressions; in particular, in the above example, we generate the expression $aa(xs, ys, xs)$ and the same program as in Example 1.[1]

[1] In some cases such let-expression elimination may be undesirable for reasons pertaining to efficiency of the generated program—but such issues are ignored in the present paper.

Again transformation proceeds in three phases, but the second phase is now more sophisticated, sometimes replacing a subtree by a new node in a generalization step.

Numerous program transformers can be cast more or less accurately in the three above mentioned phases, e.g., partial deduction [23, 26], conjunctive partial deduction [16], compiling control [10], loop absorption [31], partial evaluation of functional-logic languages [1], unfold/fold transformation of functional programs [11], unfold/fold transformation of logic programs [38], tupling [4, 29], supercompilation [39, 40], positive supercompilation [18, 35], generalized partial computation [15], deforestation [42], and online partial evaluation of functional programs [43, 33, 21].

Although *offline* transformers (i.e., transformers making use of analyses prior to the transformation to make changes in the program ensuring termination) may fit into the description with the three phases, the second phase is rather trivial, amounting to the situation in Example 1.

## 3 Abstract Program Transformers

We now formalize the idea that a program transformer is a map from trees to trees, expressing one step of transformation. We first introduce trees in a rigorous manner, following Courcelle [12].

**Definition 1.** A *tree* over a set $E$ is a partial map[2] $t : \mathbb{N}_1^* \rightarrow E$ such that

1. $\text{dom}(t) \neq \emptyset$ ($t$ is *non-empty*);
2. if $\alpha\beta \in \text{dom}(t)$ then $\alpha \in \text{dom}(t)$ ($\text{dom}(t)$ is *prefix-closed*);
3. if $\alpha \in \text{dom}(t)$ then $\{i \mid \alpha i \in \text{dom}(t)\}$ is finite ($t$ is *finitely branching*);
4. if $\alpha j \in \text{dom}(t)$ then $\alpha i \in \text{dom}(t)$ for all $1 \leq i \leq j$ ($t$ is *ordered*).

Let $t$ be a tree over $E$. The elements of $\text{dom}(t)$ are called *nodes* of $t$; the empty string $\epsilon$ is the *root*, and for any node $\alpha$ in $t$, the nodes $\alpha i$ of $t$ (if any) are the *children* of $\alpha$, and we also say that $\alpha$ is the *parent* of these nodes. A *branch* in $t$ is a finite or infinite sequence $\alpha_0, \alpha_1 \ldots \in \text{dom}(t)$ where $\alpha_0 = \epsilon$ and, for all $i$, $\alpha_{i+1}$ is a child of $\alpha_i$. A node with no children is a *leaf*. We denote by $\text{leaf}(t)$ the set of all leafs in $t$. For any node $\alpha$ of $t$, $t(\alpha) \in E$ is the *label* of $\alpha$. Also, $t$ is *finite*, if $\text{dom}(t)$ is finite. Finally, $t$ is *singleton* if $\text{dom}(t) = \{\epsilon\}$, i.e., if $\text{dom}(t)$ is singleton.

$T_\infty(E)$ is the set of all trees over $E$, and $T(E)$ is the set of all finite trees over $E$.

*Example 3.* Let $\mathcal{E}_H(V)$ be the set of expressions over symbols $H$ and variables $V$. Let $x, xs, \ldots \in V$ and $a, cons, nil \in H$, denoting $(x : xs)$ by $cons(x, xs)$ and $[]$ by $nil$. Then let $\mathcal{L}_H(V)$ be the smallest set such that $e_1, \ldots, e_n, e \in \mathcal{E}_H(V)$ implies that $\textbf{let}\ x_1{=}e_1, \ldots, x_n{=}e_n\ \textbf{in}\ e \in \mathcal{L}_H(V)$. The trees in Example 1 and 2 (ignoring labels on edges) are a diagrammatical presentation of trees over $\mathcal{E}_H(V)$ and $\mathcal{L}_H(V)$, respectively.

**Definition 2.** An *abstract program transformer* (for brevity also called an *apt*) on $E$ is a map $M : T(E) \rightarrow T(E)$.

[2] We let $\mathbb{N}_1 = \mathbb{N} \setminus \{0\}$. $S^*$ is the set of finite strings over $S$, and $\text{dom}(f)$ is the domain of a partial function $f$.

For instance, the sequences of trees in Example 1 and 2 could be computed by iterated application of some apt. How do we formally express that no more transformation steps will happen, i.e., that the apt has produced its final result? In this case, $M$ returns is argument tree unchanged, i.e., $M(t) = t$.

**Definition 3.**

1. An apt $M$ on $E$ *terminates on* $t \in T(E)$ if $M^i(t) = M^{i+1}(t)$ for some $i \in \mathbb{N}$.[3]
2. An apt $M$ on $E$ *terminates* if $M$ terminates on all singletons $t \in T(E)$.

Although apts are defined on the set $T(E)$ of finite trees, it turns out to be convenient to consider the general set $T_\infty(E)$ of finite as well as infinite trees.

The rest of this section introduces some definitions pertaining to trees that will be used in the remainder.

**Definition 4.** Let $E$ be a set, and $t, t' \in T_\infty(E)$.

1. The *depth* $|\alpha|$ of a node $\alpha$ in $t$ is:
$$\begin{aligned} |\epsilon| &= 0 \\ |\alpha i| &= |\alpha| + 1 \end{aligned}$$
2. The *depth* $|t|$ of $t$ is defined by:
$$|t| = \begin{cases} \max\{|\alpha| \mid \alpha \in \mathrm{dom}(t)\} & \text{if } t \text{ is finite} \\ \infty & \text{otherwise} \end{cases}$$
3. The *initial subtree of depth $\ell$ of $t$*, written $t[\ell]$, is the tree $t'$ with
$$\begin{aligned} \mathrm{dom}(t') &= \{\alpha \in \mathrm{dom}(t) \mid |\alpha| \le \ell\} \\ t'(\alpha) &= t(\alpha) \quad \text{for all } \alpha \in \mathrm{dom}(t') \end{aligned}$$
4. For $\alpha \in \mathrm{dom}(t)$, $t\{\alpha := t'\}$ denotes the tree $t''$ defined by:
$$\begin{aligned} \mathrm{dom}(t'') &= (\mathrm{dom}(t) \setminus \{\alpha\beta \mid \alpha\beta \in \mathrm{dom}(t)\}) \cup \{\alpha\beta \mid \beta \in \mathrm{dom}(t')\} \\ t''(\gamma) &= \begin{cases} t'(\beta) & \text{if } \gamma = \alpha\beta \text{ for some } \beta \\ t(\gamma) & \text{otherwise} \end{cases} \end{aligned}$$
5. We write $t = t'$, if $\mathrm{dom}(t) = \mathrm{dom}(t')$ and $t(\alpha) = t'(\alpha)$ for all $\alpha \in \mathrm{dom}(t)$.
6. Let $\alpha \in \mathrm{dom}(t)$. The *ancestors of $\alpha$ in $t$* is the set
$$\mathrm{anc}(t, \alpha) = \{\beta \in \mathrm{dom}(t) \mid \exists\gamma : \alpha = \beta\gamma\}$$
7. We denote by $e \rightarrow e_1, \ldots, e_n$ the tree $t \in T_\infty(E)$ with
$$\begin{aligned} \mathrm{dom}(t) &= \{\epsilon\} \cup \{1, \ldots, n\} \\ t(\epsilon) &= e \\ t(i) &= e_i \end{aligned}$$

As a special case, $e \rightarrow$ denotes the $t \in T_\infty(E)$ with $\mathrm{dom}(t) = \{\epsilon\}$ and $t(\epsilon) = e$.

[3] For $f : A \rightarrow A$, $f^0(a) = a$, $f^{i+1}(a) = f^i(f(a))$.

In the diagrammatical notation of Section 2, the depth of a node is the number of edges on the path from the root to the node. The depth of a tree is the maximal depth of any node. The initial subtree of depth $\ell$ is the tree obtained by deleting all nodes of depth greater than $\ell$ and edges into such nodes. The tree $t\{\alpha{:=}t'\}$ is the tree obtained by replacing the subtree with root $\alpha$ in $t$ by the tree $t'$. The ancestors of a node are the nodes on the path from the root to the node. Finally, the tree $e \to e_1, \ldots, e_n$ is the tree with root labeled $e$ and $n$ children labeled $e_1, \ldots, e_n$, respectively.

## 4 Example: Positive Supercompilation

We present a variant of positive supercompilation [18, 35, 36, 37] as an abstract program transformer. We consider the following first-order functional language; the intended operational semantics is normal-order graph reduction to weak head normal form.

**Definition 5.** We assume a denumerable set of symbols for variables $x \in X$ and finite sets of symbols for constructors $c \in C$, and functions $f \in F$ and $g \in G$; symbols all have fixed arity. The sets $\mathcal{Q}$ of programs, $\mathcal{D}$ of definitions, $\mathcal{E}$ of expressions, and $\mathcal{P}$ of patterns are defined by:

$$
\begin{array}{rlll}
\mathcal{Q} \ni q & ::= & d_1 \ldots d_m & \\
\mathcal{D} \ni d & ::= & f(x_1, \ldots, x_n) \triangleq e & \text{(f-function)} \\
 & | & g(p_1, x_1, \ldots, x_n) \triangleq e_1 & \\
 & & \vdots & \text{(g-function)} \\
 & & g(p_m, x_1, \ldots, x_n) \triangleq e_m & \\
\mathcal{E} \ni e & ::= & x & \text{(variable)} \\
 & | & c(e_1, \ldots, e_n) & \text{(constructor)} \\
 & | & f(e_1, \ldots, e_n) & \text{(f-function call)} \\
 & | & g(e_0, e_1, \ldots, e_n) & \text{(g-function call)} \\
\mathcal{P} \ni p & ::= & c(x_1, \ldots, x_n) &
\end{array}
$$

where $m > 0, n \geq 0$. We require that no two patterns $p_i$ and $p_j$ in a g-function definition contain the same constructor $c$, that no variable occur more than once in a left side of a definition, and that all variables on the right side of a definition be present in its left side. By vars($e$) we denote the set of variables occurring in the expression $e$.

*Example 4.* The programs in Example 1–2 are programs in this language using the short notation [] and $(x : xs)$ for the list constructors *nil* and $cons(x, xs)$.

**Definition 6.** A *substitution* on $\mathcal{E}_H(V)$ is a total map from $V$ to $\mathcal{E}_H(V)$. We denote by $\{x_1{:=}e_1, \ldots, x_n{:=}e_n\}$ the substitution that maps $x_i$ to $e_i$ and all other variables to themselves. Substitutions are lifted to expressions as usual, and application of substitutions is written postfix.

For a substitution $\theta$, base($\theta$) $= \{x \in X \mid x\theta \neq x\}$. A substitution $\theta$ is *free for* an $e \in \mathcal{E}_H(V)$ if for all $x \in$ base($\theta$): vars($x\theta$) $\cap$ vars($e$) $= \emptyset$.

As we saw in Example 2, although the input and output programs of the transformer are expressed in the above language, the trees considered during transformation might have nodes containing let-expressions. Therefore, the positive supercompiler works on trees over $\mathcal{L}$, defined as follows.

**Definition 7.** The set $\mathcal{L}$ of let-expressions is defined as follows:

$$\mathcal{L} \ni \ell ::= \textbf{let } x_1{=}e_1, \ldots, x_n{=}e_n \textbf{ in } e$$

where $n \geq 0$. If $n > 0$ then we require that $x_1, \ldots, x_n \in \text{vars}(e)$, that $e \notin X$, and that $e\{x_1 := e_1, \ldots, x_n := e_n\}$ is not a renaming[4] of $e$. If $n = 0$ then we identify the expression $\textbf{let } x_1{=}e_1, \ldots, x_n{=}e_n \textbf{ in } e$ with $e$. Thus, $\mathcal{E}$ is a subset of $\mathcal{L}$.

*Remark.* There is a close relationship between the set $\mathcal{E}$ of expressions introduced above and the set $\mathcal{E}_H(V)$ introduced in Example 3. In fact, $\mathcal{E} = \mathcal{E}_{C \cup F \cup G}(X)$. Therefore, in what follows we can make use of well-known facts about $\mathcal{E}_H(V)$ in reasoning about $\mathcal{E}$. Also, $\mathcal{L} = \mathcal{L}_{C \cup F \cup G}(X)$.

We now set out to formulate the unfolding and generalization operations mentioned in Section 2, as used in positive supercompilation. We begin with unfolding.

The following relation $\Rightarrow$ generalizes the small-step semantics for normal-order reduction to weak head normal form by propagating to the arguments of constructors and by working on expressions with variables; the latter is done by propagating unifications representing the assumed outcome of tests on constructers—notice the substitution $\{y := p\}$ in the third rule. Also, the reduction for let-expressions expresses the semantics of generalizations: that we are trying to keep things apart.

**Definition 8.** For a program $q$, the relations $e \to_\theta e'$ and $\ell \Rightarrow e$ where $e, e' \in \mathcal{E}$, $\ell \in \mathcal{L}$, and $\theta$ is a substitution on $\mathcal{E}$, is defined by:

$$\frac{f(x_1, \ldots, x_n) \triangleq e \;\in\; q}{f(e_1, \ldots, e_n) \to_{\{\}} e\{x_1 := e_1, \ldots, x_n := e_n\}}$$

$$\frac{g(c(x_1, \ldots, x_m), x_{m+1}, \ldots, x_n) \triangleq e \;\in\; q}{g(c(e_1, \ldots, e_m), e_{m+1}, \ldots, e_n) \to_{\{\}} e\{x_1 := e_1, \ldots, x_n := e_n\}}$$

$$\frac{g(p, x_1 \ldots, x_n) \triangleq e \;\in\; q}{g(y, e_1, \ldots e_n) \to_{\{y:=p\}} e\{x_1 := e_1, \ldots, x_n := e_n\}}$$

$$\frac{e \to_\theta e' \quad \& \quad \theta \text{ is free for } g(e, e_1, \ldots, e_n)}{g(e, e_1, \ldots, e_n) \to_\theta g(e', e_1, \ldots, e_n)}$$

$$\frac{e \to_\theta e'}{e \Rightarrow e'\theta}$$

$$\frac{i \in \{1, \ldots, n\}}{c(e_1, \ldots, e_n) \Rightarrow e_i}$$

$$\frac{i \in \{1, \ldots, n+1\}}{\textbf{let } x_1{=}e_1, \ldots, x_n{=}e_n \textbf{ in } e_{n+1} \Rightarrow e_i}$$

The unfolding operation in positive supercompilation is called *driving*.

[4] The notion of a renaming is defined below.

**Definition 9.** Let $t \in T(\mathcal{L})$ and $\beta \in \text{leaf}(t)$. Then

$$\text{drive}(t,\beta) = t\{\beta{:=}t(\beta)\to e_1,\ldots,e_n\}$$

where[5] $\{e_1,\ldots,e_n\} = \{e \mid t(\beta) \Rightarrow e\}$.

*Example 5.* All the unfolding steps in Examples 1–2 are, in fact, driving steps.

Next we set out to formulate the generalization operations used in positive supercompilation. In generalization steps one often compares two expressions and extracts some common structure; the ***most specific generalization***, defined next, extracts the most structure in a certain sense.

**Definition 10.** Let $e_1, e_2 \in \mathcal{E}_H(V)$, for some $H, V$.

1. The expression $e_2$ is an ***instance*** of $e_1$, $e_1 \lessdot e_2$, if $e_1\theta = e_2$ for a substitution $\theta$.
2. The expression $e_2$ is a ***renaming*** of $e_1$ if $e_1 \lessdot e_2$ and $e_2 \lessdot e_1$.
3. A ***generalization*** of $e_1, e_2$ is a expression $e_g$ such that $e_g \lessdot e_1$ and $e_g \lessdot e_2$.
4. A ***most specific*** generalization (msg) $e_1 \sqcap e_2$ of $e_1$ and $e_2$ is a generalization $e_g$ such that, for every generalization $e'_g$ of $e_1$ and $e_2$, it holds that $e'_g \lessdot e_g$.
5. Two expressions $e_1$ and $e_2$ are ***incommensurable***, $e_1 \leftrightarrow e_2$, if $e_1 \sqcap e_2$ is a variable.

*Example 6.* The following table gives example most specific generalizations $e_1 \sqcap e_2$ of $e_1, e_2 \in \mathcal{E}_H(V)$ where $(e_1 \sqcap e_2)\theta_i = e_i$ and $x, y \in V$, $b, c, d, f \in H$.

| $e_1$ | $e_2$ | $e_1 \sqcap e_2$ | $\theta_1$ | $\theta_2$ |
|---|---|---|---|---|
| $b$ | $f(b)$ | $x$ | $\{x := b\}$ | $\{x := f(b)\}$ |
| $c(b)$ | $c(f(b))$ | $c(x)$ | $\{x := b\}$ | $\{x := f(b)\}$ |
| $c(y)$ | $c(f(y))$ | $c(y)$ | $\{\}$ | $\{y := f(y)\}$ |
| $d(b,b)$ | $d(f(b), f(b))$ | $d(x,x)$ | $\{x := b\}$ | $\{x := f(b)\}$ |

**Proposition 11.** *Let $H, V$ be some sets. For all $e_1, e_2 \in \mathcal{E}_H(V)$ there is an msg which is unique up to renaming.*[6]

The following, then, are the generalization operations used in positive supercompilation; the operations are illustrated (together with driving) in Fig. 1.

**Definition 12.** Let $t \in T(\mathcal{L})$.

1. For $\beta \in \text{leaf}(t)$ with $t(\beta) = h(e_1,\ldots,e_n)$, $h \in C \cup F \cup G$, and $e_i \notin X$ for some $i \in \{1,\ldots,n\}$, define

$$\text{split}(t,\beta) = t\{\beta{:=}\textbf{let } x_1{=}e_1,\ldots,x_n{=}e_n \textbf{ in } h(x_1,\ldots,x_n)\to\}$$

---

[5] We may have $n \geq 2$ only when $t(\beta)$ contains an outermost constructor of arity $n$ with $n \geq 2$, and when $t(\beta)$ contains a call to a g-function defined by $n$ patterns with $n \geq 2$. For code generation purposes it is necessary in these cases to recall which constructor argument or which pattern each of the children $e_1,\ldots,e_n$ corresponds to, but this issue is ignored in the present paper

[6] As a matter of technicality, we shall require that if $e_1 \lessdot e_2$ then $e_1 \sqcap e_2 = e_1$. In other words, whenever $e_2$ is an instance of $e_1$, the variable names of $e_1 \sqcap e_2$ will be chosen so that the resulting term is identical to $e_1$.

2. For $\alpha, \beta \in \text{dom}(t)$ with $t(\alpha), t(\beta) \in \mathcal{E}$, $t(\alpha) \sqcap t(\beta) = e$, $t(\alpha) = e\{x_1{:=}e_1, \ldots, x_n{:=}e_n\}$, $x_1, \ldots, x_n \in \text{vars}(e)$, $e \notin X$, $t(\alpha)$ not a renaming of $e$, define

$$\text{abstract}(t, \alpha, \beta) = t\{\alpha{:=}\textbf{let } x_1{=}e_1, \ldots, x_n{=}e_n \textbf{ in } e \rightarrow\}$$

*Remark.* Note that the above operations are allowed only under circumstances that guarantee that the constructed let-expression is well-formed according to the conditions of Definition 7.

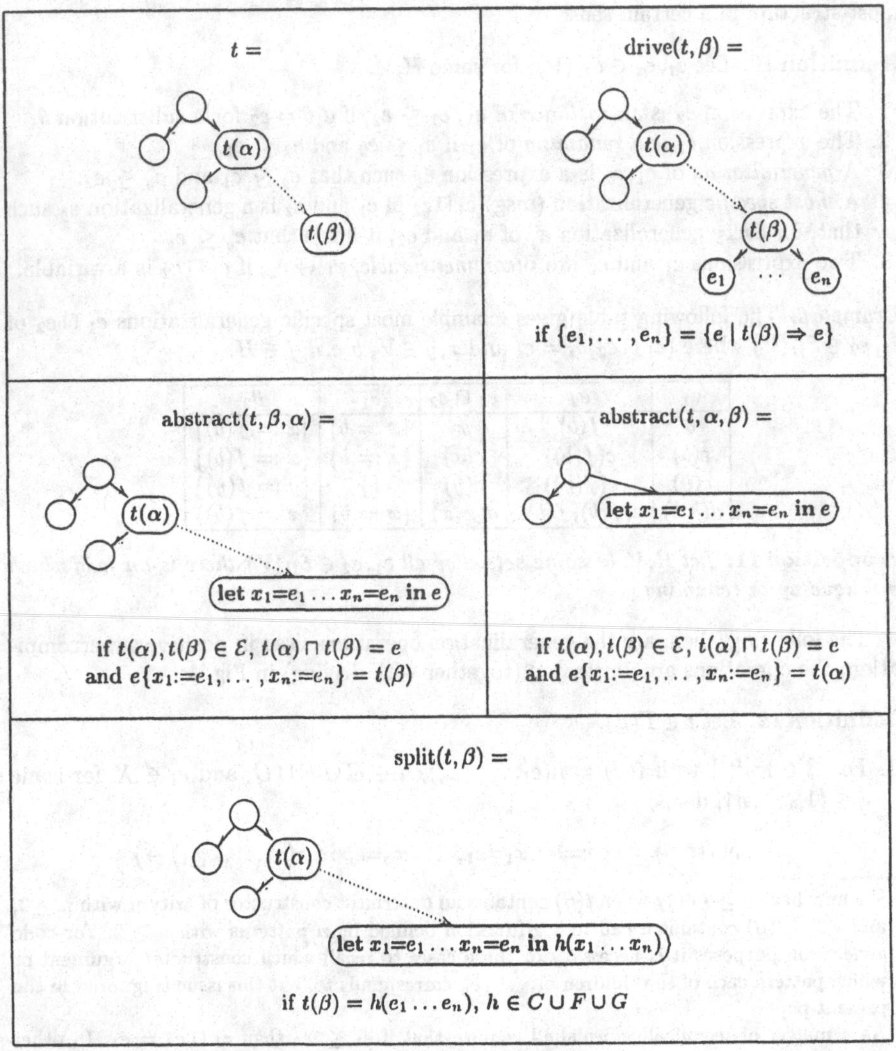


**Fig. 1.** Operations used in Positive Supercompilation

*Example 7.* The generalization step in Example 2 is an abstract step.

This completes the description of the unfolding and generalization operations in positive supercompilation. It remains to decide *when* to generalize. The following relation $\trianglelefteq$ is used for that end.

**Definition 13.** The *homeomorphic embedding* $\trianglelefteq$ is the smallest relation on $\mathcal{E}_H(V)$ such that, for all $h \in H$, $x, y \in V$, and $e_i, e'_i \in \mathcal{E}_H(V)$:

$$x \trianglelefteq y \qquad \frac{\exists i \in \{1,\ldots,n\} : e \trianglelefteq e'_i}{e \trianglelefteq h(e'_1,\ldots,e'_n)} \qquad \frac{\forall i \in \{1,\ldots,n\} : e_i \trianglelefteq e'_i}{h(e_1,\ldots,e_n) \trianglelefteq h(e'_1,\ldots,e'_n)}$$

*Example 8.* The following expressions from $\mathcal{E}_H(V)$ give examples and non-examples of embedding, where $x, y \in V$, and $b, c, d, f \in H$.

$$\begin{array}{rr} b \trianglelefteq f(b) & f(c(b)) \ntrianglelefteq c(b) \\ c(b) \trianglelefteq c(f(b)) & f(c(b)) \ntrianglelefteq c(f(b)) \\ d(b,b) \trianglelefteq d(f(b),f(b)) & f(c(b)) \ntrianglelefteq f(f(f(b))) \end{array}$$

The rationale behind using the homeomorphic embedding relation in program transformers is that in any infinite sequence $e_0, e_1, \ldots$ of expressions, there *definitely* are $i < j$ with $e_i \trianglelefteq e_j$.[7] Thus, if unfolding is stopped at any node with an expression in which an ancestor's expression is embedded, unfolding cannot construct an infinite branch. Conversely, if $e_i \trianglelefteq e_j$ then all the subexpressions of $e_i$ are present in $e_j$ embedded in extra subexpressions. This suggests that $e_j$ *might* arise from $e_i$ by some infinitely continuing system, so unfolding is stopped for a good reason.

In some cases it is desirable to unfold a node even if its label expression has some ancestor's expression embedded. In the variant of positive supercompilation studied in this paper, this is done in two situations; the first is when the expression is *trivial*.

**Definition 14.** An element of $\mathcal{L}$ is *trivial* if it has one of the following forms:

1. **let** $x_1{=}e_1, \ldots, x_m{=}e_m$ **in** $e$ where $m > 0$;
2. $c(e_1, \ldots, e_n)$;
3. $x$;

New leaf expressions, resulting from driving a node with a trivial expression, are strictly smaller than the former expression, in a certain order.

*Remark.* All non-trivial elements of $\mathcal{L}$ are, in fact, elements of $\mathcal{E}\backslash X$. Thus, the most specific generalization operation and the homeomorphic embedding relation which are defined on $\mathcal{E}_H(V)$—but not on $\mathcal{L}_H(V)$—apply to all non-trivial expressions. In particular, abstract$(t, \alpha, \beta)$ and split$(t, \beta)$ will be used only when $t(\alpha)$ and $t(\beta)$ are non-trivial.

The second situation in which we will unfold a node despite the fact that its expression has an ancestor's expression embedded, is when the the first expression gave rise to several children corresponding to different patterns (as $a(a(xs, ys), zs)$) whereas the

[7] This property holds regardless of how the sequence $e_0, e_1, \ldots$ was produced—see Theorem 41.

new expression does not give rise to several children according to different patterns (as in $a(u : a(us, ys), zs)$. In such cases, new information is available in the new expression, and it is desirable that this be taken into account by an unfolding step.

This idea is formalized by the following map $B$, which gives a *very* simple version of the *characteristic trees*, studied by Leuschel and Martens [23] and others.

**Definition 15.** Define $B : \mathcal{E} \to \mathbb{B}$ by

$$\begin{aligned} B(g(e_0, e_1, \ldots, e_m)) &= B(e_0) \\ B(f(e_1, \ldots, e_m)) &= 0 \\ B(c(e_1, \ldots, e_m)) &= 0 \\ B(x) &= 1 \end{aligned}$$

We write $e \trianglelefteq^* e'$ iff $e \trianglelefteq e'$ and $B(e) = B(e')$.

This gives us enough terminology to explain when a leaf node should be driven: if its label is trivial, or if its label is non-trivial and no ancestor has a non-trivial label which is embedded with respect to $\trianglelefteq^*$ in the leaf's label.

To formulate positive supercompilation we finally need to express when a node needs no further processing. The following will be used for that.

**Definition 16.** Let $t \in T_\infty(\mathcal{L})$. A $\beta \in \text{leaf}(t)$ is ***processed*** if one of the following conditions are satisfied:

1. $t(\beta) = c()$ for some $c \in C$;
2. $t(\beta) = x$ for some $x \in X$;
3. there is an $\alpha \in \text{anc}(t, \beta)\backslash\{\beta\}$ such that $t(\alpha)$ is non-trivial and a renaming of $t(\beta)$.

Also, $t$ is *closed* if all leafs in $t$ are processed.

Positive supercompilation $M_{ps} : T(\mathcal{L}) \to T(\mathcal{L})$ can then be defined as follows.[8]

**Definition 17.** Given $t \in T(\mathcal{L})$, if $t$ is closed $M_{ps}(t) = t$. Otherwise, let $\beta \in \text{leaf}(t)$ be an unprocessed node and proceed as follows.

```
if t(β) is trivial,
or t(β) is non-trivial and ∀α∈anc(t,β)\{β} : t(α) non-trivial ⇒ t(α) ⋬* t(β)
   then M_ps(t) = drive(t,β)
else begin
     let α ∈ anc(t,β), t(α), t(β) be non-trivial, and t(α) ⊴* t(β).
     if t(α) ≤ t(β)
         then M_ps(t) = abstract(t,β,α)
     else if t(α) ↮ t(β)
         then M_ps(t) = split(t,β)
     else M_ps(t) = abstract(t,α,β).
end
```

*Example 9.* The algorithm computes exactly the sequences of trees in Examples 1–2.

[8] A number of choices are left open in the algorithm, e.g., how one chooses among the unprocessed leaf nodes. Such details are beyond the scope of the present paper.

*Remark.* The algorithm calls abstract and split only in cases where these operations are well-defined.

The above algorithm is not the simplest conceivable version of positive supercompilation; indeed, from the point of view of termination it is somewhat involved. In Section 7 we prove that it terminates.

## 5 The Metric Space of Trees

As suggested by the examples in Section 2, termination of an online program transformer amounts to a certain form of convergence of sequences of trees. We now review some fundamental definitions and properties from the theory of metric spaces, which is a general framework for the study of convergence—see, e.g., [32]. Metric spaces have many applications in computer science—see e.g., [25, 34].

Having introduced metric spaces, we then show that the set of trees over some set can be viewed as a metric space. Early papers addressing this idea include [2, 3, 6, 7, 8, 9, 12, 27]. More recent references appear in [25, 34]. Lloyd [24] uses the metric space of trees to present complete Herbrand interpretations for non-terminating logic programs.

**Definition 18.** Let $X$ be a set and $d : X \times X \to \mathbb{R}_+$ a map[9] with, for all $x, y, z \in X$:

1. $d(x,y) = d(y,x)$;
2. $d(x,y) = 0$ iff $x = y$;
3. $d(x,y) + d(y,z) \geq d(x,z)$.

Then $d$ is a *metric* on $X$, and $(X, d)$ is a *metric space*.

*Example 10.*

1. The function $d(x,y) = |x - y|$ is a metric on $\mathbb{R}$.
2. For a set $X$, the map $d : X \times X \to \mathbb{R}_+$,

$$d_X(x,y) = \begin{cases} 0 \text{ if } x = y \\ 1 \text{ if } x \neq y \end{cases}$$

   is a metric on $X$, called the *discrete metric* on $X$.

**Definition 19.** Let $(X, d)$ be a metric space.

1. A sequence $x_0, x_1, \ldots \in X$ *stabilizes to* $x \in X$ if there exists an $N$ such that, for all $n \geq N$, $d(x_n, x) = 0$.
2. A sequence $x_0, x_1, \ldots \in X$ is *convergent* with *limit* $x \in X$ if, for all $\varepsilon > 0$, there exists an $N$ such that, for all $n \geq N$, $d(x_n, x) \leq \varepsilon$.
3. A sequence $x_0, x_1, \ldots \in X$ is a *Cauchy sequence* if, for all $\varepsilon > 0$, there exists an $N$ such that, for all $m, n \geq N$, $d(x_n, x_m) \leq \varepsilon$.

*Remark.* Let $(X, d)$ be a metric space.

[9] $\mathbb{R}_+ = \{r \in \mathbb{R} \mid r \geq 0\}$.

1. A stabilizing sequence is convergent, and a convergent sequence is a Cauchy sequence. None of the converse implications hold in general.
2. Any sequence has at most one limit.

**Definition 20.** Let $(X, d)$ be a metric space. If every Cauchy sequence in $(X, d)$ is convergent then $(X, d)$ is *complete*.

**Definition 21.** Let $(X, d), (Y, d')$ be metric spaces. A map $f : X \to Y$ is *continuous at*[10] $x \in X$ if, for every sequence $x_0, x_1, \ldots \in X$ that converges to $x$, $f(x_0), f(x_1), \ldots \in Y$ converges to $f(x)$. Also, $f : X \to Y$ is *continuous* if $f$ is continuous at every $x \in X$.

*Example 11.* Let $(X, d)$ be a metric space. Let $d_{\mathbb{B}}$ be the discrete metric on $\mathbb{B} = \{0, 1\}$. It is natural to view a predicate on $X$ as a function $p : X \to \mathbb{B}$, and say that $p(x)$ is true and false if $p(x) = 1$ and $p(x) = 0$, respectively.

Then $p$ is continuous iff for every sequence $x_0, x_1, \ldots$ that converges to $x$, the sequence $p(x_0), p(x_1), \ldots$ converges to $p(x)$.

*Remark.* Let $(X, d_X)$, $(Y, d_Y)$, and $(Z, d_Z)$ be metric spaces. If $f : X \to Y$ and $g : Y \to Z$ are both continuous, then so is $g \circ f : X \to Z$.

In the rest of this section $E$ is some set. What is the distance between $t, t' \in T_\infty(E)$? It is natural to require that trees which have large coinciding initial subtrees are close.

**Definition 22.** Define $d : T_\infty(E) \times T_\infty(E) \to \mathbb{R}_+$ by:

$$d(t, t') = \begin{cases} 0 & \text{if } t = t' \\ 2^{-\min\{\ell \mid t[\ell] \neq t'[\ell]\}} & \text{otherwise} \end{cases}$$

It is a routine exercise to verify that $(T_\infty(E), d)$ is indeed a metric space, which we call the *metric space of trees* (over $E$).

*Remark.*

1. A sequence $t_0, t_1, \ldots \in T_\infty(E)$ stabilizes to $t$ iff there exists an $N$ such that, for all $n \geq N$, $t_n = t$.
2. A sequence $t_0, t_1, \ldots \in T_\infty(E)$ converges to $t$ iff for all $\ell$, there exists an $N$ such that, for all $n \geq N$, $t_n[\ell] = t[\ell]$.
3. A sequence $t_0, t_1, \ldots \in T_\infty(E)$ is a Cauchy sequence iff for all $\ell$, there exists an $N$ such that, for all $n \geq N$, $t_n[\ell] = t_{n+1}[\ell]$.

The next result was first proved by Bloom, Elgot and Wright [7], and independently noted by Mycielski and Taylor [27] and Arnold and Nivat [3, 2].

**Proposition 23.** *The metric space $(T_\infty(E), d)$ is complete.*

The following connection between stability, convergence, and predicates does not hold in arbitrary metric spaces.

**Lemma 24.** A predicate $p$ on $T_\infty(E)$ is continuous iff for every convergent sequence $t_0, t_1, \ldots \in T_\infty(E)$ with *infinite* limit $t$, the sequence $p(t_0), p(t_1), \ldots$ stabilizes to $p(t)$.

[10] This is not the usual definition of continuity, but it is well-known that this definition is equivalent to the usual one.

## 6 Termination of Transformers

We now give a condition ensuring termination of an abstract program transformer.

The idea in ensuring termination of an apt is that it maintains some invariant. For instance, a transformer might never introduce a node whose label is larger, in some order, than the label on the parent node. In cases where an unfolding step would render the invariant false, some kind of generalization is performed.

**Definition 25.** Let $M : T(E) \to T(E)$ be an apt on $E$ and $p : T_\infty(E) \to \mathbb{B}$ be a predicate. $M$ *maintains* $p$ if, for every singleton $t \in T(E)$ and $i \in \mathbb{N}$, $p(M^i(t)) = 1$.

**Definition 26.** A predicate $p : T_\infty(E) \to \mathbb{B}$ is *finitary* if $p(t) = 0$ for all infinite $t \in T_\infty(E)$.

**Definition 27.** An apt $M$ on $E$ is *Cauchy* if, for every singleton $t \in T_\infty(E)$, the sequence $t, M(t), M^2(t), \ldots$ is a Cauchy sequence.

The following theorem gives a sufficient condition for a program transformer to terminate.

**Theorem 28.** *Let apt* $M : T(E) \to T(E)$ *maintain predicate* $p : T_\infty(E) \to \mathbb{B}$. *If*

*1. M is Cauchy, and*
*2. p is finitary and continuous,*

*then M terminates.*

Informally, the condition that $M$ be Cauchy guarantees that *only finitely many generalization steps* will happen at a given node, and the condition that $p$ be finitary and continuous guarantees that *only finitely many unfolding steps* will be used to expand the transformation tree. The first condition can be satisfied by adopting appropriate unfolding and generalization operations, and the second condition can be satisfied by adopting an appropriate criterion for deciding when to generalize.

Next we consider specific techniques for ensuring that an apt is Cauchy and that a predicate is finitary and continuous. We begin with the former.

**Definition 29.** Let $S$ be a set with a relation $\leq$. Then $(S, \leq)$ is a *quasi-order* if $\leq$ is reflexive and transitive. We write $s < s'$ if $s \leq s'$ and $s' \not\leq s$.

**Definition 30.** Let $(S, \leq)$ be a quasi-order.

1. $(S, \leq)$ is *well-founded* if there is no infinite sequence $s_0, s_1, \ldots \in S$ with $s_0 > s_1 > \ldots$
2. $(S, \leq)$ is a *well-quasi-order* if, for every infinite sequence $s_0, s_1, \ldots \in S$, there are $i < j$ with $s_i \leq s_j$.

An apt is Cauchy if it always either adds some new children to a leaf node (unfolds), or replaces a subtree by a new tree whose root label is strictly smaller than the label of the root of the former subtree (generalizes). This is how most online transformers work.

**Proposition 31.** *Let* $(E, \leq)$ *be a well-founded quasi-order and* $M : T(E) \to T(E)$ *an apt such that, for all* $t$, $M(t) = t\{\gamma := t'\}$ *for some* $\gamma, t'$ *where*

1. $\gamma \in \text{leaf}(t)$ *and* $t(\gamma) = t'(\epsilon)$ *(unfold); or*
2. $t(\gamma) > t'(\epsilon)$ *(generalize).*

*Then* $M$ *is Cauchy.*

Next we consider ways of ensuring that a predicate is (finitary and) continuous.

A family $S$ of sets is of *finite character* if each set is a member if and only if all its finite subsets are members. Adapted to families of *trees*, the definition reads:

**Definition 32.** A family $T \subseteq T_\infty(E)$ of trees is of *finite character* iff, for all $t \in T_\infty(E)$:

$$t \in T \Leftrightarrow \forall \ell \in \mathbb{N} : t[\ell] \in T$$

The following shows that a finitary predicate $p : T_\infty(E) \to \mathbb{B}$ is continuous, if the family $\{t \mid p(t) = 1\}$ is of finite character.

**Proposition 33.** *Suppose* $p : T_\infty(E) \to \mathbb{B}$ *is finitary and, for all* $t \in T_\infty(E)$,

$$p(t) = 1 \Leftrightarrow \forall \ell \in \mathbb{N} : p(t[\ell]) = 1$$

*Then* $p$ *is continuous.*

We end the section by reviewing instances of Proposition 33.

The following shows that a Cauchy transformer terminates if it never introduces a node whose label is larger than an ancestor's label with respect to some well-quasi-order. This idea is used in a number of transformers [1, 16, 23, 35, 41]

**Proposition 34.** *Let* $(E, \leq)$ *be a well-quasi-order. Then* $p : T_\infty(E) \to \mathbb{B}$,

$$p(t) = \begin{cases} 0 \text{ if } \exists \alpha, \alpha i \beta \in \text{dom}(t) : t(\alpha) \leq t(\alpha i \beta) \\ 1 \text{ otherwise} \end{cases}$$

*is finitary and continuous.*

The following shows that a Cauchy transformer terminates if it never introduces a node whose label is not smaller than its *immediate* ancestor's label with respect to some well-founded quasi-order.

**Proposition 35.** *Let* $(E, \leq)$ *be a well-founded quasi-order. Then* $p : T_\infty(E) \to \mathbb{B}$,

$$p(t) = \begin{cases} 0 \text{ if } \exists \alpha, \alpha i \in \text{dom}(t) : t(\alpha) \not> t(\alpha i) \\ 1 \text{ otherwise} \end{cases}$$

*is finitary and continuous.*

The following generalization of the preceding proposition is used in some techniques for ensuring global termination of partial deduction [26].

**Proposition 36.** *Let $\{E_1, \ldots, E_n\}$ be a partition*[11] *of $E$ and $\leq_1, \ldots, \leq_n$ be well-founded quasi-orders on $E_1, \ldots, E_n$, respectively. Then $p: T_\infty(E) \to \mathbb{B}$,*

$$p(t) = \begin{cases} 0 \text{ if } \exists \alpha, \alpha i \beta \in \text{dom}(t), j \in \{1, \ldots, n\} : t(\alpha), t(\alpha i \beta) \in E_j \;\&\; t(\alpha) \not>_j t(\alpha i \beta) \\ 1 \text{ otherwise} \end{cases}$$

*is finitary and continuous.*

The following shows that one can combine well-quasi-orders and well-founded quasi-orders in a partition.

**Proposition 37.** *Let $\{E_1, E_2\}$ be a partition of $E$ and let $\leq_1$ be a well-quasi-order on $E_1$ and $\leq_2$ a well-founded quasi-order on $E_2$. Then $p: T_\infty(E) \to \mathbb{B}$,*

$$p(t) = \begin{cases} 0 \text{ if } \exists \alpha, \alpha i \beta \in \text{dom}(t) : t(\alpha), t(\alpha i \beta) \in E_1 \;\&\; t(\alpha) \leq_1 t(\alpha i \beta) \\ 0 \text{ if } \exists \alpha, \alpha i \in \text{dom}(t) : t(\alpha), t(\alpha i) \in E_2 \;\&\; t(\alpha) \not>_2 t(\alpha i) \\ 1 \text{ otherwise} \end{cases}$$

*is finitary and continuous.*

The following shows that it suffices to apply a finitary and continuous predicate to the *interior* part of a tree.

**Definition 38.** For $t \in T_\infty(E)$, define the *interior* $t^0 \in T_\infty(E)$ of $t$ by:

$$\begin{aligned} \text{dom}(t^0) &= (\text{dom}(t) \setminus \text{leaf}(t)) \cup \{\epsilon\} \\ t^0(\gamma) &= t(\gamma) \quad \text{for all } \gamma \in \text{dom}(t^0) \end{aligned}$$

**Proposition 39.** *Let $p : T_\infty(E) \to \mathbb{B}$ be finitary and continuous. Then also the map $q : T_\infty(E) \to \mathbb{B}$ defined by*

$$q(t) = p(t^0)$$

*is finitary and continuous.*

It is not hard to see that one can replace in the proposition $\bullet^0$ by any continuous map which maps infinite trees to infinite trees.

# 7 Application: Termination of Positive Supercompilation

In this section we prove that positive supercompilation $M_{ps}$ terminates. We do so by proving that $M_{ps}$ is Cauchy and that $M_{ps}$ maintains a finitary, continuous predicate.

We first prove that $M_{ps}$ is Cauchy; the idea is to use Proposition 31. Indeed, $M_{ps}$ always either unfolds by a driving step or replaces a subtree by a new leaf whose label is strictly smaller than the expression in the root of the former subtree. In which order?

**Proposition 40.** *$M_{ps}$ is Cauchy.*

[11] That is, $E_1, \ldots E_n$ are sets with $\cup_{i=1}^n E_i = E$ and $i \neq j \Rightarrow E_i \cap E_j = \emptyset$.

*Proof.* Define the relation $\succ$ on $\mathcal{L}$ by:

$$\textbf{let } x'_1{=}e'_1,\ldots,x'_m{=}e'_m \textbf{ in } e \succ \textbf{let } x_1{=}e_1,\ldots,x_n{=}e_n \textbf{ in } e \;\Leftrightarrow\; m=0 \;\&\; n\geq 0$$

It is a routine exercise to verify that $\succeq$ is a well-founded quasi-order.

We now show that for any $t \in T(\mathcal{L})$

$$M_{ps}(t) = t\{\gamma{:=}t'\}$$

where, for some $\gamma \in \text{dom}(t)$ and $t' \in T_\infty(\mathcal{L})$, either $\gamma \in \text{leaf}(t)$ and $t(\gamma) = t'(\epsilon)$, or $t(\gamma) \succ t'(\epsilon)$. We proceed by case analysis of the operation performed by $M_{ps}$.

1. $M_{ps}(t) = \text{drive}(t,\gamma) = t\{\gamma{:=}t'\}$, where $\gamma \in \text{leaf}(t)$ and, for certain expressions $e_1,\ldots,e_n$, $t' = t(\gamma) \rightarrow e_1,\ldots,e_n$. Then
$$t(\gamma) = t'(\epsilon)$$
2. $M_{ps}(t) = \text{abstract}(t,\gamma,\alpha) = t\{\gamma{:=}\textbf{let } x_1{=}e_1,\ldots,x_n{=}e_n \textbf{ in } e\rightarrow\}$, where $\alpha \in \text{anc}(t,\gamma)$, $t(\alpha) \neq t(\gamma)$, $t(\alpha), t(\gamma) \in \mathcal{E}$ are both non-trivial, $t(\alpha) \leq\!\cdot\; t(\gamma)$, $e = t(\alpha) \sqcap t(\gamma)$, and $t(\gamma) = e\{x_1{:=}e_1,\ldots,x_n{:=}e_n\}$. Then $e = t(\alpha)$ and $t(\gamma) = t(\alpha)\{x_1{:=}e_1,\ldots,x_n{:=}e_n\}$, but $t(\gamma) \neq t(\alpha)$, so $n > 0$. Thus :
$$t(\gamma) \succ \textbf{let } x_1{=}e_1,\ldots,x_n{=}e_n \textbf{ in } e = t'(\epsilon)$$
3. $M_{ps}(t) = \text{abstract}(t,\gamma,\beta) = t\{\gamma{:=}\textbf{let } x_1{=}e_1,\ldots,x_n{=}e_n \textbf{ in } e\rightarrow\}$, where $\gamma \in \text{anc}(t,\beta)$, $t(\beta), t(\gamma)$ are both non-trivial, $t(\gamma) \not\leq\!\cdot\; t(\beta)$, $e = t(\gamma) \sqcap t(\beta)$, and where we also have $t(\gamma) = e\{x_1{:=}e_1,\ldots,x_n{:=}e_n\}$. Then $t(\gamma) \neq e$, but $t(\gamma) = e\{x_1{:=}e_1,\ldots,x_n{:=}e_n\}$, so $n > 0$. Thus:
$$t(\gamma) \succ \textbf{let } x_1{=}e_1,\ldots,x_n{=}e_n \textbf{ in } e = t'(\epsilon)$$
4. $M_{ps}(t) = \text{split}(t,\gamma) = t\{\gamma{:=}\textbf{let } x_1{=}e_1,\ldots,x_n{=}e_n \textbf{ in } h(x_1,\ldots,x_n)\rightarrow\}$ where, for some $\alpha \in \text{anc}(t,\gamma)$, $t(\alpha), t(\beta)$ are non-trivial, $t(\alpha) \trianglelefteq^* t(\gamma)$, $t(\alpha) \leftrightarrow t(\gamma)$, and also $t(\gamma) = h(e_1,\ldots,e_n)$, where $h \in C \cup F \cup G$.[12] Here $n > 0$: if $n = 0$, then $t(\gamma) = h()$, but then $t(\alpha) \not\leftrightarrow t(\beta)$. Thus,
$$t(\gamma) = h(e_1,\ldots,e_n) \succ \textbf{let } x_1{=}e_1,\ldots,x_n{=}e_n \textbf{ in } h(x_1,\ldots,x_n) = t'(\epsilon)$$

This concludes the proof. □

Next we prove that $M_{ps}$ maintains a finitary, continuous predicate.

The following result, known as *Kruskal's Tree Theorem,* is due to Higman [19] and Kruskal [22]. Its classical proof is due to Nash-Williams [28].

**Theorem 41.** *$(\mathcal{E}_H(V), \trianglelefteq)$ is a well-quasi-order, provided $H$ is finite.*

*Proof.* Collapse all variables to one 0-ary operator and use the proof in [14]. □

**Corollary 42.** *The relation $\trianglelefteq^*$ is a well-quasi order on $\mathcal{E}$.*

[12] Since $t(\gamma)$ is non-trivial, $t(\gamma)$ must have form $h(e_1,\ldots,e_n)$.

*Proof.* Given an infinite sequence $e_0, e_1, \ldots \in \mathcal{E}$ there must be an infinite subsequence $e_{i_0}, e_{i_1}, \ldots$ such that $B(e_{i_0}) = B(e_{i_1}) = \ldots$. By Theorem 41,[13] there are $k$ and $l$ such that $e_{i_k} \trianglelefteq e_{i_l}$ and then $e_{i_k} \trianglelefteq^* e_{i_l}$, as required. □

**Proposition 43.** ***$M_{ps}$ maintains a finitary, continuous predicate.***

*Proof.* Define $|\bullet| : \mathcal{E} \to \mathbb{N}$ by

$$\begin{aligned} |g(e_0, e_1, \ldots, e_m)| &= 1 + |e_0| + \ldots + |e_m| \\ |f(e_1, \ldots, e_m)| &= 1 + |e_1| + \ldots + |e_m| \\ |c(e_1, \ldots, e_m)| &= 1 + |e_1| + \ldots + |e_m| \\ |x| &= 1 \end{aligned}$$

Define $\mathrm{l} : \mathcal{L} \to \mathcal{E}$ by:

$$\mathrm{l}(\mathbf{let}\ x_1{=}e_1, \ldots, x_n{=}e_n\ \mathbf{in}\ e) = e\{x_1 := e_1, \ldots, x_n := e_n\}$$

for $n \geq 0$.

Finally, define $\sqsupseteq$ on $\mathcal{L}$ by:

$$\ell \sqsupseteq \ell' \quad \Leftrightarrow \quad |\mathrm{l}(\ell)| > |\mathrm{l}(\ell')| \text{ or, } |\mathrm{l}(\ell)| = |\mathrm{l}(\ell')| \;\&\; \mathrm{l}(\ell) \geq \mathrm{l}(\ell')$$

It is a routine exercise to verify that $\sqsubseteq$ is a well-founded quasi-order using the fact that $\leq$ is well-founded.

Consider the predicate $q : T_\infty(\ell) \to \mathbb{B}$ defined by

$$q(t) = p(t^0)$$

where $p : T_\infty(\ell) \to \mathbb{B}$ is defined by:

$$p(t) = \begin{cases} 0 \text{ if } \exists \alpha, \alpha i \beta \in \mathrm{dom}(t) : t(\alpha), t(\alpha i \beta) \text{ are non-trivial } \& \; t(\alpha) \trianglelefteq^* t(\alpha i \beta) \\ 0 \text{ if } \exists \alpha, \alpha i \in \mathrm{dom}(t) : t(\alpha), t(\alpha i) \text{ are trivial } \& \; t(\alpha) \not\sqsupset t(\alpha i) \\ 1 \text{ otherwise} \end{cases}$$

The sets of non-trivial and trivial expressions constitute a partition of $\mathcal{L}$. Also, $\trianglelefteq^*$ is a well-quasi-order on the set of non-trivial expressions (in fact, on all of $\mathcal{E}$) and $\sqsubseteq$ is a well-founded quasi-order on the set of trivial expressions (in fact, on all of $\mathcal{L}$). It follows by Proposition 37 that $p$ is finitary and continuous, and then by Proposition 39 that $q$ is also finitary and continuous.

It remains to show that $M_{ps}$ maintains $q$, i.e., that $q(M_{ps}^{*}(t_0)) = 1$ for any singleton $t_0 \in T_\infty(\mathcal{L})$.

Given any $t \in T_\infty(\mathcal{L})$ and $\beta \in \mathrm{dom}(t)$, we say that $\beta$ is *good* in $t$ if the following conditions both hold:

(i) $t(\beta)$ non-trivial $\& \; \beta \notin \mathrm{leaf}(t) \Rightarrow \forall \alpha \in \mathrm{anc}(t, \beta) \setminus \{\beta\} : t(\alpha)$ non-trivial $\Rightarrow t(\alpha) \not\trianglelefteq^* t(\beta)$;
(ii) $\beta = \alpha i \;\&\; t(\alpha)$ trivial $\Rightarrow t(\alpha) \sqsupset t(\beta)$.

[13] Recall that $\mathcal{E} = \mathcal{E}_{F \cup G \cup C}$ where $F, G, C$ are finite.

We say that $t$ is *good* if all $\beta \in \text{dom}(t)$ are good in $t$.

It is easy to see that $q(t) = 1$ if $t$ is good (the converse does not hold). It therefore suffices to show for any singleton $t_0 \in T_\infty(\mathcal{L})$ that $M^i_{ps}(t_0)$ is good for all $i$. We proceed by induction on $i$.

For $i = 0$, (i)-(ii) are both vacuously satisfied since $t_0$ consists of a single leaf.

For $i > 0$, we split into cases according to the operation performed by $M_{ps}$ on $M^{i-1}_{ps}(t_0)$. Before considering these cases, note that by the definition of goodness, if $t \in T_\infty(\ell)$ is good, $\gamma \in \text{dom}(t)$, and $t' \in T_\infty(\mathcal{L})$, then $t\{\gamma := t'\}$ is good too, provided $\gamma\delta$ is good in $t\{\gamma := t'\}$ for all $\delta \in \text{dom}(t')$.

For brevity, let $t = M^{i-1}_{ps}(t_0)$.

1. $M_{ps}(t) = \text{drive}(t,\gamma) = t\{\gamma{:=}t'\}$, where $\gamma \in \text{leaf}(t)$, $t' = t(\gamma) \to e_1, \ldots, e_n$, and $\{e_1, \ldots, e_n\} = \{e \mid t(\gamma) \Rightarrow e\}$.
   We must show that $\gamma, \gamma 1, \ldots, \gamma n$ are good in $M_{ps}(t)$.
   To see that $\gamma$ is good in $M_{ps}(t)$, note that if $t(\gamma)$ is non-trivial, then the algorithm ensures that condition (i) is satisfied. Condition (ii) follows from the induction hypothesis.
   To see that $\gamma i$ is good in $M_{ps}(t)$, note that condition (i) is vacuously satisfied. Moreover, when $\ell \Rightarrow e$ and $\ell$ is trivial, $\ell \sqsupset e$, so condition (ii) holds as well.
2. $M_{ps}(t) = \text{abstract}(t,\gamma,\alpha) = t\{\gamma{:=}\textbf{let } x_1{=}e_1, \ldots, x_n{=}e_n \textbf{ in } e \to\}$, where $\alpha \in \text{anc}(t,\gamma)$, $t(\alpha) \neq t(\gamma)$, $t(\alpha), t(\gamma) \in \mathcal{E}$ are both non-trivial, $t(\alpha) \trianglelefteq t(\gamma)$, $e = t(\alpha) \sqcap t(\gamma)$, and $t(\gamma) = e\{x_1{:=}e_1, \ldots, x_n{:=}e_n\}$.
   We must show that $\gamma$ is good in $M_{ps}(t)$. Condition (i) holds vacuously, and (ii) follows from the induction hypothesis and $\text{l}(t(\gamma)) = \text{l}(\textbf{let } x_1{=}e_1, \ldots, x_n{=}e_n \textbf{ in } e)$.

The remaining two cases are similar to the preceding case. □

Martens and Gallagher show, essentially, that an abstract program transformer terminates if it maintains a predicate of the form in Proposition 36 and always either adds children to a node or replaces a subtree with root label $e$ by a new node whose label $e'$ is in the same partition $E_j$ as $e$ and $e >_j e'$. In our setting this result follows from Propositions 31 and 36 (by Theorem 28).

Martens and Gallagher then go on to show that a certain generic partial deduction algorithm always terminates; this result follows from the above more general result. For brevity we omit the details.

*Acknowledgments.* This work grew out of joint work with Robert Glück. I am indebted to Nils Andersen and Klaus Grue for discussions about metric spaces. Thanks to Maria Alpuente, Nils Andersen, Robert Glück, Laura Lafave, Michael Leuschel, Bern Martens, and Jens Peter Secher for comments to an early version of this paper.

## References

1. M. Alpuente, M. Falaschi, and G. Vidal. Narrowing-driven partial evaluation of functional logic programs. In H.R. Nielson, editor, *European Symposium on Programming*, volume 1058 of *Lecture Notes in Computer Science*, pages 46–61. Springer-Verlag, 1996.
2. A. Arnold and M. Nivat. Metric interpretations of infinite trees and semantics of non deterministic recursive programs. *Theoretical Computer Science*, 11:181–205, 1980.

3. A. Arnold and M. Nivat. The metric space of infinite trees. Algebraic and topological properties. *Fundamenta Informaticae*, III(4):445–476, 1980.
4. R. Bird. Tabulation techniques for recursive programs. *ACM Computing Surveys*, 12(4):403–417, 1980.
5. D. Bjørner, A.P. Ershov, and N.D. Jones, editors. *Partial Evaluation and Mixed Computation*. North-Holland, Amsterdam, 1988.
6. S.L. Bloom. All solutions of a system of recursion equations in infinite trees and other contraction theories. *Journal of Computer and System Sciences*, 27:225–255, 1983.
7. S.L. Bloom, C.C. Elgot, and J.B Wright. Vector iteration in pointed iterative theories. *SIAM Journal of Computing*, 9(3):525–540, 1980.
8. S.L. Bloom and D. Patterson. Easy solutions are hard to find. In *Colloquium on Trees in Algebra and Programming*, volume 112 of *Lecture Notes in Computer Science*, pages 135–146. Springer-Verlag, 1981.
9. S.L. Bloom and R. Tindell. Compatible orderings on the metric theory of trees. *SIAM Journal of Computing*, 9(4):683–691, 1980.
10. M. Bruynooghe, D. De Schreye, and B. Krekels. Compiling control. *Journal of Logic programming*, 6:135–162, 1989.
11. R.M. Burstall and J. Darlington. A transformation system for developing recursive programs. *Journal of the Association for Computing Machines*, 24(1):44–67, 1977.
12. B. Courcelle. Fundamental properties of infinite trees. *Theoretical Computer Science*, 25:95–169, 1983.
13. O. Danvy, R. Glück, and P. Thiemann, editors. *Partial Evaluation*, volume 1110 of *Lecture Notes in Computer Science*. Springer-Verlag, 1996.
14. N. Dershowitz. Termination of rewriting. *Journal of Symbolic Computation*, 3, 1987.
15. Y. Futamura and K. Nogi. Generalized partial computation. In Bjørner et al. [5], pages 133–151.
16. R. Glück, J. Jørgensen, B. Martens, and M.H. Sørensen. Controlling conjunctive partial deduction. In H. Kuchen and D.S. Swierstra, editors, *Programming Languages: Implementations, Logics and Programs*, volume 1140 of *Lecture Notes in Computer Science*, pages 137–151. Springer-Verlag, 1996.
17. R. Glück and M.H. Sørensen. Partial deduction and driving are equivalent. In M. Hermenegildo and J. Penjam, editors, *Programming Languages: Implementations, Logics and Programs*, volume 844 of *Lecture Notes in Computer Science*, pages 165–181. Springer-Verlag, 1994.
18. R. Glück and M.H. Sørensen. A roadmap to metacomputation by supercompilation. In Danvy et al. [13], pages 137–160.
19. G. Higman. Ordering by divisibility in abstract algebras. *Proceedings of the London Mathematical Society*, (3) 2:326–336, 1952.
20. N.D. Jones. The essence of program transformation by partial evaluation and driving. In N.D. Jones, M. Hagiya, and M. Sato, editors, *Logic, Language, and Computation*, volume 792 of *Lecture Notes in Computer Science*, pages 206–224. Springer-Verlag, 1994. Festschrift in honor of S.Takasu.
21. N.D. Jones, C.K. Gomard, and P. Sestoft. *Partial Evaluation and Automatic Program Generation*. Prentice-Hall, 1993.
22. J.B. Kruskal. Well-quasi-ordering, the tree theorem, and Vazsonyi's conjecture. *Transactions of the American Mathematical Society*, 95:210–225, 1960.
23. M. Leuschel and B. Martens. Global control for partial deduction through characteristic atoms and global trees. In Danvy et al. [13], pages 263–283.
24. J.W. Lloyd. *Foundations of Logic Programming*. Springer-Verlag, 1984.

25. M. Main, A. Melton, M. Mislove, and D. Schmidt, editors. *Mathematical Foundations of Programming Language Semantics*, volume 298 of *Lecture Notes in Computer Science*. Springer-Verlag, 1987.
26. B. Martens and J. Gallagher. Ensuring global termination of partial deduction while allowing flexible polyvariance. In L. Sterling, editor, *International Conference on Logic Programming*, pages 597–613. MIT Press, 1995.
27. J. Mycielski and W. Taylor. A compactification of the algebra of terms. *Algebra Universalis*, 6:159–163, 1976.
28. C.St.J.A. Nash-Williams. On well-quasi-ordering finite trees. *Proceedings of the Cambridge Mathematical Society*, 59:833–835, 1963.
29. A. Pettorossi. A powerful strategy for deriving efficient programs by transformation. In *ACM Conference on Lisp and Functional Programming*, pages 273–281. ACM Press, 1984.
30. A. Pettorossi and M. Proietti. A comparative revisitation of some program transformation techniques. In Danvy et al. [13], pages 355–385.
31. M. Proietti and A. Pettorossi. The loop absorption and the generalization strategies for the development of logic programs and partial deduction. *Journal of Logic programming*, 16:123–161, 1993.
32. W. Rudin. *Principles of Mathematical Analysis*. Mathematics Series. McGraw-Hill, third edition, 1976.
33. E. Ruf and D. Weise. On the specialization of online program specializers. *Journal of Functional Programming*, 3(3):251–281, 1993.
34. M.B. Smyth. Topology. In S. Abramsky, D.M. Gabbay, and T.S.E. Maibaum, editors, *Handbook of Logic in Computer Science*, volume II, pages 641–761. Oxford University Press, 1992.
35. M.H. Sørensen and R. Glück. An algorithm of generalization in positive supercompilation. In J.W. Lloyd, editor, *Logic Programming: Proceedings of the 1995 International Symposium*, pages 465–479. MIT Press, 1995.
36. M.H. Sørensen, R. Glück, and N.D. Jones. Towards unifying deforestation, supercompilation, partial evaluation, and generalized partial computation. In D. Sannella, editor, *European Symposium on Programming*, volume 788 of *Lecture Notes in Computer Science*, pages 485–500. Springer-Verlag, 1994.
37. M.H. Sørensen, R. Glück, and N.D. Jones. A positive supercompiler. *Journal of Functional Programming*, 6(6):811–838, 1996.
38. H. Tamaki and T. Sato. Unfold/fold transformation of logic programs. In S.-Å. Tärnlund, editor, *International Conference on Logic Programming*, pages 127–138. Uppsala University, 1984.
39. V.F. Turchin. The concept of a supercompiler. *ACM Transactions on Programming Languages and Systems*, 8(3):292–325, 1986.
40. V.F. Turchin. The algorithm of generalization in the supercompiler. In Bjørner et al. [5], pages 531–549.
41. V.F. Turchin. On generalization of lists and strings in supercompilation. Technical Report CSc. TR 96-002, City College of the City University of New York, 1996.
42. P.L. Wadler. Deforestation: Transforming programs to eliminate intermediate trees. *Theoretical Computer Science*, 73:231–248, 1990.
43. D. Weise, R. Conybeare, E. Ruf, and S. Seligman. Automatic online partial evaluation. In J. Hughes, editor, *Conference on Functional Programming and Computer Architecture*, volume 523 of *Lecture Notes in Computer Science*, pages 165–191. Springer-Verlag, 1991.

# Realizability of Monotone Coinductive Definitions and Its Application to Program Synthesis

Makoto Tatsuta

Department of Mathematics, Kyoto University, Kyoto 606-8502, JAPAN
e-mail: tatsuta@kusm.kyoto-u.ac.jp

**Abstract.** Two realizability interpretations of monotone coinductive definitions are studied. One interpretation is defined so that a realizer of a coinductively defined predicate is the same as that of its expansion. For this interpretation, the paper proves that full monotone coinductive definitions are not sound and restricted monotone coinductive definitions are sound. The other interpreration is based on second order logic and can interpret least-upper-bound coinductive definitions, which is generalization of monotone coinductive definitions. By using these interprerations, the paper shows that a program which treats coinductively defined infinite data structures such as streams can be synthesized from a constructive proof of its specification.

## 1 Introduction

Coinductive definitions have been studied widely [17, 14, 13, 3, 15, 12, 11, 8]. Coinductive definitions formalize the greatest fixed point $X$ satisfying $X \leftrightarrow A(X)$ for a formula $A(X)$. Coinductive definitions are important since they can formalize naturally many important recursive infinite data structures such as streams, infinite lists and infinite trees. Moreover properties of these data structures such as extensional equality of streams can be also formalized by coinductive definitions. Specifications and properties of programs are formally represented in a natural way in a logical system having coinductive definitions. Coinductive definitions formalize notions semantically given by the greatest fixed point. In particular, they can formalize bisimulation of processes [9].

Program synthesis using constructive logic or type theories has been studied widely [7, 2, 5, 10, 11, 16, 17, 20, 13, 14]. The method of program synthesis using constructive logic is called constructive programming. By constructive programming, a program $f$ and the proof of its verification $\forall x(A(x) \rightarrow B(x, fx))$ are automatically produced from a constructive proof of the specification $\forall x(A(x) \rightarrow \exists y B(x, y))$ of the program, where $x$ means an input, $y$ means an output, $A(x)$ means an input condition and $B(x, y)$ means an input-output relation. By this method, we write a constructive proof to get a program instead of writing a program directly. The method integrates two separated steps of writing a program and verifying a program into a single step of writing a constructive proof. The method proposes a new programming paradigm based on the notion of proofs-as-programs.

The notion of q-realizability is the main tool for constructive programming [5, 16, 17, 20, 6]. By using q-realizability, a program and its verification proof are automatically produced from a constructive proof in the following way: From the constructive proof of $\forall x(A(x) \to \exists y B(x,y))$ and the soundness theorem of q-realizability, a realizer $e$ is produced such that $(e \;\; \mathbf{q} \;\; \forall x(A(x) \to \exists y B(x,y)))$. According to the definition of q-realizability, the realizer $e$ produces a program $f$ and a proof of its verification $\forall x(A(x) \to B(x, fx))$.

Hence realizability of coinductive definitions is important. By using the logical system having coinductive definitions and realizability, specification of programs with coinductively defined infinite data structures can be naturally represented and such programs can be produced from constructive proofs by using realizability.

Until now, realizability of coinductive definitions was studied only for the restricted case of positive formulas [17]. Positive coinductive definitions formalize the greatest fixed point $X$ satisfying $X \leftrightarrow A(X)$ for a positive formula $A(X)$. [17] studies positive coinductive definitions, which require the condition that $A(X)$ is positive with respect to $X$. [14] also studies positive coinductive definitions in a type theoretical framework.

Monotone coinductive definitions are the way to define the greatest fixed point $X$ of $A(X)$ under the monotone condition that $A(X)$ is monotone with respect to $X$. Monotone coinductive definitions are worth studying at least for the following four reasons. (1) Coinductive definitions mean the greatest fixed points. Semantically the monotone condition is sufficient to get the greatest fixed point and in this sense the positive condition is too restrictive. (2) The monotone condition is useful for program modules since it is semantical, while the positive condition is not so useful since it is syntactical. It is explained in detail in Section 6. (3) A non-positive monotone formula can be transformed into a positive formula in many cases. But the transformation loses the expansion-preserving property of realizability since transformation of a formula may change a realizer of the formula. (4) For inductive definitions, realizability of monotone inductive definitions have been already studied [19] and improved the results for the positive inductive definitions given in [6]. Realizability of monotone coinductive definitions can also improve results for positive coinductive definitions.

In this paper, we study realizability of monotone coinductive definitions and its application to program synthesis. We study two kinds of realizability interpretations of monotone coinductive definitions. One interpretation is expansion-preserving, that is, a realizer of a coinductively defined predicate is the same as that of its expansion. The other interpretation is based on second order logic.

For the expansion-preserving realizability interpretation, we present untyped theories $\mathbf{TID}_{\nu 0}$ and $\mathbf{TID}_{\nu 1}$. $\mathbf{TID}_{\nu 1}$ has full monotone coinductive definitions, while $\mathbf{TID}_{\nu 0}$ has only restricted monotone coinductive definitions. We define a q-realizability interpretation for $\mathbf{TID}_{\nu 0}$ and $\mathbf{TID}_{\nu 1}$ which is expansion-preserving. This q-realizability interpretation is an extension of the realizability in [17]. We show that the realizability interpretation for $\mathbf{TID}_{\nu 0}$ in $\mathbf{TID}_{\nu 1}$ is sound and that the realizability interpretation for $\mathbf{TID}_{\nu 1}$ in $\mathbf{TID}_{\nu 1}$ is not sound. We explain that there is no expansion-preserving realizability interpretation of full monotone coinductive definitions. The soundness proof for $\mathbf{TID}_{\nu 0}$ entails and simplifies the soundness proof for the positive case in [17] as a special case.

For the realizability interpretation based on second order logic, we present an untyped theory $\mathbf{TID}_{\nu 2}$, which has least-upper-bound coinductive definitions. Least-upper-bound coinductive definitions cover monotone coinductive definitions and are more natural when we think the meaning given by their coding. $\mathbf{TID}_{\nu 2}$ includes $\mathbf{TID}_{\nu 1}$. We define a **q**-realizability interpretation for $\mathbf{TID}_{\nu 2}$ in a second order system $\mathbf{T_2}$, using the higher order coding and **q**-realizability for second order logic [4]. We prove its soundness.

We show these two realizability interpretation can be used for program synthesis. In particular, the program extraction theorem and the stream program extraction theorem are proved by using these interpretations.

In our words, [13] and [14] also studied an expansion-preserving realizability interpretation for positive inductive and coinductive definitions in a type theoretical framework. In their words, our reresults prove the followings: For $\nu X x A\langle t\rangle$ such that $A$ may not be positive with respect to $X$, (1) the condition $(X \to Y) \to (A \to A[Y/X])$ does not imply the conservation lemma, and (2) the condition $(X \subseteq Y) \to (A \subseteq A[Y/X])$ implies the conservation lemma where $(X \subseteq Y)$ denotes $\forall x(x \in X \to x \in Y)$. The condition for (2) corresponds to the condition (MONO-Q) in our theory.

In Section 2, we define the theories $\mathbf{TID}_{\nu 0}$ and $\mathbf{TID}_{\nu 1}$ and explain that coinductive definitions are useful for program specification. In Section 3, we discuss models of $\mathbf{TID}_{\nu 1}$ and prove its consistency. In Section 4, we present the q-realizability interpretation for $\mathbf{TID}_{\nu 0}$ and $\mathbf{TID}_{\nu 1}$. We prove the soundness theorem for $\mathbf{TID}_{\nu 0}$ and show that the interpretation for $\mathbf{TID}_{\nu 1}$ is not sound. In Section 5, we present the **q**-realizability interpretation of least-upper-bound coinductive definitions. In Section 6, we explain that a program with streams can be synthesized by using these results.

## 2 Theories $\mathbf{TID}_{\nu 0}$ and $\mathbf{TID}_{\nu 1}$

We present the theories $\mathbf{TID}_{\nu 0}$ and $\mathbf{TID}_{\nu 1}$ in this section. Both are theories with $\lambda$-calculus and coinductive definitions, and based on Beeson's elementary theory of operations and numbers [1]. $\mathbf{TID}_{\nu 0}$ and $\mathbf{TID}_{\nu 1}$ differ only in the rules of coinductive definitions. These systems correspond to Martin-Löf's Type Theory with coinductive types.

In the paper, we choose $\lambda$-calculus with pairing and natural numbers as the target programming language for simplicity. We suppose that the evaluation strategy of terms is lazy or call-by-name because coinductive definitions are useful to formalize infinite objects such as streams, which are non-terminating terms.

## 2.1 Language of $\mathbf{TID}_{\nu 0}$ and $\mathbf{TID}_{\nu 1}$

The language of $\mathbf{TID}_{\nu 0}$ and that of $\mathbf{TID}_{\nu 1}$ are the same. This is based on a first order language and extended for coinductive definitions of predicates.

The constants are: $\mathbf{p}$, $\mathbf{p}_0$, $\mathbf{p}_1$, $0$, $\mathbf{s}_\mathrm{N}$, $\mathbf{p}_\mathrm{N}$, $\mathbf{d}$.

We have natural numbers as primitives, which are given by 0, the successor function $\mathbf{s}_\mathrm{N}$ and the predecessor function $\mathbf{p}_\mathrm{N}$. We also have the pairing functions $\mathbf{p}$, $\mathbf{p}_0$ and $\mathbf{p}_1$ as built-in, which correspond to **cons**, **car** and **cdr** in LISP respectively. $\mathbf{d}$ is a combinator judging equality of numbers and corresponds to an if-then-else statement in a usual programming language.

We have only one function symbol **App** whose arity is 2: It means a functional application of terms.

Terms $t$ are defined by: $t ::= x|c|\mathbf{App}(t,t)|\lambda x.t$ where $x$ stands for a variable and $c$ stands for a constant.

For terms $s$, $t$, we abbreviate $\mathbf{App}(s,t)$ as $st$. For terms $s$, $t$, we also use abbreviations $(s,t) \equiv \mathbf{p}st$, $t_0 \equiv \mathbf{p}_0 t$, $t_1 \equiv \mathbf{p}_1 t$, $t_{i_1 \ldots i_n 0} \equiv \mathbf{p}_0(t_{i_1 \ldots i_n})$ and $t_{i_1 \ldots i_n 1} \equiv \mathbf{p}_1(t_{i_1 \ldots i_n})$ for $i_j \equiv 0$ or $1$ $(1 \le j \le n)$.

The predicate symbols are: $\perp$, $\mathbf{N}$, $=$.

$\perp$ means contradiction. $\mathbf{N}(a)$ means that $a$ is a natural number. $a = b$ means that $a$ equals $b$.

We have predicate variables, which a first order language does not have. The predicate variables are: $X, Y, Z, \ldots, X^*, Y^*, Z^*, \ldots$. Each predicate variable has fixed arity. We assume that the arity of $X^*$ is $n+1$ if the arity of $X$ is $n$.

We abbreviate $\mathrm{Y}(\lambda x.t)$ as $\mu x.t$ where $\mathrm{Y} \equiv \lambda f.(\lambda x.f(xx))(\lambda x.f(xx))$.

**Definition 2.1 (Formula).**

1. If $a$, $b$ are terms, $\perp$, $\mathbf{N}(a)$, $a = b$ are formulas. We call them atomic formulas.
2. If $X$ is a predicate variable of arity $n$ and $t_1, \ldots, t_n$ are terms, $X(t_1, \ldots, t_n)$ is a formula.
3. If $A$ and $B$ are formulas, $A \,\&\, B$, $A \vee B$ and $A \to B$ are formulas.
4. If $A$ is a formula, $\forall x A$ and $\exists x A$ are formulas.
5. $(\lambda x_1 \ldots x_n.A)(t_1, \ldots, t_n)$ is a formula if $A$ is a formula and $t_1, \ldots, t_n$ are terms.
6. $(\nu X.\lambda x_1 \ldots x_n.A)(t_1, \ldots, t_n)$ is a formula where $X$ is a predicate variable of arity $n$, $A$ is a formula and $t_1, \ldots, t_n$ are terms.

$\neg A$ denotes $A \to \perp$.

The last case corresponds to coinductively defined predicates. Note that $X$ and $x_1, \ldots, x_n$ may occur freely in $A$. The intuitive meaning of the formula $(\nu X.\lambda x_1 \ldots x_n.A(X, x_1, \ldots, x_n))(t_1, \ldots, t_n)$ is as follows: Let $P$ be the predicate of arity $n$ which is the greatest solution of the equation

$$P(x_1, \ldots, x_n) \leftrightarrow A(P, x_1, \ldots, x_n).$$

Then $(\nu X.\lambda x_1 \ldots x_n.A(X, x_1, \ldots, x_n))(t_1, \ldots, t_n)$ means $P(t_1, \ldots, t_n)$.

We abbreviate a sequence as a bold type symbol, for example, $x_1, \ldots, x_n$ as $\mathbf{x}$, and $t_1, \ldots, t_n$ as $\mathbf{t}$.

**Example 2.2.** We give an example of a formula. We suppose $X$ is a predicate variable of arity 1. Then

$$(\nu X.\lambda x.x = (x_0, x_1) \,\&\, x_0 = 0 \,\&\, X(x_1))(x)$$

is a formula.

**Definition 2.3 (Abstract).**

1. A predicate symbol of arity $n$ is an abstract of arity $n$.
2. A predicate variable of arity $n$ is an abstract of arity $n$.
3. If $A$ is a formula, $\lambda x_1 \ldots x_n.A$ is an abstract of arity $n$.
4. If $(\nu X.\lambda x_1 \ldots x_n.A)(x_1, \ldots, x_n)$ is a formula, $\nu X.\lambda x_1 \ldots x_n.A$ is an abstract of arity $n$.

For a formula $A$, a predicate variable $X$ of arity $n$ and an abstract $F$ of arity $n$, the formula $A_X[F]$ denotes the formula obtained from $A$ by replacing all the occurrences of $X$ by $F$.

## 2.2 Basic Axioms and Inference Rules of $\mathbf{TID}_{\nu 0}$ and $\mathbf{TID}_{\nu 1}$

Theories $\mathbf{TID}_{\nu 0}$ and $\mathbf{TID}_{\nu 1}$ are based on intuitionistic natural deduction NJ.

We give axioms and inference rules except those of coinductive definitions in this subsection. They are usual axioms and inference rules of $\lambda$-calculus, pairing and natural numbers and we only list them here.

Axioms for Equality:

$$x = x, \tag{E1}$$

$$x = y \,\&\, A(x) \to A(y). \tag{E2}$$

Axiom for $\beta$-conversion:

$$(\lambda x.a)b = a[x := b] \tag{B1}$$

for terms $a$ and $b$, where $a[x := b]$ means the term obtained from $a$ by replacing every free occurrence of $x$ by $b$.

Axioms for Pairing:

$$\mathbf{p}_0(\mathbf{p}xy) = x, \tag{P1}$$

$$\mathbf{p}_1(\mathbf{p}xy) = y, \tag{P2}$$

Axioms for Natural Numbers:

$$\mathbf{N}(0), \tag{N1}$$

$$\mathbf{N}(x) \to \mathbf{N}(\mathbf{s_N}x), \tag{N2}$$

$$\mathbf{N}(x) \to \mathbf{p_N}(\mathbf{s_N}x) = x, \tag{N3}$$

$$\mathbf{N}(x) \to \mathbf{s_N}x \neq 0, \tag{N4}$$

$$A(0) \,\&\, \forall x(\mathbf{N}(x) \,\&\, A(x) \to A(\mathbf{s_N}x)) \to \forall x(\mathbf{N}(x) \to A(x)). \tag{N5}$$

Axioms for $\mathbf{d}$:

$$\forall xyab(\mathbf{N}(x) \,\&\, \mathbf{N}(y) \,\&\, x = y \to \mathbf{d}xyab = a), \tag{D1}$$

$$\forall xyab(\mathbf{N}(x) \,\&\, \mathbf{N}(y) \,\&\, x \neq y \to \mathbf{d}xyab = b). \tag{D2}$$

Axioms for Abstracts:

$$(\lambda \mathbf{x}.A)(\mathbf{x}) \leftrightarrow A. \tag{A1}$$

### 2.3 Inference Rules of Coinductive Definitions

We discuss inference rules of coinductive definitions. Let $\nu \equiv \nu X.\lambda \mathbf{x}.A(X)$ where $\mathbf{x}$ is a sequence of variables whose length is the arity of a predicate variable $X$ and $A(X)$ is a formula. $A(C)$ denotes the formula obtained from $A(X)$ by replacing all the occurrences of $X$ by $C$. Suppose that

$(\nu 1) \equiv \forall \mathbf{x}(\nu(\mathbf{x}) \to A(\nu))$,

$(\nu 2) \equiv \forall \mathbf{x}(C(\mathbf{x}) \to A(C)) \to \forall \mathbf{x}(C(\mathbf{x}) \to \nu(\mathbf{x}))$,

$(\mathrm{MONO}) \equiv \forall \mathbf{x}(X(\mathbf{x}) \to Y(\mathbf{x})) \to \forall \mathbf{x}(A(X) \to A(Y))$,

$$(\mathrm{MONO\text{-}Q}) \equiv \forall \mathbf{x}r(X^*(r,\mathbf{x}) \to Y^*(r,\mathbf{x})) \to \forall \mathbf{x}r((r \;\; \mathbf{q}_X[X,X^*] \;\; A(X)) \to (r \;\; \mathbf{q}_X[X,Y^*] \;\; A(X)))$$

where $X$, $Y$, $X^*$ and $Y^*$ are predicate variables, $A(X)$ is a formula and $C(\mathbf{x})$ is a formula. The formula $(e \;\; \mathbf{q}_X[X,X^*] \;\; A(X))$ denotes the realizability of the formula $A$ and is defined in Section 4.

The condition (MONO) states that the formula $A(X)$ is monotone with respect to $X$.

The condition (MONO-Q) states that the formula $(e \;\; \mathbf{q}_X[X,X^*] \;\; A(X))$ is monotone with respect to $X^*$. The formula $(e \;\; \mathbf{q}_X[X,X^*] \;\; A(X))$ means the formula obtained from the usual $\mathbf{q}$-realizability $(e \;\; \mathbf{q} \;\; A(X))$ by replacing every occurrence of the formula $(r \;\; \mathbf{q} \;\; X(x))$ by the formula $X^*(r,x)$. The condition means that the realizability $(e \;\; \mathbf{q} \;\; A(X))$ is monotone with respect to the occurrences $(r \;\; \mathbf{q} \;\; X(x))$. The condition (MONO-Q) is proved to bring the soundness of the realizability in Section 4. In words of $\mathrm{AF}_2$ [13, 14], the condition (MONO-Q) represents $X \subseteq Y \to A(X) \subseteq A(Y)$ where $X \subseteq Y$ denotes $\forall x(x \in X \to x \in Y)$.

We have 2 inference rules for $\mathbf{TID}_{\nu 0}$ and $\mathbf{TID}_{\nu 1}$ respectively. For $\mathbf{TID}_{\nu 0}$ the inference rules are as follows:

$$\frac{(\mathrm{MONO}) \quad (\mathrm{MONO\text{-}Q})}{(\nu 1)} \; (\nu R1')$$

$$\frac{(\mathrm{MONO}) \quad (\mathrm{MONO\text{-}Q})}{(\nu 2)} \; (\nu R2')$$

where $X, Y, X^*$ and $Y^*$ do not occur freely in open assumptions of deductions of the premises.

For $\mathbf{TID}_{\nu 1}$ the inference rules are as follows:

$$\frac{(\mathrm{MONO})}{(\nu 1)} \; (\nu R1)$$

$$\frac{(\mathrm{MONO})}{(\nu 2)} \; (\nu R2)$$

where $X$ and $Y$ do not occur freely in open assumptions of a deduction of the premise.

Proposition 4.13 will state that the positivity condition implies (MONO) and (MONO-Q). In fact, the set of formulas satisfying the positivity condition is a proper subset of the set of formulas satisfying (MONO) and (MONO-Q), and the set of formulas satisfying (MONO) and (MONO-Q) is a proper subset of the set of formulas satisfying (MONO). If $A(X)$ is $\bot \,\&\, \neg X$, then $A(X)$ is in the set of formulas satisfying (MONO) and (MONO-Q), but is not in the set of formulas satisfying the positivity condition. If $A(X)$ is $X \to X$, $A(X)$ is in the set of formulas satisfying (MONO), but is not in the set of formulas satisfying (MONO) and (MONO-Q).

We define a theory $\mathbf{TID}^-$ as the theory whose language is the same as $\mathbf{TID}_{\nu 1}$ and whose axioms and inference rules are only basic axioms and inference rules given in Subsection 2.2.

## 2.4 Monotone Coinductive Definitions of Predicates

We will explain how useful the coinductive definitions are to formalize properties of programs.

First, We explain the coinductive definitions. Let $\nu \equiv \nu X.\lambda \mathbf{x}.A(X)$ where $\mathbf{x}$ is a sequence of variables whose length is the arity of a predicate variable $X$ and $A(X)$ is a formula. Suppose that (MONO) and (MONO-Q) hold for the formula $A(X)$. So we can use ($\nu$1) and ($\nu$2) for $A(X)$ in each theory $\mathbf{TID}_{\nu 0}$ and $\mathbf{TID}_{\nu 1}$. We will discuss ($\nu$1) and ($\nu$2).

By ($\nu$1) and ($\nu$2),

$$\nu(\mathbf{x}) \leftrightarrow A(\nu) \qquad (\nu 1')$$

holds. This $\nu$ is the greatest solution of the equation for a predicate variable $X$: $X(\mathbf{x}) \leftrightarrow A(X)$.

Because

$$\forall \mathbf{x}(C(\mathbf{x}) \leftrightarrow A(C)) \to \forall \mathbf{x}(C(\mathbf{x}) \to \nu(\mathbf{x}))$$

holds by ($\nu$2) for any formula $C(\mathbf{x})$.

By the facility of coinductive definitions, many useful infinite recursive data structures such as streams, infinite lists and infinite trees can be defined inside the theory [17]. The coinduction principle corresponding to each data structure is derived from ($\nu$2). We will give some examples.

**Example 2.4 (Bit Stream).** We will define the predicate $BS$ which means that the argument is a bit stream. Here we suppose that a stream is represented by an infinite list constructed by pairing. One way to define the predicate $BS$ is as follows:

$$BS(x) \equiv x = (x_0, x_1) \,\&\, (x_0 = 0 \vee x_0 = 1) \,\&\, BS(x_1).$$

But it is not a definition of $BS$ in a usual sense since $BS$ appears also in the right hand side which is the body of the definition. What we want to present by this equation is the greatest solution of the recursive equation for a predicate variable $X$:

$$X(x) \leftrightarrow x = (x_0, x_1) \,\&\, (x_0 = 0 \vee x_0 = 1) \,\&\, X(x_1).$$

In $\mathbf{TID}_{\nu 0}$ and $\mathbf{TID}_{\nu 1}$ this solution can be represented by the formula

$$(\nu X.\lambda x.x = (x_0, x_1) \,\&\, (x_0 = 0 \vee x_0 = 1) \,\&\, X(x_1))(x)$$

and ($\nu 1$) and ($\nu 2$) state that this formula is actually the greatest solution of the equation. By this facility we can define $BS$ in $\mathbf{TID}_{\nu 0}$ and $\mathbf{TID}_{\nu 1}$ as follows:

$$BS(x) \equiv (\nu X.\lambda x.x = (x_0, x_1) \,\&\, (x_0 = 0 \vee x_0 = 1) \,\&\, X(x_1))(x).$$

($\nu 2$) for $BS$ represents coinduction for bit streams classified by $BS$. ($\nu 2$) represents the generalized coinduction principle.

Let $\overline{0}$ be $\mu s.(0, s)$. $\overline{0}$ represents the zero stream whose elements are all 0, that is, $\overline{0} = (0, (0, (0, \ldots)))$. By ($\nu 2$), $BS(\overline{0})$ is proved.

**Example 2.5 (Extensional Equality of Streams).** The extensional equality $s \approx t$ of two streams $s$ and $t$ is represented by coinductive definitions as follows:

$$s \approx t \equiv (\nu X.\lambda xy.x_0 = y_0 \,\&\, X(x_1, y_1))(s, t).$$

**Example 2.6 (Infinite Lists).** The predicate $InfList(x)$ which means that $x$ is an infinite (maybe finite) list of natural numbers is represented by coinductive definitions. We suppose that the empty list is represented by 0.

$$InfList(x) \equiv (\nu X.\lambda x.x = 0 \vee \exists yz(x = (y, z) \,\&\, \mathbf{N}(y) \,\&\, X(z)))(x).$$

**Example 2.7 (Infinite Trees).** The predicate $InfTree(x)$ which means that $x$ is an infinite tree is represented by coinductive definitions. We suppose that the leaf is a natural number and the node is represented by $(y, z, w)$ where $y$ is a natural number and $z$ and $w$ are infinite trees.

$$InfTree(x) \equiv$$
$$(\nu X.\lambda x.\mathbf{N}(x) \vee \exists yzw(x = (y, z, w) \,\&\, \mathbf{N}(y) \,\&\, X(z) \,\&\, X(w)))(x).$$

The theories $\mathbf{TID}_{\nu 0}$ and $\mathbf{TID}_{\nu 1}$ give a framework in which specification formulas of programs are represented in a natural way. The facility of coinductive definitions can formalize notions given by the greatest fixed point such as streams in an expressive way.

# 3 Models of $\mathbf{TID}_{\nu 1}$

We will briefly explain semantics of $\mathbf{TID}_{\nu 1}$ by giving its intended model.

We will use the well-known greatest fixed point theorem for model construction.

**Greatest Fixed Point Theorem.** Let $S$ be a set and $p(S)$ be the power set of $S$. If $f : p(S) \to p(S)$ is a monotone function, there exists $a$ such that $a \in p(S)$ and

1. $f(a) = a$,
2. For any $b \in p(S)$, if $b \subset f(b)$, then $b \subset a$.

The notation $\mathrm{gfp}(f)$ denotes the element $a$.

We will construct a model of $\mathbf{TID}_{\nu 1}$ extending an arbitrary model of $\mathbf{TID}^-$. The models of $\mathbf{TID}^-$ are the same as the models of Beeson's theory **EON** and many models of that theory are known [1]. We denote the universe by $U$.

We will define $\rho \models A$ in almost the same way as for first order logic, where $A$ is a formula and $\rho$ is an environment which assigns an element of $U$ to a first order variable and a subset of $U^n$ to a predicate variable of arity $n$. We present only the definition for the case $X(\mathbf{t})$ for a predicate variable $X$ and the case $(\nu X.\lambda\mathbf{x}.A(X))(\mathbf{t})$.

Case $X(\mathbf{t})$. $\rho \models X(\mathbf{t})$ is defined as $\mathbf{t} \in \rho(X)$.

Case $(\nu X.\lambda\mathbf{x}.A(X))(\mathbf{t})$. Define $F$ as follows:

$$F : p(U^n) \to p(U^n),$$

$$F(V) = \{\mathbf{x} \in U^n \mid \rho[X := V] \models A(X)\},$$

where $\rho[X := V]$ is defined as follows:

$$\rho[X := V](X) = V.$$

$$\rho[X := V](x) = \rho(x), \qquad \text{if } x \text{ is not } X.$$

Then $\rho \models (\nu X.\lambda\mathbf{x}.A(X))(\mathbf{t})$ is defined as $\mathbf{t} \in \mathrm{gfp}(F)$ if $F$ is monotone. $\rho \models (\nu X.\lambda\mathbf{x}.A(X))(\mathbf{t})$ is defined as false if $F$ is not monotone.

**Theorem 3.1.** *If* $\mathbf{TID}_{\nu 1} \vdash A$ *holds, then* $\rho \models A$ *holds for any environment* $\rho$.

This theorem is proved in the appendix.

**Theorem 3.2.** $\mathbf{TID}_{\nu 0}$ *and* $\mathbf{TID}_{\nu 1}$ *are consistent.*

This theorem is proved immediately from Theorem 3.1.

# 4 q-Realizability for $\mathbf{TID}_{\nu 0}$ and $\mathbf{TID}_{\nu 1}$

In this section, we give a **q**-realizability interpretation for $\mathbf{TID}_{\nu 0}$ and $\mathbf{TID}_{\nu 1}$, which is expansion-preserving.

We say a realizability interpretation is expansion-preserving if a realizer of a coinductively defined predicate is the same as that of its expansion, that is, $(e \ \mathbf{q} \ \nu(x)) \leftrightarrow (e \ \mathbf{q} \ A(\nu, x))$ holds where $\nu \equiv \nu X.\lambda x.A(X, x)$. The expansion-preserving property is important for the following reasons: (1) Since we give the same semantics to $\nu(x)$ and $A(\nu, x)$ in our model, it is naturally expected to give the same interpretation to $\nu(x)$ and $A(\nu, x)$. (2) A realizer of coinduction can give a loop structure to a synthesized program. This idea of the expansion-preserving property is also adopted in the theory $\mathrm{AF}_2$ [13, 14].

First, we give an intuitive explanation of our notion of **q**-realizability. We start with usual **q**-realizability and sketch how $(\nu X.\lambda x.A(X, x))(x)$ is interpreted. Let $\nu$ be $\nu X.\lambda x.A(X, x)$. Since we require the expansion-preserving property, it is natural to define $(e \ \mathbf{q} \ \nu(x))$ as $\nu^*(e, x)$ where $\nu^*(e, x)$ is the greatest solution of the recursive equation for a predicate variable $X^*$:

$$X^*(e, x) \leftrightarrow (e \ \mathbf{q} \ A(\nu, x))[(r \ \mathbf{q} \ \nu(y)) := X^*(r, y)].$$

where $[(r \ \mathbf{q} \ \nu(y)) := X^*(r, y)]$ of the right hand side means replacing each subformula $(r \ \mathbf{q} \ \nu(y))$ by the formula $X^*(r, y)$ in the formula $(e \ \mathbf{q} \ A(\nu, x))$. We get Definition 4.1 of our notion of **q**-realizability by describing this idea in a rigorous way. This interpretation is an extension of interpretations of positive coinductive definitions [17].

Our **q**-realizability interpretation for $\mathbf{TID}_{\nu 0}$ and that for $\mathbf{TID}_{\nu 1}$ are defined in the same way.

**Definition 4.1 (q-Realizability).** Suppose $A$ is a formula, $n \geq 0$, $X_1, \ldots, X_n$ is a sequence of predicate variables of arity $m_1, \ldots, m_n$ respectively and $F_1, G_1, \ldots, F_n, G_n$ is a sequence of abstracts of arity $m_1, m_1+1, \ldots, m_n, m_n+1$ respectively. A formula

$(e \ \ \mathbf{q}_{X_1,\ldots,X_n}[F_1, G_1, \ldots, F_n, G_n] \ \ A)$

is defined by induction on the construction of $A$ as follows.

We use the following abbreviations.

$(e \ \ \mathbf{q}' \ \ A) \equiv (e \ \ \mathbf{q}_{X_1,\ldots,X_n}[F_1, G_1, \ldots, F_n, G_n] \ \ A)$,

$(e \ \ \mathbf{q}'_X[F,G] \ \ A) \equiv (e \ \ \mathbf{q}_{X_1,\ldots,X_n,X}[F_1, G_1, \ldots, F_n, G_n, F, G] \ \ A)$,

$\mathbf{F} \equiv F_1, \ldots, F_n$,

$\mathbf{X} \equiv X_1, \ldots, X_n$.

1. $(e \ \ \mathbf{q}' \ \ A) \equiv e = 0 \,\&\, A$ if $A$ is an atomic formula.
2. $(e \ \ \mathbf{q}' \ \ X_i(\mathbf{t})) \equiv F_i(\mathbf{t}) \,\&\, G_i(e, \mathbf{t})$.
3. $(e \ \ \mathbf{q}' \ \ Y(\mathbf{t})) \equiv Y(\mathbf{t}) \,\&\, Y^*(e, \mathbf{t})$ if $Y \not\equiv X_i \quad (1 \leq i \leq n)$.
4. $(e \ \ \mathbf{q}' \ \ A \,\&\, B) \equiv (e_0 \ \ \mathbf{q}' \ \ A) \,\&\, (e_1 \ \ \mathbf{q}' \ \ B)$.
5. $(e \ \ \mathbf{q}' \ \ A \vee B) \equiv \mathbf{N}(e_0) \,\&\, (e_0 = 0 \rightarrow (e_1 \ \ \mathbf{q}' \ \ A)) \,\&\, (e_0 \neq 0 \rightarrow (e_1 \ \ \mathbf{q}' \ \ B))$.
6. $(e \ \ \mathbf{q}' \ \ A \rightarrow B) \equiv (A_{\mathbf{X}}[\mathbf{F}] \rightarrow B_{\mathbf{X}}[\mathbf{F}]) \,\&\, \forall q((q \ \ \mathbf{q}' \ \ A) \rightarrow (eq \ \ \mathbf{q}' \ \ B))$.
7. $(e \ \ \mathbf{q}' \ \ \forall x A(x)) \equiv \forall x(ex \ \ \mathbf{q}' \ \ A(x))$.
8. $(e \ \ \mathbf{q}' \ \ \exists x A(x)) \equiv (e_1 \ \ \mathbf{q}' \ \ A(e_0))$.
9. $(e \ \ \mathbf{q}' \ \ (\lambda \mathbf{x}.A)(\mathbf{t})) \equiv (\lambda r\mathbf{x}.(r \ \ \mathbf{q}' \ \ A))(e, \mathbf{t})$.
10. $(e \ \ \mathbf{q}' \ \ \nu(\mathbf{t})) \equiv \nu(\mathbf{t}) \,\&\, (\nu Y^*.\lambda r\mathbf{x}.(r \ \ \mathbf{q}'_Y[\nu_{\mathbf{X}}[\mathbf{F}], Y^*] \ \ A(Y)))(e, \mathbf{t})$ where $\nu \equiv \nu Y.\lambda \mathbf{x}.A(Y)$.

We write simply $(e \ \ \mathbf{q} \ \ A)$ if $n = 0$.

Our realizability interpretation is a usual realizability interpretation accompanied with substitution. The formula $(e \ \ \mathbf{q}_X[F,G] \ \ A)$ is obtained from the usual realizability $(e \ \ \mathbf{q} \ \ A)$ by replacing all the occurrences of $X$ by $F$ and $X^*$ by $G$. In particular, if $n = 0$, the above $(e \ \ \mathbf{q}' \ \ A)$ is exactly the same as the usual q-realizability.

The interpretation $(e \ \ \mathbf{q} \ \ A)$ corresponds to $e : A$ in type theories.

The last case of the definition is slightly changed from the definition given in [17] to prove Proposition 4.3, since ($\nu$1) and ($\nu$2) cannot be used without extra conditions (MONO) and (MONO-Q), on the other hand, the proposition is proved by using ($\nu$1) and ($\nu$2) in [17].

**Example 4.2.** We will give the interpretation of the bit stream predicate $BS(x)$ as an example. The interpretation $(e \ \ \mathbf{q} \ \ BS(x))$ is

$$BS(x) \,\&\, (\nu X^*.\lambda rx.(r \ \ \mathbf{q}_X[BS, X^*] \ \ x = (x_0, x_1) \,\&$$
$$(x_0 = 0 \vee x_0 = 1) \,\&\, X(x_1)))(e, x).$$

That is

$$BS(x) \,\&\, (\nu X^*.\lambda rx.(r_0 \ \ \mathbf{q}_X[BS, X^*] \ \ x = (x_0, x_1)) \,\&$$
$$(r_{10} \ \ \mathbf{q}_X[BS, X^*] \ \ x_0 = 0 \vee x_0 = 1) \,\&\, (r_{11} \ \ \mathbf{q}_X[BS, X^*] \ \ X(x_1)))(e, x).$$

Here we have

$(r_0 \;\; \mathbf{q}_X[BS, X^*] \;\; x = (x_0, x_1)) \equiv r_0 = 0 \;\&\; x = (x_0, x_1),$

$(r_{10} \;\; \mathbf{q}_X[BS, X^*] \;\; x_0 = 0 \vee x_0 = 1) \equiv \mathbf{N}(r_{100}) \;\&$

$\quad (r_{100} = 0 \rightarrow r_{101} = 0 \;\&\; x_0 = 0) \;\&\; (r_{100} \neq 0 \rightarrow r_{101} = 0 \;\&\; x_0 = 1),$

$(r_{11} \;\; \mathbf{q}_X[BS, X^*] \;\; X(x_1)) \equiv BS(x_1) \;\&\; X^*(r_{11}, x_1).$

Therefore the interpretation $(e \;\; \mathbf{q} \;\; BS(x))$ is

$$BS(x) \;\&\; (\nu X^*.\lambda rx.(r_0 = 0 \;\&\; x = (x_0, x_1)) \;\&\; (\mathbf{N}(r_{100}) \;\&$$
$$(r_{100} = 0 \rightarrow r_{101} = 0 \;\&\; x_0 = 0) \;\&\; (r_{100} \neq 0 \rightarrow r_{101} = 0 \;\&\; x_0 = 1)) \;\&$$
$$(BS(x_1) \;\&\; X^*(r_{11}, x_1)))(e, x).$$

**Proposition 4.3.** $\mathbf{TID}_{\nu 0} \vdash (e \;\; \mathbf{q}_\mathbf{X}[F_1, G_1, \ldots, F_n, G_n] \;\; A) \rightarrow A_\mathbf{X}[\mathbf{F}]$.

The claim is proved by induction on the construction of the formula $A$.

We will show that this interpretation works well for $\mathbf{TID}_{\nu 0}$ but goes wrong for $\mathbf{TID}_{\nu 1}$. That is, it will be shown that the interpretation for $\mathbf{TID}_{\nu 0}$ is sound but the interpretation for $\mathbf{TID}_{\nu 1}$ is not sound. The difference is brought by the additional condition (MONO-Q). In general, we cannot conclude that $(e \;\; \mathbf{q}_X[X, X^*] \;\; A)$ is monotone with respect to $X^*$ even if $A$ is monotone with respect to $X$. For such $A$, we cannot use ($\nu$1) and ($\nu$2) for $(e \;\; \mathbf{q} \;\; (\nu X.\lambda x.A)(t))$ in $\mathbf{TID}_{\nu 1}$. On the other hand, we can always use ($\nu$1) and ($\nu$2) for $(e \;\; \mathbf{q} \;\; (\nu X.\lambda x.A)(t))$ in $\mathbf{TID}_{\nu 0}$ since the additional (MONO-Q) guarantees that $(e \;\; \mathbf{q}_X[X, X^*] \;\; A)$ is monotone with respect to $X^*$.

Suppose we could define realizability $(e \;\; \mathbf{q}_2 \;\; A)$ so that $(e \;\; \mathbf{q}_2 \;\; \nu) \leftrightarrow (e \;\; \mathbf{q}_2 \;\; A(\nu))$ where $\nu \equiv \nu X.A(X)$ and (MONO-Q) does not hold for $A(X)$. Then the meaning of $(e \;\; \mathbf{q}_2 \;\; \nu)$ is a fixed point of a non-monotone function $F$ such that $(e \;\; \mathbf{q}_2 \;\; A(X))$ means $F(X^*)$. But it is hopeless in general to find a meaning of a fixed point of a non-monotone function. The next theorem shows this fact for the case of full monotone coinductive definitions.

**Theorem 4.4.** *The* $\mathbf{q}$*-realizability interpretation is not sound for* $\mathbf{TID}_{\nu 1}$*. That is, there is a formula* $A$ *such that* $\mathbf{TID}_{\nu 1} \vdash A$ *holds but* $\mathbf{TID}_{\nu 1} \vdash (e \;\; \mathbf{q} \;\; A)$ *does not hold for any* $e$*.*

This theorem is proved in the appendix.

We will show soundness of the realizability interpretation for $\mathbf{TID}_{\nu 0}$ in $\mathbf{TID}_{\nu 1}$.

**Proposition 4.5.** *For a formula* $A(X)$ *and an abstract* $C$*,*

$$(e \;\; \mathbf{q} \;\; A(X))[X := C, X^* := \lambda r\mathbf{x}.(r \;\; \mathbf{q} \;\; C(\mathbf{x}))] \leftrightarrow (e \;\; \mathbf{q} \;\; A(C))$$

*holds, where* $[X := C, X^* := \lambda r\mathbf{x}.(r \;\; \mathbf{q} \;\; C(\mathbf{x}))]$ *denotes a substitution of abstracts for predicate variables.*

This claim is proved by induction on $A$.

**Proposition 4.6.** *Let* $\nu \equiv \nu X.\lambda\mathbf{x}.A(X)$ *and suppose that* (MONO) *and* (MONO-Q) *hold for* $A(X)$*. Then*

$$\mathbf{TID}_{\nu 1} \vdash (e \;\; \mathbf{q} \;\; \nu(\mathbf{x})) \leftrightarrow (e \;\; \mathbf{q} \;\; A(\nu))$$

*holds.*

This proposition is proved in the appendix. This proposition shows that the the realizability interpretation is expansion-preserving.

We give realizers of ($\nu 1$) and ($\nu 2$) in the next two propositions.

**Proposition 4.7.** *Suppose that* $\mathbf{TID}_{\nu 0} \vdash$ (MONO) *and* $\mathbf{TID}_{\nu 0} \vdash$ (MONO-Q) *hold for a formula* $A(X)$. *Let* $\nu \equiv \nu X.\lambda \mathbf{x}.A(X)$. *Then*

$\mathbf{TID}_{\nu 1} \vdash \lambda \mathbf{x} r.r \;\; \mathbf{q} \;\; (\nu 1)$

*holds.*

This proposition is proved immediate from Proposition 4.6.

**Proposition 4.8.** *Let* $\nu \equiv \nu X.\lambda \mathbf{x}.A(X)$ *and suppose that* (MONO) *and* (MONO-Q) *hold for a formula* $A(X)$. *Then*

$\mathbf{TID}_{\nu 1} \vdash \lambda q.\mu f.\lambda \mathbf{x} r.m f \mathbf{x}(q \mathbf{x} r) \;\; \mathbf{q} \;\; (\nu 2)$

*holds where*

$\mathbf{TID}_{\nu 1} \vdash m \;\; \mathbf{q}$ (MONO).

This proposition is proved in the appendix.

**Theorem 4.9 (Soundness Theorem).** *If* $\mathbf{TID}_{\nu 0} \vdash A$, *we can get a term* $e$ *from a proof and* $\mathbf{TID}_{\nu 1} \vdash (e \;\; \mathbf{q} \;\; A)$ *holds where all the free variables of* $e$ *are included in all the free variables of* $A$.

**Proof 4.10.** By induction on the proof of $\mathbf{TID}_{\nu 0} \vdash A$. Cases are classified by the last rule applied to the proof. Cases for basic axioms and inference rules are proved in almost the same way as [17]. Case ($\nu R1'$) is proved by using Proposition 4.7. Case ($\nu R2'$) is proved by using Proposition 4.8. □

By the soundness of the realizability, we get the term existence property, the disjunction property and the program extraction theorem. Our realizability interpretation works well whenever the usual realizability works. We also get the soundness proof for **r**-realizability by modifying the definition of the realizability and the soundness proof described here so that we get consistency with some choice axioms.

**Theorem 4.11 (Term Existence Property and Disjunction Property).** *(1) If* $\mathbf{TID}_{\nu 0} \vdash \exists x A(x)$, *we can get a term* $t$ *from the proof and* $\mathbf{TID}_{\nu 1} \vdash A(t)$ *holds.*

*(2) If* $\mathbf{TID}_{\nu 0} \vdash A \vee B$, *then* $\mathbf{TID}_{\nu 1} \vdash A$ *or* $\mathbf{TID}_{\nu 1} \vdash B$ *holds.*

**Proof 4.12.** (1) Suppose $\mathbf{TID}_{\nu 0} \vdash \exists x A(x)$. By Theorem 4.9, we can get a term $e$ from the proof and $\mathbf{TID}_{\nu 1} \vdash (e \;\; \mathbf{q} \;\; \exists x A(x))$. By Definition 4.1 and Proposition 4.3, it implies $\mathbf{TID}_{\nu 1} \vdash A(e_0)$. By putting $t := e_0$, we have the claim.

(2) Suppose $\mathbf{TID}_{\nu 0} \vdash A \vee B$. By Theorem 4.9, we can get a term $e$ from the proof and $\mathbf{TID}_{\nu 1} \vdash (e \;\; \mathbf{q} \;\; A \vee B)$. By Definition 4.1, $\mathbf{TID}_{\nu 1} \vdash e_0 = 0$ or $\mathbf{TID}_{\nu 1} \vdash e_0 \neq 0$ holds, and hence $\mathbf{TID}_{\nu 1} \vdash A$ or $\mathbf{TID}_{\nu 1} \vdash B$ holds. □

We will show the discussion of the realizability given in [17] is a special case of the above discussion.

**Proposition 4.13.** *If $X$ occurs only positively in $A(X)$,* (MONO) *and* (MONO-Q) *hold.*

**Corollary 4.14.** $\mathbf{TID}_{\nu 0}$ *is an extension of* $\mathbf{TID}_{\nu}$ *presented in [17].*

If we choose an appropriate monotone realizer $m$ for $A(X)$ where $X$ is positive in $A(X)$, we get almost the same soundness proof for $\mathbf{TID}_{\nu}$ as in [17]. But the soundness proof of this paper is simpler than that for $\mathbf{TID}_{\nu}$ in [17] because of the monotone condition. The main difference of two proofs is in the proof of the case of the coinduction. This simplicity comes from the fact that we pay attention to the realizer $m$ of the monotonicity (MONO) in this paper, while in [17] we calculate concretely $\sigma^{X,f}_{A(X)}$, which corresponds to the realizer $mf\mathbf{x}$.

## 5 Theory $\mathbf{TID}_{\nu 2}$ and Its q-Realizability

In this section, we present another q-realizability interpretation, which is based on second order logic [4]. It interprets a theory $\mathbf{TID}_{\nu 2}$, which has least-upper-bound coinductive definitions, in a second order theory $\mathbf{T_2}$. It gives also a sound interpretation for $\mathbf{TID}_{\nu 1}$. The new point is to give least-upper-bound coinductive definitions, which cover monotone coinductive definitions and have natural meaning given by semantics with the second order coding.

**Definition 5.1 (Theory $\mathbf{TID}_{\nu 2}$).** The language of the theory $\mathbf{TID}_{\nu 2}$ is the same as that of $\mathbf{TID}^-$.

The axioms and inference rules of $\mathbf{TID}_{\nu 2}$ are those of $\mathbf{TID}^-$ and the following inference rule ($\nu 3$) and axiom ($\nu 2$):

$$\frac{\forall\mathbf{x}(X(\mathbf{x}) \to A(X)) \to \forall\mathbf{x}(X(\mathbf{x}) \to C(\mathbf{x}))}{\forall\mathbf{x}(\nu(\mathbf{x}) \to C(\mathbf{x}))}\ (\nu 3),$$

$$\forall\mathbf{x}(C(\mathbf{x}) \to A(C)) \to \forall\mathbf{x}(C(\mathbf{x}) \to \nu(\mathbf{x})) \qquad (\nu 2)$$

where $\nu \equiv \nu X.\lambda\mathbf{x}.A(X)$ and in the rule ($\nu 3$) the predicate variable $X$ does not occur freely in formulas $C(\mathbf{x})$ and open assumptions of a deduction of the premise.

The intended meaning of $\nu(\mathbf{x})$ is the least upper bound $\cup\{X|\forall\mathbf{x}(X(\mathbf{x}) \to A(X))\}$ with respect to the order relation $\sqsubseteq$ given by $X \sqsubseteq Y \leftrightarrow \forall x(X(x) \to Y(x))$. ($\nu 2$) means that $\nu$ is an upper bound and ($\nu 3$) means that $\nu$ is the least one.

We call the definitions of $\nu(\mathbf{x})$ by ($\nu 3$) and ($\nu 2$) *least-upper-bound coinductive definitions.* Note that monotonicity of $A(X)$ is not required here. In this sense, least-upper-bound coinductive definitions are generalization of monotone coinductive definitions.

**Theorem 5.2.** $\mathbf{TID}_{\nu 2}$ *is consistent.*

This theorem is proved in the appendix.

We use a second order theory $\mathbf{T_2}$ to give q-realizability for $\mathbf{TID}_{\nu 2}$.

**Definition 5.3 (Theory $\mathbf{T_2}$).** The theory $\mathbf{T_2}$ is defined as the theory obtained from $\mathbf{TID}_{\nu 2}$ by adding the second order universal quantifiers.

If $A$ is a formula and $X$ is a predicate variable, then $\forall X A$ is a formula.

The axioms and inference rules of $\mathbf{T_2}$ are those of $\mathbf{TID}_{\nu 2}$ and the following inference rules:

$$\frac{A(X)}{\forall X A(X)}\ (\forall^2 I), \qquad \frac{\forall X A(X)}{A(F)}\ (\forall^2 E)$$

where $A(X)$ denotes a formula, $F$ denotes an abstract of the same arity as the predicate variable $X$, $A(F)$ denotes the formula obtained from $A(X)$ by replacing all the occurrences of $X$ by $F$, and in the rule $(\forall^2 I)$ $X$ does not occur freely in open assumptions of a deduction of the premise.

**Theorem 5.4.** $\mathbf{T_2}$ *is consistent.*

This theorem is proved in the appendix.

**Proposition 5.5.** *If a formula $A(X)$ is monotone with respect to a predicate variable $X$, that is,*

$$\forall \mathbf{x}(X(\mathbf{x}) \to Y(\mathbf{x})) \to \forall \mathbf{x}(A(X) \to A(Y))$$

*holds in* $\mathbf{TID}_{\nu 2}$, *then* $\mathbf{TID}_{\nu 2}$ *proves*

$$\forall \mathbf{x}(\nu(\mathbf{x}) \to A(\nu)) \qquad (\nu 1)$$

*where* $\nu \equiv \nu X.\lambda \mathbf{x}.A(X)$.

This proposition shows that least-upper-bound coinductive definitions cover monotone coinductive definitions.

**Proof 5.6.** Assume $\forall \mathbf{x}(X(\mathbf{x}) \to A(X))$. By $(\nu 2)$, $\forall \mathbf{x}(X(\mathbf{x}) \to \nu(\mathbf{x}))$ holds. By monotonicity of $A(X)$, $\forall \mathbf{x}(A(X) \to A(\nu))$ holds. Combining it with the assumption, we have $\forall \mathbf{x}(X(\mathbf{x}) \to A(\nu))$. Hence we have $\forall \mathbf{x}(X(\mathbf{x}) \to A(X)) \to \forall \mathbf{x}(X(\mathbf{x}) \to A(\nu))$ without assumptions. By $(\nu 3)$, $\forall \mathbf{x}(\nu(\mathbf{x}) \to A(\nu))$ holds. □

**Theorem 5.7.** *If a formula $A$ is provable in* $\mathbf{TID}_{\nu 1}$, *then $A$ is provable in* $\mathbf{TID}_{\nu 2}$.

This claim is proved immediately by Proposition 5.5.

We will explain the principle of our notion of **q**-realizability defined here, before we define **q**-realizability for $\mathbf{TID}_{\nu 2}$ in $\mathbf{T_2}$. We define **q**-realizability of $\nu(t)$ by using the higher order coding and the **q**-realizability for second order logic. The least-upper-bound coinductive definitions give semantically the least upper bound $\cup\{X | X \sqsubseteq A(X)\}$, where $X \sqsubseteq Y$ denotes $\forall x(X(x) \to Y(x))$. Second order logic can code $y \in \cup\{X | P(X)\}$ by $\exists X(P(X) \& X(y))$, since, by letting $\nu(y)$ be $\exists X(P(X) \& X(y))$, (1) $P(A)$ implies $A \sqsubseteq \nu$, and (2) $\forall X(P(X) \to X \sqsubseteq C)$ implies $\nu \sqsubseteq C$. Combining them, we get the higher order coding of $\nu(y)$ by $\exists X(\forall x(X(x) \to A(x, X)) \& X(y))$. The second order existential quantifier $\exists X$ is coded by $\exists X.A(X) \equiv \forall Y(\forall X(A(X) \to Y) \to Y)$. Hence we get the coding of $\nu(y)$ by

$$\nu(y) \equiv \forall Y(\forall X(\forall x(X(x) \to A(x, X)) \& X(y) \to Y) \to Y).$$

By the realizability for second order logic, we have $(e \ \mathbf{q} \ \forall X.A(X)) \equiv \forall X X^*(e \ \mathbf{q} \ A(X))$. By using these, we define $(e \ \mathbf{q} \ \nu(y))$ by

$$(e \ \mathbf{q} \ \nu(y)) \equiv (e \ \mathbf{q} \ \forall Y(\forall X(\forall x(X(x) \to A(x,X)) \,\&\, X(y) \to Y) \to Y)).$$

**Definition 5.8 (q-Realizability for $\mathbf{TID}_{\nu 2}$).**

A q-realizability interpretation $(e \ \mathbf{q} \ A)$ of the formula $A$ is defined by induction on the construction of $A$ as follows:

1. $(e \ \mathbf{q} \ A) \equiv e = 0 \,\&\, A$ if $A$ is an atomic formula.
2. $(e \ \mathbf{q} \ X(\mathbf{t})) \equiv X(\mathbf{t}) \,\&\, X^*(e, \mathbf{t})$ if $X$ is a predicate variable.
3. $(e \ \mathbf{q} \ A \,\&\, B) \equiv (e_0 \ \mathbf{q} \ A) \,\&\, (e_1 \ \mathbf{q} \ B)$.
4. $(e \ \mathbf{q} \ A \vee B) \equiv \mathbf{N}(e_0) \,\&\, (e_0 = 0 \to (e_1 \ \mathbf{q} \ A)) \,\&\, (e_0 \neq 0 \to (e_1 \ \mathbf{q} \ B))$.
5. $(e \ \mathbf{q} \ A \to B) \equiv \forall q((q \ \mathbf{q} \ A) \to (eq \ \mathbf{q} \ B)) \,\&\, (A \to B)$.
6. $(e \ \mathbf{q} \ \forall x A(x)) \equiv \forall x(ex \ \mathbf{q} \ A(x))$.
7. $(e \ \mathbf{q} \ \exists x A(x)) \equiv (e_1 \ \mathbf{q} \ A(e_0))$.
8. $(e \ \mathbf{q} \ (\lambda \mathbf{x}.A)(\mathbf{t})) \equiv (\lambda r\mathbf{x}.(r \ \mathbf{q} \ A))(e, \mathbf{t})$.
9. $(e \ \mathbf{q} \ \nu(\mathbf{t})) \equiv \forall Y Y^* r(\forall X X^*(r \ \mathbf{q} \ \forall \mathbf{x}(X(\mathbf{x}) \to A(X)) \,\&\, X(\mathbf{t}) \to Y) \to Y \,\&\, Y^*(er)) \,\&\, \nu(\mathbf{t})$ where $\nu \equiv \nu X.\lambda \mathbf{x}.A(X)$.

**Proposition 5.9.** *Suppose that $A(X)$ is a formula and $A(C)$ is the formula obtained from $A(X)$ by replacing all the occurrences of a predicate variable $X$ by an abstract $C$. Then*

$$(e \ \mathbf{q} \ A(C)) \leftrightarrow (e \ \mathbf{q} \ A(X))[X := C, X^* := (\lambda r\mathbf{x}.(r \ \mathbf{q} \ C(\mathbf{x})))]$$

*holds.*

This claim is proved by induction the construction of $A(X)$.

**Proposition 5.10.** *$((e \ \mathbf{q} \ A) \to A)$ holds in $\mathbf{T_2}$.*

This claim is proved by induction on the construction of $A$.

We give realizers of ($\nu 3$) and ($\nu 2$) in the next proposition.

**Proposition 5.11.** *Suppose that $\nu \equiv \nu X.\lambda \mathbf{x}.A(X)$.*

*1. The rule*

$$\frac{q \ \mathbf{q} \ \forall \mathbf{x}(X(\mathbf{x}) \to A(X)) \to \forall \mathbf{x}(X(\mathbf{x}) \to C(\mathbf{x}))}{\lambda \mathbf{x} r.r(\lambda p.qp_0\mathbf{x}p_1) \ \mathbf{q} \ \forall \mathbf{x}(\nu(\mathbf{x}) \to C(\mathbf{x}))}$$

*is derivable in $\mathbf{T_2}$ where $X$ and $X^*$ do not occur freely in open assumptions of a deduction of the premise.*

*2. $(\lambda q\mathbf{x}rp.p(q,r) \ \mathbf{q} \ \forall \mathbf{x}(C(\mathbf{x}) \to A(C)) \to \forall \mathbf{x}(C(\mathbf{x}) \to \nu(\mathbf{x})))$ holds in $\mathbf{T_2}$.*

This proposition is proved in the appendix.

**Theorem 5.12 (Soundness of the Realizability for $\mathbf{TID}_{\nu 2}$).** *If a formula $A$ is provable in $\mathbf{TID}_{\nu 2}$, then we can get a term $e$ from the proof and $(e \ \mathbf{q} \ A)$ holds in $\mathbf{T_2}$.*

This theorem is proved by induction on the proof of $A$ by using Proposition 5.11.

We give a realizer of ($\nu 1$) in the next proposition.

**Proposition 5.13.** *If $m$ is a realizer of monotonicity of $A(X)$, that is,*

$$m \ \mathbf{q} \ \forall\mathbf{x}(X(\mathbf{x}) \to Y(\mathbf{x})) \to \forall\mathbf{x}(A(X) \to A(Y))$$

*holds in $\mathbf{T_2}$, then*

$$\lambda\mathbf{x}r.r(\lambda p.m(\lambda\mathbf{x}rs.s(p_0, r))\mathbf{x}(p_0\mathbf{x}p_1)) \ \mathbf{q} \ \forall\mathbf{x}(\nu(\mathbf{x}) \to A(\nu))$$

*holds in $\mathbf{T_2}$ where $\nu \equiv \nu X.\lambda\mathbf{x}.A(X)$.*

This claim is proved by calculating the realizer according to the proof of Proposition 5.5.

**Theorem 5.14 (Soundness of the Realizability for $\mathbf{TID}_{\nu 1}$).** *If a formula $A$ is provable in $\mathbf{TID}_{\nu 1}$, then we can get a term $e$ from the proof and $(e \ \mathbf{q} \ A)$ holds in $\mathbf{T_2}$.*

This theorem is proved by induction on the proof of $A$ by using Theorem 5.12 and Proposition 5.13.

By using the soundness theorem, we can prove the term existence property, the disjunction property, the program extraction theorem and so on.

**Theorem 5.15.** *(1) If $\mathbf{TID}_{\nu 2} \vdash \exists x A(x)$, we can get a term $t$ from the proof and $\mathbf{T_2} \vdash A(t)$ holds.*

*(2) If $\mathbf{TID}_{\nu 2} \vdash A \vee B$, then $\mathbf{T_2} \vdash A$ or $\mathbf{T_2} \vdash B$ holds.*

This theorem is proved in the same way as Theorem 4.11.

# 6 Application to Program Synthesis

We will explain that q-realizability of coinductive definitions can be used to synthesize programs which treats coinductively defined infinite data structures such as streams. For this purpose, both realizability interpretation for $\mathbf{TID}_{\nu 0}$ and $\mathbf{TID}_{\nu 2}$ can be used.

**Theorem 6.1 (Program Extraction).** *(1) If there exists a term $j$ such that $\mathbf{TID}_{\nu 1} \vdash \forall x(A(x) \to (j(x) \ \mathbf{q} \ A(x)))$ and $\mathbf{TID}_{\nu 0} \vdash \forall x(A(x) \to \exists y B(x, y))$, we can get a program $f$ from the proof and $\mathbf{TID}_{\nu 1} \vdash \forall x(A(x) \to B(x, f(x)))$ holds.*

*(2) The same claim holds for $\mathbf{TID}_{\nu 2}$ and $\mathbf{T_2}$.*

**Proof 6.2.** We show only the case (1). Suppose that there exists a term $j$ such that $\mathbf{TID}_{\nu 1} \vdash \forall x(A(x) \to (j(x) \ \mathbf{q} \ A(x)))$ and $\mathbf{TID}_{\nu 0} \vdash \forall x(A(x) \to \exists y B(x, y))$. By Theorem 4.9, we can get a term $e$ from the proof and $\mathbf{TID}_{\nu 1} \vdash (e \ \mathbf{q} \ \forall x(A(x) \to \exists y B(x, y)))$. By Definition 4.1 and Proposition 4.3, it implies that $\mathbf{TID}_{\nu 1} \vdash \forall x(A(x) \to B(x, (ex(jx))_0))$. Put $f := \lambda x.(ex(jx))_0$, then the claim holds. □

The next theorem holds for $\mathbf{TID}_{\nu 1}$. By the theorem, we can synthesize programs which treat streams. This theorem improves the stream program extraction theorem given in [17] by weakening required conditions.

**Theorem 6.3 (Stream Program Extraction).** *Suppose that the specification formula is* $\forall x(A(x) \to \exists y B(x,y))$,

$B \equiv \nu X.\lambda xy.\widetilde{B}(x, y_0) \,\&\, X(t, y_1)$,

*for some formula* $\widetilde{B}(x,y)$ *and some term* $t$ *in which the variable* $y$ *does not occur freely, and we have a term* $j$ *such that* $\forall x(A(x) \to (jx \;\mathbf{q}\; A(x)))$. *Then we define*

$B^{\square} \equiv \nu X.\lambda x.\exists z \widetilde{B}(x,z) \,\&\, X(t)$.

*If we have* $e$ *such that*

$e \;\mathbf{q}\; \forall x(A(x) \to B^{\square}(x))$,

*we can get a term* $F$ *such that*

$\forall x(A(x) \to B(x, Fx))$

*where*

$\mathit{filter} \equiv \mu f.\lambda x.(x_{00}, f x_1)$,

$F \equiv \lambda x.\mathit{filter}(ex(jx))$.

The theorem is proved in Appendix B.

In the specification formula $\forall x(A(x) \to \exists y B(x,y))$, $x$ means the input, $A(x)$ means the input condition, $y$ means the output stream and $B(x,y)$ means the input-output relation. The input-output relation $B(x,y)$ is restricted to the following form: (1) Each element $b$ of the stream $y$ satisfies the condition $\widetilde{B}(x',b)$ where $x'$ is usually a substream obtained from the input stream $x$. (2) If an element $b$ is decided by $\widetilde{B}(x',b)$, then the next element $c$ of the output stream is decided by $\widetilde{B}(t[x := x'], c)$. The formula $B^{\square}(x)$ means that for each input $x$ there exists some value $z$ satisfying $\widetilde{B}(x,z)$. The term $j$ means a self-realizer of the formula $A(x)$. A realizer $e$ of $\forall x(A(x) \to B^{\square}(x))$ is produced from a constructive proof of $\forall x(A(x) \to B^{\square}(x))$.

We will give examples of program synthesis by using Theorem 6.3.

**Example 6.4 (Bit Stream Transformer).** We will discuss the program which gets a bit stream and returns a stream in which each element is the alternative of the element of the input stream.

The predicate $BS(x)$ which says that $x$ is a bit stream can be represented in the theory by the facility of coinductive definitions as follows:

$BS \equiv \nu X.\lambda x.x = (x_0, x_1) \,\&\, (x_0 = 0 \lor x_0 = 1) \,\&\, X(x_1)$.

The input condition of the specification is the formula $BS(x)$.

The input-output relation of the specification is the formula $ALT(x,y)$ which is defined as follows:

$ALT \equiv \nu X.\lambda xy.(x_0 = 0 \,\&\, y_0 = 1 \lor x_0 = 1 \,\&\, y_0 = 0) \,\&\, X(x_1, y_1)$.

The specification formula is:

$\forall x(BS(x) \to \exists y ALT(x,y))$.

To produce the program by using Theorem 6.3, we prove the following formula corresponding to the specification:

$$\forall x(BS(x) \to ALT^{\square}(x)) \tag{1}$$

where

$ALT^{\square} \equiv \nu X.\lambda x.\exists z(x_0 = 0 \,\&\, z = 1 \lor x_0 = 1 \,\&\, z = 0) \,\&\, X(x_1)$.

We prove (1) in the following way here: First, we prove

$$\forall x(BS(x) \to \exists z(x_0 = 0 \,\&\, z = 1 \vee x_0 = 1 \,\&\, z = 0) \,\&\, BS(x_1)). \tag{2}$$

This is proved by letting $z$ be $\mathbf{d}x_0 010$. Secondly, by letting $C$ be $BS$ in ($\nu$2) for $ALT^{\square}$, we have

$$\forall x(BS(x) \to \exists z(x_0 = 0 \,\&\, z = 1 \vee x_0 = 1 \,\&\, z = 0) \,\&\, BS(x_1)) \to$$
$$\forall x(BS(x) \to ALT^{\square}(x)). \tag{3}$$

Finally, by (2) and (3), we get (1).

We calculate realizers corresponding to the above proofs as follows: The realizer $e_1$ corresponding to the proof of (2) is:

$$e_1 \equiv \lambda xr.((\mathbf{d}x_0 010, 0), r_{11}),$$
$$e_1 \;\mathbf{q}\; \forall x(BS(x) \to \exists z(x_0 = 0 \,\&\, z = 1 \vee x_0 = 1 \,\&\, z = 0) \,\&\, BS(x_1)).$$

The realizer $e_2$ corresponding to the proof of (3) is:

$$e_2 \equiv \lambda q.\mu f.\lambda xr.mfx(qxr),$$
$$e_2 \;\mathbf{q}\; \forall x(BS(x) \to \exists z(x_0 = 0 \,\&\, z = 1 \vee x_0 = 1 \,\&\, z = 0) \,\&\, BS(x_1)) \to$$
$$\forall x(BS(x) \to ALT^{\square}(x))$$

where

$$m \equiv \lambda fxr.(r_0, fx_1r_1).$$

The realizer $e$ corresponding to the proof of (1) is:

$$e \equiv e_2 e_1,$$
$$e \;\mathbf{q}\; \forall x(BS(x) \to ALT^{\square}(x)).$$

We get

$$e = \mu f.\lambda xr.((\mathbf{d}x_0 010, 0), fx_1r_{11}).$$

The extracted program $F$ is:

$$Fx = \mathit{filter}(ex(jx))$$
$$= \mathit{filter}(fx(\mu s.(0, s)))$$

where $f \equiv \mu f.\lambda xr.((\mathbf{d}x_0 010, 0), fx_1r_{11})$. Then we have $Fx \approx (\mu g.\lambda x.(\mathbf{d}x_0 010, gx_1))x$. This is the program we expect.

**Example 6.5 (Fibonacci Sequence).** We will produce a stream which outputs the Fibonacci sequence. We will synthesize the generalized program $F(a, b)$ which outputs a variant of the Fibonacci sequence which starts at natural numbers $a$ and $b$ instead of starting at 1 and 1.

The input is a pair of natural numbers and the input condition of the specification is the formula $\mathbf{N}(x_0) \,\&\, \mathbf{N}(x_1)$.

The input-output relation of the specification is the formula $\mathit{FIB}(x, y)$ which is defined as follows:

$$\mathit{FIB} \equiv \nu X.\lambda xy.y_0 = x_0 \,\&\, X((x_1, x_0 + x_1), y_1).$$

The specification formula is:

$$\forall x(\mathbf{N}(x_0) \,\&\, \mathbf{N}(x_1) \to \exists y \mathit{FIB}(x, y)).$$

To produce the program by using Theorem 6.3, we prove the following formula corresponding to the specification:

$$\forall x(\mathbf{N}(x_0) \,\&\, \mathbf{N}(x_1) \to \mathit{FIB}^{\square}(x)) \tag{4}$$

where

$$FIB^{\square} \equiv \nu X.\lambda x.\exists z(z = x_0) \mathbin{\&} X((x_1, x_0 + x_1)).$$

We prove (4) in the following way here: First, we prove

$$\forall x(\mathbf{N}(x_0) \mathbin{\&} \mathbf{N}(x_1) \to \exists z(z = x_0) \mathbin{\&} (\mathbf{N}(x_1) \mathbin{\&} \mathbf{N}(x_0 + x_1))). \quad (5)$$

This is proved by letting $z$ be $x_0$. Secondly, by letting $C$ be $\lambda x.\mathbf{N}(x_0) \mathbin{\&} \mathbf{N}(x_1)$ in ($\nu 2$) for $FIB^{\square}$, we have

$$\forall x(\mathbf{N}(x_0) \mathbin{\&} \mathbf{N}(x_1) \to \exists z(z = x_0) \mathbin{\&} (\mathbf{N}(x_1) \mathbin{\&} \mathbf{N}(x_0 + x_1))) \to$$
$$\forall x(\mathbf{N}(x_0) \mathbin{\&} \mathbf{N}(x_1) \to FIB^{\square}(x)). \quad (6)$$

Finally, by (5) and (6), we get (4).

We calculate realizers corresponding to the above proofs as follows: The realizer $e_1$ corresponding to the proof of (5) is:

$$e_1 \equiv \lambda xr.((x_0, 0), 0),$$
$$e_1 \;\; \mathbf{q} \;\; \forall x(\mathbf{N}(x_0) \mathbin{\&} \mathbf{N}(x_1) \to \exists z(z = x_0) \mathbin{\&} (\mathbf{N}(x_1) \mathbin{\&} \mathbf{N}(x_0 + x_1))).$$

The realizer $e_2$ corresponding to the proof of (6) is:

$$e_2 \equiv \lambda q.\mu f.\lambda xr.mfx(qxr),$$
$$e_2 \;\; \mathbf{q} \;\; \forall x(\mathbf{N}(x_0) \mathbin{\&} \mathbf{N}(x_1) \to \exists z(z = x_0) \mathbin{\&} (\mathbf{N}(x_1) \mathbin{\&} \mathbf{N}(x_0 + x_1))) \to$$
$$\forall x(\mathbf{N}(x_0) \mathbin{\&} \mathbf{N}(x_1) \to FIB^{\square}(x))$$

where

$$m \equiv \lambda fxr.(r_0, f(x_1, x_0 + x_1)r_1).$$

The realizer $e$ corresponding to the proof of (4) is:

$$e \equiv e_2 e_1,$$
$$e \;\; \mathbf{q} \;\; \forall x(\mathbf{N}(x_0) \mathbin{\&} \mathbf{N}(x_1) \to FIB^{\square}(x)).$$

We get

$$e = \mu f.\lambda xr.((x_0, 0), f(x_1, x_0 + x_1)0).$$

The extracted program $F$ is:

$$Fx = \mathit{filter}(ex(jx))$$
$$= \mathit{filter}(fx(0,0))$$

where $f \equiv \mu f.\lambda xr.((x_0, 0), f(x_1, x_0 + x_1)0)$.

Then we have the program $F(1,1)$ as the Fibonacci sequence stream. This is the program we expect, since $F(1,1) \approx (\mu g.\lambda xy.(x, gy(x + y)))11$ holds.

Monotone coinductive definitions are better fit to module programming than positive coinductive definitions. We will explain the situation by example. Suppose that a base theory $T$ can not prove that a formula $A(X)$ is transformed into a positive formula and that $A(X)$ is monotone. Suppose that by using an additional theory module $E$, $T + E$ proves that $A(X)$ is monotone and transformed into a positive formula. Suppose we can use only $T$ to prove the specification and after that, $E$ is given. In this setting, we can produce a program module $f(r)$ with a program parameter $r$ by using $T$ and when $E$ and a program $e$ are given later, $T + E$ proves that $f(e)$ is a correct program. We will compare monotone coinductive definitions with positive coinductive definitions in the setting.

(I) The monotone case. The program is produced in the following steps: (1) We make a constructive proof in $T+(\text{MONO})+(\text{MONO-Q})+(r\ \ \mathbf{q}\ \ (\text{MONO}))$. (2) We produce a program module $f(r)$ with a program parameter $r$. (3) When $E$ is given later, we prove (MONO) and (MONO-Q) in $T+E$ and find a program $m$ such that $T+E$ proves $(m\ \ \mathbf{q}\ \ (\text{MONO}))$. (4) We get a correct program $f(m)$.

(II) The positive case. The program is produced in the following steps: (1) We make a constructive proof in $T+(\nu 1)+(\nu 2)+(r_1\ \ \mathbf{q}\ \ (\nu 1))+(r_2\ \ \mathbf{q}\ \ (\nu 2))$. (2) We produce a program module $g(r_1, r_2)$ with program parameters $r_1$ and $r_2$. (3) When $E$ is given later, we find a positive formula $A_2(X)$ such that $T+E$ proves $A(X) \leftrightarrow A_2(X)$, and programs $i$ and $j$ such that $T+E$ proves $(i\ \ \mathbf{q}\ \ A(X) \rightarrow A_2(X))$ and $(j\ \ \mathbf{q}\ \ A_2(X) \rightarrow A(X))$. The form of $A_2(X)$ gives a program $e$ such that $T+E$ proves $(e\ \ \mathbf{q}\ \ (\nu 2))$ for $\nu X.A_2(X)$. (4) We get a correct program $g(i, \lambda q.e(\lambda x.q(jx)))$.

Comparing two cases, we can say monotone coinductive definitions are better fit to module programming for the following reasons: (1) The monotone case is simpler. (2) In the positive case, we need to find $A_2(X)$. (3) In the positive case, before $E$ is given, we cannot get a realizer $e$ of coinduction, which is an important part of the program module since it may give a loop structure to the program.

## References


1. M. Beeson, *Foundations of Constructive Mathematics* (Springer, 1985).
2. R.L. Constable et al, *Implementing Mathematics with the Nuprl Proof Development System* (Prentice-Hall, 1986).
3. T. Coquand, Infinite Objects in Type Theory, *LNCS* **806** (Springer, 1993) 62–78.
4. H. Friedman, On the derivability of instantiation properties, *Journal of Symbolic Logic* **42** (4) (1977) 506–514.
5. S. Hayashi and H. Nakano, **PX**: *A Computational Logic* (MIT Press, 1988).
6. S. Kobayashi and M. Tatsuta, Realizability interpretation of generalized inductive definitions, *Theoretical Computer Science* **131** (1994) 121–138.
7. P. Martin-Löf, Constructive mathematics and computer programming, In: *Logic, Methodology, and Philosophy of Science VI*, eds. L.J. Cohen et. al (North-Holland, Amsterdam, 1982) 153–179.
8. N. P. Mendler, Inductive types and type constraints in the second-order lambda calculus, *Annals of Pure and Applied Logic* **51** (1991) 159–172.
9. R. Milner, *Communication and Concurrency* (Prentice Hall, 1989).
10. C. Paulin-Mohring, Extracting $F_\omega$'s programs from proofs in the Calculus of Constructions, *Proc.* $16^{th}$ *Symp. Principles of Programming Languages* (1989) 89–104.
11. F. Leclerc and C. Paulin-Mohring, Programming with Streams in Coq, A case study: the Sieve of Eratosthenes, *LNCS* **806** (Springer, 1993) 191–212.
12. L. C. Paulson, Mechanizing Coinduction and Corecursion in Higher-order Logic, *Journal of Logic and Computation* **7** (2) (1997) 175–204.
13. M. Parigot, Recursive programming with proofs, *Theoretical Computer Science* **94** (1992) 335–356.
14. C. Raffalli, Data types, infinity and equality in system $\text{AF}_2$, *LNCS* **832** (Springer, 1993) 280–294.

15. C. Talcott, A theory for program and data type specification, *Theoretical Computer Science* **104** (1992) 129–159.
16. M. Tatsuta, Program Synthesis Using Realizability, *Theoretical Computer Science* **90** (1991) 309–353.
17. M. Tatsuta, Realizability interpretation of coinductive definitions and program synthesis with streams, *Theoretical Computer Science* **122** (1994) 119–136.
18. M. Tatsuta, Monotone Recursive Definition of Predicates and Its Realizability Interpretation, *Proceedings of International Conference on Theoretical Aspects of Computer Software*, LNCS **526** (1991) 38–52.
19. M. Tatsuta, Two realizability interpretations of monotone inductive definitions, *International Journal of Foundations of Computer Science* **5** (1) (1994) 1–21.
20. M. Tatsuta, Realizability for Constructive Theory of Functions and Classes and Its Application to Program Synthesis, *Proceedings of Thirteenth Annual IEEE Symposium on Logic in Computer Science* (1998).


# Appendix

## A Proofs

**Proof A.1 (of Theorem 3.1).** The claim is proved by induction on the proof of $A$. Cases are classified by the last rule applied to the proof. We give only two cases here, since other cases are the same as first order logic.

Case ($\nu R1$). We must show $\rho \models \forall \mathbf{x}(\nu(\mathbf{x}) \to A(\nu))$. By induction hypothesis, we have $\rho \models \forall \mathbf{x}(X(\mathbf{x}) \to Y(\mathbf{x})) \to \forall \mathbf{x}(A(X) \to A(Y))$. Define $F(V) = \{\mathbf{x} \in U^n \mid \rho[X := V] \models A(X)\}$. Then $F$ is monotone. Fix $\mathbf{t} \in U^n$ and assume $\rho \models \nu(\mathbf{t})$. Then we have $\mathbf{t} \in \mathrm{gfp}(F)$. Hence $\mathbf{t} \in F(\mathrm{gfp}(F))$. Therefore $\rho[X := \mathrm{gfp}(F)] \models A(X)[\mathbf{x} := \mathbf{t}]$. Then we have $\rho \models A(\nu)$. This shows the claim for this case.

Case ($\nu R2$). We must show $\rho \models \forall \mathbf{x}(C(\mathbf{x}) \to A(C)) \to \forall \mathbf{x}(C(\mathbf{x}) \to \nu(\mathbf{x}))$. By induction hypothesis, we have $\rho \models \forall \mathbf{x}(X(\mathbf{x}) \to Y(\mathbf{x})) \to \forall \mathbf{x}(A(X) \to A(Y))$. Define $F(V) = \{\mathbf{x} \in U^n \mid \rho[X := V] \models A(X)\}$. Then $F$ is monotone. Assume $\rho \models \forall \mathbf{x}(C(\mathbf{x}) \to A(C))$.

Assume $\mathbf{t} \in \{\mathbf{x} \in U^n \mid \rho \models C(\mathbf{x})\}$. Then $\rho \models C(\mathbf{t})$. Hence $\rho \models A(C)[\mathbf{x} := \mathbf{t}]$. Therefore $\mathbf{t} \in F(\{\mathbf{x} \in U^n \mid \rho \models C(\mathbf{x})\})$. Hence we have $\{\mathbf{x} \in U^n \mid \rho \models C(\mathbf{x})\} \subset F(\{\mathbf{x} \in U^n \mid \rho \models C(\mathbf{x})\})$ and by the definition of gfp, we get $\{\mathbf{x} \in U^n \mid \rho \models C(\mathbf{x})\} \subset \mathrm{gfp}(F)$.

We will show $\rho \models \forall \mathbf{x}(C(\mathbf{x}) \to \nu(\mathbf{x}))$. Fix $\mathbf{t} \in U^n$ and assume $\rho \models C(\mathbf{t})$. Then $\mathbf{t} \in \{\mathbf{x} \in U^n \mid \rho \models C(\mathbf{x})\}$. Therefore $\mathbf{t} \in \mathrm{gfp}(F)$. That is, $\rho \models \nu(\mathbf{t})$ holds. This shows the claim of this case. □

**Proof A.2 (of Theorem 4.4).** Let $X$,$Y$ be predicate variables of arity 0 and

$$\nu \equiv \nu X.(X \to X) \,\&\, Y,$$
$$\nu^* \equiv \nu X^*.\lambda r.(r \;\; \mathrm{q}_X[\nu, X^*] \;\; (X \to X) \,\&\, Y),$$
$$A \equiv Y \to \nu.$$

Then clearly $\mathbf{TID}_{\nu 1} \vdash A$ holds. But $\mathbf{TID}_{\nu 1} \vdash (e \;\; \mathbf{q} \;\; A)$ does not hold for any $e$. We will show it by the model given in Section 3. By Definition 4.1 we have

$$(e \;\; \mathbf{q} \;\; A) \equiv (e \;\; \mathbf{q} \;\; Y \to \nu)$$

$$\equiv (Y \to \nu) \,\&\, \forall r((r \;\; \mathbf{q} \;\; Y) \to (er \;\; \mathbf{q} \;\; \nu))$$
$$\equiv (Y \to \nu) \,\&\, \forall r(Y \,\&\, Y^*(r) \to \nu \,\&\, \nu^*(er)),$$

where

$$\begin{aligned}
\nu^* &\equiv \nu X^*.\lambda r.(r \;\; \mathbf{q}_X[\nu, X^*] \;\; (X \to X) \,\&\, Y) \\
&\equiv \nu X^*.\lambda r.(r_0 \;\; \mathbf{q}_X[\nu, X^*] \;\; X \to X) \,\&\, (r_1 \;\; \mathbf{q}_X[\nu, X^*] \;\; Y) \\
&\equiv \nu X^*.\lambda r.((\nu \to \nu) \,\&\, \forall q((q \;\; \mathbf{q}_X[\nu, X^*] \;\; X) \to (r_0 q \;\; \mathbf{q}_X[\nu, X^*] \;\; X))) \\
&\qquad \& \, Y \,\&\, Y^*(r_1) \\
&\equiv \nu X^*.\lambda r.((\nu \to \nu) \,\&\, \forall q(\nu \,\&\, X^*(q) \to \nu \,\&\, X^*(r_0 q))) \,\&\, Y \,\&\, Y^*(r_1).
\end{aligned}$$

Choose $\rho$ such that $\rho \models Y$ and $\rho[Y^*] = U^n$. Define $F$ as follows:

$$F : p(U) \to p(U),$$
$$F(V) = \{r \in U \mid \rho[X^* := V] \models (\nu \to \nu) \,\&$$
$$\forall q(\nu \,\&\, X^*(q) \to \nu \,\&\, X^*(r_0 q)) \,\&\, Y \,\&\, Y^*(r_1)\}.$$

Since $F$ is not monotone, immediately by the definition of the interpretation of $\nu^*$, $\rho[r := 0] \models \nu^*(er)$ does not hold for any $e$. Then we have

$$\rho[r := 0] \models Y,$$
$$\rho[r := 0] \models Y^*(r),$$
$$\rho[r := 0] \not\models \nu^*(er)$$

for any $e$. Therefore we have

$$\rho[r := 0] \not\models Y \,\&\, Y^*(r) \to \nu \,\&\, \nu^*(er).$$

Hence

$$\rho \not\models \forall r(Y \,\&\, Y^*(r) \to \nu \,\&\, \nu^*(er)).$$

Therefore $\mathbf{TID}_{\nu 1} \not\vdash (e \;\; \mathbf{q} \;\; A)$ for any $e$. □

**Lemma A.3.** *Suppose that* (MONO-Q) *holds for a formula* $A(X)$. *Then* $(e \;\; \mathbf{q}_X[F, G] \;\; A(X)) \to (e \;\; \mathbf{q}_X[F, \lambda r\mathbf{x}.F(\mathbf{x}) \,\&\, G(r, \mathbf{x})] \;\; A(X))$ *holds.*

This lemma is proved by induction on the construction of the formula $A(X)$.

**Proof A.4 (of Proposition 4.6).** By definition, we have $(e \;\; \mathbf{q} \;\; \nu(\mathbf{x})) \equiv \nu(\mathbf{x}) \,\&\, \nu^*(e, \mathbf{x})$ where $\nu^* \equiv \nu X^*.\lambda r\mathbf{x}.(r \;\; \mathbf{q}_X[\nu, X^*] \;\; A(X))$. By the assumption, (MONO-Q) holds for $A(X)$ with respect to $X$. Hence (MONO) holds for $(r \;\; \mathbf{q}_X[\nu, X^*] \;\; A(X))$ with respect to $X^*$. By Proposition 4.5, $(e \;\; \mathbf{q} \;\; A(\nu)) \leftrightarrow (e \;\; \mathbf{q}_X[\nu, \lambda r\mathbf{x}.\nu(\mathbf{x}) \,\&\, \nu^*(r, \mathbf{x})] \;\; A(X))$. By Lemma A.3, it is equivalent to $(e \;\; \mathbf{q}_X[\nu, \nu^*] \;\; A(X))$. It is equivalent to $\nu^*(e, \mathbf{x})$ by $(\nu 1')$ in Section 2.4, and implies $A(\nu)$ by Proposition 4.3. By $(\nu 1')$ and (MONO) for $A(X)$, we have $A(\nu) \leftrightarrow \nu(\mathbf{x})$. Hence $(e \;\; \mathbf{q} \;\; A(\nu))$ is equivalent to $(e \;\; \mathbf{q} \;\; \nu(\mathbf{x}))$. □

**Proof A.5 (of Proposition 4.8).** We assume that

$$q \;\; \mathbf{q} \;\; \forall \mathbf{x}(C(\mathbf{x}) \to A(C)). \tag{7}$$

Let

$$f \equiv \mu f.\lambda \mathbf{x} r.mf\mathbf{x}(q\mathbf{x}r).$$

We will show

$$f \;\mathbf{q}\; \forall \mathbf{x}(C(\mathbf{x}) \to \nu(\mathbf{x})) \tag{8}$$

under these conditions. This is equivalent to

$$\forall \mathbf{x}(C(\mathbf{x}) \to \nu(\mathbf{x}))\ \&$$

$$\forall \mathbf{x}r((r \;\mathbf{q}\; C(\mathbf{x})) \to \nu(\mathbf{x})\ \&\ (\nu X^*.\lambda r\mathbf{x}.(r \;\mathbf{q}_X[\nu, X^*]\; A(X)))(f\mathbf{x}r, \mathbf{x})).$$

We write $(r \;\mathbf{q}\; C(\mathbf{x}))$ as $C^*(r, \mathbf{x})$.

The first conjunct is proved by (7), Proposition 4.3 and ($\nu 2$). We will show the second conjunct:

$$\forall \mathbf{x}r(C^*(r,\mathbf{x}) \to (\nu X^*.\lambda r\mathbf{x}.(r \;\mathbf{q}_X[\nu, X^*]\; A(X)))(f\mathbf{x}r, \mathbf{x})).$$

By using the rules of NJ, this is equivalent to

$$\forall \mathbf{x}s(\exists r(C^*(r,\mathbf{x})\ \&\ s = f\mathbf{x}r) \to (\nu X^*.\lambda r\mathbf{x}.(r \;\mathbf{q}_X[\nu, X^*]\; A(X)))(s, \mathbf{x})).$$

By ($\nu 2$), it is sufficient to show

$$\forall \mathbf{x}s(\exists r(C^*(r,\mathbf{x})\ \&\ s = f\mathbf{x}r) \to$$

$$(s \;\mathbf{q}_X[\nu, \lambda s\mathbf{x}.\exists r(C^*(r,\mathbf{x})\ \&\ s = f\mathbf{x}r)]\; A(X))).$$

By using the rules of NJ, this is equivalent to

$$\forall \mathbf{x}r(C^*(r,\mathbf{x}) \to (f\mathbf{x}r \;\mathbf{q}_X[\nu, \lambda s\mathbf{x}.\exists r(C^*(r,\mathbf{x})\ \&\ s = f\mathbf{x}r)]\; A(X))).$$

We will show this. Fix $\mathbf{x}$ and $r$ and assume

$$C^*(r,\mathbf{x}). \tag{9}$$

We will show

$$(f\mathbf{x}r \;\mathbf{q}_X[\nu, \lambda s\mathbf{x}.\exists r(C^*(r,\mathbf{x})\ \&\ s = f\mathbf{x}r)]\; A(X)). \tag{10}$$

By (7),

$$\forall \mathbf{x}r(C^*(r,\mathbf{x}) \to (q\mathbf{x}r \;\mathbf{q}\; A(C)))$$

holds. Therefore by (9),

$$q\mathbf{x}r \;\mathbf{q}\; A(C) \tag{11}$$

holds.

Suppose that

$$m \;\mathbf{q}\; \forall \mathbf{x}(X(\mathbf{x}) \to Y(\mathbf{x})) \to \forall \mathbf{x}(A(X) \to A(Y)).$$

By expanding it, we get

$$\forall f(\forall \mathbf{x}((X(\mathbf{x}) \to Y(\mathbf{x}))\ \&\ \forall r(X(\mathbf{x})\ \&\ X^*(r,\mathbf{x}) \to Y(\mathbf{x})\ \&\ Y^*(f\mathbf{x}r, \mathbf{x})))$$

$$\to \forall \mathbf{x}r((r \;\mathbf{q}_X[X, X^*]\; A(X)) \to (mf\mathbf{x}r \;\mathbf{q}_X[Y, Y^*]\; A(X)))).$$

By putting

$X := C,$

$X^* := C^*,$

$Y := \nu,$

$Y^* := \lambda s\mathbf{x}.\exists r(C^*(r,\mathbf{x})\ \&\ s = f\mathbf{x}r),$

$f := f$

in this formula and using (7), Proposition 4.3, ($\nu 2$) and Proposition 4.5, we get

$$\forall \mathbf{x}r((r \;\mathbf{q}\; A(C)) \to (mf\mathbf{x}r \;\mathbf{q}_X[\nu, \lambda s\mathbf{x}.\exists r(C^*(r,\mathbf{x})\ \&\ s = f\mathbf{x}r)]\; A(X))).$$

Therefore by putting $\mathbf{x} := \mathbf{x}, r := q\mathbf{x}r$ in this formula and using (11), we get

$$(mf\mathbf{x}(q\mathbf{x}r) \;\mathbf{q}_X[\nu, \lambda s\mathbf{x}.\exists r(C^*(r,\mathbf{x})\ \&\ s = f\mathbf{x}r)]\; A(X)).$$

Therefore, by the definition of $f$, we have

$$f\mathbf{x}r \quad \mathbf{q}_X[\nu, \lambda s\mathbf{x}.\exists r(C^*(r,\mathbf{x}) \,\&\, s = f\mathbf{x}r)] \quad A(X).$$

Then (10) holds. Therefore we get (8). □

**Proof A.6 (of Theorem 5.2).** We will construct a model of $\mathbf{TID}_{\nu 2}$ extending an arbitrary model of $\mathbf{TID}^-$. We denote the universe by $U$.

We will define $\rho \models A$ in almost the same way as for first order logic where $A$ is a formula and $\rho$ is an environment which assigns an element of $U$ to a first order variable and a subset of $U^n$ to a predicate variable of arity $n$. We present only the definition for the case $\nu(\mathbf{t})$ where $\nu \equiv \nu X.\lambda\mathbf{x}.A(X)$.

We define $\rho \models \nu(\mathbf{t})$ as

$$\mathbf{t} \in \cup\{S \in p(U^n) | \rho[X := S] \models \forall\mathbf{x}(X(\mathbf{x}) \rightarrow A(X))\}$$

where $\rho[X := S]$ is defined as follows:

$\rho[X := S](X) = S;$

$\rho[X := S](x) = \rho(x), \qquad$ if $x$ is not $X$.

Then ($\nu 3$) and ($\nu 2$) hold in this model. □

**Proof A.7 (of Theorem 5.4).** A theory $\mathbf{T_2}'$ is defined as the theory obtained from $\mathbf{T_2}$ by removing the formula constructor $\nu$.

$\mathbf{T_2}'$ is clearly consistent by consistency of second order logic and the models of $\mathbf{TID}^-$.

It is sufficient to give an interpretation for $\mathbf{T_2}$ in $\mathbf{T_2}'$. An interpretation $A^\circ$ of the formula $A$ is defined by induction on the construction of $A$ as follows:

1. if $A$ is either an atomic formula or $X(\mathbf{t})$, then $A^\circ \equiv A$;
2. $(A \,\&\, B)^\circ \equiv A^\circ \,\&\, B^\circ$;
3. $(A \rightarrow B)^\circ \equiv A^\circ \rightarrow B^\circ$;
4. $(A \vee B)^\circ \equiv A^\circ \vee B^\circ$;
5. $(\forall x A)^\circ \equiv \forall x(A^\circ)$;
6. $(\exists x A)^\circ \equiv \exists x(A^\circ)$;
7. $((\lambda\mathbf{x}.B)(\mathbf{t}))^\circ \equiv (\lambda\mathbf{x}.B^\circ)(\mathbf{t})$;
8. $((\nu X.\mathbf{x}.A(X))(\mathbf{t}))^\circ \equiv \forall Y(\forall X(\forall\mathbf{x}(X(\mathbf{x}) \rightarrow A(X)^\circ) \,\&\, X(\mathbf{t}) \rightarrow Y) \rightarrow Y)$;
9. $(\forall X A)^\circ \equiv \forall X(A^\circ)$.

For an abstract $C$, $C^\circ$ is defined by $C^\circ(\mathbf{x}) \equiv (C(\mathbf{x}))^\circ$. For a formula $A(X)$ displaying all the free occurrences of a predicate variable $X$, $A^\circ(X)$ is defined by $(A(X))^\circ$. Then $(A(C))^\circ \equiv A^\circ(C^\circ)$ holds. This is proved by induction on the construction of $A$.

If a formula $A$ is proved under assumptions $A_1, \ldots, A_n$ in $\mathbf{T_2}$, then the formula $A^\circ$ is proved under assumptions $A_1^\circ, \ldots, A_n^\circ$ in $\mathbf{T_2}'$. This claim is proved by induction on a proof of a formula $A$. Cases are classified by the last rule applied to the proof. We show only the case ($\nu 3$) and the case ($\nu 2$) here.

Case ($\nu 3$). Assume

$$\forall\mathbf{x}(X(\mathbf{x}) \rightarrow A^\circ(X)) \rightarrow \forall\mathbf{x}(X(\mathbf{x}) \rightarrow C^\circ(\mathbf{x})). \tag{12}$$

We will show $\forall \mathbf{x}(\nu^\circ(\mathbf{x}) \to C^\circ(\mathbf{x}))$ under these conditions. Fix $\mathbf{x}$ and assume

$$\nu^\circ(\mathbf{x}). \tag{13}$$

We will show $C^\circ(\mathbf{x})$ under these conditions. By putting $Y := C^\circ(\mathbf{x})$ in (13), it is sufficient to show

$$\forall X(\forall \mathbf{x}(X(\mathbf{x}) \to A^\circ(X)) \,\&\, X(\mathbf{x}) \to C^\circ(\mathbf{x})).$$

We will show it. Fix $X$ and assume

$$\forall \mathbf{x}(X(\mathbf{x}) \to A^\circ(X)) \,\&\, X(\mathbf{x}). \tag{14}$$

We will show $C^\circ(\mathbf{x})$ under these conditions. By (12) and (14), we get $C^\circ(\mathbf{x})$. Then this case is proved.

Case ($\nu 2$). Assume

$$\forall \mathbf{x}(C^\circ(\mathbf{x}) \to A^\circ(C^\circ)). \tag{15}$$

We will show $\forall \mathbf{x}(C^\circ(\mathbf{x}) \to \nu^\circ(\mathbf{x}))$ under these conditions. Fix $\mathbf{x}$ and assume

$$C^\circ(\mathbf{x}). \tag{16}$$

We will show $\nu^\circ(\mathbf{x})$ under these conditions. Fix $Y$ and assume

$$\forall X(\forall \mathbf{x}(X(\mathbf{x}) \to A^\circ(X)) \,\&\, X(\mathbf{x}) \to Y). \tag{17}$$

We will show $Y$ under these conditions. By putting $X := C^\circ$ in (17) and using (15) and (16), we get $Y$. Then this case is proved. □

**Proof A.8 (of Proposition 5.11).**

1. Assume

$$q \;\mathbf{q}\; \forall \mathbf{x}(X(\mathbf{x}) \to A(X)) \to \forall \mathbf{x}(X(\mathbf{x}) \to C(\mathbf{x})). \tag{18}$$

We will show

$$\forall \mathbf{x} r((r \;\mathbf{q}\; \nu(\mathbf{x})) \to (r(\lambda p.qp_0\mathbf{x}p_1) \;\mathbf{q}\; C(\mathbf{x}))) \,\& \tag{19}$$
$$\forall \mathbf{x}(\nu(\mathbf{x}) \to C(\mathbf{x})). \tag{20}$$

(20) is proved from (18), Proposition 5.10 and ($\nu 3$).

We will show (19). Fix $\mathbf{x}$ and $r$ and assume

$$(r \;\mathbf{q}\; \nu(\mathbf{x})).$$

By the definition of q-realizability, it implies

$$\forall Y Y^* s(\forall X X^*(s \;\mathbf{q}\; \forall \mathbf{x}(X(\mathbf{x}) \to A(X)) \,\&\, X(\mathbf{x}) \to Y) \to Y \,\&\, Y^*(rs)).$$

Putting

$$Y := C(\mathbf{x}),$$
$$Y^* := \lambda r.(r \;\mathbf{q}\; C(\mathbf{x})),$$
$$s := \lambda p.qp_0\mathbf{x}p_1$$

in this formula, we get

$$\forall X X^*(\lambda p.qp_0\mathbf{x}p_1 \;\mathbf{q}\; \forall \mathbf{x}(X(\mathbf{x}) \to A(X)) \,\&\, X(\mathbf{x}) \to C(\mathbf{x})) \to$$
$$(r(\lambda p.qp_0\mathbf{x}p_1) \;\mathbf{q}\; C(\mathbf{x})). \tag{21}$$

Under these assumptions, we will show

$(r(\lambda p.qp_0\mathbf{x}p_1) \;\; \mathbf{q} \;\; C(\mathbf{x}))$.

By (21), it is sufficient to show

$\forall XX^*(\lambda p.qp_0\mathbf{x}p_1 \;\; \mathbf{q} \;\; \forall\mathbf{x}(X(\mathbf{x}) \to A(X)) \,\&\, X(\mathbf{x}) \to C(\mathbf{x}))$.

We will show it. Fix $X$ and $X^*$. By the definition of q-realizability, it is sufficient to show

$$\forall p((p \;\; \mathbf{q} \;\; \forall\mathbf{x}(X(\mathbf{x}) \to A(X)) \,\&\, X(\mathbf{x})) \to (qp_0\mathbf{x}p_1 \;\; \mathbf{q} \;\; C(\mathbf{x}))) \,\& \tag{22}$$

$$(\forall\mathbf{x}(X(\mathbf{x}) \to A(X)) \,\&\, X(\mathbf{x}) \to C(\mathbf{x})). \tag{23}$$

(23) is proved by (18) and Proposition 5.10. We will show (22). Fix $p$ and assume

$(p \;\; \mathbf{q} \;\; \forall\mathbf{x}(X(\mathbf{x}) \to A(X)) \,\&\, X(\mathbf{x}))$.

Then by (18) we have $(qp_0\mathbf{x}p_1 \;\; \mathbf{q} \;\; C(\mathbf{x}))$. □

2. We will show

$$\forall q((q \;\; \mathbf{q} \;\; \forall\mathbf{x}(C(\mathbf{x}) \to A(C))) \to (\lambda\mathbf{x}rp.p(q,r) \;\; \mathbf{q} \;\; \forall\mathbf{x}(C(\mathbf{x}) \to \nu(\mathbf{x})))) \,\& \tag{24}$$

$$\forall\mathbf{x}(C(\mathbf{x}) \to A(C)) \to \forall\mathbf{x}(C(\mathbf{x}) \to \nu(\mathbf{x})). \tag{25}$$

(25) is proved by ($\nu$2).

We will show (24). Fix $q$ and assume

$$q \;\; \mathbf{q} \;\; \forall\mathbf{x}(C(\mathbf{x}) \to A(C)). \tag{26}$$

We will show

$$\forall\mathbf{x}r((r \;\; \mathbf{q} \;\; C(\mathbf{x})) \to (\lambda p.p(q,r) \;\; \mathbf{q} \;\; \nu(\mathbf{x}))) \,\& \tag{27}$$

$$\forall\mathbf{x}(C(\mathbf{x}) \to \nu(\mathbf{x})). \tag{28}$$

(28) is proved from (26), Proposition 5.10 and ($\nu$2).

We will show (27). Fix $\mathbf{x}$ and $r$ and assume

$$(r \;\; \mathbf{q} \;\; C(\mathbf{x})). \tag{29}$$

We will show $(\lambda p.p(q,r) \;\; \mathbf{q} \;\; \nu(\mathbf{x}))$. It is sufficient to show

$$\forall YY^*s(\forall XX^*p((p_0 \;\; \mathbf{q} \;\; \forall\mathbf{x}(X(\mathbf{x}) \to A(X))) \,\&\, (p_1 \;\; \mathbf{q} \;\; X(\mathbf{x})) \to (sp \;\; \mathbf{q} \;\; Y)) \to (s(q,r) \;\; \mathbf{q} \;\; Y)) \,\& \tag{30}$$

$\nu(\mathbf{x})$.

The second conjunct is proved by (28), (29) and Proposition 5.10.

We will show (30). Fix $Y$,$Y^*$ and $s$ and assume that

$$\forall XX^*p((p_0 \;\; \mathbf{q} \;\; \forall\mathbf{x}(X(\mathbf{x}) \to A(X))) \,\&\, (p_1 \;\; \mathbf{q} \;\; X(\mathbf{x})) \to (sp \;\; \mathbf{q} \;\; Y)). \tag{31}$$

We will show $(s(q,r) \;\; \mathbf{q} \;\; Y)$. Putting $X := C(\mathbf{x}), X^* := \lambda r.(r \;\; \mathbf{q} \;\; C(\mathbf{x})), p := (q,r)$ in (31), by using Proposition 5.9, we get

$(q \;\; \mathbf{q} \;\; \forall\mathbf{x}(C(\mathbf{x}) \to A(C))) \,\&\, (r \;\; \mathbf{q} \;\; C(\mathbf{x})) \to (s(q,r) \;\; \mathbf{q} \;\; Y)$.

From (26) and (29), we have $(s(q,r) \;\; \mathbf{q} \;\; Y)$. Hence we get (24). □

## B Proof of Stream Program Extraction Theorem

We define

$$nthcdr \equiv \mu f.\lambda yx.\mathbf{d}y0x(f(\mathbf{p_N}y)x_1),$$

$$s|_n \equiv nthcdr\, n\, s,$$

$$R \equiv \mu f.\lambda yx.\mathbf{d}y0x(t[x := f(\mathbf{p_N}y)x]).$$

**Lemma B.1.** *$(r \;\; \mathbf{q} \;\; B^{\Box}(x)) \to (r|_n \;\; \mathbf{q} \;\; B^{\Box}(Rnx))$ holds.*

**Proof B.2.** Suppose $(r \;\; \mathbf{q} \;\; B^{\Box}(x))$. We will show $(r|_n \;\; \mathbf{q} \;\; B^{\Box}(Rnx))$ by induction on $n$.

Case $n = 0$ follows from the assumption.

Case $n+1$. By induction hypothesis, we have $(r|_n \;\; \mathbf{q} \;\; B^{\Box}(Rnx))$. By definition, it implies $((r|_n)_1 \;\; \mathbf{q} \;\; B^{\Box}(t[x := Rnx]))$. Hence $(r|_{n+1} \;\; \mathbf{q} \;\; B^{\Box}(R(n+1)x))$ holds. □

**Lemma B.3.** *Assume $(r \;\; \mathbf{q} \;\; B^{\Box}(a))$. Then $\forall xy(\exists n(x = Rna \;\&\; y = (\mathit{filter}\, r)|_n) \to B(x, y))$ holds.*

**Proof B.4.** By $(\nu 2)$ for $B(x, y)$, it is sufficient to show

$$\forall xy(\exists n(x = Rna \;\&\; y = (\mathit{filter}\, r)|_n) \to$$

$$\widetilde{B}(x, y_0) \;\&\; \exists l(t = Rla \;\&\; y_1 = (\mathit{filter}\, r)|_l).$$

Fix $x$ and $y$ and suppose $x = Rna \;\&\; y = (\mathit{filter}\, r)|_n$.

From Lemma B.1, $(r|_n \;\; \mathbf{q} \;\; B^{\Box}(Rna))$ holds. Therefore $\widetilde{B}(Rna, (r|_n)_{00})$ holds. Since $y_0 = ((\mathit{filter}\, r)|_n)_0 = (r|_n)_{00}$, we have $\widetilde{B}(x, y_0)$.

Let $l$ be $n+1$, then we have $t = Rla \;\&\; y_1 = (\mathit{filter}\, r)|_l$. □

**Proposition B.5.** *$(r \;\; \mathbf{q} \;\; B^{\Box}(x)) \to B(x, \mathit{filter}\, r)$ holds.*

**Proof B.6.** By putting $r := r, a := x, x := x, y := \mathit{filter}\, r$ and $n := 0$ in Lemma B.3, we have the claim. □

**Proof B.7 (of Theorem 6.3).** Fix $x$ and suppose $A(x)$. Then $(ex(jx) \;\; \mathbf{q} \;\; B^{\Box}(x))$ holds. From Proposition B.5, we have $B(x, \mathit{filter}(ex(jx)))$. Then $B(x, Fx)$ holds. Hence we have $\forall x(A(x) \to B(x, Fx))$. □

# Calculating a Round-Robin Scheduler

Matteo Vaccari[1] and Roland Backhouse[2]

[1] Department of Computing Science, Università degli Studi di Milano, via Comelico 39/41, 20135 Milano, Italy. vaccari@dsi.unimi.it
[2] Department of Mathematics and Computing Science, Eindhoven University of Technology, PO Box 513, 5600 MB Eindhoven, The Netherlands. rolandb@win.tue.nl

**Abstract.** Kropf [7] has collected together a number of problems that can be used as benchmarks for hardware verification, one of which is a bus arbiter. The function of the bus arbiter is to assign the use of a shared resource on each clock cycle to one out of $N$ subsystems that may want to use it, and in such a way that no subsystem is denied access forever. The most significant component in its implementation is a round-robin scheduler. Rather than *verify* the existing implementation of the scheduler, this paper shows how to *construct* a correct implementation from the given requirements. We make use of both point-free and pointwise relation algebra.

## 1 Introduction

Kropf [7] has collected together a number of problems that can be used as benchmarks for hardware *verification*, one of which is a bus arbiter. The function of the bus arbiter is to assign the use of a shared resource on each clock cycle to one out of $N$ subsystems that may want to use it, and in such a way that no subsystem is denied access forever.

The most significant component in the implementation of the bus arbiter is a round-robin scheduler. Rather than *verify* a given implementation of a scheduler, we consider in this paper the much more instructive problem of *constructing* a scheduler from its specification. The basis of our construction is the algebra of relations; we specify the problem within the algebra and then calculate a correct and efficient implementation.

In the next section we formulate the task and in the section thereafter we present the algebra in which our solution is presented. Subsequently, we outline our calculations and then we give the calculations in detail. The paper is concluded by a discussion of what has been achieved.

## 2 The Task

A bus arbiter is a device that should assign the use of a resource at each clock cycle to at most one out of $N$ subsystems that may want to use it, and it should do it so that no subsystem is denied access forever. More specifically, a bus arbiter is a circuit that maps a stream of $N$ boolean inputs, representing requests to use the resource, to $N$ boolean outputs, representing acknowledgements that the resource may be used[1].

Let us call the input stream *req* and the output stream *ack*. It is easier to think of $\mathbb{B}^N$ as a subset of $\{0,\ldots,N-1\}$ , so we write $n \in req.t$ to mean that the $n$-th component of *req* is high at time $t$. The specification of the arbiter, as given by Kropf [7], is then:

1. No two output wires are asserted simultaneously: for each instant $t$,
$$|\, ack.t \,| \leq 1 \ .$$
2. Acknowledge is not asserted without request:
$$ack.t \subseteq req.t \ .$$
3. Every persistent request is eventually acknowledged: there is no pair $(n,t)$ such that
$$\forall (t' : t \leq t' : n \in req.t' \ \wedge \ n \notin ack.t') \ .$$

Kropf himself suggests an implementation. The arbiter should normally grant acknowledge to the request that is lowest in index, unless there is some other wire that has been asserting its request for more than a set amount of time, in which case the latter wire is granted instead. This is accomplished as follows: at any given moment there is a privileged wire. For simplicity, we may take $t \bmod N$ to be the privileged wire at any time $t$. If wire $n$ is privileged, and is asserting a request, and it was asserting its request the previous time it was privileged, then it is acknowledged. This way any wire will be acknowledged in less than $2N$ clock cycles. In the limit case where all requests are asserted at all times, they will be granted in round-robin fashion.

One way to implement this arbiter is to construct two modules, called for instance $LT$ and $RR$, the first one granting request to the lowest index asserted in its input, and the second one implementing the round-robin algorithm. The first module is combinational, while the second one has state. Module $LT$ simply returns the lowest numbered signal that is asserted.

We focus in this paper on the development of the round-robin scheduler, $RR$. Suppose $\lhd^N$ is a function that delays an input stream by $N$ clock cycles. That is,
$$(\lhd^N.b).t \ = \ b.(t-N) \ .$$
Then, viewing $RR$ as a binary relation between output *ack* and input *req*, its specification is
$$ack\langle RR\rangle req \ \equiv \ \forall (t{::} \ ack.t \ = \ \{t \bmod N\} \cap req.t \cap (\lhd^N.req).t) \ .$$

[1] Note that we are not interested in dealing with metastability problems. Metastability is an effect that may occur whenever a signal is sampled asynchronously; what may happen is that the signal floats in a state that cannot be interpreted as a logical "true" or as a logical "false". It should be clear that this effect cannot be modelled within the framework of this paper. What we call "wire" here is a mathematical abstraction of physical wires.

The task we undertake in this paper is to construct a circuit that implements $RR$ as specified above.

## 3 Relation Algebra

We will write our specifications and our circuits in point-free relation algebra. A brief introduction to our style of relation algebra follows; for a more complete treatment see [1].

A (binary) relation over a set $\mathcal{U}$ is a set of pairs of elements of $\mathcal{U}$. For $x$,$y$ in $\mathcal{U}$ and $R$ a relation over $\mathcal{U}$, we write $x\langle R\rangle y$ instead of $(x,y)\in R$. When a relation $R$ satisfies $x\langle R\rangle y \wedge z\langle R\rangle y \Rightarrow x{=}z$ we say that the relation is *deterministic* (others prefer the term "functional"). In that case it may be considered as a function with domain on the right side and target on the left side; we denote by $R.y$ the unique $x$ such that $x\langle R\rangle y$ holds, if such an $x$ exists. The reason for this name is that we usually interpret relations as programs taking input from the right and producing output on the left. In this way a deterministic relation is interpreted as a deterministic program. We usually use the letters $f$, $g$, $h$ to stand for deterministic relations. We use the convention that "." associates to the right so that $f.g.x$ should be parsed as $f.(g.x)$ . (This is contrary to the convention used in the lambda calculus.)

Relations are ordered by the usual set inclusion ordering. Hence the set of relations forms a complete lattice. The relation corresponding to the empty set is denoted by $\perp\!\!\!\perp$, and the relation that contains all pairs of elements of $\mathcal{U}$ is denoted by $\top\!\!\!\top$. The *identity relation*, $\iota$, is defined by $x\langle\iota\rangle y \;\equiv\; x{=}y$. The composition of two relations $R$, $S$ is denoted by $R \circ S$ and defined by

$$x\langle R\circ S\rangle y \;\equiv\; \exists(z :: x\langle R\rangle z \wedge z\langle S\rangle y).$$

Composition is associative and has unit element $\iota$. The converse of a relation $R$ is written $R\cup$ and is defined by $x\langle R\cup\rangle y \;\equiv\; y\langle R\rangle x$.

A *monotype* is a relation $A$ such that $A \subseteq \iota$. An example of a monotype is $\mathbb{N}$, defined by $n\langle\mathbb{N}\rangle m \;\equiv\; n{=}m \wedge (n \text{ is a natural number})$. (Bird and De Moor [2] use the name "coreflexive" instead of monotype; another name is "partial identity".) There is a one-to-one correspondence between the subsets of $\mathcal{U}$ and the monotypes; and this makes it possible to embed set calculus in relation calculus. The *left domain* of relation $R$, denoted $R{<}$, is the least monotype $A$ such that $A\circ R = R$. As its name suggests, $R{<}$ represents the set of all $x$ such that $x$ is related by $R$ to some $y$. Similarly, the *right domain* of relation $R$, denoted $R{>}$, is the least monotype $A$ such that $R\circ A = R$.

The relation $R \vartriangle S$ (pronounced $R$ *split* $S$) is defined as the least relation $X$ such that for all $x$, $y$ and $z$,

$$(x,y)\langle X\rangle z \;\equiv\; x\langle R\rangle z \wedge y\langle S\rangle z.$$

Note that the requirement that $R \vartriangle S$ be the *least* relation satisfying the above equation in $X$ implies that there is no $y$ such that $x\langle R \vartriangle S\rangle y$ when $x$ is not a pair. That is, the left domain of $R \vartriangle S$ is a set of pairs.

In general, composition does not distribute through split. However, it is the case that

$$(R \vartriangle S) \circ T = (R \circ T) \vartriangle (S \circ T) \ \Leftarrow\ S \circ T \circ T^{\cup} \subseteq S \ . \tag{1}$$

The antecedent holds, for example, when $T$ is a deterministic relation (since then $T \circ T^{\cup} \subseteq \iota$). It also holds if $S$ is a so-called *left condition*: that is, if $S = S \circ \top\!\top$.

We define $R{\times}S$ (pronounced *R times S*) as the least relation that satisfies

$$(x, y)\langle R{\times}S\rangle(z, v) \ \equiv\ x\langle R\rangle z \wedge y\langle S\rangle v \ .$$

The following properties are easily proved:

$$\begin{aligned}(R{\times}S) \circ (T{\times}U) &= (R \circ T) \times (S \circ U)\\ (R{\times}S) \circ (T \vartriangle U) &= (R \circ T) \vartriangle (S \circ U) \ .\end{aligned} \tag{2}$$

Although the concepts of split and product are now standard, there is as yet no standard notation, Bird and De Moor [2] and the Ruby group [4, 5, 10] each using their own brand. The Ruby group, for example, would write

$$[R; S, T; U] \tag{3}$$

where we would write

$$(R \circ S) \times (T \circ U) \ .$$

This use of a comma to separate arguments is, in our view, highly inadvisable for several reasons, but in particular because of the relative size of the ",". In this example, because "," is smaller than ";" many people incorrectly read (3) as

$$[R; (S, T); V]$$

particularly when, as often happens, the author pays no consideration to spacing. The notation used in this document has been carefully chosen to enhance readability. We have also been careful to space formulae so as to automatically suggest the correct parsing of expressions to the human eye and thus minimise the need to refer to a table of precedences. Nevertheless the latter may on occasion be unavoidable, in which case table 1 should be consulted.

## 4 About circuits

Following established practice (see [3, 5, 9]) we model a circuit as a relation between arbitrary collections of ***streams***, a stream being a total function with domain the integer numbers. Abusing language somewhat, we will use the word "circuit" to mean an actual circuit, or a relation between streams as described above. Context should make clear which one is meant. We usually denote streams by small letters taken from the beginning of the alphabet.

Given a relation $R$ over $\mathcal{U}$, a relation between streams can be constructed by "lifting": $a\langle \dot{R}\rangle b \ \equiv\ \forall(t :: \ a.t\ \langle R\rangle\ b.t)$. Hence for any $R$, relation $\dot{R}$ is a circuit.

**Table 1.** Precedence of operators, from highest to lowest

| | |
|---|---|
| $^{\cup} < > ^{\sigma}$ | all unary operators |
| $.$ | function application |
| $\times \; \vartriangle$ | product, split |
| $\circ$ | relational composition |
| $\cup \; \cap$ | union, intersection |
| $= \; \subseteq$ | equality, inclusion |
| $\wedge \; \vee$ | conjunction, disjunction |
| $\Rightarrow \; \Leftarrow$ | implication, consequence |
| $\equiv$ | boolean equivalence |

Note that, for deterministic relation $f$, stream $a$ and integer $t$, $f.a.t = (\dot{f}.a).t$. We refer to this property in our calculations by the hint "lifting". Circuits can be built by relational composition and product: given $R$ and $S$, two circuits, the relations $R \circ S$ and $R \times S$ are also circuits.

A particular relation on streams is the *primitive delay*, denoted by $\partial$ and defined by

$$a\langle\partial\rangle b \;\equiv\; \forall(t :: \; a.(t+1) = b.t) \;\; .$$

The *delay* relation, written $\lhd$, is a generalisation of primitive delay to arbitrary pairings of streams. It is defined as the least fixed point of function $X \mapsto \partial \cup X \times X$:

$$\lhd \;=\; \mu(X \mapsto \partial \cup X \times X) \;.$$

Delay can be thought of informally as the union of an infinite list of terms $\lhd = \partial \cup \partial\times\partial \cup \partial\times(\partial\times\partial) \cup (\partial\times\partial)\times\partial \cup (\partial\times\partial)\times(\partial\times\partial) \cup \ldots$ . Note that $\lhd$ is deterministic.

The delay relation is polymorphic in the sense that it applies the primitive delay $\partial$ to a collection of wires, independently of the shape of the collection. Formally,

$$\iota\times\iota \circ \lhd \;=\; \lhd\times\lhd \;. \tag{4}$$

(Note that this and other properties of delays are proved in [11].)

Finally, the *feedback* of a circuit $R$, written $R^{\sigma}$, is defined by

$$a\langle R^{\sigma}\rangle b \;\equiv\; a\langle R\rangle(b,a) \;\; .$$

This definition is from Rietman [9, pages 23–25]; for $f$ a deterministic relation, the above can be written as

$$a \;=\; f^{\sigma}.b \;\equiv\; a \;=\; f.(b,a) \;\; . \tag{5}$$

We may now summarize our means of constructing circuits:

1. If $R$ is a relation then $\dot{R}$ is a circuit.

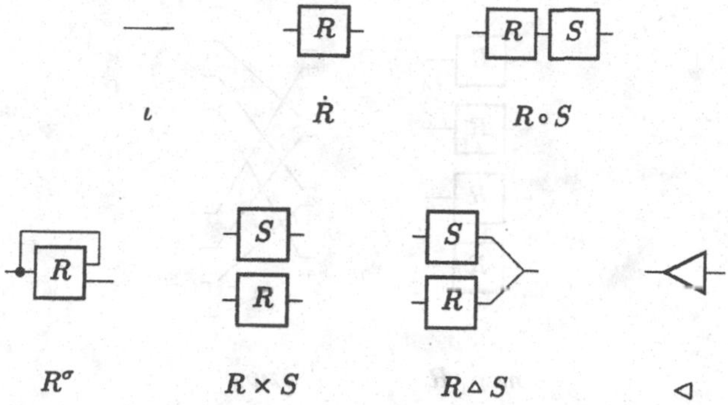


**Fig. 1.** Circuits and their pictures

2. If $R$, $S$ are circuits, then $R \circ S$, $R{\times}S$, $R \vartriangle S$ and $R^{\sigma}$ are circuits.
3. Delays are circuits.

A circuit $R$ is said to be ***combinational*** if delay does not appear in its definition.

A circuit term has an interpretation as a picture that is often useful as an aid to understanding how a circuit term is interpreted as a real circuit. Figure 1 shows the correspondence between pictures and circuit terms.

## 5 Tuples and generalised products

We now generalise the relational product to $n$-wide products. A product of a single relation is the relation itself. A product of two relations is the usual relational product. The product of $n$ relations $R_0$ through $R_{n-1}$ is $R_0{\times}(R_1{\times}(\ldots{\times}R_{n-1}))$. By adopting the convention that $\times$ associates to the right, we can write the above product as simply $R_0{\times}R_1{\times}\ldots{\times}R_{n-1}$. Corresponding to $n$-wide products we have $n$-tuples. For instance, a 3-tuple has the shape $(a,(b,c))$ for some $a$, $b$, $c$. By adopting the convention that pairing associates to the right, we write the above tuple as simply $(a,b,c)$.

The *map* operation generates the product of $n$ copies of a circuit:

$$\begin{aligned} map_1.R &= R \\ map_{n+1}.R &= R \times map_n.R \text{ for } n \geq 1 \ . \end{aligned}$$

Corresponding to the fusion law (2) we have the ***map fusion*** law:

$$map_n.(R \circ S) \;=\; map_n.R \circ map_n.S \ . \qquad (6)$$

Generalising from making $n$ copies of a circuit, we also use maps to combine $n$ possibly different circuits. The term

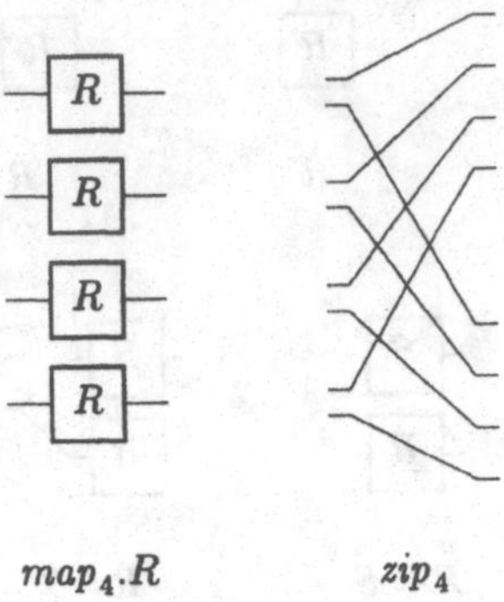


**Fig. 2.** Instances of tuple operations

$$map.(k:\ 0 \le k < n:\ R_k)$$

denotes a circuit with $n$ inputs and $n$ outputs, the relation between the $k$th input and output being determined by circuit $R_k$. Note that this more general map also obeys a fusion law like (6).

The *zip* operation is well-known in functional programming. Informally, $zip_n$ transforms a pair of $n$-tuples into an $n$-tuple of pairs. One common way to define it is:

$$\begin{aligned} zip_1.(a,b) &= (a,b) \\ zip_{n+1}.((a,b),(c,d)) &= ((a,c), zip_n.(b,d)) \ . \end{aligned}$$

The above is an acceptable relational definition, since a function is also a relation. A law about $zip_n$ is

$$\begin{aligned} & zip_n \circ map.(k:\ 0 \le k < n:\ R_k) \vartriangle map.(k:\ 0 \le k < n:\ S_k) \\ = \ & map.(k:\ 0 \le k < n:\ R_k \vartriangle S_k) \end{aligned} \tag{7}$$

the proof is by induction on $n$.

## 6 Design Steps

We recall from section 2 that our task is to construct a hardware circuit implementing the round robin scheduler $RR$ where

$$a\langle RR\rangle b \ \equiv \ \forall(t :: \ a.t \ = \ \{t \bmod N\} \cap b.t \cap (\lhd^N.b).t) \ .$$

Because our development of the round robin scheduler is quite long we begin first by giving an overview. Some of the terms used in this overview may not be completely clear at this stage. They will however be explained in full detail later.

The steps are as follows:

1. Low level specification.
   In the first step we reformulate the given specification of *RR* using tuples of booleans to represent sets. The new specification takes the form

   $$RR \;=\; \mathit{filt} \circ \mathit{intersect} \circ \iota \vartriangle \lhd^N \;. \tag{8}$$

   In this specification the definition of *RR* has been split into three components. Reading from right to left, the first component $\iota \vartriangle \lhd^N$ makes two copies of the input stream, one of which is delayed $N$ time units with respect to the other. The second component *intersect* takes two streams $b$ and $c$, each of which represents a stream of sets and computes the representation of $b \mathbin{\dot\cap} c$ (the stream whose $t$th element is $b.t \cap c.t$). In combination with the first component, this component maps input stream *req* to $req \mathbin{\dot\cap} \lhd^N.req$. Finally, the third component *filt* implements the function $(\{t \bmod N\}\cap)$. In this way the output value at time $t$ is

   $$ack.t \;=\; \{t \bmod N\} \cap (req.t \cap (\lhd^N.req).t) \;.$$

   where the bracketing shows the order in which the individual terms are computed.
2. Analysis of implementability.
   There are two advantages of a modular specification. One is ease of understanding, which is of considerable help to ensuring that the informal requirements are correctly recorded in the formal specification. The other is that it is much easier to identify potential inefficiencies in the implementation. In the second step we analyse the three components with respect to implementability.
   The *filt* component is, at first sight, a potential bottleneck. However, this turns out not to be the case. It can in fact be implemented using what is called a "cyclic multiplexer".
   The problem with the implementability of *RR* as specified by (8) is the component $\iota \vartriangle \lhd^N$. The area required for its implementation is $O(N^2)$ since it consists of $N$ delays each with arity $N$. The conclusion of this phase is thus that it is this component on which we should focus our attention.
3. Goal.
   Having analysed the source of inefficiency in (8) we can proceed to formulating the goal. Specifically, we wish to construct flip-flops $\mathit{ff}_k$ such that

   $$RR \;=\; \mathit{filt} \circ \mathit{intersect} \circ \iota \vartriangle map.(k:\; 0 \le k < N:\; \mathit{ff}_k) \tag{9}$$

   and such that each such component has at most one delay element. In this way the $O(N^2)$ area required by the component

   $$\lhd^N$$

   is replaced by the $O(N)$ area required by the component

   $$map.(k:\; 0 \le k < N:\; \mathit{ff}_k) \;.$$

   (The components are called "flip-flops" because this is a name that is commonly given to memory elements.)

4. Simplification of the goal.
The first step in the achievement of the goal is to simplify it so that it becomes more manageable. The requirement on $ff_k$ is that

$$\begin{aligned} & filt \circ intersect \circ \iota \vartriangle \lhd^N \\ = \; & filt \circ intersect \circ \iota \vartriangle map.(k:\ 0 \le k < N:\ ff_k) \end{aligned}$$

However, we show, in a series of steps, how to reduce it to

$$D_k \circ \lhd^N \;=\; D_k \circ ff_k \qquad (10)$$

(for each $k$) where

$$a\langle D_k \rangle b \;\equiv\; \forall(t:\ t \bmod N = k:\ a.t = b.t)\ .$$

Note that (10) specifies the behaviour of the flip-flop $ff_k$ only at times $t$ such that $t \bmod N = k$. At other times its behaviour is unspecified. This increased latitude (compared to the definition of $\lhd^N$ whose behaviour is specified at all instants) is what is needed to construct an efficient implementation of the circuit.

5. Construction of the flip-flops.
The final step is the construction of the components $ff_k$. Again in a series of steps, we calculate that

$$ff_k \;=\; (\lhd \circ cmx_k)^\sigma\ , \qquad (11)$$

where $cmx_k$ is a cyclic multiplexer. Thus the implementation of the flip-flop does indeed require only one delay element. The combination of (9) and (11) is then the desired implementation of the round robin scheduler.

This then is the overview. Let us now present the full details.

# 7 Low Level Specification

## 7.1 Bit Representation

Let us recall the original specification of the round robin scheduler. For input stream $b$ and output stream $a$,

$$a\langle RR \rangle b \;\equiv\; \forall(t ::\ a.t \;=\; \{t \bmod N\} \cap b.t \cap (\lhd^N.b).t)\ .$$

As is usual we choose to represent a subset of a set of $N$ elements by a sequence of $N$ bits. A stream of subsets of $\{0,\ldots,N-1\}$ is represented by an $N$-tuple of boolean streams. Let $a$ be such an $N$-tuple. We denote the $k$-th stream in $a$ by $a_k$; the set that $a$ represents at time $t$ is $\{k \mid 0 \le k < N \;\wedge\; a_k.t = true\}$.

The intersection operator on sets is then translated into the conjunction operator mapped over the $N$ input wires. The implementation of the relation $R$ where

$$a\langle R \rangle b \;\equiv\; \forall(t ::\ a.t \;=\; b.t \cap (\lhd^N.b).t)$$

is easily derived. Specifically, we have:

$$\begin{aligned}
& \forall(t :: a.t = b.t \cap (\lhd^N.b).t) \\
\equiv \quad & \{ \text{ representation of sets as sequence of } N \text{ bits } \} \\
& \forall(t,k : 0 \le k < N : a_k.t \equiv b_k.t \wedge (\lhd^N.b_k).t) \\
\equiv \quad & \{ \text{ definition of } \mathit{map} \} \\
& \forall(t :: a.t = (\mathit{map}_N.\wedge).(b.t, (\lhd^N.b).t)) \\
\equiv \quad & \{ \text{ definition of } \mathit{zip} \} \\
& \forall(t :: a.t = (\mathit{map}_N.\wedge).((\mathit{zip}_N.(b, \lhd^N.b)).t)) \\
\equiv \quad & \{ \text{ lifting, definition of split and composition } \} \\
& a = (\mathit{map}_N.\dot{\wedge} \circ \mathit{zip}_N \circ \iota \vartriangle \lhd^N).b \ .
\end{aligned}$$

Whence

$$R = \mathit{intersect} \circ \iota \vartriangle \lhd^N$$

where

$$\mathit{intersect} = \mathit{map}_N.\dot{\wedge} \circ \mathit{zip}_N \ .$$

It follows that

$$RR = \mathit{filt} \circ \mathit{intersect} \circ \iota \vartriangle \lhd^N \qquad (12)$$

where the component *filt* must satisfy the requirement:

$$a\langle \mathit{filt} \rangle b \equiv \forall(t :: a.t = \{t \bmod N\} \cap b.t) \ .$$

### 7.2 Implementing the Filter Component

With the exception of *filt*, it is clear that all components in (12) can be implemented directly. In this section we consider how *filt* is implemented.

In terms of the bit representation *filt* must satisfy:

$$\begin{aligned}
a\langle \mathit{filt} \rangle b \equiv \quad & \forall(t,k : t \bmod N = k : a_k.t = b_k.t) \\
& \wedge \forall(t,k : t \bmod N \ne k : a_k.t = \mathit{false})
\end{aligned} \qquad (13)$$

In software, *filt* would be implemented with a straightforward if-then-else statement. In Ruby the full generality of an if-then-else statement is typically shunned. In this case, however, the full generality is not needed and the component can be implemented using a so-called cyclic multiplexer [8].

For each $k$, $0 \le k < N$, the cyclic multiplexer $cmx_k$ has two input streams and one output stream. Its function is to copy the input value in the first stream to the output at times $t$ such that $t \bmod N = k$ and to copy the input values from the second stream to the output stream at all other times. Formally,

$$\begin{aligned}
a\langle cmx_k \rangle (b,c) \equiv \quad & \forall(t : t \bmod N = k : a.t = b.t) \\
& \wedge \forall(t : t \bmod N \ne k : a.t = c.t) \ .
\end{aligned}$$

In practice, a cyclic multiplexer can be implemented by a combination of a counter and a so-called demultiplexer, using techniques that can be found in any circuit design textbook; see for instance Katz [6]. More discussion on the implementation of *filt* is in [11].

Comparing the definition of *filt* with that of $cmx_k$ it is clear that *filt* can be implemented by pairing each of the $N$ bits of the input stream with a stream of *false* bits and passing each pair of bits to the corresponding cyclic multiplexer. That is,

$$filt \;=\; map.(k:\ 0 \leq k < N:\ cmx_k \circ \iota \vartriangle K_F)\ . \tag{14}$$

where $K_F$ is a circuit that ignores its input and constantly outputs the value $F$ (false).

In conclusion, the combination of (12) and (14) is a correct implementation of the round-robin scheduler.

## 8 Efficiency Analysis and the Goal

One advantage of a modular specification like (12) is that it simplifies the task of identifying potential inefficiencies. We need only examine each component in turn.

Assuming that a cyclic multiplexer has an efficient implementation, it is clear that the two components *filt* and *intersect* have efficient implementations. The bottleneck in the implementation is in fact the component $\lhd^N$. Note that the input arity of this component is $N$ since the input stream is in fact a stream of $N$ bits. The total area required for its implementation is thus $O(N^2)$. On the other hand, it seems plausible that an $O(N)$ implementation can be found for $RR$ (although not the component $\lhd^N$) since at any stage only $N$ bits need to be recorded. Specifically, at any time $t$ it suffices to record the value of the $k$th input bit only at the last time that it was privileged.

We can express our intuition about the memory component that is required as follows. For each input bit $k$ we replace the $\lhd^N$ component by a memory element $ff_k$, "ff" standing for "flip-flop" (this being the name often given by circuit designers to memory elements). That is, we wish to design $ff_k$ such that

$$\begin{aligned} & filt \circ intersect \circ \iota \vartriangle \lhd^N \\ = \ & filt \circ intersect \circ \iota \vartriangle map.(k:\ 0 \leq k < N:\ ff_k)\ . \end{aligned}$$

Moreover, the implementation of the flip-flops should involve at most one delay element.

## 9 Simplifying the Goal

In the following discussion it will be useful to introduce the name *specRR* for the term

$$filt \circ intersect \circ \iota \vartriangle \lhd^N$$

and *impRR* for the term

$$filt \circ intersect \circ \iota \vartriangle map.(k:\ 0 \leq k < N:\ ff_k)\ .$$

The goal is to derive $ff_k$ such that $specRR = impRR$. In this section we simplify the goal by splitting it up into separate requirements for the individual flip-flops and by eliminating the "$map.\dot{\wedge}$" term in the definition of *intersect*. We begin by splitting the goal up.

Observe first that $zip \circ \iota \vartriangle \lhd^N$ and $zip \circ \iota \vartriangle map.(k:\ 0 \leq k < N:\ ff_k)$ can be written as maps. Specifically,

$$\begin{array}{ll} & zip_N \circ \iota \vartriangle \lhd^N \\ = & \{ \quad \text{arity of } zip \quad \} \\ & zip_N \circ map_N.\iota \times map_N.\iota \circ \iota \vartriangle \lhd^N \\ = & \{ \quad \text{fusion, polymorphism of } \lhd\text{: (4)} \quad \} \\ & zip_N \circ map_N.\iota \vartriangle map_N.\lhd^N \\ = & \{ \quad (7) \quad \} \\ & map_N.(\iota \vartriangle \lhd^N) \ . \end{array}$$

Similarly,

$$zip_N \circ \iota \vartriangle map.(k:\ 0 \leq k < N:\ ff_k) = map.(k:\ 0 \leq k < N:\ \iota \vartriangle ff_k)$$

Substituting these terms back into the definitions of *specRR* and *impRR*, we conclude that $ff_k$ must satisfy

$$\begin{array}{l} map.(k ::\ cmx_k \circ \iota \vartriangle K_F) \circ map_N.\dot{\wedge} \circ map_N.(\iota \vartriangle \lhd^N) \\ = map.(k ::\ cmx_k \circ \iota \vartriangle K_F) \circ map_N.\dot{\wedge} \circ map.(k ::\ \iota \vartriangle ff_k) \ . \end{array} \tag{15}$$

Thus, by map fusion and introducing the abbreviation $\varphi_k$ where, by definition,

$$\varphi_k \;=\; cmx_k \circ \iota \vartriangle K_F \ , \tag{16}$$

we have obtained individual requirements on each flip-flop. Specifically, we require that

$$\forall(k:\ 0 \leq k < N:\ \varphi_k \circ \dot{\wedge} \circ \iota \vartriangle \lhd^N \;=\; \varphi_k \circ \dot{\wedge} \circ \iota \vartriangle ff_k) \ . \tag{17}$$

In order to remove the spurious conjunction we observe that $\varphi_k$ satisfies

$$\varphi_k \circ \dot{\wedge} \;=\; \dot{\wedge} \circ \varphi_k \times \varphi_k \ . \tag{18}$$

(We leave the proof to the reader.) Hence we may rewrite (17): for all $k$, $0 \leq k < N$:

$$\begin{array}{ll} & \varphi_k \circ \dot{\wedge} \circ \iota \vartriangle \lhd^N \;=\; \varphi_k \circ \dot{\wedge} \circ \iota \vartriangle ff_k \\ \equiv & \{ \quad \text{above property of } \varphi_k \quad \} \\ & \dot{\wedge} \circ \varphi_k \times \varphi_k \circ \iota \vartriangle \lhd^N \;=\; \dot{\wedge} \circ \varphi_k \times \varphi_k \circ \iota \vartriangle ff_k \\ \equiv & \{ \quad \text{fusion} \quad \} \\ & \dot{\wedge} \circ \varphi_k \vartriangle (\varphi_k \circ \lhd^N) \;=\; \dot{\wedge} \circ \varphi_k \vartriangle (\varphi_k \circ ff_k) \\ \Leftarrow & \{ \quad \text{Leibniz} \quad \} \\ & \varphi_k \circ \lhd^N \;=\; \varphi_k \circ ff_k \ . \end{array}$$

So we have reduced the specification of $ff_k$ from (15) to

$$\varphi_k \circ \lhd^N \;=\; \varphi_k \circ ff_k \;. \tag{19}$$

One further simplification is possible. Recalling the definition of $\varphi_k$ (equation (16)):

$$\varphi_k \;=\; cmx_k \circ \iota \vartriangle K_F$$

and the definition of $cmx_k$

$$\begin{aligned} a\langle cmx_k\rangle(b,c) \equiv \quad & \forall(t:\ t \bmod N \;=\; k:\ a.t \;=\; b.t) \\ & \wedge \forall(t:\ t \bmod N \;\neq\; k:\ a.t \;=\; c.t) \end{aligned}$$

it is clear that $cmx_k$ ignores the first component of its input stream whenever $t \bmod N \neq k$. As a consequence, $\varphi_k$ ignores its input stream entirely whenever $t \bmod N \neq k$. We can express this formally by introducing the relation $D_k$ defined by

$$a\langle D_k\rangle b \;\equiv\; \forall(t:\ t \bmod N \;=\; k:\ a.t \;=\; b.t) \;.$$

Two input streams are related by $D_k$ whenever they are equal for all times $t$ such that $t \bmod N \;=\; k$; at all other times no relation between the two streams is required. Thus the fact that $cmx_k$ ignores the first input stream whenever $t \bmod N \neq k$ is expressed by the equation:

$$cmx_k \circ D_k \times \iota \;=\; cmx_k \;,$$

and the fact that $\varphi_k$ ignores its input stream entirely whenever $t \bmod N \neq k$ is expressed by the equation:

$$\varphi_k \circ D_k \;=\; \varphi_k \;.$$

The verification of the former equation follows by straightforward pointwise reasoning. The derivation of the latter equation proceeds as follows:

$$\begin{aligned}
& \varphi_k \\
= \quad & \{ \quad \text{definition of } \varphi_k \quad \} \\
& cmx_k \circ \iota \vartriangle K_F \\
= \quad & \{ \quad \text{above} \quad \} \\
& cmx_k \circ D_k \times \iota \circ \iota \vartriangle K_F \\
= \quad & \{ \quad \text{fusion} \quad \} \\
& cmx_k \circ D_k \vartriangle K_F \\
= \quad & \{ \quad K_F = K_F \circ D_k \} \\
& cmx_k \circ D_k \vartriangle (K_F \circ D_k) \\
= \quad & \{ \quad (1),\ K_F \text{ is a left condition} \quad \} \\
& cmx_k \circ \iota \vartriangle K_F \circ D_k \\
= \quad & \{ \quad \text{definition of } \varphi_k \quad \} \\
& \varphi_k \circ D_k \;.
\end{aligned}$$

Substituting this equation in (19) we obtain the final simplification to the requirement on the flip-flops.

$$\begin{array}{ll} & \varphi_k \circ \triangleleft^N \;=\; \varphi_k \circ \mathit{ff}_k \\ \equiv & \quad \{ \quad \text{above} \quad \} \\ & \varphi_k \circ D_k \circ \triangleleft^N \;=\; \varphi_k \circ D_k \circ \mathit{ff}_k \\ \Leftarrow & \quad \{ \quad \text{Leibniz} \quad \} \\ & D_k \circ \triangleleft^N \;=\; D_k \circ \mathit{ff}_k \;. \end{array}$$

In summary, the requirement on $\mathit{ff}_k$ is:

$$D_k \circ \triangleleft^N \;=\; D_k \circ \mathit{ff}_k \;. \tag{20}$$

## 10 Construction of the Flip-Flops

From the definition of $D_k$ it is clear that (20) specifies the behaviour of $\mathit{ff}_k$ only at times $t$ such that $t \bmod N = k$; at all other times there is complete latitude in its behaviour. It is this latitude that we now exploit.

The component $\triangleleft^N$ can be seen as a memory element that stores $N$ input values. This is because its implementation demands that the input value at each time $t$ is recorded for use at time $t{+}N$ after which it can be discarded. From (20) it is clear, however, that it suffices to record the input value only at times $t$ such that $t \bmod N = k$, that is once every $N$ clock beats. The crucial step in the calculation of $\mathit{ff}_k$ below is thus to replace the function mapping $t$ to $t{-}N$ by a function that is constant for $N$ time intervals. A well known example of such a function is the function mapping $t$ to $t \operatorname{div} N$. But this function does not suffice because of the additional requirement that the function's value should equal $t{-}N$ when $t \bmod N = k$. Noting that

$$(t \operatorname{div} N) * N \;=\; t - t \bmod N$$

is the clue to discovering the appropriate function.

Since it occurs twice in the following calculation it is useful to begin by observing that, in general, for arbitrary function $f$

$$a\langle D_k \circ f\rangle b \;\equiv\; \forall(t\text{: } t \bmod N = k\text{: } a.t = (f.b).t) \;.$$

This is because

$$\begin{array}{ll} & a\langle D_k \circ f\rangle b \\ \equiv & \quad \{ \quad \text{composition and one point rule} \quad \} \\ & a\,\langle D_k\rangle\, f.b \\ \equiv & \quad \{ \quad \text{definition of } D_k \quad \} \\ & \forall(t\text{: } t \bmod N = k\text{: } a.t = (f.b).t) \;. \end{array}$$

Now,

$$
\begin{array}{ll}
 & a\langle D_k \circ \lhd^N \rangle b \\
\equiv & \{ \quad \text{above, definition of } \lhd^N \quad \} \\
 & \forall(t\colon t \bmod N = k\colon a.t = b.(t-N)) \\
\equiv & \{ \quad \text{This is the crucial step discussed above.} \\
 & \quad\ \ \text{We replace "}t-N\text{" using the property of} \\
 & \quad\ \ \text{modular arithmetic:} \\
 & \quad\ \ t \bmod N = k \ \Rightarrow\ N-1 = (t-k-1) \bmod N \quad \} \\
 & \forall(t\colon t \bmod N = k\colon a.t = b.(t-1-(t-k-1) \bmod N)) \\
\equiv & \{ \quad \text{Define } f\!f_k \text{ by} \\
 & \quad\ \ (f\!f_k.b).t = b.(t-1-(t-k-1) \bmod N) \quad \} \\
 & \forall(t\colon t \bmod N = k\colon a.t = (f\!f_k.b).t) \\
\equiv & \{ \quad \text{above} \quad \} \\
 & a\langle D_k \circ f\!f_k \rangle b \ .
\end{array}
$$

We have thus calculated a functional specification of $f\!f_k$:

$$(f\!f_k.b).t = b.(t-1-(t-k-1) \bmod N) \ .$$

The construction of an implementation for $f\!f_k$ amounts to verifying that the function mapping $t$ to $t-1-(t-1-k) \bmod N$ is indeed constant over $N$ time intervals. To be precise, we explore when $(f\!f_k.b).(t+1)$ equals $(f\!f_k.b).t$:

$$
\begin{array}{ll}
 & (f\!f_k.b).(t+1) \\
= & \{ \quad \text{definition} \quad \} \\
 & b.(t-(t-k) \bmod N) \\
= & \{ \quad \bullet \ \ \text{Suppose } (t-k) \bmod N \neq 0 \text{ . Then} \\
 & \quad\ \ (t-k) \bmod N = (t-k-1) \bmod N + 1 \quad \} \\
 & b.(t-((t-k-1) \bmod N + 1)) \\
= & \{ \quad \text{arithmetic} \quad \} \\
 & b.(t-1-(t-k-1) \bmod N) \\
= & \{ \quad \text{definition} \quad \} \\
 & (f\!f_k.b).t \ .
\end{array}
$$

Thus if $(t-k) \bmod N \neq 0$, $(f\!f_k.b).(t+1) = (f\!f_k.b).t$. Also, if $(t-k) \bmod N = 0$, it is obvious that $(f\!f_k.b).(t+1) = b.t$. So $f\!f_k.b$ is defined by the following equations:

$$
\begin{array}{ll}
(f\!f_k.b).(t+1) = (f\!f_k.b).t & \text{if } (t-k) \bmod N \neq 0 \\
(f\!f_k.b).(t+1) = b.t & \text{if } (t-k) \bmod N = 0 \ .
\end{array}
$$

We recognize in these equations a combination of the cyclic multiplexer and a feedback. Indeed,

$$f\!f_k.b \equiv m.(b, f\!f_k.b)$$

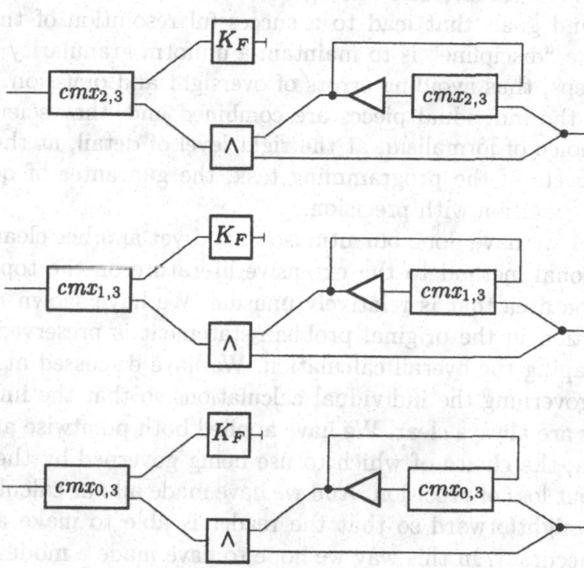


**Fig. 3.** An instance of (22)

where

$$(m.(b,c)).(t+1) = c.t \text{ if } (t-k) \bmod N \neq 0$$
$$(m.(b,c)).(t+1) = b.t \text{ if } (t-k) \bmod N = 0 \ .$$

By (5) this equivales $f\!f_k = m^\sigma$ where, as is obvious from the definitions of the cyclic multiplexer and delay, $m = \lhd \circ cmx_k$. Thus,

$$f\!f_k \ = \ (\lhd \circ cmx_k)^\sigma \ . \qquad (21)$$

In summary, the implementation of $RR$ we have come to is

$$RR \ = \ \mathit{filt} \circ map_N.\dot{\wedge} \circ zip_N \circ \iota \vartriangle map.(k:\ 0 \leq k < N:\ f\!f_k) \ ,$$

or equivalently, exploiting (7)

$$RR \ = \ \mathit{filt} \circ map_N.\dot{\wedge} \circ map.(k:\ 0 \leq k < N:\ \iota \vartriangle f\!f_k) \ , \qquad (22)$$

where $f\!f_k$ is defined by (21) and *filt* is defined by (14). A picture of (22) is in figure 3.

## 11 Discussion

Programming has been variously described as an "art", a "craft", a "discipline", a "logic" and a "science". In this paper we have tried to illustrate the calculational style of programming at work. The "art" of calculation lies in the way the original problem is dissected into manageable chunks, the "craft" is formulating the heuristics and goals that lead to a successful resolution of the individual calculations. The "discipline" is to maintain a uniform granularity in executing calculational steps, thus avoiding errors of oversight and omission. The "logic" lies in the way the individual pieces are combined and, the "science" is making the right choice of formalism, at the right level of detail, at the right time. In all these aspects of the programming task, the guarantee of quality is the combination of concision with precision.

In this paper we have done our utmost to add yet another clear illustration of the calculational method to the extensive literature on the topic, this time in an application area that is relatively unusual. We have shown how the natural decomposition in the original problem statement is preserved and indeed exploited in shaping the overall calculation. We have discussed at some length the heuristics governing the individual calculations so that the immediate and long-term goals are always clear. We have applied both pointwise and point-free relation algebra, the choice of which to use being governed by the concern for concision without loss of precision. And we have made all our calculational steps explicit and straightforward so that the reader is able to make an easy local check of their accuracy. In this way we hope to have made a modest but lasting contribution to the mathematics of program construction.

**Acknowledgement** Thanks go to Tom Verhoeff and Peter Veltkamp for their comments on a draft of this paper.

## References

1. Chritiene Aarts, Roland Backhouse, Paul Hoogendijk, Ed Voermans, and Jaap van der Woude. A relational theory of datatypes. Available at `ftp://ftp.win.tue.nl/pub/math.prog.construction/book.dvi`, December 1992.
2. Richard S. Bird and Oege de Moor. *Algebra of Programming*. Prentice-Hall International, 1996.
3. Avra Cohn and Mike Gordon. A mechanized proof of correctness of a simple counter. In K. McEvoy and J.V. Tucker, editors, *Theoretical Foundations of VLSI Design*, Cambridge Tracts in Theoretical Computer Science. Cambridge University Press, 1990.
4. Geraint Jones. Designing circuits by calculation. Technical Report PRG-TR-10-90, Programming Research Group, Oxford University Computing Laboratory, April 1990. Available at `http://www.comlab.ox.ac.uk/oucl/users/geraint.jones/publications`.
5. Geraint Jones and Mary Sheeran. Circuit design in Ruby. In Jørgen Staunstrup, editor, *Formal Methods for VLSI Design. IFIP WG 10.5 Lecture Notes*. North-Holland, 1990. A revised version is available at `http://www.comlab.ox.ac.uk/oucl/users/geraint.jones/publications`.
6. Randy H. Katz. *Contemporary Logic Design*. Addison-Wesley, 1994.
7. Thomas Kropf. IFIP WG10.5 benchmark circuits for hardware verification. Available at `http://goethe.ira.uka.de/hvg`, 1996.

8. Wayne Luk. Systematic serialisation of array-based architectures. *Integration*, 14(3):333–360, 1993. Available at `ftp://ftp.comlab.ox.ac.uk/pub/Documents/techpapers/Wayne.Luk`.
9. Frans Rietman. *A Relational Calculus for the Design of Distributed Algorithms*. PhD thesis, University of Utrecht, 1995.
10. Robin Sharp and Ole Rasmussen. An introduction to Ruby. 2nd edition. Technical report, Dept. of Computer Science, Technical University of Denmark, 1995. Available at `ftp://ftp.it.dtu.dk/pub/Ruby/intro.ps.Z`.
11. Matteo Vaccari. *Calculational Derivation of Circuits*. PhD thesis, Dipartimento di Informatica, Università degli Studi di Milano, 1998. Available at `http://eolo.usr.dsi.unimi.it/~matteo`.

# Author Index

# Lecture Notes in Computer Science

For information about Vols. 1–1340

please contact your bookseller or Springer-Verlag

.Vol. 1341: F. Bry, R. Ramakrishnan, K. Ramamohanarao (Eds.), Deductive and Object-Oriented Databases. Proceedings, 1997. XIV, 430 pages. 1997.

Vol. 1342: A. Sattar (Ed.), Advanced Topics in Artificial Intelligence. Proceedings, 1997. XVII, 516 pages. 1997. (Subseries LNAI).

Vol. 1343: Y. Ishikawa, R.R. Oldehoeft, J.V.W. Reynders, M. Tholburn (Eds.), Scientific Computing in Object-Oriented Parallel Environments. Proceedings, 1997. XI, 295 pages. 1997.

Vol. 1344: C. Ausnit-Hood, K.A. Johnson, R.G. Pettit, IV, S.B. Opdahl (Eds.), Ada 95 – Quality and Style. XV, 292 pages. 1997.

Vol. 1345: R.K. Shyamasundar, K. Ueda (Eds.), Advances in Computing Science - ASIAN'97. Proceedings, 1997. XIII, 387 pages. 1997.

Vol. 1346: S. Ramesh, G. Sivakumar (Eds.), Foundations of Software Technology and Theoretical Computer Science. Proceedings, 1997. XI, 343 pages. 1997.

Vol. 1347: E. Ahronovitz, C. Fiorio (Eds.), Discrete Geometry for Computer Imagery. Proceedings, 1997. X, 255 pages. 1997.

Vol. 1348: S. Steel, R. Alami (Eds.), Recent Advances in AI Planning. Proceedings, 1997. IX, 454 pages. 1997. (Subseries LNAI).

Vol. 1349: M. Johnson (Ed.), Algebraic Methodology and Software Technology. Proceedings, 1997. X, 594 pages. 1997.

Vol. 1350: H.W. Leong, H. Imai, S. Jain (Eds.), Algorithms and Computation. Proceedings, 1997. XV, 426 pages. 1997.

Vol. 1351: R. Chin, T.-C. Pong (Eds.), Computer Vision – ACCV'98. Proceedings Vol. I, 1998. XXIV, 761 pages. 1997.

Vol. 1352: R. Chin, T.-C. Pong (Eds.), Computer Vision – ACCV'98. Proceedings Vol. II, 1998. XXIV, 757 pages. 1997.

Vol. 1353: G. BiBattista (Ed.), Graph Drawing. Proceedings, 1997. XII, 448 pages. 1997.

Vol. 1354: O. Burkart, Automatic Verification of Sequential Infinite-State Processes. X, 163 pages. 1997.

Vol. 1355: M. Darnell (Ed.), Cryptography and Coding. Proceedings, 1997. IX, 335 pages. 1997.

Vol. 1356: A. Danthine, Ch. Diot (Eds.), From Multimedia Services to Network Services. Proceedings, 1997. XII, 180 pages. 1997.

Vol. 1357: J. Bosch, S. Mitchell (Eds.), Object-Oriented Technology. Proceedings, 1997. XIV, 555 pages. 1998.

Vol. 1358: B. Thalheim, L. Libkin (Eds.), Semantics in Databases. XI, 265 pages. 1998.

Vol. 1359: G. Antoniou, A.K. Ghose, M. Truszczyński (Eds.), Learning and Reasoning with Complex Representations. Proceedings, 1996. X, 283 pages. 1998. (Subseries LNAI).

Vol. 1360: D. Wang (Ed.), Automated Deduction in Geometry. Proceedings, 1996. VII, 235 pages. 1998. (Subseries LNAI).

Vol. 1361: B. Christianson, B. Crispo, M. Lomas, M. Roe (Eds.), Security Protocols. Proceedings, 1997. VIII, 217 pages. 1998.

Vol. 1362: D.K. Panda, C.B. Stunkel (Eds.), Network-Based Parallel Computing. Proceedings, 1998. X, 247 pages. 1998.

Vol. 1363: J.-K. Hao, E. Lutton, E. Ronald, M. Schoenauer, D. Snyers (Eds.), Artificial Evolution. XI, 349 pages. 1998.

Vol. 1364: W. Conen, G. Neumann (Eds.), Coordination Technology for Collaborative Applications. VIII, 282 pages. 1998.

Vol. 1365: M.P. Singh, A. Rao, M.J. Wooldridge (Eds.), Intelligent Agents IV. Proceedings, 1997. XII, 351 pages. 1998. (Subseries LNAI).

Vol. 1366: Z. Li, P.-C. Yew, S. Chatterjee, C.-H. Huang, P. Sadayappan, D. Sehr (Eds.), Languages and Compilers for Parallel Computing. Proceedings, 1997. XII, 428 pages. 1998.

Vol. 1367: E.W. Mayr, H.J. Prömel, A. Steger (Eds.), Lectures on Proof Verification and Approximation Algorithms. XII, 344 pages. 1998.

Vol. 1368: Y. Masunaga, T. Katayama, M. Tsukamoto (Eds.), Worldwide Computing and Its Applications — WWCA'98. Proceedings, 1998. XIV, 473 pages. 1998.

Vol. 1370: N.A. Streitz, S. Konomi, H.-J. Burkhardt (Eds.), Cooperative Buildings. Proceedings, 1998. XI, 267 pages. 1998.

Vol. 1371: I. Wachsmuth, M. Fröhlich (Eds.), Gesture and Sign Language in Human-Computer Interaction. Proceedings, 1997. XI, 309 pages. 1998. (Subseries LNAI).

Vol. 1372: S. Vaudenay (Ed.), Fast Software Encryption. Proceedings, 1998. VIII, 297 pages. 1998.

Vol. 1373: M. Morvan, C. Meinel, D. Krob (Eds.), STACS 98. Proceedings, 1998. XV, 630 pages. 1998.

Vol. 1374: H. Bunt, R.-J. Beun, T. Borghuis (Eds.), Multimodal Human-Computer Communication. VIII, 345 pages. 1998. (Subseries LNAI).

Vol. 1375: R. D. Hersch, J. André, H. Brown (Eds.), Electronic Publishing, Artistic Imaging, and Digital Typography. Proceedings, 1998. XIII, 575 pages. 1998.

Vol. 1376: F. Parisi Presicce (Ed.), Recent Trends in Algebraic Development Techniques. Proceedings, 1997. VIII, 435 pages. 1998.

Vol. 1377: H.-J. Schek, F. Saltor, I. Ramos, G. Alonso (Eds.), Advances in Database Technology – EDBT'98. Proceedings, 1998. XII, 515 pages. 1998.

Vol. 1378: M. Nivat (Ed.), Foundations of Software Science and Computation Structures. Proceedings, 1998. X, 289 pages. 1998.

Vol. 1379: T. Nipkow (Ed.), Rewriting Techniques and Applications. Proceedings, 1998. X, 343 pages. 1998.

Vol. 1380: C.L. Lucchesi, A.V. Moura (Eds.), LATIN'98: Theoretical Informatics. Proceedings, 1998. XI, 391 pages. 1998.

Vol. 1381: C. Hankin (Ed.), Programming Languages and Systems. Proceedings, 1998. X, 283 pages. 1998.

Vol. 1382: E. Astesiano (Ed.), Fundamental Approaches to Software Engineering. Proceedings, 1998. XII, 331 pages. 1998.

Vol. 1383: K. Koskimies (Ed.), Compiler Construction. Proceedings, 1998. X, 309 pages. 1998.

Vol. 1384: B. Steffen (Ed.), Tools and Algorithms for the Construction and Analysis of Systems. Proceedings, 1998. XIII, 457 pages. 1998.

Vol. 1385: T. Margaria, B. Steffen, R. Rückert, J. Posegga (Eds.), Services and Visualization. Proceedings, 1997/1998. XII, 323 pages. 1998.

Vol. 1386: T.A. Henzinger, S. Sastry (Eds.), Hybrid Systems: Computation and Control. Proceedings, 1998. VIII, 417 pages. 1998.

Vol. 1387: C. Lee Giles, M. Gori (Eds.), Adaptive Processing of Sequences and Data Structures. Proceedings, 1997. XII, 434 pages. 1998. (Subseries LNAI).

Vol. 1388: J. Rolim (Ed.), Parallel and Distributed Processing. Proceedings, 1998. XVII, 1168 pages. 1998.

Vol. 1389: K. Tombre, A.K. Chhabra (Eds.), Graphics Recognition. Proceedings, 1997. XII, 421 pages. 1998.

Vol. 1390: C. Scheideler, Universal Routing Strategies for Interconnection Networks. XVII, 234 pages. 1998.

Vol. 1391: W. Banzhaf, R. Poli, M. Schoenauer, T.C. Fogarty (Eds.), Genetic Programming. Proceedings, 1998. X, 232 pages. 1998.

Vol. 1392: A. Barth, M. Breu, A. Endres, A. de Kemp (Eds.), Digital Libraries in Computer Science: The MeDoc Approach. VIII, 239 pages. 1998.

Vol. 1393: D. Bert (Ed.), B'98: Recent Advances in the Development and Use of the B Method. Proceedings, 1998. VIII, 313 pages. 1998.

Vol. 1394: X. Wu. R. Kotagiri, K.B. Korb (Eds.), Research and Development in Knowledge Discovery and Data Mining. Proceedings, 1998. XVI, 424 pages. 1998. (Subseries LNAI).

Vol. 1395: H. Kitano (Ed.), RoboCup-97: Robot Soccer World Cup I. XIV, 520 pages. 1998. (Subseries LNAI).

Vol. 1396: E. Okamoto, G. Davida, M. Mambo (Eds.), Information Security. Proceedings, 1997. XII, 357 pages. 1998.

Vol. 1397: H. de Swart (Ed.), Automated Reasoning with Analytic Tableaux and Related Methods. Proceedings, 1998. X, 325 pages. 1998. (Subseries LNAI).

Vol. 1398: C. Nédellec, C. Rouveirol (Eds.), Machine Learning: ECML-98. Proceedings, 1998. XII, 420 pages. 1998. (Subseries LNAI).

Vol. 1399: O. Etzion, S. Jajodia, S. Sripada (Eds.), Temporal Databases: Research and Practice. X, 429 pages. 1998.

Vol. 1400: M. Lenz, B. Bartsch-Spörl, H.-D. Burkhard, S. Wess (Eds.), Case-Based Reasoning Technology. XVIII, 405 pages. 1998. (Subseries LNAI).

Vol. 1401: P. Sloot, M. Bubak, B. Hertzberger (Eds.), High-Performance Computing and Networking. Proceedings, 1998. XX, 1309 pages. 1998.

Vol. 1402: W. Lamersdorf, M. Merz (Eds.), Trends in Distributed Systems for Electronic Commerce. Proceedings, 1998. XII, 255 pages. 1998.

Vol. 1403: K. Nyberg (Ed.), Advances in Cryptology – EUROCRYPT '98. Proceedings, 1998. X, 607 pages. 1998.

Vol. 1404: C. Freksa, C. Habel. K.F. Wender (Eds.), Spatial Cognition. VIII, 491 pages. 1998. (Subseries LNAI).

Vol. 1406: H. Burkhardt, B. Neumann (Eds.), Computer Vision – ECCV'98. Vol. I. Proceedings, 1998. XVI, 927 pages. 1998.

Vol. 1407: H. Burkhardt, B. Neumann (Eds.), Computer Vision – ECCV'98. Vol. II. Proceedings, 1998. XVI, 881 pages. 1998.

Vol. 1409: T. Schaub, The Automation of Reasoning with Incomplete Information. XI, 159 pages. 1998. (Subseries LNAI).

Vol. 1411: L. Asplund (Ed.), Reliable Software Technologies – Ada-Europe. Proceedings, 1998. XI, 297 pages. 1998.

Vol. 1413: B. Pernici, C. Thanos (Eds.), Advanced Information Systems Engineering. Proceedings, 1998. X, 423 pages. 1998.

Vol. 1414: M. Nielsen, W. Thomas (Eds.), Computer Science Logic. Selected Papers, 1997. VIII, 511 pages. 1998.

Vol. 1415: J. Mira, A.P. del Pobil, M.Ali (Eds.), Methodology and Tools in Knowledge-Based Systems. Vol. I. Proceedings, 1998. XXIV, 887 pages. 1998. (Subseries LNAI).

Vol. 1416: A.P. del Pobil, J. Mira, M.Ali (Eds.), Tasks and Methods in Applied Artificial Intelligence. Vol.II. Proceedings, 1998. XXIII, 943 pages. 1998. (Subseries LNAI).

Vol. 1417: S. Yalamanchili, J. Duato (Eds.), Parallel Computer Routing and Communication. Proceedings, 1997. XII, 309 pages. 1998.

Vol. 1418: R. Mercer, E. Neufeld (Eds.), Advances in Artificial Intelligence. Proceedings, 1998. XII, 467 pages. 1998. (Subseries LNAI).

Vol. 1422: J. Jeuring (Ed.), Mathematics of Program Construction. Proceedings, 1998. X, 383 pages. 1998.

Vol. 1425: D. Hutchison, R. Schäfer (Eds.), Multimedia Applications, Services and Techniques – ECMAST'98. Proceedings, 1998. XVI, 531 pages. 1998.

Vol. 1427: A.J. Hu, M.Y. Vardi (Eds.), Computer Aided Verification. Proceedings, 1998. IX, 552 pages. 1998.

Vol. 1430: S. Trigila, A. Mullery, M. Campolargo, H. Vanderstraeten, M. Mampaey (Eds.), Intelligence in Services and Networks: Technology for Ubiquitous Telecom Services. Proceedings, 1998. XII, 550 pages. 1998.